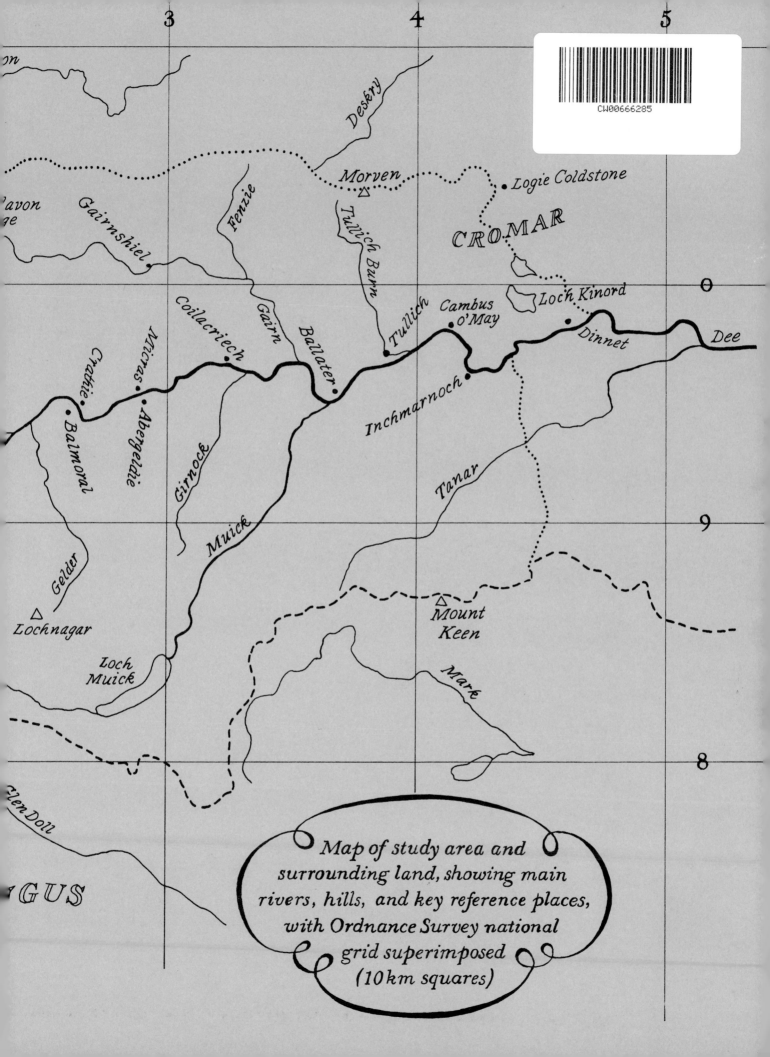

3    4    5

Deskry

Morven · Logie Coldstone

'avon
ge    Gairnshiel ·    Fenzie    Tullich Burn    CROMAR

0

Coilacriech    Gairn    Ballater    Tullich    Cambus o'May    Loch Kinord

Micras    Dinnet    Dee

Crathie    Abergeldie    Girnock    Inchmarnoch

· Balmoral    Muick    Tanar

9

Gelder

△    Mount
Lochnagar    Keen

Loch
Muick    Mare

8

Glen Doll

'GUS

Map of study area and
surrounding land, showing main
rivers, hills, and key reference places,
with Ordnance Survey national
grid superimposed
(10 km squares)

# THE PLACE NAMES OF UPPER DEESIDE

# THE PLACE NAMES OF UPPER DEESIDE

*by*

## Adam Watson & Elizabeth Allan

*Institute of Terrestrial Ecology,*
*Banchory, Kincardineshire*

With the assistance of staff of the School of Scottish Studies,
University of Edinburgh

ABERDEEN UNIVERSITY PRESS

First published 1984
Aberdeen University Press
A member of the Pergamon Group

© Adam Watson and Elizabeth Allan 1984

The University of Aberdeen Development Trust
is pleased and proud to be associated with this volume

**British Library Cataloguing in Publication Data**

Watson, Adam, *1930–*
    The place names of Upper Deeside.
    1. Names, Geographical—Gaelic—Dictionaries
    2. Names, Geographical—English—Dictionaries
    3. Dee, River, Valley (Grampian, Scotland)—
    Gazetteers
    I. Title    II. Allan, Elizabeth
    914.12′4    DA880.D4

    ISBN 0-08-030403-6

Photographs by Adam Watson

Printed in Great Britain
The University Press
Aberdeen

# LIST OF SPONSORS

Publication of this book was made possible by generous financial support from

BP Petroleum Development Ltd
The Braemar Royal Highland Society
The British Academy
The Cairngorm Club
The Carnegie Trust for the Universities of Scotland
The Deeside Field Club
The Etchachan Club
The Gaelic Society of Inverness
The MacRobert Trusts
The North East Mountain Trust
The Rotary Club of Banchory-Ternan
The Royal Society of Edinburgh
The Scottish Arts Council
Scottish Malt Distillers Ltd (Royal Lochnagar Distillery)
The University of Aberdeen Development Trust

# ACKNOWLEDGEMENTS

Above all we thank the many local folk who welcomed us to their homes and gave much unpublished information (Table 4 lists their names). Without them the study would have been merely a desk job, sifting largely extinct information that was very dubious to interpret because of the lack of pronunciations, and finding nothing about living cultures today.

J E M Duff and A Watson began the study in 1973, and E Allan took part from 1974. In early 1976, after finding himself unable to give the time needed, John Duff insisted that he no longer be regarded as an author, although he has continued to show an interest in the study.

Many librarians assisted, particularly J M Smethurst and staff at the University of Aberdeen and Miss E Cuthbert at Windsor Castle; Sir Rennie Maudslay, formerly Keeper of the Privy Purse, made enquiries about the royal libraries. Mr D G Moir, Royal Scottish Geographical Society, helped us to find an old map, and Dr J C Stone, L McLean and J S Doverty showed us maps at the Department of Geography, University of Aberdeen. We thank the staff of the Scottish Record Office and the National Library of Scotland. Mr Fleming, Ordnance Survey, Edinburgh, kindly made available the original OS object name books.

We thank A W Barbour, Mrs J Bruce, A A C Farquharson, J Gordon, M Humphrey, W G McHardy and A Ramsay for allowing us to study estate maps and papers, and Fathers C T Stanley and J Morrow and Rev J A K Angus baptism registers and other church papers.

Several people with professional experience of place names and of Gaelic and Scots linguistics took much time from their own research to read the typescript and make valuable comments. We are deeply grateful to R D Clement (Linguistic Survey of Scotland, School of Scottish Studies, University of Edinburgh), I A Fraser (Scottish Place-names Survey, School of Scottish Studies), D MacAulay (Head of the Department of Celtic, University of Aberdeen), D Murison (formerly of the Scottish National Dictionary Association), and Professor W F H Nicolaisen (Department of English, General Literature & Rhetoric, State University of New York at Binghamton, formerly at the School of Scottish Studies) for all that they did on behalf of this study. I A Fraser also encouraged and advised us at the start, loaned maps, and discussed the project at all stages, and Professor Nicolaisen kindly wrote the foreword.

We are grateful to Art Ó Maolfabhail in charge of the Irish place-names survey, Ordnance Survey, Dublin, for useful discussion on place-name studies. Dr J MacInnes, School of Scottish Studies, made some valuable suggestions on derivations after a seminar at the School.

We thank Dr J P Dempster (Institute of Terrestrial Ecology) for his interest and for allowing some typing to be done in ITE time. The Carnegie Trust for the Universities of Scotland gave a grant for expenses in the first two years. Financial support for the book was generously provided by a number of organisations which are listed at the front of the book.

Jenny Watson generously gave time to design the jacket.

# FOREWORD

There can be few more fascinating topics than the study of place names. While names provide orientation and a sense of location in the current landscape, they are also evocative of cultural continuity and of past human endeavour, and speak of the history that has created the present. They are reminders of people and languages long dead and of our indebtedness to them. Frequently no longer meaningful in terms of contemporary speech, they challenge laymen and scholars alike to reveal their secrets. In their regional variations, they are as representative of the spirit of an area as any dialect word or pronunciation, or any house type or field pattern.

During the last few decades, students of place names have raised the standards of the art considerably, and it is perhaps not surprising therefore that there have, on the whole, been fewer publications on the names of Scottish places than during the preceding three quarters of a century. It is simply no longer possible to publish lists of local names and their alleged 'meanings', without extensive field work and a systematic scrutiny of relevant early sources. There is a new responsibility towards the public which earlier authors on the subject did not always possess.

It is particularly gratifying that the present study of place names in Upper Deeside meets to the full these new criteria and expectations. There are ten years of painstaking field work behind the authors' presentation, and their findings are based on a conscientious examination of both manuscripts and written sources and on countless interviews with the people of Deeside on whose roadsides, rivers, farms and mountains these names occur. Whenever outside expertise or advice was required they have availed themselves of it and their book shows persuasively the benefits derived from co-operation within a community of scholars. At the same time, it has not lost the immediate freshness, even delight, of the discovery of unrecorded names or of pleasing confirmation of a hunch by those whose oral tradition has kept these names alive.

*The Place Names of Upper Deeside* is a sound book in every sense. In both scope and attention to detail, it surpasses everything published in Scotland so far. May the love, the patience, the rigour, and the energy which have gone into its making find a favourable echo not only on Deeside and in the Scottish north-east but wherever place names are considered important signposts to the past.

W F H Nicolaisen

# CONTENTS

*To the folk of Upper Deeside*

# INTRODUCTION

Place names are an important part of the identity and culture of local communities, and their meanings and associations interest many people. They can also tell us much about history, ecology, social changes, language and dialect.

In this book we document information on place names in Upper Deeside, most of it gained from interviews with local people. Many of them regretted the extinction of old names and languages, and welcomed the opportunity to have their own knowledge recorded. The study was done intermittently in our spare time during 1973–83. All known published maps, books and other publications on the area were searched, unpublished maps and papers in archive collections on the area at Register House, the Windsor Royal Archives, the University of Aberdeen and all estate offices, and all graveyards in the area.

We are both native speakers of the Aberdeenshire type of lowland Scots, and this made it easier to gain the confidence and wholehearted cooperation of informants. One of us (Elizabeth Allan) was born and brought up in the area, and Adam Watson has had a lifelong association with it, so that both of us were personally well known to many Deeside folk before the study began. We attended evening classes in Gaelic, in order to get a better basis for reliable derivations of Gaelic place names.

The study produced a large number of previously unpublished place names. In the course of the work we discovered the last known native speaker of the Deeside dialect of Gaelic, and this led to a detailed study of Aberdeenshire Gaelic (Watson & Clement 1983). We also found previously unpublished Gaelic poems from the area (Watson 1983).

As we had no experience of place-name study until 1973, we sought help from professional workers on place names and linguistics who encouraged us and gave much help and advice at every stage.

The main part of the book is an alphabetical list of place names. To help readers wishing to find out the names of former habitations in particular parts of the area, we also give these separately in Appendix 2.

# STUDY AREA AND METHODS OF COLLECTION

## Study area

This covers two adjacent parishes in west Aberdeenshire: Glenmuick, Tullich and Glengairn, and Crathie–Braemar. The area has three electoral registers (Glenmuick & Ballater; Crathie; and Braemar) and one district ward (Upper Deeside). It stretches from Dinnet to the top of the Cairngorms. As most of the land is moor and hill, the human population has always been small, and each parish covers a larger area than the average Scottish parish.

## Land use

Place names reflect past and present land use, and our list gives many examples. We now describe land use briefly, to help put the list in perspective; Nethersole-Thompson & Watson (1981) give fuller descriptions.

High hills are a barrier to the north, west and south, and moorland formerly barred easy access to the east. Despite the difficult terrain, however, nationally-important north–south routes over the passes developed centuries ago, being much shorter than alternative routes round the hills. Many of Scotland's famous Mounth roads and other cross-country hill tracks are in our study area (the Mounth, Capel Mounth, Tolmount, Monega, Cairnwell, Ca, Camock, Bealach Dearg, Lairig an Laoigh, Lairig Ghru, Glen Feshie-Geldie-Tilt).

Treeless deer 'forest' occupies most of the high land, with grouse moors covering most of the lower slopes. Upper Deeside contains some of Scotland's best known deer forests and largest estates (Invercauld, Balmoral and Mar), and some of the best known grouse moors (Glen Muick, Corndavon, Micras and Gairnshiel). It holds some of the finest Scottish relics of Old Caledonian pine and birch forest at Mar, Ballochbuie and Glen Tanar. Coniferous woods have been planted on some of the lower moorland. Salmon fishing brings in much revenue, and there is one whisky distillery.

Farming has been confined to patches of fertile soil on the lower parts of the valleys. In the 1800s, people were cleared from several glens to make way for more deer, but in most glens the farms have become deserted because people left voluntarily. Only the better, accessible farmland at low altitudes is now ploughed. Very few farmers own their farms, and there are fewer tenant farmers than formerly; the landowners now work many farms on their own account with paid staff.

The area's western part in the Cairngorms has been less modified by man than any other large part of Britain because of its high altitude, harsh climate, and infertile soils. Now part of the Cairngorms National Nature Reserve, it is internationally important for its arctic-like plant and animal life. There are four other National Nature Reserves, ten Sites of Special Scientific Interest, and one Scottish Wildlife Trust Reserve within the study area. Furthermore, most of it lies inside 'National Scenic Areas', with scenery of outstanding national value.

Upper Deeside has long been famed for its scenic beauty, healthy air, and associations with royalty, and is very popular with people touring Scotland. It is one of the best parts of Scotland for mountaineering, hill walking, and cross-country skiing. Facilities for downhill skiing have been developed at the Cairnwell (the so-called 'Glenshee' ski ground), one of Scotland's four ski centres. Tourism and its services have now replaced agriculture as the main occupation.

## Language

The place names show few definite traces of Pictish, the Celtic language of north Scotland before Gaelic came from Ireland. Most place names even in lower Deeside are of Gaelic origin. People west of Dinnet still spoke Gaelic until 1500–1600, but Gaelic has since been replaced by lowland Scots and English (Watson & Clement 1983). Only a few folk brought up west of Ballater have any Deeside Gaelic left, and none uses it fluently. Most local people speak lowland Scots. They learn English as a secondary language at school, and incidentally at home through radio, television, newspapers and books. They use it in ordinary conversation only when talking to foreigners, English people, and Scots who do not understand lowland Scots speech or choose not to use it. Lowland Scots has predominated for centuries at the east end of the area, and similarly Gaelic at the west end until its fairly recent decline and now precipitate collapse. Lowland Scots names occur most commonly in the east and least in the west; and conversely Gaelic died soonest in the east and latest in the west. The area is unusual in Scotland for its history of Gaelic and lowland Scots as the two main languages.

## Past studies

Upper Deeside has been well covered by past studies of place names, in the books by Macdonald (1899) and Alexander (1952) on place names in Aberdeenshire. Diack's (1944) book about inscriptions on standing stones included a collection of names from the area, and Seton Gordon's books on natural history and the hill country included more names from here than from other parts of Scotland. We therefore expected to discover few unpublished names, but in fact we found many.

## Methods of collection

The widely-accepted early methods of Joyce (1869) and Watson (1926) were used, along with the standard modern methods reviewed by Nicolaisen (1979). We concentrated throughout the study on visiting people who had lived locally all their lives. The total number of local residents seen was 260. Some lived in surrounding areas such as Speyside, and gave a few boundary names not heard from Deeside folk. A collection of the place names of an area can never be complete. More informants provide more names, and informants seen repeatedly may give further names on return visits. We halted the collection when we had asked for the names of every field, ruin, hill, corrie, stream, and wood, and when over half the new informants were producing no further names for our list. By then we had searched all graveyards in Upper Deeside, all maps and papers pertaining to the study area in Register House and other archive collections at estate offices and charter rooms, the central and university libraries at Aberdeen, the National Library of Scotland, and other sources given below in the References section.

During each interview we asked whether informants knew names and locations shown on maps and other documents. If they did not, we offered only the first letter or syllable as a prompt. Only after this did we show them the OS (Ordnance Survey) map to get precise locations. Next we asked them for names of other obvious features such as small hillocks and river pools which were not on maps. Few of them were accustomed to reading maps, so if they pointed to a location on the map we checked with further questions, asked for places to be shown from window or garden, and took many people out to field and hill. We recorded pronunciations and key parts of interviews with tape-recorders, and made notes.

Informants who had forgotten some names often recalled them on later visits. On return visits we mentioned names since heard from others, to check whether the current informant knew them. This indicated relatively how widely known the names were. Where only one person or family had given a name, or an informant was uncertain about a name or location, we always checked particularly carefully with other people.

All parts of the area were visited to see whether our derivations of the name fitted the appearance of the places. Every place in the list whose approximate or precise location is known was visited by Adam Watson and many by Elizabeth Allan also.

## BRIEF GUIDE TO USE OF MAIN LIST

Below we use one name from the list as an example to explain the main layout of information, followed by a few explanatory notes.

**Allt Glas-choille** (OS, 3, 311032), burn of green wood. Burn of Glasschoil (I), Alt-glas-choile (R14). Also the Glas-choille Burn (A, C), ðɪˈglasçəlˈbʌrn. North-east of Gairnshiel.

| | |
|---|---|
| Allt Glas-choille | Gaelic name as on current OS (Ordnance Survey) map |
| OS | On current OS map |
| 3 | Rank (scale 1–6) for reliability of Gaelic derivation (see Table 1) |

| | |
|---|---|
| 311032 | Precise location by map reference |
| burn of green wood | English translation |
| Burn of Glasschoil | Spelling in early record |
| (I) | Source of early record, in this case Invercauld map (see Table 2 for abbreviations) |
| Alt-glas-choile | Spelling in another early record |
| (R14) | Another source (see Table 2) |
| Also | Indicates alternative name for the same place |
| the Glas-choille Burn | Alternative name |
| A | Published source for alternative name (see Table 2) |
| C | Common, alternative name known to over 7 of our informants |
| ðɪˈglasçɔlˈbʌrn | Pronunciation using phonetic symbols (Table 3) |
| North-east of Gairnshiel | Description of approximate location, occasionally giving other information |

*Other notes*

* Name not published previously, to our knowledge.

An OS Gaelic name with no phonetics attached and no other sources has no rank given to it because of this lack of other evidence.

Pairs of capital initials other than OS, such as JB and CMcI, show initials of informants who gave interesting Gaelic pronunciations or a story with the name. Table 4 gives informants' names.

An incomplete map reference, such as 38-02- means that we have located the relevant kilometre square but not the exact spot to the nearest 100 metres. Some locations are deduced by eliminating known alternatives. For example, if we knew the names and locations of three out of four farm ruins in a glen, another farm name in an old record for that glen obviously referred to the fourth set of ruins. Where we give a grid reference for this, we add 'by elimination'.

If we give phonetic pronunciations from Alexander beside those from our informants, Alexander's follows ours, in parentheses, like this (...(A)). Where our informants gave two versions, e.g. Tom an t-Sidhein (F, 148916), tǫmˈtʃiən, tǫmˈʤiɐn (Sch), Sch refers to the second, and F to the first.

'As above' means that the name is pronounced as in the previous name in the list.

U—name known to 1–3 of our informants, F—known to 4–6.

?—tentative suggestion for a Gaelic word in a particularly doubtful case.

### The definite article, and the names' alphabetical positions

Names in some earlier place-name lists appear in alphabetical order according to the Gaelic article (with Am Mullach under A, but Mullach under M). We ignore the definite article (A', Am, An, An t-, Na, The) in deciding where to enter a name in our alphabetical list.

### Examples of Gaelic and English definite article

*Lowland Scots or English names, and partly Gaelic names*

OS—Callater Burn
Local use—the Callater Burn
Our list—(The) Callater Burn (OS)

*Mainly or wholly Gaelic names*

(i)  OS—Coire Mor, Clais Mhor
Local use— the Coire Mor, the Clais Mhor.
Our List—(An) Coire Mor (OS), (A') C(h)lais Mhor (OS); the extra An, A', h, etc in parentheses do not affect the name's position in the alphabetical list.

(ii)  Names not on OS map
Local use—the Coire Mor, the Allt Mor, the Clais, the Claigionns.
Our list—An Coire Mor, An t-Allt Mor, A' Chlais, Na Claignean. These are classic Gaelic forms, whereas the phonetics show actual pronunciations (ðɪˌkǫrˈmoːr, etc).

### Gaelic derivations

One should be sceptical about any Gaelic derivations in areas like Upper Deeside where local Gaelic speech has virtually died out. In such areas the all-important original vernacular Gaelic pronunciation of place names is no longer available in common use as a reliable indication of most derivations. With simple names such as Allt Mor and Coire Beag, Gaelic words and their English translations are obvious. However, many derivations are doubtful, and we could not find even a possible meaning for some names. We have graded these differences by ranking the reliability in our opinion of Gaelic forms and their English translations (Table 1). Ranks put an approximate order of likelihood on these and provide a standard for comparison, by defining the estimated degree of probability of the derivations.

We could not rank Gaelic names given on OS maps in cases where we had no other evidence such as old spellings of the name or local pronunciations. We do not rank or translate partly-Gaelic names such as Clochanyell Burn and Cnap o the Coire an t-Slugain; readers can find them under Clochanyell and Coire an t-Slugain. In Braes o Begarry, however, we give the Gaelic for Begarry and a rank and translation, as Begarry does not appear separately in the list.

## Lowland Scots names

Here we relied on local knowledge of lowland Scots by informants and ourselves. One of us (EA) was brought up at Ballater inside the study area, and AW at Turriff in Buchan. We used the Scottish National Dictionary and Jamieson's dictionary for deciding probable meanings of a few words not known to us. Spellings follow the standard forms in the Scottish National Dictionary, for example Auld, Stane, Puil and Wuid, and not Aal, Steen, Peel and Wid as one often sees in Aberdeenshire writings. Local people may prefer these Aberdeenshire forms. However, we feel that one should not flout standard SND spellings for Scots words while accepting standard Oxford Dictionary spelling for English words. As every Scots place name heard by us also appears in phonetics, this shows local pronunciations beyond any doubt.

When translating lowland Scots names to English, we use the convention Scots Auld = old. We do not rank Scots names, because their meanings are nearly always certain. To save space, where names with the same word occur in succession, such as the Auld X, the Auld Y, and so on, we give the English meaning only for the first. In a very few names whose language of origin is uncertain, any translation offered must be speculative.

## Abbreviated place names

Ghillies do use the full names of fishing pools such as the Jock Robertson Puil, but more often say just Jock Robertson, except where the abbreviated form would be confusing, as in the Brig Puil and the Lodge Puil. We omit these short forms, except for double abbreviations as in Little Thorny, which we give under the Little Thorny Buss Puil. As people shorten very few other names, such as Coilies for Coilacriech, we give all of them under the full name.

### TABLE 1. RANKS FOR RELIABILITY OF GAELIC FORMS

1. Given by locally-reared Gaelic speakers in areas where Gaelic is still dominant (none in this book).

2. Given by locally-reared Gaelic speakers in areas where Gaelic is not dominant, and meaning given by them without hesitation.

3. We found no other dictionary form. The form that we give fits the nature of the place or at least is not opposed to it, and also fits local pronunciation or old spellings.

4. Other dictionary forms that we found for part or all of the name do not fit the place or the local pronunciation or old spellings as well as the form that we have chosen.

5. Other dictionary forms that we found for part or all of the name fit the place or at least are not opposed to it, and also fit the local pronunciation or old spellings, so the form which we have chosen is merely the one that we think is the most likely possibility. Where there is evidence for making this choice (nature of the place, conclusions from studies elsewhere, etc), this evidence is given.

6. We found no dictionary form for part or all of the name, but we give the name here in Gaelic-type spelling, based on local pronunciation or old spellings.

In names with two or more words, the rank refers to the most doubtful word. Example: alt'kul. Even though Allt on its own would rate 3, Allt Cul gets 5, because the sound 'kul could represent either Cul or Cuil. In cases where no phonetics are given because no local pronunciation is known, Gaelic forms and translations are likely to be more doubtful. Names beginning Inbhir of . . . might equally well be given as Scots Inver (same meaning as Gaelic Inbhir = mouth), and similarly with Spideal (Spittal), and Sron of . . . (Strone). Ruighe can mean a shiel building, a cattle-run, or a slope or reach of land; we use shiel if ground inspection showed a building, but otherwise use cattle-run or slope.

### TABLE 2. ABBREVIATIONS OF SOURCES FROM WRITTEN RECORDS

| | | | |
|---|---|---|---|
| A | W Alexander | Ande | Anderson 1889 |
| Aa | W Alexander notes | Ano | Anonymous 1973 |
| Ab | Aboyne | Anon | Anonymous 1924, 1928 |
| Ad | Adair | Anony | Anonymous 1955 |
| Af | A S Fraser 1973 | Anonym | Anonymous 1856 |
| Afr | A S Fraser 1977 | Ap | Abergeldie papers, from M |
| Aj | Aberdeen Journal | Ar | Arrowsmith |
| Al | H Alexander | As | Astor |
| Ale | Alexander 1925 | At | Atholl map 1780, Blair Castle |
| All | Allan 1925 | Ath | Atholl map 1823 |
| Am | Abergeldie map | Asr | Aberdeen sasines, from A |
| An | Antiquities, Robertson 1847 | Av | Avery |
| And | Anderson 1922 | | |

| | |
|---|---|
| B | Balmoral map |
| Ba | Bacon |
| Bal | Balfour's Collection, in Robertson 1843 |
| Be | Bellamore ledger |
| Bg | Book of Braemar Gathering |
| Bl | Blundell |
| Bla | Blaeu |
| Blm | British Library maps |
| Br | Braemar Guide |
| Bre | Bremner 1931 |
| Brem | Bremner 1933 |
| Bro | Brown 1869 |
| Brow | Brown 1885 |
| Brown | Brown 1831 |
| Brown 1 | Brown 1835 |
| Bs | Balmoral stalkers' map |
| Bu | Burn in Cj |
| Bul | Bulloch, refers to 1614 |
| Bur | Burn, An Gaidheal |
| | |
| C | Common, heard from over 7 informants |
| Ca | Carta Jacobi etc (1564), in Robertson 1804 |
| Ce | Census records New Register House |
| Cg | Congregation of Gairnside |
| Ch | Christie |
| Cj | Cairngorm Club Journal |
| Cm | Cairngorm Club map |
| Cp | Crathie presbytery |
| Cpb | Crathie parish books |
| Cr | Catholic register Braemar |
| Crev | Celtic Review |
| Crg | Catholic register Glen Gairn |
| Cro | Chamberlain Rolls, Thomson 1817–45, from M |
| Crom | Crombie 1861 |
| Cromb | Crombie 1875 |
| | |
| D | Diack |
| Da | Diack notes |
| Dav | Davidson |
| Df | Deeside Field |
| Di | Dinnie |
| Dil | Dilworth 1956 |
| Dms | Diack ms |
| Drc | Diack Revue Celtique |
| Dro | Diack notes to Robertson |
| Du | Duff 1978 |
| Duf | Duff 1981 |
| Dug | Duguid 1931 |
| Dw | Dwelly |
| | |
| E | Erskine |
| Ed | Edward |
| Er | Electoral register |
| | |
| F | Few, heard from 4–6 informants |
| Fa | Farquharson map, Nat. Library of Scotland |
| Fi | Fife |
| Fo | Forbes 1872 |
| | |
| G | GD in Scottish Record Office |
| Ga | Gaffney |
| Gf | G Fraser |
| Gi | Gibb |
| Gib | Gibson |
| Gl | Grampian Regional Council |
| Gle | 'Glenmore' (D Shaw) |
| Gler | Glen Tanar Right of Way |
| Gm | Grant & Murison |

| | |
|---|---|
| Go | Gordon map, Nat. Library of Scotland |
| Gr | Grant 1861 |
| | |
| H | Huntly Rental Book |
| Ha | Harper |
| Hi | Historical Papers, Allardyce |
| Hr | Huntly rental mss, from M |
| Hu | Humphrey |
| | |
| I | Invercauld map, RHP 3897 in Register House list |
| Im | Other Invercauld maps |
| In | Innes map, Abergeldie Castle |
| Inn | Innes 1854 |
| Inne | Innes 1845 |
| Io | Invercauld other papers |
| Iop | Invercauld other, poems probably 1814–17 |
| Is | Invercauld shooting map, RHP 3330 in Register House List |
| | |
| J | Joyce |
| Ja | Jackson |
| Jam | Jamieson |
| Je | Jervise |
| Jo | Johnston, or map in Mg |
| | |
| K | Keith |
| Ke | Keddie |
| Kn | Knox map 1831 |
| Ky | Kyd |
| | |
| L | Logie |
| Le | Ledger, Mill of Auchendryne |
| Lp | Legal papers |
| Ly | Lyall |
| | |
| M | Macdonald 1899 |
| Ma | Marlee map, RHP 3896 in Register House list |
| Mac | MacKinlay |
| Mb | MacBain 1890 |
| Mc | Mackintosh |
| McC | McConnochie 1898 |
| McC 1891 | McConnochie 1891 |
| McC 1895 | McConnochie 1895 |
| McC 1896 | McConnochie 1896 |
| McC 1923 | McConnochie 1923 |
| McC 1932 | McConnochie 1932 |
| Mco | M'Coss |
| Md | Macdonald Collection maps |
| Me | Mar Estate |
| Mf | Macfarlane's Geog. Coll., 1736, Mitchell, also Robertson 1847 |
| Mg | MacGillivray |
| Mi | Michie 1908 |
| Mi 1877 | Michie 1877 |
| Mic | Michie 1896 |
| Mil | Milne 1912 |
| Miln | Milne 1908 |
| Milne | Milne 1897 |
| Ml | Macleod |
| Mm | Mar map |
| Mo | Moll map |
| Moi | Moir 1975 |
| Mp | MacPherson 1906 |
| Mpj | MacPherson, J von Lamont |
| Ms | M Smith |
| Mu | Murray |
| | |
| N | Nicolaisen 1976 |
| Ni | Nicolaisen 1960 |

| | |
|---|---|
| Nic | Nicolaisen 1961 |
| Ne | Neil 1947 |
| Nei | Neil 1933 |
| Nw | Nethersole-Thompson & Watson |
| O | Ogston |
| Od | Ó Dónaill |
| Opr | OPR (Old Parochial Registers) |
| OS | Ordnance Survey |
| OSn | Ordnance Survey Object Name Books |
| P | Parker |
| Pa | Paul |
| Pb | Poll Book, Stuart |
| Pe | Pennant |
| Pj | Press & Journal |
| Po | Pont map, National Library of Scotland |
| Pr | Parish registers, from A |
| R | RHP in Register House plans |
| Ra | RA in Royal Archives, Windsor Castle Library |
| Ram | Royal Archives map |
| Rc | Revue Celtique |
| Re | Reg. Episc. Aberd., C Innes, from M |
| Rg | RMS in Reg. of Great Seal, J M Thomson, from M |
| Ri | Records of Invercauld, Michie 1901 |
| Rj | Ruddiman Johnston map, Dinnet Estate |
| Rlh | Rentaill of the Lordschipe of Huntlye, Stuart 1849 |
| Rli | Rental of Lands etc of Invercauld |
| Ro | Robertson map |
| Rob | Robertson 1933 |
| Robe | Robertson 1798 |
| Ros | Ross |
| Roy | Roy, British Library maps |
| Rt | Reid & Tewnion |
| S | Stirton |
| Sc | Scott |
| Sch | School of Scottish Studies, tape-recordings |
| Scr | Scrope |
| Sd | Scottish Development Department |

| | |
|---|---|
| Sg | Seton Gordon 1925 |
| Sg 1948 | Seton Gordon 1948 |
| Sgs | Scottish Gaelic Studies |
| Sh | Service of Heirs, Retours, Thomson 1811–16, from A |
| Si | Sissons |
| Sim | Sim |
| Simp | Simpson 1947 |
| Simps | Simpson 1929 |
| Simpso | Simpson 1943 |
| Sin | Sinton |
| Sm | A Smith |
| Sto | Statistical Account (Old), Sinclair |
| Stob | Stobie map 1783 |
| Stu | Stuart 1865 |
| Stua | Stuart 1874 |
| Stuar | Stuart 1877 |
| T | Transactions of the Gaelic Society of Inverness |
| Ta | Taylor |
| Tay | Taylor map |
| Tayl | A & H Tayler 1932, 1933 |
| Tayle | A & H Tayler 1928 |
| Th | Thomson map |
| U | Uncommon, heard from 1–3 informants |
| V | Victoria 1868 |
| Va | Valuation Book, Anonymous 1802 |
| Vd | A View of the Diocese of Aberdeen 1732, in Robertson 1843 |
| Vi | Victoria 1884 |
| Vr 1, 2, 3, 4 | Valuation Roll 1860 Lamont & Fimister, 70, 80, 92 Russell |
| W | Watson 1926 |
| W 1904 | Watson 1904 |
| Wa | A Watson 1975 |
| Wade | Wade map |
| Wav | Waverley Press map, Anonymous 1972 |
| Wi | Wills |
| Wy | Wyness |

Numbers e.g. T30, 107 (Trans. of the Gaelic Society of Inverness, Vol. 30, page 107), refer to volume and page, or years (list below). Pairs of capital letters other than OS show the initials of the informants who gave unusually interesting information such as a Gaelic pronunciation or a story with the name; their full names can be found by referring to Table 4.

*Abbreviations for years*

| | | | | | | | | | | | |
|---|---|---|---|---|---|---|---|---|---|---|---|
| Ab | 1 | 1474 | Ab | 18 | 1675 | Anon | 3 | 1605 | Ce | 5 | 1881 |
| | 2 | 84 | | 19 | 6 | | 4 | 32 | | 6 | 91 |
| | 3 | 1501 | | 20 | 9 | | 5 | 3 | Cpb | 1 | 1730 |
| | 4 | 3 | | 21 | 80 | | 6 | 5 | | 2 | 8 |
| | 5 | 7 | | 22 | 6 | | 7 | 8 | | 3 | 82 |
| | 6 | 14 | Aj | 1 | 1666 | | 8 | 40 | | 4 | 8 |
| | 7 | 35 | | 2 | 1706 | | 9 | 9 | | 5 | 1825 |
| | 7a | 6 | | 3 | 15 | | 10 | 50 | | 6 | 6 |
| | 8 | 52 | | 4 | 6 | | 11 | 4 | | 7 | 9 |
| | 9 | 3 | | 5 | 68 | | 12 | 6 | | 8 | 32 |
| | 10 | 99 | | 6 | 89 | | 13 | 9 | | 9 | 3 |
| | 11 | 1607 | | 7 | 1819 | Blm | 1, 1a | 1750 | | 9a | 43 |
| | 12 | 14 | | 8 | 1906 | | 2 | 1 | | 10 | 65–71 |
| | 13 | 20 | | 9 | 10 | | 3 | 3 | Cr | 1 | 1703 |
| | 14 | 35 | | 10 | 1 | Ce | 1 | 1841 | | 2 | 4 |
| | 15 | 38 | Ande | | 1656 | | 2 | 51 | | 3 | 5 |
| | 16 | 39 | Anon | 1 | 1602 | | 3 | 61 | | 4 | 6 |
| | 17 | 69 | | 2 | 4 | | 4 | 71 | | 5 | 7 |

*Abbreviations for years contd.*

| | | |
|---|---|---|
| Cr | 6 | 1708 |
| | 7 | 9 |
| | 8 | 10 |
| | 9 | 1 |
| | 10 | 2 |
| | 11 | 3 |
| | 12 | 4 |
| | 13 | 5 |
| | 14 | 6 |
| | 15 | 7 |
| | 16 | 8 |
| | 17 | 9 |
| | 18 | 20 |
| | 19 | 1 |
| | 20 | 2 |
| | 21 | 3 |
| | 22 | 4 |
| | 23 | 5 |
| | 24 | 6 |
| | 25 | 7 |
| | 26 | 8 |
| | 27 | 9 |
| | 28 | 30 |
| | 29 | 1 |
| | 30 | 2 |
| | 31 | 3 |
| | 32 | 4 |
| | 33 | 5 |
| | 34 | 6 |
| | 35 | 7 |
| | 36 | 8 |
| | 37 | 9 |
| | 37a | 40 |
| | 38 | 2 |
| | 38a | 3 |
| | 39 | 4 |
| | 40 | 5 |
| | 41 | 6 |
| | 42 | 7 |
| | 43 | 8 |
| | 44 | 9 |
| | 45 | 50 |
| | 46 | 1 |
| | 47 | 2 |
| | 48 | 3 |
| | 49 | 4 |
| | 50 | 6 |
| | 51 | 96 |
| | 52 | 7 |
| | 53 | 1803 |
| | 54 | 6 |
| | 55 | 14 |
| | 56 | 36 |
| | 57 | 39 |
| | 58 | 51 |
| Crg | 1 | 1771 |
| | 2 | 86 |
| | 3 | 97 |
| | 4 | 9 |
| | 5 | 1800 |
| | 6 | 1 |
| | 7 | 3 |
| | 8 | 8 |
| | 9 | 10 |

| | | |
|---|---|---|
| Crg | 10 | 1814 |
| | 11 | 5 |
| | 12 | 6 |
| | 13 | 20 |
| | 14 | 4 |
| | 15 | 7 |
| | 16 | 8 |
| | 17 | 9 |
| | 18 | 30 |
| | 19 | 1 |
| Dms | 1 | 1284 |
| | 2 | 1559 |
| | 3 | 1600 |
| | 4 | 20 |
| | 5 | 36 |
| | 6 | 8 |
| | 7 | 17th century |
| | 8 | 1663 |
| | 9 | 4 |
| | 10 | 5 |
| | 11 | 9 |
| | 12 | 81 |
| | 13 | 86–91 |
| | 14 | 1700 |
| | 15 | 8 |
| | 16 | 14 |
| | 17 | 1700–30 |
| | 18 | 1715–16 |
| | 19 | 1730 |
| | 20 | 2 |
| | 21 | 5 |
| | 22 | 44 |
| | 23 | 6 |
| | 24 | 61 |
| | 25 | 89 |
| G | 1 | 1535 |
| | 1a | 1611 |
| | 2 | 3 |
| | 2a | 4 |
| | 3 | 5 |
| | 4 | 20 |
| | 5 | 30 |
| | 6 | 2 |
| | 7 | 8 |
| | 8 | 9 |
| | 9 | 80 |
| | 10 | 2 |
| | 11 | 96 |
| | 12 | 7 |
| | 13 | 1718 |
| | 14 | 23 |
| | 15 | 4 |
| | 16 | 5 |
| | 17 | 6 |
| | 18 | 40 |
| | 19 | c.1750 |
| | 20 | 2 |
| | 21 | 6 |
| | 22 | 8 |
| | 23 | 66 |
| | 24 | 73 |
| | 25 | 8 |
| | 26 | 81 |
| | 27 | 3 |

| | | |
|---|---|---|
| G | 28 | 1785 |
| | 29 | 9 |
| | 30 | 1806 |
| | 30a | c.1812 |
| | 31 | 1815 |
| | 32 | 7 |
| | 33 | 1813–42 |
| | 34 | 1827 |
| | 35 | 66 |
| | 36 | 7 |
| Im | 1 | Early, undated |
| | 2 | prob. 1700s |
| | 3 | 1743 |
| | 4 | c.1750 |
| | 5 | 1775 |
| | 6 | Undated |
| | 7 | 1787 |
| | 8 | prob. late 1700s |
| | 9 | 1798 |
| | 10 | 1810 |
| | 11 | 1826 |
| Inn | 1 | 1497 |
| | 2 | 1506 |
| | 3 | 31 |
| | 4 | 1677 |
| Inne | | 1275 |
| Io | 1 | 1620 |
| | 2 | 32 |
| | 3 | 3 |
| | 4 | 4 |
| | 4a | 1632 or 1662 |
| | 5 | 1662 |
| | 6 | 4 |
| | 7 | 81 |
| | 8 | 2 |
| | 9 | 3 |
| | 10 | 99 |
| | 11 | 1702 |
| | 12 | 7 |
| | 13 | 8 |
| | 14 | 10 |
| | 15 | 3 |
| | 16 | 26 |
| | 17 | 7 |
| | 18 | 30 |
| | 19 | 1 |
| | 20 | 2 |
| | 21 | 4 |
| | 22 | 5 |
| | 23 | 9 |
| | 24 | 43 |
| | 25 | 4 |
| | 25a | 18th century |
| | 26 | 1752 |
| | 27 | 4 |
| | 28 | 6 |
| | 29 | 7 |
| | 30 | 60 |
| | 31 | 1 |
| | 32 | 2 |
| | 33 | 3 |
| | 34 | 4 |
| | 35 | 5 |
| | 36 | 6 |

| | | |
|---|---|---|
| Io | 37 | 1767 |
| | 38 | 8 |
| | 39 | 9 |
| | 40 | 70 |
| | 41 | 2 |
| | 42 | 3 |
| | 43 | 4 |
| | 43a | prob. late 1700s |
| | 44 | 1778 |
| | 45 | 81 |
| | 46 | 3 |
| | 47 | 6 |
| | 48 | 7 |
| | 49 | 8 |
| | 50 | 9 |
| | 51 | 90 |
| | 52 | 1 |
| | 53 | 2 |
| | 53a | 3 |
| | 54 | 4 |
| | 55 | 5 |
| | 56 | 6 |
| | 57 | 7 |
| | 58 | 8 |
| | 59 | 9 |
| | 60 | 1800 |
| | 60a | 1 |
| | 61 | 2 |
| | 62 | 5 |
| | 63 | 6 |
| | 64 | 7 |
| | 65 | 8 |
| | 66 | 9 |
| | 67 | 10 |
| | 68 | 2 |
| | 69 | 6 |
| | 70 | 8 |
| | 71 | 9 |
| | 73 | 23 |
| | 74 | 8 |
| | 75 | 32 |
| | 76 | 41 |
| | 77 | 51 |
| | 78 | 4 |
| | 79 | 5 |
| | 80 | 8 |
| | 81 | 1912 |
| Lp | 1 | 1733 Io |
| | 2 | 85 Me |
| | 3 | 1843 G |
| | 4 | 8 G |
| | 5 | 56 Io |
| Mc | 1 | 1620 |
| | 2 | 8 |
| | 3 | 32 |
| | 4 | 3 |
| | 5 | 4 |
| | 6 | 42 |
| | 7 | 7 |
| | 8 | 9 |
| | 9 | 61 |
| | 10 | 2 |
| | 11 | 4 |
| | 12 | 6 |

*Abbreviations for years contd.*

| | | |
|---|---|---|
| Mc | 13 | 1675 |
| | 14 | 9 |
| | 15 | 80 |
| | 16 | 3 |
| | 17 | 93 |
| | 18 | 1732 |
| | 19 | 3 |
| | 20 | 7 |
| | 21 | 46 |
| | 22 | 7 |
| | 23 | 52 |
| | 24 | 61 |
| | 25 | 72 |
| | 26 | 80 |
| Md | 1 | 1854 |
| | 2 | 63 |
| | 3 | c.1856–63 |
| | 4 | 1856 |
| | 5 | 1800s |
| | 6 | 1883 |
| | 7 | 4 |
| | 8 | 4 |
| | 9 | 1880s |
| | 10 | 1880s |
| | 11 | late 1800s |
| | 12 | late 1800s |
| Me | 1 | 1673 |
| | 2 | 92 |
| | 3 | 99 |
| | 4 | 1707 |
| | 5 | 26 |
| | 6 | 30 |
| | 7 | 1 |
| | 8 | 2 |
| | 9 | 3 |
| | 10 | 6 |
| | 11 | 46 |
| | 12 | 51 |
| | 13 | 6 |
| | 14 | 7 |
| | 15 | 64 |
| | 16 | 76 |
| | 17 | 82 |
| | 18 | 4 |
| | 19 | 9 |
| | 20 | 1809 |
| | 21 | 34 |
| | 22 | 35 |
| | 23 | 69 |
| | 24 | late 1800s |
| Opr | 1 | 1719 |
| | 1a | 21 |
| | 1b | 2 |
| | 1c | 3 |
| | 1d | 5 |
| | 1e | 8 |
| | 2 | 9 |
| | 3 | 43 |
| | 4 | 4 |
| | 5 | 5 |
| | 6 | 9 |
| | 7 | 51 |
| | 8 | 3 |
| | 9 | 4 |

| | | |
|---|---|---|
| Opr | 9a | 1700s, probably mid 1750s |
| | 10 | 1756 |
| | 11 | 8 |
| | 12 | 60 |
| | 13 | 4 |
| | 14 | 5 |
| | 15 | 6 |
| | 16 | 8 |
| | 17 | 9 |
| | 18 | 70 |
| | 19 | 2 |
| | 20 | 3 |
| | 21 | 4 |
| | 21a | 6 |
| | 22 | 7 |
| | 23 | 80 |
| | 24 | 1 |
| | 24a | 3 |
| | 25 | 4 |
| | 25a | 5 |
| | 26 | 7 |
| | 27 | 8 |
| | 28 | 9 |
| | 29 | 90 |
| | 30 | 1 |
| | 31 | 2 |
| | 32 | 3 |
| | 33 | 4 |
| | 34 | 5 |
| | 35 | 8 |
| | 36 | 9 |
| | 37 | 1801 |
| | 38 | 2 |
| | 38a | 3 |
| | 38b | 4 |
| | 39 | 5 |
| | 40 | 6 |
| | 41 | 8 |
| | 41a | 12 |
| | 41b | 3 |
| | 41c | 4 |
| | 41d | 6 |
| | 41e | 8 |
| | 42 | 9 |
| | 43 | 20 |
| | 44 | 1 |
| | 45 | 2 |
| | 46 | 3 |
| | 47 | 25 |
| | 47a | 6 |
| | 48 | 7 |
| | 49 | 8 |
| | 50 | 9 |
| | 51 | 30 |
| | 52 | 1 |
| | 53 | 2 |
| | 54 | 3 |
| | 55 | 5 |
| | 55a | 7 |
| | 56 | 9 |
| | 57 | 40 |
| | 58 | 1 |

| | | |
|---|---|---|
| Opr | 59 | 1842 |
| | 60 | 4 |
| | 61 | 7 |
| | 62 | 9 |
| | 63 | 51 |
| | 64 | 2 |
| | 65 | 3 |
| R | 1 | 1725 |
| | 1a | c.1735 |
| | 2 | mid 1700s |
| | 2a | 1700s |
| | 2b | 1773 |
| | 3 | 88 |
| | 4 | 90 |
| | 5 | prob. late 1700s |
| | 6 | c.1800 |
| | 7 | 1808 |
| | 8 | 9 |
| | 9 | 26 |
| | 10 | 6 |
| | 11 | 6 |
| | 12 | 7 |
| | 13 | 7 |
| | 14 | 8 |
| | 14a | 1825–66 |
| | 15 | 1864 |
| | 16 | 7 |
| | 17 | late 1800s |
| | 18 | 1895 |
| Ra | 1 | 1732 |
| | 2 | 3 |
| | 2a | 1733–35 |
| | 3 | 1735 |
| | 4 | 81 |
| | 5 | 5 |
| | 6 | 6 |
| | 7 | 94 |
| | 8 | 1804 |
| | 9 | 9 |
| | 10 | 24 |
| | 11 | 9 |
| | 12 | 32 |
| | 13 | 4 |
| | 14 | 47 |
| | 15 | 8 |
| Ri | 1 | 1563 |
| | 2 | 1620 |
| | 3 | 32 |
| | 4 | 3 |
| | 4a | 5 |
| | 5 | 50 |
| | 6 | 8 |
| | 7 | 60 |
| | 8 | 7 |
| | 9 | 75 |
| | 9a | 6 |
| | 10 | 81 |
| | 11 | 3 |
| | 12 | 95 |
| | 13 | 6 |
| | 14 | 9 |
| | 15 | 1702 |
| | 16 | 5 |
| | 17 | 7 |

| | | |
|---|---|---|
| Ri | 18 | 1708 |
| | 19 | 9 |
| | 20 | 21 |
| | 21 | 6 |
| | 22 | 31 |
| | 23 | 34 |
| | 23a | 7 |
| | 23b | 9 |
| | 24 | 40 |
| | 24a | 5 |
| | 24b | 9 |
| | 25 | 52 |
| | 26 | 9 |
| | 27 | 60 |
| | 28 | 2 |
| | 29 | 5 |
| | 30 | 6 |
| | 31 | 9 |
| | 32 | 72 |
| | 32a | 4 |
| | 33 | 7 |
| | 34 | 81 |
| | 34a | 2 |
| | 35 | 3 |
| | 36 | 7 |
| | 37 | 8 |
| | 38 | 96 |
| | 39 | 8 |
| | 39a | 1806 |
| | 40 | 11 |
| Rli | 1 | 1681 |
| | 2 | 3 |
| | 3 | 91 |
| | 4 | 5 |
| | 5 | 8 |
| | 6 | 9 |
| | 7 | 1707 |
| | 8 | 11 |
| | 9 | 2 |
| | 10 | 3 |
| | 11 | 4 |
| | 12 | 21 |
| | 13 | 3 |
| | 14 | 34 |
| | 15 | 40 |
| | 16 | 6 |
| | 17 | 8 |
| | 18 | 61 |
| | 19 | 3 |
| | 20 | 5 |
| | 21 | 6 |
| | 22 | 70 |
| | 23 | 1797–1798 |
| S | 1 | 1451 |
| | 2 | 1529 |
| | 3 | 38 |
| | 4 | 9 |
| | 5 | 64 |
| | 6 | 1632 |
| | 7 | 5 |
| | 8 | 51 |
| | 9 | 5 |
| | 10 | 94 |
| | 11 | 1701 |

*Abbreviations for years contd.*

| S | 12 | 1707 | S | 17 | 1741 | S | 23 | 1825 | Tayl | | 1667 |
|---|----|------|---|----|------|---|----|------|------|---|------|
| | 13 | 10 | | 18 | 88 | | 24 | 31 | Vr | 1 | 1860 |
| | 14 | 5 | | 19 | 9 | | 25 | 2 | | 2 | 9 |
| | 14a | 8 | | 20 | 90 | | 26 | 1834–8 | | 3 | 79 |
| | 15 | 9 | | 21 | 3 | | 27 | 40 | | 4 | 92 |
| | 16 | 20 | | 22 | 1814 | | | | | | |

From the Old Caledonian forest, looking up Glen Lui to the November snow on Carn Crom (left) and the conical Derry Cairngorm (right). A typical scene in the glens of Mar, below the Cairngorms.

## TABLE 3. PHONETIC SCHEME

Most phonetic sounds below refer to the accompanying English words as spoken in English by locally-reared and locally educated people in Upper Deeside. The words in parentheses are as spoken by such people in Scots, or in Gaelic as spoken by the very few locally-reared and locally-educated people in Upper Deeside who still use or recently used some of the local Gaelic dialect, and other sounds in French, German, and RP ('received pronunciation' or educated southern English (O'Connor 1973)).

*Vowels*

| | |
|---|---|
| a | f<u>a</u>t |
| ɑ | w<u>a</u>st (Scots), ch<u>a</u>rm (RP) |
| ɐ | between a and ʌ, loch<u>a</u>n (Scots) |
| æ | between a and ɛ, p<u>a</u>t (RP) |
| ɛ | m<u>e</u>t |
| ɜ̈ | h<u>e</u>r |
| e | t<u>a</u>ke |
| ẹ | between ɛ and e, sn<u>e</u>ck (Scots) |
| ə | gard<u>e</u>ner, bitt<u>e</u> (German) |
| i | sh<u>ee</u>p |
| ɪ | m<u>i</u>d |
| ɔ | p<u>o</u>t |
| ọ | between ɔ and o, b<u>o</u>nnie (Scots) |
| o | b<u>o</u>ne |
| œ | ɛ with lips rounded, p<u>eu</u>r (French) |
| ʊ | o with lips spread, c<u>ao</u>chan (Gaelic) |
| u | r<u>oo</u>t |
| ɯ | u with lips spread |
| ʌ | s<u>u</u>n |

*Diphthongs*

| | |
|---|---|
| ae | h<u>igh</u> |
| ai | h<u>igh</u> (RP) |
| au | ar<u>ou</u>nd (RP), gr<u>au</u> (German) |
| ei | b<u>ei</u>nne (Gaelic) |
| ɛi | h<u>ei</u>ght |
| əi | <u>o</u> the (Scots) |
| iɐ | l<u>ia</u>th (Gaelic) |
| iɔ | <u>ia</u>sgair (Gaelic) |
| iɯ | sl<u>ia</u>bh (Gaelic) |
| ɔi | b<u>oy</u> (RP) |
| oi | b<u>oy</u> (Scots) |
| ou | bh<u>o</u>gha (Gaelic) |
| ʌu | ar<u>ou</u>nd |
| uɐ | r<u>ua</u>dh (Gaelic) |
| uə | f<u>ua</u>r (Gaelic) |
| ui | b<u>ui</u>dhe (Gaelic) |

Where these combinations are not diphthongs but are pronounced as two vowels with a hiatus between them, . is inserted between them to distinguish from diphthongs. Other combinations such as ei, ia, oe and oi are pronounced as two separate vowels with a hiatus between them, so a . between them is unnecessary.

### Consonants

| | | | |
|---|---|---|---|
| ʤ | <u>j</u>et | h | breathing sound |
| ŋ | si<u>ng</u> | ṇ | syllabic n in Gair<u>n</u>, between gern and gerən; also |
| ɲ | bei<u>nn</u>e (Gaelic) | | occurs with l, m, r and other consonants |
| ʃ | <u>sh</u>un | ' | (upper position) primary stress on the following |
| ʧ | <u>ch</u>in | | syllable |
| θ | <u>th</u>ing | ͵ | (lower position) secondary stress on the following |
| ð | <u>th</u>is | | syllable |
| ʒ | mea<u>s</u>ure | : | long vowel (after the vowel in question) |
| ç | <u>h</u>eich (Scots), i<u>ch</u> (German) | · | (upper position) half-long vowel (after the vowel in |
| χ | lo<u>ch</u>, Ba<u>ch</u> (German) | | question) |
| ɣ | <u>ch</u> in loch voiced, a<u>gh</u>aidh (Gaelic) | . | (lower position) between two vowels or consonants, |
| j | <u>y</u>ou | | (a) to avoid ambiguity in pronunciation, as in the |
| hw | <u>wh</u>en | | Cowie Burn ðɪˈkʌu.iˈbʌrn, (b) to show a hiatus |
| ḅ, ḍ, g̣ | labial, dental, palatal, tending towards p, t, k (Gaelic) | | between two vowels that usually form a diphthong but |
| ļ | palatised liquid l (Gaelic) | | in this case are pronounced as two separate vowels. |

*Alexander* (differences from our scheme)

| | |
|---|---|
| ȫ | French p<u>eu</u>r |
| . | same as our : |

*Macdonald*

In Macdonald's pronunciations, an accent shows which syllable is stressed, and 'at the same time the quantity of the vowel—the grave accent (à) denoting the broad, and the acute accent (á) the short, vowel sound'.

## TABLE 4. LIST OF INFORMANTS

| Name of informant | Area for which the informant gave names | Name of informant | Area for which the informant gave names |
|---|---|---|---|
| Charles A Abel | Balmoral | Shirley Esson | Cromar |
| Edward M S Adams | Ballater | Alwyne A C Farquharson | Invercauld |
| Joy F Adams | Ballater | William S Farquharson | Inchmarnoch |
| Alexander Anderson | Inchmarnoch | Ronald A Finnie | Crathie |
| Elizabeth J Anderson | Don march | Charles Forbes | Glen Tanar, Inchmarnoch |
| Emily Anderson | Don march | Gordon Forbes | Glen Gairn |
| Harry J Anderson | Glen Gairn | Jane Forbes | Glen Gairn |
| Isabella Anderson | Glen Muick | Kenneth I Forbes | Glen Muick |
| John Anderson | Don march | William Forbes | Mar |
| Robert Anderson | Don march | William J R Forbes | Glen Muick, Glen Gairn |
| Alison J Angus | Crathie | Amy S Fraser | Glen Gairn |
| James A K Angus | Crathie | Charles J Fraser | Bridge of Gairn |
| Jean Bain | Upper Deeside | Constance G Fraser | Glen Muick |
| Jeannie M Bain | Dinnet | Dan Fraser | Glen Muick |
| Robert Bain | Crathie, Glen Gairn | David A Fraser | Glen Gairn |
| Alexander K Bernard | Braemar | Ernest L Fraser | Crathie |
| Annie Bey | Abergeldie | Ernest S Fraser | Crathie |
| Maggie J Bisset | Balmoral | Isabel Fraser | Glen Muick, Cromar |
| Robert Bisset | Balmoral, Cromar | Isobel M Fraser | Crathie |
| Robert Bruce | Glen Tanar | Margaret A Fraser | Glen Gairn |
| Allan Brodie | Glen Tanar | Thomas Fraser | Glen Muick |
| Mary W Brodie | Glen Tanar | Margaret Gibb | Glen Gairn |
| Christina H Calder | Bridge of Gairn | David W Gill | Corndavon, Crathie |
| Agnes M Cameron | Ballater, Glen Gairn | James Gillan | Glen Gairn, Crathie |
| Donald Campbell | Braemar | William Gillanders | Glen Gairn, Dinnet, Cromar |
| Mabel I Campbell | Braemar | Lewis Gillies | Ballater |
| George Cassie | Glen Muick | Louise M Gillies | Ballater |
| Jean E Cassie | Glen Muick, Inverey | Douglas J A Glass | Inchmarnoch |
| Robert C V Cook | Bovaglie | Douglas L Glass | Inchmarnoch |
| Elsie Coutts | Abergeldie | Frank Goldie | Tullich |
| Elizabeth A W Coutts | Inchmarnoch | Ann Gordon | Dinnet, Crathie |
| Francis Coutts | Inchmarnoch | Charles Gordon | Dinnet |
| James Coutts | Abergeldie | Elizabeth Gordon | Dinnet |
| Jane A Coutts | Cromar | George Gordon | Abergeldie, Balmoral |
| Joseph D Coutts | Balmoral | James Gordon | Glen Gairn |
| Walter Coutts | Glen Gairn, Crathie | John H S Gordon | Abergeldie |
| Gordon Croll | Ballater, Glen Muick | Mabel Gordon | Birkhall |
| James Cruickshank | Abergeldie | Seton P Gordon | Upper Deeside |
| Margaret Cruickshank | Abergeldie | Sheila I W Gordon | Corriemulzie |
| Helen Cummings | Gairnshiel | Alexander J Grant | Corndavon |
| Alexander Davidson | Glen Esk march | Alexandra E Grant | Corndavon |
| Alexander Dempster | Mar | Annie B Grant | Braemar |
| Alexander Dempster Jun. | Mar | Charles Grant† | Mar |
| Douglas Dempster | Mar | Elizabeth Grant | Crathie |
| Charles Downie | Crathie | Heather Grant | Mar |
| Euphemia Downie | Bridge of Gairn | Ian A Grant | Mar |
| Jane B Downie | Glen Gairn, Crathie | Joseph Grant | Braemar |
| William M Downie | Crathie, Glen Gairn, Ballater | Joseph Grant | Braemar, Clunie, Callater |
| Alexander B Duguid | Glen Gairn | Margaret J Grant | Crathie, Mar |
| George Duguid | Cromar | Seumas Grant | Spey march |
| Margaret J Duguid | Cromar | William Grant | Mar |
| Robert Duthie | Mar | William Grant | Glen Gairn |
| James Emslie | Glen Clunie, Callater | Ann K Greig | Bridge of Gairn, Morven |
| Alexander Esson | Cromar | Eliza Grubb | Inchmarnoch |
| Edward Esson | Balmoral | James Harper | Crathie |
| Ian A Esson | Crathie | John E Harper | Crathie |
| James Esson | Glen Girnock, Glen Muick | John Henderson | Glen Gairn, Crathie, Tullich |
| Jessie A Esson | Glen Muick | Margaret Henderson | Cromar |
| John Esson | Glen Feardar, Glen Gairn, Crathie | Robert A Henderson | Glen Gairn, Crathie, Tullich, Glen Clova march |
| Margaret Esson | Cromar | | |
| Mary M Esson | Crathie | James G Hepburn | Dee |
| Robert Esson | Cromar | J M Marcus Humphrey | Dinnet, Cromar |

| Name of informant | Area for which the informant gave names | Name of informant | Area for which the informant gave names |
|---|---|---|---|
| William Ironside | Spey march | Constance Morgan | Mar |
| William D Irvine | Dinnet | Jack Morgan | Mar |
| John W Jolly | Abergeldie | John Morgan | Mar |
| Ada R Kellas | Cromar | Mary Morgan | Mar |
| Agnes Kellas | Cromar | Bella Morrice | Inchmarnoch |
| James C Kellas | Cromar | Brock Nethersole-Thompson | Spey march |
| Andrew L Kemp | Crathie | Carrie Nethersole-Thompson | Spey march |
| Margaret J Kennedy | Girnock | Desmond Nethersole-Thompson | Spey march |
| John Leitch | Balmoral | James Niven | Don march |
| May H Leslie | Cromar | Mrs Niven | Don march |
| William Leslie | Glen Gairn | Bert Osler | Glen Esk march |
| Elizabeth Lobban | Mar | James Oswald | Glen Tanar, Dee |
| William Lobban | Mar | Derek P Petrie | Invercauld |
| Dolina Macdonald | Spey march | James R Phillips | Braemar |
| George C Mackie | Glen Gairn | Marie S Phillips | Braemar |
| James C Mackintosh | Corndavon, Crathie | Charles Pithie | Tullich |
| Helen M S Mackintosh | Crathie | Euphemia Pithie | Tullich |
| Peter Mackintosh | Mar | James D Porter | Dinnet, Cromar |
| John P Main | Clunie, Callater | Lily Porter | Dinnet, Cromar |
| Flora R Malcolm | Bridge of Gairn | Stanley Pottinger | Braemar |
| Frederick Malone | Glen Gairn | William Potts | Glen Esk and Clova marches |
| James McCartney | Mar, Braemar | Alexander Rae | Mar |
| Morag G McCartney | Mar, Braemar | Alexander Ramsay | Mar |
| Alastair McDonald | Cromar | Ernest Rattray | Glen Gairn |
| Alexander J McDonald | Mar, Invercauld, Braemar | Jane M Reid | Tullich |
| Belle McDonald | Braemar | Evelyn M M Reid | Bridge of Gairn |
| Donald McDonald | Mar, Invercauld, Braemar, Dee | James Reid | Bridge of Gairn |
| Elsie M McDonald | Cromar | George Rettie | Glen Gairn, Crathie |
| Harold McDonald | Ballater | Albert Robertson | Inchmarnoch, Dee |
| Helen McDonald | Mar, Braemar | John B Robertson | Glen Muick |
| Jessie M McDonald | Mar, Braemar | Margaret Robertson | Glen Clova march |
| Annie McDougall | Mar | Percy Robertson | Glen Muick |
| Charles McDougall† | Mar | Ronald Robertson | Glen Muick |
| William McDougall | Mar | David H Rose | Abergeldie, Braemar |
| James McGillivray | Inchmarnoch | Elizabeth B Rose | Mar, Braemar |
| Alastair J McGregor | Braemar | John M Rose | Birkhall |
| Colin McGregor | Inchmarnoch, Glen Tanar | Marjory J Rose | Birkhall |
| James D McGregor† | Braemar | David R Ross | Cromar |
| Mary A McGregor | Inchmarnoch, Glen Tanar | William Ross | Glen Gairn, Tullich |
| William L McGregor† | Balmoral | Eileen C S Scott | Mar |
| Andrew McGrory | Braemar | Robert L Scott | Mar |
| Agnes McHardy | Braemar | Robert E Shaw | Glen Clunie |
| Charles McHardy | Braemar | William J Sim | Glen Muick |
| Donald McHardy† | Balmoral | Colin G Simon | Cromar |
| Colin F McIntosh | Braemar, Invercauld, Dee | Leslie P Simon | Cromar |
| George P McIntosh | Braemar, Mar, Dee | Phyllis M Simon | Cromar |
| Alexander McLachlan | Braemar | Bella Simpson | Tullich |
| Ian A McLaren | Corriemulzie, Mar | Helen H Simpson | Tullich |
| Marie-Ann C W McPherson | Invercauld | Arthur Smith | Dee |
| Thomas McPherson | Invercauld, Dee | Lily Smith | Glen Gairn |
| Charles Melvin | Dinnet, Dee | John C Stammers | Mar, Braemar |
| William Merchant | Abergeldie | Frederick Stephen | Dee |
| Mary J Metcalfe | Mar | George Stewart | Cromar |
| Alexandra R Michie | Glen Muick | James Stewart | Glen Muick |
| Charles S Michie | Tullich | James Stewart | Cromar, Balmoral |
| Valerie M Michie | Ballater | Ruby Stewart | Cromar |
| William C Michie | Ballater | J Strang | Glen Tanar |
| Charles A Middleton | Bridge of Gairn | George Sturton | Ballater |
| Charles Milne | Glen Tanar, Inchmarnoch | Graham Sturton | Glen Gairn, Tullich, Ballater |
| Dolly Mitchell | Tullich | William C Thain | Invercauld |
| James Moir | Glen Esk march | | |
| Catherine Morgan | Mar | | |

| Name of informant | Area for which the informant gave names | Name of informant | Area for which the informant gave names |
|---|---|---|---|
| Albert A Thomson | Crathie, Balmoral | Louise R Watt | Birkhall |
| Gordon C Thomson | Crathie, Balmoral | Hugh D Welsh† | Braemar |
| Annie J S Tough | Bridge of Gairn | James F Williams | Dinnet, Cromar |
| James Troup | Don march | Bryan P Wright | Glen Gairn |
| Alexander Walker | Glen Tanar | Charles A Wright | Balmoral, Abergeldie, Glen Muick, Braemar, Dee |
| Elizabeth A Watt | Inchmarnoch, Dinnet | | |
| George S Watt | Inchmarnoch, Dinnet | Elizabeth J Wright | Upper Deeside |
| James G Watt | Birkhall | John Wright | Callater |

† Died before our study began in 1973.

# DETAILED GUIDE TO USE OF MAIN LIST

This section gives extra details not covered in the brief guide above. We discuss topics below in the order in which they arise for a given name in the list.

## Which names are included and excluded

Apart from exceptions noted below, we include all names found; local people do not separate 'important' from 'less important' names, and any such division by us would be subjective and arbitrary.

*Excluded:*

1. Names invented and used by only one family.
2. Non-specific names such as the Curling Pond, the Golf Course and the Churchyard, and estate names of houses such as the Stables, Gardener's Cottage, and Bridge Lodge (which can be found in electoral registers, valuation rolls, and postal records).
3. Hotels.
4. Postal and current OS names of streets, dwellings, and other buildings in villages or scattered hamlets, unless they retain a former name that is not elsewhere in the list (as in Ford House). The villages or hamlets are:—Dinnet (west to Clarack), Cambus o' May (hotel west to Glencolstane), Inchmarnoch, Ballater (out the Braemar road as far as the Pass of Ballater road), the foot of Girnock around Littlemill, Abergeldie (Khantore north to Mains of Abergeldie), Balmoral-Crathie (from the distillery north by Easter Balmoral and Aspenholm to Crathie, east to Fergach Cottages, and west to Tynabaich and houses around Balmoral Castle), Balnault-Inver (Balnault Cottages west to Hamewith), Braemar (south to Golf Club House, north to Braemar Castle, west to the top of Chapel Brae), and Inverey (Craigview west to Pinewood). Many house names alter with change of ownership, sometimes replacing local traditional names. A study of place names should not be confused with a house directory, and we saw no point in giving information available in electoral registers, valuation rolls, and postal records.
5. In rural areas, postal and current OS names of inhabited houses and other buildings where these have been built in the last twenty years or where new owners have ignored former OS names or locally-used names and have invented new names in English, lowland Scots, or Gaelic. However, we checked all Gaelic names of rural houses carefully, in case they were genuine old names. One can tell new Gaelic names of houses in Deeside by their contrived construction (Darroch Learg) or spelling (Sluiemohr, Tigh na Rosan), or by their classic Gaelic spelling even though local written Gaelic has died out (An Grianan, Tom Meann).
6. Roads and paths going to places in the list and named after these places (Balmenach road, Creag nam Ban path). Many of these names change according to one's position, the main road west of Ballater being the Braemar road or Crathie road, but east of Braemar the Ballater road, Crathie road, or Aberdeen road.
7. Hundreds of rock, snow, and ice climbs, described in the Scottish Mountaineering Club's Climbers' Guides.
8. Grouse butts and drives, tracks bulldozed for shooters, huts for shooters and fishers, and 'beats' on hill and river, unless these names refer to a local feature whose name does not appear in the list, or unless the name describes the butts, drives etc themselves (as in the Juniper Butts). Grouse moors cover big tracts of Upper Deeside, and about every mile or two a line of butts faces a drive over part of the moor. These lines have their own names, mostly after hills or other features that also appear in the list. Fishers name the salmon fishings on Dee by sub-divisions based largely on estate boundaries. Three maps by Parker, Scott and Waverley Press show most of them; we give other, unpublished ones below in italics. (From east to west on the north side lie the fishings of the Dinnet Water, the Monaltrie Water, the Morven Water, the Lower Invercauld Water, the *Crathie Beat* of the Invercauld Water from Balmoral Bridge up to the Bridge of Dee, then on both sides the *Clunie Water* or the *Private Water* up past Invercauld House to the Mar march. From east to west on the south side are the Glen Tanar Water, the Cambus o' May Water (locally the Cambus Water, ðɪ'kamɐs'watɛr), the Glenmuick Water, the Birkhall Water, the Abergeldie Water, and the Balmoral Water.)
9. All names of fields if these involve field numbers from OS maps, or other numbers such as park 1 and park 2, and general names for all fields on each farm, as in the Deecastle Parks.
10. Names with Davoch (the Davoch of Sterin, Quarter Davoch of Aberarder) in old books and documents, referring to measures of land rather than place names, except for one—the Half Dabhach—that survives as a currently-used place name.
11. Cairns on hills whose names are in the list (the Ben Macdui cairn).
12. Doubtful, erroneous and bogus names (in Appendix 1).

## Places with more than one name

1. *A place with an OS name and another name.* We give details under the OS name even if we think it incorrect, as this is the name that people will see on current maps. We add the other name as a separate entry, and ask readers to look under the OS name for details.

2. *Villages or inhabited houses.* These appear under the OS name or electoral-register name. In the same entry we include any Gaelic names for the place.

3. *Places other than current habitations, and not on current OS maps.* We enter Gaelic names and lowland Scots or English names separately in the list if both exist, but include details under the Gaelic entry; the lowland Scots or English entry gives a cross-reference to the Gaelic one.

4. *Inhabited houses named after a closely adjacent feature (such as a burn or hillock) which also has the same name.* The two places usually have different grid references, so we give two entries. We exclude cases where the house has been named in the last twenty years.

5. *Places sharing part of the same name.* Example:—Easter Micras and Wester Micras. Other such cases are East, Mid and West; North and South; Upper, Middle and Lower or Nether; Fore and Back; Big and Little; Muckle and Little; and Meikle (OS) and Little. We give separate entries for each of these, and in some cases for the word that they share (as in Micras), if local people use it in a collective sense.

6. *Two or more alternative names for one place.* Example:—Allt Coire Buidhe, the Burn o Coire Buidhe, and the Coire Buidhe Burn, the first being usually the OS form, and the last usually the current form. We give the current one a brief entry in the list, but provide all details under the OS form. We do not put the second of the above three forms in a separate entry; nobody will find it in OS maps and very few will know it as a current local name, so we include details under the first form.

## Spelling of the name

*Removal of Gaelic a' by elision.* Where local pronunciations, books, or other papers provide no evidence that the genitive definite article occurs before a masculine noun, we omit it. Example:—Spelling in old records Dellachork, we give Dail a' Choirce; old spelling Dalchork, we give Dail Choirce, omitting the a' which often disappears in pronunciation, due to elision.

*Names in current 1:10000 or smaller-scale OS maps.* We enter them in our list as spelled in these maps, even if we believe the map name incorrect. If the OS name differs from local usage, we classify this in the following five ways, using 'from', 'locally', 'should be', 'classic form' and 'printers' errors':—

1. *From.* The OS name has incomplete spelling. Example:—Allt na Cloch (OS), from Allt na Cloiche.

2. *Locally.* The OS name differs slightly from local usage. (a) Example:—Carn na Drochaide (OS), locally Carn Drochaide—the current local pronunciation (and also early records in some cases) indicates no article na, so the OS form is probably incorrect. (b) In other cases the current local pronunciation has probably changed due to the local Gaelic grammar dying out, so the OS form may well be correct; if so, we say so. One can sometimes see various stages in the dying of the local grammar, for instance Allt a' Choire Ghuirm (OS), Allt Choir Ghorm (D in A), and now Allt Coire Gorm, and occasionally more recent changes as the Allt . . . Burn.

3. *Should be.* Example:—Coire an Fhir Bhogha, should be Coire Cadha an Fhir Bhogha. The OS form is incorrect in more than the minor way indicated in 2(a), for example, with at least one erroneous word other than an article.

4. *Classic form.* Example:—Allt a' Choire Bhoidheach, classic Gaelic form would be Allt a' Choire Bhoidhich.

5. *Printers' errors.* We have corrected all obvious printers' errors, such as Coire na Sqreuchaig, but do not mention them as such; printers' errors in one map edition usually do not occur in editions before or after.

*All other names.* We enter these in the list not necessarily as spelled in the OS 1869 map, other publications, or unpublished papers, but according to our decisions based on the name's local pronunciation and probable derivation.

We spell Gaelic names according to classic Gaelic form. Some nouns have different genders in different parts of the Highlands. Therefore, where a noun's gender in Deeside Gaelic can no longer be checked, the local usage today may possibly not be incorrect. Nevertheless, local people tend to drop cases and genders as Gaelic dies (Dorian 1976). For example, Beinn Mhor and A' Chlais become Beinn Mor and the Clais, and with some such common nouns the correct gender in Deeside Gaelic is known. Probably some less common words in names heard by us have also changed like this, and in such cases we give the form as in classic Gaelic. However in all such cases we add the original spelling or the phonetic pronunciation, so that readers can work out their own interpretations from the original data. In other cases the local pronunciation could represent either a genitive or dative singular, or other alternatives of case and number; we usually do not give these alternatives.

We break with tradition by spelling in Gaelic instead of lowland Scots or English for all names (except those in current OS maps) where the words are obviously Gaelic but where we do not know and cannot deduce the original spellings. Thus, we use some Gaelic spellings (such as Allt Bheidhneig) that appear in no Gaelic dictionary, but then the numerous English phonetic equivalents that often occur in maps and books, such as Bynack, Ballochan or Etchachan appear in no English dictionary either. We see no point in anglicising when it adds no information to do so. Similarly, we spell in lowland Scots instead of English for all names (except those in current OS maps) where most local people pronounce them in Scots, such as the Fuird Road.

When spelling according to classic Gaelic form, we follow Dwelly's dictionary. In some cases such as Ruighe and Sidhean, we spell as in the OS (1973) booklet 'Place Names on Maps of Scotland and Wales'; these changes accord with the preferred modern usage of Gaelic linguists. Our spellings of lowland Scots words rely on the Scottish National Dictionary by Grant & Murison, and of English words on the Oxford English Dictionary. Where we could not tell easily which language a name came from, we spell it in a somewhat phonetic form as if it were lowland Scots; most names of this sort occur in the eastern part of our study area, where lowland Scots predominates.

## References to sources of information

1. *Current OS 1:10000 and smaller-scale maps.* Example:—Allt Mor (OS). The name appears in current OS maps. If we give OS, with no other reference, we have found no other information about it; therefore, either the name has died out in local use or never existed

locally. If local people use a very different name for the same place we say so; such a difference casts doubt on the authenticity of the OS name.

2. *Early OS maps.* Example:—Allt Liath (OS 1869). The name is in the OS 1869 map but not in current OS maps.

3. *Other publications and unpublished papers.* We refer to these by abbreviations such as (A) for Alexander's book (see list in Table 2). If (A) follows the only phonetic symbols given, we have not heard the name locally, and so it has probably become extinct since Alexander's book (1952), or maybe even many years earlier when he did his field work.

4. *Informants.* Table 4 lists these.

### Location of the name

For map references from the national grid, we do not use letters such as NN and NO before the six-figure reference, because in no case does the same reference appear twice in our study area. For every location we laid a plastic transparent grid on maps at 1:10000 or 1:25000 so as to measure eastings and northings accurately to the nearest 100 m. If the six-figure point did not fall precisely on the location and might be confused with a second location, we added words such as 'north of'. For each stream we chose a point where the reference fell exactly on the stream, but for a big area such as a corrie we give a reference roughly in the middle of it. Phonetic symbols without a grid reference indicate that local informants remember the name but not the location.

Previous writers on place names in west Aberdeenshire did not give exact locations by map references or detailed descriptions, and this was also the case for numerous places mentioned in other documents. Many of these places are no longer commonly known, but we succeeded in tracing some of them by asking local people. We worked out many others by making a thorough examination of the area on foot. In such cases we put 'probably' before the grid references, unless there was no doubt. (For instance, Diack wrote of An Deamhas (the shears), a place in Glen Ey that 'looks like a set of sheep shears'. When we went there, we noticed a hillside with obvious indentations in the shape of a pair of sheep shears, which we had not noticed on aerial photographs or OS maps.) By these methods we have been able to identify the locations of numerous places no longer known by local people. Where old documents give place names without locations, we feel that it is worth making a major effort on the ground to locate them, as the record will then be more complete and satisfying.

### Pronunciation of the name by locally-reared people

For each name we give the usual phonetic sound as spoken by local people, except in cases where 'as above' means that the name is pronounced as in the previous name in the list. We add major variants, especially those spoken by informants who gave most names and other information. With names unknown to local folk today, we include spellings as in the original sources. These give a rough indication of what the pronunciation might have been. With these basic data provided, readers can decide about our Gaelic spellings and derivations for themselves.

We based our phonetic scheme (Table 3) on the International Phonetic Association (1963), with a few additions by ourselves in consultation with R D Clement and D Murison.

Where a place has two or three names, such as Allt Coire Buidhe, the Burn o Coire Buidhe, and the Coire Buidhe Burn, we give phonetics for the first, but for only one of the others.

We give Alexander's phonetic forms either for names not heard by us, or for names heard by us but with interesting extra information on pronunciation noted by him. He used fewer phonetic symbols than us, and did not show secondary stress. His phonetics for a few place names differ from ours. Ours are from informants using the local vernacular speech. In these cases, Alexander's agree with the more genteel pronunciations sometimes heard by us from other people who habitually speak English. Alexander relied on memory, after a long time. In 1945 he wrote, 'The sounds represented here are, as nearly as memory serves, those which the writer was accustomed to hear in the district from good Gaelic speakers of the last generation' (CCJ 15, 265). In 1952 he stated, 'It is now too late to hear the Braemar names used in Gaelic speech; but it is not too late to set down particulars of them as they were when the language was spoken there. . . . I have drawn largely on my own recollections of numerous contacts with Gaelic speakers of the district during the earlier part of the present century'. Our phonetic forms rest on memory only where informants had already died before the study began in 1973 (shown by a cross in the list in Table 4).

### Meaning of the name

#### Gaelic names

We used Dwelly's dictionary, and rarely Ó Dónaill's Irish dictionary. We give literal translations where possible, for example, Allt a' Choire Ghuirm or burn of the green corrie. A commoner type, Allt Coire Buidhe, usually becomes the Burn of Coire Buidhe or the Coire Buidhe Burn when anglicised, but we translate as burn of yellow corrie. Occasionally we refer to place-name studies in Scotland and Ireland, or publications on Gaelic language and folklore, where these help to elucidate Deeside names and their meanings.

### Early spellings or changes in the name

After the name's probable meaning, we give spellings as in early records, if these differ from the name entered in the alphabetical list. In some cases we add the year, but mostly use abbreviations to save space. Readers can find the year by taking the abbreviation in parentheses after the early spelling, and then looking it up under Table 2 or the References. To save space, we saw no point in duplicating all old spellings in Macdonald's book, but we do give a few key spellings from publications, and a larger selection from unpublished records found by ourselves. In a few cases where a name has changed in an interesting way over the centuries we provide a more complete account of successive spellings and years. We do not repeat all spellings from major books such as Alexander (1952). If our entry shows no published source and is not marked * (unpublished), the source can be found in Alexander or in our Addenda (p. 191).

# THE PLACE NAMES OF UPPER DEESIDE

# MAIN LIST OF PLACE NAMES

**Aberarder** (C, 213937), ˌabër'ardër, Scots (C) ˌe̥bër'e̥rdër, from Obair Ardair (3), ˌo̥bər'a:rdər (Sch), mouth of high water. Obaràrdair (Iop), Abererdor (Inn 4), Abrerdar (Cpb 9a). Low ground where Felagie Burn meets Feardar, including farmland there and part of the glen to the west up to Middleton of Aberarder. See Feardar Burn.

**Aberdeen Cottage** (OS, C, 377964), ˌe̥bër'din'ko̥tədʒ. Smith's house (R) in 1790 was on same site as present cottage. East of Ballater.

**Aberdeen Haugh\*** (R7, 14, C, 219926), ˌe̥bër'din'ha·χ. Formerly a grassy area with signs of cultivation, now under trees. An Alexander Aberdeen at Invercauld was mentioned in 1770 (Opr). East of Invercauld Bridge.

**Abergairn** (OS, C, 355974), ˌabër'gern̥, Scots (C) ˌe̥bër'gern̥, from Obair Ghàrain (5, A), ɔpər'garan (A), mouth of Gairn, see River Gairn for meaning. Obergharain (Gr), Abirgarny, Abirgerny (Inn 1), Abyrgardin (Inn 2), Abergardin (Inn 3), Abergaran (D). Formerly Wester Abergairn. Easter and Wester Aber Gardynes (Ab 12) and Abergairn Wester and Easter (Gr 60). A farm in lower Glen Gairn.

**The Abergairn Bank\*** (F, 354976 and 355975), ðıˌe̥bër'gern̥ 'baŋk. A collective name for two fields, the Red Croft and the Sheep Fank Park, on a hillside in Glen Gairn.

**Abergairn Castle** (OS, C, west of 359974), ˌabër'gern̥'kasəl. Gairn Castle (Brown 1), Castle Gairn (Gr). Also Baile an Lochain Castle (F), bɐ'lo̥χɐn'kasəl. Ruin north-west of Ballater.

**Abergeldie** (C), ˌabër'ge̥ldi, Scots (C) ˌe̥bër'ge̥ldi, from Obair Gheallaidh (3, Mp, D, A), ɔpər'juli (A), ˌo̥bər'jauli (Sch), mouth of Geldie or bright one, see Allt Gheallaidh. Aberzaldie (Anon 1), Abiryeldie, Aberzeldie in 1654 (Mf), Aberyeldy (R 1, Stuar), Opper-yūlli, yūllyi (D). Flat area around Abergeldie Castle.

**The Abergeldie Approach\*** (U, 289953), ðıˌabër'ge̥ldiˌa'protʃ. Private road to Abergeldie Castle.

**The Abergeldie Brig\*** (C, 287953), ðıˌe̥bër'ge̥ldi'brıg. Suspension bridge over Dee.

**Abergeldie Castle** (OS, C, 287953), ˌabër'ge̥ldi'kasəl. Formerly the Castle of Abergeldie (Brow). East of Crathie.

**Abergeldie Ferry** (Wy, c. 285953). Former ferry over Dee.

**The Abergeldie Opening\*** (U, 298954), ðıˌe̥bër'ge̥ldi'opn̥ën. Where the farmland of Abergeldie opens out to the west, as one goes up the road near Corby Hall.

**Abhainn Coich\*** See Quoich Water.

**Abhainn Feith Ardair\*** See Feardar Burn.

**Abhainn Garain\*** See River Gairn.

**The Ach a' Cheiridh Brig\*** (C, 088863), ðıˌa'çi·ri'brıg. A footbridge over Ey Burn beside the former farm of Ach a' Cheiridh (erroneously Auchelie (OS)).

**Achadh na Creige** (OS, 245927), field of the crag. A field on the derelict farm of Cinn na Creige in lower Gelder, below a crag.

**Ach a' Ghiubhais** (3, c. 202906), field of the fir. Achighouse, Ahighouse (Pb), Ach chighuis (R 1), Ach a' ghiuthais (D in A). A former farm east of Invercauld Bridge.

**Ach a' Mhadaidh** (3, 051926), field of the dog or wolf. Achavadie (Roy, Sg). Ruin of a farm in Glen Lui.

**Ach an Daimh\*** (3, 363002), field of the ox or stag. Auchindow (G 30), Achdaw (R 1, G 33). A former farm up Tullich Burn.

**Ach an Fhearainn\*** (3, U, 348926), aχ'ne̥rën, field of the land. A field in lower Glen Muick.

**Ach an Sgeich** (3, C, 167930), ˌaχən'ske̥ç (nasal e), field of the hawthorn. Achinscench (Fa), Auchinskench (Ri 17), Achinskeach (Mc 24), Ach-in-skēch (D). A former farm beside Invercauld.

**Ach an Sgeich Park\*** (165930). Auch na skaink Park (R 7). A group of fields at Invercauld.

**Ach an t-Sabhail** (3, C, 279005), ˌaχən'tʌul̥, field of the barn. Achan t'sabhail (Iop), Achintowl (R 1), Auchintoul (OS 1869). A former farm west of Gairnshiel.

**The Ach an t-Sabhail Park\*** (U, 279004), ðıˌaχən'tʌul̥'park. A field west of Gairnshiel.

**Ach Chadha\*** (4, probably 364016), field of the narrow pass. Achā (R 1), Acha, Auchaw, Achaw (G 19, 30, 33), Achas Upper and Nether (Mc 9). One document (G) gives Achas once and Acha or Auchaw many times, referring to the same place. Nearly all references gave Acha etc without an s at the end. As there were two places, Upper and Nether, the s was probably an English plural. A former farm up Tullich Burn.

**Ach Chòis** (3), field of the hollow. Achós or Achósh about Tullich (D).

**Ach Eich** (4, 292007), field of horse. Acheech (I, Ro). A former farm beside Gairnshiel.

**Ach Eich an Easa** (5, c. 200904), horse field of the cascade. Ach ich nes (Fa), Achichinness or Ballach Buoy (Cr 16), Auchichinness, Auchichness, Achichneas (Io 16, 17, 51), Auchichness (Ri 27), Achichness (Me 3). The meaning is doubtful, see Beinn nan Ciochan for more details. A former farm about the site of Garbh Allt Shiel, east of Invercauld Bridge.

**Ach Latharn** (6, 186012), field of ? mire, Latharn has been suggested speculatively as from Lath = mire (W 122). Auchlaarne (Io), Achlarne (Ri 17). On upper Gairn.

**Ach na Creige** (3, U, 340892), ˌaχnɐ'kreg, field of the crag. 'Auchoilzies, Upper and Neither Auchnacraig' (Ri 10) is probably an error and should have read 'Auchoilzies Upper and Neither, Auchnacraig' as there were two Aucholzies but only one Ach na Creige. A former farm in Glen Muick.

**Ach nan Cuithe Iomlan** (4, C, 192956), ˌaχnɐ'gɯimlən, field of the full cattle-folds or snow-drifts. Achnaguimalen (Roy), Auchnichuymalin, Achnancoimlin (Cr 27, 35), Auchnaguiumlan (Rli 19), Auchnagoimlan (I). A former farm up Feardar.

**The Ach nan Cuithe Iomlan Birks\*** (U, 191954), ðıˌaχnɐ 'gɯimlən'bërks. A scattered few birches in Glen Feardar.

**Ach nan Saighdear** (3, probably c. 129822), açnɐ'dadʒɐr (A), field of the soldiers. Auchnadadger (A). A former house at the Baddoch.

**Ach Uanan\*** (3, F, 321911), aχ'ɯɑnɐn, field of lambs, with Uanan probably a variant genitive plural. Auchuanan (G 5), Auchquhanan (In, Am). A slope of fertile grassland in Glen Girnock.

**The Admiral Tree\*** (F, 430927), ðı'admırəl'tri. A tree beside the road up Glen Tanar.

**(An) Aghaidh Gharbh** (OS, 2, F, 960904), ˌnʌɣi'garo, ðıˌʌgi 'garo, the rough face. An ughi gharu (D in A). A boulder-strewn slope on Beinn Bhrotain.

**Ailbhean** (3). An old name for the river at Braemar. The Legend of St Andrew tells of Chondrochedalvan, meaning bridge-end of Alvan. At this point, Clunie rushes between steep rocks, so the name probably comes from Ail = stone or rock, as in several other similar river names such as Allan, Elvan and Alvain (W 467–9).

**An t-Ailean** See An t-Ailean Mor.

**An t-Àilean** (3, 263016), the green. The Alin (D). A bog west of Gairnshiel.

**Àilean Choich** (6, F, 120910), between ˌalɐnˈχoɩç and ˌalɐnˈχuəç (JB), green of the Quoich, for meaning see Quoich Water. Alanchoich (R 1), Alen-chōich (D). The big flat area east of where Quoich joins Dee.

**An t-Àilean Mór** (2, F, 135915), ðɪˌalɐnˈmoːr, the big green. The Allan More (R 2). N d alen (D), ˈdalɐn, ˌdalɐnˈmoːr (Sch) come from An t-Àilean and An t-Àilean Mór. The flat marshy ground west of Braemar.

**Àilean nan Cearc*** (3, C, 140913), ˌalɐnɐˈgërk, green of the hens. A green west of Braemar, below a house now called Greenfield. Also the Green Field (F), ðɪˈgrinˈfild.

**Àilean nan Cearc** (3, C, 140912), as above. Allanagirk (OS 1869). Also now Greenfield (Er, C) ˈgrinˈfild. Hen Field, Henfield (Le, an address in Braemar area) was probably here. A house west of Braemar.

**Àilean Torr na h-Aibhne*** (3, 296959), green of mound of the river. Allan Tornahan (I). A grassy patch beside a hillock, east of Crathie.

**The Ailtridh Burn*** See the Balnault Burn.

**Ais an Tulaich*** (5, U, 342941), ˌaʃənˈtële, hill of the hillock; Tulach often becomes Tilly in lowland north-east Scotland (N). Hill of Ashentilly (In, Am). A little top on a hill ridge in lower Glen Muick.

**The Aisle** (OS, C, 268002), ðɪˈɛiˑl. Also MacDonald's Aisle (Cj 2). A family burial place for the MacDonalds, former landowners of Rineten near Gairnshiel.

**Aitionn Mór** (3, D, probably north-west of 266030), big juniper (D). Near the Sleach, west of Gairnshiel.

**Alehouse of Abergairn.** Ailhouse of Abergarden (Ab 8). A former place in lower Glen Gairn, with its own small area of farmland.

**Allanaquoich** (OS, C, 120914), ˌalɐnˈkoɩç, a farm taking its name from Ailean Choich, the big flat area where Quoich joins Dee. Alleinchoigh (G 18), Ellanaqueich (Roy), Alenchoich (Fa), Alanchoich (R 1). Also Muckle Allanaquoich or Easter Allanaquoich. Mikkel Allenaquoich, Big Alanquoich (Cr 5, 47), Easter Allanaquoich (Mc 19), Eister Alenquoich (Anon 9).

**The Allanaquoich Boat** (F, 128910), ðɪˌalɐnˈkoɩçˈbot. Allanquoich Boat (Wy). Former ferry over Dee west of Braemar.

**The Allanaquoich Burn*** (F, 120915), ðɪˌalɐnˈkoɩçˈbʌrn. West of Braemar.

**The Allanaquoich Plantin*** (F, 123917), ðɪˌalɐnˈkoɩçˈplantɪn. A coniferous plantation west of Braemar.

**Allanaquoich's Shiels*** (035975). Allanquoich's Sheals (Io 19). In Glen Derry.

**Allanmore** (OS, C, 138919), ˌalɐnˈmoˑr. Ellanmorre (Pb), Alen mor (Fa), Ellanmor (Roy), Allan More (I). A cottage and former farm west of Braemar, named from the nearby An t-Ailean Mor.

**The Allanmore Burn*** (C, 138918), ðɪˌalɐnˈmoˑrˈbʌrn. Drained burn at Allanmore.

**Allan's Corrie*** (F, 322792), ˈalɐnzˈkọre. Named after Sir Allan Mackenzie, a former owner of Glenmuick Estate. South-east of Loch Muick.

**The Aller Island*** (I, 356943), Scots Aller = alder. 'Island' in Upper Deeside is frequently an anglicised version of Eilean or riverside-field. Now the Dorsincilly Haugh* (U), ðɪˌdọrsən ˈsële'haˑχ. A field in lower Glen Muick.

**The Aller Island*** (I, 360946), the alder riverside-field. A field in lower Glen Muick.

**Allie Ritchie's Cottage*** (U, south of 322008), ˈaleˈrɪtʃizˈkọtədʒ. A former house near Ardoch in Glen Gairn.

**The All-mhad Barn*** (5, F, 237947), ðɪˈalˌmadˈbarn, the wolf rock. Allmhadadh (Dw) is an alternative of Madadh-allaidh = wolf. Madadh was Mad in Deeside Gaelic (D), and Barn is often used in Speyside and Deeside for a big rock. Alla-mhadadh = fierce fox is another slight variant. A big boulder north-east of the Inver, with a cave under it.

**Allt a' Bhealaich Bhuidhe** (OS, 171825 is wrong location, should be main burn at 172836 and its west fork higher up at 170822, 171825 is Alltan Tarsuinn) now Allt Bealach Buidhe (3, U), ˌaltˌbalɐχˈbui, burn of yellow pass. Ault Byallach Buie (I). Also the Ballochbuie Burn (F), ðɪˌbalɐχˈbuiˈbarn. Also the Easter Allt Bealach Buidhe, ðɪˈistɛrˌaltˌbalɐχˈbui (U), pairing with the Wester Allt Bealach Buidhe. Runs into Callater.

**Allt a' Bhò** (OS, 350044), should be Allt Bhó (3, F), OS form is not classic Gaelic form and does not fit the local pronunciation, altˈvouː, burn of cows. West of Morven.

**Allt a' Bhreabair** (OS, 3, C, 343050), altˈvrɐpër, burn of the weaver. Allt na Breabair (M). Local Gaelic was Bhreabair, not Bhreabadair. Also the Weaver's Burn (C), ðɪˈwivërzˈbʌrn. Near Morven Lodge.

**Allt a' Chaorainn*** See Easter Kirn.

**Allt a' Chaorainn*** See Wester Kirn.

**Allt a' Chaorainn** (OS, 4, F, 923851), ˌaltɐˈχuːrən (CG), now alt ˈχuˑrən, burn of the rowan. Also Allt a' Chaorainn Bàideanaich (3), Badenoch Allt a' Chaorainn. Ald Chuirn Badenoch (Roy), distinguishing it from Ald Chuirn Allich (Roy), Allich from Athallaich (3) = Atholl, on the Perthshire side. Sometimes now shortened to the Caorainn, ðɪˈkuˑrən (F). The Cairn (Ros). Also the Silach crom (Go) from the Sileach Crom (4), the crooked oozing one; when Alexander wrote that this was the same as 'the present Allt an t-Seilich, a tributary of the Geldie some miles to the west', he must have meant Allt a' Chaorainn, as it was the burn shown on Gordon's map. Roy's much more detailed map shows Shelochcrom as the burn at 996845 south of Bynack Lodge above Allt an t-Seilich, so Gordon's location was probably an error. In Glen Geldie.

**Allt a' Chaorainn Baideanaich*** See Allt a' Chaorainn.

**Allt a' Chlaiginn** (OS, 3, F, 193836), altˈçlagən, (altaˈhlagən (A)), burn of the rounded hillock. Claigionn (genitive Claiginn) in place names often means the 'best field of arable land on a farm' (Dw), but not here, as there is no farmland. Also Wester Allt a' Chlaiginn. Wester Ault chlaggan (I). See Easter Allt a' Chlaiginn, which is a different burn that runs into Callater slightly further west than the Wester Allt a' Chlaiginn. This paradox is explained by the fact that 'down' to Braemar people was usually east, down Deeside, and so Sios or east was sometimes used in other valleys like Glen Callater for places that were downstream but in fact further west. In upper Glen Callater.

**Allt a' Chlaiginn** (OS, 3, F, 302830), as above, burn of the rounded hillock. The comment about Claigionn in the previous name applies here also. Alt Clagin (R 6), Ault chlaggan (I), Allt Thlaggan (Bs). Crosses the Capel Mounth track near Loch Muick.

**Allt a' Chlair** (OS, 3, F, 121892), altˈχlaːr, burn of the flat ground. Also the Allt a' Chlair Burn (C), ðɪˌaltˈχlaˑrˈbarn. West of Braemar.

**Alltachlair** (OS, C, 118899), as above, often shortened now to aˈχlaːr (C) or aˈflaːr (F). Ruin of a farm beside the above burn.

**The Allt a' Chlair Haughs*** (U, 116899), ðɪˌaltˈχlaˑrˈhaˑχs. Below Corriemulzie.

**The Allt a' Chlair Pool*** See Poll Allt a' Chlair.

**Allt a' Choire Bhoidheach** (OS, A, 236843), altkɔre'vɔjaç (A), classic form would be Allt a' Choire Bhòidhich (3), burn of the beautiful corrie, more recently Allt Coire Bòidheach (U), ˌaltˌkɔr'buˑɔç. Also the Coire Boidheach Burn (F), ðɪˌkɔr 'buˑɔç'bʌrn. Burn of Corbuyach (Am). On south side of Lochnagar.

**Allt a' Choire Chlachaich** (OS, 095776), should be Allt Coire na Cùlath (5, U), altˌkɔrnə'kulɐ, burn of corrie of the back place (note Culach = back place (W 1904, 109)), Culach = boar has a short *u*. Ault cor na Cula (I), Allt na Cula (A). At the head of Baddoch Burn.

**Allt a' Choire Dhuibh** (OS, 018931), burn of the black corrie. Also the Black Corries Burn (F), ðɪ'blak'kɔrez'bʌrn. In Glen Luibeg.

**Allt a' Choire Dhuibh** (OS, 205870), burn of the black corrie. West of Lochnagar.

**Allt a' Choire Ghuirm** (OS, 084970), burn of the green corrie, now Allt Coire Gorm (3, U), ˌaltˌkɔr'gɔrəm. On Beinn a' Bhuird.

**Allt a' Choire Ghuirm** (OS, 3, 166879), burn of the green corrie; now Allt Coire Gorm (U) as above. Also Burn of Wester Corry Goram (I). As Gaelic declined, aspiration disappeared and so did the genitive form of the adjective; Allt Choir Ghorm (D in A), and now Allt Coire Gorm, as above. Also the Coire Gorm Burn (U), ðɪˌkɔr'gɔrəm'bʌrn. In lower Glen Callater.

**Allt a' Choire Mhóir** (OS, 980994), burn of the big corrie, more recently Allt Coire Mór (2, A, U), ˌaltˌkɔr'moːr. In the Lairig Ghru.

**Allt a' Choire Odhair** (OS, 2, F, 974957), ˌaltˌχɔ'rʌuṛ, burn of the dun corrie. Allt choir odhair (D in A). Beside the Corrour Bothy in Glen Dee.

**Allt a' Choire Yaltie** (OS, 130851), from Allt a' Choire Ghealtaidh (6, C), ˌaltˌkɔr'jalti, burn of the corrie of the ? white place (see Coire Yaltie). Ault Yaultie (I). In Glen Clunie.

**Allt a' Chùil Riabhaich** (OS, 5, A, 172795), ˌalthul'riɔç (A) is a general name for two burns. This burn is Allt Cùl Riabhach Beag (5), burn of little brindled back. Ault Culriach Beg (I). Also the Ptarmigan Brae Burn (U), ðɪ'tarmɪgən'breˑ'bʌrn. North-east of the Glas Maol, forming a pair with Allt Cul Riabhach Mor.

**Allt a' Chuirn Dheirg** (OS, 2, U, 098869), ˌaltɐˌχurn'jɛrək, burn of the red hill. Allt a chuirn yerrek (D). Runs off the Carn Dearg into lower Glen Ey.

**Allt a' Gharbh-choire** (OS, 161803), burn of the rough corrie, more recently Allt Garbh-choire (3, U), alt'garçɔre. Ault Garra Chorry (I). Also the Garbh-choire Burn (C), ðɪ'garçɔre 'bʌrn. North of the Glas Maol.

**Allt a' Gharbh-choire** (OS, 970985), burn of the rough corrie, more recently Allt Garbh-choire (2, A, U), as above. Also the Garbh-choire Burn (C), as above. Garrachory B. (Ro). Between Cairn Toul and Braeriach. Formerly (K, Mg) also referred to the continuation south to the junction with the Geusachan Burn.

**Allt a' Gharbh Choire** See Garchory Burn.

**Allt a' Ghillin** (5), burn of the horse, or Ghil-eòin = of the white bird. Allazealzean (Io 37), Altuzealzean (G 23, Io 40a, Ri 34), Altazulzean (Io 59), Altazealzean (G 23, Io 26). Note old Scots ʒ was a *y* sound. A pendicle in Glen Gairn, along with Torbeg, presumably named after a burn near Torbeg.

**Allt a' Ghlas-choire** (OS, 261887), should be Allt Coire Glas (3, F), ˌaltˌkɔr'glas, burn of green corrie. Although recorded as Allt ghlaschoire (D in A), it is now Allt Coire Glas; moreover, the OS name for the corrie—Coire Glas—is

inconsistent with the OS name for the burn. Also the Coire Glas Burn (F), ðɪˌkɔr'glas'bʌrn. In Glen Gelder.

**Allt Ainneartaidh*** (5, U, 348010), alt'anɐrte, burn of force. A steep rough burn up from Lary in Glen Gairn.

**Allt air Chùl*** (3, 165781), back burn. Ault-er-chul (I). North of the Glas Maol.

**Allt air Chùl*** (3, 173963), back burn. Ault-er-Chul (I). Also the Sanctuary Burn (U), ðɪ'saŋtjəri'bʌrn. North of Invercauld.

**Allt a' Mhadaidh** (OS, 3, A, U, 055933), alt'vat, burn of the dog or wolf. Pronounced Altaváddie (M). Runs into Allt a' Mhadaidh-allaidh in Glen Lui.

**Allt a' Mhadaidh-allaidh** (2, C, 057922), ˌaltˌvɐt'ale, ˌaltˌb̥ət'gale, burn of the wolf. Allt vat alli (D). See name below. Also the Wolf Burn (U), ðɪ'wulf'bʌrn. In Glen Lui.

**Allt a' Mhadaidh-allaidh** (2, F, 058923), as above. Alt Vattigally (Roy) and Ault vad gaullie (Im 3) suggest a variant Allt Mhad-gallaidh, note Badenoch variant Mada-galluidh = wolf (MacBain 1894). In recent Braemar Gaelic the entire second syllable of Madadh = dog was not sounded (D), but note Allt Mhadadh allaidh with the dh in Mhadadh 'a guttural spirant voiced' (Dro). Some people still pronounce Allt a' Mhadaidh-allaidh as ˌaltˌb̥ət'gale or ˌaltˌpɪt'gale, perhaps a relic of the old pronunciation. A former farm in Glen Lui.

**Allt a' Mhaide** (OS, 2, C, 142833), alt'vitʃ, burn of the piece of wood, referring to a small bridge with a plank or log (CMcI). Ault Vait (I), Allt a vetsh (D). In Glen Clunie.

**Allt a' Mhaide** (3, U, 312877), as above, burn of the piece of wood. Altavait (G 35), Aldvetch (In, Am). A former farm beside the burn Allt Vitch in upper Glen Muick.

**Allt a' Mhaide** (3, 256014), burn of the piece of wood. Altdavyde (Mc 4), Aldavaid (Ri 21), Alt-bhidse (R 3), Ault Matt (I), Altavaitch (M). Lower part of the Wester Sleach Burn west of Gairnshiel.

**The Allt a' Mhaide Brig*** (C, 140835), ðɪˌalt'vitʃ'brɪg. A road bridge in Glen Clunie.

**The Allt a' Mhaide Path*** (F, 147832), ðɪˌalt'vitʃ'paθ. In Glen Clunie.

**Alltamhait** (OS, C, 140834), alt'vitʃ, from Allt a' Mhaide, alt 'vɛtʃ (Sch). Altamytt (Cr 28), Altmhaid (Io 52, 53), Altvaid (Fa, R 1), Ault Vait (I), Aldmhaide (Gr 85). Ruin of a former farm beside the burn of Allt a' Mhaide in Glen Clunie.

**Allt a' Mhóir Ghrianaich** (OS, 105840), should be Allt Meòir Ghrianaich (3, U), ˌaltˌmjur'grianəç, burn of sunny stream-branch. Allt Meoir Grianach (OSn), Allt meoir ghrianaich (D), Allt myor grianich (D in A), Allt a' Mheoir Ghrianaich (A). Also now the Creag an Fhuathais Burn (F), ðɪˌkreg 'nuˑəʃ'bʌrn. In mid Glen Ey.

**Allt a' Mhuilinn*** (3, 184910), burn of the mill. AultaMulin (R 7). A man-made diversion from Allt na Claise Moire taking water to a former mill at the present Invercauld estate office.

**Alltan a' Chadha Leathain*** (4, 180835), burnie of the broad pass. Ault-na-ha-lain (I, R 13). Above Loch Callater.

**Allt an Aghaidh Mhilis** (OS, 2, U, 064990), ˌaltɐnˌʌgi' . . . , burn of the sweet face, referring to a fertile grassy hillside. West of Beinn a' Bhuird.

**Allt an Aitinn** (OS, 3, A, U, 139988), is a general name for two burns. This one is Allt an Aitinn air Bheul (3), fore burn (literally burn in front) of the juniper. Aultn Aiten-er-vail (I). This burn and Allt an Aitinn air Chul run in opposite directions off the same hill near Ben Avon. They have been forgotten, but Allt an Aitinn is still remembered, ˌaltn'aχtjən (U), burn of the juniper.

**Allt an Aitinn** (OS, 3, A, 201821), altan'ahtjən (A), burn of the juniper. Aultn Aiten (I), Aultin Aiten (R 13). In upper Callater.

5

**Allt an Aitinn air Bheul\*** See Allt an Aitinn.

**Allt an Aitinn air Chùl\*** (3, 124982), back burn (literally burn on the back) of the juniper. Aultn Aiten-er-Chul (I). See Allt an Aitinn air Bheul. Beside Ben Avon.

**Allt an Beal** (OS, 066866), classic form Alltan Beal (5, A), altan 'bjal (A), burnie of broom (from Bealaidh) or of a pass (from Bealach). Beul = mouth or fore is unlikely as its pronunciation in Braemar Gaelic is be̜l, not bjal. South-west of Inverey.

**An t-Alltan Buidhe** (2, F, 044852), ðɪˌaltɐn'b̜ui, the yellow burnie. South-west of the Linn of Dee.

**An t-Alltan Buidhe\*** (3, F, 094827), as above, the yellow burnie. In upper Glen Ey.

**Allt an Da Chraobh Bheath** (OS, 3, U, 220846), ˌaltn̩'da·'χru·vi, classic form Chraobh-bheithe, burn of the two birch trees. As the lowest part of the burn is at 880 m, this must have been unusually high for trees. No trees have been there this century, and today's high deer stocks would put paid to any seedlings that did try to grow there. Also Burn of Carn an t-Sagairt. Burn of Cairntaggart (In). West of Lochnagar.

**Allt an Dà Chaorainn\*** (3, 186024), burn of the two rowans. Aultn Da churn (I). Chuirn would not fit, as there are no cairns or screes there. South of Loch Builg.

**Alltan Dearg\*** (3, 193904), red burnie. Aultan Derg (R 7). In Ballochbuie Forest.

**Allt an Dearg** (OS, 286838) classic form An t-Alltan Dearg (3, C), ðɪˌaltn̩'dʒerg, the red burnie. Altan derg (Im 1). At Loch Muick.

**Alltan Dearg\*** (3, 205805), red burnie. Ault Derg (I), Aultn Derg (R 13). At the head of Callater.

**(An t-) Alltan Dearg** (OS, 3, U, 030882), ðɪˌaltɐn'dʒerək, the red burnie. West of the Linn of Dee.

**The Alltan Dearg Brig\*** (F, south-west of 290834), ðɪˌaltn̩'dʒerg 'brɪg. A bridge at Loch Muick.

**An t-Alltan Domhain** See Allt Domhain.

**Allt an Droighnean** (OS, 208809) classic form Allt an Droighinn (3), burn of the thorn. Also Easter Allt an Droighinn. Easter Aultn Droin (I). Pairs with Wester Allt an Droighinn. At the head of Callater.

**An t-Alltan Dubh\*** (3, 164827), the black burnie. Aultan Du (R 13). Also the Black Burn (U), ðɪ'blak'bʌrn. South-west of Loch Callater.

**Allt an Dubh-choire** (OS, 3, U, 137800), ˌaltn̩'duçri, burn of the black corrie. Also the Dubh-choire Burn (U), ðɪ'duçri'bʌrn. The upper part of Allt Chronaidh, north of the Cairnwell.

**Allt an Dubh-ghlinne** (OS, 2, A, U, 070966), ˌaltɐn'duˌglɐn, burn of the black glen. Also the Dubh-Ghleann Burn (C), ðɪ'duˌglɐn'bʌrn, has been the Duglen Water (McC 1896). Runs into Quoich.

**Allt an Dubh-loch** (OS, 3, C, 260821 and 224834), ˌaltn̩'duˌlɔχ, burn of the black loch. Second OS location is incorrect; Allt an Dubh-loch is below the loch and the Back Latch above it (C), ðɪ'bak'latʃ, Scots Latch = stream. Water of the Duloch (I) below the loch, the Black Latch Burn (Io 34, I) above it. The Latch of Dowloch (Io 36). Also the Dubh-loch Burn (C) ðɪ'duˌlɔχ'bʌrn. B. of Duloch (Ro). West of Loch Muick.

**Allt an Dubh-Lochain** (OS, 3, F, 104994), ˌaltn̩'duˌlɔχɐn, burn of the black tarn. On Beinn a' Bhuird.

**Allt an Dùin\*** (3, 237954), burn of the hillock. Alt'n Duin (R 3). West of Crathie.

**Allt an Earb** See Allt na h-Earba.

**Allt an Eas Bhig** (OS, 140997), locally Allt Easaidh Beag (3, A, U), ˌalt̩ˌese'b̜eg, little rapidly-falling burn (note Easaidh was a genitive of Easach (W 1904, 182)). Essie Beg (I). Also the Little Easaidh (C), ðɪ'lɛ̈tɐl'ese. This, and the adjoining Allt an Easaidh Mhoir cannot be Burn of the Little Waterfall and

Burn of the Big Waterfall, as there is no obvious single waterfall, little or big. Both burns are steep and swift, with numerous small waterfalls. Allt an Eas Bhig is merely the smaller of the two burns, a point that is still kept by the current names the Little Easaidh and Muckle Easaidh. The most reasonable interpretation is that Easaidh means simply a steep rushing burn (note Easach = a dark, deep, rocky stream (Dw), and Essy in Inverness-shire is from a locative of Easach = water-fall stream, rapidly falling stream (Mb)). Essie (Hi). On Ben Avon.

**Allt an Eas Mhóir** (OS, 154000), locally Allt Easaidh Mór (3, A, U), ˌaltˌese'mo·r, big rapidly-falling burn (see above). Essie More (I). Also the Muckle Easaidh (C), ðɪ'mʌkəl'ese, and the Big Easaidh (C). The Big Essie (A). On Ben Avon.

**Alltan Imire\*** (3, U, 090881), ˌaltɐn'ëmër, burnie of ridge. In lower Glen Ey.

**Allt an Leathaid** (OS, 090878), altan'ljaçt (A) suggests Allt an Leachd (3), burn of the declivity, see Cnapan Dubh Coire an Leachd. In lower Glen Ey.

**Allt an Loch** (OS, 3, A, 196820), altən'lɔχ (A), burn of the loch. Runs into Loch Callater.

**Allt an Loch\*** See Allt Loch Vrotachan.

**Allt an Lochain Buidhe\*** (3, U, 251832), ˌaltn̩ˌlɔχɐn'bui, burn of the yellow tarn. West of Loch Muick.

**Allt an Lochain Uaine** (OS, 2, C, 960983), ˌaltn̩ˌlɔχɐn'uɐn, burn of the green tarn. On Cairn Toul.

**Allt an Lochain Uaine\*** (2, U, 005979), as above, burn of the green tarn. On Ben Macdui.

**Allt an Lochain Uaine** (OS, 029985), burn of the green tarn, locally now Allt Lochan Uaine (2, M, A, C), ˌaltˌlɔχɐn'uɐn. The fine old poem Allt an Lochain Uaine, by Uilleam Smith of Rynuie in Strath Spey, was named after this burn.

**Alltan Lochan Mór\*** (2, U, 093843), ˌaltn̩ˌlɔχɐn'mo·r, burnie of big tarn. In mid Glen Ey.

**Alltan na Beinne** (OS, 2, C, 080979), ˌaltn̩ɐ'b̜iˌn, burnie of the hill. Altanabin (Ri 22), Altnapin (R 10) shown for Carn Allt na Beinne. On Beinn a' Bhuird.

**An t-Alltan Odhar\*** (3, F, 194888), ðɪˌaltn̩'ʌur̩, the dun-coloured burnie. In Ballochbuie Forest.

**Alltan Odhar** (OS, 061822), from An t-Alltan Odhar (3, A), now the Alltan Odhar (2, C), ðɪˌaltɐn'ʌur̩, the dun burnie. Altanour (Fa), d alltan aur (D). In upper Glen Ey.

**An t-Alltan Odhar** (3, D, 100843), the dun burnie. In mid Glen Ey.

**The Alltan Odhar Brig\*** (F, 192891), ðɪˌaltn̩'ʌur'brɪg. A bridge in Ballochbuie Forest.

**The Alltan Odhar Ridge\*** (F, 192869), ðɪˌaltn̩'ʌur'rɪdʒ. In Ballochbuie Forest.

**Allt an Ruighe\*** (3, U, 350916), ˌaltən'ri·, burn of the slope. A little burn in Glen Muick.

**Allt an Ruighe\*** See Eilean Dearg Toll Dubh.

**Alltan Seileach** (OS, 3, U, 060840), ˌaltən'ʃiləç, willow burnie. West of Glen Ey.

**An t-Alltan Seileach** (3, D, 093833), the willow burnie. The Altan Sealach, the Aultan Shellach (Io 79). In mid Glen Ey.

**Alltan Sleibh** (OS, 253040), should be Alltan Sliabhach (3), burnie of moor (or mountainous) place. Alt Sliach (R 16). Becomes Wester Sleach Burn lower down. Note Sleach is from Sliabhach = moor place (2, JB). North-west of Gairnshiel.

**Allt an Stuic Ghiubhais** (OS, 3, A, 054810), altstuhk'juʃ (A), burn of the stump or root of fir, more recently also Allt Stoc Ghiubhais (2, D, U), ˌaltˌstɔk'juɪʃ. Refers to the lower continuation at 066812 as well (IG). At the head of Glen Ey.

**Alltan Taibhse\*** (3, U, 378990), ˌaltən'ta·z, burnie of ghost. Up the Tullich Burn near Ballater.

**Alltan Tarsuinn** (3, U, 161991), ˌaltən'tarsən, cross burnie. Alltan tarsin (A 283) probably same burn. A characteristic of the burns with Tarsuinn is that they go straight down a slope and approximately at a right angle into a different burn below. South-east of Ben Avon.

**Alltan Tarsuinn*** (3, 160807), cross burnie. Aultan Tarcen (I). In upper Clunie.

**Alltan Tarsuinn** (OS, U, 090966), ˌaltən'tarsɛin, cross burnie. The burn in Avalanche Gully on Beinn a' Bhuird.

**Alltan Tarsuinn*** (3, U, 171825), ˌaltən'tarsən, cross burnie. Aultn Tarcen (I). In upper Callater.

**Alltan Tarsuinn*** (3, U, 117812), as above, cross burnie. Aultn Tarcen (I). In lower Baddoch.

**Alltan Tarsuinn*** (3, 085787), cross burnie. Aultn Tarcen (I). In upper Baddoch.

**Alltan Tarsuinn*** (3, 133954), cross burnie. Aultn Tarcen (I). In Gleann an t-Slugain.

**Allt an Tobair*** See Cairnwell Burn.

**Allt an t-Seilich*** (3, U, 108955), ˌaltən'tiliç, burn of the willow. In upper Quoich.

**Allt an t-Seilich** (OS, 003850), burn of the willow. Locally usually the Seileach (4, A, C, discussion in A 371), ðɪ'ʃiləç, a shortening as in the Caorainn for Allt a' Chaorainn. Sometimes Alltan Seileich (U), ˌaltən'siləç, suggesting burnie of willow. Early maps gave:—Schelach Vren (Po), from Seileach Bhronn (4), willow–one of Bhronn or of bulges, Coire Bhronn and Allt Bhronn being nearby; Silach wren (Go) and Silach vren (Bla) as above; and Silich Vren (Mo). Auldnalochvron (At), Auld Shilochvran (Stob, Kn), and Ault Shilochvran (Ro) from Allt Seileach Bhronn. Possibly from Sileach = oozing one. Roy's map gives Shelochuren (obviously Shelochvren) as the burn at 005852 to the east of Allt an t-Seilich. Sometimes the Seileach Burn (F), ðɪ'ʃiləç 'bʌrn. The Shilloch Burn (A). North of Glen Tilt.

**Allt an t-Seilich*** (2, U, 085868), ˌaltən'dʒiliç, burn of the willow. Beside the former farm of Ruighe an t-Seilich in Glen Ey.

**Allt an t-Seilich** (3, A, ? 117950), altən'tʃɛləç (A), burn of the willow. Allt an jellich (D in A). In Gleann an t-Slugain.

**Allt an t-Sionnaich** (OS, 2, C, 087861), alt'juniç, burn of the fox. Aldennach (Roy) shown too far west, Allt yunnach, djunngach (D in A). In lower Glen Ey.

**Allt an t-Sionnaich** (OS, 2, C, 018871), as above, burn of the fox. Aultannich (Im 3). Allt Shionnach (D) suggests burn of foxes. South of the White Bridge in Glen Dee.

**Allt an t-Slugain** (OS, 3, D, A, 138945), burn of the gullet. Allt an lukan (D). Also Burn of the Sluggan (I), now the Slugan Burn (C), ðɪ'slʌgən'bʌrn. Water of Sluggan (Ro), Sluggan Water (Mg map). In Gleann an t-Slugain.

**Allt an t-Slugain** See Sluggan Burn.

**Allt an t-Sneachda** (OS, 330883), from Allt an t-Sneachdaidh (3, U), ˌaltən'drɛçte, burn of the snow. Ault Dreachkie (I), Auld Drechty (M). Also the Snowy Burn (U), ðɪ'snoe'bʌrn. In upper Glen Muick.

**Allt an t-Sneachda** (OS, 2, A, F, 101962), ˌaltən'drɛçk, burn of the snow. Also the Snowy Corrie Burn (A), and the Snowy Burn (F), ðɪ'snoe'bʌrn. In Glen Quoich.

**The Allt an t-Sneachda Brig*** (F, 328888), ðɪˌaltən'drɛçte'brɪg. A bridge in Glen Muick.

**Allt an Tulaich** See Doulich Burn.

**Allt an Tuim Bhàin** (OS, 3, A, U, 101861), ˌaltən̩ˌduim'va·n, burn of the white hillock. In Glen Ey.

**Allt an Uisge** (OS, 3, F, 327870), ˌaltən'usk, ˌaltən'jusk, (altan 'uʃk (A)), burn of the water. Altinusk (R 6), Aultn Uishk (I). Also the Uisge Burn (Gib) and the Whisky Burn (Gib). In upper Glen Muick.

**Allt Bad a' Mhonaidh** (OS, 160008), should be Allt Bad Tomaigh (3, U), ˌaltˌpɪt'ome, burn of clump of knoll or tuft place, with Tomaigh from Tomaich = oblique case of Tomach = knoll place. Ault Bat Toumie (I), Allt Pit-omie (A), pɪt'omi (A). Allt bad Thomaidh, or burn of Thomas's clump was suggested (A), but numerous cases of Toum on the Invercauld maps refer to hillocks (i.e. Tom). South-east of Ben Avon.

**Allt Bad an Laoigh** (3, 241989), burn of clump of the calf. Ault Bad-am Lui (map in Mg). Also Bad an Laoigh Burn. Badan-lui Burn (R 3). North of Crathie.

**Allt Bad Creiceal*** (3, 196010), burn of clump with a wheezing sound. Ault Bat Craikel (I). Also Wester Kirn, but the Wester Kirn also includes the main burn running into Gairn. South of Loch Builg.

**Allt Bad na h-Earba*** (3, 388029), burn of clump of the roe deer. Altpatnaharp (Io 20). Also the Burn of Bad na h-Earba. The Burn of Badenyarb, the Burn of Badnaharb (Io 20). Also the Stripe of Bad na h-Earba. The Stryp of Badnearb (Io 20). Some regarded it as continuing down to the ford, where the map shows Rashy Burn (OS). South-east of Morven.

**An t-Allt Beag** (3, A, U, 322046), ðɪˌalt'bɛg, the little burn. Forms a pair with the Allt Mor in Glen Fenzie.

**Allt Beag*** See Little Burn.

**Allt Beag*** (3, U, 143899), alt'bɛg, little burn. Ault Beg (I). On Morrone south of Braemar.

**Allt Beag*** (3, 122803), little burn. Ault Beg (I). In the lower Baddoch.

**Allt Beag*** (3, 161805), little burn. Ault Beg (I). On Carn an Tuirc north of the Glas Maol.

**Allt Bealach Buidhe** See Allt a' Bhealaich Bhuidhe.

**Allt Bealach Buidhe*** (3, 163809 and 159805), burn of yellow pass. Ault Ballach Buie (I). Note that the above burn and this one run down opposite sides of Am Bealach Buidhe, the pass at 167815. Also the Wester Allt Bealach Buidhe (U), ðɪ 'wɛstër ˌalt'balɐx'bui, or ðɪ'wɒstër etc, pairing with the Easter Allt Bealach Buidhe. Runs off Carn an Tuirc into the upper Clunie.

**Allt Beart an Tuairneir*** (3, 235018), burn of lathe of the turner. Ald Beairt an-Tuairnear, Altpersanduarnar or Turner Burn, Altpersanduarnar (R 3, 5, 9) suggests there was formerly a clump of birches there, but no trees now. Near Corndavon Lodge.

**Allt Beinn Iutharn** (OS, C, 060794), should be Allt Beinn Fhiùbharainn (3), ˌaltˌbɛn'jurn̩, but ˌaltˌbɛn'jurɪn̩ from those with most Gaelic, burn of hill of the edge-point (see Beinn Iutharn). Also the Burn of Beinn Fhiubharainn. Burn of Benurin (Io 79), the Burn of Beinurn (Lp 5). In Glen Ey.

**Allt Bhardaidh*** See Glenbardy Burn.

**Allt Bhearn-uisge*** See Allt Coire Fhearneasg.

**Allt Bheidhneig** See Bynack Burn.

**Allt Bhronn** (OS, 3, F, 017849), alt'vrɔin, but alt'vrɔn from best informants; (alt'vrɔn, palatal *n* (A)), burn of bulges. Allt vronn (D in A). Near Bynack Lodge.

**Allt Bhrot-choin** (5, U, 140947), alt'vrɒtəçən, burn of the mastiff. Alt vrotachan (Im 2), Altvrotochan (Io 63), Ault Brotachin (I). In Gleann an t-Slugain.

**Allt Bhruid or Bhruidh** (5, D, A, U, 148802), alt'brui, (alt'vritʃ (A)), burn of ? the raging (note N 178 under Burn of Brown). Allt Bhruididh (OS 1869), Allt Vrúidje (M). Allt vrui (D) suggests Bhruidh. Vrúidje became Vrui probably by lenition. Becomes Uisge Bhruidh lower down. The suggested meaning fits the name of the glen—Gleann Bruthainn, which is like the name Glen Brown at Bridge of Brown. Also formerly Burn of Bruthainn. Burn of Bruin (Im 2). North of the Cairnwell.

**Allt Blàr nam Marbh*** (3, 374017), burn of moor of the dead. Altblarnamarrow (G 33). Also the Burn of Blar nam Marbh. The Burn of Blarnamarrow (Io 20). Extends from 368021 where Wheel Burn joins main burn, down to 377016. South of Morven.

**Allt Boruiche** (OS, 100790) is incorrect, as the stress falls on the *u* (A, U), ˌaltˌbəˈruɪç or ˌaltˌpəˈruɪç, and so Boruiche must be two words. Probably Allt Both Fhraoich (5), burn of heather hut. Auld porich (Ra 3). In the upper Baddoch.

**Allt Bothan Dubh*** See Blacksheil Burn.

**Allt Briste-amhaich*** (3, 197813), burn of break neck. Ault Priesh-auich (I), Ault Prish Auich (R 13). Runs over cliffs in upper Callater.

**Allt Cac Dubh** (OS, 073798), burn of black shit, should be Cadhach Dubh (5), black passageway. Also the Burn of Cadhach Dubh. The Burn of Caachdhu (Lp 5), Caagh Dhu (R 16), Ca'ach dubh (D). Note Hills of Cadhach Dubh nearby. In upper Glen Ey.

**Alltcailleach** (OS, 347921), from Allt Chailleach (3, A, C), alt ˈhɛiləç, burn of old women. Auldchaliach (G 5), Auldchylach, Altachallach (Io 7, 33), Auldhallich (Ab 19), Aldchallach (In), other similar old forms in M, Allt Chyllich (M). Former farm in Glen Muick, now a house. Upper Balachalioch (Roy) was shown on roughly the same location, and was probably an error for Upper Allt Chailleach.

**The Alltcailleach Brig*** (C, 346919), ðɪˌaltˈhɛiləçˈbrɪg. A bridge in Glen Muick.

**Alltcailleach Forest** (OS, 335925). Wrong spelling, as above.

**Allt Carn a' Mhaim** (OS, 3, C, 005960), ˌaltˌkarnɐˈvɛim, burn of hill of the pass. Also the West Grain of Luibeg (Fi). In Glen Luibeg.

**Allt Carn Bhathaich** (OS, 063840), locally Allt Carn Bhac (3, U), ˌaltˌkarnˈvɑːχ, burn of hill of banks, but old note Carn Vaich (Gr) would suggest Bhàthaich = of the shelter. Runs from Carn Bhac into Connie, west of Glen Ey.

**Allt Chaidear*** (3, 146846), cadgers' burn, or Allt Chaideir, burn of the cadger. Ault Chatcher (I). In Glen Clunie.

**Allt Chailleach*** (3, U, 159905), altˈχaləç, burn of witches, also said to mean burn of old women, or of nuns. Ault Chalich (I). Also the Witches' Burn (U), ðɪˈwɛtʃɪzˈbʌrn. South-east of Braemar.

**Allt Chala** (5, D, 174925), burn of the hard water (5, same word as in Callater). Allt Challa (Gr), Allt Chall (D). See A 303. Beside Invercauld House.

**Allt Chalmanaich*** (4, U, 024888), altˈχalɐmniç, burn of pigeon place. Near the White Bridge in Glen Dee.

**Allt Cheann-bhuilg** (3, 127950), burn of the bag-head. See Gleann an t-Slugain. See A 376. Allt chanlic (D). The main head-water of Allt an t-Slugain north-west of Invercauld.

**Allt Chernie** (OS, U, 361900), from Allt ? Cheatharnaich (5), ˌaltˈçjarne, (altˈhjerne (A)), burn of ? the soldier. Ald Chirn (G 5), Ault churnie (I), pron. Chăǒ-ărnich (M). In mid Glen Muick.

**Allt Chernie*** (west of 349907). Altchurnak, Althurnach (Opr 46, 50b). Former farm in Glen Muick.

**Allt Chlacharraidh*** (5, 380018), burn of stones. Auldchlachary (Io 20), Alt clachary (G 33). Went from 377016 east to 386018 and north to 388022, and some said it went further north, where the map shows Rashy Burn (OS). South-east of Morven.

**Allt Chli** See Feardar Burn.

**Allt Choltair*** (3, 115815), burn of the ploughshare. Ault Choulter (I). Cuts a fairly straight line down a steep hillside up the Baddoch.

**Allt Choltair** (3, probably 103823), burn of the ploughshare.

Allt chollter, ploughshare (D). Like the above burn, this one cuts a straight line down a steep hillside, in a side-glen leading into mid Glen Ey.

**Allt Cholzie** (OS, 344905), from Allt Choille (3, A, F) altˈχɔili, altˈχɔlji (U), burn of woods. Ald Chuily (G 5), Alt Chuillie (Im 1), Ault chulzie (I). Burn of Aucholzie (A). Lower part is now the Aucholzie Burn, higher part the Drum Cholzie Burn (F). In mid Glen Muick.

**Allt Chonnaidh** See Allt Connie.

**Allt Chraichidh** See Crathie Burn.

**Allt Chrithich*** See Coilacriech Burn.

**Allt Chronaidh** (5, 142810), burn of the little hollow or of the dark brown place (Cron has both meanings in Irish names (J), note also Ardchronie in Ross-shire W 1904, 3). Crònan = low murmuring, is another possibility (see Coire Chronaidh). Burn of Aultchronie (Md 1), Ault chronie (I), Allt chroni (D). The lower part of the burn whose upper part is Allt an Dubh-choire. North of the Cairnwell.

**Allt Chruinneachtaidh** See Allt Connachty.

**The Allt Chruinneachtaidh Ridge*** (U, 350886), ðɪˌaltˈkrunɐχteˈrɪdʒ, a ridge near the above burn, in mid Glen Muick.

**Allt Clach nan Taillear** (OS, 2, F, 981975), ˌaltˌklaχnənˈdaˑljər, burn of stone of the tailors. Also Allt nan Tàillear (3, Gordon 1921, 1951), burn of the tailors. Also the Tailors' Burn (A, F), ðɪˈtelɛrzˈbʌrn. See Clach nan Taillear. In the Lairig Ghru.

**Allt Clais an t-Sabhail** (OS, 3, F, 951962), ˌaltˌklaʃənˈdʌuḷ, burn of hollow of the barn. On Cairn Toul.

**Allt Clais Chàil*** (2, U, 087833), ˌaltˌklaʃˈhaːl, burn of hollow of the kale. In upper Glen Ey.

**Allt Clais Fhearnaig** (OS, 3, U, 077936), ˌaltˌklaʃˈjaˑrnək, burn of hollow of the little alder. In Glen Quoich.

**Allt Clais Mhadaidh** (OS, 2, F, 988930), ˌaltˌklaʃˈvate, burn of hollow of the dog or wolf. In Glen Dee opposite Glen Geusachan.

**Allt Clais na Firich*** (3, U, 074940), ˌaltˌklaʃnɐˈfiriç, burn of hollow of the moor. In Glen Quoich.

**Allt Clais nam Balgair** (OS, 3, C, 060980), ˌaltˌklaʃnəmˈbalɐgɛr, burn of hollow of the foxes. In the Dubh-Ghleann.

**Allt Clais nam Marbh*** (3), burn of hollow of the dead. Auldclashni and Blairnamarrow (G 19). Probably near Allt Blar nam Marbh, south of Morven.

**Allt Clais nan Cat*** (3, U, 141940), ˌaltˌklaʃnɐˈgat, burn of hollow of the cats. Also Burn of Clash na gaat (I). Runs into Gleann an t-Slugain.

**Allt Clais nan Gamhainn** (3, 111866), burn of hollow of the stirks. Allt clais na gamhann (D). South of Corriemulzie.

**Allt Cnapan an Laoigh*** (3, U, 993839), ˌaltˌkrapanɐˈluː, burn of little hillock of the calf. Also the Cnapan an Laoigh Burn (U), ðɪˌkrapanɐˈluˑˈbʌrn. Near Bynack Lodge.

**Allt Cnoc Biorach*** (3, 103793), burn of sharp hill. Ault Knock Birach (I). In the upper Baddoch.

**Allt Coire an Dà Bheinn*** See Corndavon Burn.

**Allt Coire an Fhir Bhogha** (OS, 044970), should be Allt Coire Cadha an Fhir Bhogha (3, C, see also A 219), ˌaltˌkɔrˌkanˌjərˈvouː, burn of corrie of pass of the archer. Also the Burn of Cadha an Fhir Bhogha. The Burn of Cainferbow (Io 19). Note Cadha an Fhir Bogha nearby. In Glen Derry.

**Allt Coire an t-Sabhail*** (3, U, 975974), ˌaltˌkɔrnˈdʌuḷ, burn of corrie of the barn. Cairn Toul Burn (Cm). On Cairn Toul.

**Allt Coire an t-Sagairt** (OS, 3, 188009), burn of corrie of the priest. The Corndakart (Coire an t-sagairt) burn (A 283). South of Loch Builg.

**Allt Coire an t-Saighdeir** (OS, 3, U, 980965), ˌaltˌkɔrṇˈdɔidʒɛr, burn of corrie of the soldier. On Cairn Toul.

**Allt Coire an t-Seilich** (3, A, probably 108955), altkɔrnˈdʒɛləç

(A), burn of corrie of the willow. Probably same as Allt an t-Seilich. A tributary of Quoich, location not given (A).

**Allt Coire an t-Seilich** (OS, 3, F, 948850), ˌaltˌkọrənˈʤeliç, burn of corrie of the willow. In Glen Geldie.

**Allt Coire an t-Slugain*** (3, U, 280904), ˌaltˌkọrn̩ˈlugən, burn of corrie of the gullet. Also the Burn o Coire an t-Slugain (U), now the Coire an t-Slugain Burn (F), ðɪˌkọrn̩ˈlugənˈbʌrn. In Glen Girnock.

**Allt Coire an t-Slugain** (OS, 295022), burn of corrie of the gullet. Also the Slugan Burn (C), ðɪˈslugənˈbʌrn. The Sloggan Burn (A). Near Gairnshiel.

**Allt Coire an t-Sneachda** (2, F, 100972 and 096970), ˌaltˌkọrn̩ ˈdrẹç, burn of corrie of the snow. Aldcorryandreachk (Roy), Alltcorriedraughty at the burn of the snow quarry (Me 15), Ault cor-n-Dreachk (I). Allt coirach an drechk, burn of the snowy corries (D in A 140) indicates the collective name Coireach for the two adjacent corries; for other examples see Na Coireach Bhuth and Coireach na Moine. On Beinn a' Bhuird.

**Allt Coire an t-Sneachda** (2, A, U, 960920), ˌaltˌkọrn̩ˈdreçk, burn of corrie of the snow. Allt corr 'n drechk (D in A). On Beinn Bhrotain.

**Allt Coire Bhearnaist** (OS, 051844), should be Allt Coire Bhearn-uisge (3, F), ˌaltˌkọrˈvjarnˌuəʃk, or more often now ˌaltˌkọrˈvjarnəʃ, burn of corrie of the water gap. At the head of Allt Connie, west of Glen Ey.

**Allt Coire Bhrochain*** (3, U, 961992), ˌaltˌkọrˈvrọχɐn, burn of corrie 'where everything is in little bits' (see C. Bhrochain). On Braeriach.

**Allt Coire Breac*** (3, 200817), burn of speckled corrie. Alt Corbreachk (R 14). Also Burn of Coire Breac. Burn of Conbreach (Ro), Burn of Corbreachk (I), Corbreach Burn (Mg). At the head of Callater.

**Allt Coire Buidhe*** (3, 151863), burn of yellow corrie. Ault Cor Buie (I). In Glen Clunie.

**Allt Coire Buidhe*** (2, U, 062895), as above, burn of yellow corrie. Also the Coire Buidhe Burn (U), ðɪˌkọrˈbuiˈbʌrn, or the Burn o Coire Buidhe (U). South of the Linn of Dee.

**Allt Coire Cadha an Fhir Bhogha** See Allt Coire an Fhir Bhogha.

**Allt Coire Cath nam Fionn** (OS, 954939), should be Allt Coire Cadha nam Fiann (5, U, see also D 171), ˌaltˌkọrˌkaˑnɐˈvjʌŋ, burn of corrie of pass of the crowberries, or of the Fingalians. In Glen Geusachan.

**Allt Coire Chais** See Corrie Chash Burn.

**Allt Coire Chrid** (OS, 3, F, 129829), probably should be Chrit, ˌaltˌkọrˈçritʃ, burn of corrie of crofts, Crit = Croit (Dw). Sometimes Allt Chrid (A, U). Usually now the Coire Chrid Burn (F), ðɪˌkọrˈçritʃˈbʌrn. At the Baddoch.

**Allt Coire Craoibh an Òir*** (2, U, 027939), ˌaltˌkọrˌkrin̩ˈọˑr, burn of corrie with (or of) the tree of the gold. Also the Coire Craoibh an Oir Burn (C), ðɪˌkọrˌkrin̩ˈọrˈbʌrn. In Glen Luibeg.

**Allt Coire Cùl Dorch*** (3, U, 104779), ˌaltˌkọrˌkulˈdorɐχ, burn of corrie of dark back. West of the Cairnwell.

**Allt Coire Dhà Thom*** (3, 272036), burn of corrie with two hillocks. Ault Cor-ga-Houm (I), Ault Corr-ga-Houm (R 12). North-west of Gairnsheil.

**Allt Coire Eiteachan*** See Coire Etchachan Burn.

**Allt Coire Feuragaidh*** (3, 159911), burn of grassy corrie (? from Feur = grass). Ault Cor Feragie (I). Also the Corrie Feragie Burn (C), ðɪˌkọreˈfẹrəgiˈbʌrn. Beside Braemar.

**Allt Coire Fhearneasg** (OS, 106813), should be Allt Coire Bhearn-uisge (3, A, D in A, U), ˌaltˌkọrˈvjarnəʃ, burn of corrie of the water gap. Ault Vyarn Uishk (I), Aultvarnesk

(Io 79), Allt corr vyarnisk (D). Also the Big Corrie Burn (F), ðɪˈbɪgˈkọreˈbʌrn. Up the Baddoch.

**Allt Coire Fionn** (OS, 153789), should be Allt Fionn-choire (3, M, U), altˈfjançəre, burn of white corrie. Ault Fyaun na chorry, Ault Fyaun na Chor (I). Also the Fionn-choire Burn (C), ðɪˈfjançəreˈbʌrn. Incorrectly said to be a tributary of Geusachan (A). On the north side of the Glas Maol.

**Allt Coire Ghiuthais** (OS, 3, A, 171864), altkɔrˈjuʃ (A), burn of corrie of the fir. Pronounced Yewaish (M). Also Allt Loch Phadruig. Ault Loch Patrick (I). Also Allt Giuthas. Altguise (Io 43a). In Glen Callater.

**Allt Coire Glas** See Allt a' Ghlas-choire.

**Allt Coire Lic*** (3, U, 291011), ˌaltˌkọrˈlik, burn of corrie at a slope. Also the Coire Lic Burn (U), ðɪˌkọrˈlikˈbʌrn. Near Gairnshiel.

**Allt Coire Mhiadain*** (3, 155990), burn of corrie of the green. Ault Cor Viaten (I). Also the Coire Mhiadain Burn (U), ðɪ ˌkọrˈvitənˈbʌrn. South of Ben Avon.

**Allt Coire na Cìche** (OS, 110974), burn of corrie of the pap. On Beinn a' Bhuird.

**Allt Coire na Cloiche** (OS, 277018), burn of corrie of the stone. Near Gairnshiel.

**Allt Coire na Cloiche** (OS, 183004), burn of corrie of the stone. Also the Coire na Cloiche Burn (A). South of Loch Builg.

**Allt Coire na Cloiche** See Megen Burn.

**Allt Coire na Còinnich*** (3, 166811), burn of corrie of the moss. Ault-cor-na-Cuanich (I). Cuanich certainly means moss here, as the burn is also the Foggy Burn (U), ðɪˈfọgiˈbʌrn, and Aberdeenshire Scots Foggy means mossy. On Carn an Tuirc north of Glas Maol.

**Allt Coire na Cùlath*** (5, U, 006897), ˌaltˌkọrnɐˈkulɐ, burn of corrie of the back place. Cùil = corner is possible instead of Cùl = back, but Cul is more likely in such cases (W 1904, 109; J 3, 240). In mid Glen Dee.

**Allt Coire na Culath** See Allt a' Choire Chlachaich.

**Allt Coire na Feadaige*** (3, 104785), burn of corrie of the golden plover. Auld corrie na fatack (Ra 3), Ault-Cor-na faitack (I). A good place for golden plovers in summer still. West of the Cairnwell.

**Allt Coire na h-Eaglais** (3, U, 305974), ˌaltˌkọrnɐˈhẹklɪʃ, burn of corrie of the church. Allt Coir' na h-eaglais (D) said to be 'the burn at Rinavaich', below the corrie, but this is now Allt na h-Eaglais. East of Crathie.

**Allt Coire na h-Oisinn*** (3, U, 288909), ˌaltˌkọrnɐˈhọʃən, burn of corrie of the nook. Also the Burn o Coire na h-Oisinn (U), ðɪˈbʌrnɐˌkọrnɐˈhọʃən. Burn of Cornyhoshan (In). Now usually the Coire na h-Oisinn Burn (F). In Glen Girnock.

**Allt Coire na Lairige** (OS, 3, U, 130838), ˌaltˌkọrnɐˈlaˑrɪg, burn of corrie of the hill pass. Ault Cornalarick (I). In upper Clunie.

**Allt Coire na Meanneasg** (OS, 145875), should be Allt Coire na Mion-easga or Allt Coire nam Mion-easg (3, U, other evidence under Coire na Meanneasg), ˌaltˌkọrnɐˈminəsk, burn of corrie of the little bog or of the little bogs. In mid Glen Clunie.

**Allt Coire nam Freumh** (OS, 3, 281033), burn of corrie of the roots. Ault Corna Freaue (I). Also the Tulloch Burn (F), ðɪ ˈtʌləçˈbʌrn. North of Gairnshiel.

**Allt Coire nam Muillear*** (3, 269046), burn of corrie of the millers. Ault Corr-na-Mhuluir (R 12). Also Burn of Coire nam Muillear. Burn of Cor-na-mhu luir (I). North-west of Gairnshiel.

**Allt Coire na Mòine*** (3, U, 102942), ˌaltˌkọrnɐˈmọn, burn of corrie of the peat moss. In Glen Quoich.

**Allt Coire nan Clach*** (3, 101999), burn of corrie of the stones. Ault-Cor-na Clach (I). Shown at 111991 (I) on the site of Allt

Dearg (OS), but Allt Dearg is really the burn coming off Cnap a' Chleirich at 104000. On Beinn a' Bhuird.

**Allt Coire nan Imireachan** (OS, 3, A, U, 340040), ˌaltˌkọrnən 'ımrəçən, burn of corrie of the ridges. Suggestions of 'flittings' for Imireachan (M) seem fanciful. West of Morven.

**Allt Coire nan Ràgh*** (3, U, 121871), ˌaltˌkọrnən'raːɣ, burn of corrie of the rafts (i.e. tree roots, note A 221). South-east of Corriemulzie.

**Allt Coire na Saobhaidhe** (OS, 3, U, 250870), ˌaltˌkọrnɐ'sıvi, burn of corrie of the fox's den. Also the Coire na Saobhaidhe Burn (F), ðıˌkọrn'sıvi'bʌrn. On Lochnagar.

**Allt Coire na Sgreuchaig** (OS, 149896), locally Allt Sgreuchaig (3, D in A, A, CMcH), alt'skreçək, burn of screeching one (e.g. an owl). Ault Scraichaig (I). Also now the Sgreuchaig Burn (F), ðı'skreçətʃ'bʌrn. Above Braemar Golf Course.

**Allt Coire Odhar*** (3, 149783), burn of dun corrie. Ault-Cor-Our (I). East of Cairnwell.

**Allt Coire Ruairidh** (OS, 2, U, 071994), ˌaltˌkọ'ru·əri, burn of Rory's corrie. Note Rory also appears in another Allt Coire Ruairidh 1 km to the north in Banffshire, and in Inchrory of Glen Avon. On Beinn a' Bhuird.

**Allt Coire Spùtan Dearg*** (2, U, 007980), ˌaltˌkọrˌsputɐn'ʤɛrək, burn of corrie of red spouts. On Ben Macdui.

**Allt Coire Sùilean Dubha*** (3, U, 098935), ˌaltˌkọrˌsulṇ'ḍu, burn of corrie with black eyes (i.e. springs). Also the Coire Suilean Dubha Burn (U), ðıˌkọrˌsulṇ'du'bʌrn. In Glen Quoich.

**Allt Coire Uilleim Mhóir** (OS, 226830), burn of Muckle Willie's corrie. Also the Little Black Latch (I), now the Back Latch (A, C), ðı'bak'latʃ. West of Loch Muick.

**Allt Cosaig** See Cossack Burn.

**Ault Connachty** (OS, 351890), should be Allt Chruinneachtaidh (5, U), alt'krunɐχte, burn of ? possibly from Cruinn = round, Cruinneachd = of convexity, or Chruinneachaidh = of the gathering. Ault chrunachty (I). In mid Glen Muick.

**Allt Connie** (OS, 073866), from Allt Chonnaidh (5, D in A, A, U), alt'χọne, burn of the firewood or of the dog stream (note W 442). Pronounced Chònie (M). Also the Connie Burn (Br, U), ðı'kọne'bʌrn, usually now the Connie (C). South-west of Inverey.

**Allt Creag Phadruig** (OS, 2, F, 045899), ˌaltˌkreg'fa·rək, burn of Patrick's rock. Also the Creag Phadruig Burn (F), ðıˌkreg 'fa·rək'bʌrn. West of the Linn of Dee.

**Allt Creag Phadruig*** See Allt Phadruig.

**Allt Cristie Beag** (OS, 044865), from Allt Criosdaidh Beag (5, D in A, A, U), ˌaltˌkriəstji'beg, little burn of swift one, or of Christie (a personal name), or of a Christian. Also the Little Criosdaidh (C), ðı'lëtəl'kristi. South-west of Inverey.

**Allt Cristie Mór** (OS, 051860), from Allt Criosdaidh Mór (5, F), ˌaltˌkriəstji'mo·r, big burn of swift one, or of Christie (a personal name), or of a Christian. Ald Christich (Roy). Note hill of Christie (Scr). Also the Big Criosdaidh (C), ðı'bıg 'kristi. South-west of Inverey.

**Allt Cùl** (OS, 5, U, 181959), alt'kul, back burn. Also the Broken Brig Burn (U), ðı'brokən'brıg'bʌrn. North of Invercauld.

**Allt Cùl Raineich*** (5, 164848), burn of back (place) of fern. Ault Culrannich (I). In Glen Callater.

**Allt Cul Riabhach Beag*** See Allt a' Chuil Riabhaich.

**Allt Cùl Riabhach Mór*** (5, 173789), burn of big brindled back. Ault Culriach more (I). East of the Cairnwell.

**Allt ? Daimheag*** (6, 344892), burn of ? possibly from Damh = stag, or personal name Diack. Ault Diack (I). In Glen Muick.

**Allt Damhaidh Beag and A.D. Mor** See Allt Dhaidh Beag and A.D. Mor.

**Allt Darrarie** (OS, C, 311847), from Allt Dairiridh (4), alt 'darəre, burn of loud rattling noise, which fits it well. Altarerie (R 6), Ault Darrarie (I). In Glen Muick.

**An t-Allt Dearg** (2, A, U, 121904), ðıˌalt'ʤɛrək, the red burn. Also the Arderg Burn (C), ðıˌard'ʤɛrək'bʌrn. West of Braemar.

**(An t-) Allt Dearg** (OS, 3, U, 104000), as above, the red burn. See also Allt Coire nan Clach. Flows through reddish patches of granite gravel. At the head of Quoich.

**Allt Dearg*** (3, 150877), red burn. Aulderge (Im 3), Auldierg (Rli 23). A former farm in Glen Clunie.

**An t-Allt Dearg*** (3, U, 149877), ðıˌalt'ʤɛrək, the red burn. In Glen Clunie.

**The Allt Dearg Pool*** See Poll Allt Dearg.

**Allt Deas** (OS, 4, C, 385880), alt'ḍes (C), alt'ẹs, ald'ẹs (F, older folk), south burn, probably Allt Eas = waterfall burn (Dms), but note Ault Dess (I). This name covers the top three burns and the main one below (I). At the head of Glen Tanar.

**Allt Dhàidh Beag** (OS, 980881), should be Allt Damhaidh Beag (5, M, D, A, C), ˌaltˌdavi'beg, little burn of stag stream. Pronounced Allt Davy Beg (M). Note that Daimhidh (Allt Daimheidh (OS)), a tributary of Ardle, 'is from damh, an ox, stag' (W 442). 'Burn of Davy' was suggested by some local people (D), but no other place-name evidence of a David in this area. Daibhidh Beag given by keepers (OSn). Little davie fl. (Go) with fl. presumably Latin fluvius = river, Davvy-beg (Roy), Davy Beg (Ro). Also the Little Damhaidh (C), ðı'lëtəl 'davi. In Glen Geldie.

**Allt Dhàidh Mór** (OS, 964880), should be Allt Damhaidh Mór (5, M, D, A, C), ˌaltˌdavi'mo·r, big burn of stag stream. See above. Davvy-mor (Roy), Davy More (Ro), Daibhidh Mor given by keepers (OSn). Also the Big Damhaidh or Muckle Damhaidh (C), ðı'mʌkəl'davi. In Glen Geldie.

**The Allt Dhaidhs**, from the Allt Damhaidhs (F), ðıˌalt'daviz. The Alt Davies (S). Often the Damhaidhs (C). The Delvys, the Dalvys (Fi). A collective name for the burns Allt Dhaidh Beag and Mor in Glen Geldie.

**Allt Dobharaidh*** (3, 377013), burn of little water (note W 453-6). Altdourie or burn of Tullich (G 33), Burn of Altdowry (R 4) shown south of the North Deeside Road. Runs into Tullich Burn near Ballater, but formerly was also the present Tullich Burn.

**Allt Domhain** (OS, 151820), should be An t-Alltan Domhain (3, D, A, F), ðıˌalten'dọn, the deep burnie. Aultn Don (I). In upper Clunie.

**Allt Dorch*** (3, 180014), dark burn. Ault Dorach (I). South of Loch Builg.

**Allt Dourie** (OS, 165957), from Allt Dobharaidh (3, C), alt 'dʌuri, alt'ḍauri (Sch), alt'duri or duəri (A), burn of little water (note W 453-6). Pronounced Alltdùrie (M). Aldourie (Fa), Ault Uarie (I), Allt ouri, allt douri, allt durie (D in A). Beside Invercauld.

**Alltdourie** (OS, 167931), locally the Alltdourie Ferm (C), ðıˌalt 'dʌuri'fẹṛm, or the Hame Ferm (C), ðı'hem'fẹṛm. Alltdourie Home Farm (Er). Near Invercauld.

**The Alltdourie Burn*** (U, 165930), ðıˌalt'dʌuri'bʌrn. Beside Alltdourie Cottage, see below.

**Alltdourie Cottage** (OS, C, 167929), alt'dʌuri or alt'dʌuri 'kọtəʤ. Altdowrie (Io 75). Near Invercauld.

**The Alltdourie Cottage Boat** (Gf, 165923). Also the Factor's Boat (Wy). Former ferry over Dee at Invercauld.

**Alltdourie Pool** See Upper Boat Pool.

**Allt Dowrie** (OS, 352899), from Allt Dobharaidh, meaning as above. Ault Duarie (I). Lower part is now the Cadger Burn (F), ðı'kaʤɛr'bʌrn. Aldourea also shown as a house (Roy) on lower part of burn, probably same as Upper Aucholzie. In Glen Muick.

**Allt Dubhag*** (3, U, 154910), alt'duɐk, burn of little black one. Ault Duack (I). Also the Dubhag Burn (C), ðɪ'duɐk'bʌrn. Formerly burn of Duack (Ra 5). South of Braemar.

**Allt Dubh-allt*** (4), burn of dark burn, possibly Allt Dubhailt, burn of gloom. Altdualt (Me 3), Altadowelt, Altduald (Io 12, 19). In Glen Gairn, probably about Glen Fenzie.

**Allt Dubh-choire** See Duchrie Burn.

**Allt Duibh-leathad*** (3, 383028), burn of dark slope, possibly Dubh-leathad of same meaning. Auldoulitt (Io 20). Also the Duibh-leathad Burn. The Duileat Burn (Io 20). Also the Duileat Stryp (Io 20). South of Morven.

**Allt Duisgan** (OS, 317038), from Allt Dubh-easgainne (3, A, C), alt'duəskɪn, burn of black little bog. In Glen Fenzie.

**The Allt Duisgan Moss*** See Moine Allt Duisgan.

**Allt Eacartach** (3, U, 046868), alt'ekɐrtɐχ, hostile burn. Allt Eagartach, Allt an Eas Eagartach, altənjɛs'ɛkərtaç (A). A steep burn south-west of Inverey.

**Allt Feith an t-Salachair** See Feindallacher Burn.

**Allt Feith Ardair** See Feardar Burn.

**Allt Feurglaidh** See Sleach Burn.

**Allt Fhionnaidh** See Glenfenzie Burn.

**Allt Fileachaidh** (OS, 320861), probably from Allt Filleachaidh (5, C), alt'filəçi, burn of ? from Filleadh = a fold, plait. Alt filickie (R 6). In Glen Muick.

**The Allt Fileachaidh Brig*** (C, 314871), ðɪ,alt'filəçi'brɪg. A bridge in Glen Muick.

**Allt Fionn-choire** See Allt Coire Fionn.

**Allt Garbh** (OS, 980912), should be An Garbh-allt (2, F), ðɪ 'garɐwɐlt, the rough burn. Note that the OS name for the corrie—Coire Gharbh-uillt—fits An Garbh-allt but not Allt Garbh. On Beinn Bhrotain.

**Allt Garbh*** (3, 157890), rough burn. Ault Garraw (I). In lower Glen Clunie.

**Allt Geallaidh** See Geldie Burn.

**Allt Ghealain*** (4, 278956), burn of the sparrow. Ault Yalin (I). Also the Fergie Burn (U), ðɪ'fɛrgi'bʌrn. East of Crathie.

**Allt Gheallaidh** (3, D, U, 282939), alt'jʌuli, burn of the Geldie or bright one. The top part of the burn that gave the name to Abergeldie Castle. See Geldie Burn.

**Allt Ghealldair** See Gelder Burn.

**Allt Gille Geal*** (3, 229879), burn of white lad. Ault Gillie Gyall (R 7). Becomes Allt Bothan Dubh or Blacksheil Burn (OS) only lower down, so the Blacksheil Burn is incorrect for the upper part. On Lochnagar.

**Allt Giubhais** (3), burn of fir. Ault Guish (I) at 200952 and 210947. The upper part of the Feardar Burn. Ault Guish (Ro). Ault Guish (Mg map) is shown as the main burn at 198953 as well as the westward burn up by Allt Cul.

**Allt Giubhasachain** See Geusachan Burn.

**Allt Giuthas*** See Allt Coire Ghiuthais.

**Allt Glas** (OS, 242027), should be An Fhéith Ghlas (3), the green bog-stream. N Fhea Glass (R 3), Fea Glas (I), Fae Glass (R 12). Near Corndavon Lodge.

**Allt Glas-choille** (OS, 3, 311032), burn of green wood. Burn of Glasschoil (I), Alt-glas-choile (R 14). Also the Glas-choille Burn (A, C), ðɪ'glasçəl'bʌrn. North-east of Gairnshiel.

**Allt Glas-leathad** See Allt Glas-neulach.

**Allt Glas-neulach** (OS, 010839), should be Allt Glas-leathad (2, F), alt'glas,lɛt, burn of green slope. Aldglasseild (Roy), Alt Glasheild (Ar). Note Carn Glas-leathad nearby. Near Bynack Lodge.

**Allt Griogair*** (5, 140859), Gregor's burn. Grugair = surly fellow is possible but seems less likely. Note Carn Ghriogair is only 3 km south-west. Ault Grugar (I). In Glen Clunie.

**Allt Iarnaidh** (OS, 2, F, 992897), alt'iərni, burn of iron. In mid Glen Dee.

**Allt Leac Dubh*** (3, 189880), burn of black slope. Ault Leak du (R 7). Also the Clais Bhalgaire Burn (F), ðɪ,klaʃ'valəgër 'bʌrn. Above Ballochbuie Forest.

**Allt Leth-allt** See Dalvorar Burn.

**The Allt Leth-allt Pool*** See Poll Leth-allt.

**Allt Leum an Easain** (OS, 954897), locally Allt Leum Easan (2, A, F), ,alt,lem'ɛsɐn, burn of waterfall leaps, with Easan probably a variant genitive plural. Note also Allt nan Leum Easain near the Linn of Dee. In Glen Geldie.

**(An t-) Allt Liath** (OS 1869, 2, U, 060978), ðɪ,alt'liɐ, the grey burn. In the Dubh-Ghleann.

**Allt Liath-choire Beag*** (3, 174969), burn of little grey corrie. Ault Lia chorry Beg (I). Also the Little Liath-choire Burn (U), ðɪ'lɛtəl'liəçəre'bʌrn. At the west end of Feardar.

**Allt Liath-choire Mhór** (OS, 3, 170992), classic form Allt Liath-choire Mór, burn of big grey corrie. Allt Liath Choire (A), alt 'liəhər (A). Also the Muckle Liath-choire Burn (A 283, U), ðɪ 'mʌkəl'liəçəre'bʌrn. South-east of Ben Avon.

**Allt Lochan nan Eun** (OS, 3, U, 215870), ,alt,lɔχənən'je·n, burn of tarn of the birds. Burn of Lochnanean (Ro, R 7). Top part south of Sandy Loch also the Burn o Lochan nan Eun (U), now the Lochan nan Eun Burn (F). West of Lochnagar.

**Allt Loch Kander** (OS, 195814), from Allt Loch Ceanndair or Ceanndobhair (3, C), ,alt,lɔχ'kjandër, burn of head-water loch. In Glen Callater.

**Allt Loch nan Stuirteag*** (3, U, 946956), ,alt,lɔχnɐ'stjurtək, burn of loch of the black-headed gulls. In Glen Geusachan.

**Allt Loch Phadruig*** See Allt Coire Ghiuthais.

**Allt Loch Vrotachan** (OS, 110790), from Allt Loch Bhrot-choin (3, C), ,alt,lɔχ'vrɔtəçən, burn of loch of the mastiff. Also Allt an Loch (3), burn of the loch. Aultn Loch (I). The Allt Loch Vrotachan Burn is sometimes now heard (U), a good example of repetition due to anglicisation. North-west of the Cairnwell.

**Allt Luachrach*** (3, 148810), burn of rushes. Ault Luachrich (I). North of the Cairnwell.

**Allt Meadhonach*** (3, 163776), middle burn. Ault mainach (I). The middle one of three burns on the north side of the Glas Maol.

**Allt Meadhonach*** See Corndavon Burn.

**Allt Meadhonach*** (3, 140857), middle burn. Ault Mainach (I). The middle one of three burns at Coireyaltie in Glen Clunie.

**Allt Mòine Rumaich*** (3, 288966), burn of peat-moss of marsh. Ault moin Rumich (I). North-east of Crathie.

**Allt Mór*** (3, U, 328044), alt'mo·r, big burn. Forms a pair with Allt Beag in Glen Fenzie.

**Allt Mór** (3, U, 363974), as above, big burn. Alltmore (OS 1904). A former farm on west side of the burn, named after the burn (see below). Near the Pass of Ballater.

**An t-Allt Mor*** See Loin Burn.

**An t-Allt Mór*** (3, 122800), the big burn. The Auldmore (Ra 3), Ault more (I). In the Baddoch.

**The Allt Mor Park*** (U, 363973), ðɪ,alt'mo·r'park. A field near the Pass of Ballater.

**Allt na Bà Cuirc** (4, F, 045957), ,altnɐ,pə'kurk, burn of the ? cow with a top-knot. Allt na Pacuirc (A). See Caochan na Ba Cuirc. In Glen Derry.

**Allt na Beinne Brice** (OS, 049960), burn of the speckled hill. In Glen Derry.

**Allt na Beithe** (OS, 299879), burn of the birch. In upper Glen Muick.

**Allt na Buidheannaich*** (3, north of 188995), burn of the yellow place. Ault na Buinich (I). Top of Cula Burn on Culardoch.

**Allt na Buidheannaich*** See Buidheanach Burn.

**Allt na Caillich** (OS, 345915), should be Allt Chailleach (3, F), alt'hɛiləç, alt'çɛiləç (JS), burn of old women. In Glen Muick.

**Allt na Cailliche*** (3, U, 085830), ˌaltnɐˈkaləç, burn of the old woman, named from the upright rock A' Chailleach in upper Glen Ey. A variant is Alltan Cailleach (3, U), ˌaltənˈkaljɐχ, burnie of old woman.

**Allt na Caimeath*** (3, 279995), burn of the bent place. Ault na Coima (I), the Kyma (D). A burn north-east of Crathie, taking a big bend in its upper part.

**Allt na Clais Coire na Feadaige*** (3, 108781), burn of the hollow of corrie of the golden plover. Auldnaclash corrie na fatack (Ra 3). In upper Baddoch.

**Allt na Claise Finne*** (3, 091789), burn of the white hollow. Ault-na-Clash Fyin (I). In upper Baddoch.

**Allt na Claise Móire** (OS, 175990), burn of the big hollow, now Allt Clais Mór (3, U), ˌaltˌklaʃˈmoːr. Also the Clais Mhor Burn (F), ðɪˌklaʃˈmoˑrˈbʌrn. South-east of Ben Avon.

**Allt na Claise Móire** (OS, 178903), meaning as above. Also the Clais Mhor Burn (A, C), as above. South-east of Braemar.

**Allt na Cloch** (OS, 440913), from Allt na Cloiche (3, F), ˌaltnɐˈklɔiç, burn of the stone. In Glen Tanar.

**The Allt na Cloch Brig*** (U, 437930), ðɪˌaltnɐˈklɔiçˈbrɪg. A bridge in Glen Tanar.

**Allt na Coille** (OS, 257977), burn of the wood. Also Dam Burn (R 3), the Burn o the Dam (F), ðɪˈbʌrnɪðɪˈdam. North of Crathie.

**Allt na Conair** (OS, 3, 386892), altənˈkɔnər (A), burn of the path, with Alltan Conaire as a variant (3, A). Altangonar (Io 60a), the Burn of Altingonner (Ri 29). Ault-na-Connar (I), Ault na Connar (Io 34). See Burn of Coinneach. In upper Glen Tanar.

**Allt na Creige Leith** (OS, 335956), burn of the grey rocky hill. Now the Strathgirnock Burn (F), ðɪˌstraθˈgɜrnɐkˈbʌrn. West of Ballater.

**Allt na Criche** See March Burn.

**Allt na Culaidh** See Wheel Burn.

**Allt na Culaidh** See Queel Burn.

**Allt na Culath** See Cula Burn.

**Allt na Cùlath*** (5, U, 005892), ˌaltnɐˈkulɐ, burn of the back place. In Glen Dee.

**Allt na Dabhaich** See Vat Burn.

**Allt na Damhaireich*** (3, U, 050861), ˌaltnɐˈdʌuriç, burn of the rutting. Note Carn Damhaireach opposite to it. South-west of Inverey.

**Allt na Déisinneachd*** (3, U, 380890), altˈʤɛsnɐχ, burn of ugliness, Allt Déisinneach would be ugly burn. Ault-na-Jesnach (I). At the head of Tanar.

**Allt na Duibhre** (OS, 021841), locally An Duibhir (3, A, C), ðɪˈduivər, the dark one. The Duiver (M). Dubh Mheur = black finger stated (A), but does not fit the pronunciation. East of Bynack Lodge.

**Allt na Giubhsaich** (OS, 3, C, 285855), ˌaltnɐˈgjusɐç, burn of the fir wood. Also often Allt Giubhasach (3, C), altˈgjusɐχ, burn abounding in fir, especially among older local people who know the place best. Both spellings appear in old records, but nearly all refer to Allt Giubhasach:—Auld Gewschawche (Ap), Auldguishach (Pr), Aldjusach (In, Am), Alltguisach (K), Altnagiuthasach (V), Altguisach (Cpb 10). In upper Glen Muick.

**Allt-na-giubhsaich** (OS, C, 298858), as above. Also formerly called the Hut (F), ðɪˈhʌt. The Hutt (In, Am), Aultgusach Hut (Ce 3). A shooting lodge beside the above burn.

**Allt na Glaic** (OS, 3, 333023), classic form Glaice, burn of the hollow. Pronounced Allt Glac (M). Also the Glac Burn (A, U), ðɪˈglakˈbʌrn. West of Morven.

**Allt na Goibhre*** (3, 212951), burn of the goat. Ault na Goir (I). In Glen Feardar.

**Allt na h-Eaglais** See Easter Micras Burn.

**Allt na h-Earba** (3, 157939), burn of the roe. Ault na herap (I), Alltan Earb (A), altanˈɛrəb (A). In Gleann an t-Slugain.

**Allt na h-Earba** (OS, 106929 should be at 110931, also burn lower down to Quoich, 2, C), ˌaltnɐˈhɛrɐþ, burn of the roe.

**Allt na h-Easgainne*** (3, U, 080882), ˌaltnɐˈhɛskən, burn of the little bog. South-west of Inverey.

**Allt na h-Easgainne Fraoich*** (3, C, 025973), ˌaltnɐˌhɛskənˈfruiç, burn of the heather boglet. In Glen Derry.

**Allt na Làirige** (3), burn of the pass. Alt na Lairic (Iop), Allt na Lairic (T 33), location not known, probably refers to Lairig south of Corndavon Lodge.

**Allt na Lairig Ghru** (OS, 973987), from Allt na Làirige Dhrù (3), burn of the hill pass of the Dhru (i.e. the stream Dhru on the Rothiemurchus side).

**Allt na Meadhonaidh*** (5, U, 173994), ˌaltnɐˈmene, burn of the middle place (note the burn is in a central position in relation to several burns running into it). In upper Gairn.

**Allt na Megein** See Megen Burn.

**Allt nam Mèirleach** (3, A, U, 135783), ˌaltnɐˈmjaˑrlɐχ, burn of the thieves. Ault na myarlach (I). Allt nam meirleach (D in A 146), but note that all cases with this name have the pronunciation as above, therefore Meàrlach in local Gaelic, not Mèirleach. Near the Cairnwell.

**Allt na Mòine** (OS, 172997), burn of the peat moss. South-east of Ben Avon.

**Allt na Mòine** (OS, 3, 283971), burn of the peat moss. Ault na Moin (I). East of Crathie.

**Allt na Mòine** (3, A, U, 106929), is the burn incorrectly marked Allt na h-Earba (OS), ˌaltnɐˈmoˑn, burn of the peat moss. In Glen Quoich.

**Allt nan Clach Geala** (OS, 053815), locally Allt nan Clachan Geala (2, D, U), ˌaltnɐˈglaχɐnˈjal, burn of the white stones, with Clachan probably a variant genitive plural. Also the White Stane Burn (C), ðɪˈhwɛitˈstinˈbʌrn. In upper Glen Ey.

**Allt nan Coinnlean** (4, D, A, 115850), burn of the fir candles, with Coinnlean probably a variant genitive plural. Allt na gonaln (D). In mid Glen Ey.

**Allt nan Còsag*** (3, 367906), burn of the little crevices. Aldnacosag, Aldnacosaig (G 5). In Glen Muick.

**Allt nan Cuigeal*** (3, U, 406947), ˌaltnɐˈgwigəl, burn of the distaffs. Sometimes now the Allt nan Cuigeal Burn (U), ðɪˌaltnɐˈgwigəlˈbʌrn. South of Pannanich.

**Allt nan Deanntag** See Rintarsin Burn.

**Allt nan Easan*** See Allt nan Leum Easain.

**The Allt nan Easan Brig*** (U, south of 040895), ðɪˌaltnənˈjɛsɐnˈbrɪg. In Glen Dee.

**Allt nan Gamhainn** (3, U, 290002), ˌaltnɐˈgʌu.ən, burn of the stirks. Also the Allt nan Gamhainn Burn (U), and the Stirkies' Burn (F), ðɪˈstɜrkezˈbʌrn. Near Gairnshiel.

**Allt nan Laogh** (3, D, 109829), burn of the calves. Aldinlui (Roy). In mid Glen Ey.

**Allt nan Leum Easain** (OS, 3, 041901), classic form would be Allt nan Leum Easan, locally Allt Leum Easan (2, F), ˌaltˌlemˈɛsɐn, burn of waterfall leaps, with Easan probably a variant genitive plural. Sometimes Allt nan Easan (3, U), ˌaltnənˈjɛsɐn, burn of the waterfalls. West of the Linn of Dee.

**Allt nan Sgalan*** (4, 197972), burn of the sheltered places, the Scallan (I) being a corrie on Culardoch. Ault-na-Scalan (I). Also the Culardoch Burn (F), ðɪˌkəlˈardɔçˈbʌrn.

**Allt nan Taillear** See Allt Clach nan Taillear.

**Allt na Ruigh Gile** (OS 1869, 258892), burn of the white shieling. Ruighe Geal was a shieling beside this burn in Glen Gelder.

**Allt na Slaite** (OS, 110852), burn of the wand. Locally is usually Allt Shlat (3, D, A, C), altˈlaχt, burn of wands. Aldinslat (Roy). In mid Glen Ey.

**Allt Phàdruig** (OS, 3, C, 173852), alt'fɑˑrək, Patrick's burn. A variant is Allt Creag Phadruig, burn of Patrick's rock. Ault Craig Patrick (I). In Glen Callater.

**Allt Phouple** (OS, 170008), from Allt Phubuill (3), alt'fupəl, (al 'fʌpəl and alt'fɔpəl (A)), burn of the booth. Ault Fuple (I), Allt Phobil (D in A). The Shiels of Allt Phouple lie near the foot of the burn. South-east of Ben Avon, on the upper Gairn.

**The Allt Phouple Haugh**\* (U, 179008), ðɪˌalt'fupəl'haˑχ. A haugh by the upper Gairn.

**Allt Poll Bhàt** (OS, 067957), from Allt Poll Bhàthaidh (4, note A 352), ˌalt̩ˌpɒl'vaˑ, burn of pool of the drowning. In the Dubh-Ghleann.

**Allt Preas nam Meirleach** (OS, 010937), locally Allt Preas nam Meàrlach (2, C), ˌaltˌprɛsnɐ'mjaˑrlɐχ, burn of copse of the robbers. In Glen Luibeg.

**Allt Roinn a' Bhàthaich** (4, 367022, Little Burn (OS) there should be at 361031), burn of land-portion of the byre. Aultrinnavaich, Auldtrinnavaich (Io 20). Also the Burn of Roinn a' Bhathaich. The Burn of Rinnavaich, Burn of Rinavauch (Io 20), Burn of Reinavaig (G 33). Extends from 368026 down to 368021 where Wheel Burn runs in, south-west of Morven.

**Allt Ruigh na Cuileige** (OS, 268037), should be Allt Ruighe nan Cuileag (3, D, A), altruina'gulək (A), burn of shiel of the flies, now shortened to the Allt Ruighe (U), ðɪˌalt'rui. Ault Rie na Geuluk (R 12), Allt-Ru-na-Cuileage (OSn). North-west of Gairnshiel.

**Allt Salach** (OS, 350032), should be Féith Salach (3, A), fe'salaç (A), dirty bog-stream. West of Morven.

**Allt Seileach** (OS, 236007), willow burn. Also Sauchy Burn, Sauchen Stripe (R 9). Scots Sauch = willow. Near Corndavon in Glen Gairn.

**Allt Sgàirdeach**\* (5, 253963), squirting burn, or Sgàirteach = roaring. Ald Scardich (R 3). North of Crathie.

**Allt Sgreuchaig**\* (3, U, 133954), alt'skreçək, burn of screeching one (e.g. an owl). In Gleann an t-Slugain.

**Allt Sgreuchaig** (3, A, U, 072875), as above, burn of screeching one. Alt Scrichack (Fa) shown nearby on lower Connie. South-west of Inverey.

**Allt Sheanacheann**\* (4, 230027), burn of wise men. Alt Sheanachan (R 3), Althaunachan (R 9). At Corndavon in Glen Gairn.

**Allt Sheangan**\* (3, 371008), burn of ants. Althaingin, Auldhangine, Auldheangie, Auldeangin (Io 20). Up the Tullich Burn.

**Allt Shìos na Mòine** (3, D, 093818), east burn of the peat-moss. In Braemar Gaelic, Sìos and Suas were used for east and west, as well as down and up. In upper Glen Ey.

**Allt Shlat** (3, 102852), burn of wands. Altalat, Aultlat (Me 18, 21), Altalait (Mi). A former farm in Glen Ey, named after the nearby burn (see Allt na Slaite).

**Allt Shuas na Mòine** (3, D, 082814), west burn of the peat-moss. See name two up.

**Allt Sliabhach**\* See Wester Sleach Burn.

**Allt Sròn nam Fiadh** (OS, 122800), burn of nose of the deer. North-west of the Cairnwell.

**Allt Stiùbhart**\* (3, U, 127811), alt'stjuˑərt, Stewart's burn. Ault Stewart (I). Farquharson of Invercauld in 1733 mentioned 'now deceased John Stewart Alias Tyarn in Rienluig in Baddoch' (Ra); Tyarn here would be Tighearn = master or proprietor. A burn in the Baddoch.

**Allt Tarsuinn** (OS, 3, U, 135961), alt'tarsən, cross burn. Aultn Tarcen (I), Allt tarshing (D in A). In Gleann an t-Slugain.

**Allt Tom a' Bhealaidh** (OS, 4, 240035), burn of hillock of the broom. Ault Toum Byall (R 12). Pronounced Allt Tombally (M). Near Corndavon in Glen Gairn.

**Allt Tòn na Gaoithe** (OS, 2, C, 030890), ˌaltˌtɒnɐ'gui, burn of bottom of the wind. West of the Linn of Dee.

**Allt Vitch** (OS, 302875), from Allt a' Mhaide (3, C), alt'vitʃ, burn of the stick. Allt VATSH or VETSH (A 1954). In upper Glen Muick.

**The Allt Vitch Brig**\* (F, 303875), ðɪˌalt'vitʃ'brɪg. A bridge in Glen Muick.

**The Allt Vitch Moss**\* See Ceap Mad.

**(The) Altanour Lodge** (OS, C, 082823), ðɪˌaltən'aurˌlɒdʒ, named from the nearby burn An t-Alltan Odhar in upper Glen Ey. Also Alltanodhar Shieling (Anon).

**The Altanour Wuid**\* (C, 082824), ðɪˌaltn̩'aur'wɪd. The wood at Altanour Lodge.

**The American Gairdens**\* (U, east of 287948), ðɪˌa'mɛrəkən 'gɛrdənz, ? from Gaelic Meuragan = small branches. A patch with trees near Abergeldie.

**The Ancient Way** (O 123, Wy 71). An old route used by soldiers at the Battle of Culblean, possibly now the road from Cambus o' May to Ordie via the north-west corner of Loch Davan.

**The Angel's Peak** See Sgor an Lochain Uaine.

**Annag's Parkie**\* (U, 149916), 'anɛks'parke, Gaelic Annag (3) = Annie, Scots Parkie = little field. A former field at Braemar, now council houses there.

**Annie Bremner's Cottage**\* (U, 338996), 'ane'brɛmɛrz'kɒtədʒ. A former house in Glen Gairn.

**Annie Keir's Well**\* (U, south of 304963), 'ane'kirz'wɛl. East of Crathie.

**Anthony's Cast** (Wav, F, 331963), 'anθəniz'kast, after an Anthony Crossley who fished there in the 1930s. Also the Island Puil (F), ðɪ'ɛilənd'pil. A pool in Dee, west of Ballater.

**Aoineadh Mhèirleich**\* (5, F, 304944), locally Mheàrlaich, ɪn 'vaˑrliç, steep promontory of the thief, possibly Eang = point or Aonach = hill. Invarlich (Bs). A slope near Abergeldie.

**Aonach Geal**\* (5, 342969), white moor, or Eanach Geal (5), white wet meadow. Ennach Gyall (I). A field on north side of the road west of the Bridge of Gairn, not wet now.

**The Approach**\* (C, 372953 and 371951), ðɪˌa'protʃ. A name for either one of two private drives up to House of Glenmuick. To older folk the Braichlie Approach, ðɪ'breçleˌa'protʃ, as the House of Glenmuick was previously called Braichlie House. Note Approach Lodge at Abergeldie, and Balmoral (Vr 3).

**Ardach**\* (3, 308016), high place. Ardoch (Roy). A building, probably a former farm, north-east of Gairnshiel. The same map shows Ardoch Pinzey (presumably Finzey or Fenzie) at the present Ardoch at 322009.

**Ard-achaidh** (3, 156920), high field. Ardichi (Cr 19), Ardochie (Ri 22). Note Ardachaidh (T 30, 104) on Findhorn, and Ardachy, highfield (T 31, 102) near Dornoch. A former farm near Braemar.

**Ard-achaidh Park**\* (156921). Ardachy Park (I). A field near Braemar.

**Ardach Fionnaidh**\* See Ardoch.

**Arderg** (OS, 121904), from An t-Ard Dearg (3, C), ðɪˌar'dʒɛrək, ar'dʒɛrg (Sch), the red height. The Ard yerrag, Ardyeirrag (Cr 27, 29), nar'jɛrəg (Sch) from An Ard Dhearg suggesting a feminine noun. A former farm west of Braemar.

**The Arderg Boat** (120905). The Ardearg Boat (Wy). Former ferry over Dee east of Mar Lodge.

**The Arderg Burn** See An t-Allt Dearg.

**The Arderg Fuird**\* (U, 119904), ðɪˌar'dʒɛrək'fjurd. A former ford over Dee east of Mar Lodge.

**The Arderg Haugh**\* (U, 123906), ðɪˌar'dʒɛrək'haˑχ. Flat grassland by Dee, west of Braemar.

**Arderg Pool** See Poll Allt Dearg.

**Ardgairn** (OS, C, 348978), ard'gern̩, from Ard Gharain (5), height of the Gairn (see River Gairn). Now a house near the Bridge of Gairn.

**Ardmeanach** (OS, 354948), from Ard Meadhonach (3, C), ard 'mɛnɐχ, middle height. Ardemenach (Io in 1681), Easter Aurdmenach (Ri 28). E^r Ardmanoch (Roy) was at the site of the present Ardmeanach, and W^r Ardmanoch near the present Dorsincilly. A house, formerly a farm, in lower Glen Muick.

**Ardmeanach*** (355947 and 356946). Two fields (Am) at Ardmeanach in lower Glen Muick.

**Ardmeanach Croft**. Ardemenach Croft (Ab). Possibly the same as Croft of Wester Ardmeanach.

**The Ardmeanach Smiddie*** (C, north-east of 354948), ðɪˌard 'mɛnɐχ'smɪdi. A former smithy, now a shed, west of Ballater.

**Ardmohr** (Er, C, 153912), from An t-Ard Mór (3, F), ðɪˌard 'moˑr, the big height. Now a house at Braemar.

**(The) Ardoch** (OS, C, 322009), ðɪ'aˑrdɐç, from An t-Ard-achaidh (3), the high field. Ardochie (Pb, Tayl 1932), Ardachy (Ri 21), Ardichi (Cr 8), Ardach (H). Some of these spellings may refer to a different Ardoch in Glen Gairn. One map (Ro) gives the Ardoch at 322009 as Ardoch Pinzey (presumably Ardach Fionnaidh, Fenzie Ardoch), and a second Ardoch about 308016. A deserted farm in Glen Gairn.

**(The) Ardoch** (OS, C, 263956), as above, from An t-Ardach (2, JB), ðɪ'aːrdɐχ, the high point. Ardach (Opr 18). Shown at 263953 (R 8) in 1809. A farm at Crathie.

**Ardoch Cottage*** (Ce 5). Former habitation beside Ardoch near Crathie.

**The Ardoch Wuid*** (F, 264954), ðɪ'aˑrdɐç'wɪd. A wood near Crathie.

**The Arns of Culsh*** (346982), Scots Arns = alders. The Arns of Cults (Io 47). On west bank of lower Gairn.

**The Arrowmaker's Well** (McC 1891, 208838), after an arrowmaker in mid 1600s, also referred to in Creag an Fhleisdeir. On Lochnagar.

**The Aspenholm Wuid*** (F, 269944), ðɪ'aspən'hom'wɪd, after the nearby house Aspenholm, probably from Scots Howm = low-lying ground on banks of river. Also the Aspen Wuid (U), ðɪ'aspən'wɪd. Near Crathie.

**The Aspen Wuid*** See the Aspenholm Wuid.

**Àthan Ghiubhais*** (3), little ford of the fir. Anhuish (Opr 4). Former habitation in Crathie–Braemar parish, possibly beside Timber Fuird west of Braemar.

**An Àthan Leathan** (3, probably 075897), the broad little ford. N ā'an lyean (D). A ford over Dee near Inverey.

**Àthan Phuill** (4, F, 290955), a·n'ful, ɑ·n'fuḷ from best informant, little ford of the pool. There is no evidence for Diack's derivation Athan Fuill = bloody ford, which is unlikely in any case. A ford on Dee near Abergeldie.

**The Athan Phuill Park*** (F, 292954), ðɪˌa·n'ful'park. Also Middpark (Am). A field at Abergeldie.

**The Athan Phuill Puil** (F, 292956), ðɪˌa·n'ful'pil. Ann-Foul (P). A pool in Dee, beside the above ford. Pairs with Little Athan Phuill.

**Àthan Uisge Ghàrain Shuas** (5, probably 212020), little ford of water of the upper Gairn or crying one. In an old Braemar poem (T 33, 17).

**Àth Mhagairle*** (3, west of 036975), ford of ? testicles. Avagerill, the Ford of Avagril (Io 19), ford of Avagrill (Me 11). In Glen Derry.

**Auchallater** (OS, C, 156883), a'χalətɛr, from Ach a' Chaladair (3), field of the hard water. Pronounced Callater, occasionally Callter (M). Auchinquhillater in a 1564 charter (Ca) suggests Achan = small field. Achaladar (Cr 3). Also Upper

Auchallater, Wester Auchallater. Upper Achaladar, Wester Achaladar (Cr 33, 34). Farm in Glen Clunie.

**The Auchallater Brig*** (C, 156882), ðɪˌa'χalətɛr'brɪg. Road bridge beside above farm.

**The Auchallater Haughs*** (F, 156890), ðɪˌa'χalətɛr'haˑχs. Flat riverside lands north of Auchallater, on east side of Clunie.

**Auchelie** (OS, 088863), should be Ach a' Chéiridh (4, C), a'çiːri, (aç'eri (A)), field of the waxy place or duskiness. Auchachere (Mc 3), Acherie (Fa), Achery (Cr 46), Ach Cherie (Opr 38), Aucherrie (OS 1869), Ach cherri (D). Note Baile-cheiridh in Ross-shire (W 1904, 41). A former farm in lower Glen Ey.

**The Auchelie Moss Road*** (U, 080860), ðɪˌa'çi'ri'mɒs'rod. An old track to a peat moss in Glen Ey, near the house of Auchelie (see above).

**Auchendryne*** Auchindryne (Me 15). A former farm at Braemar, went along with Fife Arms Hotel, was opposite hotel.

**Auchendryne** (OS, C, 149915), ˌaχən'drɛin, from Ach an Droighinn (3), field of the thorn. The part of Braemar village west of Clunie.

**The Auchendryne Land*** See Lower Auchendryne.

**Auchnacraig Hill** (OS, 339894), açnə'kreg (A). Also the Craig Hill (C), ðɪ'kreg'hɛl, often the Craig (C). Hill of Aucholzie (I), Acholzie Craigs (Crom). See Ach na Creige. In mid Glen Muick.

**Auchnerran** (OS, 417031), from Ach an Fhearainn (3, C), aχ 'nɛrɛn, field of the land. Auchinerren (G 9), Achanaran (Pb), Achenerran (H). Also South Auchnerran (F), 'suθˌaχ'nɛrɛn, pairs with North Auchnerran. A house near Logie Coldstone.

**Auchnerran Cottage*** See the Fit o the Toon.

**The Auchnerran Moss** (C, 426035), ðɪˌaχ'nɛrɛn'mɒs. The Moss of Auchinaran (Ri 32). A peat moss near the above farm.

**Aucholzie** (OS, C, 344906), from Ach Choille (3), usually a'hwɛili, but a'χɔili, a'χɔlji from best informants; (aç'ɔlji with palatal *l* (A)), field of woods. Achullye (Io 4) in 1634, Owhaille (Bla), Achaqhuaile, Achaquhuoile (Ab 1), Achoily, Achoillie (R 1, 6), Achülyi, as in coille, ach-chuall (D). Probably also Nether Aucholzie. Neither Auchoilzie (Ri 14). Also Mains of Aucholzie (Ri 29, I). A farm in mid Glen Muick.

**The Aucholzie Brig*** (C, 343900), ðɪˌa'hwɛili'brɪg. A bridge in Glen Muick.

**The Aucholzie Burn*** (F, 343903), ðɪˌa'hwɛili'bʌrn. The lower part of Allt Cholzie in mid Glen Muick.

**Aucholzie Craigs** See Auchnacraig Hill.

**The Aucholzie Fit Brig*** (F, 343908), ðɪˌa'hwɛili'fɛt'brɪg. A former bridge over Muick.

**The Aucholzie Wuid*** (F, 345900), ðɪˌa'hwɛili'wɪd. A wood in lower Glen Muick.

**Auchtavan** (OS, 204955), from Ochdamh Mheann (4, C), ˌaχtə 'vjaˑn, eighth part of kids (i.e. part of a davoch or former measure of land), as in Auchtyfardle (W 201), or Ach Dà Mheann, field of two kids. Achidavand (Fa), Achtamheann (Io 53), Achtavainn (Cr 26), Auchtivian (Rli 23). Shown at 206956 to east of present house (I). Ach da mhunng, 2 kids (D) fits pronunciation less well. A former farm in Glen Feardar, now a house.

**The Auchtavan Auld Park*** (U, 208955), ðɪˌaχtə'vjaˑn'aˑl'park, Scots Auld = old, a field beside the above house.

**The Auld Arderg Road*** (U, north of 123904), ðɪˌa·l'ar'dʒɛrək 'rod. A former cart track west of Braemar.

**The Auld Ballater Road*** (F, 350980), ðɪˌa·l'balətɛr'rod. The former road to Ballater down the east side of Glen Gairn.

**The Auld Ballater Road** (F, 432009), ðɪˌa·l'bɑ·ltɛr'rod. The Old

Ballater Road (O). Also called the General Wade Road (U), but Wade was not here. Also the Culblean Road (U), ðɪˌkəl'blin'rod. Also Mar's Road (Mil), after the Earl of Mar in 1431. A drove road (Gf) from Tullich to Cromar.

**The Auld Boat Puil** (F, 240941), ðɪ'aˑl'bot'pil. Old Boat (Sc). A pool in Dee, on Invercauld side. On Balmoral side it is called the Carnaquheen Puil (F), ðɪˌkɛrnɐ'çwin'pil. Cairnaquheen (Sc).

**The Auld Braes Road*** (U, 430020) ðɪ'aˑl'brez'rod. A path from the Braes o Cromar via Raebush to join the Auld Ballater Road behind Boggerfool.

**The Auld Brig*** (F, 266942), ðɪ'aˑl'brɪg. To younger folk the Suspension Brig (F), ðɪˌsəs'pɛnʃən'brɪg. Also the White Brig (U), ðɪ'hwɛit'brɪg. Bridge of Crathie (Vr 1). A bridge over Dee near Balmoral, was there before the present wide road bridge at Balmoral was built.

**The Auld Brig o Dee** See Bridge of Dee.

**The Auld Brig o Dee Puil*** (F, 187909), ðɪ'aˑl'brɪgɐ'diˑ'pil. In Dee below the hump-backed Bridge of Dee at Invercauld.

**The Auld Brig o Inver*** (F, west of 233937), ðɪ'aˑl'brɪgɐ'ɪnvɐr. A bridge at the Inver.

**The Auld Brig Puil** (F, 186909), ðɪ'aˑl'brɪg'pil. Old Bridge Pool (A). On Balmoral side is called the Brig Pot (U), ðɪ'brɪg'pɒt, Scots Pot = deep pool. A pool in Dee, south-east of Invercauld.

**The Auld Cairnwell Road*** (F, 145791), ðɪ'aˑl'kɛrnˌwɛl'rod. Parts of the old military road that were not used for the current line of the road.

**Auld Clais an Fhraoich*** See Clais an Fhraoich.

**The Auld Cragan Road*** (F, 108898), ðɪ'aˑl'kragən'rod. East of Mar Lodge.

**The Auld Dam*** (F, 421959) ðɪ'aˑl'dam. A former dam, now a wet patch, near Inchmarnoch.

**The Auld Derry Brig*** (F, 040934), ðɪ'aˑl'dɛre'brɪg. Former road bridge at Derry Lodge.

**Auld Derry Lodge*** (U, 042942), 'aˑl'dɛre'lɒʤ. Also the Derry Shiel. The Dairy Sheal (Fi). A former shooting lodge in Glen Derry.

**The Auld Derry Lodge Road*** (U, 044934), ðɪ'aˑl'dɛre'lɒʤ'rod. An old track to a former lodge in Glen Derry.

**The Auld Drove Road*** (U, 366982), ðɪ'aˑl'drov'rod. An old track north of Ballater, formerly a drove road.

**The Auld Fuird*** (U, 214920), ðɪ'aˑl'fjurd. A former ford over Dee, at Ballochbuie Forest.

**The Auld Groddie Brig*** See the Morven View Brig.

**The Auld House o the Etnach*** (U, south of 413917), ðɪ'aˑl 'husiðɪ'ɛtnɐχ. Old Etnach (Gler). Also the Shepherd's Bothy (F), ðɪ'ʃɛpɛrdz'bɒθe. A former house and farm in Glen Tanar.

**The Auld Hut*** (U, 418981), ðɪ'aˑl'hʌt. Probably was Easterton earlier. Ruin of a former croft at Cambus o' May.

**The Auld Lary Road*** (U, 341010), ðɪ'aˑl'leˑre'rod. A track from Wester Morven to Lary, used before the present road was built.

**The Auld Lime Quarry*** (U, 275938), ðɪ'aˑl'lɛim'kware. A disused quarry near Balmoral.

**The Auld Line** (C, 361962) ðɪ'aˑl'lɛin. The Old Line (Gl). Also Lovers' Walk (Wy), but this is not a local name. A track from Ballater to the Bridge of Gairn, made for a proposed railway line to Braemar.

**The Auld Luibeg Brig*** (F, 038933), ðɪ'aˑlˌlui'bɛg'brɪg. Former bridge near Derry Lodge.

**The Auld Manse*** (C, 316006), ðɪ'aˑl'mans. A former manse east of Gairnshiel.

**Auld Mary's*** See Bellamore.

**Auld Mary's Park*** (F, 414963), 'aˑl'merez'park. A field east of

Pannanich, beside the ruin of Bellamore, named after old Mary Ewen the last inhabitant, who died in the 1890s. Also the Bellamore Park (Dms).

**Auld Meggie's*** (U, 311014), 'aˑl'mɛgiz. A former house east of Gairnshiel.

**The Auld Mill*** (F, 269017), ðɪ'aˑl'mël. In Glen Gairn.

**The Auld Regions*** (U, 299962), ðɪ'aˑl'riʤɪnz. A name at the Lebhall for the former site of the house and farm buildings further uphill. East of Crathie.

**The Auld Road*** (U, 266944), ðɪ'aˑl'rod. An old road between the North and South Deeside Roads at Crathie, which existed before the present road crossing at Balmoral Brig.

**The Auld School*** (C, north of 300011), ðɪ'aˑl'skul. Former school, now a house, near Gairnshiel.

**The Auld Schoolhouse** See Dalphuil.

**The Auld Schoolhouse Park*** (F, 449994), ðɪ'aˑl'skulˌhus'park. A field beside a former school at Loch Kinord.

**The Auld Sean Spittal Brig*** See Drochaid an t-Seann-spideil.

**The Auld Sgairneach Road*** (F, 296900), ðɪ'aˑl'skarnjɐχ'rod. An old track in Glen Girnock.

**The Auld Sleach Brig*** (F, 266015), ðɪ'aˑl'sliɐç'brɪg. A former footbridge over Gairn near Gairnshiel.

**The Auld Toll House*** (U, 405980), ðɪ'aˑl'tɒlˌhus. Also Colonel Jock's (F), ˌkʌrnəl'ʤɒks, after Colonel Jock Sandison who lived there. This house, which is no longer visible, stood west of Cambus o' May where the Auld Ballater Road from Logie Coldstone meets the North Deeside Road.

**The Auld Tom Bad a' Mhonaidh Road*** (U, 291914), ðɪ'aˑlˌtam ˌpɪt'funi'rod. A track from Girnock to Balmoral, used before the present road was built.

**The Auld Walls*** (F, 362925), ðɪ'aˑl'wɑːz, Scots = old walls. A collective name for old ruined houses and enclosures at Loinn Mor in lower Glen Muick.

**The Auld Wifie's Housie Park*** (U, 429045), ðɪ'aˑl'wɛifiz'husi 'park, Scots for the field of the old woman's little house. A field near Logie Coldstone, named after a former little house in the field.

**Aultonrea** (OS, 354918), from Allt an Ruighe (3, C), ˌaltən'riː, burn of the slope. Aultanruie (Io 7), Auldinruiff (G 4), Altinrui (Mc 15), Altownrie (Ri 14), Allt an rui (D). A farm in lower Glen Muick.

**The Aultonrea Birks*** (U, 352918), ðɪˌaltən'riˑ'bërks. Birch wood in lower Glen Muick.

**The Aultonrea Wuid*** (F, 355915), ðɪˌaltən'riˑ'wɪd. A plantation in lower Glen Muick.

**Avalanche Gully** (Sd, 088964), the steep gully of Alltan Tarsuinn on Beinn a' Bhuird, scene of an avalanche that killed two walkers and buried another for a day in 1964.

**Am Bac** (3, D, 103880), the ridge. A broad ridge south of Corriemulzie.

**Am Bac*** (3, 144882), the ridge. The Baack (I). A broad ridge in lower Glen Clunie.

**The Back Burn*** See Little Burn.

**The Back Coire Buidhe*** See Coire Buidhe air Chul.

**The Back Coire Buidhe Burn*** (U, 277872), ðɪ'bakˌkɒr'bui'bʌrn. In Glen Gelder.

**The Back Corrie*** (Fi, U, 020956), ðɪ'bak'kɒre. North-west of Derry Lodge.

**The Back Corrie Burn*** (U, 020958), ðɪ'bak'kɒre'bʌrn. North-west of Derry Lodge.

**The Back Latch** See Allt Coire Uilleim Mhoir.

**The Back o the House Puil*** See Mary's Cottage Puil.

**The Back o the Wuid Butts*** (U, 265010), ðɪ'bakɪðɪ'wɪd'bʌts. Grouse butts west of Gairnshiel.

**The Back o the Wuid Butts*** (U, 231025), as above. Near Corndavon Lodge.

**The Back Park*** (U, 422037), ðɪˈbakˈpark. A former field near Logie Coldstone.

**The Back Parkie*** (U, east of 260956), ðɪˈbakˈparki. A tiny field in a wood north-west of Crathie.

**Back Rashes*** See North Auchnerran.

**The Back Road*** (C, 085900), ðɪˈbakˈrod. Right of way road on north side of Dee from Linn of Dee past Claybokie, Mar Lodge, Allanaquoich, Alltdourie and Invercauld to the Keiloch.

**The Back Road*** (C, 351945), as above. Public road up west side of lower Glen Muick.

**The Back Road*** (U, 406041), as above. A path behind fields west of Logie Coldstone.

**The Back Wuid*** (C, 444000), ðɪˈbakˈwɪd, sometimes the Back Wuid o Kinord (U). A wood beside Loch Kinord.

**Bad a' Chabair** (3, U), badˈhabër, clump of the pole. Bad Chaber (Im 1), Baddochaber (Cp). Near Moine Bad a' Chabair in upper Girnock.

**The Bad a' Chabair Moss** See Moine Bad a' Chabair.

**The Bad a' Chabair Stane*** See Clach Mhor Bad a' Chabair.

**Bad a' Chàirr*** (5), clump of the bog, possibly Bad a' Chuir, clump of the turn. Either would fit the place well. Badaquhar, Badachurr, Badchurr (Io 20). About top of Culsten Burn, south-east of Morven.

**Bad a' Challain** (3), clump of the noise. Bad-a-chuilein in an old Braemar poem (T 33, 17), but original notes (Iop) Bad-a-chailein suggest Chailein = of the seedling or prickle; however, see Carn Bad a' Challain. Probably near Carn Bad a' Challain on Brown Cow Hill.

**Bad a' Chròthain*** (3), clump of the sheep-fold (note Mb 269). Sheiling of Badachrone (G 1a). In Glen Callater.

**Bad a' Mheig Wood*** (4, 109910), clump of the cry, Uig = nook is less likely as it is usually a coastal term. Badiwick Wood (Fa). On the slope between Mar Lodge and Glen Quoich.

**Am Badan*** (3, U, 090948), ðɪˈbadɐn, ðɪˈbatɐn, the little clump. A clump of old firs in Glen Quoich.

**Bad an Easa*** (3, 075893), clump of the waterfall. Badnēss silva (Go), Wood of Bad in ess (Fa), Bydeness, Baidness (Me 13, 18). Note Creag Bad an Eas. A wood shown (Fa) as stretching from Inverey to the Linn of Dee.

**Bad an Iasgair*** (3, U, 153935), ˌbadɐnˈiskər, clump of the fisher (i.e. probably a heron or other fishing bird). Now in a plantation north of Braemar.

**The Bad an Iasgair Wuid*** (U, 155932), ðɪˌbadɐnˈiskərˈwɪd. North of Braemar.

**Bad an Laoigh** (3, c. 238988), clump of the calf. Badenlui (D). A 'mossy brow' (D) north of Crathie.

**Bad an Laoigh Moss*** (3, 240991), Badan lui Moss (R 3). A peat-moss north of Crathie.

**Bad an Lòin** (3, 271983), clump of the marsh. Bad'n Loin (R 3), Battenloan (D). South-west of Gairnshiel.

**Badan Seilich** (4, 313891), little clump of willow. Badinscolich (R 6), Badinshalloch (Io 60a, A). Former shielings on hill ground west of the Linn of Muick.

**Bad an t-Seabhaig*** (3, F, 037940), ˌbadɐnˈʤuɪk, ˌpadɐnˈʤuɪk, clump of the hawk. Patenduig (R 10). Near Derry Lodge.

**The Bad an t-Seabhaig Path*** (F, 037942), ðɪˌpadɐnˈʤuɪkˈpaθ. An old stalkers' path from the Derry on to Carn Crom.

**Bad an t-Suidhe*** (4, 054925), clump of the ? level shelf. Badintoy (Go). A former farm in Glen Lui.

**Bad an Tuairneir*** (4, 253922), clump of the turner. Bad an t-Suirn = clump of the kiln does not fit as the place is not on or beside farmland. Bad an durna (B). In Glen Gelder.

**Bad Charn** See Renatton.

**(The) Baddoch** (OS, C, 132828), ðɪˈbadəç, from A' Bhadach (3), the place of clumps. The Battach (Cr 34), A' bhadaich (D). A disused farm up Glen Clunie.

**The Baddoch** (A, C), as above, a general name for the area around the above farm, including the grazings in the glen and hills to the south-west. This was obvious in earlier maps also (R 14).

**The Baddoch Brig*** (F, 130822), ðɪˈbadəçˈbrɪg. Bridge over Baddoch Burn.

**(The) Baddoch Burn** (OS, C, 120805), ðɪˈbadəçˈbʌrn. Also Water of Baddoch. Water of Badach (Fa), Water of the Baddoch (Ro). A tributary of the Clunie.

**The Baddoch Fit Brig*** (U, 131828), ðɪˈbadəçˈfɛtˈbrɪg. A foot bridge at Baddoch.

**The Baddoch Plantin*** (F, 136827), ðɪˈbadəçˈplantɪn. A recent coniferous plantation at the Baddoch.

**Bad Eadar Allt** (3, c. 280994), clump between burns. Bad eadarallt (D). South-west of Gairnshiel.

**Bad Fiantaige** (4, C, 256989), badˈfjantɪk, clump of crowberry. Bad feandaig, Baudfantack, Blairfiantick, Badfaintaig (R3, 5, 6a, 14), Balfentaig (OS 1869). Crowberries grow commonly on the damp parts of the moor there. Note Tom na Fiantaige, crowberry knoll, in Dorback on Spey (T 41, 232). Fionntag = the little white one, a stream at Moy in Inverness-shire (T 30, 112) does not fit as the stream below Bad Fiantaige is the Coulachan Burn. A former farm north of Crathie.

**Am Bad Leathan** (3, 388915), the broad clump. Badlien (Ri 29), the Badlean (I). South-east of Ballater.

**Bad Leathan** (3, probably 25-03-), broad clump. Bad leathan, broad clump (D). Near the Sleach north-west of Gairnshiel.

**Am Bad Liath*** (3, 222959), the grey clump. The Batlia (I). North-west of the Inver.

**Bad ? Luachair*** (3), clump of rushes. Badlouklare (Me 5). A former grazing in Glen Gelder.

**Bad na Ban** (OS, 410930), classic form would be Bad nam Ban (3), badnəˈban (A), clump of the women. Part of a peat-moss south-east of Ballater.

**Bad na Beinne** (OS, 3, C, 390034), ˌbadnɐˈbin, clump of the hill. On south side of Morven.

**Bad na Beinne** (3, 221044), clump of the hill. Badnabine (Io 15), Bad na-bein (R 14), Badnabane, a grazing on the upper Gairn (A).

**Bad na h-Earba*** (3, about Rashy Burn), clump of the roe deer. Badnaharb (Io 20). Badinyearb, Badenyarb (G 19) suggest Badan Earba = little clump of roe deer. South-east of Morven.

**Bad nam Barraigh** (3), clump of the crops, from Barr + ach = crop place. Badnabarrie (D), Barrie in this name means cultivated pieces where crops had been grown (D). In the area about Gairnshiel, to judge from the name's position in Diack's list.

**Bad nam Boghta*** (5, 397974), clump of the swathes of hay. Pitnabucht (Io 58), Potnabucht (R 4). Possibly Scots Boucht = sheep-fold, but part-Gaelic part-Scots names are unusual. On farmland at Tullich.

**Bad nan Coileach*** (3, 192903), clump of the cocks (i.e. woodcocks, note 'Burn of Badnaculach or Woodcocks Burn' (R 7)). Badnaculach (R 7). In Ballochbuie Forest.

**Bad nan Cuigeal** (3, U, 405946), ˌbadnɐˈgwigəl, clump of the distaffs. South of Pannanich.

**Bad nan Cuileag** (OS, 3, 213974), badnəˈgulak (A), clump of the flies. Badna culack (I), Bad na gulig (D). Shown as 'green spots' at 212967 (I). North-west of Crathie.

**Bad nan Dearcag** (OS, 208969), clump of the little berries. West of Crathie.

Snow corries and avalanche tracks in Coire an Lochain Uaine of Ben Macdui lie below the peak named Stob Coire Sputan Dearg by climbers.

**Bad nan Laogh*** (4, c. 244017), clump of the calves, Laoch = of champions unlikely (see Carn Bad nan Laogh). Badnaloach (G 3), Badnoloach (Me 3). East of Corndavon Lodge.

**Bad Phlaid** (3), clump of cultivated plots. Badflad (Ri 17, Me 3). A former shieling on upper Gairn.

**Bad Ruighe an Uillt** (3, c. 270027), clump of shieling of the burn (see Ruighe an Uillt). Bad-Renald (Blaeu's map shows this as a hill near the head of Gairn), Badronnald (Io 2), Badronuald (Me 3). A former grazing on upper Gairn.

**The Bads o Ben Avon*** (U), ðɪˌbadzɐˌbɛnˈaːn. A local name for the tors of Ben Avon. Suggests that Bad can mean a projecting rock on top of a hill. Note Bad = top cluster, hair on the upper part of the head (Dw).

**The Ba Field*** (U, 425045), ðɪˈbaːˈfild. Scots Ba = ball, perhaps where ball games were played. There is a Ba Muir (OS) on moorland at Glass, Huntly. An area of rough grassland and bog near Logie Coldstone.

**Baideal Uarach*** (3, 282930), pillar of time or weather. Badelwarrach (In, Am). On a prominent high ridge south-east of Crathie.

**Baile a' Cheòthaich*** (3, U, 295953), bɐlˈçjɔχ, farm-town of the mist. Balchich (Opr 63). Balecloich (Roy), Balachloich (Opr 6) suggest Baile Cloiche, farm-town of a stone. Blelachlioch (Am), Bualtchach (1962 deed at Abergeldie Castle). Also the Three Neuk Park (U), ðɪˈθriˈnjukˈpark, Scots Neuk = corner. A former farm, now a field, near Abergeldie.

**Baile a' Chlaiginn** (3, c. 151913), farm-town of the infield. Bellachlaggan (Ri 22), Bell i chleughan hard by the old castle of Braemar (Cr 3). A former farm.

**Baile a' Mhuilinn** (3), farm-town of the mill. Baile vuiln (A). Now the Milltoun (C, 319002), ðɪˈmɛltən. A former house east of Gairnshiel, where the West and East Milton Burns meet.

**Baile a' Mhuilinn*** (2, U, 087887), balˈvulən, farm-town of the mill. Also the Milltoun o Inverey (U), ðɪˈmɛltnɐˌɪnvɛrˈɛiˑ. Milntown of Inverey (Me15). A former farm at the foot of Glen Ey.

**Bailean Dabhaich** (3), little farm-town of the davoch (i.e. area of land). Bellundavach ('Balmenach')—a pendicle of Balmoral (Mc), suggests that Baile Meadhonach and Bailean Dabhaich in 1662 had recently become one farm, possibly having referred to different farms that became joined.

**Baile an Eilein** (3, C, 152913), bɐlˈnɛlən, farm-town of the riverside-field. Ballinneillan, Bellin-neillan (Cr 31), Ballanellan (Opr 37). A former farm south of Braemar, now refers to a group of fields.

**Baile an Eilein*** (3), farm-town of the riverside-field. Bellin neillan in the grounds of Dalmore (Cr 30), Balnelean (Me 15). A former farm at Mar Lodge.

**Baile an Lochain** (3, F, 359972), bɐˈlɔχɐn, farm-town of the tarn. Ballinlochan (Io 20), Ballenlochan (Cr 44), Ballochan (H, OS 1904). No tarn now, but ground to the east is boggy and might well have held a tarn before being drained. A former farm above the Pass of Ballater.

**Baile an Lochain Castle*** See Abergairn Castle.

**The Baile an Lochain Park*** (U, 358972), ðɪˌbɐˈlɔχɐnˈpark. Also one of two Tom Meann Parks. A field at west end of Pass of Ballater.

**Baile an Lòin** (3, A, U, 153898), ˌbalənˈlon, farm-town of the wet meadow. Balanloin (Cr 35), Baileloin, Ballnloan (Opr 9), Balnloan (I), Bail an Lon, town of the gutters (D). A former farm, now part of Braemar Golf Course.

**Baile an Lòin*** (3, c. 108902), farm-town of the wet meadow. Ballinlon (Roy). A former farm east of Mar Lodge.

**Baile an Torraidh** (3, U, 360941), ˌbalənˈdore, farm-town of the little hill. Balindorie (Rli 19), Belindorie (Ri 14). A former farm south of Ballater.

**Baile an Torraidh*** (3, C, 361945), ˌbɛlənˈdore. A name used for a house in the 1930s–1940s, now demolished. Near the above place.

**Baile an Tuim** (3, F, 112892), ˌbalənˈduim, farm-town of the hillock. Balintuim (OS 1869). A former farm on the south side of the road immediately east of the bridge at Corriemulzie.

**Baile an Uird** (3, probably 18-91-), farm-town of the round hill. Balnourd (Vd), Balanard (E), Balnaurt (Mp). Site of a former chapel near the Keiloch at Invercauld.

**Baile Cloiche*** See Balgairn.

**Baile Meadhonach*** (3, 141845), middle farm-town. Ruins of Balmainack (I). A former farm in mid Glen Clunie, about half way between the former farms of Coireyaltie and Coirenalarig.

**Baile Meadhonach** (3, U), bɐlˈmɛnɐχ, middle farm-town. Balmurrel with pendicle thereof called Balmenach and the lands of Inveryelder (Mc 6), pendicles of Bellamanach and Abergelder (Mc 11), Balminach (Ra 15). A former farm near Balmoral.

**(Am) Baile Mór** (3, F, 413041), ðɪˌbɛlɐˈmoˑr, big farm-town. Ballamore (OS 1869). A former farm near Logie Coldstone.

**The Baile Mor Park*** (U, 413043), ðɪˌbɛlɐˈmoˑrˈpark. Also the Roadside Park (U), ðɪˈrodˈsɛidˈpark. A field west of Logie Coldstone.

**Baile-na-coille** (OS, C, 261943), from Baile na Coille (2), ˌbalnɐˈkɛil, farm-town of the wood. A modern house at Balmoral, named after farm named below.

**Baile na Coille** (2, F, 259946), as above. Belnakyle (Opr 33), Bailnacoill (Cpb 8), Balnacoil (B). Former farm at Balmoral.

**The Baile-na-coille Park*** (F, north-west of 261944), ðɪˌbalnɐˈkɛilˈpark. A field at Balmoral.

**Baile na Mòine*** (3), farm-town of the peat-moss. Bellnamuin in the Davoch of Aberrarder (Cr 22). A former farm in Glen Feardar.

**Baile na Mòine*** (3), meaning as above. 'Bellnimuin o're against the Dupprach (parish of St Andrews Braemar)' (Cr 24) shows a former house Baile na Moine west of the Linn of Dee or at Braemar Golf Course on east side of Clunie.

**Baile nan Critheach** (3, U, probably 349974), ˌbɛlɐˈkrih, farm-town of the aspens. Belenocrith (Asr). See Muileann Chritheannaich which stood nearby, and Coilacriech. A former farm near the foot of Glen Gairn, now the house Glengarden.

**Baile nan Gabhar** (3, U, 160931), ˌbalnɐˈgʌvˌər, ˌbalnənˈgau.ər (Sch), farm-town of the goats. Ballnagabhar or goats town (Opr 41b), Balnagour (I). A former farm near Invercauld.

**Baile nan Taobhanach*** (3), farm-town of the rafters. Bellnitouvenach, Bellni-touvennach very near Dalmor's house, Ball nan tuanach, Bailnotuanach, Ballnantuanach (Cr 30, 31, 44, 48, 50). A former farm near Mar Lodge.

**Baile Nighinne** (3, F, 406046), bɐlˈniˑn, daughter's farm-town. Bolnean (Pb), Balnain, Bealnean (G 18, 28), Bilnean (Io 39), Benean (H). A former farm west of Logie Coldstone.

**Am Baile Nodha** (3, F, 347911), ðɪˌbɐlˈnoː, the new farm-town. Bellino, Bellno (Ri 8, 27), Balnoe (I). A former farm in Glen Muick.

**The Bailey Brig*** (C, 328890), ðɪˈbeliˈbrɪg. A bridge in mid Glen Muick, demolished late 1982.

**The Bailey Brig*** (C, 276013), as above. Also the Tulloch Brig (F), ðɪˈtʌləçˈbrɪg. West of Gairnshiel.

**Balanreich** (OS, C, 342969), ˌbalənˈriaç, ˌbalɛnˈriç from best informants, balənri.ç (A), from Baile an Fhraoich (2), farm-town of the heather. Ballenreich, fhraoch (D). Balnruich (I, Ro) a former farm at 341968 on the Braemar side of the Balanreich Burn, on the upper side of the main road. Balanreich is now a big house west of Ballater.

**The Balanreich Burn*** (C, 345969), ðɪˌbalənˈriəçˈbʌrn. Burn of Balnruich (I). Burn beside above house.

**The Balanreich Loch*** (U, 341969), ðɪˌbalənˈriəçˈlɔχ. An artificial loch west of Bridge of Gairn, beside the house of Moine-na-vey, which is not a local name. Also the Moine-na-vey Loch (U), ðɪˌmɔɪnɐˈveˈlɔχ.

**Bald Horse Stripe*** See Feith Preas an Eich Bhlair.

**Balgairn** (OS, C, 351971), bɐlˈgerṇ, from Baile Ghàrain (5), farm-town of the Gairn, (see River Gairn for meaning). Said to be an invented name (A), but this was incorrect, as it appears as Ball Garden (farm) in 1815 (I), exactly on the site of the present Balgairn, as Bellgairden (Io) in 1786, and as Balgairn (Io) in 1798 and 1851. The former Tom Bealaidh was near here. Also formerly Baile Cloiche (3), farm-town of stone. Ballacloich (Im) in 1726, Ballachloich (Io) in 1763, Balachloich (Opr) in 1769. A farm west of Ballater.

**The Balgairn Puil** (C, 352966), ðɪˌbɐlˈgerṇˈpil. Balgairn (Sc). In Dee, near the Gairn entry.

**Balhalloch** (OS, C, 331961), bɐlˈhɛiləç, from Baile Chailleach (3), farm-town of old women. Ballachalloch (Aj1), Ballachylach (Opr 4), Ballachallaiche (Io 41), Balchailach (R 1), Ballichailliach, Bailechaileach (Cpb 1, 4), Bellachailach (Ap), Ballachalich (I), common speech Balhóllak (M), Balchŏllăĭk (Da). Balachaileach (M) is recorded as a separate name but is obviously the same place. Balquhollie (Abergeldie) (Gr xiv) is probably the same place. Balach mor (Roy) suggests big Balhalloch, and he gives Upper Balachalioch in Glen Muick. A farm west of Ballater.

**Balhennie** (OS, C, 406043), bɐlˈhɛne, balˈhɛne from one brought up there, from Baile ? Chuinnidh (5), farm-town of champions, as in Dalwhinnie in Inverness-shire. Bellhangie (G 28), Belhenny (H), Bal-henni (D). A former farm near Logie Coldstone.

**The Balhennie Plantin*** (F, 406045), ðɪˌbɐlˈhɛneˈplantɪn. A plantation west of Logie Coldstone.

**The Balhennie Ruighe na Beinne*** (U, south-west of 407044), ðɪˌbɐlˈhɛneˌrʌneˈbɛn. Pairs with the Groddie Ruighe na Beinne. A field west of Logie Coldstone.

**Balindory** (OS, C, 419959), ˌbalənˈdore, ˌbɛlənˈdore, from Baile an Torraidh (3), farm-town of the small hill. Belndorrie (H), Ballindory of Inchmarnoch (Opr 24). Other old spellings (A 170). The original Balindory was further west (Dms). A house near Inchmarnoch.

**Balintober** (OS, C, 365942), ˌbalənˈtobër, from Baile an Tobair (3), farm-town of the well. Balintober (Rli 19). Also Muckle Balintober. Muckle Bellintober (Io 34, 50), Meikle Ballentober (I). Also Upper Balintober. Oper Bellintober (Io 9). Formerly a farm, now a house south-west of Ballater.

**Balintobers** (Ab 19). A former collective name for the two former farms Muckle and Little Balintober, later Balintober and Littleton. Bellintobers (Io 50). South-west of Ballater.

**Balintuim** (OS, C, 153894), ˌbalənˈtuəm, from Baile an Tuim (2), ˌbalənˈṭuim (Sch), farm-town of the hillock. Bellniduym (Cr 33), Balln Duim (I). A former farm south of Braemar, now a house, beside a prominent steep hillock.

**Balintuim East*** (U, 154896), ˌbalənˈtuəmˈist. A field in Glen Clunie, includes former field An Ton Fail and other ground.

**The Balintuim Quarry*** (F, 152895), ðɪˌbalənˈtuəmˈkware. South of Braemar.

**Balintuim South*** (U, 154894), ˌbalənˈtuəmˈsuθ. A field in Glen Clunie.

**Balintuim West*** (U, 153896), ˌbalənˈtuəmˈwɛst. A field in Glen Clunie, includes former field Lios Mor and other ground.

**(The) Ballabeg** (OS, C, 414038), ðɪˌbɛlɐˈbɛg, from Am Baile Beag (3), the little farm-town. Bellabeig (Anon 10), Bellabegg (H). This was formerly Lower Ballabeg, Upper Ballabeg being another farm further up the burn (JK). A house near Logie Coldstone, formerly a farm.

**The Ballabeg Burn*** (U, 413036), ðɪˌbɛlɐˈbɛgˈbʌrn. Lower part of Coinlach Burn near above farm.

**The Ballabeg Park*** (U, 412037), ðɪˌbɛlɐˈbɛgˈpark. A field west of Logie Coldstone.

**Ballachan Inbhir Eidh** (6), walls of Inverey (Gr). Ballachan Enbhireidh (Gr). At Inverey Castle.

**Ballachlaggan** (OS, C, 222940), from Baile a' Chlaiginn (3), bɐlˈçlagən, farm-town of the infield. Bellechlagan (Fa), Bella-chleughan (Cr 33), Balachlagan (R 14). A former farm at Aberarder west of Crathie.

**The Ballachlaggan Brig*** (F, 225937), ðɪˌbɐlˈçlagənˈbrɪg. A bridge in Glen Feardar.

**Ballachrosk** (OS, C, 342985), ˌbalɐˈχrɒsk, bɐlɐˈfrɒsk, ˌbalɐˈχrɒʃk, from Baile a' Chroisg (3), farm-town of the crossing, after a nearby ford over Gairn. Ballacroish (Im 3), Belachroisk (Opr 19), Ballachroisht (I), Balchroisk (R 14), Balcroist (Io 77), Balchroisg (D). A house in lower Glen Gairn, formerly a farm.

**The Ballachrosk Brae*** (C, 342991), ðɪˌbalɐˈχrɒskˈbre·. A hill on the road north of Ballachrosk.

**The Ballachrosk Brig*** (C, 342985), ðɪˌbalɐˈχrɒskˈbrɪg. A bridge in Glen Gairn.

**The Ballachrosk Burn*** (C, 340985). ðɪˌbalɐˈχrɒskˈbʌrn. Burn of Ballachroisk (I). In lower Glen Gairn.

**The Ballachrosk Fuird*** (U, south-west of 343993), ðɪˌbalɐˈχrɒskˈfjurd. A former ford north-west of Bridge of Gairn.

**Ballater** (OS, C, 370960), ˈbalətër, but ˈbɑ·ltër by some old people, from Bealdair or Bealadair (5), in Gaelic Byalter (D), Be'alter or Be'halter (M), Beal'tair, Bealadair (W in Dw), ˈbjaltər (Sch). Baladar (Bl) in 1704, Ballader (Aj) in 1716. Up to the end of the 18th century, Ballater was a name not at the present town but at the east end of the Pass of Ballater, where the Ballater Burn is today. Dair possibly = water, referring to the Ballater Burn. Beal might suggest Bealach = pass, as the Pass of Ballater is such a striking feature and the pass was formerly called Creagach Bhealdair. However Diack stated that the Gaelic pronunciation of Ballater lingered on the l, as the current ˈbɑ·ltër of some old people also does. In 1790 the name was being used for farmland at about 375966 (R 4), at least 1 km north-east of the centre of Ballater town today. The present Monaltrie House was then Ballater House, and the present Ballater town did not exist. Balater (Roy) in 1747 shown as a building at the present Monaltrie House.

**Ballaterach** (OS, 421960), from Baile Leitreach (3, C), bɐˈlɛtrëç, farm-town of slope. Pronounced Ballétrach (M). In Gaelic Bal-lēthterach, bal-iatrach (D). The OS name is a distortion of the local pronunciation. Ballaitrich (Rli 21), other old spellings in (M). South of Cambus o' May.

**The Ballaterach Burn*** (C, 420960), ðɪˌbɐˈlɛtrëçˈbʌrn. At Inchmarnoch.

**The Ballaterach Burn Brig*** (C, 423962), ðɪˌbɐˈlɛtrëçˈbʌrnˈbrɪg. A road bridge at Inchmarnoch.

**The Ballaterach Corrie*** (F, 418950), ðɪˌbɐˈlɛtrëçˈkɒre. The Corrie o Ballaterach when he was a boy (AR). South of Ballaterach.

**The Ballaterach Golf Course*** (F, 418957), ðɪˌbɐˈlɛtrëçˈgɒlfˌkors. Two fields on Ballaterach; a former farmer played golf there.

**The Ballaterach Hill*** (F, 418948), ðɪˌbɐˈlɛ̤trɛ̈ç'hël. A big area of hill, used as a grazing.

**(The) Ballater Burn** (OS, C, 380973), ðɪˈbalətër'bʌrn. Burn of Ballater (R 4). Burn coming out of the east end of the Pass of Ballater.

**Ballater House** See Monaltrie House.

**Ballater House Farm*** See Farm of Ballater.

**Ballater Village Lands*** (Io in 1807). The sections of land rented out during the expansion of Ballater in its early years as a new, planned village.

**(The) Ballochbuie Burn** (OS, C, 210904), ðɪˌbaləç'bui'bʌrn. A burn in Ballochbuie Forest.

**The Ballochbuie Burn*** See Allt a' Bhealaich Bhuidhe.

**Ballochbuie Forest** (OS, 210900). In Gaelic was Frith Bhealaich Bhuidhe (3), deer forest of the yellow pass. Fridh vyalich vui (D). The OS map misleadingly shows this name as a wood, but the word Forest in Upper Deeside always referred in past maps and papers, and in current speech, to a deer forest, not a forest of trees. See the Wuid o Ballochbuie.

**(The) Balloch Plantation** (OS, C, 198948), ðɪˈbaləç'plantɪn, ðɪ 'beiləç,plan'teʃən. A wood north of Invercauld, named after the nearby Am Bealach.

**The Ballroom Park*** (F, 094899), ðɪˈbalˌrum'park. A narrow field beside the Ballroom at Mar Lodge.

**Balmenach** (OS, C, 362977), from Baile Meadhonach (3), bɐl 'mɛnɐχ, middle farm-town. Ballamenach (Io 16). A farm above the Pass of Ballater.

**The Balmenach Burn*** (F, 363975), ðɪˌbɐl'mɛnɐχ'bʌrn. Lower part of Loin Burn.

**The Balmenach Corrie*** See Coire Mor.

**Balmoral** (C), bəl'mọrəl, bə'mọrəl, also bə'mʌrl (A), from Both Mhoir-ail (4), in Gaelic Bă-vŏr-ăl, sometimes Bal-vorar or bă-voră (D), ba'vorɐl (Sch), hut of the big spot (i.e. spot of ground), see Balmoral Castle. Bouchmorale (Cro) in 1451, Ballmorall (Cr 19), Balmurral (R 3, 5), Balmurrel (Mc 6). Much has been written (M, D, A) on the possible meaning of Balmoral, though little evidence is available. We think Both Mhoir-ail is the most likely (note J 239; Mb 182; W in T 30, 113). Both Mhoir Thul(aidh), hut of the big hillock, is also a possibility. Other suggestions such as Mór Choille, and Morail = magnificent, do not fit the local pronunciation. The o was short in local Gaelic (D) and in current local pronunciation is not long as in current Gaelic Mór = big, so the Mhoir or Mhor here may indicate an ancient form. Balmoral is a general name for the low ground on the opposite side of the Dee to Crathie, including the village and the castle. See Easter Balmoral.

**The Balmoral Approach*** (U, 260949), ðɪˌbəl'mọrəla'protʃ. A private road to Balmoral Castle.

**The Balmoral Brig** (C, 262949), ðɪˌbəl'mọrəl'brɪg, Balmoral Bridge (Gf). The road bridge at Balmoral.

**Balmoral Castle** (OS, C, 255951), bəl'mọrəl'kasəl. Formerly Castle of Balmoral (Cromb), the Castle of Balmoral (S). The castle stands on a place formerly called Both-mhorail, east of which was Bail-mhoirir (MP), see under Easter Balmoral.

**The Balmoral Cottages** (C, 257951), ðɪˌbəl'mọrəl'kọtədʒɪz, Balmoral Cottages (Crom).

**Balmoral Forest** (OS, C), bəl'mọrəl'fọrëst. A large area of deer forest south of Balmoral.

**Balmore** (OS, C, 216943), bɐl'mọ·r, from Baile Mór (3), big farm-town. Beilemor (Fa), Bail mor of Aberarder (Cr 48), Ballmore (I). Ballamoor (S 14a), Ballamore, Bellamore (Cpb 2) show an extra a in the middle, as in Bellamore at Inchmarnoch. Also Easter Balmore (Vr 2), paired with Wester. A former farm near the Inver.

**The Balmore Brig*** (F, 217944), ðɪˌbɐl'mor'brɪg. A bridge in Glen Feardar.

**The Balmore Hill*** (U, 210942), ðɪˌbɐl'mor'hël. Hill grazing above Balmore.

**Balnaan** (OS, C, 285005), bɐl'naːn, bəl'naːn, (bal'na.n (A)), from Beul an Âthain (4), mouth of the little ford, possibly Baile an Athain, farm-town of the little ford (D in A). Belnaan (R 14). A former farm west of Gairnshiel, beside a shallow part of Gairn with former ford.

**Balnacroft** (OS, C, 285944), ˌbalnə'krọft, ˌbɐlnə'krọft, from Baile na Creit (3), farm-town of the croft. Belnacroft (Aj) in 1666, Bal na creitsh (D in A). A former farm at Abergeldie, now a name for nearby houses.

**Balnagower Cottage** (OS, C, 157930), ˌbalnə'gʌu.ër'kọtədʒ. A house near Invercauld.

**Balnalan** (OS, Mc25, C, 229943), bəl'nalën, bɐl'nɛlən, from Baile an Âilein (4), farm-town of the meadow, or Eilein = of streamside field. Ballenaillan, Ballanneallan (Io 49, 50), Bailanalain (Cpb 4), Belnalan (R 14), Bal nalin (D in A). A former farm near the Inver.

**The Balnalan Park*** (U, 229942), ðɪˌbɐl'nɛlən'park. A field near the Inver.

**Balnault** (OS, C, 244946), bɐl'nalt, (bal'nult (A)), from Baile an Uillt (3), farm-town of the burn. Balnuilt (R 14), Bal n uiltsh (D). A farm west of Crathie, beside a burn.

**The Balnault Burn*** (F, 242946), ðɪˌbɐl'nalt'bʌrn. Formerly Ailtridh Burn (6), see Monaltrie for meaning. Rivulet called Altry (Wi), the Burn of Altry (Io 34), Altrie Burn (R 3), Monaltrie Burn (Vi). Near the above farm.

**Balno** (OS, C, 321004), bɐl'noː, from Baile Nodha (3), new farm-town. Belnoe (H). A farm in Glen Gairn.

**The Balno Burn*** (F, 322005), ðɪˌbɐl'no·'bʌrn. East of Gairnshiel.

**Balno Cottage*** (Ce 6). Former habitation beside Balno in Glen Gairn.

**Balnoe** (OS, I, C, 214938), bɐl'noː, from Am Baile Nodha (3), the new farm-town. Belno (Fa), the Bellno (Cr 22). Also Newtown Aberarder (Opr 26). A former farm at Aberarder west of the Inver.

**The Balnoe Brig*** (F, 214938), ðɪˌbɐl'no·'brɪg. A bridge in Glen Feardar.

**The Balnoe Burn*** (U, 220938), ðɪ'bɐl'noː'bʌrn. The lower part of Felagie Burn, west of the Inver.

**The Balnoe Park*** (U, 218939), ðɪˌbɐl'noː'park. A field at Balnoe.

**The Balno Fuird*** (F, west of 317004), ðɪˌbɐl'noː'fjurd. A ford in Gairn.

**The Balno Wuid*** (F, 320006), ðɪˌbɐl'noː'wɪd. A wood east of Gairnshiel.

**The Bankie Puil*** (C, 405977), ðɪ'baŋki'pil. Green Bank (Ly). A pool in Dee, west of Cambus o' May.

**Bannerman's Brae*** (C), 'banërmənz'bre·. A hill on a road at south-west corner of Church Square in Ballater.

**Bard Mór** (3), big meadow. A name at Braemar (D).

**The Bard of Gleney*** (Io 79, 091834), Gaelic Bard (3) = park.

**Bards of Gleney*** (Io 79, 097842), Bard (3) = park. Also the Glen Ey Park. Gleney Park (Io 79). A former grazing enclosed by a stone dyke, extending for over 1 km.

**Barglass** (OS, C, 413030), bər'glas, blər'glas, glas now often glɛs, from Blàr Glas (3), green field. Blairglesse (Ab) in 1676, Barglass (H), Blairglass (R 17). A former farm near Logie Coldstone.

**(The) Barglass Burn** (OS, C, 415032), ðɪˌbər'glas'bʌrn. Beside above farm.

**The Barn Park*** (U, 414037), ðɪ'barn'park. A field west of Logie Coldstone.

**The Barns**\* (F, 156013), ðɪ'barnz. A rough hillside on Ben Avon between Allt Phouple and Allt Bad a' Mhonaidh, said to be called the Barns because it holds deep snow-drifts.

**The Barns o Cnap a' Chleirich**\* (U), ðɪ'barnzɐ‚knap'çlɪrɪç. Collective name for tors north-east of Beinn a' Bhuird.

**The Barns of Beinn a' Bhuird** (Miln). Tors.

**The Barns of Ben Avon** (Miln). See Sabhalan Beinn Athfhinn.

**Barrack Ground**\* See the Castle Park.

**The Barrack Yard** See the Castle Park.

**The Barr Yard**\* (Dms, west of 438967, by elimination), Gaelic Bàrr (3) = crop. Small piece of land at Deecastle farm near Inchmarnoch.

**Bàta an Duinidh** (5, 466984), boat of the Dinnet. Bat an dunie (D). Boat of Dinnet (Be). Former ferry over Dee.

**Bàta Poll Chollaig** (5, 344965), boat of Polhollick. Bat poll-chollaik (D). Boat of Poulchollick (I). Former ferry over Dee.

**The Battery**\* (F, 070865), ðɪ'batɐre. Note Carn Damhaireach or Top of the Battery is the summit to the south-west. A hill slope between Connie and Cristie, near Inverey.

**Am Bealach** (3, A, U, 179948), ðɪ'balɐχ, the pass. A pass between Invercauld House and Glen Feardar.

**Am Bealach** (3, OS 1869, C), ðɪ'beiləç, the pass. The Baillach, the Biallach (Cr 31, 47), Bealach (Opr 38), an old farm. One map (I) gives Upper and Lower Balloch and the whole area of both farms as Balloch, and notes 'The Cyards' (presumably tinkers) as being at Lower Balloch. Former farmland north-east of Invercauld.

**Am Bealach**\* (3, U, 170933), ðɪ'beiləç, the pass. A narrow stretch that had not been planted with trees, but is now planted. Near Invercauld.

**Am Bealach Buidhe** (3, Mp, C), ðɪ‚balɐç'bui, in Gaelic m‚bjalɐχ 'bui (JB, Sch), the yellow pass. 'M byalloch bui (D). A general name for the open ground around 203905 east of Garbh Allt Shiel in Ballochbuie Forest. Note Achichnes or Ballach Buoy (Cr 16), and Parks of Ballochbuie (R 7) show that the name used to refer to a farm. The Bealach here probably means a passage or crossing low down, not a high pass over the hills, and Bealachodhar (below) is another example of this. The name Bealach Buidhe is often used also for Connachat Cottage further east. Balloch bui (Roy) is shown above the wood east of the Falls of Garbh Allt.

**(Am) Bealach Buidhe** (OS, 3, C, 173839), as above, the yellow pass. The OS map marks the name on the old Bealach Buidhe path, but the actual Bealach or top of the pass is at 167815. In Glen Callater.

**Am Bealach Buidhe**\* (3), the yellow pass. Ballach buy (Fa) shown about the top of the Feindallacher Burn, probably the pass at 195845 south-east of Creag an Loch, leading from Ballochbuie Forest over to Loch Callater. Another Am Bealach Buidhe is between Loch Callater and the Cairnwell, and a third beside Garbh Allt Shiel in the Dee valley. Possibly all three lay on one route over the hills.

**(Am) Bealach Dearg** (OS, 3, C, 181984), ðɪ‚beilɐχ'ʤɛrg, ðɪ ‚bjalɐχ'ʤɛrəg (JB), the red pass. Ballachjarg (Fi), Balloch Dearg (I). Note the Little Bealach Dearg also. An old track over Culardoch, on a route from Tomintoul to Braemar.

**The Bealach Dearg Road**\* See Rathad Bealach Dearg.

**Bealach Eadar Dhà Chreagan**\* (3, 122975), pass between two rocks. Balloch-eter-a-Chragan (Roy). Between Quoich and Gairn.

**Bealachodhar** (OS, 316867), from Bealach Odhar (3, F), ‚bɛlɐχ 'ʌuɽ, dun-coloured passage. Byalloch Our (Io 65). Byallach Our (I), farm buildings at 316871 and 315869. Byallachour (Ram 3) shown as a house at about 314871. An area in upper Glen Muick.

**The Bealach Plantin**\* (F, 170934), ðɪ'beiləç'plantɪn. A wood near Invercauld House.

**Bealach Ruadh**\* (3), red pass. Ballochruadh (Io 79). In Glen Ey, quite likely from Ey to Coirenalarig in Glen Clunie.

**The Bealachs** (U, 190935), ðɪ'beiləçs. Ballocks (Ro). A collective name for the enclosed former farmland at Upper and Lower Bealach north-east of Invercauld.

**The Bealach Wuid**\* (C, 194935), ðɪ'beiləç'wɪd. A birch wood north-east of Invercauld.

**Beal Ghabhar**\* (3, 224942), passageway of goats, from Bealach. Bial Gour (I). A field in Glen Feardar.

**The Bee Hillock**\* (U, north of 289947), ðɪ'bi'hɛlëk. Near Abergeldie, bees kept there formerly.

**Beinn a' Bhuilg**\* See Creag Bhalg.

**Beinn a' Bhuird** (OS, North Top (OS) at 092006, South Top (OS) at 090979), should be Beinn Bòrd (2, C), bɛnɐ'bɔ·rd, bɛn'bɔ·rd (JB), table-hill (see D, A). Bini bourd (Bla), Binnavordy (Hi), Binnybuart (Ra 5), Ben Vurde (Roy), Binnyboard (Fi), Bein-na-Board (I), Beinn-na-Baird (Ro), Benabord (R 10). In Gaelic Binn Burd, table mountain; 'Beinn a' Bhuird is wrong, as the a is only a euphonic a, not the article' (Mp). Ping burd, ping ya burd, ping a burd (D). A big hill above Glen Quoich, with a flattish high plateau.

**Beinn a' Chaorainn** (OS, 3, C, 045013), bɛn'hu·rən, (pin'hörɪn with both n's palatal (A)), hill of the rowan. Ben Chuirn (Roy), Binnachuirn (R 2a), Ping hörinn (D). OS name criticised, as rowan 'is quite inapplicable' (A), but this ignored the fact that trees once grew at much higher altitudes than today (note Allt an Da Chraobh Bheath high on Lochnagar). Also North Top (R 2b). A hill at the top of Glen Derry.

**Beinn a' Chaorainn Bheag** (OS, 3, 057017), little hill of the rowan. Also South Top (R 2b). Also the Little Beinn a' Chaorainn (C), ðɪ'lëtəl‚bɛn'hu·rən. Beside the above hill. Note the Beinn a' Chaorainns (C), a collective name for the above two hills.

**Beinn Bhreac** (OS, 3, C, 059971), ben'vrɛ·çk, speckled hill. Binnyvreach (Fi). Pronounced Vrehk, tending towards Vrack (A). A hill with speckled screes, north of Derry Lodge.

**Beinn Bhrotain** (OS, 3, C, 954923), bɛn'vrɔtɐn, hill of the mastiff. Binwrodin (Fa), Binny-wroten (Fi), Beinn-na-Vrotan (Ro), Ping vrottan (D). A big hill above Glen Dee.

**Beinn Chraimeal** (6), hill of the ? crease, possibly from Cramb = squeeze or Cramasgadh = creasing. Bing ya Chraimal (D), Air mulach Binne Chraimeal, Ben Chraimeal (D). Appears in a Gaelic song 'The Lass of Braegarrie', referring to places near Corriemulzie. Note Bin Chrombie (Mo) for high tops along the county boundary between Ey and Clunie, and Meall Chrombaig (OS) near Fealar Lodge, Perthshire.

**Beinn Gharbh** (3, 156773), rough hill. Ben Garrow (Th, Kn). The top of Meall Odhar on the south side, a place with rough screes. East of the Cairnwell.

**Beinn Iutharn Bheag** (OS, 065791), should be Beinn Fhiùbharainn Bheag (3, W 1916), ‚bɛn‚jurɲ'bɛg but ‚beiɲ jurɲ'vɛg from those with most Gaelic (F), little hill of the edge-point. Iutharn does not fit the local pronunciation. Ben Euarn beg (Roy), Ben urn Beg (I). Binn uirinn bheag (D), Ping yuring, Ping yurnn vek (D in A, note the ng and the nn which Diack used for referring to a palatal n, as in Beinn or Fhiubharainn, but not as in Iutharn). Also the Little Beinn Fhiubharainn (C), ðɪ'lëtəl‚bɛn'jurɲ. Little Benurin (Io 79). At the head of Glen Ey.

**Beinn Iutharn Mhór** (OS, 046793), should be Beinn Fhiùbharainn Mhór (3, W 1916), ‚bɛn‚jurɲ'mo·r, but ‚bei‚ɲ ‚jurɲ'vo·r from those with most Gaelic, (F), big hill of the edge-point. See above. Bin Neur (Bla, L), Ben Euarn mor

(Roy), Binn uirinn Mhor (D). Also the Big Beinn Fhiubharainn (C), ðɪˈbɪɡˌbɛnˈjurn̩. Also Muckle Beinn Fhiubharainn. Meickle Benurin (Io 79). At the head of Glen Ey. Note the Beinn Iutharns (C), a collective name for the above two hills.

**The Beinn Iutharns Corrie*** (C, 060790), ðɪˌbɛnˈjurn̩zˈkọre. The big corrie between the above two hills.

**Beinn Mheadhoin** (OS, 025017), should be Beinn Meadhon (2, C), bɛnˈmeːn, middle-hill. Binnimain (R 2a), Biny Main (Fi), Ben Mean (Ar), Beinamean (Scr), Bennamain—Beinn Mheadhoin is known only to the map (Mp), Ping mein, main, pingi mēin (D). A big hill at the top of Glen Derry, in the middle between Loch Avon and Glen Derry. The summit at 025017 is in Banffshire, but the hill comes into Aberdeenshire.

**Beinn nan Cìochan** (3, U), ˌbɛinˌnənˈkiɔçɛn, hill of the paps, with Ciochan probably a variant genitive plural (see Allt nan Clach Geala for another example). The old name for the Lochnagar massif including the White Mounth, and also (Ed) for the rest of the hill ridge forming the boundary between Angus and Aberdeenshire. The Little Pap and Meikle Pap are current names of hills in this massif. Bine-chichnes (Go), Bin Chichnes, Bin-chichins (Bla), Binchichins, Hichins (Ed), Bin chichins (Mo), Binn Chioch (Dro), Ben Chichins (A), Beinn nan Cichean (Sg 199). Ben Chichins suggests an anglicised plural the Beinn Chiochans, from Beinn Chiochan, hill of paps. The Forrest of Beinichichness (Io 63) suggests again Beinn Chiochans with a svarabhakti *i* or a slender *n*, but Beinn Chioch an Easa, paps hill of the cascade, seems possible. The construction looks similar to Achichneas lower down in the same Forest, which we have interpreted as Ach Eich an Easa but might be Ach Chioch an Easa.

**Am Beitheachan** (3, C, 090951), ðɪˈbeːχɛn, ðɪˈbeːɐχɐn, the little birch place. Forrest of Beachan (Go), Beachan (Bla), the Beachan (Roy), Bechan (R 10). Cha teid mi 'n a Bheachan, I'll go not to the birch clump (Sin). Now refers to a big area of firs in Glen Quoich, an area almost devoid of birches today. Presumably, birch at one time had been as usual a pioneer tree colonising open ground, and was later succeeded by fir.

**The Beitheachan Burn*** (C, 104955), ðɪˈbeːχɛnˈbʌrn. Burn of Bechan (R 10). Note Water of Beachin (Ri 27). Water Beachan (Fa) is a semi-Gaelic construction suggesting Uisge Beitheachan. Part of Quoich Water in the area of Am Beitheachan.

**The Beitheachan Wuid*** (C, 095950), ðɪˈbeːχɐnˈwɪd. Beachin Wood (Fa). A big area of natural old firs in Glen Quoich (see Am Beitheachan).

**Beitheach Park*** (3, 255956), Beitheach = birch-place, Scots Park = field. Baich Park (R 6a). A birch wood near Crathie.

**Bellamore** (OS 1869, C, 415964), ˌbɛlɐˈmoːr, balɐˈmoːr (U), from Baile Mór (3), big farm-town. Bellamoir (Dms 8). Also Auld Mary's (F), ˈaˑlˈmɛˑrez. Note Maynes of Bellamore (Dms 10), the Mains of Bellamore (G 15). A former farm near Inchmarnoch. It covered a big area (Dms), hence the name Baile Mor = big farm-town.

**(The) Bellamore Craig** (OS, C, 404963), ðɪˌbɛlɐˈmoˑrˈkreg. Craig of Bellamore (Dms). A rocky hill above Bellamore.

**The Bellamore Park*** See Auld Mary's Park.

**Bellaneye** (OS, C, 083894), ˌbɛlɐnˈɛiˑ, from Bealan Eidh (6), ˈbjalɐnˈɛiˑ (F), little passage of Ey (see Ey Burn for meaning). A house at Inverey.

**The Bell Brae** (A, C, 421965), ðɪˈbɛlˈbreˑ, a hill on the road between Inchmarnoch and Pannanich, named after a bell there which called worshippers to a former chapel nearby.

**The Bell Hole** (F, 423965), ðɪˈbɛlˈhol. Bell Peel (A). A pool in Dee, near the Bell Brae south of Cambus o' May.

**Bell Puil** See the Bell Hole.

**The Bell Wall*** (F, south-east of 419967), ðɪˈbɛlˈwaˑl. A well near Inchmarnoch, between road and river.

**Ben Avon** (OS, 132018 (summit)), from Beinn Athfhinn (4, Sin, C), bɛnˈaːn, possibly hill of Athfhinn (i.e. very bright one, referring to the river), or perhaps from Abhainn = river (Sgs 9, 136), from an earlier Abona = river (Ni). A' h'-Fhinn, water of Fingal (Gle). In Gaelic Ping auinn, ping auing (D 188); Diack noted that Abhainn was pronounced av-eng (short) and Avon was auw-eng. The Fingalian reference (Gle) seems possible, as there is a ford called Ath nam Fiann, ford of the Fingalians, on the River Avon. Another possibility suggested to us instead of the Ath in Athfhinn is Abha as in River Awe or Obha as in Loch Awe, probably originally Abha, from obsolete Gaelic = stream, river (W). Obha would agree with the *auw* in Diack's Gaelic pronunciation. Ben Awn (Roy). The easternmost high hill in the Cairngorms, to the south of Glen Avon.

**Benjie's Rig*** (U, south of 329958), ˈbɛndʒizˈrɪg. A strip of ground on lower Girnock, on north side of South Deeside Road.

**Ben Macdui (Beinn Macduibh)** (OS, 4, Mp, C, 989989), ˌbɛnˌmɐçˈdui, ˌbɪnˌmaχˈdui (Sch), hill of Macduff. Ben MacDuff (Po), Ben Mach Dui (Roy), Binny Machdui, Biny-Macdou (Fi), Bhin-na-mach on-daidh, now Bhin Macduff (Laing). A Duff or Fife family owned the Aberdeenshire part of Ben Macdui for centuries until it was sold to a Swiss family in the early 1960s. The highest hill in the Cairngorms.

**Benton's Brae*** (C, 252955), ˈbɛntənzˈbreˑ. A hill on a road west of Crathie, named after a local man.

**The Bents*** (F, 374970), ðɪˈbɛnts, ðɪˈbɪnts. A piece of gravelly ground with bent vegetation north-east of Ballater.

**Besom Jimmy's Cave*** (F, south-west of 266953), ˈbizʌmˈdʒimiz ˈkeˑv. A cave in the rocks behind Crathie school, formerly used by 'Jemmy Sim' (Dav), a traveller who sold besoms (Scots = brooms).

**Beul-àth na Làirige Dhrù** (3, JB, on the Luibeg, probably 015939) ˈbelɐnɛˌlɑˑrɪgˈgruː, ford-mouth of hill pass of the Dru (see Lairig Ghrù). Beul-ath na Lairg Dhruthadh or ford of the Lairig Ru (D in Rc 39, 154). Also the Sands Fuird, (F), ðɪˈsaˑnzˈfjurd, after the nearby Sands o Lui. Also the Fuird o the Lairig Ghru (U), ðɪˈfjurdɪðɪˌlɑˑrɪgˈgruˑ heard of, but location uncertain. In Glen Luibeg.

**A' Bhó Dhonn** See Brown Cow Hill.

**Bhonich** (OS, 199966), from A'Bhuidheannach (3, U), ðɪˈbunjɐç, the yellow place. A hill in Glen Feardar.

**A' Bhruach** (3, D, 142906), the bank. This and other Bruach names may be Bruthach = brae. Brae on the road above Woodhill at Braemar.

**A' Bhruach Chorrach*** (3, U, 300964), ðɪˌbrɔˈχɔrɐχ, the steep bank. A steep bank in a field east of Crathie.

**A' Bhruach Ruadh** (3, U, 276950), ðɪˌbrɔχˈroiˑ, the red bank. A' bhruthach ruadh (D). A gravelly river bank east of Crathie.

**A' Bhruach Ruadh*** (3, U, 100923), ðɪˌbruɐχˈruɐ, the red bank. A gravelly bank in Glen Quoich.

**A' Bhruach Ruadh*** (3, U, north of 082899), as above, the red bank. Also the Red Brae (U), ðɪˈrɛdˈbreˑ. A gravelly bank west of Mar Lodge.

**A' Bhruach Ruadh*** (3, U, 154889), as above, the red bank. Also the Red Brae (F). A gravelly bank on Clunie Water.

**A' Bhruach Ruadh** (3, U, 280930), now ðɪˌbrɔχˈroiz, the red bank. A gravelly bank south-west of Abergeldie.

**A' Bhruach Ruadh*** (2, U, 072896), ðɪˌbruɐχˈruɐ, the red bank. Also the Red Brae (C), ðɪˈrɛdˈbreˑ or ðɪˈridˈbreˑ. A gravelly bank west of Inverey.

**A' Bhuidheannach\*** (3, U, 185975), ðɪˈbunjaχ, the yellow placc. Buyanach in Glen farder (G 3). A big grassy area south of Culardoch.

**A' Bhuidheannach\*** (3, U, 187995), as above, the yellow place. A grassy area north-west of Culardoch.

**A' Bhuidheannach** (3, C, 355051), as above, the yellow place. A vunyach (D). A big grassy area around the head of Deskry north-west of Morven, now largely under planted conifers. Mostly outside the area covered in this book but comes up to the edge of it.

**A' Bhuidheannach\*** (3, U, 193997), ðɪˈbuənjɐχ, the yellow place, after the colour of the rough grass there. On Culardoch.

**A' Bhuidheannach\*** (3, 190970). The Bowinnach (Io 60). A former grazing in Glen Feardar, covering much of the basin drained by Stable Burn and the upper Feardar Burn. The hill Bhonich (OS) to the east probably comes from the same name.

**A' Bhuidheannach Bheag\*** (2, CG, 968954), əˌvuˑənjɐχˈvȩk, the little yellow place. A grassy slope on Cairn Toul.

**A' Bhuidheannach Mhor** See Buidheanach of Cairntoul.

**Bield\*** Scots = sheltered place. Beild (Io 54). A former farm in Glen Gelder. Fielie (Me 5) in a list of grazings in Gelder may possibly be the same, but handwriting obscure.

**Big Allanaquoich\*** See Allanaquoich.

**The Big Beinn Iutharn** See Beinn Iutharn Mhor.

**The Big Bruach Ruadh Puil** (F, 279951), ðɪˈbɪgˌbroχˈroiˈpil. Big Broch Roy (P). Also the Lower Bruach Ruadh Puil (F), ðɪ ˈloͻr etc. Pairs with Little, and Middle and Upper. A pool in Dee east of Crathie.

**The Big Caochan Duird\*** See Caochan Duird Mor.

**The Big Caochan Ruadh\*** See An Caochan Ruadh Mor.

**The Big Caorainn\*** See Easter Kirn.

**The Big Corrie\*** (F, 108810), ðɪˈbɪgˈkȩre. An English stalking tenant's name for the complex of corries between Sgor Mor and An Socach in Glen Clunie, because he could not pronounce the Gaelic names.

**The Big Corrie\*** (U, east of 190875), as above. Pairs with the Little Corrie. In Ballochbuie Forest.

**The Big Corrie Burn\*** See Allt Coire Fhearneasg.

**The Big Dam\*** (F, 265935), ðɪˈbɪgˈdam, the upper pond supplying water to the distillery at Balmoral.

**The Big Damhaidh Corrie\*** (U, 942922), ðɪˈbɪgˈdaviˈkȩre, with Damhaidh referring to a stream. The corrie at the top of Allt Dhaidh Mor.

**Big Donal\*** (U, 437969), bɪgˈdͻnəl, as in Scots pronunciation of Donald. Pairs with Little Donal. A field south of Muir of Dinnet.

**The Big Dooker\*** See the Dooker.

**The Big Drive Butts\*** (U, 235032), ðɪˈbɪgˈdraevˈbʌts. Grouse butts near Corndavon Lodge.

**The Big Dubh-bhruach Pool\*** See Upper Dubh-bhruach Pool.

**The Big Dyke\*** (Io 79, probably 127818). In the Baddoch.

**The Big Howe\*** (U, 418029), ðɪˈbɪgˈhʌuˑ. A hollow near Logie Coldstone.

**The Big Howe Burn\*** See the Howe Burn.

**Big Inverey\*** See Meikle Inverey.

**The Big Nose** See An t-Sron.

**The Big Ord\*** (F, 425001), ðɪˈbɪgˈȩrd, Ord (3) = round hill. Forms a pair with the Little Ord, west of Loch Davan.

**The Big Park** See Cook's Park.

**Big Poll a' Bhior\*** See Poll a' Bhior.

**The Big Puil\*** (U, 437005), ðɪˈbɪgˈpil. A pool near Loch Davan.

**The Big Sean-bhaile Puil** (F, 337962), ðɪˈbɪgˈʃȩnˌvɐlˈpil. Big Shenval (Wav). Pairs with the Little Sean-bhaile Puil. See the Sean-bhaile Puil. In Dee east of Coilacriech.

**The Big Stane\*** (U, north-east of 343974), ðɪˈbɪgˈstin. A boulder north-west of Bridge of Gairn.

**The Big Stane\*** (Γ, 185911), as above. A boulder carrying a measure for water-levels, at Invercauld Bridge.

**Big Stane o' Carn Beag** (OS, 409943). A boulder on the hill south of Cambus o' May. This name is on OS 1: 10000, but OS 1: 50000 incorrectly gives Rocking Stone.

**The Big Stane Puil** (F, north of 185911), ðɪˈbɪgˈstinˈpil. Big Stone Pool (Ly). A pool in Dee at Invercauld, named after the nearby Clunie Stane.

**The Big Thorny Buss Puil** (C, 390967), ðɪˈbɪgˌθȩrneˈbʌsˈpil. Big Thorny Bush (Sc). A pool in Dee north-east of Ballater, pairs with Little.

**The Birch Tree Pool\*** (F, 057896), ðɪˈbȩrʧˈtriˈpul. In Dee, west of Linn of Dee.

**The Birk Bush\*** See Preas Bad Smeorach.

**Birkenhillock\*** (U, 443997), ˌbȩrkənˈhȅlȅk, a birch-clad hillock above Loch Kinord.

**Birkhall** (OS, C, 349936), bȩrkˈhaːr, birch haugh, Scots Haugh = riverside meadow. Earlier name was Sterin (M) from Stairean (3, U), stȩrn, stepping stones. 'The stepping-stones are now removed, but are well remembered by old people' (M). Birkhall (Ri 34a), Birchhall (I), the House of Birkhall (Brown 1835). A house in lower Glen Muick, presumably named after the nearby haugh.

**Birkhall Cottage** (OS, 348939), should be Sterinbeg (Am, D, Er, C), ˌstȩrnˈbȩg, from Stairean Beag (3), little place of stepping stones. A former farm, now a house, in lower Glen Muick.

**The Birkhall Drive\*** (C, 350939), ðɪˌbȩrkˈhaˑˈdraev. A road in lower Glen Muick.

**The Birkhall Fit Briggie\*** (F, 350935), ðɪˌbȩrkˈhaˑˈfȅtˈbrɪgi, Scots = little foot bridge. In lower Glen Muick.

**The Birkhall Haugh\*** See Dail Bhreac.

**The Birkhall Haughie\*** (U, south of 350935), ðɪˌbȩrkˈhaˑˈhaχe. A field in lower Glen Muick.

**The Birk Puil** (C, 454981), ðɪˈbȩrkˈpil. Birch Pool (P). In Dee, west of the Bridge at Dinnet.

**The Birks\*** See the Tomidhus.

**The Birks Park\*** (U, south of 273948), ðɪˈbȩrksˈpark. A field beside a birch wood, at Crathie.

**The Birk Tree Puil\*** (U, 341961), ðɪˈbȩrkˈtriˈpil. A pool on north side of Dee, west of Bridge of Gairn.

**The Birk Wuid\*** See the Garbh-allt Birk Wuid.

**The Birk Wuid Road\*** (U, 071907), ðɪˈbȩrkˈwɪdˈrod. A track near Mar Lodge.

**The Bittie\*** (F, 245007), ðɪˈbȅte, Scots = the small bit. The grassy area below the stone dyke south-east of Corndavon Lodge.

**The Bittie\*** (U, 241007), as above. Bitty (Io 77), the Bittie (R 12). A former shepherd's house south-east of Corndavon Lodge.

**The Bittie Park\*** (U, 240001), ðɪˈbȅteˈpark. A field west of Gairnshiel.

**Black Boat** (A). A pool in Dee. Black Boat unknown to our informants, probably an error for the Black Shed Puil.

**Black Bothy** (OS, 923868). Also Bothan Dubh Geallaidh (3), black bothy of Geldie. Boandū Geoldie (Fa). Also the Black Sheal (Fi). Site of a former stalkers' bothy in upper Glen Geldie.

**The Black Brig** See An Drochaid Dhubh.

**The Black Brig\*** (F, 242008), ðɪˈblakˈbrɪg. The bridge over Gairn at Daldownie.

**The Black Brig\*** (C, 317004), as above. A footbridge over Gairn near Balno.

**The Black Brig Brae\*** (U, 063914), ðɪˈblakˈbrɪgˈbreˑ. A hill on the road in Glen Lui.

**The Black Brig Plantin\*** (C, 065915), ðɪˈblakˈbrɪgˈplantɪn. A plantation in Glen Lui.

**(The) Black Burn** (OS, F, 387920), ðɪˈblakˈbʌrn. A burn on the hill south-east of Ballater. A characteristic of all the Black Burn names is that these burns run through peaty ground and so the water tends to be dark.

**(The) Black Burn** (OS, C, 290817), as above. A big burn on the south side of Loch Muick.

**(The) Black Burn** (OS, C, 398890), as above. A burn running off Mount Keen, in Glen Tanar.

**The Black Burn\*** See An t-Alltan Dubh.

**The Black Burn\*** See An Fheith Dhubh.

**The Black Burn Brig\*** (C, 289822), ðɪˈblakˈbʌrnˈbrɪg. A bridge at Loch Muick.

**Blackburn Cottage\*** (C, 079896), ˈblakˌbʌrnˈkɒtədʒ. Now the Inverey Youth Hostel, this house was formerly named after the Black Burn (JB).

**The Black Burn Flats\*** (U, 280810), ðɪˈblakˈbʌrnˈflats. A peaty plateau studded with pools, south of Loch Muick.

**The Blackcocks' Howe\*** See Preas Bad nan Coileach-dubha.

**The Blackcocks' Wall\*** (U, south-west of 303937), ðɪˈblakˌkɒks ˈwɑ·l. A well in Glen Girnock.

**The Black Corrie\*** See An Dubh-choire.

**The Black Corries\*** See Coire Dubh.

**The Black Corries** See Na Coireachan Dubha.

**The Black Corries Burn\*** See Allt a' Choire Dhuibh.

**The Black Crags\*** (U, 402028), ðɪˈblakˈkragz. A rocky place by the Roar Road east of Morven.

**The Black Crags Wall\*** (U, 402028), ðɪˈblakˈkragzˈwɑ·l. A well below a rocky stretch east of Morven.

**(The) Black Craig** (OS, F, 434944), ðɪˈblakˈkreg. A hill south-east of Cambus o' May.

**(The) Black Craig** (OS, F, 431904), as above. Sometimes called the Red Craig (U), ðɪˈrɛdˈkreg, with the Red Craig (OS) to the west as the Etnach Red Craig (U), ðɪˈɛtnɐχˈrɛdˈkreg. In upper Glen Tanar.

**The Black Craig\*** (Bs, F, 300873), ðɪˈblakˈkreg. A crag in Glen Muick.

**Black Fir Stripe\*** (R 3, 240003). A stripe (small burn) above Daldownie in Glen Gairn.

**The Black Fold\*** (I, 343984). A field near Ballachrosk in Glen Gairn.

**The Black Gate\*** (U, 326005), ðɪˈblakˈget. A gate on a road west of Inverenzie in Glen Gairn.

**Black Geallaig** See Geallaig Hill.

**(The) Black Hill** (OS, 311824), locally the Black Hill o the Spittal (C), ðɪˈblakˈhëlɪðɪˈspëtəl. Also Black Hill of Ault Darrarie (I). A hill near Loch Muick. A characteristic of the Black Hill and Black Hillock names is that these places are dark in colour because of the heather growing there.

**Black Hill\*** See Meall an t-Slugain.

**(The) Black Hillock** (OS, F, 243022), ðɪˈblakˈhëlɛk. Also Tom-bell and Tom na-beallidh (R 3), from Tom Bealaidh (3), broom hillock. Also Black Know (R 12), Scots Know = knoll. A hill east of Corndavon Lodge in Glen Gairn.

**The Black Hillock\*** (I, 351928). A hillock south of Brochdhu in lower Glen Muick.

**The Black Hillock\*** (Io 20, 366971). In Pass of Ballater.

**The Black Hillock of Garbh-choire\*** See Tom Dubh Garbh-choire.

**Black Hillocks of Creag Liath\*** (240896). Black Hillocks of Craig lia (B). In Glen Gelder.

**The Black Hill of Clais Muice\*** (339882). The Black Hill of Clashmuick (I). A hill in Glen Muick.

**(The) Black Hill of Mark** (OS, C, 325814), ðɪˈblakˈhëlɐˈmark. A hill south-east of Loch Muick.

**The Black Hill o the Spittal\*** See Black Hill.

**Black Know\*** See Black Hillock.

**The Black Latch\*** See Allt an Dubh-loch.

**The Black Lump of the Hunt Hill\*** See Hunt Hill.

**(The) Black Moss** (OS, C, 411938), ðɪˈblakˈmɒs. A peat-moss on the hill south-east of Ballater.

**The Black Muir\*** (U, 263000), ðɪˈblakˈmir̩. A dark heathery moor west of Gairnshiel.

**The Black Neuk Puil** (A, C, 404976), ðɪˈblakˈnjukˈpil, Scots = black corner. Black Neuk (A). A pool in Dee near Cambus o' May.

**Black Park\*** (I, 303016). A rough field near Gairnshiel.

**Black Park** (OS, 375947). A hillside, now part of a plantation near Ballater. All the Black Park names refer to enclosed areas of rough pasture, which probably got their names from having much heather and so being dark in colour.

**The Black Park\*** (F, 294939), ðɪˈblakˈpark. A rough hillside enclosed inside a stone dyke near Abergeldie.

**The Black Park\*** (U, 166933), as above. Now a plantation north of Alltdourie at Invercauld.

**The Black Park\*** (Io 50). Where Balmoral folk once 'cast divots'. Probably an area of infertile peaty ground near Balmoral Castle.

**The Black Park\*** (U, 130915). Also the Black Ward (R 2), Scots Ward = area of pasture enclosed by a dyke. West of Braemar.

**Black Pool\*** (R 4, 385966). A former pool, now dry land, east of Ballater.

**The Black Rock Puil\*** (F, 335963), ðɪˈblakˈrɒkˈpil. A pool in Dee, with a big rock in the middle. East of Coilacriech.

**The Black Shed\*** (F, 234936), ðɪˈblakˈʃɛd. A former cattle shed near the Inver.

**The Black Shed\*** (F, 079899), as above. A former tarred shed for feeding deer, west of Mar Lodge.

**The Black Shed\*** (F, south of 057898), as above, west of Linn of Dee.

**The Black Shed Puil\*** See the Ploughboy Puil.

**The Black Sheds\*** (F, south-east of 103897), ðɪˈblakˈʃɛdz, former tarred sheds for holding mowers for a golf course at Mar Lodge.

**(The) Blacksheil Burn** (OS, C, 220883), ðɪˈblakˈʃilˈbʌrn. Also Allt Bothan Dubh (3), burn of black bothy. Ault Bohan du (R 7). North-west of Lochnagar.

**The Black Shiel\*** See Am Bothan Dubh.

**The Black Shiel\*** See Black Bothy.

**The Black Shiel** (Cj 1, 257). Near the source of Gairn, on north side.

**The Black Shiel\*** See An Ruighe Dubh.

**The Black Slugan of the Candlic** See An Slugan.

**(The) Black Spout** (OS, C, 246859), ðɪˈblakˈsput. Also Muckle Spout (B). A big gully filled with scree on Lochnagar.

**The Black Spout** (Wa, F, 232825), as above. More recently, climbers have called it Central Gully. A wide gully filled with scree on Creag an Dubh-loch.

**Black Stripe** (OS, 350870). The Black Stripe (I). A burn in Glen Muick.

**The Black Ward\*** See the Black Park.

**The Black Wuid\*** (U, 295957), ðɪˈblakˈwɪd. A small wood east of Crathie.

**The Black Wuid Park\*** (U, 296958), ðɪˈblakˈwɪdˈpark. A field beside the above wood.

**The Blaeberry Face\*** (U, 197981), ðɪˈblebərɛˈfes. A slope on the south side of Culardoch, with much blaeberry due to its being a notable place for snow accumulation.

**Blairglass** (OS, C, 259999), blərˈglas, from Am Blàr Glas (2), the green field. Blarglass, Blair Glass (R 3, 6a), 'M blar glas (D in A). Often now changed to blərˈglɛs (C), showing the influence of Aberdeenshire Scots, in which the English word

Glass is pronounced glęs. A former farm now a house, north of Crathie.

**Blàr Charraid** (3, U, 357926), blɐˈχarəʤ, often changed now to bɐlˈharəʧ, field of conflicts. Blackaridge (Roy), Blackharage (Ri 14), Blarcharrage (Mc 15), Bla-chárridge (M), Blacharraj (D), Blacharrage (A). A former farm in lower Glen Muick.

**Blar Glas** (OS, 198945), green moor. A grassy flattish area, now in a plantation. In Glen Feardar.

**Blàr nam Marbh**\* (3, 378018), moor of the dead. Blarnamarrow (G 19, Io 20), Blarnamarra (Io). Extends from 379022 east to 382022 and south-west to the lower part of Allt Blar nam Marbh. South of Morven.

**The Blind Burn**\* See Rashy Burn.

**The Blue Cairn of Morven** (A, 389043), or the Blue Cairn (U), ðɪˈbluˈkjarn. The Blue Cairn (Mco, As). A top with screes on east shoulder of Morven, conspicuous from Cromar and Strathdon (A).

**The Blue Cairns**\* (U, 125810), ðɪˈbluˈkernz. Stony patches up the Baddoch.

**(The) Blue Corrie** (OS, F, 318813), ðɪˈbluˈkore. The Blue Corry (I). A green, grassy corrie south-east of Loch Muick, so was probably An Coire Gorm originally, with Gorm = green, but in this case mistranslated to blue (Gorm usually = blue, less often = green).

**The Blue Corrie Burn**\* (F, 318816). In the above corrie.

**The Blue Plaid**\* (C, south of 419008), ðɪˈbluˈpled, sometimes just the Plaid. A prominent rock west of Loch Davan.

**The Blue Rock**\* (Fi, 980926). A cliff in Glen Dee.

**The Blue Rock**\* (U, 311971), ðɪˈbluˈrɒk. A rock west of Coilacriech Inn.

**The Blue Rock**\* (F, 329856), as above. In upper Glen Muick.

**The Blue Rock Ridge**\* (U, 330855), ðɪˈbluˈrɒkˈrɪʤ. A long ridge from the above place up to the top of the hill.

**The Blue Stane**\* (C, north of 405040), ðɪˈbluˈstin, sometimes the Blue Stane o Morven or the Blue Stane o Balhennie, ðɪˈbluˈstinɐˈmʌrˌvən or ðɪˈbluˈstinɐˌbɐlˈhɛne. A prominent stone on the hillside above Balhennie near Logie Coldstone.

**The Bluidy Hillocks**\* (F, 983853), ðɪˈblidiˈhɛlɛks, Scots Bluidy = bloody. Hillocks up the Bynack Burn.

**Boat Clachanturn**\* Boat Clachinturn (Opr 21). Former habitation east of Balmoral.

**Boat Croft**\* (Rli 19). Near Inverchandlick Cottage at Braemar, presumably beside the boat ferry that formerly crossed the river there.

**Boat Croft**\* Boatcroft, Crofts for the Boatman (Io 58), probably the same as Coble Croft. A former croft comprising East Croft and West Croft at Balnault, west of Crathie.

**The Boat Farm**\* See Boat Town.

**Boatie's** (Mi, north-east of 289955). A former house inhabited by a boatman nicknamed Boatie, beside a former Boat over Dee east of Crathie.

**Boatland**\* See Boat Town.

**Boat of Ballater** (Wy). Former ferry over Dee beside present Brig o Ballater.

**The Boat of Carn na Cuimhne**. The Boat of Carnachuimne (Ri 34). Probably same as Boat of Monaltrie. East of the Inver. This name and others below refer to former ferries over the river.

**Boat of Clachanturn**\* (I, 275946). Former ferry over Dee east of Balmoral.

**Boat of Dalmochie** (378964). Boat of Dalmuickeachie (Wy). Former ferry over Dee north-east of Ballater, same crossing as at Cobletoun of Dalmochie.

**Boat of Dinnet** See Bata an Duinidh.

**Boat of Inverchandlick**\* Boat of Inverchanlig, Boat (Cr 33, 42). A former habitation near Braemar, beside Inverchandlick.

**The Boat of Monaltrie** (Wy, 245944). Former ferry over Dee west of Crathie.

**The Boat of Monaltrie**\* (Cr 8). Boat House (Io 77). A former house at Monaltrie west of Crathie, ruins removed for field clearance.

**Boat of Polhollick** See Bata Poll Chollaig.

**Boat Pool** See McDougall's Boat Pool.

**The Boat Puil** (C, west of 420977), ðɪˈbotˈpil. Boat Pool (P). A pool in Dee near Cambus o' May, on south-west bank; top end of the Brig Puil.

**The Boat Puil** (F, 344966), as above. A pool in Dee, down from the Polhollick Brig west of Ballater. Boat Pool (P).

**The Boat Puil** (C, 463983–467984), as above. Boat Pool (P), Boatie (A). A long pool in Dee, below the bridge at Dinnet.

**The Boat Puil** (F, 360957), as above. Boat Pool (Sc). A pool in Dee, north-west of Ballater.

**The Boat Puil**\* (C, 248947), as above. A long pool in Dee south-west of Balmoral.

**The Boat Puil**\* (F), as above. A pool in Dee above Invercauld, a collective name for two pools, see under Upper and Lower Boat.

**The Boat Puil Park**\* (F, 167923), ðɪˈbotˈpilˈpark. A field at Invercauld.

**The Boat Road**\* (F, 342961), ðɪˈbotˈrod. West of Ballater.

**The Boat Road** See the Fuird Road.

**The Boat Road** (Gf, 469990). On south side of the burn at Mill of Dinnet.

**The Boat Road** (Act 1776, Gf, 378965). Former road from Tullich to near site of present Aberdeen Cottage, about line of present main road.

**Boat Town**\* (Io, 245945), sometimes Boat Town of Monaltrie (Io 42). Also Boatland (Im 8), also the Boat Farm (Io 58). A former farm at Balnault, near a former ferry on Dee.

**The Bobbie Puil** See the Three Bobbies.

**The Bobbin Mill**\* (C, 406979), ðɪˈbɒbɪnˈmɛl. Also Turning Mill (R 15). A former mill for making bobbins, beside Turnerhall where the wood turners presumably lived. West of Cambus o' May.

**The Bockie Howe**\* (C, 352930), ðɪˈbokeˈhʌuˑ, Scots = goblin hollow. A hollow by a sharp bend in the road up Glen Muick.

**The Bockie Howe**\* (U, 310965), as above. A hollow by the road west of the Coilacriech Inn.

**The Bockie Howe Brae**\* (U, 351930), ðɪˈbokeˈhʌuˈbreˑ. A hill on a road in Glen Muick.

**The Bockie's Drain**\* (U, 100895), ðɪˈbokezˈdren. A small stream near the Victoria Bridge at Mar Lodge.

**The Bockie's Howe**\* (U, 436006), ðɪˈbokezˈhʌuˑ. A hollow on the road near Loch Davan.

**Bod an Deamhain** See the Devil's Point.

**Bod an Diabhail** See the Devil's Point.

**The Bog** See the Lang Bend.

**Bog Allaidh**\* (4, U, 318868), bɒgˈale, wild bog. Bog Alry (I). A boggy area in Glen Muick.

**Bog an Roil** (3, U, 345894), ˌbɒgənˈrol, bog of the roll of hay or grass. Boginroll (Ri 14). A former farm in mid Glen Muick.

**Bog an Roil Park**\* (344895). Bogn-roll Park (I), formerly Park of Boginroll (Io 36). A grassy area inside a stone dyke beside the above farm.

**Bog Chroisg**\* (4, 378934), bog of the crossing. Bog Chroish (I). Coire Chrasgaidh was nearby. On the hill south of Ballater.

**Bog Farral**\* (4, F, 269016), bɒgˈfarəl, high bog (note W 1904, 98); it stands on a bank south of the more recent ruined house of Renatton. A former farm north-east of Gairnshiel.

**Boggerfool** (OS, C, 432010), from Bogar Phuill (4, note W 1904,

25), ˌbɔgər'ful, wet place of the pool. There is a big pool only 200 m to the east. Now a house near Loch Davan.

**Bogha Cloiche\*** (3, 035855), bow of stone. Bow Cloich (Im 5, Io 25a). A hill east of Bynack Lodge.

**Bogingore** (OS, C, 432995), ˌbɔgən'gor, from Bogan Corra (4), little bog of heron. Bogangore (Opr 46). A former farm near Loch Kinord, now a house.

**Bogingore Cottage\*** (U, 432997), ˌbɔgən'gor'kɔtədʒ. A former house near Loch Kinord.

**Bog na Muice** (3, 340034), bog of the pig. Bognamuick (D). A former house west of Morven.

**The Bog of Baile Nodha** (350914). Bog of Balnoe (I), the Boge (Rli 13), Bog (Ro, Ram 3). A former farm in Glen Muick.

**(The) Bog of Cairn Nairvie** (OS, U, 429931), ðɪ'bɔgɐˌkern'nervi. Often the Bog o Nairvie (F), ðɪ'bɔgɐ'nervi, or now the Nairvie Bog. A boggy area in Glen Tanar.

**The Bog of Glencoldstone\*** (G 17, 388013). South of Morven.

**The Bog o the Trimmlin Tree\*** (Dms, 459988). In a place-name jingle, probably referring to aspen (i.e. Scots Trimmlin = trembling). Where Dinnet village now is.

**The Bog o Tulach Folmaidh\*** (U, 418959), ðɪ'bɔgɐˌtəl'folme. The site of the present Balindory was formerly called Bog of Tilfolmie (Dms). Near Inchmarnoch.

**The Bog Park\*** (C, 352945), ðɪ'bɔg'park. A former damp field, later a wood, in lower Glen Muick.

**The Bog Park\*** (U, 299958), as above. A wet field east of Crathie.

**The Bog Park\*** (U, 414036), as above. A field west of Logie Coldstone.

**The Bog Park\*** See Tarr nam Mothar.

**The Bog Road\*** (U, 303855), ðɪ'bɔg'rod. A former path through bogs in upper Glen Muick, now a road; it had this name before the road was made.

**Bog Ròmach** (3, F, 361970), bɔg'rɔmɐχ, shaggy bog. Bogromach (R 17, D). A former house at the Pass of Ballater.

**Bog's Well Puil** (C, 320967), bɔgz'wel̩'pil. A pool in Dee, near Coilacriech. Bog's Well (P).

**Bond's Brig\*** (C, 099846), 'bɔndz'brɪg. In upper Glen Ey.

**Bond's Hut\*** (C, 099846), 'bɔndz'hʌt. A hut in upper Glen Ey, named after a former shooting tenant.

**The Bonnet Puil** (C, west of 405977), ðɪ'bɔnët'pil. Bonnetty (A). A pool in Dee, near Cambus o' May.

**Bonn Uaine** (4, 336889), green bottom. Bon Ewin (I), Bonewen (M). A former field in mid Glen Muick.

**The Boolin Green** (Gib, F, 312780), ðɪ'bulənˌgrin. A grassy patch on a hilltop south of Loch Muick, half in Aberdeenshire and half in Angus. Here, men from Glen Muick, Lethnot and Clova used to meet to contest in throwing large round stones or bools (Scots = bowls).

**Am Borr Dubh\*** (4, U), ðɪˌbɔr'du·, the black knob, Borr now obsolete Gaelic (Dw). Possibly Am Barr Dubh = the black top. A hill near Auchtavan in Glen Feardar.

**Bothan Coire Odhar\*** See the Corrour Bothy.

**Am Bothan Dubh\*** (3, U, 213884), ðɪ'bɔɐn'du·, the black bothy. Also the Black Shiel (F), ðɪ'blak'ʃil. A shiel north-west of Lochnagar.

**Bothan Dubh Geallaidh\*** See Black Bothy.

**Bothan Dubh-ghleann\*** (2, JB, 074953), ˌbɔɐn'du·ˌglauŋ, bothy of dark glen. A former bothy in the Dubh-Ghleann.

**Bothan Eitidh** (5, F, 336034), ˌbɔɐn'jɛte, bɔɐn'ɛte, stormy bothy. Eitidh = dismal is a possibility, though it has a longer *e* than in the present pronunciation. Bothanyettie (R 17, OS 1869), Boan-nyeti, bo-en-yeti (D in A). A former farm west of Morven.

**Am Bothan Leathan** (3), the broad bothy. The Bothan Leathan (Gr 150). In Glen Geldie, probably the pair of roadside ruins (very broad when seen from road) north-west of 014881, at a place with no fields.

**The Bottom House\*** See Ruigh nan Clach.

**The Bouchts\*** (C, 087885), ðɪ'bʌ·χts, Scots = sheep pens. In Glen Ey.

**The Bouchts\*** (C, 311014), as above. In Glen Gairn.

**Bourtree Haugh\*** Scots Bourtree = elder. Bortree Haugh (Ce 4). Former habitation in Cromar.

**Bovaglie** (OS, C, 302920), bə'vagli, from Both Mhàglaich (4), bothy of the arable field place. Early spellings suggest that *Both* and *Baile* have both been used, with *Both* first (Botwaglach in 1358, Bogvaglich in 1607), Balbaglie (Aj) in 1666, Bavaglech in 1698, Bovaglaig (R 1) in 1725), then *Baile* more often (Bellvauglich in 1738, Bavaglack (Io) in 1764, Belvaglich in 1782, Bavaglie (Opr) in 1799, Balvagly (In) in 1806, Balvagley (Ro) in 1822, Balvagly (Am) in 1848, and Balvaglie (Vr 1) in 1860), and the *Bo* or *Ba* sound again more recently; names without references above have full references elsewhere (M). In Gaelic Pavacli, Ba-vaglyk (D), Ba-bhaglaig, Ba-vack-laic (D in A). A former farm in upper Glen Girnock.

**The Bovaglie Burn\*** (C, 301916), ðɪˌbə'vagli'bʌrn. In Glen Girnock.

**The Bovaglie Gate\*** (U, 309919), ðɪˌbə'vagli'get. In Glen Girnock.

**The Bovaglie Roadie\***(U, south-east of 307926), ðɪˌbə'vagli'rodi. A path from Bovaglie over the hill to the Camlet in Glen Girnock.

**Bovaglie's Plaid\*** See the Bovaglie Wuid.

**The Bovaglie Wuid\*** (C, 301920), ðɪˌbə'vagli'wɪd. Bovaglie's Plaid (U), bə'vagliz'pled, the name of one of Scott Skinner's fiddle tunes, is also known locally as the wood that 'haps (shelters) Bovaglie ferm like a plaid'. In Glen Girnock.

**Bowie's Stone** (Brown, c. 185911). A former stone which prevented timber being floated down Dee, and which was partly blown up by a former factor Mr Bowie. Above Invercauld Bridge.

**Bowman's Cairn\*** See Carn an Fhir Bhogha.

**Bowman's Moss** See Moine Chruinn.

**Brackley Burn** (OS, 376944), locally the Braichlie Burn (C), ðɪ 'breçle'bʌrn. South of Ballater.

**Braegarrie** (OS, C, 108891), brə'ga·re, from Bràigh Gharaidh (3), upper ground of the dyke. Braidh-gharaidh, Braigh-gharaigh (Opr 44), Bray Garré (Cr), Bry-ghāri 'dyke' (D). A former farm at Corriemulzie.

**Braehead** (Vr, C, 284942), bre'hɛd. A former farm near Abergeldie.

**Braehead Cottage** (OS, C, 419967), bre'hid'kɔtədʒ, bre'hɛd 'kɔtədʒ. A house east of Pannanich.

**Braehead Cottage** (OS, C, 389976), as above. Also Braehead Cottages (OS, C) on south side of road, poor's houses (Vr 2) and was still known locally (C) as the Puirs' House (i.e. poorhouse) up to about 1940, ðɪ'pirz̩ˌhus. Tullich Cottages (Er). At Tullich Kirk north-east of Ballater.

**The Braehead Hill\*** (U, 390990), ðɪˌbre'hid'hël. Hill grazing of the former farm of Braehead of Tullich.

**Braehead of Tullich** (OS, C, 390977), bre'hidɐ'tʌləç, commonly bre'hid. A house east of Ballater.

**The Braeheads\*** (C), ðɪˌbre'hɛdz. A collective name for three fields, Upper, Middle and Lower Braehead at Inchmarnoch.

**Braemar** (OS, C, 150915), brə'ma:r, from Bràigh Mharr (6, U), brae'va:r, brə'va:r (Sch), upland of Marr (see Mar). Pry-vārr (D). A village, used to be a district name (D, A), with the village called Baile a' Chaisteil, or Castleton (often the Castleton of Braemar).

**Braemar Castle** (OS, C, 156924), brə'maːr'kasəl. The *t* sound in Castle is still heard among older people, 'kaˑstəl. Castle and Barrock Ground (Rli 19), the Castle of Braemar (Ke), the Castle of Mar (E). Also An Caisteal (3, Sch), n'gaˑstjəl, the castle. The Duke's Castle (Vd).

**Braenaloin** (OS, C, 280000), ˌbrɪnɐ'lɛin, ˌbrɛnɐ'lɛin (U), from Bràigh na Loinne (3), upper ground of the enclosure. Braeloyn (Opr 15), Braenaloighn (R 14, Io 77). A house west of Gairnshiel.

**The Braenaloin Birks**\* (F, 282003), ðɪˌbrɪnɐ'lɛin'bërks. A birch wood near Gairnshiel.

**The Braenaloin Brae**\* (C, 280999), ðɪˌbrɪnɐ'lɛin'breˑ. A hill on the road from Gairnshiel to Crathie.

**The Braenaloin Brig** (C, 280000), ðɪˌbrɪnɐ'lɛin'brɪg. Bridge of Braenaloin (I), Braenaloin Bridge (Pj). In Glen Gairn.

**(The) Braenaloin Burn** (OS, C, 281996), ðɪˌbrɪnɐ'lɛin'bʌrn.

**The Braenaloin Corrie**\* See Coire Chuilinn.

**Braeneach** (OS, C, 257964), brə'niˑɪç, from Bràigh an Fhiadhaich (3), upper ground of the deer-hunting. Diack suggested wild (upper ground), but this would not give the *n* sound, which most likely indicates the article in front of a noun. Brayneighs suggests a plural (Me 3), Braeniach (Roy), Braneighich (Cr 48), Braidh neach (R 3), Bry-nyiuich (D). A former farm north of Crathie.

**Braeneach Cottage**\* Braneoch Cottage (Ce 5). Former habitation beside Braeneach near Crathie.

**The Braeneach Park**\* (U, 258964), ðɪˌbrə'niˑɪç'park. A field north of Crathie.

**The Brae of Mar** See Braigh Mharr.

**The Brae Park**\* (U, 293958), ðɪ'bre'park. Includes the Upper Haugh and Dail Iaruinn, and steep ground. A field with a steep bank, east of Crathie.

**Braeriach (Braigh Riabhach)** (OS, C, 953999), commonly bre'riˑɒç but brae'riːaχ to older people on Spey and brae'riˑɐχ on Dee, from Am Bràigh Riabhach (2, W in Dw, Sg), the brindled upland. The old stalkers called it the Braeriach (SGo). The second-highest hill in the Cairngorms.

**The Braeriach Plateau** (Mu, F, 940989), ðɪˌbrae'riˑɒç'plato. Not a local name, except by a few people who have picked it up from hill walkers.

**(The) Braes** (OS, F, 427041), ðɪ'breˑz, Scots = hill slopes or banks. Locally the Braes refers to miles of ground south-west of Logie Coldstone, and the house is the Auld Schoolhouse o the Braes (U), ðɪ'al'skulˌhusəi'brez, often now Auld Braes Schoolhouse (C). A house near Logie Coldstone. See the Braes o Cromar.

**Braeside**\* Braesyde (Io 7). A former farm in lower Glen Muick, near Braichlie.

**Braeside** (Er, C, 354970), ˌbre'sɛid. A house at Bridge of Gairn.

**Braes Manse** (OS, 426041), locally the Free Manse o the Braes (C), ðɪ'fri'mansiðɪ'breˑz. A house near Logie Coldstone.

**(The) Braes o' Begarry** (OS, C, 407941), ðɪ'brezɐbə'gaˑre. The origin of Begarry is doubtful; one possibility is Both Gharaidh (5), bothy of the dyke (there is an old dyke and ruin at the north end of the defile). A steep defile on Pollagach Burn south-east of Ballater, refers to the steep hillsides on both sides of the burn.

**The Braes o Cromar** (C), ðɪ'brezɐkrə'maːr, often just the Braes (C). Braes of Cromar (R 1, A), the Braes of Cromar (Mic). Also the Braes o Mar (F), ðɪ'brezɐ'maːr. Also Bruthachan Crò Mharr (6), braes of sheep-fold of Marr. Bruchan crā-vār (D), in Inverey crō-vār. A general name for the uncultivated ground west and south-west of Logie Coldstone, and for other such areas above the more fertile lower ground in the bottom of the Howe o Cromar.

**The Braes of Bad nan Cuileag**\* (213964). The Braes of Badnaculack (I). A hill slope west of Crathie.

**Braes of Gairn**\* See Braes of Glengarden.

**Braes of Glengarden** (S 332). Also Braes of Gairn (Cr 43). Glen Garden was formerly often printed for Glen Gairn. The upper part of Glen Gairn above Gairnshiel.

**Braes of Inverenzie**\* (Crg 11). A former habitation in Glen Gairn.

**Braes of Mark**\* (I, 371875). Slopes at the head of Tanar, which also run down to the county boundary above Glen Mark in Angus.

**Braes of Prony**\* See An Coire Beag.

**Braes of the Glas-choille**\* (301037). Braes of the Glass Choil (I). The whole face on the west side of Allt Glas-choille, north-east of Gairnshiel.

**The Braes o Mar**\* See the Braes o Cromar.

**The Braes o' Mar** (Bg, C), ðɪ'brezɐ'maːr. A collective name for the Braemar area from about Invercauld westwards, with Braes used in its lowland Scottish sense of hillsides. Possibly arose as a misunderstanding of the Brae of Mar. See the Brae of Mar, where the word Brae came from a different origin and had a different meaning.

**The Braes o the Glas Allt** (F, 275827), ðɪ'brezɪðɪ'glasəlt. The Braes of Glas Allt (McC 1891, 54). Hillsides above Glas-allt Shiel at Loch Muick.

**Braeview** (Df 1962, C, 144905), bre'vjuˑ. A former farm, now a house, near Braemar.

**Bràghad ? Tabain** (5), neck of tub, or Bràigh = upland. Braidàbin pronounced quite like Breadalbane, and the site of an 'old place' in Glen Muick parish (M), presumably a former house.

**Braichlie** (D, C, 372946), 'breçle, from Breaclach (5), speckled place, or Breac-thulach, speckled hillock (see W 1904; T 34, 265). Baron Bhrachlich, Baron of Brachlie (Gr) in a Gaelic peom suggests an original ending *ach* later turning to *ie*, as often occurred in north-east Scotland. In Gaelic Prē-ich-lĕ, Prechli (D). Braechlay (Io 77). The alternative spelling Brackley, as in Brackley Burn (OS) and the ballad the Baron of Brackley refers to this area. Breaclach, perhaps pronounced 'breɐχle originally, may have given rise to 'breçle and 'brakle. A name for the general area around the house named by an owner as the House of Glenmuick but formerly called Braichlie House. Braichlie Road, a street in Ballater, continues the name.

**Braichlie** (Vr 1). See Mains of Braichlie.

**The Braichlie Brig**\* (C, 368949), ðɪ'breçle'brɪg. Note formerly Bridge of Braichly (Opr 41e) was a house there. A road bridge south of Ballater.

**Braichlie Castle** (McC 1891, C, 372946), 'breçle'kasəl. The Castle of Brachlie (Gr). A former castle south of Ballater on the site of the present House of Glenmuick (Pa).

**The Braichlie Corrie**\* (U, 383942), ðɪ'breçle'ḵọre. Corry of Breachley (I). The corrie above the House of Glenmuick.

**The Braichlie Corrie Burn**\* (U, 380944), ðɪ'breçle'ḵọre'bʌrn. The higher part of Brackley Burn south-east of Ballater.

**The Braichlie Park**\* (F, 370948), ðɪ'breçle'park. A field south of Ballater, part of what was formerly Park of Braichlie.

**The Braichlie Wuid** (C, 375946), ðɪ'breçle'wɪd. Wood of Breachley (I), Brackley Wood (Gf). A wood on the Glen Muick side of Ballater.

**Bràigh Chraichidh**\* (6), upland of the Crathie or ? shaking place. Braechrachie (Opr 9a). Former habitation probably north of Crathie, maybe same as Ruighe Chreichidh.

**(The) Braid Cairn** (OS, C, 426873), ðɪ'bred'kerṇ, often the Braid Cairns (C). Braid Cairns (Th, Jo). A broad-backed hill south of Glen Tanar.

**Bràigh Coire Caochan nan Laogh** (OS, 959815), upland of corrie of streamlet of the calves. South of Glen Geldie.

**Braigh Dhe** See Upper Deeside.

**Bràigh Dhunaidh** (3), brɛ'duni (A), upper ground of the little hill. Braedownie (A), Bry-ghuni (D). In Glen Gairn.

**Bràigh Mharr** (6, D), Pry-varr (D), upland of Marr. The original name of the Braemar district, Marr being an old province including much of Deeside and part of Donside, as in Cromar and Midmar. Also Inverey in Brae of Marr (Io 12), the Brae of Marr (Lp 5), the Brae of Mar (Stua), usually referring to inhabited high ground in the Braemar area. Upper Mar or Bra of Mar (Mf).

**Bràigh nan Garbh-choire** (3, probably 940982), upland of the rough corries. Brae-na-garrachor (Mg) shown as the high ground south-west of Loch nan Stuirteag, but seems more likely to be the high plateau west of the Garbh Choire Mor. Garrachorry Hill (Crom). On Braeriach.

**Bràigh Raonach*** (4, U, 309932), brae'ru·nəç, meadowy upland. A stony bank in Glen Girnock.

**Am Branndair** (3, 116868), 'the "brander", tangled roots in a peat moss are so called' (D). The flattish bottom of a corrie south of Corriemulzie.

**Am Branndair*** (3, 370023), the place of tangled roots (see name above). The Brander (Io 20). Extended south of footpath from Wheel Burn to the east of Doulich Burn, south of Morven.

**Am Branndair*** (3, 361015), the place of tangled roots (see two names above). The Brander (G 19). See Peter's Hill and Burn of the Branndair. South-west of Morven.

**The Breakneck Falls** See Eas Allt Briste Amhaich.

**The Breem Hillock*** (U, 419034), ðɪ'brim'hëlëk, Scots Breem = broom. Near Logie Coldstone.

**Bremner's Brae*** See the Stranlea Brae.

**Breunalach*** (3, U, 352940), 'brɛnəlɐχ, stinking place. Brenelach (Am). A field in Glen Muick.

**Brew Croft of Tullich*** (G 13). Note Brewlands there also. A former farm at Tullich, probably near Tomnakeist.

**The Brew House*** (U, north of 405041), ðɪ'bru'hus. A former building for brewing, with a small stream running through it. East of Morven.

**Brewlands** (G 29, Me 13). Browlands (Mc 26). A former farm at Tullich, possibly same as Brew Croft, and probably near Tomnakeist; a public house once stood nearby at the Stile of Tullich.

**The Brew Toft*** (Io 39), English Toft = homestead. A piece of farmland near Mill of Dinnet, near a former alehouse on a much-used ferry route across Dee.

**Bridge Cottage*** (C, 322969), 'brɪg'kɒtədʒ. Old Toll House (Ce 5). A former toll house on north side of road at Coilacriech.

**Bridge End*** (Ce 5). Former habitation at Inverey, not Victoria Bridge, probably near Brig o Ey.

**Bridgefoot** (OS, C, 413040), brɪg'fët. The original Bridgefoot (OS 1869) was at the present steading, with Baile Mor just north of the present house at Bridgefoot. A farm near Logie Coldstone.

**Bridgefoot** (Vr, C, west of 368949), as above. Bridgefoot of Braichlie (Opr 47). A house near Ballater.

**Bridge House*** (C, east of 371956), 'brɪdʒ'hʌus. A house at the bridge over Dee at Ballater. Probably the former house of Bridge of Ballater (Opr 36) was the same house.

**Bridgend** (OS, C, 428039), brɪg'ɛnd. A house near Logie Coldstone.

**Bridgend** (OS, C, south of 260953), as above. Bridgend of Lawsie (Opr 18, R 3). A former farm at Crathie, below the road.

**Bridgend** (C, 353970), as above, beside the Bridge of Gairn. Brigend (G) in 1639, Bridgend of Gairn (Er). Also Ceann na Drochaide (3), end of the bridge. Ceann na droichead (D). A former croft, now a house.

**Bridgend** (Er, C, 326958), as above. Bridgend of Girneck (Opr 32). At the foot of Glen Girnock.

**Bridgend*** (R 4, west of 372956). Also Bridgend of Ballater (G 8). House at the north end of the bridge at Ballater, shown in 1790 (R), until recently a farm house (see Corn Eilean).

**Bridgend Cottages** (OS, C, 365947), brɪg'ɛnd'kɒtədʒɪz. Bridge-end (I). Also Bridgend of Muick (Io 43, Be). A former farm at the foot of Glen Muick.

**Bridgend of Ailtridh*** (6, 244945). Bridgend of altrie (R 3), Bridgend of Altran (Opr 29). Altrie is the same word as in the nearby Monaltrie, and sounds the same as the Altrie near Old Deer, which occurs in the Book of Deer as Alteri (dative) and Alterin (accusative), and is probably from the word Ailtere, contracted to Ailtre by syncope (Ja). The meaning is unknown, but may be from Ail = stone. A former farm at Balnault west of Crathie on both sides of the road, west of the burn.

**Bridgend of Ballater*** See Bridgend.

**Bridgend of Bush** (OS 1869, C, 254964), 'brɪgɛndɐ'bʌs, 'brɪgɛndɐ'buʃ. Bridge of the Bush (Crg 19). Also formerly Ruighe Iomlan Cùldair (5, C), 'rʌmlën'kutɐr, full cattle-run of back water, possibly Coltair = of ploughshare, perhaps Scots Rummlin Cooter = rumbling ploughshare. Rumbling Culter (A). A former farm, now a house called Heath Cottage (OS), north of Crathie.

**Bridgend of Castleton*** See Kindrochit.

**Bridgend of Lawsie*** See Bridgend.

**Bridgend of Muick*** See Bridgend Cottages.

**Bridge of Ballater*** See Bridge House.

**Bridge of Braichlie*** (Opr 46). Bridge of Braechlay (Io 77). A former house probably beside Bridgefoot, near Ballater.

**Bridge of Crathie** See the Auld Brig.

**Bridge of Crathie** (Gf, 260953). A largely ruined bridge over Crathie Burn, just north-east of the present bridge; it carried the old North Deeside Road.

**(The) Bridge of Dee** (OS, 186909), locally the Auld Brig o Dee (Mi, C), ðɪ'a·l'brɪgɐ'di·. A hump-backed bridge built about 1752 for the Perth–Fort George military road, not a Wade bridge as sometimes stated.

**Bridge of Dee Croft*** (R 7, 186910). Later became the toll house at the Bridge of Dee near Invercauld.

**Bridge of Dinnet** (Gf, 469990). A former bridge east of Dinnet, which carried the old North Deeside Road at that point.

**The Bridge of Gairn** (Gf, C, 352971), ðɪ'brɪgɐ'gern̩. Near Ballater.

**Bridge of Gairn** (OS, Opr 55a, C, 353971), ˌbrɪgɐ'gern̩. Houses beside Bridge of Gairn.

**The Bridge of Gairn Brae*** (F, 355970), ðɪ'brɪgɐ'gern̩'bre·. A hill on a road north-west of Ballater.

**(The) Bridge of Glendui** (OS, U, 437931), ðɪ'brɪgɐˌglɒn'dui, now the Glendui Brig (C). In Glen Tanar.

**(The) Bridge of Muick** (OS, I, C, 366948), ðɪ'brɪgɐ'mëk. Near Ballater.

**The Bridge Park*** (I, 351971). A field at the foot of Glen Gairn.

**The Bridge Rig*** (Io 18). A piece of farmland on the former Mill Croft of Inver, presumably beside the bridge over the burn.

**The Bridle Path*** (F, 416023), ðɪ'brɛidəl'paθ. A former path, now a bulldozed road, south-west of Logie Coldstone.

**The Brig Bittie*** (U, north-west of 367948), ðɪ'brɪg'bëte. A small field in lower Glen Muick, between Muick and road.

**Brighton Pier*** (F, north of 380965), ˈbrɛɪtənˈpiər. A small jetty for fishing in Dee, north-east of Ballater.

**The Brig o Ballater** (C, 372956), ðɪˈbrɪgɐˈbalətër. The Bridge of Ballater (Gf). Also the Royal Bridge, as inscribed on the parapet, opened by Queen Victoria in 1855. Bridge over Dee, at Ballater.

**The Brig o Bush*** See the Piper Brig.

**The Brig o Dee** See Invercauld Bridge.

**The Brig o Ey*** See Drochaid Eidh.

**The Brig o Girnock** (F, 326957), ðɪˈbrɪgɐˈgërnɐk. Bridge of Girnicke (Io 9), Bridge of Girnoc (Simp). Usually now the Girnock Brig (F), or the Littlemill Brig (C), ðɪˌlɛ̈təlˈmɛ̈lˈbrɪg. At the foot of Glen Girnock.

**The Brig o Girnock*** (F, 293909), as above, usually now the Girnock Brig (C). On road from Balmoral to upper Glen Muick.

**The Brig o Inver*** (C, 233937), ðɪˈbrɪgɐˈɪnvër. A bridge west of Crathie.

**The Brig o the Dam*** (C, 299015), ðɪˈbrɪgɪðɪˈdam. The former dam is now a marsh on the Gairnshiel side of the bridge.

**The Brig o the Dam*** (C, 258970), as above. On the Gairnshiel road north of Crathie.

**The Brig Park*** (U, 318004), ðɪˈbrɪgˈpark. A field in Glen Gairn.

**The Brig Park*** (F, 296008), as above. A field beside the bridge at Gairnshiel.

**The Brig Park*** (U, 241940), as above. A field at Invergelder.

**The Brig Pot*** See the Auld Brig Puil.

**The Brig Puil*** (F, 185911), ðɪˈbrɪgˈpil. A pool in Dee above Invercauld Bridge.

**The Brig Puil** (C, south-east of 420977), as above. Bridge Pool (P). Also the Pot (A). A pool in Dee above the bridge at Cambus o' May.

**(The) Broad Cairn** (OS, C, 240816), ðɪˈbrɒdˈkern. The Broad Cairn (I), Broad Carn (R 16). A hill west of Loch Muick.

**Broad Cast** (Wav). On a map of fishing pools on Dee, west of Dinnet Bridge. Not known to our informants, who said if it really is a pool name it can only be the tail end of the Logie Puil.

**The Broad Puil** (F, 216925), ðɪˈbrɒdˈpil. Broad Pool (Wav). A pool on Dee, south-west of Inver.

**The Broad Stripes*** (I, 373885). Several little burns at the head of Tanar.

**Brochdhu** (OS, C, 350932), brɒχˈduˑ, from Bruach Dhubh (3), black bank. Broughdow (Ri). A house in Glen Muick.

**Brockie's Pond*** (C, south-east of 364954), ˈbrɒkezˈpɒnd. On the Golf Course at Ballater, now drained, named after a Mr Brockie who once lived near there.

**Broilleach Garbh*** (3, 179932), rough breast. Broilach Garrow or Rough Breast (R 7). A rough part of the hillside above Invercauld House.

**The Broken Brig*** (C, 150910), ðɪˈbrokənˈbrɪg. A former bridge on Clunie at Braemar.

**The Broken Brig*** (F, 179961), as above. A bridge on the Bealach Dearg Road north of Invercauld.

**The Broken Brig Burn*** See Allt Cul.

**Broom Bank*** (CMcI, 148913), brumˈbaŋk. A bank with broom, now also the name of a house nearby (Er, C), at Braemar.

**Broom Hill** (OS, F, 278798), brumˈhɛ̈l. A hill south of Loch Muick.

**The Broon Coo** See Brown Cow Hill.

**Brown Cow Hill** (OS, 229044), locally the Broon Coo (C), ðɪ ˈbrunˈkuː, sometimes shortened by the same people to the Coo. Previously A' Bhó Dhonn (3, D), the brown cow. Bow Gouln (Roy), Bo-dhonn, Bowown, Bovown or Brown Cow,

Bo dhonn (R 3, 5, 9, 14), Vo ghunn (D). The Broon Coo carries a big snow-drift far into the summer on its south face. Seton Gordon wrote that this was the Brown Cow's White Calf, and told us that the old Balmoral stalkers used this name. More recently, people spoke of the Broon Coo and her White Calf (F), ðɪˈbrunˈku.ənërˈhwɛɪtˈkɑˑf, as long as the snow still lasted. See the Calf and the White Calf. The Broon Coo is a big brown hill east of Ben Avon.

**The Brown Stone*** (U, 184916), ðɪˈbrʌunˈston. A boulder on north bank of Dee near Invercauld.

**Bruach Bhuidhe*** (3, U, 284915), brɒχˈbui, yellow bank. Broughbuie (In, Am). A bank on a hillside in upper Girnock.

**Bruach Dhearg*** (3, 153879), red bank. Bruach Derg (I, R 13). A bank on the east side of Clunie Water, near Auchallater.

**Bruach Dhobhrag** (4), bank of little stream (note W in Crev 7, 364). 'Brochgowrak market at Dalliefour and later at Scurriestone; a good authority says Bruach Gowrich' (D). At foot of Muick.

**Bruach Dhubh** (OS, U, 302044), from A' Bhruach Dhubh (3), ðɪ ˌbruɐχˈduˑ, the black bank. The Brough Du (I). A peat-moss north-east of Gairnshiel.

**Bruach Dhubh*** (3, U, 415959), brɒχˈdu, black bank. Brochdhu (Dms). A former farm near Inchmarnoch.

**Bruach Droighinn*** (3, U, 150914), bruɐχˈdrɛin, bank of thorn. Now the house of Bruachdryne opposite the Post Office at Braemar (Er, C).

**Bruach Mhór** (OS, 092960), from A' Bhruthach Mhór (2, C), ðɪ ˌbruɐχˈmoˑr (in Gaelic aˈvruaçˈvor (A)), the big brae. A steep hillside on Beinn a' Bhuird.

**Bruach na Mòine** (3, D, 266017), bank of the peat-moss. Near the Sleach north-west of Gairnshiel.

**Bruach nam Pilear*** (4, WD, 301963), ˌbrɒχnɐˈpɪljɐr, bank of the pillars. Immediately above the former church and burial ground east of Crathie. A stone pillar still stands on the site.

**Bruach nam Preas*** (3, C, 304015), ˌbrɒχnɐˈbrɛs, bank of the copses. A steep bank near Gairnshiel.

**The Bruach nam Preas Park*** (F, 305016), ðɪˌbrɒχnɐˈbrɛsˈpark. Field at above bank.

**The Bruach Ruadh Brae*** (C, 072896), ðɪˈbruɐχˈruɐˈbreˑ. A hill on the road west of Inverey, on top of the steep bank A' Bhruach Ruadh.

**The Bruach Ruadh Burn*** (U, 070895), ðɪˌbrɒχˈruɐˈbʌrn. East of the Linn of Dee.

**(The) Bruntlan Burn** (OS, F, 317950), ðɪˈbrʌntlɐnˈbʌrn, Scots Brunt = burnt (i.e. the burnt-land burn (note A)). In Glen Girnock.

**Bruntland or Burnt land*** (notes by M in OSn, 319951). Fields in Girnock.

**Bruthachan Cro Mharr** See the Braes o Cromar.

**(Am) Buachaille Bréige** (OS, 3, U, 023854), ðɪˌbuˈçɐlˈbrɛk, the false shepherd. A bhuachaille bhreige (D in A) suggests a feminine form. A cairn east of Bynack Lodge.

**(Am) Buailteach** (OS, 3, C, 277933), ðɪˈbultʃɐç, the summer hut. Gaelic pronunciation Buailtyeach (M). Na bualltshich (D) suggests the plural, which in classic Gaelic form would be Na Buailteachean. A former farm near Balmoral.

**The Buailteach Brae*** (C, 275933), ðɪˈbultʃɐçˈbreˑ. A hill on the road near above place.

**The Buailteach Burn*** (C, 278931), ðɪˈbultʃɐçˈbʌrn. Near Abergeldie.

**The Buailteach Burn Brig*** (U, 280927), ðɪˈbultʃɐçˈbʌrnˈbrɪg. A bridge near Abergeldie.

**The Buailteach Corrie*** (F, 275925), ðɪˈbultʃɐçˈkɒre. Corrie near Abergeldie.

**The Buailteach Road*** (U, 283940), ðɪˈbultʃɐçˈrod. A track up

Geldie Burn from Catanellan to the Buailteach near Abergeldie.

**The Buailteach Wall**\* (U, 275931), ðɪˈbultʃɔçˈwɑ·l. A well south-west of Abergeldie.

**Buailtean na Cailliche Beathraiche** (3, 319020 and 320021), cattle folds of the wild old woman. Buailtean na Caillich-Beathraiche (Gr 61). Three circles made of stones in Glen Fenzie, according to legend said to be the cattle folds of the famed Cailleach Bheathrach. See Tigh na Cailliche Beathraiche.

**Buaran Dubh** (3, D, 254025), black gutter. A burn north-west of Gairnshiel.

**The Bucket Mill** (U, 288955), ðɪˈbʌkёtˈmёl. A former mill for making buckets at Micras. This has been mis-interpreted (A 190) as a Buckie Mill.

**The Buckets Puil**\* See the Streams o the Boat Puil.

**(The) Buidheanach Burn** (OS, F, 959950), ðɪˈbuˑənjɐҳˈbʌrn. Also Allt na Buidheannaich (3, U), ˌaltnɐˈbuˑənɪç, burn of the yellow place. Runs off Cairn Toul into Glen Geusachan on north side of glen.

**Buidheanach of Cairntoul** (OS, 960952), locally the Buidheannach or the B. of Cairn Toul. From A' Bhuidheannach (3, F), ðɪˈbuˑənjɐҳ, the yellow place. A' Bhuidheannaich (SGo). Formerly A' Bhuidheannach Mhór (3), the big yellow place. A vunyach vor (D). Often called the Boirneach or the B. of Cairn Toul, from A' Bhoirneach (4, C), ðɪˈbouˑrnjɐҳ or ˈbuˑrnjɐҳ, in Gaelic a' vörnjaç (A), A' bhaornyach, a' bheoirneach, supposed to be Buidhernach meaning yellowness (D), but possibly from the word Boirneach or rocky place (J 3, 147). Also the Muckle Buidheannach (CG), ðɪˈmʌkəlˈbuˑənjɐҳ, Muckle Boonyach (A). A south-facing grassy slope on Cairn Toul, but with many big tracts of granite boulder fields.

**The Bulwark Pool**\* (F, 036891), ðɪˈbulwʌrkˈpul. A pool in Dee, beside an old bulwark west of the Linn of Dee.

**The Bulwarks**\* (Fi, C, 090898), ðɪˈbulwʌrks. Bulwarks along Dee, near Mar Lodge.

**The Bumbee Puil** (F, 381965), ðɪˈbʌmˈbiˈpil. Bumble Bee (P), Bumbee (A). A pool on Dee, east of Ballater.

**Bun Allaidh** (3), bunˈali (A), wild bottom-land. Bunailie (A). In Glen Gairn.

**Bun Fhiodhaich**\* (3, F, 193907), bʌnˈjuˑɪç, bottom-land of shrubs. Binuech (Fa), Bunnuich (Cr 17), Bun Uich (R 7). A former farm on a flat area east of Invercauld.

**The Bun Fhiodhaich Haugh**\* (F, 193906), ðɪˌbʌnˈjuɪçˈhaˑҳ. The grassy haugh where the above farm stood.

**The Bun Fhiodhaich Puil** (F, 191906), ðɪˌbʌnˈjuɪçˈpil. Benuich (Wav). A long pool on Dee beside the above haugh.

**Bùrn Dubh Ach Eich an Easa**\* (3, 211912), black water of horse field of the cascade. Burn Dow Auchichnes (Im 6). Lower part of Ballochbuie Burn, east of Invercauld Bridge.

**Burnfoot Cottage** (OS, 368948), locally Burnfoot, bʌrnˈfut (C). Near Ballater.

**The Burn o Bad Fiantaige**\* (U, 261990), ðɪˈbʌrnɐˌbadˈfjantɪk, often now the Bad Fiantaige Burn. Part of the Coulachan Burn west of Gairnshiel.

**The Burn o Ceap Mad**\* (U, 293887), ðɪˈbʌrnɐˌkɛpˈmad. Burn of Capmawd (In, Am). In Glen Girnock.

**The Burn o Coire na h-Oisinn**\* See Allt Coire na h-Oisinn.

**The Burn of Ach Chadha**\* (371016). The Burn of Acha, the Acha Burn (G 19, Io 20). South of Morven.

**Burn of Aultonrea**\* See Burn of Tom nam Buachaillean.

**The Burn of Bad a' Chairr**\* (388017). The Burn of Badachurr (Io 20). South-east of Morven.

**Burn of Bad nan Coileach**\* (188902). Burn of Badnaculach or Woodcocks Burn (R 7). In Ballochbuie Forest.

**Burn of Ballaterach** (A 355). The lower part of the Pollagach Burn south of Cambus o' May (A).

**Burn of Blar nam Marbh**\* See Allt Blar nam Marbh.

**Burn of Bruthainn**\* See Allt Bhruid.

**The Burn of Cadhach Dubh** See Allt Cac Dubh.

**Burn of Caich** See Quoich Water.

**Burn of Carn an t-Sagairt**\* See Allt an Da Chraobh Bheath.

**(The) Burn of Clachanyell** (OS, U, 453913), ðɪˈbʌrnɐˌklɔҳɐnˈjɛl, now the Clachanyell Burn (F). In Glen Tanar.

**Burn of Claigionn Mor**\* (363917). Burn of Claggan-more (I). In Glen Muick.

**Burn of Clais Bhinn**\* See West Milton Burn.

**(The) Burn of Clais-ean-Toul** (OS, U, 407899), ðɪˈbʌrnɐˌklaʃən ˈtul, now the Clais-ean-Toul Burn (F). Burn of Clashintuill (R 6). See Clais an t-Sabhail. In Glen Tanar.

**The Burn of Coinneach**\*, Coinneach (3) = moss, or Kenneth. Burn of Coinach or Mackenzie's burn (Dms), at the Linn of Tanar on the north side, so is almost certainly the same as Allt na Conair.

**Burn of Coire Breac** See Allt Coire Breac.

**Burn of Coire Buidhe**\* (235907). Burn of Corrybuie (Ra 15). The top part of the Connachat Burn west of Balmoral.

**(The) Burn of Coire Meacan** (OS, 404921), should be the Burn of Coire Muilcinn (CM), or now the Coire Muilcinn Burn (F), ðɪˈbʌrnɐˌkɔrˈmulʃən. In Glen Tanar.

**Burn of Coire nam Muillear**\* See Allt Coire nam Muillear.

**Burn of Coire Poll Randaidh** (252048). Burn of Cor-Pol-Rauntich (I), Burn of Corr-pol-Rauntich (Ro), Burn of Corr Pol Rauntich (R 12), Burn of Polranty (A). North-west of Gairnshiel.

**(The) Burn of Corn Arn** (OS, 402949), from the Burn o Coire an Eirbhein (U), ðɪˈbʌrnɐˌkɔrˈnernṇ, or now the Coire an Eirbhein Burn (F). See Corrienearn. South-east of Ballater.

**Burn of Dubh-choire**\* See Corrie Burn.

**Burn of Easter Coire Gorm**\* See Millstone Burn.

**The Burn o Ferrowie**\* (U, 313794), ðɪˈbʌrnɐˌfëˈrʌu.i, now often the Ferrowie Burn (F). South of Loch Muick.

**Burn of Garbh Allt**\* See Garbh Allt.

**(The) Burn of Garbh Choire** (OS, U, 397911), ðɪˈbʌrnɐˈgarçəre, now often the Garbh Choire Burn (F). In Glen Tanar.

**The Burn of Glen Colstane**\* See Culsten Burn.

**Burn of Glendui** (OS, 431937), now the Glendui Burn (F), ðɪˌglɛnˈduiˈbʌrn. In Glen Tanar.

**Burn of Lebhall**\* (299965). Burn of Leaval (I). The Lebhall Burn (F, 299961), ðɪˈlɛvəlˈbʌrn, also now refers to a branch lower down by the farm. At Micras.

**The Burn of Logie** See Red Burn.

**Burn of Milltown**\* (Im 4, I, 160930). Bottom part of Allt an t-Slugain near Invercauld.

**Burn of Mohamed** (OS, 330835), should be the Burn o Mahomet (U) or now the Mahomet Burn (F), ðɪˈbʌrnɐˌmɐ ˈhọmёt. This is the north fork at 330835, not the main part below the fork as on the OS map. The Tammie Burn is the south fork, and Tammie's Stripe the main burn below the fork. Note not Mohamed as on OS, but Mahomet. Possibly MacThomaid = Thomson. East of Loch Muick.

**Burn of Moine Eun**\* (360932). Burn of Moinain (I). In lower Glen Muick.

**Burn of Preas Dubh**\* See East Milton Burn.

**(The) Burn of Redshank** (OS, U, 452899), ðɪˈbʌrnɐˌridˈʃaŋk, now the Reid Shank Burn (F). Refers not to Redshank the bird, but to a reddish-coloured shank, Scots Shank = broad ridge. In Glen Tanar.

**Burn of Roinn a' Bhathaich**\* See Little Burn.

**Burn of Roinn Bheag**\* See Garchory Burn.

**Burn of Stair nan Gall**\* (250878), Stair nan Gall (3) = stepping

Signs from map names that make some local people change pronunciations away from the old vernacular forms.

The house of Tomrichton at Braemar, named after the nearby hillock Tom Reachdan.

The Tink, a Ballater pub, is near the Tinkies' Park where formerly tinkers regularly camped. Craig Coillich rises beyond.

stones of the foreigners. Burn of Stair-na-gall (B). North of Lochnagar.

**The Burn of the Branndair*** See Doulich Burn.

**The Burn of the Branndair*** (363015). The Burn of Brander (G 19, Io 20), Burn of the Brander (G 33). Upper part of the Burn of Ach Chadha. South-west of Morven.

**Burn of the Buidheannach*** (193968). Burn of the Buinach (I). On south side of Culardoch, north of Invercauld.

**Burn of the Dail a' Choirce*** (171916). Burn of the Dalechork (R 7). Opposite Invercauld.

**Burn of the Latch*** See Allt an Dubh-loch.

**(The) Burn of (the) Mosstown** (OS, F, 427046), ðɪˈbʌrnɪðɪ ˈmǫstən, often now the Mosstown Burn (C). Near Logie Coldstone.

**Burn of Tom nam Buachaillean*** (360915). Burn of Toum na buachlin (I). Also Burn of Aultonrea. Burn of Altonree (Roy). In Glen Muick.

**Burn of Wester Coire Gorm*** See Allt a' Choire Ghuirm.

**The Burn o Searraidh*** (U, west of 292932), ðɪˈbʌrnɐˈʃare, ? from Seàrraidh (4) = of cutting. A burn near Abergeldie.

**The Burn o the Dam*** See Allt na Coille.

**The Burn o the Graves*** (U, 312787), ðɪˈbʌrnɪðɪˈgrevz, often now the Graves Burn (F). South-east of Loch Muick.

**The Burn o the Lair*** (F, 314787), ðɪˈbʌrnɪðɪˈler. Runs off the Lair of Aldararie south-east of Loch Muick.

**The Burn o Vat** See Vat Burn.

**(The) Burn o' Vat** (OS, C, 429997), ðɪˌbʌrnɐˈvat. A house near Loch Kinord.

**The Burn o Vat Brig*** (C, 429996), ðɪˌbʌrnɐˈvatˈbrɪg. A bridge near Loch Kinord.

**Burnside** (OS 1869, 343027). A former house west of Morven.

**Burnside*** (Io in 1807). A former farm on the old Monaltrie estate, near Balnault.

**Burnside** (OS, C, 421038), bʌrnˈseid, sometimes Burnside o Whitehouse, ˈbʌrnˈseidɐˌhweitˈhus. A deserted house near Logie Coldstone.

**Burnside** (Er, C, 264942), as above. House opposite shop at Easter Balmoral.

**Burnside** (OS 1869, C, 418035), as above, sometimes Burnside o Auchnerran (F), bʌrnˈseidɐˌaχˈnerën. Also Strawberry Cottage (U), ˈstrabəreˈkǫtədʒ. A house near Logie Coldstone.

**Burnside*** (I, 368944). Now the Lang Park (F), ðɪˈlaŋˈpark. A field south of Ballater.

**Burnside of Braichlie**. Burnesyde de Braichlie (Ab 19). A former farm south of Ballater, probably near 368948 at Burnfoot.

**Burnside of Greystone*** (Io 76). A former farm east of Crathie.

**The Burnt Craig*** (I, 335980). A small crag above lower Glen Gairn.

**Bush Crathie** (OS, 255963), and Bush Lawsie, two errors in recent OS maps but not in earlier ones up to the 1930s. Should be the Bush (C), ðɪˈbuʃ, Scots ðɪˈbʌs, from Am Preas (3) = the copse. M bress, am preas (D). A farm north of Crathie.

**Butan Sasunnach** (3, 151916), English butts. Putan Sassenich (Gr 179). A bank on the west side of Clunie, at Braemar, site of a minor battle with occupying troops after the 1745 Jacobite rising (Gr).

**Butchart's Corrie** (Pj, C, 130789), ˈbutʃɑrtzˈkǫre. A skiers' name for a snow-holding corrie near the Cairnwell, named after Col H Butchart, one of the early Aberdeen skiers.

**The Butler's Walk*** (C, 369947), ðɪˈbʌtlërzˈwaˑk. Probably refers to a butler for the former Braichlie House, now called the House of Glenmuick. South of Ballater.

**The Bynack** (C), ðɪˈbeinək, from Am Beidhneag (6), meaning unknown. Bynack (Fi), Baynock (Mc 18), Bainoch or Beynoch (V). The sound is the same as in the prominent hills

of Bynack south of Nethybridge on Speyside (note D 193). Bynack is a general name for the large area around Bynack Lodge. Mathieson suggested (T 41, 237) Beinneag or little peak for the Bynack at Strath Nethy. The pronunciation of the Bynack in Strath Nethy was recorded by Diack as Binn bynaic, and Diack's Allt vynaic (below) suggests that Beidhneag is a masculine noun, and the name Beidhneag Beag for the smaller hill below Beinn Beidhneig agrees with this. See An Crasg Binneach for a similar-looking word.

**(The) Bynack Burn** (OS, C, 000856), ðɪˈbeinəkˈbʌrn. Burn of Baynock (Io 21), Water of Bainaick (Fa), Water of Bynack (Ro). Also Allt Bheidhneig (6). Alt Bainac (L), Auld Bynag (At), Auld Baynaig (Stob), Allt vynaic (D). See above name. Runs into Geldie.

**(The) Bynack Lodge** (OS, C, 000856), ðɪˈbeinəkˈlǫdʒ. Glenbaynoch Lodge (Vr 2). North of Glen Tilt.

**The Bynack Shiel** See An Cro Chlach.

**The Cabrach** (OS, 3, F, 284937, should be at 284933 (GG), with the Lower Cabrach at 284937), from A' Chabrach (3, F), ðɪ ˈkabrəç, the place of Cabars or poles. A' chabrich (D in A). South of Abergeldie.

**Cabrach Hill** (OS 1869, 283930). Near above place.

**The Cabrach Wuid*** (F, 285931), ðɪˈkabrəçˈwɪd. A wood south of Abergeldie.

**Cac Carn Beag** (OS, 240863), should be Cadha Chuirn Beag (3), now Cadha Charn Beag (GG), or Cadha Carn Beag (F), ˌkaˌχernˈbeg, little steep of the stony hill (with Carn meaning a stony hill). Cadha on Speyside and Deeside refers in some names to a steep place (as in the OS booklet on place names (OS 1973)), and not to any obvious pass or way (e.g. Cadha Mor and Cadha Beag on Creag Dhubh south of Aviemore, An Cadha at the Inver and at the Bynack, and Cadha Carn Beag. The OS Cac, meaning shit, does not fit the local pronunciation or old records of the name in books and maps. Further discussion below under Cac Carn Mor, and elsewhere (A). Also the Little Cadha Chuirn (C), ðɪˈlëtəlˈka ˈχern. Little Cacurn (Ra 15), Little Ca-cairn (B). On Lochnagar.

**Cac Carn Mór** (OS, 245857, locally refers to the summit area of Lochnagar, the culmination tor of which was probably Carn nan Gabhar and is now incorrectly Cac Carn Beag (OS)), should be Cadha Chuirn Mór (3), big steep of the stony hill (see above), now Cadha Charn Mór (U), or Cadha Carn Mór (F), ˌkaˌχernˈmoˑr, often just the Cadha Carn. Cuchurn (In), Ca chuirn (K), Loch-na-gar Cacurn (Ro), Cacurn, Ca-Ciorn (R 7, 16). Also the Muckle Cadha Chuirn (F), ðɪˈmʌkəlˈkaˈχern. Big Cacurn (Ra 15), Muckle Ca-cairn (B).

**The Cadger Brig*** (F, 347906), ðɪˈkadʒërˈbrig. A bridge in Glen Muick.

**The Cadger Burn*** (F, 348904), ðɪˈkadʒërˈbʌrn. The lower part of Allt Dowrie in mid Glen Muick.

**An Cadha** (3, U, 278032), ðɪˈkaˑ, the pass. The Ca (D). An old route from Gairn to Corgarff.

**An Cadha*** (3, C, 011860), as above, the steep place (see Cac Carn Beag above). A hill opposite Bynack Lodge.

**An Cadha*** (3, 219933), the steep place (see notes under Cac Carn Beag above). The Ca 'Steep hill' (I). A hillside overlooking the Inver.

**Cadha an Fhir Bhogha*** (3, U, 043977), ˌkaɲərˈvouˑ, pass of the archer. Cainferbow (Io 19). An easy way up to the great deer moss east of Glen Derry.

**Cadha an Fhir Bhogha** (3, c. 097848), steep hill of the archer. Cadha an fhir-bhogha = archer's crossing (D). A steep hillside in upper Glen Ey.

**Cadha an Fhir Bhogha*** See Carn an Fhir Bhogha.

**Cadha Clann Ailein*** (3, 278039), pass of Clan Allan. Ca Clan Allan (I). A part of the route of An Cadha from Gairn to Corgarff. The Clan Allan from upper Strath Don often raided Deeside.

**An Cadha Dubh*** (3, U, 372977), ðɪˌkaˈduˑ, the dark pass. A hollow offering a good way up the hill above the Pass of Ballater, between screes and cliffs on both sides.

**Cadha Dubh Burn*** (372977). Cadow Burn (R 4). A small burn at the above hollow.

**The Cadha Face*** (F, 007860), ðɪˈkaˑˈfes. A hill face opposite Bynack Lodge.

**An Cadha Mór** (3, 260048), the big pass. The Ca More about the Camag (D), n ga mor (D in A). The second of the two main ascents on the Camock Road, an old route from Gairn via Tom Odhar and Camock Hill to Cock Bridge on Don.

**Cadha nam Fiann** (5, 948929), pass of the crowberries or of the warriors or Fingalians. Ca na vyunng (D). A pass between Beinn Bhrotain and the Monadh Mor.

**The Cadha Road** (U), ðɪˈkaˑˈrod. The Ca' road (Moi). Path on An Cadha from Gairn to Corgarff.

**Cadha Shiorram*** (3), pass of sheriffs. The words Ca Hiram or Lass Rock (R 7) cover an area from 177914 to 178915 where there is a large rock at the roadside. Lass from Laws, Scots pronunciation laˑz, or formerly, with Gaelic influence, laˑs. A gully with a big rock below, east of Braemar.

**Cadha Shìos Féith Laoigh*** (3, 181029), east (or down) pass of bogstream of the calf. Ca hias-Fea-luie (I). A hollow near Loch Builg, offering a way over to Feith Laoigh in Banffshire. Pairs with name below.

**Cadha Shuas Féith Laoigh*** (3, U, 169018), kaˈhuəsˌfəˈlui, west (or up) pass of bogstream of the calf. See above name.

**(The) Caenlochan National Nature Reserve** (OS, C, 165770), locally the Caenlochan Reserve (F), ðɪˈkaənˈlɔχənˌrɪˈzɛrv, from Cadha an Lochain (3), pass of the tarn. Caenlochan is on the Angus side of the Glas Maol, but the reserve extends into Aberdeenshire.

**Caich** (6, 110960), referring to Quoich Water, for meaning see Quoich Water. Moor ground called Caich (I), referring to the moors east of the uppermost firs in Glen Quoich. Forest of Caich (frequent notes in Ri 34, referring to a grazing). Grazing and Plantations of Caich (R 7) referred to ground near the foot of Gleann an t-Slugain, now under woods, so Caich was obviously a very big area. Although Caich might seem a different word from Quoich, the key evidence showing it is the same is that the Quoich Water in the north-eastern, top part of the Quoich woods was Burn of Caich (I) in 1807–9, with the same map giving Glen Quoich and also 'Moor ground called Caich'. Glens of Quoich and Water of Caich (Me 12), Glenquoich of Caich, Glenquoich or the Glen of Caich (Lp 2). Also there is a note on 'the sheallings of Milntown of Invercauld in Glenquoich of Caich' (Ra 5), and two on 'the Water of Beachan, commonly called Uskaich' and 'the Water of Beachin, called Usquikaich' (i.e. Uisge Caich). Also, one map (Ro) gives Burn of Caich for the top part and R. Quich for the bottom. Obviously the name of the grazing was taken from the stream name and eventually was used for a much bigger area including ground even in a different glen. This happens quite frequently with names of grazings, e.g. the Auchallater grazing now goes right to the top of the Glas Maol and the Tolmount.

**The Caimeath** See Allt na Caimeath.

**The Caimeath Road** (3, 182941), from A' Chaimeath = the bend place. The Kymah Road (A 169). An old track to Aberarder from the Bealach Dearg road, branching off near the highest point between Invercauld and Feardar.

**The Cairn*** See An Carn.

**Cairnagour Hill** (OS, 325057), no Hill locally, from Carn nan Gabhar (3, C), ˌkernɐˈgʌu.ər, ˌkjarnɐˈgʌuɾ, hill of the goats. At the top of Glen Fenzie.

**Cairn Bannoch** (OS, C, 223826), kernˈbjɐnəç, from Carn a' Bheannaich (3), hill of the point. Carnabanack (G 5), Cairn-na-bannock (I), Carn vyunnich (D). A flattish-topped hill west of Loch Muick, with the actual summit in the form of a small but prominent point.

**Cairndoor Hill** (OS, 304027), no Hill locally, from Carn Dobhar (4, C), kernˈdor, dark hill. Carn dhoir (R 14), Carn dobhar (D). Near Gairnshiel.

**Cairn Geldie** (OS, C, 996885), kernˈgɛldi, (karnˈjʌuli (A)), from Carn Gheallaidh (3, A), hill of the Geldie. Carn Geouley (Roy), Carn yolli (D in A), yulli (D). In Glen Geldie.

**(The) Cairngorm Mountains** (OS). Not a local name, as the words Mountain and Mountains are not used for local hills. Locally the Cairngorms on both Spey and Dee, ðɪˌkern ˈgɔrmz. The hill range between Braemar and Aviemore, named after Cairn Gorm, from An Carn Gorm (3, F), nˌkarn ˈgɔrəm, kærnˈgɔrm (C) on Spey, the blue hill, above Strath Spey. Sometimes shortened to the Gorms by some hill walkers.

**(The) Cairngorms National Nature Reserve** (OS). A large reserve covering much ground in Inverness-shire and Banffshire as well as Aberdeenshire.

**Cairn Hillock** (OS, 369885), should be Carn na h-Iolaire (3, C), ˌkernɐˈhɛlɛr, hill of the eagle. Carn na huilir (G 5), Cairn-na-Heulre (I), Cairn Hillar (Mg). Rocks at 365893 also called Cairn-na-Heulre (I), probably in error as the same map also gave that name for the top of the hill. A hill in Glen Muick.

**Cairn Lochan** (OS, 985026), from Carn Lochain (2, F), karn ˈlɔχən (F), kærnˈlɔχən (C, on Spey), hill of a tarn. A hill north of Ben Macdui, whose summit lies outside Aberdeenshire but whose south-western corner is inside.

**Cairn Nairvie** (OS, C, 421931), kernˈnervi, karnˈnervi and kjarn ˈervi from best informants. From Carn an Eirbhidh (3), hill of the dyke. A big stone dyke enclosing former farmland runs below Cairn Nairvie, at Etnach in Glen Tanar. The words Airvie and Nairvie are still known locally, referring to big stone dykes partially made of earth, like the one at Etnach (CM, JO).

**Cairn of Claise** (OS, 185789), from Carn na Glaiseath (5, C), ˌkernɐˈglaʃɐ, hill of the green grassy place. Cairn-na-Clasha (Ro, R 13, 17), Carn na glashi (D). A hill north-east of the Glas Maol.

**The Cairn of Claise Dyke*** (F, 186790), ðɪˌkernɐˈglaʃɐˈdɛik. A stone dyke at unusually high altitudes east of Glas Maol.

**(The) Cairn of (the) Gowal** (OS, 228817), ðɪˌkernɪðɪˈgʌu.əl, which fits Cairn-na-Goul (I), from Carn a' Ghobhail (3), hill of the fork. Probably named after the burn below (Burn of Gowal) in upper Glen Clova. A hill west of Loch Muick.

**The Cairn of Monaltrie** See Carn Moine an Tighearn.

**The Cairn of Morven*** The Cairn of Morvine (Io 20). The upper stony slopes of Morven.

**Cairn of the Darach*** (360964). Cairn of the Darrach (G 19). A cairn on east side of Dee near Ballater, marking an old estate boundary.

**The Cairn o Morven** See the Muckle Cairn.

**The Cairn o the Bockie** (331023), Scots Bockie = goblin. The Cairn o' the Bokie (Dil). Where a lost woman and her daughter were once found dead (Dil). A group of rocks at north side of a track near Wester Morven.

**The Cairns*** (F, 264834), ðɪˈkernz. A hillside with many boulders, by the Glas Allt above Loch Muick.

**The Cairns*** (I, 365920). A stony piece of moor in Glen Muick.

**Cairn Sawvie** (OS, 212045), from Carn na Saobhaidhe (3, C),

ˌkernɐ'sivi, hill of the fox's den. Carn saovi, carn na sevi (D in A). A hill near Corndavon, the west part of Brown Cow Hill.

**The Cairns of Cùl nan Gad** (OS, 322874). Cairn of Culnagad (I). Now the Cairns (F), ðɪ'kernz̩. Stony hillside in upper Glen Muick.

**Cairn Toul** (Carn an t-Sabhail) (OS, 3, C, 963972), karn'dauḷ (U), kern̩tʌul (C), hill of the barn (i.e. probably referring to the hill's shape). In Gaelic Carn 'n t-sabhail (Mp), Cairntoull (Fa). Cairn Toul or Prospect Cairn (Gi 75), presumably from Carn an t-Seallaidh, but the pronunciation does not fit this. Divle's Cairn (Fi), i.e. presumably Carn an Diabhail, but this also would not fit the local pronunciation. Also Sabhal Beinn Macduibh (3), barn of Ben Macdui. Soul bin Mac Duff (Go). The third highest hill in the Cairngorms; all of it lies in Aberdeenshire.

**The Cairnwell** (OS, C, 135774), ðɪ'kern̩ˌwɛl, stress in local speech is on Cairn (A), from An Carn Bhalg (3), karnə'valəg (A), the hill of bags (i.e. round-shaped hill (D)), always spoken of as the Cairnwall (Sg 1948). In Gaelic Carn Bhalg, carn valluk, the hill of pimples, from the rocky protruberances on the south face (Mp), Carnwallak (M), Garn-vallak, n garn bhalg (D). Carnavalage (Bal), Carnwallak (Bla), Cairnbalg (Fa), Cairnwall, Carnavalage (Vd), Carnvallag (Roy), the Carnvalg (Hi). Always had the definite article, in Gaelic and English (D). The presence of definite article and stress not on the last noun may be explained by this being a compound noun, An Carn-bhalg, the bag hill or bulge hill, where the article is attached to the first noun, the second noun is aspirated, and the stress can sometimes fall upon both nouns. A hill between Clunie and Glen Shee.

**The Cairnwell** (A, C, 141776), as above. The Cairnwell Pass (Gf). Name of the pass between Braemar and Glen Shee under the above hill.

**(The) Cairnwell Burn** (OS, C, 144790), ðɪ'kern̩ˌwɛl'bʌrn. Also Allt an Tobair (3), burn of the well, (referring to Tobar Chuirn). Aultn Douper (I). At the Cairnwell.

**The Cairnwell Pass** See the Cairnwell.

**The Cairnwell Road** (C), ðɪ'kern̩ˌwɛl'rod. Road across the Cairnwell from Glen Clunie to Glen Shee.

**(The) Cairnwell Ski School** (OS, C, 139781). At the ski grounds on the Cairnwell.

**The Cairt Shed Park*** (U, 418033), ðɪ'kɛrt'ʃed'park. A field near Logie Coldstone.

**An Caisteal*** See Braemar Castle.

**Caisteal Cnoc** See Knock Castle.

**Caisteal Inbhir Eidh*** See Inverey Castle.

**Caisteal na Caillich** (OS, 3, C, 282875), ˌkasəlnɐ'kaljəç, castle of the old woman or witch. A rocky top east of Lochnagar.

**Caisteal na Coille*** (3, U, 296960), ˌkastəlnɐ'keil, castle of the wood. A hillock and steep, wooded bank east of Crathie.

**Caitir Fhrangach's Cairn** (C, 299947), 'kēte'raŋkiz'kjarn. On Creag nam Ban (rocky hill of the women) near Abergeldie Castle. Kitty Rankie (i.e. Caitir Fhrangach or French Kate) was said to have been burned here as a witch (Gr 47). The name is known to Gairnside people (e.g. AC) as well as in the main Dee valley.

**Caitir Fhrangach's Hole*** (U, 287953), 'kēte'raŋkiz'hol. A tiny door at Abergeldie Castle, leading to a cell reputed to have held Caitir Fhrangach (see name above).

**Calder's Cottary** See Muirtown of Ach Eich an Easa.

**Calder's Croft** See Muirtown of Ach Eich an Easa.

**Calder's Prop*** (F, north-west of 290929), 'kaldɛrz'prop. A cairn south of Abergeldie, where a Mr Calder was found dead around 1896.

**The Calf*** (F, 246046), ðɪ'kɑːf. This name often goes along with the bigger Brown Cow Hill to the west, i.e. the Broon Coo an the Calf. The whole hill of which Carn Bad a' Challain is the top, north of Corndavon. (Not the same as White Calf.)

**The Calfies' Park*** (U, 275951), ðɪ'ka·fez'park, Scots Calfies = calves. A field at Crathie.

**(The) Callater Burn** (OS, C, 164864), ðɪ'kalətər'bʌrn, often now the Callater (C), from Caladair (3), hard water. In Gaelic Caladair (Mp), N gallater, callter (D). Also Uisge Chaladair (3, U), uʃ'kalətër, water of the Callater. Uisge challater (D). Water Caleter (Fa). Joins Clunie south of Braemar.

**The Callater Park*** See Inbhir Uisge.

**Callum's Cast** (Sc, C, north-east of 370951), 'kaləmz'kast. A pool in Dee, at Ballater.

**Camasadh Gead*** (4, 449978), bend of small bit of arable land. Note Camasach and Camasaigh are other forms meaning a bend, in Irish names (J 3, 161). Camasa gate was at the river beside Dinnet House (Dms). In a place-name jingle.

**Camas na Ciste** (3, 153898), bend of the coffin. Cames ne kist (Fa), Camminikist, Camnikist, Cammisnikist, Cammisnikisht (Cr 4, 4, 8, 16), Camishnakist (Roy), Camusnakist (Ri), Camasakist (Ri 25). Camisnaciste or Balanloin (Cr 35) shows that these two habitations were at the same place, but Camas na Ciste was also a small estate covering a much bigger area. A former farm at a river-bend of Clunie south of Braemar. Historical details elsewhere (S).

**Camas na Ciste** (3), bend of the coffin. The 'neighbouring estate of Tullich or Cambus-na-cist (i.e. the bend of the river at the pass)' (Ha 12). The river formerly swept in a big horn or bend nearer the Pass of Ballater than today, as is obvious from an early map (R 4).

**Camas Odhar*** (3, near 315870) dun bend. Camisour (Io 53). A former farm near Bealachodhar in Glen Muick.

**The Cam-bhruach Pool*** (U, 000868), ðɪ'kambrəç'pul, after nearby A' Cham-bhruach. In Geldie.

**The Cambus Brae*** (U, 421977), ðɪ'kamɐs'bre·. A hill on the road at Cambus o' May.

**The Cambus Brig*** (C, 421976), ðɪ'kamɐs'brig. Also the Gordon Bridge (Rt). The white suspension bridge at Cambus o' May.

**The Cambus Fuird** (U, 422973), ðɪ'kamɐs'fjurd. The Cambus Ford (Gf). A former ford over Dee at Cambus o' May.

**Cambus House** (Bre, F, 421978), 'kamɐs'hus. Former name for what is now the Cambus o' May Hotel.

**Cambus o' May** (OS, C, 417981), locally with no *b*, ˌkamɐsɐ 'mɛi·, often shortened to the Camas, from Camas a' Mhaigh (3), bend of the plain. Camasmay (G 8), Camasamay (Opr 4), Cammisnimey hard by Tullich (Cr 9), other old spellings elsewhere (M), Camas vei, vēĭ (nasal) (D). An area with several houses and a former railway station beside a big bend in the Dee valley east of Ballater. Formerly a farm.

**The Cambus o' May Walkway** (Pj). A track from Ballater to Cambus o' May along the former Deeside railway line.

**The Cambus Parks*** (F, 416981, 418980, and north of 413982), ðɪ'kamɐs'parks. Three fields at Cambus o' May.

**The Cambus Quarries** (Bre, C, 399988), ðɪ'kamɐs'kwarez. TomnaKiest Quarries (Ce 5). Disused quarries west of Cambus o' May.

**Cameron's Well** (Cj 2, 114, south-west of 280858). A well beside a track to Lochnagar, on north side of the track.

**(The) Camlet** (OS, C, 308931), ðɪ'kamlët, from An Cam-leathad (3), the curved slope. Chamlatsh (D) indicates a genitive Cham-leathaid as in ... of the Camlet. Camlett (Rg) in 1607, Camislet (Aj 1) might suggest Camas = a bend, Camlet (Ap) in 1677. A former farm on a curved slope in Glen Girnock.

**The Camlet Birks*** (U, 312929), ðɪ'kamlët'bërks. A birch wood in Glen Girnock.

**The Camlet Brig*** (F, 311926), ðɪˈkamlɛ̈tˈbrɪg. A bridge in Glen Girnock.

**The Camlet Burn*** (F, 312926), ðɪˈkamlɛ̈tˈbʌrn. In Glen Girnock.

**The Camlet Park*** (U, 305921), ðɪˈkamlɛ̈tˈpark. A field in Glen Girnock.

**The Camock** (Wa, F), ðɪˈkamək. See below.

**Camock Hill** (OS, 265051), no Hill locally, from Carn na Camaig (3, C), ˌkernɐˈχamək, hill of the crook. Kearn-Cammock (Blm 1a), Cairn na Camaik (I), Cairn na Camack (R 12), Carn a Chamaic (Mg). A hill on the old route of the Camock from Gairn to the Cock Bridge on Don.

**The Camock Road** (C, 260049), ðɪˈkaməkˈrod, incorrectly the Camus Road (Moi). Path on above route.

**Campbell's Cairn*** (U, north-west of 286831, above road), ˈkambəlzˈkern̩. A former cairn built on a boulder by a keeper who stayed at Glas-allt Shiel; cairn later broken down by a snow avalanche.

**The Canadian Brig*** (C, 073896), ðɪˌkəˈnedjənˈbrɪg. A bridge, now with only the ends still in position, made by Canadian lumbermen west of Inverey during the second world war.

**The Canadian Camp*** (C, 071899), ðɪˌkəˈnedjənˈkamp. The site of a sawmill and lumber camp beside the above bridge.

**The Canadian Camp Pool*** See Poll na Bruaich Ruaidhe.

**Candacraig** (OS, C, 339997), ˌkandiˈkreg, (kjanaˈkreg (A)), from Ceann na Creige (3), end of the rocky hill. Cannacraig (G 20), Cean na craig (Cr 34), Ceann-na-craige (Iop). Cyunng na crek, cinn na crek (D in A); the latter and Kinacraig (I) indicate occasional use of the dative Cinn = at end of. At the north-west end of a steep hillside with screes. The site of the house at Candacraig was formerly called the Chapel or the Chapel House (C), ðɪˈtʃapəlˈhus. A former farm, now a house, in Glen Gairn.

**The Candacraig Brig*** (C, 338997), ðɪˌkandiˈkregˈbrɪg. A bridge in Glen Gairn.

**(The) Canup** (OS, C, 239929), ðɪˈkarəp, from A' Chairb (4), the bent ridge of a girth-saddle, or Cainb (A), hemp. Konep (Roy), Cannape (B), Carrop (V). A hill near Balmoral.

**The Canup Quarry*** (U, 241927), ðɪˈkarəpˈkware. In lower Gelder, produced the stone for Balmoral Castle.

**(Na) Caochanan Bàna** (OS, 3, U, 001957), nəˌkʊχɐnənˈbɑːn, the white streamlets. On Carn a' Mhaim north-west of Derry Lodge.

**(Na) Caochanan Ruadha** (OS, 3, U, 940884), nəˌkʊχɐnənˈruɐ, now the Caochan Ruadhs (C), ðɪˌkɔχɐnˈruɐz, the red streamlets. This is a collective name for several streams in parallel, including An Caochan Ruadh Mor and Beag. The OS map is incorrect in labelling one stream with this collective, plural name. In upper Glen Geldie.

**An Caochan Bàn*** (3, F, 985882), ðɪˌkɔχɐnˈb̪ɑːn, the white streamlet. In Glen Geldie.

**An Caochan Bàn*** (3, U, 980854), as above, the white streamlet. Up Bynack Burn.

**Caochan Beith*** (3, 203856), streamlet of birch. Cychan Bae (R 7). Now the Little Taggart Burn (F), ðɪˈlɛ̈təlˈtagɛrtˈbʌrn. South of Ballochbuie Forest.

**Caochan Bheithe** (OS, 049916), classic form would be Bheith, not Bheithe, locally An Caochan Beithe (3, U), ðɪˌkɔχɐnˈbeː, the birch streamlet. N gaochan beithe (D in A), i.e. An Caochan Beithe, suggests that Beith here was used in an adjectival sense (see T 27, 40; 34, 269 and 47, 319 for similar examples from Kintyre, Breadalbane and Bernera). Other Braemar examples are Caochan Fearn, Dail a' Choirce, and Eilean Fearn. A burn in Glen Lui.

**Caochan Dùird Beag*** (3, F, 017855), ˌkʊχɐnˌdurtʃˈb̪ɛg, little streamlet of humming. Forms a pair with Caochan Duird Mor. Also Little Caochan Duird (F), ˈlɛ̈təlˌkɔχɐnˈdurtʃ. Near Bynack Lodge.

**Caochan Dùird Mór*** (3, F, 013857), ˌkʊχɐnˌdurtʃˈmoːr, big streamlet of humming. Also Big Caochan Duird (F), ˈbɪgˌkɔχɐnˈdurtʃ. Near Bynack Lodge.

**An Caochan Dubh*** (3, U, 960838), ðɪˌkɔχɐnˈduˑ, the dark streamlet. In upper Glen Geldie.

**An Caochan Fearn** (3, 147904), the alder streamlet. N gaochan fyarn (D), shows the definite article (see Caochan Bheithe above). A little burn flowing into Clunie near Braemar.

**Caochan na Bà Cuirc*** (4, 036977), streamlet of the ? cow with a top-knot. Kichanabacuirk (Io 19). In Glen Derry.

**Caochan na Còthaiche** (OS, 3, U, 995975), ˌkɔχɐnɐˈkɔˑɪç, streamlet of the spongy place. On Ben Macdui.

**Caochan na Cuairte** (OS, 3, 962824), kõhənnaˈkuɛrʃtʃ (A), streamlet of the circle. Runs in a semi-circle in the upper Bynack.

**Caochan nan Spòld** (3, U, 013970), ˌkɔχɐnɐˈspɔˑl, streamlet of the haunches. Caochan na Spolda (SGo). A favourite place for deer on Derry Cairngorm.

**(An) Caochan Odhar** (OS, 3, U, 260902), ðɪˌkɔχɐnˈʌur̩, the dun streamlet. Cachanour (B). In Glen Gelder.

**Caochan Roibidh** (OS, 3, C, 980923), ˌkɔχɐnˈrɔpe, Robbie's streamlet. Off Beinn Bhrotain into Glen Dee.

**An Caochan Ruadh Beag*** (3, U, 945880), ðɪˌkʊχɐnˌruɐˈb̪ɛg, the little red streamlet. Also the Little Caochan Ruadh (F), ðɪ ˈlɛ̈təlˌkɔχɐnˈruɐ. In upper Geldie.

**An Caochan Ruadh Mór*** (3, U, 941881), ðɪˌkɔχɐnˌruɐˈmoːr, the big red streamlet. Also the Big Caochan Ruadh (F), ðɪˈbɪg ˌkɔχɐnˈruɐ. In upper Geldie.

**Caochan Tachaidh*** (3, F, 028864), ˌkɔχɐnˈtaχe, ˌkʊχɐnˈtaχeɪɲ from best informant suggests Tachainn, streamlet of choking, from Tachd. A burn in the lower Geldie.

**Caochan Tachaidh Beag*** (3, F, 020870), ˌkʊχɐnˌtaχeˈb̪ɛg, little streamlet of choking (see name above). Also Little Caochan Tachaidh (F), ˈlɛ̈təlˌkɔχɐnˈtaχe. In the lower Geldie.

**Caochan Tarsuinn** (3, A), kahənˈtarsən (A) recorded as being in Braemar parish, but unfortunately Alexander did not publish details about locations for any of his names.

**Caochan Tarsuinn*** (3, 237826), cross streamlet. Kichan tarsen (R 6). Also the Latch of the Dubh-loch, Scots Latch = stream. The Latch of the Duloch (I). Runs at a right angle straight into the Dubh-loch from the south.

**An Caolach*** (3, 185916), the narrow place. The Keilach (Im 4). A former field near Invercauld, at the narrowest part of the Invercauld haughs between Balnagower Cottage and Invercauld Bridge.

**An Caol-bhad*** (4, U, 325923), ðɪˈkɛlvət, the narrow spot. At a little hollow between Girnock and Muick.

**An Caol-bhad*** (4, 144901), the narrow spot. The Cul Vatt (I). A narrow hollow on Morrone, next to Coire Chaol-bhaid.

**The Capel Mounth** (A, C, 297801), ðɪˈkepəlˈmʌnθ, from Monadh Chapall (3), Mon Chapil (D), hill or mounth of horses. Alexander wrote that this was not an adequate meaning. In Gaelic Mon-cheapail (Alexander 1942). As the Capel Mounth was an easier route for horses than most of the mounth roads, this meaning seems quite likely. Even before the present bulldozed tracks along the route were made, the Capel Road was a very good way for hill ponies.

**The Capel Pass** (Ri). The pass over to Clova by the Capel Mounth.

**(The) Capel Road** (OS, C, 296799), ðɪˈkepəlˈrod, from Rathad Chapall (3), road of horses. Rathad chapuill, rat-chapul (D). See above name. Was formerly a good path from Glen Clova to Loch Muick, now largely replaced by tracks bulldozed since the 1950s.

**The Captain's Road*** (C, 256986), ðɪˈkaptənzˈrod. An old road north of Crathie.

**An Car** (OS, 3, C, 125904), ðɪˈkaˑr, nˈgaːr (Sch), the turn. An car, the turn or bend (Mp), N garr: like carr an ratsh, bend of the road (D). A small hill where the aspect of the hillside below Morrone turns from north to north-west. Also refers to the bend on the road west of Braemar, at 125907.

**An Car** (3, U, 143905), as above, the turn. An gar (D). A high point above Braemar, where the slope turns abruptly.

**Car an Rathaid*** (3, U, 298966), ˌkarənˈratʃ, turn of the road. A sharp bend on an old track east of Crathie.

**The Caravan Park*** (U, 311008), ðɪˈkarəvɐnˈpark. A field with a caravan, east of Gairnshiel.

**The Car Hill** (128908). The Carr Hill (Brow). Hill at An Car and Carr Cottage west of Braemar.

**The Car Linn** (U, north of 135911), ðɪˈkaˑrˈlën, Scots Linn = narrow, rocky place with fast water. The Carr Linn (Mg 150, Crom, McC 1895). A small waterfall west of Braemar, near An Car.

**Car Lòchaidh** (4, 440989), dark turn. Car-lochie (A). A former house at Loch Kinord, at a point where the main aspect of the loch shoreline turns from facing north to facing north-east.

**Carlochy** (OS, C, 453986), ˌkɐrˈlɒχe. A house at Dinnet, which preserves the above name.

**An Carn*** (3, 335989), the cairn. Carn (R 14). Also the Cairn (I). A little rocky top above the mouth of Glen Gairn.

**Carn a' Bhacain** (OS, 3, 291043), indicates hill of the little bank. Pronunciations suggest Carn a' Bheachdain: ˌkarnɐˈvjaχtən (C), ˌkjarnɐˈvjaχtən (F), (karnaˈvaçtən (A)), hill of the watching. Older maps seem more consistent with the OS form:—Cairn Bachkan (I), Carn Bachkan (R 12), Cairn Bhaichan (R 16). However, there may well have been interchange here, because the original pronunciation of words spelt chd was χk, though it has become χt later. North of Gairnshiel.

**Carn a' Bhealaidh** (OS, 330933), hill of the broom. South-west of Ballater.

**Carn a' Bhùtha*** (3, 384933), hill of the tent or anthill. Carn na-vue (I). Bhutha here refers to a tent-like or anthill-like shape, like a little point on a flattish hill. Another Carn a' Bhutha above Fealar Lodge in Perthshire is a good example, giving an excellent description of this remote hilltop. A little point on the hill above Ballater.

**Carn a' Chlarsaich** (OS, 069780), hill of the harp. At the very top of Glen Ey, with the actual summit just inside Perthshire.

**Carn a' Choin Ruaidh*** (3, 371934), hill of the red dog. Cairn-na-chon-ruie (I). A little top above Ballater.

**Carn a' Choire Bhoidheach** (OS, 3, U, 227846), classic form would be Bhòidich, ˌkernɐˌkɒrˈbuaç, hill of the beautiful corrie. Cairn of Cur Buyach (In, Am), Cairn of Corbreach (Ro, map in Mg). Also the Heid o the White Mount (F), ðɪ ˈhidɪðrˈhwɛitˈmʌnθ. On Lochnagar.

**Carn Afluimeirg** (6, 456983). Two cairns called Afflumurock (Brown 1), Cairns called Afflumrock (Gr), Cairn Flumerick (A), ˈflʌmrək (A). ? possibly Carn Ach Lumadheirg, cairn of field of deep river channel, with Ach becoming Af as is common in Deeside. A cairn near Dinnet.

**Carn a' Gheòidh** (OS, 3, C, 107767), karnˈjɒi, hill of the goose. Carn Eoie (R 14), Cairn Yeoie (M), Carn Yoi (D in A). West of the Cairnwell.

**Carn Allt an Aitinn** (OS, 3, U, 135993), ˌkernˌaltˈnaχtjən, hill of burn of the juniper. Carn alt an achtsing (D). On Ben Avon.

**Carn Allt na Beinne** (OS, 076965), should be Carn Alltan na Beinne, as it rises above Alltan na Beinne (OS), hill of streamlet of the hill. On Beinn a' Bhuird.

**Carn Allt Shlat** (3, D, U, 114861), ˌkarnˌaltˈlaχt, hill of burn of wands. In Glen Ey.

**Carn a' Mhaim** (OS, 3, Sin, C, 994952), ˌkarnɐˈvɛim, hill of the pass (W J Watson in Sg 1948). Cairn a Vime (Fi), the Cairn of the Mam (Sin). West of Derry Lodge, rises above the Lairig Ghru pass.

**The Carn a' Mhaim Ridge*** (U, 993955), ðɪˌkarnɐˈvɛimˈrɪdʒ. Not a local name except by a few people who have picked it up from hill walkers. The entire long ridge connecting Carn a' Mhaim to Ben Macdui.

**Carn an Alltan Dhuibh*** (3, 157820), hill of the black burnie. Cairn Aultan-duie (I), Carn Aultan Duie, Carn Aultan dhuie (R 13, 14). A broad hill south-west of Loch Callater, part of Carn Dubh.

**Carn an Daimh** (OS, 298871), hill of the stag. In Glen Muick.

**Carn an Dubh-loch*** (3, U, 233823), ˌkarnənˈduˌlɒχ, hill of the black loch. Also the Cairn o the Dubh-loch (U), ðɪˈkernɪðrˈduˌlɒχ. West of Loch Muick.

**Carn an Fhidhleir** (OS, 3, C, 905842), karnˈiˑlër, hill of the fiddler. Karn Iler hill or the fidlars cairn (Po), Cairneelar (K), Carn eelar (D). Has been called Carn an Fhidhleir Féithisidh (3), i.e. of Feshie or boggy-haugh, distinguishing it from the nearby Carn an Fhidhleir Lorgaidh. Carn an Fhidhleir Feisidh (Cj 11). Above upper Glen Geldie.

**Carn an Fhir Bhogha** (OS, 4, 120990, also refers to the 1089 m hilltop at 122992), hill of the archer. Can er vow (Im 3), Ca-ner-vow (I), Caner bhu (R 14), and perhaps Conor Mor (OS 1869) suggest Cadha an Fhir Bhogha = way of the archer, but Bowman's Cairn (Im 3), a hill called Bowman's Cairn, and Cairnervow (Io 25a, 63) suggest that the OS form may be correct. It is shown as a steep hillside on one map (I) but on others is the hilltop. On Ben Avon.

**Carn an Fhithich*** (3, 098888), hill of the raven. 'Hill called Cornenich opposite to Mar Lodge' (Ra 5). A hilltop above Creag an Fhithich near Inverey.

**Carn an 'Ic Duibhe** (OS, 051907), should be Carn an Uidhir (3, U), ˌkarnənˈtujər, hill of the traveller. Leachd nan Uan (M), Leac an Uidhear (D in A), ūiar (D), should be Uidhir, Leac = slope. Carn an t-Uidhear (A); the t sound may have crept in to ease pronunciation. A hill north of the Linn of Dee.

**Carn an Leth-Allt** (OS, 3, U, 053884), ˌkarnənˈljɛɐlt, hill of the half-burn (i.e. steeper on one side than the other). Caurn leault (Im 3), Caurn Leault (Io 25a). See under Dalvorar Burn. West of the Linn of Dee.

**Carn an Ruighe Riabhaich*** (3, 358017), hill of the brindled shiel. Rising ground, the Cairn of the Ririach (Io 20), Cairn of Rea Reach (G 17). A low hill south-west of Morven.

**Carn an t-Sagairt** (C), kernˈtagërt, in Gaelic karnˈdagërtʃ (JB). A collective name for Carn an t-Sagairt Beag and Mor near Lochnagar. Carnintaghird (G 5).

**Carn an t-Sagairt Beag** (OS, 2, C, 217849), ˌkernˌtagërtˈbɛg, little hill of the priest, Gaelic pronunciation ˌkarnˌdagërtʃˈbɛg (JB). Also Little Carn an t-Sagairt (F), ˈlɛtəlˌkernˈtagërt. Little Cairn Taggart (A 1954). The priest was said to be the same one as at the Priest's Well at Loch Callater, below Carn an t-Sagairt (McC 1891). A hill west of Lochnagar.

**Carn an t-Sagairt Mór** (OS, 3, C, 208843), ˌkernˌtagërtˈmoˑr, big hill of the priest. See above. Also Muckle Carn an t-Sagairt (F), ˈmʌkəlˌkernˈtagërt. East of Loch Callater.

**Carn an t-Seilich** (3), karnˈdʒɛləç (A), hill of the willow. Carn nan Seileach . . . should be spelt Carn an t-seilich (A), but Alexander erred here with his sole entry for Carn nan Seileach, as the only Carn nan Seileach so far documented in Upper Deeside is in Glen Ey (OS). Carn an t-Seilich may have been a local name for Carn na Craoibhe Seileich (OS) or some other hill in that area.

**Carn an Tuirc** (OS, 3, C, 174805), kern̩'tʌrk, hill of the boar, sometimes shortened to Turk (C), tʌrk. Cairn Duirk (I, R 14), Carn Duirk (R 13), Cairn-Duirk (Ro), Carn durk (D). Boars appear often in Fingalian mythology (Campbell 1972), and this may be the association here, as nearby Glen Shee definitely has Fingalian names (Ben Gulabin and Tom Diarmaid). A hill south of Loch Callater.

**Carn an Tuirc Beag** (3,185813), little hill of the boar. Carn Duirk Begg (R 13), Carn Tuirc bheag (Mg 148). Also Little Carn an Tuirc (C), 'lɛ̈təl̩ˌkern̩'tʌrk. Little Cairn Turc (V). A spur of the above hill.

**(The) Carn an Tuirc Hut** (OS, C, 173810). A ski hut built in the late 1950s, now demolished.

**Carn an Uidhir** See Carn an 'Ic Duibhe.

**Carn Aosda** (OS, 134792), should be Carn Aoise (3, F), karn'ʊʃ, (karn'nö̈ʃ (A)), hill of old age. Cairn Nuish (I), Carn naosh, 'old age' (D), see also other notes (A). Also Moses' Cairn (CMcI), 'mozız'kern̩. North of the Cairnwell.

**(The) Carn Aosda Hut** (OS, C, 130786). A ski hut near the above hill.

**Carnaquheen** (OS, C, 242943), ˌkernɐ'çwin. See Carn na Cuimhne, from which Carnaquheen comes. A house west of Crathie.

**The Carnaquheen Puil** See the Auld Boat Puil.

**Carn Bad a' Challain** (3, F, 245046), ˌkern̩ˌpɪt'χalën (F), ˌkern ˌpɪt'χaljɪn (WL), hill of clump of the noise. Carn Bad Challain, Cairnbadachallan, Cairn Bad Challen, Carn a' challan (R 3, 9, 12, 14), Cairn bad chalan or C. pit chalan (D). An eastward extension of Brown Cow Hill.

**Carn Badan Seileach*** (3, 143022), hill of willow clumps. Carn Battan Shellach (R 2a), also note the Bads o Ben Avon. A broad ridge on Ben Avon.

**Carn Bad nan Dearcag*** (3, 208969), hill of clump of the little berries. In the same place as Bad nan Dearcag (OS). Carn-Batnan-derkaig (I). A little top above Glen Feardar.

**Carn Bad nan Laogh*** (4, 240017), hill of clump of the calves (see Bad nan Laogh). Carn Badenlua, Cairnbadenlua, Carn-badenlua (R 3, 5, 14). A little top near Corndavon Lodge.

**Carn Beidhneig** See Carn Greannach.

**Carn Beinne** (4), hill or cairn of mountain, possibly Beann = corner. Carnben (S 8), Carnbean, Cairnbian, Cairnbean (Io 14, 14, 74), Cairnbeann (Me 20). A grazing that went with Braeneach north of Crathie.

**Carn Bhac** (OS, 3, C, 041828), karn'vaːχk, hill of banks, but Carn Vaich (Gr) and Allt Carn a' Bhathaich (OS) would suggest Bhàthaich = of the shelter. Carn vahk (D). Carries some peat banks at unusually high altitude. West of Glen Ey.

**Carn Bhithir** (OS, 077868), from Carn a' Bhior (2, A, C), karn 'viˑr̩, hill of the sharp point. Carn Bhir, Carn a' Bhir (D). The hill sends a narrow ridge to the north-east towards Inverey.

**Carn Blàir Rèidh** (3, 379939), hill of level ground. Cairn-Pla-raie (I), Cairn of Blaraye (Mg). A small top at a flattish stretch of heathery ground south-east of Ballater.

**Carn Bòrd*** (3, 285872), table hill, probably the same construction as in Beinn Bord (Beinn a' Bhuird). Cairn-na-Bourd (B). A flat top on the same site as Conachcraig (OS), but Conachcraig is really a general name for the whole hill group between Coire na Ciche and Inchnabobart in Glen Muick.

**Carn Bràigh an Uillt*** (3, 179887), hill of upland of the burn. Carn-Braen Uilt (I), Carnbraen Uilt, Carn Braen alt, Carn Baen-Ult (R 7, 14, 16). South-east of Braemar.

**Carn Buachaille Bréige*** (3, 080784), hill of false shepherd. Cairn-bua-chil-a-breac (I), Cairn-buachil-breck, Carn Buchal a-Breach (R 14, 16). A hill with a cairn which was

presumably the false shepherd (i.e. like a man in the distance). Above the head of the Baddoch Burn.

**Carn Chaol-bhaid*** (4, 292038), hill of the narrow spot. Cairn Chulvat (I), Carn chulbhat (R 14). North of Gairnshiel.

**Carn Chrionaidh** (OS, 135810), should be Carn a' Chronaidh (5), hill of the little hollow or of the dark brown place or of the low murmuring (see Coire Chronaidh). Cairn Chronie (I) at 131793, also Carn na Chronie (I) about the OS location, so obviously the name covers the whole ridge from the OS location up to the top west of Carn Aosda. Carnachronie (Ra 3), Cairn Chronie (R 14). South of the Baddoch.

**Carn Clach-mhuilinn*** (3, 272045), hill of millstones. Carn-clach-Mhulin (R 14). Cairn Clach-n-Mulun (R 12), Cairn Clachn Mulun (I) suggest a variant Carn Clachan-muilinn, of millstones. Also the Millstone Cairn (A). North-west of Gairnshiel.

**Carn Cloich-mhuilinn** (OS, 969907), should be Carn nan Clach-mhuilinn (3, U), ˌkarnɐˌglaχ'vulən, (karnklaç'vuljən (A)), hill of the millstones. Carn na glachan muiln, na clach vuln (D). Also the Millstone Hill (A, C), ðɪ'mɛ̈lˌstɒn'hël. A stony spur of Beinn Bhrotain.

**Carn Coire an Eirbhein*** See Corrienearn.

**Carn Creagach** (OS, 069830), karn'hrɛkaç (A), rocky hill. In Glen Ey. Said to be in Glen Geusachan (A), where there is a Coire Creagach, but probably an error for Glen Ey.

**Carn Crom** (OS, 2, C, 023954), karn'krọm, curved hill. Carn Croum (Fi). A hill in a curve above Luibeg.

**Carn Cruinn** (OS, 092810), round hill. A round-shaped hill in upper Glen Ey. Also Mullach Cruinn (3, D).

**Carn Dairiridh*** (4, 323785), hill of Darrarie (see Allt Darrarie). Cairn of Ault Darrarie (I), Carn Dararie (R 16). South of Loch Muick.

**Carn Damhaireach or Top of the Battery** (OS, 3, F, 059859), karn'dʌuriç, rutting hill. Carn taurich, rutting (D in A). South-west of Inverey.

**(An) Carn Dearg** (OS, 2, U, 096865), ðɪˌkarn'ʤɛrək, the red hill. In Glen Ey. This name usually indicates reddish screes or rocks.

**(An) Carn Dearg** (OS, 2, U, 124931), as above, the red hill. North-west of Braemar.

**(An) Carn Dearg** (OS, 2, U, 035874), as above, the red hill. South-west of the Linn of Dee.

**Carn Dearg** (3), red hill. Cairn Derig (At, Ath), Crⁿ Derig (Kn). Summit part of Beinn Iutharn Mhor, south-west of Glen Ey.

**Carn Dearg** (OS, 319983), red hill. Above Coilacriech.

**Carn Dearg** (OS, 3, U, 177027), karn'ʤɛrək, red hill. 'Top of the Red Cairn of Loch Bulg' (R 2a), Caern Derg (R 14), Red Cairn (map in Mg). Near Loch Builg.

**Carn Dearg*** (3, 199939), red hill. Carn Derg (I). A small top north-east of Invercauld House.

**Carn Dearg*** (3, 120788), red hill. Cairn Derg (I); Sron nam Fiadh (OS) is the nose further out. North-west of the Cairnwell.

**Carn Dearg*** See Creag Dearg.

**Carn Dearg** (3, U, south of 242960), karn'ʤɛrg, red hill. Carn-jerik (D). North-west of Crathie.

**Carn Dearg*** (3, 302996), red hill. Cairn Derg (I). South of Gairnshiel.

**Carn Dearg*** (3, 258025), red hill. Cairn Derg (I). A little top north-west of Gairnshiel.

**Carn Drochaid** (OS, 165016), hill at bridge. Presumably named after a bridge on River Gairn below. A footbridge stands there today, near where the Bealach Dearg Road comes off Culardoch down to the valley bottom.

**Carn Dubh** (OS, 3, F, 162819), karn'duˑ, black hill. A predominantly heathery hill, in contrast to the grassier hills to the south, hence Dubh = black. Also now the Hare Hill

(F), ðɪˈherˌhël, as many hares live on it (see Carn na Greine). South-west of Loch Callater.

**Carn Dubh*** (3, 381925), black hill. Carn Dhu (R 16). Between Carn Leuchan and Craig Vallich, about a mile from Carn Leuchan to judge from the map (R). South of Ballater.

**Carn Dubh an Eagail*** (3, 363938), black cairn of fear. Cairn-du-necal (I). A small patch of dark rocks above the Mounth Road in Glen Muick.

**Carn Eag Dhubh** (OS, 3, 123973), hill of black notch. Cairn Eig-Du (I), Carn Eigh-Dhu (R 14). Both these maps give the location of Carn Eag Dhubh at Carn na Craoibhe Seileich (OS), and the hill at 123973 is Hill of Aultn Aiten (I), i.e. of Allt an Aitinn. Neither Alexander nor we found any local people who knew the name Carn na Craoibhe Seileich. South of Ben Avon.

**Carn Eas** (OS, 127989), from Carn an Easa (3), karnˈnjɛs (C), hill of the waterfall. Carn an yess (D). There is a steep burn just to the east, and the burn Allt an Eas Bhig is to the north-east. On Ben Avon.

**Carn Elrig Beag** (OS, 093935), from Carn Eileirig Beag (3, U), ˌkarnˌɛlrɪkˈbɛg, little hill of the deer-trap. In Glen Quoich.

**Carn Elrig Mór** (OS, 096944), from Carn Eileirig Mór (3, U), ˌkarnˌɛlrɪkˈmoːr, big hill of the deer-trap. In Glen Quoich.

**Carn Etchachan** (OS, 003009), from Carn Éiteachan (6, F), karnˈɛˌtʃɛχɛn, hill of ? expansive place, see under Coire Etchachan. Above Loch Etchachan.

**Carn Fiaclach** (OS, 3, U, 103970), karnˈfiəklɛχ, toothed hill. Cairn Fiachlach (I), Carn Fhiaclachd (R 14). Has a tooth-like shape when seen from Glen Quoich.

**Carn Fiaclach** (OS, 3, R 7, C, 220891), as above, toothed hill. A rocky point above Ballochbuie Forest.

**Carn Fiaclach** (OS, F, 309054), as above, toothed hill. A sharp point above the top of the Gairnshiel–Corgarff road.

**Carn Fiaclach** (OS, 2, U, 983906), as above, toothed hill. Carnfiachlach (Roy). A sharp point south-east of Beinn Bhrotain, forming a pair with Carn Fiaclach Beag.

**An Carn Fiaclach** (3, U, 134899), nˌgarnˈfiəklɛx, the toothed hill. N garn fiaclach (D). A sharp hillock west of Braemar.

**Carn Fiaclach Beag** (OS, 2, U, 989903), ˌkarnˌfiəklɛχˈbɛg, little toothed hill. A sharp little point south-east of Beinn Bhrotain.

**Carn Ghille Ruadh** (3, U, 053822), ˌkarnˈgilˈruɛ, hill of the red-haired lad. Carn Ghill' rua (D). In upper Glen Ey.

**Carn Ghriogair** (OS, 3, 115831), karnˈgrigər (A), hill of Gregor. Cairn Grigor (I) is shown at 121837, and the top at 115831 is shown on that map but without a name. Carn grigach (Da). In upper Glen Clunie.

**Carn Gille gun Thriubhas** (2, U, 960815), ˌkarnˌgilgənˈhruʃ, cairn of lad without trousers. Carn kill kun hrūsh (D). Alexander wrote of a tale 'of a Braemar Jacobite, compelled to wear trews after the '45, who took them off here and walked trouserless'. This is the cairn at the top of Braigh Coire Caochan nan Laogh. At the top of the Bynack Burn.

**Carn Glas-leathad*** (3, U, 009833), ˌkarnˈglasˌlët, hill of grey slope. Near the Tilt-Bynack march.

**An Carn Gorm** See the Derry Cairngorm.

**An Carn Gorm Beag** See the Little Cairngorm.

**Carn Greannach** (OS, 3, 950822), karnˈgrenɔç (A), rough hill. Cairnbaynock (Io 21, Mc 18), Cairn Baynock, Cairnbaynoch, Cairnbynoch (Me 13, 16, 19) and Cairnbunnoch (Ath) from Carn Beidhneig (6), hill of Bynack. Cairn-brennoch (At) and Cairn Brennoch (Kn, Mg) suggest something different, but Mg also gives Brennoch Water for Bynack Burn. A stony hill at top of Bynack.

**Carn Grianach*** (3, 115825), sunny hill. Cairn Grianich (I). This is on the site of Sgor Mor (OS), but the OS location is

incorrect and should refer to the rocks 1 km to the east, above the Baddoch.

**Carn Leac Dubh*** (3, 071928), karnˈlɛçt (U), hill of dark slope. Caurn lechkadow (Im 3), Caurn Lechkadow (Io 25a). North of Linn of Dee.

**Carn Leuchan** (OS, C, 380911), from Carn Fhliuchan (4), kjarnˈluχɛn (U), kernˌluχən (C), hill of wet spots. Cairnlichan (G 22). South of Ballater.

**(An) Carn Liath** (OS, 2, U, 036867), ðɪˌkarnˈliɛ, the grey hill. Alexander (1952) incorrectly wrote that this should be Carn Leth-allt, but that is a top nearer the Linn of Dee. Carn LEEa (A 1954). South-west of the Linn of Dee.

**Carn Liath** (OS, 3, F, 165977), as above, the grey hill. Hill of Lia Chorry Beg, Top of Lia Chorry Beg (I), the Liath-choire (A, F). A hill north of Invercauld.

**Carn Loinn Aitinn*** (3, 364863), hill of enclosure of juniper. Carnloinaitne (G 5). A small hilltop south-east of Linn of Muick.

**Carn Lunndan*** (3, probably 062948), hill at marshy ground, or at green place, or at green marshy place (see also Meall an Lundain). Cairnaluntan (Me 15) might suggest Carn an Lunndain, hill of the . . ., but may well involve the middle svarabhakti *a* simply to make speech easier. Hilltop at Meall an Lundain, possibly the name refers to the stony ground on top of the Meall. A hill north-east of Derry Lodge.

**Carn Meadhonach** (3, 238046), middle hill. Carn-meanoch, Carn Mainach (R 3, 12), Cairnmenach (D). A top in the middle between Brown Cow Hill and Carn Bad a' Challain.

**Carn Mhaide*** See Creag Liath.

**Carn Mhuillidh Mór*** (4, 301032), big hill fit for driving a mill, as in Corriemulzie. Cairn Vullie-more (I), Carn bhuil mhoir (R 14). A little top north of Gairnshiel.

**Carn Mòine an Tighearn** (OS, 3, 227969), hill of peat-moss of the proprietor. Hill of Cairnmongiran, Carn-moine n' tighearn (R 9, 14). The Cairn of Monaltrie (A). Also now the Mains o Monaltrie Cairn or the Mains Cairn, ðɪˈmenzɛˌmọn ˈaltriˈkerṇ or ðɪˌmenzˈkern (F). Prominent hill above Monaltrie, Crathie, with extensive peat-mosses behind it.

**Carn Mór** (OS, 2, U, 103872), karnˈmoːr, big hill. South-east of Inverey.

**Carn Mór** (OS, 2, U, 030903), as above, big hill. West of the Linn of Dee.

**Carn Mór** (3), big cairn or hill. Carnemore (Pb), Carnmore (G 20), Cairnmoir (Cr 51, Ab 19). A former farm at the foot of Gairn, on east side of river.

**Carn na Cailliche** (3, 176826), hill of the old woman. Carn na caillich (Mg 148). Above Loch Callater.

**Carn na Craoibhe Seileich** (OS, 130966), classic Gaelic form would be Seilich, hill of the willow tree. Neither Alexander nor we found any local people who knew this name. See Carn Eag Dhubh. South of Ben Avon.

**Carn na Crìche** (OS, 3, A, U, 110946), ˌkernɛˈkriç, cairn of the boundary. Also the March Cairn (Me 24, U), ðɪˈmertʃˈkern. On the boundary between Mar and Invercauld, east of Glen Quoich.

**Carn na Crìche** (3, Wa, U, 938982), as above, cairn of the boundary. Also the March Cairn (Cj 1, McC). A cairn on the Braeriach plateau, where three parishes meet.

**Carn na Cuimhne** (OS, 241942), should be Carn na Coinnimh (3), local pronunciation ˌkernɛˈçwin, cairn of the assembly. Carn na Coinniudh (R 3), Carn-na-coinniudh (Ro), Cairn-a-cuimhue (Brown 1835), Carn a' Chuimhne (Gr), Carn a chuing (slightly nasal), remembrance would be cuinn, not ng (D). The usual spelling of Carn na Cuimhne means cairn of remembrance, but Alexander (1931) and Diack (1944) doubted this derivation. The cairn was for long a meeting place for the Farquharsons in times of battle (see Go 201), and the name was the war-cry of the Clan Farquharson. Cairn of the assembly is less romantic than cairn of remembrance, but does describe what the cairn was used for.

**Carn na Drochaide** (OS, 127938), locally Carn Drochaide (2, C), karnˈdrɔχɪt, (karnˈdrɔχɪtʃ (A)), in Gaelic karnˈdrɔχt (U), hill of bridge. Carndrochit (Me 12), Cairn Drochaide (Gr), Cairndrochet (Ri 22), Cairndrochat (Io 63), Carn Drochit, Carn Droughd (R 14, 16), Carn droychat (D). North-west of Braemar.

**Carn na Drochaide** (OS, 3, 125861, should be the cairn at 132868 directly above Fraser's Brig in mid Glen Clunie (U); 125861 is Meall gun Aon), as above, hill of the bridge. See Meall gun Aon for further evidence.

**Carn na Feithe Seileach*** See Fasheilach.

**Carn na Feòraig** (4, U, 235970), ˌkarnɐˈfjɔrək, cairn of the grassy spot. Carn na feorag, squirrel cairn (A 205). A cairn north-west of Crathie.

**Carn na Gréine** (OS, 149815), hill of the sun. South of Glen Clunie. The slope below is Leathad Grianain, slope of the sunny spot. Also the Hare Hill (A, F), ðɪˈheṛˈhɛl, as many hares live on it. This name covers the hill ground nearby, including Carn Dubh. South-east of Baddoch.

**Carn na h-Eileirige** See Meikle Elrick.

**Carn nam Blàithean*** (4, 219959), hill of the little flowers. Carn Na mplaithen (R 3). North-west of the Inver.

**Carn na Moine** (OS, 2, A, U, 061878), ˌkarnɐˈmǫn (U), (karnə ˈmon, final *n* palatal (A)), hill of the peat-moss. South of the Linn of Dee.

**Carn na Mòine*** (3, 163893), hill of the peat-moss. Carn na Moin (I). A small top south-east of Braemar.

**Carn nan Clach-mhuilinn** See Millstone Cairn.

**Carn nan Cnap*** (3, 164898), hill of the knobs. Carn-na-Knap (I). A hilltop with rocky bumps, south-east of Braemar.

**Carn nan Damh*** (3, 178784), hill of the stags. Cairn-n-dau (I). North-east of the Glas Maol.

**Carn nan Dearcag*** (2, JB, 173875), ˌkarnənˈdʒɛrkɐg, stony hill of the little berries. A name for the whole of the first big hill up Glen Callater on the east side; note Creag na Dearcaige (OS) for a rock on this hill.

**Carn nan Gabhar** (3, 244861), cairn of the goats, carn nan gobhar (D). The highest top of Lochnagar (D), probably just the tor and other rocks where the indicator now stands; see Cac Carn Mor for the whole summit area.

**Carn nan Sac** (OS, 3, A, 119770), karnənˈsahk (A), hill of the sacks (i.e. referring to bulges on the surface of the hill). West of the Cairnwell.

**Carn nan Seileach** (OS, 074854), hill of the willows. Above lower Glen Ey.

**Carn nan Sgliat** (OS, 167903). A better Gaelic spelling, which would also fit the local pronunciation better, would be Carn nan Sglèat (3, C), ˌkarnɐnˈsklɛtʃ, karnˈsklɛtʃ, hill of the slates. Carn na skletsh, Carn skletsh (D), karnˈsklɛtʃ (A). Has an old slate quarry on the top (A). South-east of Braemar.

**Carn nan Sian*** (4, 312989), hill of the storms. Car-na-shien (I), Carn-a-shien (R 14). An exposed top sticking out from Geallaig Hill towards Gairnshiel.

**Carn nan Slòigh*** (4, 295997), possibly a variant genitive plural with *gh* not sounded, hill of the peoples. Cairn na sloich (I), Carn 'a-sloich (R 14). A little top above Gairnshiel.

**Carn nan Tri Crìoch** (2, Wa, U, 981017), ˌkarnɐnˈtriˈkriɐç, cairn of the three boundaries. A cairn where Aberdeenshire, Banffshire and Inverness-shire meet on the hill of Cairn Lochan north of Ben Macdui.

**Carn Rèidh, Carn Ruadh** or **Carn na Roinne**. Carnerein (Rli 6),

Cairn Ray (Ri 14), Cairnroy (Ap) in 1766. A pendicle of Aucholzie in Glen Muick.

**Carn Seumas Mór na Pluice*** (3, U, 082823), ˌkarnˌʃemɐsˈmoˑrnɐ ˈpluχk (SGo), cairn of big James of the fat cheek. James McKenzie of Dalmore was killed there by Lochaber caterans about 1726–27 (Ri). In upper Glen Ey.

**Carn Sùilean Dubha*** (3, 112944), hill with black eyes (i.e. springs). On top of the hill called Cairnsulendoo (Ra 4), Cairnsulendow, or the cairn with the black eyes (Ra 5), Cairnsuillendu (Io 63). East of Glen Quoich, on the Mar–Invercauld boundary. Holds the cairns of Carn na Criche and Old Shelter Cairn.

**Carn Tiekeiver** (OS, 176022 should be at 182020; 176022 is part of Carn Dearg), from Carn Tigh 'Ic Iomhair (3, U), ˌkarnˌtɛi ˈkiˑvɛr, hill of house of MacIvor. Carn Daie Kiaver (I), Caern dhaie-Khiabher (R 14). The house probably refers to one of the old ruins by Gairn, below the hill. South of Loch Builg.

**Carn Ulie** (OS, 197044), from Carn Ulaidh Mór (3), big hill of treasure. Carn Yulie more (I), Carn ulaidh Mhoir (R 14), Carn Yulie Mor (Io 34). Above Loch Builg.

**The Carpet Roadie*** (U, 419971), ðɪˈkarpɛtˈrodi. A moss-covered track near Cambus o' May.

**The Car Prop** (Ky, C, 125904), ðɪˈkarˈprɔp. A landmark cairn at An Car, west of Braemar.

**The Car Prop Road*** (C, 130905), ðɪˈkarˈprɔpˈrod. A track west of Braemar.

**An Càrr*** (3, F, 032898), ðɪˈkaːr, the rough hillside or rock. A rocky face west of the Linn of Dee.

**An Càrr*** (3, 183934), the rough ground. The Carr (I). A rocky top north-east of Invercauld.

**Càrrach Mór*** (3, 202010 and 197016), big boggy place. Carach-more—'mossy ground' (I), Carach Mhoir (R 14). A boggy area south of Loch Builg.

**The Carr Burn*** (F, 026897), ðɪˈkaˑrˈbʌrn. The upper part of Allt Ton na Gaoithe, runs beside the face of An Carr, west of the Linn of Dee.

**Carr Cottage** (OS, C, 127908), ˈkarˈkǫtədʒ. Named after An Car, the bend on the road and hillside near the cottage. Opposite the mouth of Quoich.

**The Car Rocks*** (F, 125907), ðɪˈkaˑrˈrɔks. Rocks below the road west of Braemar.

**An Càrr Odhar** (3, F, 176943), ðɪˌkəˈrʌuṛ, the dun-coloured rough ground. Gaar Our 'building' (I), Carour, Carrour (Io 75, 77), Carower (Mg). The G sound in Gaar was probably due to eclipsis after the article An. A former shepherd's house north of Invercauld.

**The Carr Odhar Wuid*** (F, 178947), ðɪˌkəˈrʌuṛˈwɪd. A wood near the above place.

**Carr's Drive** (S, 186899). Car's Drive (R 7). A road in Ballochbuie Forest, made in the late 18th century by the Invercauld laird's wife Margaret Carr (Ri).

**The Car Wuid*** (C, 126907), ðɪˈkaˑrˈwɪd. Carr Wood (Ra 14). Wood beside An Car, west of Braemar.

**The Castle Fuird*** (U, 157926), ðɪˈkastəlˈfjurd. A ford over Dee near Braemar Castle.

**The Castle Fuird Road*** (U, 155923), ðɪˈkastəlˈfjurdˈrod. A track outside fence on west side of Braemar Castle ground, to a ford over Dee.

**Castlehill*** Castellhill (Io). A former house in 1832 on the Invercauld part of Glen Gairn, and hence not at Abergairn Castle. Possibly same as Castlehill east of Ballater. Probably near Rineten.

**Castlehill** (OS, C, 396979), ˈkasəlˈhɛl. A house, named after the hillock below.

**The Castle Hill*** (U, 397979), ðɪˈkasəlˈhɛl, sometimes the Castle Hillock (U), ðɪˈkasəlˈhɛlɛk. A hillock east of Ballater.

**The Castle-hill** See Tom Meann.

**The Castle Hillock Park*** (U, 398979), ðɪˈkasəlˈhëlëkˈpark. A field near Tullich.

**The Castle Housie*** (JS, 335922), ðɪˈkasəlˈhusi, Scots Housie = little house. Ruin of a building south-west of Ballater, used in the production of illicit whisky (JS).

**The Castle Island** See the Muckle Island.

**Castle of Ceann na Coille** See Deecastle.

**The Castle of Invercauld** See Invercauld House.

**The Castle of Kinord** See the Peel of Kinord.

**The Castle o Kindrochit** (F, 151913), ðɪˈkastələˌkɪnˈdroχët, usually now Kindrochit Castle (C). The castell of Kindrocht (Rg) in 1634, the King's Castle of Kindrocht (Vd). At Braemar.

**The Castle Park*** (U, 360974), ðɪˈkasəlˈpark. A former rough field from 359976 down to 361970, now mostly a wood. Near Abergairn Castle.

**The Castle Park*** (F, 252948), as above. A field near Balmoral Castle.

**The Castle Park** (Gr, F, 156923), as above. Also the Barrack Yard (Gf). Barrack Ground (Im 4). Ground around Braemar Castle.

**The Castle Park*** (Dms 435970). Also the Park of Ceann na Coille. The Park of Kanakyle (Dms 13). A large area, now several fields the Lang Haugh, Torraidh Siol and Coble Haugh, named after a former castle at Deecastle west of Dinnet.

**Castle Park*** (Im 4, 156926). A field beside Braemar Castle.

**The Castle Parks*** (F, 152923), ðɪˈkasəlˈparks. Three fields between the Old Toll House and the wood at Braemar Castle; the middle one was formerly Cook's Park.

**The Castle Puil** (F, 255952), ðɪˈkasəlˈpil. Castle (Sc). A pool in Dee, beside Balmoral Castle.

**The Castle Puil** (F, 158925), as above. Castle (A). A pool in Dee, near Braemar Castle.

**(The) Castleton** (OS, C, 152915), ðɪˈkasəltən. A former name, still often used, for the village of Braemar. The Castletoune (Cr 12), Casteltown (Io 75). A translation of Baile a' Chaisteil (2, F, Sch), balˈχastjəl, farm-town of the castle. Often it was called the Castleton of Braemar, with the word Braemar referring to the district.

**Castleton Ferry** (149925). Castletown Ferry (Wy). Former ferry over Dee at Braemar.

**The Castleton Haugh** (F, 152921), ðɪˈkasəltənˈhaˑχ. The Haugh of Castletown (Sto), Castletown Haugh (I). A field near Braemar.

**The Castletoun** (U, 359974), ðɪˈkasəltən. Castletoun (H), Castletoun of Glengarden (Io 20). A former farm at Abergairn Castle near Ballater.

**Castletoun of Knock*** Castelltoune of Cnock (G 5). A former farm probably at Muckle Knock near Ballater.

**Castle William*** (I, 270959), possibly from Caisteal Uillne (3), castle on a corner. A rock on a corner of a hill north of Crathie. Another such name, possibly of the same derivation, is Castle Wilson, a rocky pinnacle in Glen Carvie, Strath Don.

**Cata na Cailliche** (3, west of 276016), sheep-cot of the old woman. Catnakylyach (D). A former house and cot west of Gairnshiel.

**Cata na Coille Móire*** (4, JS, 333904), ˌkatnɐˌkɛiliˈmoˑr, sheep-cot of the big wood. In mid Glen Muick.

**Cata nan Gabhar** (3, probably north-west of 264021), sheep-cot of the goats. Cat na gabhar, the sheepfold (D). North-west of Gairnshiel.

**Catanellan** (OS, F, 283942), katˈnjɛlən, (katənɛlɛn (A)), from Cata an Eilein (3), sheep-cot of the streamside field. Catneilin (Cpb 9). A former farm near Abergeldie, now a house.

**Catanellan Croft*** (284942). Cattenellan Croft (Ce 6). Former habitation near Abergeldie.

**The Caterans' Graves*** (U, 139782), ðɪˈketərənzˈgrevz, Scots Caterans = cattle thieves. The Catterine's Graves (Md 1). Former graves from the Battle of the Cairnwell in 1644 (Gr), still visible as hollows until the ski developments in 1962, now on the site of the cess-pit hut for the ski cafe.

**The Caterans' Hollow** (U, 140782), ðɪˈketərənzˈhọlɐ. The Katrin's Howe (Ta), referring to the Battle of the Cairnwell. On the Cairnwell pass.

**Catharine's Drive*** (R 7, 178934). A road above Invercauld House.

**The Cats' Cairn*** (U, 362001), ðɪˈkatsˈkern̩. A rocky place good for wild cats, north of Ballater.

**The Cauldron*** (I, 238942). A rough, stony hillside near the Inver.

**The Cauld Spring*** (U, 453913), ðɪˈkaˑlˈsprɪŋ, Scots Cauld = cold. On north side of a ford in Glen Tanar.

**Cavan's Burn*** (F, east of 156910), ˈkavənzˈbʌrn. Lower part of Corrie Feragie Burn at Braemar.

**Cavan's Park*** See A' Mhoine Mhor.

**The Cave*** (U, south-east of 087870), ðɪˈkeˑv. A deep pool between rocks south of the Colonel's Bed in Glen Ey.

**Ceann a' Gharaidh*** (3, probably near 398970), end of the dyke. Candagarie (Io 7). A former farm near Pannanich east of Ballater.

**Ceann an t-Sean-bhaile*** (3, 30-01-), end of the old farm-town. Khenghenwill (Opr in 1720), Keanshannavil (Rli 23), Keannsheanbhail (Io 52). A former farm near the Shenval at Gairnshiel.

**Ceann an t-Sean-bhaile** (3, 223936), end of the old farm-town. Ceannantenaval, Ceanantenbhail, Ceannantenval (Cr 40, 41, 42), Kaun Shanval (I), Keanshanbhal (R 14), Canshanvell a pendicle of Shanvell (Ri 17). A former farm near the Inver.

**An Ceann Caol** (3, U, 987972), ðɪˌkjaunˈkʊl, the tapering extremity. Ceann Caol (Sg). A narrow ridge connecting Carn a' Mhaim to Ben Macdui.

**Ceann Crionn Carn a' Mhaim** (OS, 989964), little end of hill of the pass. On the west face of Carn a' Mhaim (Cj 1), south of the above.

**Ceann na Coille** See Deecastle.

**Ceann na Coille*** (3, 124915), end of the wood. Kenakyle (Roy), Ceannacoil of Alanquoich, Cean na coill (Cr 38, 45), Kanachyle (R 2) on the site of the house Cairn na Drochaide (OS). West of Braemar.

**The Ceann na Coille Ford** (434968). The Ceann-na-Coille (Dee Castle) ford (Gf). A former ford over Dee, south-west of Dinnet.

**Ceann na Creige** (3, F, 242944), ˌkandɐˈkreg, (kjanaˈkreg (A)), end of the rocky hill. Ceann na Craig (R 3). Formerly Upper Ceann na Creige. Upper Canacraig (Io 58). A former farm north-east of the Inver, at the end of the rocks on Craig Nordie.

**Ceann na Creige** See Candacraig.

**Ceann na Drochaide** See Bridgend.

**Ceann na Dalach** (3, 09-89-), head of the haugh. Cionn na dallach, Ceann na dallach (Cr 37a, 38), Kandalach (Me 15), Kindalloch (Gr). A former habitation, and chapel (Vd), near Mar Lodge.

**The Ceapach*** (3, U, 178916), ðɪˈkẹpəç, likely to have been A' Cheapach originally, the tillage plot. Kebech (Im 4). Also Park of the Ceapach. Park of the Cabich (R 7), Park of Kebich (Io 45). A former field at Invercauld.

**The Ceapach Puil** See Poll Cheapaich.

**Ceapachs*** (4, 392976), tillage plots, an anglicised plural from Ceapach. Capachs (R 4). On farmland north-east of Ballater.

**Ceap Mad*** (4, U, 300876), kapˈmad. A peat-moss with many fir roots and stumps, so Ceap = a stump is likely, and Mad the shortened Braemar Gaelic form of Madadh, i.e. stump place of dog or wolf. Capmawd (In, Am). Also the Allt Vitch Moss (F), ðɪˌaltˈvitʃˈmọs. In upper Glen Muick.

**Na Cèarr-lannan*** (3, C, 322956), ðɪˈkjarlənz, the awkward, left, or astray enclosures. Carland (Ce 3). Former houses with small isolated enclosures in Glen Girnock, now overgrown with trees.

**The Cearr-lannan Road*** (F, 322957), ðɪˈkjarlənzˈrod. In Glen Girnock.

**Ceathramh Caiseag*** (5, C, 290948), kërˈkasɐk, possibly quarter of land ? with weed stems. Craig Hassach (Am). A piece of land once cultivated but now a wood, near Abergeldie.

**The Ceathramh Caiseag Road*** (U, 291948), ðɪˌkërˈkasɐkˈrod. An old track from the Den Burn below Creag nam Ban to Corby Hall.

**The Centre Golf Course*** (F, 099898), ðɪˈsɛntërˈgọlfˌkors. A field at Mar Lodge.

**Centre Gully** (Sd, 163776). A ski-run down Allt Meadhonach on the Glas Maol.

**The Centrical Kirk** (Dug, 370958). Also the Meer, Moor, or Muir Kirk (Dug), from the fact that it was built on what was a moor. Former names for the big church in the centre of Ballater.

**The Cess Pool*** (F, 276947), ðɪˈsɛsˌpul. A pool in Dee near Crathie, named possibly after an old field drain that entered there.

**A' Chailleach** (OS, 2, F, 087828), ðɪˈχaljɐχ, now sometimes ðɪˈkɛiləç, (aˈhaljaç (A)), the old woman. An upright rock in upper Glen Ey.

**A' Chamag** (3, F, 259035), ðɪˈkamɐk, the crook. The Camag (D). An old route from Gairn to Cock Bridge over Camock Hill.

**Chamber Croft*** (I, 361947). A field at the foot of Glen Muick.

**A' Cham-bhruach*** (2, U, 000869), ðɪˈkamˌbruɐç with *u* sound almost gone, the bent brae. A hill on the road up Geldie.

**Chapel Brae** (C, 147914), ˈtʃapəlˈbreˑ. Chapel Hill (Mp). A hill in Braemar, named from the Catholic chapel that used to be there.

**Chapel Croft*** (I, 343906). A field in Glen Muick.

**Chapel Croft** See Creit an t-Seapail.

**Chapel Croft of Aucholzie** Chappelcroft, Chapel Croft of Auchulzie (Io 36, 53), Chapel Croft (Ri 29). Near Aucholzie in Glen Muick, probably c. 343906.

**Chapel Croft of Inverey** (north of 087892). Chapell Croft de Inuerre (Ca), Chapelcroft of Innerrey (G 2).

**Chapel Gate*** (F, east of 148915). Former name of the house now called Piedmont, near chapel at Braemar.

**The Chapel Glebe*** (F, 148917), ðɪˈtʃapəlˈglib. Farmland formerly used for the nearby chapel. Possibly the same as Creit an t-Seapail. At Braemar.

**Chapel House*** (Ce 3). Former habitation near Ardoch in Glen Gairn.

**The Chapel House** See Candacraig.

**(The) Chapel House** (OS, C, 437967), ðɪˈtʃapəlˈhus, a house south-west of Dinnet.

**Chapel Ma-Chalmaig*** (3, 287946). Chapel Mo-chalmag (Dms), St Colm's Chapel (A, C), sɪntˈkomzˈtʃapəl. Note Poll Ma-Chalmaig nearby. Above Abergeldie.

**Chapel Ma-Dheoir** (3, C, 301962), ˌtʃapəlmɐˈjọr, Chapel Mayore (A), i.e. St Mayore. At Micras east of Crathie.

**The Chapel of the Seven Maidens** (087894). The Chappell of the Seven Maidens (Vd, E). Named after St Donald's seven or nine daughters (Fo), see Nine Maidens' Well. At Inverey.

**Chapel Park** (S, probably 217943). A field at Balnoe in Aberarder, with old graves nearby.

**The Chapel Park** (S, F, 286946), ðɪˈtʃapəlˈpark. Chappel Park (Am). Beside a former chapel above Abergeldie.

**The Chapel Park*** (U, 240952), as above. A field west of Crathie.

**The Chapel Park*** (U, 301962), as above. A field containing the remains of a former church east of Crathie.

**The Chapel Parks*** (U, two fields at 339996 and 341995), ðɪ ˈtʃapəlˈparks. The field at 339996 also has the name Roinn a' Chaibeil. Beside a former chapel in Glen Gairn.

**Charlie Clais Bhacaidh's*** (U, 297968), ˌtʃarleˌklaʃˈvaˑχez. Site of a house beside Clais Bhacaidh east of Crathie, whose last inhabitant was called Charlie Clais Bhacaidh.

**Charlie Clais Bhacaidh's Road*** (U, 298966), ˈtʃarleˌklaʃˈvaˑχez 'rod. A track east of Crathie.

**Charlie Leys' Butts*** (U, 260030), ˈtʃarleˈlɛizˈbʌts. Also the Tom Leys Butts (U), ðɪˌtamˈlɛizˈbʌts, named after a nearby hill (see Tom Odhar). Grouse butts north-west of Gairnshiel, named after the man who built them.

**Charlie Milne's Cairn*** (F, 410930), ˈtʃarleˈmëlzˈkern̩. Refers to an accident where Charlie Milne, father of our informant Charlie Milne, was shot. In Glen Tanar.

**A' Charraig*** (3, U, 293967), ðɪˈkarɐk, the pinnacle. A stony point at the top of a hill east of Crathie. This name, the one below, and Tullochmacarrick are three interesting examples of Carraig, a name common in Ireland and south-west Scotland, but rare in the north-east.

**A' Charraig Dhuibh*** (3, U, 392985), ðɪˌkarɐkˈdui, at the black pinnacle. A prominent stony hillock east of Ballater.

**Charter's Chest** (OS, north-west of 178914), locally the Charter Chest (C), ðɪˈtʃartërˈtʃɛst. The Laird of Cluny's Charter Chest (Ke). A recess in the rock on Creag Clunie opposite Invercauld, where Farquharson hid his estate charters when he joined the 1715 Jacobite rebellion.

**(The) Chest of Dee** (OS, C, 013886), ðɪˈtʃɛstɐˈdi. Formerly Ciste Dhé (3, D, U), kiʃtˈjeˑ, chest of the Dee, recently the Kist (U), ðɪˈkëst, Scots = chest. Rocky pools in Glen Dee. Note Pol Dee (Mi xxxiv) from Poll Dé (3), pool of Dee, which was probably at Ciste Dhe to judge from the description.

**Chinatown*** (C, 244945), ˈtʃɛinəˌtʌun. Local name for Balnault Cottages (OS) west of Crathie.

**A' Chioch** (OS, 3, F, 098987), ðɪˈkiiç, (aˈhiɐç (A)), the pap. Keich (I, R 14). A big tor on Beinn a' Bhuird.

**A' Chioch Bheag** See Little Pap.

**A' Chioch Mhor** See Meikle Pap.

**A' Chlach Ghlas** See Greystone.

**A' Chlais*** (3, U, 280930), ðɪˈklaʃ, the hollow. South-west of Abergeldie.

**A' Chlais*** (3, U, 233941), as above, the hollow. A former house beside a hollow near the Inver.

**A' Chlais Fhionn*** (3, U, 095787), ðɪˌklaʃˈiˑn, the white hollow (see Allt na Claise Finne). A grassy hollow, looking pale against the darker, more heathery hillside. At the head of the Baddoch Burn.

**A' Chlais Mhór*** (3, F, 178982), ðɪˌklaʃˈmoˑr, the big hollow. On Culardoch.

**A' Choinneach*** (3, U, 308962), ðɪˈkɛinəç, the mossy place. A flat area at Micras.

**A' Choire Shreap*** (4, F, 237907), ðɪˌkọrˈrɛip, ˌkoreˈrɛip, the corrie you have to climb, possibly Shreup = of contentions. Corrie Ripe (Bs). West of Glen Gelder.

**A' Chraoibh Fhiodhag** (3, 147905), (? at) the tree of bird-cherries. Chrui yu-ak, the hagberry tree (D) possibly indicates Craobh in the dative case. Above Braemar.

**A' Chreag Bheag*** See Little Craig.

**A' Chreag Bheag*** (3, 158902), the little rocky hill. The Craigvegg (Io 25a), Craig Veck (I). South of Braemar.

**A' Chreag Mhór\*** (3, 330967), the big rocky hill. The Meikle Craig (I), Craeg Mhoir (R 14). East of Coilacriech.

**A' Chreit** (3, 144906), the croft. Chreitsh, a field (D). Above Braemar.

**A' Chruinn-mhoine** See Moine Chruinn.

**A' Chulath** See the Coolah.

**Cill Ma-Thatha** (3, 353970), church of St Tatha or Tua. Cill Mo-Thatha (W 298), Cill Măchă (D). The former name of Glengairn Church, or Church of Glen Garden (I). Also St Mungo's Chapel (M). The fair of Féill Ma-Thatha (Feill ma cha (D)) was held nearby, at Torr Darach.

**Cill Nachlan** (3, A 404, 390975), church of St Nathalan. Also St Nathalan's Chapel (M). Now the Tullich Kirk (C), ðɪˈtʌləç ˈkërk, formerly the Kirke of Tilliche (Vd). North-east of Ballater.

**The Cinder Path** (Rt, C, 372965), ðɪˈsɪndërˈpaθ. A path from the games park at Ballater to Monaltrie House, surfaced with cinders possibly from the nearby railway station. Formerly part of a kirk road from Easter Morven to Ballater.

**Cinn a' Gharaidh** (3, 438987), at end of the dyke. Kinnagarry, end of the dike (A 311). A former croft near Loch Kinord.

**Cinn an t-Socaidh\*** (3, U, 088780), kɪnˈtʌke, at end of the snout, from Socach, like Easaidh from Easach (W 1904, 182). A slope above the head of the Baddoch Burn.

**The Cinn an t-Socaidh Bothy\*** (U, 089781), ðɪˌkɪnˈtʌkeˈbɔθe. A ruin on the above slope.

**Cinn Drochaide** See Kindrochit.

**Cinn na Creige\*** (3, 246925), at end of the crag. Kinacraig (B). A former farm in Glen Gelder.

**Cioch Lodge** See Slugain Lodge.

**The Circular Path\*** (F, 365969), ðɪˈsërkjəlërˈpaθ. The Circular Track (Gl). Goes round Craigendarroch at Ballater.

**The Circular Track** See above name.

**Ciste Dhe** See Chest of Dee.

**Clach a' Bhodaich** (3, 201934), stone of the old man. Clach i voittich (Cr 34), Clacha-vottich (I), Clachavotich (Ra 6), Clachbhotich (R 14), Clachbottach (Vr 1). Clashbattock (M), klaʃˈvotəç (A) and Clash-vottach 'carle's howe' (D) refer to the same place. Thus, Clach a' Bhodaich changed in sound to Clais Bhodaich and possibly even Clashbattock. A former farm west of the Inver.

**Clach a' Chléirich** (OS, 3, C, 114992), klaχˈçliˈrɪç, stone of the clergyman. West of Ben Avon.

**Clach an Dubhagain\*** (5, U, 124896), ˌklaχənˈdʌgən, stone of the deep gulf. A stone in the birch wood east of Corriemulzie, below a cliff.

**Clach an Fhithich** (3, 424005), stone of the raven. Clashneach (O) might suggest Clais, but Ogston described it as a huge erratic block (i.e. a boulder). Near Loch Davan.

**Clachan Frìthe\*** (3, 314867), little stone of deer forest. Clachin frie (R 6). A stone marking a former estate boundary in upper Glen Muick.

**The Clachan of Bogingore**. The Clachan of Bogangore (Aj 8). A collective name for former houses at and near Bogingore near Dinnet.

**The Clachan of Loinahaun** (Af). Former houses at Loinahaun west of Gairnshiel.

**The Clachan o' the Micras** (Mil). A collective name for a former large group of scattered houses east of Crathie.

**Clach an Reachdan\*** (3, 140976), stone of the statute. Clachn Raichten (I). A stone near the source of Gairn.

**Na Clachan Reamhar\*** (3, F, 222927), ðɪˌklaχenˈruˈr̩, the thick stones. A group of stones in Dee, at pool below.

**The Clachan Reamhar Puil** (F, 222927), ðɪˌklaχenˈrur̩ˈpil. Clachanrar (A) mistakenly placed above the Invercauld Bridge. A pool in Dee, near the Inver.

**The Clachan Reamhar Road\*** (U, 221926), ðɪˌklaχenˈrur̩ˈrod. Near the above pool.

**Clach an Stalcair\*** (3, 301825), stone of the hunter. Clachin Stalker (R 6). On the plateau above Loch Muick.

**Clach an t-Sagairt\*** (3, U, 180844), ˌklaχənˈtagërt, stone of the priest. Beside the Priest's Well at Loch Callater.

**Clach an t-Seallaidh** (2, U, 034004), ˌklaχenˈdʒɔl or ˌklaχenˈdjɔl, stone of the view. Clachandeouley (Roy). Clach an Duile (Sg), stone of the view, was probably an incorrect inference from the local pronunciation and meaning. A stone at the top of the Lairig an Laoigh, with a fine view down to Glen Avon and Glen Derry. Allt an t-Seallaidh runs to the north.

**Clachanturn** (OS, C, 277947), ˌklaχenˈtʌrn, from Clach an t-Sùirn (4), stone of the kiln. Clach-an-durn (D). A farm west of Abergeldie.

**The Clachanturn Puil** (F), ðɪˌklaχenˈtʌrnˈpil. Clachanturn (P). A collective name for pools in Dee from Fence End to Cess Pool.

**Clachan Yell** (OS, 3, C, 446911), ˌklɔχɐnˈjẹl, from Clachan Geala (3), white stones. A stony hill in Glen Tanar.

**The Clachan Yell Burn** See Burn of Clachanyell.

**An Clacharan** (3, 099880), the pavement. N glacharan (D). A place with screes, south-west of Corriemulzie.

**Clach Choutsaich** (OS, C, 143019), klaχˈkutsɪç, from Clach a' Chuitseich (McC in Cj), Coutts' stone. Clach Chutsich (R 14). Also formerly Invercauld's Stables from deer ponies being taken there (McC 1896). A big tor on Ben Avon.

**Clach Chrò\*** (3, I, 157928), stone of sheep-cots. Opposite Braemar Castle.

**Clach Cùrra\*** (4, 388974), stone of end. Clach cur (R 4, Io 58). On farmland at Tullich, no big stone now, presumably removed for field clearance.

**Clachdhu** (OS, 160001), from Clach Dhubh, black stone. A rocky top on Ben Avon.

**Clach Dhubh\*** (3, 206983), black stone. Clach dhuth (R 3). A prominent stone north-west of Crathie.

**Clach Dhubh Bad na Beinne\*** (3, 232038), black stone of clump of the hill. Clach du Badnapien (R 12). North of Corndavon Lodge.

**Clach Fhaobharaidh** (3, 456982), klaçˈʌuri (A), ? Clach fhaobhair, a sharpening stone (A). A former ford on Dee, west of Dinnet.

**Clach Gheinne** (3, 148924), stone of the wedge. Clach yenn 'wedge' (D). Where Clunie meets Dee.

**Clach Mhadaidh** (3, CMcI, 197813), klaχˈmadi, stone of the fox or wolf. Clach mhaduibh (Mg 146). A big boulder below the cliffs up from Loch Callater.

**Clach Mholach\*** (3, 231040), rough stone. Clach-mholach (R 3). North of Corndavon Lodge.

**Clach Mhór Bad a' Chabair** (OS, 3, 294889), big stone of clump of the pole. Also the Muckle Stane o Bad a' Chabair, ðɪˈmʌkəlˈstinɐˌbadˈhabër (F), see A 159, now usually the Bad a' Chabair Stane (C), sometimes the Muckle Stane (F). A big stone at the side of the road from Inchnabobart to Balmoral.

**Clach Mhór Ruighe na Sròine\*** (3, north-east of 243997), big stone of cattle-run of the nose. Clach-mhore Rie' na Stroine, Clachvoirinistroan—Mickle Ston of the Roof of the Nose (R 3, 5). South of Daldownie on the upper Gairn.

**Clach nam Bó\*** (3, 244966), stone of the cows. Clach na'm Bo (R 3). North-west of Crathie.

**Clach nan Sealladh** (3, probably south-east of 318012), stone of the views. Clachnaschoul (Dil). Near Ardoch in Glen Gairn.

**Clach nan Taillear** (OS, 2, C, 983965), ˌklaχnənˈdaːljër, stone of the tailors. Clach-nan-talairean (Gle) indicates a variant genitive plural Taillearan. Also the Tailors' Stane (F), ðɪ

Ruins of the former farm of Dail nam Fiadh in Glen Ey, where people were evicted in a clearance in the mid 1800s. The remains of the birch wood of Coille Phiobair are in the background.

The ruined Street at Loinahaun, a row of houses by River Gairn (left centre), with Geallaig Hill beyond.

'telẽrz'stin. The Tailors' Stone (A). The legend is that, in the late 18th century, three tailors once wagered they would dance a reel at Rothiemurchus and another in Mar on the same day, but perished here in the snow on the way to Mar. A group of stones·in the Lairig Ghru.

**Clach Sgonnach*** (3, south-west of 154877), lumpish stone. Clach Sconnach (Io 43a). A stone in lower Glen Clunie.

**Clach Thogalach** (2, A, U, north-east of 032934), klaχ'hɔglɐχ, stone of the lifting. Used for trials of strength. The old legend is that a Braemar man outdid the Rothiemurchus men there after the planning meeting for the 1715 Jacobite rising (Gr 120). In Glen Luibeg.

**Cladach** (3, 389973), stony place. Claddach or Claddich (D). A field at Tullich east of Ballater.

**Cladh Bhotaichidh*** (4, U, south of 218946), klat'vɔtɐχe, mound of little old man. In Glen Feardar.

**Clagganghoul** (OS, C, 212915), ˌklagən'gu·l, from Claigionn nan Gual or Claigionn Ghual (3), ˌklʊgən'ɣuɐl (Sch), rounded hillock of the coals or of coals (i.e. hard black peats, note W 1904, 95). Claggan na Gual (R 7), Clyganaghuail (Io 75), Claggan-na-ghoul (Vr 4), Cluggan-a-gual (D). A house west of the Inver.

**The Clagganghoul Puil*** (F, 212914), ðɪˌklagən'gul'pil. In Dee, near above house. Also the Maclaren Puil (F), ðɪˌmək'lerɐn 'pil, often Maclaren's (F). McLarens (Wav).

**The Clagganghoul Quarry** (Gf, 211915). A former quarry which provided stone for the Invercauld Bridge.

**An Claigionn*** (3, 187913), the rounded hillock. The Claggan (R 7). Near Invercauld Bridge.

**Claigionn Dubh** See Na Claignean.

**Claigionn Gainmheach*** (3, 392978), sandy hillock. Clagingannich (R 4). A gravelly hillock at Tullich north-east of Ballater.

**An Claigionn Mór** (3, U, 367920), ðɪˌklagən'mo·r, the big rounded hillock. Clavinmore (Ab 22). A broad hillock in lower Glen Muick.

**Claigionn Mullaich** (3, A, U, 279946), ˌklagən'mulɐç, rounded hillock of eminence. Claggenmuloch (Am). A hillock near Abergeldie.

**Claigionn na Caithriseachd*** (4, 225952), hillock of the watching. Clugan na Carasich (I). North of the Inver.

**The Claigionn Road*** (C, 282946), ðɪ'klagən'rod. Runs below Claigionn Mullaich from Clachanturn to Balnacroft, near Abergeldie.

**The Claigionns Wuid*** (U, 289949), ðɪ'klagənz'wɪd. Clagans Wood (Am). A little wood at Abergeldie, beside hillocks called the Claigionns (see Na Claignean).

**The Claigionns Wuid*** (F, 441998), as above. A birch wood at Loch Kinord, beside an area called the Claigionns (see Na Claignean).

**Na Claignean*** (3, 343972), the in-fields. Claggan (Ip), Claggans (Opr 44). Formerly Claigionn Dubh (3), dark in-field. Clagandu (Io 9), Claggandow (Im 3), also given an anglicised plural Claggandous (Io 58), over and nether Claigendows (A 397). Probably Nether Claigendows was the same field as Easter Claignean, and Over Claigendows the same field as Wester Claignean. A former farm west of Bridge of Gairn.

**Na Claignean** (3, 343972), classic Gaelic for the anglicised plural the Claigionns (A, U), ðɪ'klagənz, the in-fields. Na clughan (D). A collective name for Easter and Wester Claignean, fields west of Bridge of Gairn.

**Na Claignean** (3, 439998), classic Gaelic for the Claigionns (A, F), as above, the rounded hillocks. Beside Loch Kinord.

**Na Claignean*** (3, 289948), classic Gaelic for the Claigionns (U), as above, the rounded hillocks. At Abergeldie.

**Clais an Fhraoich** (3, C, 314010), ˌklaʃən'riiç, hollow of the heather, or Auld Clais an Fhraoich (U), 'a·lˌklaʃən'riiç. Clashinruich (Io), Clashin Ruich (I), Clashendrich (Bl). Clashinruich (OS) is a recent house at 313014. A former farm east of Gairnshiel.

**Clais an t-Sabhail** (5, A 212, U, 401901), ˌklaʃən'tul, (klaʃən 'tʌul (A)), hollow of the barn, but possibly Clais an Tuill = hollow of the hole, as a map about 1800 gives Burn of Clashintuill (R 6). In upper Glen Tanar.

**Clais an t-Sabhail** (3, Sg, F, 952963), ˌklaʃɐn'dʌul, hollow of the barn. On Cairn Toul.

**Clais an t-Seilich*** (2, U, 063840), ˌklaʃɐn'dʒiliç, hollow of the willow. West of Glen Ey.

**Clais Bad a' Mhonaidh*** (3, U, 297041), ˌklaʃˌpɪt'vuni, hollow of clump of the hill. Clashpatavunie (I). North of Gairnshiel.

**Clais Badan Eagarach*** (3, 310990), hollow of little clump of trees in rows. Clash Badneckrach (I). South of Gairnshiel.

**Clais Bain*** (3, 389973), hollow of fallow or vacant ground. Clashbain (Io 58), Clash bain (R 4). On farmland north-east of Ballater.

**Clais Balgaire*** (3, U, 317983), klaʃ'balɐgẽr, hollow of fox. North of Coilacriech.

**Clais Beithe*** (3, U, 312907), klaʃ'be·z, hollow of birch. Claishinbea (G 5) suggests Claisean = hollows and the z sound in the pronunciation indicates an anglicised plural. In Glen Girnock.

**Clais Bhacaidh*** (4, U, 298967), klaʃ'va·χe, hollow at crooked place. Bhacaidh is an old locative of Bhacach (W 1904, 90). A crooked hollow east of Crathie. Another possible meaning is hollow of the obstruction, as the hollow is steep-sided and rough.

**Clais Bhalgaire*** (3, F, west of 190875), klaʃ'valɐgẽr, hollow of the fox, or (Bhalgair) of foxes. In Ballochbuie Forest.

**The Clais Bhalgaire Burn** See Allt Leac Dubh.

**Clais Bheag nan Oighreag** (3, north of 144899), little hollow of the cloudberries. Clais mhor nan erak, hollow of averins; clais bheag of same (D). On Morrone.

**Clais Bhinn*** (5, 305990), hollow of hills. Clash-vien (I). On Geallaig Hill south of Gairnshiel.

**Clais Bhrodainn** See Clais Rathadan.

**The Clais Bhrodainn Burn*** (F, 279857), ðɪˌklaʃ'vrɔtɐn'bʌrn. Runs into Allt na Giubhsaich in upper Glen Muick.

**Clais Bhrodainn's Cairn*** (F, 272861), ˌklaʃ'vrɔtɐnz'kern. Clais Clashrathan's Cairn (McC 1891). An interesting anglicisation. A cairn where the path from the Glas Allt meets the path from Allt-na-giubhsaich to Lochnagar.

**Clais Bhùtha** (5, 248980), klaʃ'vu: (U), hollow of the cot. Bhó = cows is a possibility (see Na Coireach Bho). Tombady and Clashvoue, two knaps (D), but the two knaps are the Upper and Lower Tom Bhadaidh, with Clais Bhutha between them. A hollow north of Crathie, with an old shieling or cot in it.

**Clais Bràidean*** (3, U, 287854), klaʃ'pratɐn, hollow in mountains, or possibly referring to horse-collars or pack-saddles (note A 395 and see Lairig Bhraighdean). From Allt-na-giubhsaich on to Lochnagar, and would be a good way for a horse.

**The Clais Braidean Burn*** (U, 280848), ðɪˌklaʃ'pratɐn'bʌrn. In the above hollow.

**Clais Branndair*** (3, 302051), hollow of place of tangled roots (see note under Am Branndair). Clash Braunter (I). At the top of the road between Gairnshiel and Don.

**Clais Capaill*** (4), hollow of a mare. Written as Clashcathbuil and interpreted as 'hollow where battle was struck'! (Io 81). Near Invercauld House, to the north.

**Clais Chàil** (2, D, U, 086835), klaʃ'ha:l, hollow of the kail (D). In Glen Ey.

**Clais Chàil** (4, 284045), hollow of the kail. Clais chall (D). North-west of Gairnshiel.

**Clais Challtuinn\*** (3, U, 262994), klaʃˈχaltən, hollow of hazels. West of Gairnshiel.

**Clais Chaol** (3, D, 144903), narrow hollow. On Morrone.

**Clais Chaol** (3, D, 075826), narrow hollow. In upper Glen Ey.

**Clais Choltair** (3, D, 097825), hollow of the ploughshare. In upper Glen Ey.

**Clais Cleithe** (5, F, 278888), klaʃˈkleˑz, hollow of lurking. Clash Cleith (Bs), Clais Cley, klashˈkleɪ (A). Usually now called Clais Cleiths, suggesting an anglicised plural. In upper Girnock.

**The Clais Cleithe Burn\*** (U, 280888), ðɪˌklaʃˈklezˈbʌrn.

**Clais Còinnich\*** (3, south of 356955), hollow of moss. Clashconick (G 35). A hollow west of Ballater.

**Clais Còinnich** (3, south of 355955), hollow of moss. Clashkonack (Ri 28), Clashconnach (Rli 23), Clais conich (Ap). A former farm west of Ballater.

**Clais Doimhne** (3, U, 063872), klaʃˈɖɛin, hollow of depth. Clash Dine (A 235). A hollow running far up a steep hillside south-west of Inverey.

**Na Claisean** (3, 355935). The Clashes, previously Na Claisean, the furrows (Mg). A rocky hollow in Glen Muick.

**Claisean Beithe\*** (3, 246968), little hollow of birch. Clashinbae, Clashenbae (R 5, 9). North-west of Crathie.

**Claisean Beithe\*** (3, 359015), little hollow of birch. Clashinbea twice (Io 20), Claishinbea, Clasbea (G 5, 19). South-west of Morven.

**Claisean Dorch\*** (3, U, 328928), ˌklaʃənˈdɔrəç, dark little hollow. Above Glen Girnock.

**Claisean Mhadaidh** (3, 283017), little hollow of the wolf or dog. Clashn Vattie (I), Clais a mhaduidh (Mg). North of Gairnshiel.

**An Claisean Mór** (2, C, 058907), ðɪˌklaʃɐnˈmoːr, the big hollowlet. Glashan Mor (Anonym). In Glen Lui.

**The Claisean Mor Burn\*** (U, 060908), ðɪˌklaʃɐnˈmoˑrˈbʌrn. In Glen Lui.

**Claisean Slugain\*** (3, 290031), little hollow of gullet. Clash-na-Sluggan (R 12), Clashn Sluggan (I). North of Gairnshiel.

**The Clais-ean-Toul Burn** See Burn of Clais-ean-Toul.

**Clais Féithe** (3, south of 261023), hollow of bog-stream. Clais feith (D). At the Sleach north-west of Gairnshiel.

**Clais Fhearnaig** (OS, 3, C, 070933), klaʃˈjaˑrnək, hollow of the alder place. Clashyairnack, Clashʒernak (Me 2, 3), Clash Yarnoch (Im 3), Clash yarrnaig (D). Note Fearnaig = a place of alders (W 1904, 184). Also the Little Glen (Si). A hollow with some boggy patches, between Lui and Quoich.

**The Clais Fhearnaig Dam\*** (U, 073936), ðɪˌklaʃˈjaˑrnəkˈdam. A dam to make a loch in the above hollow.

**The Clais Fhearnaig Green\*** (U, 077937), ðɪˌklaʃˈjaˑrnəkˈgrin. A grassy slope in Glen Quoich.

**The Clais Fhearnaig Loch\*** (C, 070934), ðɪˌklaʃˈjaˑrnəkˈlɔχ. An artificial loch in the above hollow.

**The Clais Fhearnaig Plantin\*** (F, 080930), ðɪˌklaʃˈjaˑrnək ˈplantɪn. A plantation in Glen Quoich.

**Clais Ghiubhas** (3, C, 274894), klaʃˈjuːz, hollow of firs. A hollow which still has a few old firs. In upper Girnock.

**The Clais Ghiubhas Burn\*** (U, 278895), ðɪˌklaʃˈjuˑzˈbʌrn. In upper Girnock.

**Clais Lighe\*** (4, U, 348945), klaʃˈliˑ, hollow of flood, possibly Liath = grey. In lower Glen Muick.

**The Clais Lighe Burn\*** (U, 349945), ðɪˌklaʃˈliˈbʌrn. See above.

**Clais Meadhonach\*** (3, 231948), middle hollow. Clash Mainach (I). The middle hollow in a series of three hollows north of the Inver.

**Clais Mhadaidh** (3, A, U, 988932), klaʃˈvate, hollow of the wolf or dog. Clashmaddie (Roy), Clais a' Mhadaidh (Sg). In Glen Dee.

**Clais Mhadaidh\*** (3, U, 059927), as above, hollow of the wolf or dog. In Glen Lui.

**Clais Mhèirleach\*** (3, 218964), local form Mheàrlach, hollow of thieves. Clash Myarlach (I). North-west of the Inver.

**(A') C(h)lais Mhór** (OS, 3, C, 172898), ðɪˌklaʃˈmoˑr, (in Gaelic klaʃˈvor (A)), the big hollow. Clash Mor (R 7). South-east of Braemar.

**The Clais Mhor Burn\*** See Allt na Claise Moire.

**Clais Mhór nan Oighreag** (3, east of 143897, extends northwards), big hollow of the cloudberries. Clais mhor nan erak, hollow of averins (D). On Morrone.

**Clais Muice\*** (4, 327956), hollow of pig. Clachmuick (Roy). See name below. West of Ballater.

**Clais Muice** (4, south-west of 329957), hollow of pig. Clash Muck (A). Former habitation west of Ballater.

**Clais Muice\*** (4, U, 337886), klaʃˈmëk, hollow of pig. Clashmuick (I). A hollow in Glen Muick.

**Clais Muice** (4, U, 338888), as above. Clashmuick (I, Ro, Ram 3). A former farm in Glen Muick.

**Clais na Firich\*** (3, C, 066941), ˌklaʃnɐˈfirɪç, hollow of the moor. East of Derry Lodge.

**Clais nam Balgair** (3, A, U, 057983), ˌklaʃnɐmˈbalɐgër, hollow of the foxes. North-east of Derry Lodge.

**Clais nam Mèirleach** (2, F, 009937), locally Meàrlach, ˌklaʃnɐ ˈmjaˑrlɐχ, hollow of the thieves. Clais nam Meirleach (Sg). In Glen Luibeg.

**Clais nam Mèirleach\*** (3, U, 137783), as above, hollow of the thieves. Near the Cairnwell.

**Clais na Mnatha\*** (3, 233947), hollow of the woman. Clachd-na-mnath (R 3), Clash na Vra (I). North of the Inver.

**Clais na Nathrach** (3, 086876), hollow of the adder. Clais na narrach, serpents (D). In Glen Ey.

**Clais nan Cat** (OS, 3, 139935), hollow of the cats. Clashna gaat (I), Clash na gaat (R 14). Clais a' Chait, klaʃˈhatʃ (A), but the earlier references agree with the OS form. North of Braemar.

**Clais nan Cat** (OS, 3, U, 255049), ˌklaʃnəˈgat, hollow of the cats. Clash-na-ghaat (I), Clash na Gaat (R 12), Clais na gat, cats' clash (D). A hollow north-west of Gairnshiel.

**Clais nan Gamhainn\*** (3, U, 112868), ˌklaʃnɐˈgʌu.ən, hollow of the stirks. Near Corriemulzie.

**Clais Òtraich\*** (3, 231950), hollow of dirt. Clash Utrach (I). North of the Inver.

**The Clais Park\*** (U, 232941), ðɪˈklaʃˈpark. A field near the Inver, beside A' Chlais.

**Clais Poll Bhàthaidh** (4, F, 057958), ˌklaʃˌpɔlˈvaː, hollow of pool of the drowning. In the Dubh-Ghleann.

**Clais Rathadan** (OS, 3, 277856), locally usually Clais Bhrodainn (3, F), klaʃˈvrɔtɐn, hollow of the mastiff, but ˈrɔtɐn also heard (U). 'The sound suggests Clais Radan, rat gully' (A), klaʃˈrɔtən, klaʃˈratən (A) but 19th century references—Clash Brodan (In, Am) and Clash Vrodan (B) agree with the usual present local form. On the way up to Lochnagar from Glen Muick.

**Clais Sgòr na h-Iolaire\*** (3, 122954), hollow of rock of the eagle. Clash Scur na Heulre (I). In Gleann an t-Slugain.

**Clais Thomais** or **Lag Thomais** (3, south-west of 302965), Thomas's furrow or hollow. Clash Homish or Lack Homish (D 199), a former house east of Crathie.

**Clàrach\*** (3, Io 34), flat place. A former farm on Invercauld, probably near the present Clarag Pool and Clerach Cottages west of Balmoral.

**(The) Clarack** (OS, C, 451987), ðɪˈklarɐk, from Clàrach (3), flat place or Clàrag (3), little flat place. Clarach in 1686 (M), Clarag (R 1, Opr 8). A farm near Dinnet.

**The Clarack Loch\*** (C, 454989), ðɪˈklarɐkˈlɒχ. A loch at Dinnet.

**The Clarack Wuid\*** (F, 452985), ðɪˈklarɐkˈwɪd. Wood of Claritt (Roy). Wood on both sides of main road at Clarack near Dinnet. Roy showed it on Ord Hill, but locally this is now the Ord Wuid.

**Clarag** See Gordon's Clarag.

**The Clarag Puil** (F, south of 185912), ðɪˈklarɐkˈpil. Clàrag (3) = little flat place. Clarick (A). A pool in Dee, at the lower end of the Invercauld flat lands.

**The Clarag Puil** (F, 245944), as above. Clàrag (3) = little flat place. Clerach (A). A pool on Dee, at a flat stretch of land west of Balmoral.

**Clashie's\*** (U, 312012), ˈklaʃez. A former field east of Gairnshiel, named after the nearby Clais an Fhraoich.

**Clashinruich** (OS, 313014), from Clais an Fhraoich (3), ˌklaʃənˈruːɪç (F), ˌklaʃənˈriəç (C), hollow of the heather. Clash-an-raoch 'heather' (D). A house in Glen Gairn, named after a former farm nearby; comments by A and D may refer to the farm.

**The Clashinruich Burn\*** (U, 312012), ðɪˌklaʃənˈriəçˈbʌrn. East of Gairnshiel.

**Claybokie** (OS, C, 086900), kləˈboːki, from Cladh Bhòcaidh (3), mound of the spectre. Clobokaick (Fa), Clabockaig (Roy), Clabockaig, Clabockaid, Clabochcaig (Cr 36, 36, 39), Clabocaidh (Gr). In Gaelic Clă-bóchkie (M), Cla-bhochki (D in A). A house west of Mar Lodge.

**The Claybokie Park\*** (Ra 11, U, 087898), ðɪˌkləˈboˑkiˈpark. A field at Claybokie.

**The Claybokie Sand Hole\*** (U, 082900), ðɪˌkləˈboˑkiˈsanˈhol. A sand quarry west of Mar Lodge.

**The Clay Hole\*** (U, south-west of 367948), ðɪˈkleˈhol. A former quarry in lower Glen Muick.

**The Clay Hole Park\*** (U, 367947), ðɪˈkleˈholˈpark. A field south of Ballater.

**Clayholes\*** (Io 75 in 1832). In a list of former habitations in Glen Girnock, along with Bovaglie, Camlet and Loinveg.

**The Clay Park\*** (F, 282941), ðɪˈkleˈpark. A field south-west of Abergeldie.

**Cleikumin** (A, C, 438012), ˌklikəmˈɛn. Cleekimin (Ce 3). The same name occurs at a former farm near Lumphanan, Cleikhimin Pot (a pool on Don (A)), a broch at Clickhimin (pronounced ˌklɪkəmˈɛn) near Lerwick in Shetland, and a house at Cleikiminn north of Stanley near Perth and also in East Lothian, see Cleikum (Gm), note similar names Clinkumin and Clinkum's. These locations suggest that it is of lowland origin. Several people said it was locally thought to mean the place where you took in the horse's traces up the little brae on the road to the east (i.e. Scots Cleek them in = snatch them in), but this was offered so hesitantly that it may be a popular invention to explain a rather odd name. An area beside Loch Davan.

**Cleikumin** (U, east of 438012), as above. The Cleikum Inn (O). See name above. A former house near Loch Davan.

**The Cleikumin Brig\*** See the Glendavan Brig.

**The Cleikum Muir** (O, U, 437012), ðɪˈklikəmˈmir̩. The Cleikum moor (A). A former moor, now under trees, beside Loch Davan.

**The Cleikum Muir Bridge** See the Glendavan Brig.

**Clerach Cottages** (OS, 244942), locally the Clarag Cottages (C), ðɪˈklarɐkˈkɒtədʒɪz, same name as the nearby pool west of Balmoral.

**Clinkamin of Tullochcoy\*** (Opr 17). See Cleikumin, which looks a similar name. A former habitation near the Inver.

**Clinkum's** (Mi, north-east of 289955 on south side of road), Scots Clinkum = bellman. See Cleikumin and Clinkamin of Tullochcoy. A former inn east of Crathie, beside a ford and former Boat across Dee.

**An Cluainidh\*** (3, 184914), at the meadow. A dative form from Cluain = a meadow (Mb), probably was masculine at Braemar (see Creag Clunie). The Clunie (Im 4). A former field near Invercauld.

**Clunie** See Clunie Cottage.

**Clunie Bank** (Er, C, 149907), ˌkluniˈbaŋk. A steep hillside above Clunie Water, south of Braemar.

**The Clunie Brig** (C, 151914), ðɪˈkluniˈbrɪg. The Bridge of Cluny (Cromb). Bridge over Clunie, at Braemar.

**Clunie Cottage** (OS, C, 182913), ˈkluniˈkɒtədʒ, named after An Cluainidh (3), at the plain. Clonye (Ca), the Clunie (Im 4), Clunie (R 14), Clinny (Opr 41a), a former farm at Invercauld, on a big flat grassy area. Note this is a different Clunie or plain from the one in Glen Clunie. Cluny-on-the-Dee (Tayle). Also Clunie Lodge (Sch), ˈkluniˈlœdʒ. Near Invercauld Bridge.

**Clunie Lodge\*** See Clunie Cottage.

**The Clunie Park\*** (U, 184912), ðɪˈkluniˈpark. The Parks of Clunie (Rli 19). A grassy area, formerly a field, near Clunie Cottage.

**Clunieside\*** (C, 150910), ˌkluniˈsɛid. A name to describe any place along either side of Clunie Water south of Braemar, usually as far up as the Golf Course, though sometimes as far as Auchallater.

**(The) Clunie Stane** (OS, C, 183912). ðɪˈkluniˈstin, formerly the Muckle Stane o the Clunie (U), ðɪˈmʌkəlˈstinɪðɪˈkluni. The Muckle Stane o' the Clunie (Brow). Also Erskine's Stane (Bro, U), ˈɛrskənzˈstin. A big boulder by the roadside beside Invercauld Bridge.

**Clunie Water** (OS, 151905), now the Clunie (C), ðɪˈkluni, formerly Water of Cluny (Io 75). For meaning see Clunie Cottage. In Gaelic Uisge Chluainidh (3), uʃkˈçluɐni (JB), uisg chluani (D), Cluanaidh (Cluan-i) the meadow land through which the river flows, afterwards used for the name of the river (Mp). The form ˈɡluɐni (Sch) suggests eclipsis from An Cluainidh. Cluanaidh (Sto), Cliny (Fi). The river at Braemar. This Clunie and the Invercauld one refer to two different plains. The lower part at Braemar was also called Ailbhean many centuries ago.

**An Cnagan Cruinn\*** (3, U, west of 148906), ðɪˌkrakɐnˈkrun, the round little knob. A stony hillock near Braemar.

**The Cnapach\*** (3, F, 409037), ðɪˈknapɐχ, the knobby place, note feminine A' Chnapaich = the knobby land in Badenoch Gaelic (Mb). A field in Cromar, with a ruin at its top end.

**The Cnapach\*** (3, C, 408038), as above. A former house at the top of the above field.

**Cnapach\*** (3), knobby place. Knappack (Io 33). A former farm near the Inver.

**Cnap a' Chléirich** (OS, 2, C, 108003), knapˈçliˑrɪç, knob of the clergyman. Capuchlerich (I, R 14). A top above the upper Quoich. The whole hill is Meall Tionail.

**Cnap a' Choire Bhuidhe** (OS, 3, C, 229900, should be at 230902, 229900 is Meall Coire Buidhe), ˌknapɐˌkɒrˈbui, knob of the yellow corrie. Probably should be Scots form Knap o Coire Buidhe, as OSn got Nap.a.Coir.Buidh. Note also Little Cnap a' Choire Bhuidhe. A knob west of Glen Gelder.

**Cnapan an Laoigh** (OS, 995840), should be Cnapan nan Laogh (3, C), ˌkrapɐnɐˈluː, little knob of the calves. Cnapan na laogh, nan laogh (D in A). North of Glen Tilt.

**The Cnapan an Laoigh Burn** See Allt Cnapan an Laoigh.

**The Cnapan an Laoigh Hillocks\*** (U, 999839), ðɪˌkrapɐnɐˈluˑˈhɛlɛks. South of Bynack Lodge.

**(An) Cnapan Beag** (OS, 3, 932889), the little knoblet. An Cnapan Beag (D in A 217). Forms a pair with (An) Cnapan Mor. In Glen Geldie.

**Cnapan Coire Dubh\*** (3, 203863), little knob of black corrie. Knapan Corry Du, Knapan Cor-Dhu (R 7, 14). Above Ballochbuie Forest.

**Cnapan Damhaidh** See Duke's Chair.

**An Cnapan Dubh\*** (3, U, 174817), ðɪˌkrapɐnˈduˑ, the little black knob. Crappan Du (I), Crappan Dhu (R 14). South of Loch Callater.

**Cnapan Dubh Coire an Leachd\*** (3, 137949), little black knob of corrie of the declivity. Crapan-du-Corn-n-lachk (I), Crapan Dhu Cor'n-leicht (R 14). In Gleann an t-Slugain.

**Cnapan Fhéith Bheag Bhàn** (2, A, U, 961851), ˌknapɐnˈeˌvɐg ˈvaˑn, little knob of the little white bog-stream, ˌknapnɐˈfe ˌvegˈvaˑn (U) is also heard, suggesting classic form Cnap na Féithe Bige Bàine, meaning as above. Forms a pair with the name below. In Glen Geldie.

**Cnapan Fhéith Mhór Bhàn** (2, A, U, 953848), ˌknapɐnˈeˌvor ˈvaˑn, little knob of the big white bog-stream. See above name.

**(An) Cnapan Garbh** (OS, 2, C, 980864), ðɪˌkrapɐnˈgaro, (grapan ˈgaru (A)), the rough little knob. In Glen Geldie.

**Cnapan Loch Tilt** (OS, C, 996828), from Cnapan Loch Teilt (6), ˌkrapɐnˌlɔχˈtëlt, little knob of Loch Tilt (meaning of Teilt is unknown).

**(An) Cnapan Mór** (OS, 2, C, 939908), ðɪˌkrapɐnˈmoːr, the big knoblet. An cnapan, grapan, mor (D in A 217). In Glen Geldie.

**Cnapan na Buachailleachd** (3, A, U, 966867), ˌkrapɐnɐˈbuaçɐlɐχ, little knob of the herding. In Glen Geldie.

**Cnapan nan Clach** (OS, 3, C, 982846), ˌkrapɐnɐˈglaχ, little knob of the stones. Up Bynack Burn.

**Cnapan Nathraichean** (OS, 223889), ˌknapɐnˈɛrəçën (C), OS form means little knob of adders. Alexander noted the Gaelic pronunciation as Crahpan Naarihen, and the Scottish pronunciation as Cnapan Naerihen. However, his Gaelic pronunciation does not agree with early records, which are nearer the current pronunciation:—Knapan eracher and Little Knapan eracher (R 7), Knapan Eracher (R 14), Carpanercher (Ra 15), Knapaneracher (B), Knapan-eracher (R 16). The evidence suggests that the OS name is incorrect and should be Cnapan Fhearchair (3), Farquhar's little knob. Note that the area was part of the Farquharson lands before Queen Victoria bought it. Moreover, adders in Deeside have seldom been noted above 450 m and the highest record is from 690 m (Nw), whereas Cnapan Nathraichean is 824 m. Five old maps show this name as a little knob at 229885, and moreover the hill at 223889 is so big that it would be unlikely to be called a Cnapan. Pairs with Little Cnapan Nathraichean. A hill north-west of Lochnagar.

**Cnapan Or** (OS, 996885), from Cnapan Òir (2, F), ˌkrapɐnˈɔːr, (grapan ˈor (A)), little knob of gold. There is an old legend of gold buried here (Sg, see Craobh an Oir). At the top of Cairn Geldie.

**Cnap Coire an t-Slugain** (3, U, 271904), ˌknapˌkɔrnˈlugən, knob of corrie of the gullet. Noted vaguely by Alexander (219). Also the Cnap o the Coire an t-Slugain (F), ðɪˈknapɪðɪˌkɔrn ˈlugən. In Glen Girnock.

**Cnap Coire na h-Oisinn\*** (U, 273912), ˌknapˌkɔrnɐˈhoʃən, knob of corrie of the nook. Above Glen Girnock.

**Cnap Lochan nan Corra\*** (3, 172892), knob of tarn of the herons. Knap Lochan na Gurr (I). On a hilltop south-east of Braemar.

**Cnap na Clais Giubhais** (OS, 274898), knob of the fir hollow. Note Clais Ghiubhas nearby. In upper Girnock.

**Cnap na Cùile** (OS, 4, U, 307921, should be at 306924), ˌknapnɐ ˈkul, knob of the corner. Cnap Cuail (Mg 238) would suggest Cuail = of a faggot. In Glen Girnock.

**The Cnap o the Coire an t-Slugain** See Cnap Coire an t-Slugain.

**Cnap of Back Coire Buidhe\*** (3, 275871), from Gaelic Cnap (3) = knob, or borrowing into Scots. Knap of Back Corbuie (B). In Glen Gelder.

**The Cnaps\*** (393940), from Gaelic Na Cnapan (3) = the knobs, or borrowing into Scots. The Knaps (I). Rocky knobs south-east of Ballater.

**(The) Cnaps of (the) Blue Corrie** (OS, U, 319811), ðɪˈknapsɪðɪ ˈbluˌkọre, probably borrowing into Scots as above. Hillocks south-east of Loch Muick.

**Cnoc\*** (3, 223941), knoll, or borrowing into Scots. Knock (I), Knock of Aberarder (Opr 29, 41c). A former farm beside a hillock, near the Inver.

**Cnoc\*** (3, R 14, 265996), knoll. A hillock north of Crathie.

**Cnoc** See Cnoc Mharcaich.

**An Cnoc\*** (3, 262022), the knoll. The Knock (I). A hillock at the Sleach north-west of Gairnshiel.

**Cnoc a' Bhranndair\*** See Peter's Hill.

**Cnoc a' Chuitseich\*** (3, 154887), knoll of Coutts. Knockcouts, Knockachoutich (Opr 43, 49), Knock Coutsich (I), Croch chuotsich (Ce 1). A former farm south of Braemar.

**Cnoc Àgaidh** (3, D in Rc 39, 168), knoll of ox. Agaidh is generally an obsolete form but at Braemar 'a work stot is akich, a two-year old bullock is aku' (D in A). In Braemar parish (D).

**Cnoc a' Mhadaidh\*** (3, 265972), hill of the dog or wolf. Cnochd 'a mhadie, Cnoc Maidhe (R 3, 14). North of Crathie.

**Cnocan\*** (3, 281011), little knoll. Knockan (I). A hillocky field west of Gairnshiel.

**An Cnocanaidh Cruinn\*** (3, U, south of 297967), ðɪˌknọkɐne ˈkrun, the round little hillocklet. Possibly a double diminutive (little hillocklet), but possibly a svarabhakti vowel, i.e. an extra vowel sound inserted between Cnocan and Cruinn to make pronunciation easier. East of Crathie.

**Cnocan Aitinn\*** (3, U, 276006), ˌknọkɐnˈitən, little knoll of juniper. A bank running up from behind Auchintoul to behind Rineten, near Gairnshiel. Still has many junipers.

**Cnocan Aitinn** (3, U, 268998), ˌknọkɐnˈatən, little knoll of juniper. Cnockanatan (Io 75), Knockanatun, juniper (D). A former house beside a hillock, west of Gairnshiel. Still has many junipers.

**Cnocan Aitinn** (3, 254021), little knoll of juniper. Cnocan Aitionn, juniper hill (D). Also the Juniper Hill (U), ðɪˈdʒunəpër ˈhël. At the Sleach north-west of Gairnshiel.

**Cnocan an t-Sabhail** (3, north of 148905), little knoll of the barn. Cnocan n daul, barn hillock (D). Near Braemar.

**An Cnocan Dubh** (3, U, west of 147904), ðɪˌknọkɐnˈduˑ, the black little knoll. Cnocan dubh (D). Culminates above the house named after it (see below). Near Braemar.

**An Cnocan Dubh** (3, U, 147904), as above, the black little knoll. Cnocan-Dubh (Ha). A former croft, often called the Cnocan (C). Near Braemar.

**Cnocan Dubh** (3, F, 352924), ˌknọkɐnˈduˑ, black little knoll. Cnockindow (Opr 23). A former farm on the east side of the road up Glen Muick.

**The Cnocan Dubh Brig\*** (U, 352923), ðɪˌknọkɐnˈduˑˈbrɪg. A bridge in Glen Muick.

**The Cnocan Dubh Burn** (F, 351924), ðɪˌknọkɐnˈduˑˈbʌrn. The Burn of Knockendow (Rli 23), the Knockandhu Burn (D). Beside the above ruin.

**The Cnocan Dubh Park\*** (U, west of 352924), ðɪˌknọkɐnˈduˑ ˈpark. Includes the former fields of Cross Butts and Creag Mollachdaidh. In lower Glen Muick.

**Cnoc an Fhuarain** (3, 145907), knoll of the well. Cnoc nuaran, well hillock (D). On Morrone.

**Cnocan Mór** (OS, 199941), big hillock. Above Glen Feardar.

**Cnocan na Gaoithe** (3, 261019), little knoll of the wind. Cnocan na gaoith (D). North-west of Gairnshiel.

**Cnocan nan Corra** (4, south-west of 263018), little knoll of the herons. Cnocan na gorr, heron's hill (D). North-west of Gairnshiel.

**Cnocan nan Corra\*** (4, 227938), little knoll of the herons. Knockan na Gore (I). A hillock in a field near the Inver.

**Cnocan Riabhach** (3, F, 322953), ˌknọkɐn'riˑəç, brindled little knoll. Knockanriach (Opr 29), Knockanrioch (A). A former farm on east side of Girnock, beside a prominent hillock.

**Cnoc Bhreabair\*** (3, WD, 299967), knọk'vrepɐr, knoll of the weaver. East of Crathie.

**An Cnoc Biorach\*** (3, U, 103792), ðɪˌknọk'piˑrəç, the pointed knoll. In the upper Baddoch.

**Cnoc Chadail** (3, 086878), knoll of the sleep. Crochk chadil, sleepy hillock, with story of a man put to sleep under it for seven years and released by fairies (D). We have recently heard this legend also (JB). In lower Glen Ey.

**Cnoc Chalmac** (OS, 3, F, 266007), krọk'aˑlmɐχ, hill of St Colm, or of little Malcolm. West of Gairnshiel.

**Cnoc Chalmac\*** (3, 269006), see above. Cnock-chalmack (Crg 18). A former habitation west of Gairnshiel, on above hill.

**Cnoc Cheann-bhuilg** (4), knoll of the head-bag (referring to the stream). Crochauli (Mf), Crochanli (Gr), Knock-a'-andlic (Mp). The former chapel of St Bride's near Braemar. Across Dee, opposite the parish church (Mp), i.e. beside Inverchandlick.

**Cnoc Choltair\*** (3, 102818), hill of the ploughshare. Knock Choulter (I), Knoc Choulter (R 14). Looks into Baddoch and Ey.

**Cnoc Dubh** (OS, 3, C, 420991), knọk'duˑ, black hill. Knockdow (Io 20). A dark, heather-covered hill east of Ballater.

**Cnoc Dubh\*** (3, 109894), black knoll. Knockdow (Im 3). Near Corriemulzie.

**Cnoc Dubh\*** (3), black knoll. Knockdow (Opr late 1700s). A former habitation near Corriemulzie, probably beside the above hillock.

**Cnoc Dubh\*** (3, 144875), black knoll. Knock Du (I). A rounded heathery hillock south of Braemar.

**Cnoc Dubh\*** (3, U, 411044), knọk'duˑ, black knoll. A heathery hillock, now under fir trees, west of Logie Coldstone.

**Cnoc Dubh** (3, C, 409043), as above, black knoll. Knockdhu (OS 1869). Knockindow (Io in 1732) suggests Cnocan Dubh (3), black little knoll. A former house beside above knoll.

**Cnoc Dubh\*** (3, 138834), black knoll. Knock Du (I). In Glen Clunie.

**Cnoc Dubh\*** (3, 138833), black knoll. Knock Du (I). A field in Glen Clunie, beside above hillock.

**The Cnoc Dubh Park\*** (F, 410042), ðɪˌknọk'du'park. A field west of Logie Coldstone.

**The Cnoc Dubh Wuid\*** (U, 411044), ðɪˌknọk'du'wɪd. West of Logie Coldstone.

**Cnoc Mharcaich\*** (3, 158890), knoll of the horseman. Knock Varkich (I, R 13). Also Cnoc. Knock (Im 3, Ri). A former farm south of Braemar, beside a hillock above it, at 158891 just west of the road.

**Cnoc Mhuiceann** (3), knoll of baldmoneys (see Croft Muickan). Cnoc-Muicean by the Cluny (Gr 21). Presumably beside Croft Muickan at Braemar.

**Cnoc na Ceardaich\*** (3, north-west of 248971), knoll of the smithy. Cnochd na cardich (R 3). A little hillock north of Crathie.

**Cnoc na Cloiche Duibhe\*** (3, 211976 on R 3 and probably 206984 on R 14, but both part of the same hill), knoll of the black stone. See Meallan Clach Dhubh. Cnochd na-clach-

dhuth, Cnoc-na–clach dhu (R 3, 14). A knoll on the hills north-west of Crathie.

**Cnoc na ? h-Éide\*** (5, 923868), knoll of the tribute, possibly Cnocan Shéid, little knoll of blowings (e.g. windy). Knoc na hide (Go). Old shielings in upper Glen Geldie.

**Cnoc nam Buachaillean\*** (3, south-west of 252958), knoll of the herdsmen, with Buachaillean probably a variant genitive plural. Cnochd na buachailean (R 3). A knoll north-west of Crathie.

**Cnoc nam Mèirleach\*** (3, U, 148914), ˌknọknɐ'mjaˑrlɐχ, local form Meàrlach, knoll of the thieves. A rocky hillock, also now the name of a nearby house. Near the road into the Games Park at Braemar.

**Cnoc nam Mult** (3, west of 083893), knoll of the wethers. Cnoc nam muilt (A 353), knoknaMOOLTSH (A 1954). At Inverey.

**Cnoc nan Gabhar\*** (3, 266985), knoll of the goats. Cnochd-na-Gour, Cnoc na-gaobhr (R 3, 14). Above the Crathie–Gairnshiel road.

**Cnoc na Teididh** (3, 058919), knoll of the wild fire. Krocht na tete (Im 3), Knocknatete (Me 15), Knockinted (Roy, Ar). A former farm in Glen Lui.

**Cnoc of Braichlie\*** Gaelic Cnoc (3) = knoll, or Scots borrowing Knock. Knock of Braichly (G 19). Near Ardmeanach south-west of Ballater, possibly same as the Knock (OS).

**Cnoc Ruighe na h-Aon Oidhche\*** (3, 277984), hill of shieling of the one night. Knock-Rie-na-han-Oich (I), Cnoc-rie-na chan-Oich (R 14). Now (U) knọk'hɪnri, knọk'hɪnrɪç, an unusual anglicisation. South-west of Gairnshiel, above shiels at 280996 and 270985, and Shiel of the Herds of Lawsie.

**The Coal Mossie\*** (F, 434011), ðɪ'kol'mọse. The Coal Moss (U). A bog near Loch Davan, which offered hard, black, coal-like peats.

**Coble Croft\*** (Io 41). At Balnault, probably same as Boat Croft.

**Coble Croft** Cowbill Croft (Ca). At Braemar, probably at the former ferry below Inverchandlick Cottage.

**Coble Croft\*** Coblecroft (Io 41). Probably was at Clachanturn west of Abergeldie.

**Coble Croft** (Ab 19, G 13). At Cobletoun of Tullich east of Ballater.

**The Coble Haugh\*** (U, 437971), ðɪ'kobəl'haˑχ. A field south-west of Dinnet.

**Coble Seat of Tullich** Coble Seatt of Tullich (G 13). Different from Cobletoun and Coble Croft. Cobletown alias Cobleseat (Me 13), but other papers (G 13) show it as different, probably two habitations close together. East of Ballater.

**The Cobles Puil** (C, 438972), ðɪ'kobəlz'pil. Cobbles (A). Cobble (P) and Cobbie (Sc) are incorrect. A pool in Dee south-west of Dinnet.

**Cobletoun** (Mc 26, 377964). Cobletoun of Tullich (Mc 7), Cobletown (M), Cobletown of Tullich (Gf 177). Beside a former ferry, east of Ballater.

**Cobletoun of Ballater\*** Cobbletown of Ballater (Io in 1802). Probably was opposite the Cobletoun of Dalmochie (see below and Cobletoun Park).

**The Cobletoun of Dalmochie** (378964). Cobbletown of Dalmuchie (Opr 34). The Cobbletown of Dalmuchie (Dug); a boat plied from here, about Pannanich Lodge on south side of Dee, to about site of Aberdeen Cottage on north side. Former habitation near Ballater.

**Cobletoun of Monaltrie\*** Cobletown of Monaltrie (Opr 29). A former habitation near Balnault.

**Cobletoun Park\*** (375965). Cobletown Park (R 4). A field east of Ballater.

**(The) Cock Cairn** (OS, C, 463886), ðɪ'kọk'kern, ðɪˌkọ'kern (JO). Often the Cock Cairns (F). Cockcairns (Th), Cock

Cairn (Jo). Possibly a similar name to Cac Carn on Lochnagar. In Glen Tanar.

**The Cock's Neck*** (C, south-east of 350930), ðɪˈkɔksˈnɛk, said to be because the bends in the road look like a cock's neck. Also formerly the Mill of Sterin Brae (U), ðɪˈmëlɐˈstɛrn̩ˈbreˑ. A steep hill with sharp bends on a road in lower Glen Muick, at the narrowest part of the glen.

**Coilacriech** (OS, 323969), from Coille a' Chrithich (3, C), ˌkɛilɐˈçriç, (kɛiləˈkriç (A) was an error), wood of the aspen. Note Slat ghlas de'n chritheach, a green rod of aspen (Dw 851). Kyle-a-chreech (I), Coill a chrich, the last clearly for chrithich, aspen trees are cruin cri (D). A former farm, and area around an inn, locally often called Coillies, ˈkɛiliz. West of Ballater.

**The Coilacriech Brae*** (C, 325968), ðɪˌkɛilɐˈçriçˈbreˑ. A hill on the road west of Ballater.

**(The) Coilacriech Burn** (OS, C, 320975), ðɪˌkɛilɐˈçriçˈbʌrn. Also Allt Chrithich (3), burn of the aspen. Ault Chreech (I).

**The Coilacriech Wuid*** (C, 318970), ðɪˌkɛilɐˈçriçˈwɪd, often the Coillies Wuid. The big wood at Coilacriech.

**Coille Ailmhaigh** (3, 205925), wood of stony plain. Kyle Alvie (heath and birch wood) (I), Kiel Albhie (R 14), Kilalvie (A 331). East of Invercauld.

**Coille Ailmhaigh Side*** (210928). Kyle Alvie Side (I). A hillside east of Invercauld.

**Coille Bhantrach** (3, 205913), wood of widows or widowers. Kyl fan trach (Fa), Kyle Fantrach (Roy, Ar), Kalfantrach (Io 63). South-west of the Inver, but Roy shows it, more vaguely, as about the top of Craig Leek.

**Coille na Dubh-bhruaich** (3, 156904), wood of the black bank. Coille na Dubraich (D). Also the Dubh-bhruach Wuid (U), ðɪˈduˌbrɐχˈwɪd. The Dubrach Wood (Aj 9). A birch wood south of Braemar.

**Coille Phìobair** (2, U, 098857), kʊlˈfiḅёr, wood of the piper, or of pipers. A Lamont family, locally nicknamed Piper, once lived at the farm nearby. Coire Phiobair given probably in error (A). A birch wood in Glen Ey.

**The Coillich Puil** (C, 371952), ðɪˈkɛiləçˈpil, Cailliche a better spelling, see Craig Coillich. Coilach (A, Sc), Kynoch (P) is incorrect. A pool on Dee above the bridge at Ballater.

**The Coillies Straight*** See the Lang Straucht.

**(The) Coinlach Burn** (OS, 393034), ðɪˈkɛinləçˈbʌrn (F), sometimes the Coinlach (U), from Coinnleach (3) = of candles, referring to fir roots which abound in the peat. Old Deeside folk call the resinous roots 'fir candles' because they make good tapers for lighting fires. The Cunliach Burn (G 19). Locally now the Roar Burn (C), ðɪˈrɔrˈbʌrn, and further down on the Cromar farmlands the Howe Burn (C), ðɪˈhʌuˈbʌrn.

**The Coinneach Park*** (U, 306962), ðɪˈkɛinəçˈpark. A field at Micras, named after A' Choinneach.

**The Coinneach Puil** (C, 305962), ðɪˈkɛinəçˈpil, named after the nearby A' Choinneach. Cainnach (M), Coynach (A, Sc). A pool in Dee west of Coilacriech, at Micras.

**(Na) Coireachan Dubha** (OS, 3, 093807), the black corries. A collective name for the two corries Coire Moine Mor and Beag. The corries-dhu or Black Corries (Lp 5). In upper Glen Ey.

**Na Coireachan Dubha*** (3), see above. The corries-dhu (Lp 5). Also Black Corries (Lp). This name referred to a grazing centred on the above two corries, but extending north almost to Creag an Fhuathais and south to Beinn Iutharn Bheag.

**Na Coireachan Dubha** See An Coire Dubh.

**Coireach Bhùth** (5, C), kɔreˈvuː or ðɪˌkɔreˈvuˑz (anglicised plural), corries of cots. Bhó = of cows is a possibility, as the Braemar Gaelic pronunciation of words with a long *o* tended towards a *u* sound, as in An Stoban Biorach (see also Allt a' Bhò). A collective name for the corries between Carn an Tuirc and Sron na Gaoithe, well known to farmers as a fertile hill grazing. Korry vow (Po), Corribhudhs (Io 52), Corry Vue (I, R 13), Corryvooe (Hi), Corrie Bhu (Gr 180), Corrach voo (D), corrach gives a collective sense (D). Corie Bhue (R 14) shows it clearly as the group of three corries north-west, west, and south-west of Cairn of Claise, and Corie Wows (Fa) includes also the corries leading up to the Cairnwell.

**Coireach Bhùth*** (5). Corryvow (Cr 47). A former habitation in summer, probably a shieling, in above corries.

**Coireach na Mòine*** (3, 083806 and 093816), corries of the peat-moss. Corrachnamoin (Io 16, Rli 19). A combined name for the two corries Coire Moine Beag and Coire Moine Mor in upper Glen Ey.

**Coire a' Chuirn Dheirg*** (3, U, 097868), ˌkɔrɐˌχurnˈjɛrək, corrie of the red hill. On An Carn Dearg in Glen Ey.

**Coire air Chùl*** (3, U, 166781), ˌkɔrёrˈχuˑl, back corrie, air Chùl = behind. On the Glas Maol.

**Coire air Chùl*** (3, 102812), back corrie. Cor-er-Chul (I), Cor-er-chuil (R 14). Looks into the Baddoch.

**Coire Aiteachan Carn an t-Sabhail** (6, 965975). Coire Aiteachan Carn Toul (Bur). 'A is sounded long', Aiteachan thought to mean place with junipers; on Cairn Toul below the 4241 top. There are no junipers there, and Burn noted that the pronunciation was the same as in Etchachan and in Ruigh-aiteachain of Glen Feshie, so it probably has the same meaning as Coire Etchachan, in this case Coire Etchachan of Cairn Toul.

**Coire Allt a' Chlair** (OS, 3, F, 125885), ˌkɔrˌaltˈχlaːr, corrie of burn of the flat ground. West of Braemar.

**Coire Allt a' Mhaide*** (3, U, 157833), ˌkɔrˌaltˈvitʃ, corrie of burn of the stick. Cor Ault Vait (I), Corr Ault Vait, Corie Ault Bhait (R 13, 14). Also the Allt a' Mhaide Corrie (U), ðɪˌaltˈvitʃˌkɔre. In Glen Clunie.

**Coire Allt an Aitinn** (OS, 212827), corrie of burn of the juniper. East of Loch Callater.

**Coire Allt an Droighnean** (OS, 214814), classic form would be Coire Allt an Droighinn (see Allt an Droighinn), corrie of burn of the thorn. In upper Callater.

**Coire Alltan na Beinne*** (3, U, 081982), ˌkɔrˌaltnɐˈḅeiːn, corrie of burnie of the hill. On Beinn a' Bhuird.

**Coire Alltan Odhar*** (3, U, 197879), ˌkɔrˌaltn̩ˈʌur, corrie of dun burnie. Cor Aultan-our (R 7). Above Ballochbuie Forest.

**Coire Allt an t-Sionnaich*** (3, U, 025858), ˌkɔrˌaltˈjuniç, corrie of burn of the fox. Possibly Coire Allt Shionnach, corrie of burn of foxes (see Allt an t-Sionnaich). South of the White Bridge in Glen Dee.

**Coire Allt Beag*** (3, 127801), corrie of little burn. Cor Ault Beg (I). In the Baddoch.

**Coire Allt Chailleach*** (3, U, 159904), ˌkɔrˌaltˈχaləç, corrie of burn of witches, old women, or nuns. South-east of Braemar.

**Coire Allt Leth-allt** See Dalvorar Corrie.

**Coire Allt Luachrach*** (3, 149810), corrie of burn of rushes. Cor Ault Luachrach (I). North of the Cairnwell.

**Coire Allt na h-Earba*** (3, F, 115935), ˌkɔrˌaltnɐˈhɛrɐḅ, corrie of burn of the roe. In lower Glen Quoich.

**Coire Allt na Mòine*** (3, 284969), corrie of burn of the peat-moss. Cor-Alt-na-Moin (I), Cor Alt na Moin (R 14). North-east of Crathie.

**Coire Allt Sgreuchaig** See Coire na Sgreuchaig.

**Coire Allt Sgreuchaig*** (3, U, 069876), ˌkɔrˌaltˈskreçək, corrie of burn of screeching one (e.g. owl). South-east of Inverey.

**Coire Allt Shlat*** (3, 108850), corrie of burn of wands. Corie ault-lat (Io 79). In Glen Ey.

**Coire Allt Stiubhart*** (3, U, 128808), ˌkɔrˌaltˈstjuˑərt, corrie of Stewart's burn. Up the Baddoch.

**Coire an Alltain Odhair** (3, U, 057826), ˌkɔrˌaltɐnˈʌur̩, corrie of the dun burnie. Corr n alltan odhar (D). In upper Glen Ey.

**Coire an Dà Bheinn** (3, U, 225033), ˌkɔrənˈdaˑvən, corrie of the two hills. Coir-an-tamuil in an old Gaelic poem (T 33, 18), but original manuscript (Iop) gives Coir-an-tamhain, Tamhain = of the body; however, first *a* in Tamhain is short, not long as in Diack's notes (see name below) and in the phonetics of this name. A corrie in upper Glen Gairn.

**Coire an Dà Bheinn** (3). Corintavan (Io 22), Corndaven (Roy), Corintavin (Ano), Corindavan (R 1), Corintaven (Io 60), Corandaven (Mg 206) used in error for the hill Culardoch, see also name above. Corr n dāvăn (D) without stating what the location was, Davan interpreted locally as da mheann = two kids (D in A), but this does not fit the pronunciation. A former farm below the above corrie, about the site of the present Corndavon Lodge.

**Coire an Daimh Mhoile** (OS, 247844), corrie of the hummel stag. Also the Hummel Corrie (C), ðɪˈhʌməlˈkɔre. On Lochnagar.

**Coire an Deamhais*** (3, U, 077825), ˌkɔrn̩ˈdjeɪʃ, eɪ nasal, corrie of the shears. See note under An Deamhais. In upper Glen Ey.

**Coirean Domhain*** (3, 240041), deep little corrie. Corrindoun (Io 15), Corry Doune (R 12). Note Corndoun Burn (OS 1869), later changed mistakenly to Corndavon Burn. North-east of Corndavon Lodge.

**Coirean Domhain** (3). A shieling Corrintoune (Asr). See above.

**Coirean Domhain Burn** See Corndavon Burn.

**Coire an Dubh-loch*** (3, U, 232833), ˌkɔrn̩ˈduˌlɔχ, corrie of the black loch. Also the Dubh-loch Corrie (F), with earlier variation the Corrie o the Dubh-loch (U), ðɪˈkɔreɪðɪˈduˌlɔχ. West of Loch Muick.

**Coire an Dubh-lochain** (OS, 3, F, 095994), ˌkɔrn̩ˈduˌlɔχən, corrie of the black tarn. Cor-du-Lochan (I). Also Coire an Loch (A), kɔrnˈlɔχ (A). On Beinn a' Bhuird.

**Coire an Easaidh Bhig*** (3, U, 128002), ˌkɔrˌn̩eseˈbeg, corrie of the little waterfall one (see Allt an Eas Bhig). Cor of the Little Essie (I). On Ben Avon.

**Coire an Easaidh Mhóir*** (3, U, 140010), ˌkɔrˌn̩eseˈmoˑr, corrie of the big waterfall one. On Ben Avon.

**Coire an Fhèidh** (OS, 093850), should be Coire nam Fiadh (3, C), ˌkɔrnɐˈvio, corrie of the deer. Coir na fiadh, na viu (D). In mid Glen Ey.

**Coire an Fhiadhaich*** (4, 186939), corrie of the deer-hunting. Cor Neach (I). North-east of Invercauld.

**Coire an Fhiadhaich*** (4, 333984), corrie of the deer-hunting. Cor Neach (I), Cor neach (R 14). In lower Glen Gairn.

**Coire an Fhir Bhogha** (OS, 044975), should be Coire Cadha an Fhir Bhogha (3, C), ˌkɔrˌkanjərˈvouː, corrie of pass of the archer. Coir' cadha an fhir-bhogh (D). East of Glen Derry.

**Coire an Fhuarain Mhóir** (3, A, U, 059872), ˌkɔrˌnuɐrənˈvoːr, corrie of the big well. South of the Linn of Dee.

**Coire an Iomaill*** (3, 274964), corrie of the limit. Cor-n-Iemal (I). Above Crathie, runs up to the limit of the former Invercauld Estate.

**Coire an Laoigh** (OS, 152847), locally Coire Laoigh (3, F), kɔr ˈlui, corrie of calf. Cor Luie (I). Also the Newbigging Corrie (U), ðɪˌnjuˈbɪgənˈkɔre. In Glen Clunie.

**Coire an Leachd*** (3, U, 134953), kɔrn̩ˈlɛçt, corrie of the declivity. In Gleann an t-Slugain.

**Coire an Loch*** (3, 119782), corrie of the loch. Corn Loch (I). Also the Loch Corrie (F), ðɪˈlɔχˈkɔre. North-west of the Cairnwell.

**Coire an Loch** See Coire an Dubh-lochain.

**Coire an Lochain Bhig** (3, 091840), corrie of the little tarn. Corr an lochan bheag (D). In upper Glen Ey.

**Coire an Lochain Buidhe** See Coire an Loch Bhuidhe.

**Coire an Lochain Mhóir** (3, 092844), corrie of the big tarn. Corr an lochan mhor (D). In upper Glen Ey.

**Coire an Lochain Uaine** (OS, 3, C, 957977), ˌkɔrn̩ˌlɔχɐnˈuɐn, corrie of the green tarn. On Cairn Toul.

**Coire an Lochain Uaine** (3, Sg, C, 002983), as above, corrie of the green tarn. On Ben Macdui.

**Coire an Lochain Uaine** (OS, 025985), locally Coire Lochan Uaine (2, C), ˌkɔrˌlɔχɐnˈuɐn, corrie of green tarn. In Glen Derry.

**Coire an Loch Bhuidhe** (OS, 244836), corrie of the yellow loch. Curlochbuy (In). Also An Coire Buidhe (3, F), ðɪˌkɔrˈbui, the yellow corrie. South of Lochnagar.

**Coire an Tobair** (OS, 3, C, 938842), ˌkɔrn̩ˈdoupɐr, corrie of the well. In Glen Geldie.

**Coire an t-Sabhail** (OS, 3, U, 965972), ˌkɔrn̩ˈdʌul̩, corrie of the barn. On Cairn Toul.

**Coire an t-Sagairt** (OS, 3, A, 188009), kɔrənˈtagərt and kɔrən ˈdagərtʃ (A), corrie of the priest. South of Loch Builg.

**Coire an t-Sagairt** (OS, 960912), corrie of the priest. On Beinn Bhrotain.

**Coire an t-Saighdeir** (OS, 3, U, 964967), ˌkɔrənˈdɔiʤɛr, (kɔrən ˈdaʤər (A)), corrie of the soldier. Coir' na saighdearan (D in A). Also the Soldier's Corrie (Ky, F), ðɪˈsolʤɛrzˈkɔre. On Cairn Toul.

**Coire an t-Searraich*** (3), corrie of the colt. Coirnjarroch, coire searrach 'colt' (Cp). Near Crathie.

**Coire an t-Seilich** (OS, 3, F, 948843), ˌkɔrənˈʤeliç, corrie of the willow. Corrie Sheiloch (Ros). In Glen Geldie.

**Coire an t-Seilich*** (3, U, probably 109955), ˌkɔrənˈtiliç, corrie of the willow. In Glen Quoich.

**Coire an t-Sìdhein*** (3, U, 086881), ˌkɔrn̩ˈʤiˑn, corrie of the fairy hillock. Holds the prominent hillock of Sidhean Chorr, in lower Glen Ey.

**Coire an t-Slugain** (OS, 3, C, 273903), ˌkɔrn̩ˈlugən, (kɔran ˈtlukan (A)), corrie of the gullet. In upper Girnock.

**Coire an t-Slugain** (OS, 3, U, 292029), ˌkɔrənˈlugən (kɔran ˈtlukan (A)), corrie of the gullet. Also the Slugan Corrie (U), ðɪˈslugənˈkɔre. North of Gairnshiel.

**Coire an t-Sneachda** (3, A, F, 095975), ˌkɔrn̩ˈdreç, corrie of the snow. Corry-n-dreach (I). A collective name for the two corries Ear and Iar-choire Sneachdach, on Beinn a' Bhuird. Also the Snowy Corrie (Al, F), ðɪˈsnoeˈkɔre.

**Coire an t-Sneachda** (OS, 3, 959920), corrie of the snow. Also the Snowy Corrie (F), as above. Holds one of the longest-lying snow beds on the Braemar side of the Cairngorms. On Beinn Bhrotain.

**Coire an Turaraidh** (4, 373920), corrie of the rattling, probably from Turaraich = rattle, disorder. Cor-n-Durarie (I), Carntorrarie and Moss sixeklike, Corrie of Cairntonararie (Ri 14). Also the Yowe Corrie (JS), Scots Yowe = ewe. South of Ballater.

**Coire Bad an Lòin*** (3, 274981), corrie of clump of the marsh. Cor Badnlone (I). South-west of Gairnshiel.

**Coire Beag*** (3, 215962), little corrie. Corry Beg (I). In Glen Feardar.

**An Coire Beag*** (2, F, 355983), ðɪˌkɔrɐˈbeg, the little corrie. In lower Glen Gairn.

**An Coire Beag** (3, F, 353979), ˌkɔreˈbeg, to oldest folk ˌkɔrɐ ˈbeg, the little corrie. Former farms, see Lower and Upper Coire Beag. An coir beag (Da). Also Braes of Prony. Braes of Pronny or Corybegg (Crg 13), Brae of Prony (Opr 17). Near Bridge of Gairn, below the above corrie. Corrybeg (OS 1904).

**Coire Beag** (3, 293033), little corrie. Corriebeg, Corybeg (Ri 21,

37), Cor Beg (I), Corr Beg (R 12). A small corrie north of Gairnshiel, almost part of the bigger Coire an t-Slugain.

**Coire Beag*** (3, U, 339878), ˌkọre'bẹg, little corrie. In Glen Muick.

**The Coire Beag Burn** (C, 354980), ðɪˌkọre'bẹg'bʌrn. Corrybeg Burn (OS 1904). Near Bridge of Gairn.

**The Coire Beag Road*** (U, 350980), ðɪˌkọre'bẹg'rod. The old road from the east side of Glen Gairn towards Abergairn.

**Coire Bhearnaist** (OS, 045834), should be Coire Bhearn-uisge (3, F), ˌkọr'vjarnˌuəʃk, kọr'vjarnəʃ, (kɔr'vjarnəs, and kɔr 'vurnɛʃk (A)), corrie of the water gap. See Coire Fhearneasg, where the present pronunciation is the same as for Coire Bhearnaist but where there is clear evidence from an old map that the name should be Coire Bhearn-uisge, corrie of the water gap. Coire Bhourneasg (OS 1869). West of Glen Ey.

**Coire Bhó*** (3, U, 352053), ˌkọre'vouː, corrie of cows. West of Morven.

**Coire Bhothain Mhóir*** (3, probably 074821), corrie of the big hut. Cor-bhoan-more (Io 79). In upper Glen Ey.

**Coire Bhraineich*** (5, 099887), corrie of the ? front. Corrievranoch (Me 15). South of Mar Lodge.

**Coire Bhrochain** (OS, 2, C, 956996), kọr'vrọχɐn, corrie where 'everything is in little bits' (JB). A corrie whose floor is filled with scree, on Braeriach.

**Coire Bhronn** (OS, 030850), probably from Coire a' Bhrothain (5, C), kọr'vrɔin, but kọr'vrɔɲ from best informants; (kọre 'vron, palatal *n* (A)), corrie of the sultry heat. Cory Vren (Po), Corri Wran (Fa), Coire-a-bhrothain (Gr 12). Also includes the burn to the south. East of Bynack Lodge.

**Coirebhruach** (OS, 405897), see name below. A hillside in upper Glen Tanar.

**Coirebhruach** (C, 404896), ˌkọre'vraχ, from Còrr Bhruach (5), point of banks. Coirvroche (Hr), Corywrauch (Ap), Corrywrach (H), Cornabruich (Cr 31), Corrybruach (Crg 2), Corryvruach (Opr 20), Corrie Vrach (Ri 20), Cory bruoch (R 1), Corryvrac—Coire-bhreac (Mg), Corrie Vruach (V), Corrie Vrack (A), in Gaelic Coire vrechk (D), in other words evidence for both Breac (speckled) and Bruach (bank). There is no corrie there, just a hillside leading down to a haugh by the burn. However the OS name (see name below) is at the eastern extremity of a steep Bruach or bank running west past the Shiel of Glentanar, so it is more likely to be Còrr Bhruach = point or end of banks (note T 30, 109). In any case, Coire Bhreac does not fit as Coire is masculine and so the form would have been Coire Breac as in other cases; if anything, aspiration has tended to be dropped on Deeside, and not added. A former habitation in upper Glen Tanar.

**Coirebhruach** (C, 406896), as above. The early spellings above refer to this former settlement in upper Glen Tanar. Once a public house (Gf) serving travellers coming over the Mounth.

**The Coirebhruach Brig*** (F, south-west of 407896), ðɪˌkọre'vraχ 'brɪg. A footbridge in Glen Tanar.

**The Coirebhruach Fuird*** (U, south-west of 407896), ðɪˌkọre 'vraχ'fjurd. A ford over Tanar on the Mounth Road.

**The Coirebhruach Park*** (F, 405895), ðɪˌkọre'vraχ'park. A field in Glen Tanar.

**Coire Bhuth** See Na Coireachan Bhuth.

**(An) Coire Boidheach** (OS, 3, C, 235843), ðɪˌkọr'bu.əç, the beautiful corrie. A wide, gently-sloping corrie with good grazing for deer, south-west of Lochnagar.

**Coire Bòidheach** (3, A, 105975), kɔr'bɔjəç (A), beautiful corrie. On Beinn a' Bhuird.

**The Coire Boidheach Burn*** See Allt a' Choire Bhoidheach.

**Coire Breac** (3, Wa, 207808), speckled corrie. Cor Breachk (I).

The big corrie north-west of Tolmount, at the head of Glen Callater.

**(An) Coire Buidhe** (OS, 3, C, 226904), ðɪˌkọr'bui, the yellow corrie. Corbuie (R 7). Also the Muckle Coire Buidhe. The Muckle Cor Buie (Io 78). West of Glen Gelder. Note that all the cases of Coire Buidhe involve corries with patches of rough, little-grazed grassland, standing out conspicuously against predominantly heathery slopes nearby.

**(An) Coire Buidhe** (OS, 3, Sg, A, U, 101980), as above, the yellow corrie. Corbuie (I). On Beinn a' Bhuird.

**(An) Coire Buidhe** (OS, 2, F, 989845), as above, the yellow corrie. West of Bynack Lodge.

**(An) Coire Buidhe** (OS, 3, U, 295885), as above, the yellow corrie. At the top of Glen Girnock.

**An Coire Buidhe*** (2, F, 061889), as above, the yellow corrie. Above the Linn of Dee.

**An Coire Buidhe*** (3, U, 151863), as above, the yellow corrie. Cor Buie (I). In Glen Clunie.

**Coire Buidhe*** (3, 122794), yellow corrie. Cor Buie (I). Up the Baddoch.

**Coire Buidhe*** (3, 182852), yellow corrie. Cor buie (I). Above Loch Callater.

**An Coire Buidhe** See Coire an Loch Bhuidhe.

**Coire Buidhe*** (3, 012830), yellow corrie. Corrybui (Roy). Corrie drained by Dubh Alltan Beag south of Bynack.

**Coire Buidhe air Bheul*** (3, U, 293877), kọr'buiɾ'vel, front yellow corrie, air Bheul = before, in front. Curbuie (In, Am). Also the Fore Coire Buidhe (C), ðɪ'forˌkọr'bui. North of Loch Muick.

**Coire Buidhe air Chùl*** (3, U, 276872), kọr'buiɾ'χul, back yellow corrie, air Chùl = behind. Also the Back Coire Buidhe (C), ðɪ 'bakˌkọr'bui. Back Corbuie (B). In upper Glen Gelder.

**An Coire Buidhe Beag*** (3, U, 222908), ðɪˌkọrˌbui'bẹg, the little yellow corrie. Also the Little Coire Buidhe (U), ðɪ'lëtəlˌkọr 'bui. The Little Corbuie (Io 78, B). South-west of Balmoral.

**The Coire Buidhe Burn** See Allt Coire Buidhe.

**The Coire Buidhe Burn*** (U, 246834), ðɪˌkọr'bui'bʌrn. Burn of Curlochbuy (In). West of Loch Muick.

**The Coire Buidhe Burn*** (U, 230909), ðɪˌkọr'bui'bʌrn. Cor-buie burn (Io 78). West of Balmoral.

**The Coire Buidhe Rocks*** (U, north of 062890), ðɪˌkọr'bui'rọks. A small stretch of rocks near Linn of Dee.

**Coire Caochan na Còthaiche*** (3, U, 995976), ˌkọrˌkọχɐnɐ'koˑɪç, corrie of streamlet of the spongy place. On Ben Macdui.

**Coire Caochan nan Spòld*** (3, U, 014972), ˌkọrˌkọχɐnɐ'spɔˑl, corrie of streamlet of the haunches. On Derry Cairngorm.

**Coire Caochan Roibidh** (OS, 969926), locally Coire Roibidh, (2, A, U), kọr'rọpe, Robbie's corrie; Caochan Roibidh is the burn. In Glen Dee.

**Coire Cath nam Fionn** (OS, 951930), should be Coire Cadha nam Fiann (5, D, A, F), ˌkọrˌkaˑnɐ'vjʌŋ, corrie of pass of the crowberries, or of the warriors or Fingalians. In Glen Geusachan.

**Coire Ceanndair** See Coire Loch Kander.

**Coire Challtuinn*** (3, U, 130927), kọr'χaltən, corrie of hazels. The Allanmore Corrie (F), ðɪˌalɐn'moˑr'kọre. North-west of Braemar.

**Coire Chaol-bhaid** (4, 143900), corrie of the narrow spot. Coir chaolvat (D). On the north side of Morrone.

**Coire Chaorach*** (3, 288820), corrie of sheep. Cor churach (I). On the south side of Loch Muick.

**Coire Chrasgaidh*** (3, 385937), corrie of the little crossing. Corr Chraskie (I). Above Ballater, offering a good route across to the Pollagach Burn and Glen Tanar.

**Coire Chreag Chais*** See Corrie Chash.

**Coire Chrid** (OS, 3, F, 122828), probably Chrit or Chruit, kọr

51

'çritʃ, corrie of crofts. Note Crit is a form of Croit (Dw), a croft. Cor Chree (I, R 14). Above the Baddoch crofts. Also Forbes' Corrie (F), 'fǫrbz'kǫre, after a former inhabitant of the Baddoch.

**Coire Chronaidh** (5, 135806), corrie of the little hollow or of the dark brown place (Cron has both meanings in Irish names (J), note Ardchronie in Ross-shire, W 1904, 3). A derivative of Crònan = low murmuring is another possibility as it was recorded as Coire Chroni, corrie of echoes (Gr 224). North of Dubh-choire on Carn Aosda, north of the Cairnwell.

**Coire Chuil** (OS, 5, U, 973825), kǫr'χuˑl, corrie of the back. On the upper Bynack.

**Coire Chuilinn** (5, 284987), corrie of the ? holly. Corriecholding, Coriquholing (Me 3), Corriequholdich (Ri 21), Cor Choulan (I), Cor Choullan (R 14), Cor-whoolan, Kor-whoolyan (D). Probably not Challtuinn as this is given as Chaldin elsewhere in the same maps (I). Now the Braenaloin Corrie (F), ðɪ ˌbrɪnɐˈlɛinˈkǫre. Formerly Cory of Braeloighne (Io 79). A corrie on the north-west side of Geallaig Hill near Gairnshiel.

**Coire Clachach** (OS, 096774), should be Coire na Cùlath (5, F), ˌkǫrnɐˈkulɐ, corrie of the back place (see Allt Coire na Culath). Alexander gave this name but thought it was on the Perthshire side. At the head of the Baddoch.

**Coire Clach-mhuilinn** (3, 271047), corrie of millstone. Coir clach vuln, millstone corry (D). The upper, gentle slope above Coire nam Muillear, north-west of Gairnshiel.

**Coire Clach nan Taillear** (OS, 988980), corrie of stone of the tailors, locally Coire nan Tàillear (2, Sg, A, F), ˌkǫrnɐn 'daˈljər, corrie of the tailors. Also the Tailors' Corrie (F), ðɪ 'telɛrz'kǫre. A big corrie on the south side of Ben Macdui.

**Coire Clais an t-Sabhail*** (3, U, 955965), ˌkǫrˌklaʃɐnˈdʌuḷ, corrie of hollow of the barn. On Cairn Toul.

**Coire Clais Bhinn*** (3, 303988), corrie of hollow of hills. Corie clash bhien (R 14). On Geallaig Hill south of Gairnshiel.

**Coire Clais Mhór*** (3, 175901), corrie of big hollow. Corie Clashmore (R 14). South-west of the Invercauld Bridge.

**Coire Craobh an Oir** (OS, 027945), locally Coire Craoibh an Òir (2, Gr, Sg, A, C), ˌkǫrˌkrɪṇˈǫˑr, corrie with (or of) the tree of the gold. Coir' craoi nor (D) and kǫrkröiˈnor (A). North-west of Derry Lodge.

**The Coire Craoibh an Oir Burn*** See Allt Coire Craoibh an Oir.

**Coire Creagach** (OS, 3, C, 944946), kǫr'krɪkɐχ, rocky corrie. A rocky and stony corrie in Glen Geusachan.

**Coire Cùl Dorch** (5, A, F, 104777), ˌkǫrˌkul'dorɐχ, corrie of dark back. Also the Cul Dorch Corrie (F), ðɪˌkul'dorɐχ'kǫre. At the head of the Baddoch, including the ground further down to the Baddoch Burn, and now covers Coire na Feadaige also.

**Coire De** See An Garbh Choire.

**Coire Dhà Thom*** (3, 273038), corrie with two hillocks. Cor-ga-Houm (I), Corr-ga-Houm (R 12). North-west of Gairnshiel.

**Coire Dhonnachaidh Taillear** (OS, 934842), corrie of tailor Duncan, locally Coire an Tàilleir (3, A, C), kǫrṇ'daˈljər, corrie of the tailor. In upper Glen Geldie.

**An Coire Dìreach** (3, U, 150806), ðɪˌkǫr'ʤiˑrɐç, the straight corrie. Coire Diridh, straight corrie (A). A narrow, long straight corrie running up a hillside north of the Cairnwell.

**(An) Coire Dubh** (OS, 2, U, 010924), ðɪˌkǫr'duˑ, the black corrie. The name was used collectively for two corries, including the one to the east at 024926. Also the Black Corries (C), ðɪ'blak'kǫrez. In Glen Luibeg.

**Coire Dubh** (3, A, 235965), kǫr'du (A). Black corrie. North-west of Crathie.

**An Coire Dubh** (3, A, C, 213858 and 222864), locally now the anglicised plural the Coire Dubhs, ðɪˌkǫre'duˑz, the black

corrie. Corrie Doos, Coireachan Dubh (A 1954) suggests Na Coireachan Dubha (3), the black corries. A collective name for two corries west of Lochnagar, respectively Muckle Coire Dubh and Little Coire Dubh.

**Coire Etchachan** (OS, 023999), from Coire Éiteachan (6), kǫr'ɐˑtʃɐχɐn, kǫr'ɐˑtjɐχɐn (F), kǫr'ɐtʃǝçǝn (C), corrie of ? expansive place. Eitachan (R 2a), Etakin, Etakan (Fi), Etagan (Mg), Etchan (V), Etichan (Gi), Ētshachan, ētsh-cheann (D). Note also Coire Aiteachan on Cairn Toul with the same pronunciation. Coire Etchachan is a corrie at the head of Glen Derry, with Loch Etchachan above it, also a well known name because of the Etchachan Club, an Aberdeen-based mountaineering club. The usual derivation is from Aitionnach = abounding in junipers, with the *n* and *ch* sounds transposed as in Ruigh-aiteachain in Glen Feshie (Mb 280). The word is pronounced in the same way in both places. Ruigh-aiteachain is certainly a place abounding in big juniper bushes, and the vegetation in Coire Etchachan has a higher proportion of dwarf juniper than any other place of similar area on the Derry beat on the Aberdeenshire side of the Cairngorms. Against this, however, is the fact that Etnach in Glen Tanar retained the original Aitionnach without transposition. Also, the word Etnach was well known in Deeside, as the Deeside Scots for juniper berries was etnach berries (Dms). Furthermore, Coire Aiteachan has no juniper. More important, the initial vowel in Etchachan, Aiteachan and Aiteachain is long, not short as in Aitionn or Aitionnach, and the *j* in the pronunciation above indicates an initial *e*, not *a*. The best fit is Éiteachan, as in Allt Chill Eiteachan, Allt Eiteachan, An Fheill Eiteachan and Tobar na h-Eiteachan in Ross-shire (W 1904). It seems improbable that transposition from Aitionnach would have occurred in all these cases, and in any case this can be rejected with Tobar na h-Eiteachan, where the word is a noun and not an adjective. Watson grouped these tentatively with Carn Éite in Ross (Carn Eige (OS)), and suggested a possible link with Éite or Éiteadh, meaning stretching or extending. Éiteach = root of burnt heath can probably be rejected; Coire Aiteachan, Loch Etchachan and Carn Eite, along with most of Coire Etchachan, are at high altitudes with such scanty vegetation that a heather fire would scarcely be possible. Éiteag = white quartz stone does not fit any of the places, as none of them has white stones in abundance. Watson's suggestion of a link with Éite or Éiteadh seems quite likely, giving Etchachan as Éiteachan or extending place (i.e. expansive or with much space). This fits all the Etchachan cases well; Coire Etchachan is a big spacious corrie and Loch Etchachan also imparts a feeling of great space, as does Coire Aiteachan. Ruigh-aiteachain lies on an expansive flattish tract along the bottom of Glen Feshie, beside an unusually wide and long flood-plain of shingle. Carn Eite is the highest hill in Ross-shire, and Allt Eiteachan and Tobar na h-Eiteachan are also places giving a sense of great space.

**(The) Coire Etchachan Burn** (OS, C, 030997), ðɪˌkǫr'ɐtʃǝçǝn 'bʌrn. Also Allt Coire Éiteachan (6, U), ˌaltˌkǫr'ɐˑtʃɐχɐn, burn of corrie of ? expansive place. In the above corrie.

**Coire Féith Ghille*** (3, U, 238870), ˌkǫrˌfe'hil, corrie of bog-stream of the lad. On Lochnagar.

**Coire Fhearneasg** (OS, 108810), should be Coire Bhearn-uisge (3, F), kǫr'vjarnǝʃ, corrie of the water gap. Cor Vyarn Uishk (I). See Allt Coire Fhearneasg. Up the Baddoch.

**Coire Fionn** (OS, 160787, should be at 161772 going north as far as 161782), should be Am Fionn-choire (3, C), ðɪ'fjançǝre, the white corrie. Fyaun-na-Chorry (I), Fiean Chorrie (R 14), Fian Chory (V), Fionn Choire (M, A). Also the Horseshoe Corrie (F), ðɪ'hǫrs'ʃu'kǫre, because of its shape. A cold, north-facing corrie on the Glas Maol, with much pale grass, holding deep snow in early summer.

**Coire Gharbh-uillt** (OS, 2, 979911), corrie of the rough burn. On Beinn Bhrotain.

**Coire Ghiuthais** (OS, 172863), corrie of the fir. Tom Giubhais is nearby. In lower Glen Callater.

**(An) Coire Glas** (OS, 3, F, 251878), ðɪˌkɔrˈglas, the green corrie. The Coire Glas east of Carn Liath (A) is obviously an error for the Coire Glas at 251878 east of Creag Liath. In Glen Gelder.

**The Coire Glas Burn**\* See Allt a' Ghlas-choire.

**(An) Coire Gorm** (OS, 3, F, 173879), ðɪˌkɔrˈgɔrɔm, the green corrie. This name covers two corries, Wester Coire Gorm at 173879 and Easter Coire Gorm to the north at 167883. Wester Corry Goram (I). Translated as blue corrie (A) but the place has green grassy patches on an otherwise dark heathery hillside. In lower Glen Callater.

**An Coire Gorm**\* (2, C, 062966), as above, the green corrie. Has a wide strip of green in summer, due to predominant mat grass growing on a notable snow-accumulation area. On Beinn Bhreac above the Dubh-Ghleann.

**(An) Coire Gorm** (OS, 2, C, 085973), as above, the green corrie. A grassy corrie that stands out against the bare, gravelly, surrounding slopes; it is grassy for the same reason as above. On Beinn a' Bhuird.

**Coire Gorm** (OS, 314787), green corrie. A grassy high corrie south of Loch Muick.

**Coire Iain Daibhidh**\* (2, U, 123874), ˌkɔrˈiənˈdevi, corrie of Ian Davy. South-east of Corriemulzie.

**Coire Laoigh** See Newbigging.

**Coire Lic** (3, U, 290018), kɔrˈlik, corrie at a slope. Cor Liechk (I), Corleek or Corry-leichk (D). A corrie on a uniform slope, without the usual hollow. At Gairnshiel.

**The Coire Lic Burn**\* See Allt Coire Lic.

**Coire Lochan nan Eun** (OS, 3, C, 230856), ˌkɔrˌlɔχənənˈjeˑn, corrie of lochs of the birds. The plural Lochan or lochs is not an error for Loch nan Eun, as the present Sandy Loch was formerly also called Loch nan Eun (R 7). West of Lochnagar.

**Coire Loch Kander** (OS, 189810), locally Coire Ceanndair or Ceanndobhair (3, C), kɔrˈkjandër, corrie of head-water. Gaelic kyaunder, cyanner (D). See Loch Kander. In upper Glen Callater.

**Coire Meacan** (OS, 405922), should be Coire Muilcinn (4, C), kɔrˈmulʃən, (kɔreˈmɛlhən (A)), corrie of baldmoney (a plant flowering in grassy spots on the hill). Corimialachin, Corrymealachin (Io 17, 60a), Corremealachine (Ri 29), Cornamalchone, Correnmalchen (Dms 6), Coire Melhen (A). Above Etnach in upper Glen Tanar.

**Coire Mhallachaidh**\* (3, 224948), corrie of the cursing. Cor Valachie (I). Near the Inver.

**Coire Mhiadain** (3, U, 157984), kɔrˈvitən, corrie of the green. Cor Viaten (I), Cor-viatan (vee-atan) (A). South of Ben Avon.

**The Coire Mhiadain Burn** See Allt Coire Mhiadain.

**Coire Mhon Ruaidh**\* (3, 136864), corrie of the red hill. Cor Von Ruie (I). Now anglicised to Coire Munro (U), ˌkɔreˌmʌnˈro. In mid Glen Clunie.

**Coire Mhuillidh** (3, U, 113890), kɔrˈvuˑlji, corrie of the mill, i.e. fit for driving a mill. Corrymulie (Im 3). The corrie that gave the name to the nearby houses of Corriemulzie.

**Coire Mòine Beag** (3, A, 095815), kɔrˈmon with palatal *n* (A), little corrie of peat-moss. Also was probably Coire Shìos na Mòine, down corrie of peat-moss, pairing with name below. See also Coireachan Dubha. In upper Glen Ey.

**Coire Mòine Mór** (3, A, 085805), see name above, big corrie of

peat-moss. Also Coire Shuas na Mòine (3), up corrie of the peat-moss. Corie-huas-na-moan (Io 79). In upper Glen Ey.

**(An) Coire Mór** (OS, 2, U, 986993, 980996 on OS 1869), ðɪˌkɔr ˈmoːr, the big corrie. Also Coire Mór na Làirige (3), big corrie of the pass. Coire mhor na Lairige (Gordon 1921). On Ben Macdui, above Lairig Ghru.

**An Coire Mór**\* (3, 365985), the big corrie. Currymore (G 19), the Corriemore (Io 20). Now the Balmenach Corrie (U), ðɪˌbɛlˈmɛnɐχˈkɔre. Pairs with An Coire Beag, near Pass of Ballater.

**Coire Mor na Lairige** See Coire Mor.

**The Coire Muilcinn Burn** See the Burn of Coire Meacan.

**Coire na Caillich** (OS, 2, F, 080833), ˌkɔrnɐˈkaləç, now sometimes ˌkɔrnɐˈkɛiləç, corrie of the old woman. The old woman is the rock of A' Chailleach below this corrie in upper Glen Ey.

**Coire na Camaig**\* (3, 262042), corrie of the Camag or crook. Cor-na-Camaik (I). North-west of Gairnshiel. The Camag (anglicised Camock) is an old drove road from Sleach on Gairn over to Cock Bridge on Don.

**Coire na Cìche** (OS, 3, C, 098985), ˌkɔrnɐˈkiç, corrie of the pap, referring to the rock A' Chioch. Cor-na-Keich (I). On Beinn a' Bhuird.

**Coire na Cìche** (OS, 3, C, 269867), as above, corrie of the pap. Cor na Keich (B). North-east of the Meikle Pap on Lochnagar.

**The Coire na Ciche Burn**\* (F, 270870), ðɪˌkɔrnɐˈkiçˈbʌrn. In the above corrie.

**Coire na Cloiche** (OS, 3, 281023), corrie of the stone. Cornacloich (D). North-west of Gairnshiel.

**Coire na Cloiche** (OS, 027967), should be Coire nan Clach (2, A, C), ˌkɔrnɐˈglaˑχ, corrie of the stones. Coir' na glach (D). The most stony corrie in Glen Derry.

**Coire na Cloiche** (OS, 3, A, 183006), kɔrnɐˈkloəç (A), corrie of the stone. A big boulder stands on the upper rim of this corrie on Culardoch.

**Coire na Cloiche** (3, A, C, 305900), ˌkɔrnɐˈklɔiç, corrie of the stone. A corrie in Glen Girnock with boulders on its rim.

**The Coire na Cloiche Burn**\* See Allt Coire na Cloiche.

**The Coire na Cloiche Burn** See Allt Coire na Cloiche.

**Coire na Còinnich** (3, Wa, 174810), corrie of the moss. More evidence under Allt Coire na Coinnich. Cor-na-Cuanich (I), Corr na Cuanich (R 13). On Carn an Tuirc south of Loch Callater.

**Coire na Còrr-thulaich**\* (4, 144883), corrie of the Coldrach or of the great hillock. Coire na Corr-thulaich is not classic Gaelic form, but Diack noted one Gaelic pronunciation of the Coldrach as masculine and two as feminine, indicating the break-down of the language. Cor na-Coldrich (I). Possibly was Coire nan Còrra-thulach, corrie of the great hillocks. Also the Coldrach Corrie (F), ðɪˈkoldrɔçˈkɔre. See the Coldrach. In lower Glen Clunie.

**Coire na Creige**\* (3, U, corrie probably at 242928), ˌkɔrnɐˈkreg, corrie of the rock. Cornacraig (Opr 47a), the Crofts and Cornacraig (Ra 7). A former habitation south-west of Balmoral, possibly same as Cinn na Creige.

**Coire na Cuairte**\* (3, F, 953827), ˌkɔrnɐˈkuərst, corrie of the circle. Caochan na Cuairte makes a semi-circular loop as it runs out of this corrie at the head of Bynack Burn.

**Coire na Culath**\* See Coire Clachach.

**Coire na Cùlath**\* (5, F, 008899), ˌkɔrnɐˈkulɐ, corrie of the back place. In mid Glen Dee.

**Coire na Culath** See Corrie Cula.

**The Coire na Culath Burn** See Cula Burn.

**Coire na Feadaige**\* (3, 112776), corrie of the golden plover. Cor-na-Faitack (I). West of the Cairnwell.

**Coire na Fìonaige*** (3), corrie of the crowberry. Corrienafionick (Me 5). A former grazing in Glen Gelder.

**Coire na Fuath-chlais** (4, C, 131894), ˌkọrnɐˈfuɐˌçlɐʃ, corrie of the spectre hollow. Coire-na-fua'-chlash (Mp). A corrie south-west of Braemar, mistakenly printed Coire nam Muc (OS). The Clais referred to may be the rocky furrow at 130901, which leads into the corrie from the east.

**Coire na h-Eaglais** (3, A, U, 304974), ˌkọrnɐˈhɛklɪʃ, corrie of the church. Cor-na-Hecklish (I), Coreklish (D), Corr Eaglais (A). The church is the former Chapel Ma-Dheoir east of Crathie.

**Coire na h-Easgainne Fraoich** (3, F, 024975), ˌkọrnɐˌhɛskən ˈfru ç, corrie of the heather boglet. Coire Easgann Fhraoich, corrie of the eel of the heather, i.e. lizard (Sg 1948). On Derry Cairngorm.

**Coire na h-Oisinn** (OS, 3, F, 280912), ˌkọrnɐˈhoʃən, corrie of the nook. Cornahoshan (Cp), Cornyhoshan (In). In upper Glen Girnock.

**The Coire na h-Oisinn Burn*** See Allt Coire na h-Oisinn.

**Coire na Làirige** (2, F, 967001), ˌkọrnɐˈlaːrɪk, corrie of the hill pass. In the Lairig Ghru. Coire Ruadh is the name by people on the Mar side, and Coire na Lairige by people on the Spey side. Coire an Lairig (Al).

**Coire na Lairige** (OS, 3, C, 126840), ˌkọrnɐˈlaˑrɪg, corrie of the hill pass. Cor-na-Larick (I). Also McHardy's Corrie (F), mɐk ˈardizˌkọre, after a former keeper who lived at the house of Coirenalarig. The hill pass was an old track from Coirenalarig over to Glen Ey.

**Coirenalarig** (OS, C, 136836), as above. From Coire na Làirige, see above name. Cornilarick (Fa), Corrinlarge, Coirrinlairg, Corrinlairg (Cr 8, 27, 31), Cornalarick (I, R 14). A former farm in upper Glen Clunie.

**The Coirenalarig Brig*** (C, 136834), ðɪˌkọrnɐˈlaˑrɪgˈbrɪg. A bridge in Glen Clunie.

**The Coirenalarig Haughs*** (F, 140840), ðɪˌkọrnɐˈlaˑrɪgˈhaˑχs. Formerly the Haugh of Coirenalarig. The Haugh of Cornalairg (Io 65). A big stretch of flat grassland in Glen Clunie.

**Coire na Loinne*** (3, 212961), corrie of the enclosure. Cor-na-line (I). The Loin is a former farm below the corrie, north-west of the Inver.

**Coire na Meanneasg** (OS, 139873), should be Coire na Mion-easga or Coire nam Mion-easg (3, F), ˌkọrnɐˈminəsk, (kɔrna ˈmɛnəs with palatal *n* (A)), corrie of the little bog or of the little bogs. Cor-na-minesk (I). In mid Glen Clunie.

**Coire nam Fiadh*** (3, 095857), corrie of the deer. Corri ne fiey (Fa), Corrynafiach (Roy), Cornafea (Me 8). A former farm in Glen Ey, named from the corrie above it (Coire an Fheidh (OS), which should be Coire nam Fiadh).

**Coire nam Freumh** (OS, 3, U, 282037), ˌkọrnɐˈvrev, (kɔrnaˈvreu (A)), corrie of the roots. Cor-na-Freaue (I), Corr na Freaue, Cor na Freaue (R 12, 14), Cornavraeive (D). North-west of Gairnshiel.

**Coire nam Freumh** (OS, 122869), should be Coire nan Ràgh (3, C), ˌkọrnənˈraːɣ (U), ˌkọrnənˈraˑ ŋ, (kɔrnənˈrau with nasal *r* (A)), corrie of the rafts (i.e. tree roots, note A 221). Curnarau (Io 79), Corronarrou, Coronorau, Corinaraw (Me 3, 3, 9). Cor nan dhrau, nan ragh (D). South-east of Corriemulzie.

**Coire nam Monadh*** (4, ?258979), corrie of the moors. Possibly Coirean Monaidh, little corrie of moor. Cormomoney, Cornomomy, Commomony (Io 14, 17, 74). In old legal papers went with Blairglass north of Crathie.

**Coire nam Muc** (OS, 2, C, 131894, should be at 136902, 131894 is Coire na Fuath-chlais), ˌkọrnɐˈmuk (C), ˌkọrnɐˈmuχk (Sch, U), corrie of the pigs. Cornamuc (Me 3). West of Braemar.

**The Coire nam Muc Birk Wuid** (C, 135905), ðɪˌkọrnɐˈmukˈbërk ˈwɪd, or the Coire nam Muc Wuid (C). Corino-muck silva (Go), wood of Corrynamuk (Mc 3). West of Braemar.

**Coire nam Muillear** (3, 268045), corrie of the millers. Cor na Mhu luir (I), Corr-na-Mhuluir, Cor-na-mhuiluir (R 12, 14), Coire na ma Lui-yer (D). Carn Clach-mhuilinn, hill of millstone, is nearby. North-west of Gairnshiel.

**Coire na Mòine*** (3, U, 103943), ˌkọrnɐˈmọn, corrie of the peat-moss. In Glen Quoich.

**Coire na Mòine*** (3, 133859), corrie of the peat-moss. Cor-na-moin (I). In mid Glen Clunie.

**Coire na Mòine*** (3), corrie of the peat-moss. Corry na moan (Roy). Shown covering the two corries Coire Moine Beag and Coire Moine Mor in upper Glen Ey.

**Coire na Mucraich*** (3, 223962), now Coire Mucraich (C), kọr ˈmukrɐç, corrie of the pig place. Cor-na-muchrie (I). Now commonly used to refer to the hill behind, at about 218967 and to the east. North of the Inver.

**Coire na Muice*** (3, U, 233040), ˌkọrnɐˈmëk, corrie of the pig. Near Corndavon Lodge.

**Coire nan Cìchean*** (3, U, 261864), ˌkọrnɐˈkiçən, corrie of the paps, with Cichean probably a variant genitive plural. Below the Meikle Pap on Lochnagar.

**Coire nan Clach** (OS, 3, A, U, 096002), ˌkọrnɐˈglaχ, corrie of the stones. Also the Stony Corrie (U), ðɪˈstoneˈkọre. A stone-filled corrie on Beinn a' Bhuird.

**Coire nan Coinnlean*** (4, U, 115843), ˌkọrnaˈgɔnlən, corrie of the fir candles (i.e. fir roots), with Coinnlean probably a variant genitive plural. In mid Glen Ey.

**Coire nan Craobh-bheithe*** (3, F, 220847), ˌkọrnɐˈkruˑvi, corrie of the birch trees. A corrie west of Lochnagar, with the burn Allt an Da Chraobh Bheath running out of it.

**Coire nan Imireachan** (OS, 3, U, 337044), ˌkọrnɐnˈimrəçən, corrie of the ridges. See Allt Coire nan Imireachan. West of Morven.

**Coire nan Roinn** (5, probably 275992, by elimination), corrie of the divisions. Corynynraun, Corrynynrawan (Me 3), Corrinrawns, Corrynanraw (Io 14), Corrynynrawne (Mc 5). Near Gairnshiel.

**Coire nan Taillear** See Coire Clach nan Taillear.

**Coire na Poite*** (3, F, 284850), ˌkọrnɐˈpọtʃ, corrie of the pot. South-west of Allt-na-giubhsaich near Loch Muick.

**Coire na Poite** (OS, 2, C, 003949), as above, corrie of the pot. Corrapot (Fi). In Glen Luibeg.

**The Coire na Poite Burn*** (U, 010947), ðɪˌkọrnɐˈpọtʃˈbʌrn. In the above corrie.

**Coire na Saobhaidh** (OS, 2, C, 027957), ˌkọrnɐˈsʊvi (U), ˌkọrnɐˈsiˑvi (C), corrie of the fox's den. In Glen Derry.

**Coire na Saobhaidhe** (OS, 3, C, 246867), kọrn̩ˈsɪvi, corrie of the fox's den. Has been anglicised to Coire Fox (U) in the past, ˌkọreˈfọks. On the north side of Lochnagar.

**The Coire na Saobhaidh Burn*** (U, 030957), ðɪˌkọrnɐˈsiviˈbʌrn. In Glen Derry.

**Coire na Sgreuchaig** (OS, 3, A, 143893), kɔrnaˈskrekɐç and krɔnəˈskrehək (A), corrie of the screeching one (e.g. the owl). Also Coire Allt Sgreuchaig (3, U), ˌkọrˌaltˈskreçək. Cor-na-Scraichaig (I), Coir allt sgreuchag (D). South of Braemar.

**(An) Coire Odhar** (OS, 2, C, 971956), n̩ˌkọrˈau.ər (U), ðɪˌkọ ˈrʌur (C), the dun corrie. Coroor (Fi). On Cairn Toul.

**An Coire Odhar*** (3, F, 148779), as above, the dun corrie. Cor Our (I). East of the Cairnwell.

**An Coire Odhar*** (3, U, 092779), as above, the dun corrie. At the head of Baddoch Burn.

**Coire of Corn Arn** (OS, 397944), from the Corrie o Coire an Eirbhein (3, C), ðɪˈkọreɐˌkọrn̩ˈern̩, a repetitive anglicisation which has arisen probably because kọrˈnern̩ is now used for the hill behind, and not for the corrie. See Corrienearn. South-east of Ballater.

**Coire Poll Randaidh** (OS, 245051), from Coire Poll Ranntaich (3, C), ˌkɔrˌpɒlˈranti, corrie of divided pool (the pools in the corrie are on flat ground close to the Strathdon march). Corr-pol-Ranntich (Ro), Cor-Pol-Rauntie (I), Corr Pol Rauntich, Cor'n-pol-Rauntie (R 12, 14). North-west of Gairnshiel.

**Coire Preas Dubh\*** (3, 319989), corrie of dark copse. Corry of Press Du (I), Corie press dhu (R 14). North of Coilacriech.

**(An) Coire Ruadh** (OS, 2, U, 967001), ðɪˌkɔrˈruɐ, the red corrie. In the Lairig Ghru. Called Coire na Lairige by people on the Spey side of the Cairngorms.

**Coire Ruairidh** (OS, 2, C, 083003), kɔˈruɐre, Rory's corrie. Sometimes given a repetitive anglicisation to the Coire Ruairidh Corrie (U), ðɪˌkɔˈruɐreˈkɔre. On Beinn a' Bhuird.

**Coire Sean\*** (3, 217041), old corrie. Corry Shin (R 12). Also the Shenalt Corrie (F), ðɪˈʃɛnɒltˈkɔre. The Easter Shenalt (i.e. Sean-allt) runs out of this corrie north-west of Corndavon.

**Coire Sgòran** (3, 142902), corrie with little peak, or Coire Sgòrain = corrie of little peak. Coir' sguran (D). On north side of Morrone, near a rock called An Sgoran.

**Coire Sputan Dearg** (OS, 2, M, C, 005987), ˌkɔrˌsputɐnˈdʒɛrək, classic form would be Coire Spùt Dearga, corrie of red spouts. Corryspouten darrick (Roy). Coir' na sput yerrk (D) and Corr-spoot-yerrick (A), kɔrsputˈyɛrək (A), indicate Coire an Spùta Dheirg and Coire Spùta Dheirg, corrie of the red spout. Corr-spootan-jerrick (A) indicates Coire Spùtan Dearga, corrie with red spouts. A corrie on Ben Macdui with red-tinged screes in its widest gullies.

**Coire Sùilean Dubha\*** (3, F, 097934), ˌkɔrˌsuln̩ˈdu, corrie with black eyes (i.e. springs). In Glen Quoich.

**The Coire Suilean Dubha Burn** See Allt Coire Suilean Dubha.

**Coire Uchdain** (3), corrie of hillock. Carrieauchtane (Bul). A former croft at Lary in Glen Gairn.

**Coire Uilleim Mhóir** (OS, 3, U, 229824), ˌkɔrˌwɛləmˈmoʳr, corrie of Muckle Willie. Also Muckle Willie's Corrie (C), ˈmʌkəlˈwɛlezˈkɔre. McConnochie's (1891) story about the murder of Muckle Willie was later retracted by him (Cj 12, 14). West of Loch Muick.

**Coire Yaltie** (OS, 131852), from Coire Ghealtaidh (6, C), kɔr ˈjalti (Sch, C), (kɔrˈjɛlti (A)), corrie of ? the white place (see Allt a' Choire Yaltie). Cor Yaultie (I), Cor altie (R 14), Cor-yallti (D), Corr yelti (D in A). In Glen Clunie.

**Coireyaltie** (OS, C, 142854), as above. Corghealtie (Io 52), Corgaltie (Crg 6), Coirghealty (Opr 32), Cor Yaultie (I), Corie alte (R 14). A former farm below the above corrie.

**Coit an t-Seachrain\*** (3, probably 23-93-), boat of the wandering. Coytintechran (Io 18). A piece of farmland on the former Mill Croft of Inver, presumably beside a boat on Dee.

**Coldrach** (OS, C, 239952), ðɪˈkoldrəç, see name below. Both names changed by metathesis. Coirlarach, Cordlach, Coldrach, Corlarach, Corlaroch (Io 11, 18, 25, 47, 65), Coldrach of Munaltrie (G 21), Colrach (Aj 6), Collrach (Opr 1b, c), Collarach, Corlarich (Opr 1d, e). Former farm north of the Inver.

**The Coldrach** (C, 152883), as above, from An Còrr-thulach (4), the great hillock. Corlarache (Me) in 1699. The origin and changes in this name are evident (Cr):—Cordillach in 1705, 1718, 1721, 1725; Coirluch in 1726; Corrlach in 1723 and 1727. Corlaroch in 1752 (Io); Corlarach 1723, 1758 (Opr); Collorach 1768 (Io). Corlerach (Fa), Corlorak (ASr), Corlaroch, Colrach (Ri 25, 31), Corlarach (R 1), Coldrach (I), Coldrach (R 14), Goldroch (Md 1); in Gaelic N golldrach, chollrich, a chorlraich (D), the first masculine and the other two feminine, an uncertainty suggesting the

breakdown of the language (D), ˈgɔldrɐχ (Sch) suggests eclipsis after the article An. The Coldrach is a general name for the area as well as for a former farm in lower Glen Clunie (see Mains of the Coldrach).

**The Coldrach Brae\*** (F, 154886), ðɪˈkoldrəçˈbreˑ. A hill on a road in Glen Clunie.

**The Coldrach Brig** (C, 152882), ðɪˈkoldrəçˈbrɪg. Bridge of the Coldrach (Io 14), Coldrach Bridge (Bg). A road bridge in lower Glen Clunie.

**(The) Coldrach Burn** (OS, C, 231957), ðɪˈkoldrəçˈbʌrn. North of the Inver.

**(The) Coldrach Burn** (OS, C, 140881), as above. In lower Glen Clunie.

**The Coldrach Corrie\*** See Coire na Corra-thulaich.

**Coldrach North\*** (U, east of 154888), ˈkoldrəçˈnɔrθ. A field in Glen Clunie.

**The Coldrach Pot\*** (C, 154882), ðɪˈkoldrəçˈpɒt, Scots Pot = deep pool. A rocky pool on the lower Clunie Water.

**The Coldrach Pot Brig\*** (F, west of 154882), ðɪˈkoldrəçˈpɒtˈbrɪg. Former footbridge on Clunie.

**The Coldrach Plantin\*** (F, 153887), ðɪˈkoldrəçˈplantɪn. A plantation south of Braemar.

**Coldrach South\*** (U, 154885), ˈkoldrəçˈsuθ. A field in Glen Clunie including the former field Creit an Easa and other land.

**Coldrach West\*** (U, 152884), ˈkoldrəçˈwɛst. A field in Glen Clunie.

**Colin's Brig\*** (U, 171851), ˈkɔlɛnzˈbrɪg. In Glen Callater.

**Collie's Brae\*** (C, west of 150915), ˈkɔlezˈbreˑ. A hill on a road beside Collie's former shop in Braemar.

**Colonel Jock's\*** See The Auld Toll House.

**The Colonel's Basin** (Brow, 087871). A smooth hollow stone in the bed of the stream at the Colonel's Bed in Glen Ey.

**The Colonel's Bed** (OS, C, 087871), ðɪˈkʌrnəlzˈbɛd. Also Leabaidh Choirneil (2, JB), ˌljɛpeˈχʌrnəl, bed of the colonel. A rocky shelf in lower Glen Ey.

**Colonel's Cave** (OS, 080884). Near Inverey.

**The Colonel's Cave** (C, 087871), ðɪˈkʌrnəlzˈkeˑv. Farquharson's Cave (Mg). The Rebel's Cave (Ke). Cave holding the Colonel's Bed in Glen Ey.

**The Commando Bivvies\*** (U, 990988), ðɪˌkəˈmandoˈbɪviz. Numerous stone bivouacs between top of Ben Macdui and Sappers' Bothy, made by Commandos in 1942–44.

**The Commando Brig\*** (C, 135912), ðɪˌkəˈmandoˈbrɪg. Site of a footbridge west of Braemar, made by Commandos about 1944.

**The Commutation Road** (Gf, 268952). Part of the old North Deeside Road east of Crathie, and also part of the Kirk Road from Wester Micras. Commutation roads were paid for by an early type of rate assessment, based on commuting the statute labour of residents into a sum proportional to their annual rental. Part of the Commutation Road also ran on the line of the present main road from Mill of Inver to just east of Invercauld Bridge; there it cut south of the house opposite the private gates to Invercauld, and on to the Bridge of Dee.

**Conachcraig** (OS, 285872), from Conachreag (3, C), ˈkɔnɐχrek, high rocks, or combination of rocks (note W 1904, 91). Conachrek (D). Alexander was mistaken in putting the stress on the last syllable, as in kɔnəˈhrɛk (1952), and connach CREK (1954). A big hill in upper Glen Muick, with broken cliffs and some small rocks on the lower slopes, and with small tors and rocky patches on its several hilltops, so either of the two meanings suggested would fit.

**The Conical Hillocks\*** (C, 205895), ðɪˈkɔnəkəlˈhɛlɛks. In Ballochbuie Forest.

**The Conical Hillocks*** (F, 185872), as above. At the top of Glen Beg, south of Ballochbuie Forest.

**The Connachat Brig*** (F, 218919), ðɪˈkɔnɐχɐtˈbrɪg. A bridge west of Balmoral.

**(The) Connachat Burn** (OS, C, 222916), from Còinneachaig (3), ðɪˈkɔnɐχɐtˈbʌrn, (ˈkɔnjòhat (A)), mossy place. March Burn of Cainnachaig (Im 3), Burn of Coinachaig (R 7), Kynachack (Ri 17). Also often known locally as the Bealach Buidhe Burn (F), ðɪˌbalɐçˈbuiˈbʌrn. A burn running through a peaty forest-bog south-west of the Inver.

**Connachat Cottage** (OS, C, 217919), usually the Connachat locally, ðɪˈkɔnɐχɐt. Coinachaig (R 7), Coinachag (Io 77). Also often known locally as the Bealach Buidhe (see Am Bealach Buidhe).

**The Connie Burn** See Allt Connie.

**The Conservancy Plots*** (C, 034935, 042943, 040939, 039954), ðɪ ˌkɔnˈsɛrvɐnsiˈplɔts. Deer-proof fences put up to encourage natural regeneration of trees in Glen Derry.

**The Coo and the Calf** (F, 274945), ðɪˈku.ənðɪˈkɑ·f. A pool in Dee near Crathie, named after a big and a little stone projecting out of the water.

**The Coo Hill** (A, C, 162903), ðɪˈkuˈhël. The Cow Hill (Ale, A). The lower part of Carn nan Sgliat next to Braemar.

**Cook's Park*** (I, 154923). Note 'Mr Cook for the Big Park' near Braemar Castle (Rli 19).

**The Coolah** (OS, 112768), ðɪˈkulɐ, from A' Chùlath (5, D), the back place. Chula (D). A little plateau west of the Cairnwell, mostly on the Perthshire side but comes up to the Aberdeenshire boundary.

**Cooper's Gate*** (U, 305875), ˈkupɐrzˈget. At edge of a wood in upper Glen Muick.

**Cooper's Hut*** (C, 148800 on west side of road), ˈkupɐrzˈhʌt. Former hut near Cairnwell, used by a Rhynie sheep farmer.

**The Coos' Park*** (U, 217943), ðɪˈkuzˈpark, Scots Coo = cow. West of Inver, probably same as Chapel Park.

**The Coos' Park*** (U, 353920), as above. A field in lower Glen Muick, includes the former field of An Dubh-bhruach.

**The Coos' Park*** (U, 303919), as above. A field in Glen Girnock.

**The Coos' Roadie** (Dug). A former path from Ballater village through the wood to Monaltrie, probably about where the railway station was later built, and leading to what is now the Cinder Path.

**Corbie Bush*** (R 4, 381972), Scots Corbie = crow, rook. North-east of Ballater.

**Corbie Craw*** (F, south-west of 417038), ˈkɔrbiˈkraː, Scots = carrion crow. A hillock west of Logie Coldstone.

**The Corbie Craw Park*** (U, 416038), ðɪˈkɔrbiˈkraˈpark. A field beside the above hillock.

**Corby Hall** (OS, 299955), ˈkɔrbiˈha: (C), ˈkɔrbiˈha·χ (C), from Scots Corbie = crow, Haugh = riverside-field. May have referred to rooks, which have had a rookery nearby since at least 1890. Corby Ha' (Mi), Corbiehaugh (private road-sign pointing to house). Houses east of Abergeldie.

**Corby Hall*** (F, 295954), as above. Also East Park (Am), and the Lower Haugh (U), ðɪˈloɐrˈha·χ. A field at Abergeldie.

**The Corby Hall Burn*** (F, 296954), ðɪˈkɔrbiˈha·ˈbʌrn or ðɪˈkɔrbi ˈha·χˈbʌrn (F). Near Abergeldie.

**The Corby Hall Puil** (F, 298955), ðɪˈkɔrbiˈha·ˈpil. Corbyhaugh (P), Corbie Ha (A), Corbie's Haugh (Sc). In Dee east of Abergeldie Castle.

**The Corn Arn Burn** See Burn of Corn Arn.

**Corndavon** (C), kɔrn̩ˈdavɐn, ˌkɔrɐn̩ˈda·vɐn (U), a general name for a big area centred on Corndavon Lodge (see below). For derivation see Coire an Da Bheinn.

**(The) Corndavon Burn** (OS, C, 228025), ðɪˌkɔrn̩ˈdavɐnˈbʌrn.

Also Allt Coire an Dà Bheinn (3), burn of corrie of the two hills. Ault Corn Davin (R 12), including the lowest part beside Corndavon Lodge, which is also now the Kennel Burn. West of Gairnshiel.

**Corndavon Burn** (OS, 245034), an error for Corndoun Burn (OS 1869), from Coirean Domhain Burn. Allt Meadhonach (3), middle burn, is the lower part of this burn. Ald meanoch (R 3). North-west of Gairnshiel.

**Corndavon Lodge** (OS, C, 228021), kɔrn̩ˈdavɐnˈlɔdʒ. West of Gairnshiel.

**The Corndavon Wuid*** (C, 227022), ðɪˌkɔrn̩ˈdavɐnˈwɪd. A wood at Corndavon, now mostly gone.

**Corn Eilean** (4, C, a general name for the fields north-east of Ballater that lie about half way between Monaltrie House and Eastfield of Monaltrie), kɔrnˈɛlən, horn or bend of riverside-fields. Conellan, Cornellan (Io 58, 69), Coirneilain (Cpb 5), Cornellan (M). A map in 1790 (R 4) shows Conellan as a small area at 379971, and Conellan Park as the entire field (which still exists) centred on 377968; the two were separated by a stretch of moory or marshy ground. This poor ground is shown clearly on this map as a big horn extending from just west of the present Ballater sewage works north to the Ballater Burn and then round by Eastfield of Monaltrie back to the present course of Dee just west of a big island at 388967. The map says 'Swampy, covered with Bushes, presumed old Tract of the Dee'. Much of the course of this horn is still marshy, permanently so along the Ballater Burn, and parts of the fields alongside it still become waterlogged in wet weather. The river obviously flowed along this horn formerly, and there is a pair of Eileans or riverside-fields opposite one another, on either side of the horn. The Con of Conellan was possibly an error for Corn in the map; certainly Con-eilean meaning high Eileans or combination of Eileans can be rejected, as the emphasis then would have been on Con, and not, as it is, on the *Ei* of Eilean. Abercorn in Linlithgow 'is the only derivative of *corn*, a horn which has survived in Scotland' (W 461), but this may be another. However, Corran was pronounced Corn in Braemar Gaelic (Dro), so Corran = a sickle, point of land, is a possibility. Within living memory, Cornellan was a separate farm attached to the Invercauld Arms Hotel, with the steading just west of 372956, locally called the Steading (C), ðɪˈstɛdən, but is now part of Eastfield. The farm was often called the Hotel Ferm (C), ðɪˈhəˈtɛlˈfɛrm.

**The Cornice Run** (Sd, 161771). A ski run on the Glas Maol.

**The Corn Rigs of the Branndair*** (374026). 'Ground above that rode that has the form of Cornrigs is called the Corn Riggs of the Brander' (Io 20). South of Morven.

**The Cornyard Bittie*** (U, 354942), ðɪˈkɔrnˈjardˈbëte. A raised patch of ground in lower Glen Muick.

**The Cornyard Park*** (U, 419032), ðɪˈkɔrn̩ˈjardˈpark. A field near Logie Coldstone.

**The Cornyard Park*** (U, north of 414038), as above. Now amalgamated with the Corbie Craw Park. A field west of Logie Coldstone.

**Corrach** (OS, 407877), should be An Coireleach (3, C), ðɪ ˈkɔrlɐχ, ? the corrie place. Corlach (Mg), the Corlach (D, A). A big corrie on the north side of Mount Keen, so probably derived from Coire = corrie.

**Corrach Diùbhaidh*** (5), ? useless bog. Corrauchdeū (G 8). A former croft near Bridge of Gairn on east side of Gairn.

**Corrie Burn** (OS, 330923), lower part now the Fountain Burn (C), ðɪˈfʌuntɪnˈbʌrn. Also Burn of Dubh-choire. Burn of Duckery (Am). In lower Glen Muick.

**The Corrie Burn*** (F, 419954), ðɪˈkɔreˈbʌrn. Above Ballaterach, south of Cambus o' May.

The derelict farm of Glen Fenzie near the Glen Gairn–Corgarff road has been deserted since the 1920s.

Still a farm, Tomnakeist lies near the North Deeside Road east of Ballater, with the old workings of the Cambus Quarries behind.

**Corrie Chash** (OS, 260813 is wrong location, should be 264814), from Coire Chàis (3, C), ko̱r'ha·ʃ, corrie of the difficulty. Also Coire Chreag Chàis (3), corrie of rocks of the difficulty. Corri Chraig Caise (R 6), Corri chrag Chais (Im 1), Cor Chaash (I). A steep corrie at the top of Loch Muick.

**(The) Corrie Chash Burn** (OS, C, 267816), ðɪˌko̱r'ha·ʃ'bʌrn. Also Allt Coire Chàis (3, A), altko̱re'haʃ (A), burn of corrie of the difficulty. In the above corrie.

**Corrie Cula** (OS, 187995), from Coire na Cùlath (5, U), ˌko̱rnɐ'kulɐ, corrie of the back place. Cor na Cula (A 283). South of Loch Builg.

**Corrie Feragie** (OS, C, 160912), ˌko̱re'ferəgi, from Coire Feuragaidh (3), grassy corrie (? from A' Feurachaidh = grazing or feeding), ko̱r'fe̱rɐgi (Sch). Cor Feragie (I), Corrie Fergie (A), Coire ferigi (D in A). A grassy corrie, now mostly under planted trees, beside Braemar village.

**Corrie Feragie** (OS, 155910), as above. Corfergie, Corrifergy (Io 75). A former house (1832) near Braemar, now a youth hostel on this site.

**The Corrie Feragie Burn\*** See Allt Coire Feuragaidh.

**The Corrie Feragie Pond\*** (C, 162914), ðɪˌko̱re'ferəgi'po̱nd. Beside Braemar.

**The Corrie Feragie Wuid** (C, 158911), ðɪˌko̱re'ferəgi'wɪd. The Wood of Coripherige (Ri 27). Near Braemar.

**Corriemulzie** (OS, C, 112892), ˌko̱re'mu·lji, but usually now ˌko̱re'mulzi, from Coire Mhuillidh (3, F), ko̱r'vu·lji, ko̱r'vuːlji (Sch), corrie of the mill, i.e. fit for driving a mill. Curvoyley (Tayl), Corrymulzie (Me 3), Corimuinlie (Fa), Corriemun̠lzie (Io 12), Cormulzi (Cr 8), Corry Muillie (Roy), Coirmuilly (R 1), Cormulie (I). In Gaelic Coire mhuillidh, corr vullyie, probably mill corrie (Mp), Corr-vullyi (D), ko̱r'vulji (A). 'Properly muinnlidh for muilnidh from muileann' (C M Robertson, quoted by Da). A small settlement east of Inverey.

**The Corriemulzie Brig\*** (C, 112893), ðɪˌko̱re'mulzi'brɪg. As above.

**(The) Corriemulzie Burn** (OS, C, 110875), ðɪˌko̱re'mulzi'bʌrn. As above.

**Corriemulzie Cottage** See Mar Lodge.

**The Corriemulzie Dam** (F, 111891), ðɪˌko̱re'mulzi'dam. Also the Dynamo Dam (F), ðɪ'dɛinəmo'dam. A dam formerly used for hydro-electricity when Mar Lodge was at Corriemulzie.

**The Corriemulzie Dynamo House\*** (U, 111896), ðɪˌko̱re'mulzi 'dɛinəmo'hus. Ruined building that formerly held a dynamo for hydro-electricity at Corriemulzie.

**The Corriemulzie Fit Brig\*** (F, 112893), ðɪˌko̱re'mulzi'fe̱t'brɪg. A former footbridge at Linn of Corriemulzie.

**The Corriemulzie Wuid\*** (C, 111894), ðɪˌko̱re'mulzi'wɪd. Corriemulzie Wood (Ra 14).

**Corrienearn** (OS, 393950), from Coire an Eirbhein (3, C), ko̱rn 'e̱rn̩, corrie of the little dyke. This name on the OS map refers to a hilltop south-east of Ballater, and the corrie below it is Coire of Corn Arn. Corrienearn is pronounced as Cor Nairn, and Coire of Corn Arn as the Corrie of Cor Nairn. The earliest record is the Cairn of Correnervine (Ri) in 1765, referring to the hilltop now erroneously named Pannanich Hill (OS), and 'the sky of Correnervine' to the top of the ridge between Glas Choire and Coire of Corn Arn, now named Corrienearn (OS). Skay of Corinervin and Cairn of Corinervine (G 22) confirm this. This suggests that the root of the name is Coire an Eirbhein, with the Eirbhein or little dyke possibly referring to the old dyke at the bottom of the corrie. Similarly, a map about 1800 (R 6) shows Cairn Cornanernen for the hilltop and Skay Cornanernen. Cornanernen indicates that the *bh* or *v* sound in Eirbhein had by that time been dropped, subsequently becoming Cor Nairn (Cor-n-ern (I) and ko̱rn'ern̩ currently), with the Cairn

of Corrienairn (G 32) in 1817. The two references to Cairn of Correnervine and Cairn Cornanernen as the hilltop indicate that Pannanich Hill (OS) was Carn Coire an Eirbhein, with Coire an Eirbhein referring to the corrie to the east (Coire of Corn Arn (OS)) and Sky Coire an Eirbhein referring to the hilltop Corrienearn (OS). Alexander noted that the sound ko̱r 'nern applied to the corrie and to the top behind it. This might seem far-fetched if it were an isolated case, but it has happened in at least three other cases in Aberdeenshire, at Coire na Mucraich near Crathie, and at Little Corr Riabhach and Meikle Corr Riabhach at the Lecht (above the two corries Little Coire Riabhach and Muckle Coire Riabhach). Another similar example is that the Cuidhe Crom on Lochnagar, referring to a snow-wreath in a corrie, also became used for the hilltop behind. A poem in 1776 (Simps) mentioned Cairn-earn as the hill. Diack (ms) noted that Cornearn was the hill south-west of Bellamore and that the Corrienearn of the map 'is a made-up form'. We could say the same for Corn Arn (OS), which is beginning to be used by younger gamekeepers who see it on the maps. We have found ko̱rn'ern in common use for the whole hill from Corrienearn (OS) south to 391936 where it was placed on an early map of Glen Muick (I). This sound is used by a few people for the corrie also. To clear up this confusion, Corrienearn (OS) should be replaced by Sky Coire an Eirbhein, Pannanich Hill (OS) by Carn Coire an Eirbhein, Coire of Corn Arn (OS) by Coire an Eirbhein, Shank of Corn Arn (OS) by the Shank of Coire an Eirbhein, Burn of Corn Arn (OS) by Burn of Coire an Eirbhein, and Pannanich Hill (OS) should refer to the 507 m top south-east of Craigs of Pannanich.

**The Corrie o Creag nan Gall\*** (F, 264921), ðɪˈko̱reɐˌkregnɐ'ga·l. A small corrie south of Balmoral.

**Corrie of Cairn Gorm of Derry** (Cj 2, 218, 020977). North-west of Derry Lodge.

**(The) Corrie of Lochnagar** (OS, C, 253856), ðɪˈko̱reɐˌlo̱χnə'ga·r. Also the Muckle Corrie o Lochnagar (U), ðɪˈmʌkəlˌko̱reɐ ˌlo̱χnə'ga·r. Muckle Corrie of Lochnagar (B). Note the Little Corrie of Lochnagar.

**(The) Corrie of the Chokestone Gully** (Ms, U, 950977), ðɪ 'ko̱reɪðɪ'tʃok ˌsto̱n'gʌle. A climbers' name for a small corrie between Cairn Toul and Braeriach, which forms almost a part of the bigger Garbh Choire Mor. Not in local use.

**Corrie of Tom Loisgte\*** (172871). Corry of Toum Loishk (I). In Glen Callater.

**The Corrie o the Bittie\*** (U, 240002), ðɪ'ko̱reɪðɪ'be̱te, Scots Bittie = small bit. The Bittie was a building and small area of grass. A corrie south-east of Corndavon Lodge.

**The Corrie o Tom nam Buachaillean\*** (U, 364910), ðɪ'ko̱reɐ ˌto̱mnɐ'baχlən. The corry of Toum-na-Buachlin (I). In lower Glen Muick.

**(The) Corrour Bothy** (OS, C, 981958), ðɪˌko̱'rʌu̯r'bo̱θe. Also Bothan Coire Odhar (2, U), ˌbo̱ɐnˌko̱r'au.ər, bothy of dun corrie. Below Coire Odhar on Cairn Toul.

**The Corrour Brig\*** (C, 984956), ðɪˌko̱'rʌu̯r'brɪg. A footbridge over Dee, beside the Corrour Bothy.

**Còsag** (3, 269998), little crevice. Coshack (D). A hollow west of Gairnshiel.

**Còs Choille\*** (3, 387963), hollow of woods. Coschill (Roy). East of Ballater.

**Cossack\*** (Io 75, 267998, by elimination), from Còsag (3), little crevice. Cosag (Cr 41). A former house west of Gairnshiel, different from the nearby Cnocan Aitinn.

**(The) Cossack Burn** (OS, C, 264001), ðɪ'ko̱sɛk'bʌrn. Also Allt Còsaig (3), burn of little crevice. Ault Cosaick (I). West of Gairnshiel.

**The Cot Hillocks\*** (U, 386976), ðɪˈkot̞ˈhëlëks. Hillocks with ruins of dry-stone cots, near Tullich.

**The Coths** (D, 371975). 'Knaps where the lead mines are' (D). Coathe (R 4). A steep rocky gap on the hillside above the Pass of Ballater.

**The Cots of Tomnakeist\*** (399982, on west side of burn). The Coats of Tomnakeist (Io 20). West of Cambus o' May.

**Cots on the Commonty\*** (R 4, 404980). West of Cambus o' May.

**The Cottage\*** See Mar Lodge.

**The Cottage Brae\*** See the Mar Brae.

**The Cottar House o the Crofts\*** See Crofts Cottage.

**The Cottar House o the Newton\*** (U, 254954), ðɪˈkot̞ërˈhusəi ˈnjutən. Also the Newton Cottage (U), ðɪˈnjutənˈkot̞ədʒ. Newton Cottage (Io 77, Vr). Now the Leys of Newton (Er), a recent name invented by a householder. At Crathie.

**The Cottar Mossie\*** (F, 397947), ðɪˈkot̞ërˈmǫse, or the Cottars' Moss (U), ðɪˈkot̞ërzˈmǫs. A poor-quality peat-moss for the cottars, south of Pannanich.

**Cottoune\*** (Dms 10). In 1665, probably a pendicle of Tom Darach east of Pannanich.

**Cot Toun of Auchnerran\*** Coattoun of Acheneran (G 15). Presumably beside Auchnerran, near Logie Coldstone.

**(The) Coulachan Burn** (OS, C, 261990), ðɪˈkuləçɛnˈbʌrn, (ˈkuləgən (A)), from An Cùlachan (5), ? the little back place. Locally taken to be cuileagan, midges (A). Note Culachin (I) for the burn at 264993, with Water of Culachin (I) lower down at 276002. West of Gairnshiel.

**The Coulachan Corrie\*** (U, 248986), ðɪˈkuləçɛnˈkǫre, an area at the head of the above burn.

**(The) Cowie Burn** (OS, C, 410883), ðɪˈkʌu.iˈbʌrn, probably Collaigh (3), from Coll = hazel, as in Presscow 'hazel wood' (A 311), or Moscow near Kilmarnock (W 378). On Mount Keen.

**The Coyles of Muick** (OS, A, C, 329911), ˌðɪˈkɛilzɐˈmëk. The OS map gives this name as a hilltop, which is locally the Coyle (C), from A' Choille (4), the wood. Quoil (In, Am), Coial (Mg 239), A' choill, A hyll (D), the wood. The Coyles of Muick is a name referring not to the Coyle as on the OS map, but to the group of three hills so prominent from Ballater, including the Coyle, Meall Dubh and Craig of Loinmuie (D, A, C). Our oldest informants in Glen Muick did not use this collective anglicisation. Note the Coial Peaks (Mg 247) and the Coil Hills (Mi 107), suggesting how the current collective name probably originated. A group of hills south-west of Ballater.

**The Cradle Brig\*** (U, 286953), ðɪˈkredəlˈbrɪg. A former crossing of Dee at Abergeldie, using a movable cradle.

**The Cradle Puil** (C, 285953), ðɪˈkredəlˈpil. The Cradle (Sc). A pool on Dee, beside Abergeldie.

**Crà Eilein** (3, 437001), fold of (or at) lochside land. Cra-Ellan (A 311). Note Crà is a variant of Crò (W 1904, 5), and Eilean in Deeside often means a piece of flat land beside water, often not on an island. At Loch Kinord.

**The Craft\*** (U, 324005), ðɪˈkraft, Scots = croft. A field in Glen Gairn.

**The Crafts o Bridgefoot\*** (F, 410040), ðɪˈkraftsɐˈbrɪgˈfët, often the Crafts Park (F), ðɪˈkraftsˈpark. Named after former small crofts. Also the Rams' Park (U), ðɪˈramzˈpark. A field west of Logie Coldstone.

**(The) Cragan** (OS, Fa, Me 11, C, 110902), ðɪˈkragən, from An Creagan (3), the little rock. There is a little exposure of bedrock on a nearby ridge to the east. A house east of Mar Lodge.

**The Cragan Brae\*** (C, 113905), ðɪˈkragənˈbre·. A hill on a public road near Mar Lodge.

**The Cragan Ditch\*** (C, 112901), ðɪˈkragənˈdëtʃ. A back-water of Dee, east of Mar Lodge.

**The Cragan Golf Course\*** (C, 110900), ðɪˈkragənˈgǫlfˌkors, officially was the Royal Cragan Golf Course. A former course, now a field, east of Mar Lodge.

**The Cragan Loch\*** See Lochan a' Chreagain.

**The Cragan Park\*** See the Druim a' Chreagain Park.

**The Cragan Park\*** (116906). The Craggan Park (Ra 11). Formerly good farmland, but became boggy after the Quoich flood in 1829.

**The Cragan Plantin\*** (U, 116905), ðɪˈkragənˈplantɪn. A plantation east of Mar Lodge.

**The Cragan Pool** (U, 114901), ðɪˈkragənˈpul. Craggan Pool (Ly). A pool in Dee east of Mar Lodge.

**(The) Craggan** (OS, C, 357972), ðɪˈkragən. Craigs (Ce 1). A house near Bridge of Gairn, below the rocky ridge called the Craggans.

**Craggan Hill** (OS, 317858), should be the Craggan (C), as above, from An Creagan (3), the little rock. The Craggan (I). In upper Glen Muick.

**The Craggan Park\*** (F, 357971), ðɪˈkragənˈpark. A field below a house called the Craggan, near Bridge of Gairn.

**Craggan Rour** (OS, C, 182928), ˌkragɛnˈro·r, from Creagan Reamhar (3), thick little rocky hill. Craggan Raur (R 7), Cragan rōr (D). The rocky hill above Invercauld (A, C).

**(The) Craggans** (OS, C, 358977), ðɪˈkragənz, from Na Creaganan or Na Creagain (3), the little rocks. Na Creagain, the Craggans (Mg 198). A rocky ridge near Bridge of Gairn.

**The Crags\*** (U, 387984), ðɪˈkrags. A rocky area above Tullich, north-east of Ballater.

**Craig Coillich** (OS, C, 379955), kregˈkɛiləç, from Creag Cailliche (4), witch's rocky hill. Craig-o-the-Kyloch (Mg 290), Craig of the Kyloch (OS 1869), Craig Chailleach i.e. the witch's crag (Ha). These references, along with the Witch's Stone, the Howe o the Cailleach and the Coillich pool on Dee, which are all close together below Craig Coillich at Ballater, indicate that the name is Creag Cailliche. Older people understood the name to refer to the more rocky hill behind the OS location, at 385951 (JS). On south side of Dee at Ballater.

**The Craig Coillich Mast\*** (C, 379955), ðɪˌkregˈkɛiləçˈmast. A TV mast near Ballater.

**The Craig Coillich Wuid\*** (C, 375955), ðɪˌkregˈkɛiləçˈwɪd. A wood on the above hill.

**Craig Derry** (OS, C, 048980, should be at 043979), kregˈdɛre, from Creag Doire (3), rocky hill of Derry.

**The Craig Derry Face\*** (C, 040978), ðɪˌkregˈdɛreˈfes. A hill face with screes, above Glen Derry.

**Craig Doin** (OS, C, 220912), kregˈdɛin, from Creag Doimhne (3), cliff of depth. Craigdyne (Io 78), Craig Doyne, Creag Doine (R 7, 14), Craig Daign (V). N grekan tong (D) was probably an error of location for An Creagan Domhain nearby on the other side of Dee. A cliff south-west of the Inver.

**The Craig Doin Prop\*** (C, 219911), ðɪˌkregˈdɛinˈprǫp. A cairn commemorating Queen Victoria's purchase of Ballochbuie Forest to save it from being felled.

**The Craig Doin Wuid\*** (C, 223914), ðɪˌkregˈdɛinˈwɪd. On the above hill.

**Craigendarroch** (OS, C, 366965), from Creag an Daraich (3), ˌkregənˈdaraç, rocky hill of the oak wood. One of the very few oak woods in Deeside still grows on the lower slopes above Ballater. Craig of Ballater (Ro). North of Ballater.

**Craig Gowan** (OS, C, 255941), kregˈʌu.ən. A hill above Balmoral, the same name as the nearby Creag a' Ghobhainn

59

(OS), rocky hill of the smith. This name refers to the whole hill. Craiggowan (B).

**Craig Gowan House** (OS, C, 262940), kreg'ʌu.ən'hus. Below the above hill.

**The Craig Hill** See Auchnacraig Hill.

**Craighuie** (OS, C, 265950). A house at Crathie, named from the rock behind it (see Creag na Gaoithe).

**Craig Leek** (OS, C, 185931), kreg'lik, krɪk'lik (U), from Creag Lice (3), rocky hill of slab. Craigleach (Io 63), Craig Lichk (I, R 7), Creag Liechk (R 14), Crek lichk (D). A hill with a cliff of smooth rock, east of Invercauld.

**Craig Megen** (OS, C, 316898), kreg'mẹgən, from Creag Megein (3), rocky hill of bog place. See Megen. Craig Megan (In). In mid Glen Muick.

**Craig Moseen** (OS, 268826), should be Creag na Sìne (4), ˌkregnɐ'ʃin (A, C), rocky hill of the stormy weather. Craignasin (In). An exposed rocky corner of hill above Loch Muick.

**Craig Nordie** (OS, C, 235945, should be at 239943; 235945 is Meall Mor), kreg'nọrdi, from Creag an Òrduigh (3), rock of the command. Craiginordie (Io 18), Craig n ordu, Craignorthie (R 3, 9), Crek-norte (D). Although Macdonald dismissed the early OS form Creag an Orduigh in favour of Creag an Ordain (Ordain = of little round hill), and Alexander more tentatively agreed, there was no evidence for Ordain. In fact, the early form Craig n ordu (R 3 in 1788), in addition to the current pronunciation, indicate that the early OS name was correct. Note also 'Creag an Orduigh . . . locally corrupted to Craig Nortie' (McC 1895, 127). The name makes sense in view of the close vicinity of Carn na Cuimhne, the assembly cairn for the Farquharson clan in times of trouble; it stands only 200 m below the rock of Creag an Orduigh. A rocky little hill north-east of the Inver.

**(The) Craignordie Wood** (OS, C, 238942), ðıˌkreg'nọrdi'wɪd. North-east of the Inver.

**Craig of Ballater** See Craigendarroch.

**The Craig of Balmoral**. The Craig of Balmorrall (Mc 10). ? same as Creag a' Ghobhainn.

**(The) Craig of Coirebhruach** (OS, C, 396896), ðı'kregɐˌkọre 'vraχ. In upper Glen Tanar.

**Craig of Inchnabobart** (OS, 304881). Craig Inchbobart (F), ˌkreg.ɪnʃ'bọbërt indicates an original Creag Inis Bó-bard (3), rocky hill of river-meadow of cow enclosure. Hill of Inchbobart (Crom). In upper Glen Muick.

**(The) Craig of Loinmuie** (OS, C, 332920), ðı'kregɐˌlɪn'mui. Craig Linmuie (In) indicates that the name was originally Creag Loinn Muighe (3), rocky hill of enclosure of field. South-west of Ballater.

**Craig of Prony*** Craig of Pronie (Opr 17). A former habitation in lower Glen Gairn.

**(The) Craig of (the) Prony** (OS, C, 353988), ðı'kregɪðı'prone, from Creag Phronnaich (3), rocky hill of the Prony or of the thing broken in small fragments, probably referring to the hill's many stony screes. Craig Phroni (Mg). See Prony. North of the Bridge of Gairn.

**Craig of the Greystone*** (I, 292964). A rocky top east of Crathie, Sron Dubh (OS) being the whole hill-nose.

**(The) Craig of the Knock(s)** (OS, C, 354955), ðı'kregɪðı'nọks, or the Knocks Craigs (F). Little Cairn (I), Craig of the Knocks (Mg 52), Craig-knock (Mg 259). There are several Knocks or small hills (Gaelic Cnoc) in the area. A rock outcrop west of Ballater.

**(The) Craig of the Linn** (OS, C, 328896), ðı'kregɪðı'lën. A rocky hill above the Linn of Muick.

**(The) Craig of Tulloch** (OS, C, 282016), ðı'kregɐ'tʌləç, from

Creag Thulaich (3), rocky hill of the Tulloch (i.e. of Tullochmacarrick), with Tulach = a hillock. Craig Hullach (I). North-west of Gairnshiel.

**Craigrae Beg** (OS, 424942), ˌkreg.re'bẹg (U), from Creag Rèidh Bheag (3), little level rocky hill. Creag reidh, smooth craig (A). A hill south of Cambus o' May.

**The Craigs** See the Pass of Ballater.

**Craigs of Ballater*** See Pass of Ballater.

**The Craigs of Braichlie** (Sm, 369935 by elimination). Rocks south of Ballater.

**(The) Craigs of Pannanich** (OS, C, 387961), ðı'kregzɐ'panɐnıç. Cliffs east of Ballater.

**The Craigs of Richarkarie** (298014). The Craigs of Reacharchrie (Mg 213). Rock outcrops near Gairnshiel.

**Craig Vallich** (OS, C, 377927), kreg'valəç, from Creag a' Bhealaich (3), rocky hill of the pass. Craigivallach (Ri 14), Craig Vyallich (I). The pass leads the Mounth Road from Ballater over a col at about 380920 towards Glen Tanar.

**The Craig Walk*** (C, 105894), ðı'kreg'wɑ·k. Also Princess Walk (Br). A track west of Corriemulzie, below the cliff of Creag an Fhithich.

**Cranee** (P, C, 452979), 'krani, 'kra'ni·, ? Scots Cran = top, Ee = eye, or Gaelic Crann = tree. A pool in Dee west of the bridge at Dinnet.

**Crannach Hill** (OS, 385999), locally the Crannach (3), with no Hill (A, C), ðı'kranɐχ, likely to have been A' Chrannach originally, the place of trees. The Krynyach (D). A hill north-east of Ballater.

**The Crannog Island** See the Little Island.

**Craobh —*** (3, U, south-east of 065913), kru —, tree —. Informant could not remember second part of name. A big fir in Glen Lui.

**Craobh an Òir** (2, Sg, C, 025942), krin̩'ọ·r, tree of the gold. An old fir on Carn Crom near Luibeg. The old story is that Mackenzie, laird of Dalmore (formerly Mar Lodge), hid stolen gold under this tree, and later put it near the top of Cairn Geldie, under a big stone with the figure of a horse's shoe carved on it (Sg).

**Craoibh na Croiche** (3, 101895), (? at) tree of the gallows. Crui na croich (D) possibly indicates the dative case. Also the Hangman's Tree (C), ðı'haŋmənz'tri. Also the Gallows Tree (Sg). East of Inverey.

**An Crasg Binneach*** (3, 300051), the hilly crossing-place, or Beinneach = full of hills. Grass paywnich, Graspywnich, Grasspywnich, (I), Gras-pienich, Gras-Pienac (R 14, 16). Near the top of the road from Gairnshiel to Corgarff.

**Crathie** (OS, C, 264949), 'kra·θe, in Gaelic Cra-hy (A), 'kreçi (Sch), from Craichidh or Creichidh (6, both forms used in local Gaelic, e short as in Creag (D)). Crachy in 1706 (Aj). Older forms of the name (A) add no new evidence except the forms Creythyn and Creychyn which help to explain Crathienaird (below). Another Crathie, in upper Badenoch, is Craichidh in Gaelic (Mb), as in the Deeside Crathie. There is another Crathie near Meigle, a Crathes near Banchory, Craichie at Forfar, Crachie at Dufftown, and Crichie at Kintore and Old Deer. Cray in Glenshee and Loch Achray in the Trossachs are Crathaidh and Loch Ath-chrathaidh in Gaelic, the latter probably meaning loch of ford of the shaking (W), and to be compared with Irish Crathaidhe or Creathaidhe, a quaking bog (J, 3). These are probably all variations of the same name (Mb, A). The most likely possibility is a variation of Crathach or Crathaidh = shaking place, in the sense of a bog, possibly referring to the bogs of Moine Chraichidh on the hill up Crathie Burn.

**(The) Crathie Burn** (OS, C, 249968), ðı'kraθe'bʌrn. Also Allt Chraichidh (6, U), alt'çra·χe, burn of the Crathie, for meaning see above name. Alltchrachag (Me 4), Altochrachay (Io 12), Ald Chrathie, Burn of Crathie (R 3, 9), Alt Craichie (Vi).

**Crathie Cottage\*** See Crystalls.

**Crathie Cottages\*** (Be, U), 'kraθe'kɒtədʒɪz. Collective name for houses near church at Crathie.

**Crathie Ford** (Wy, 261950). Former ford over Dee.

**Crathienaird** (OS, C, 257958), ˌkraθe'nerd, to older people Crichienaird (C), ˌkrɪçe'nerd, ˌkrɪçi'nerd, from Creich an Airde (6), Crathie of the high place. In Gaelic Crechinērd, crechin-artsh (D). Creichinaird (Crg 2), Craichenaird (Pb). See Crathie above. A farm near Crathie.

**Crathienaird Village\*** Crathinard Village (Ce 4). Former group of houses at Crathienaird near Crathie.

**Crathie Shiel\*** See Ruighe Chreichidh.

**The Craw Island\*** (C, 172919), ðɪ'kra·'ɛilənd, Scots Craw = rook. An island on Dee at Invercauld, with a rookery.

**The Craws' Tree\*** (U, 317000), ðɪ'kra·z'tri. A birch used by crows for nesting, south-east of Gairnshiel.

**The Craw Wuid\*** (U, 353949), ðɪ'kra·'wɪd, Scots = rook wood. Former rookery in lower Glen Muick, now nest on north side of road.

**The Craw Wuid\*** (F, 291953), as above. At Abergeldie.

**Creag a' Chait** (OS, 172958), locally Creagan Chat (3, F), ˌkregən'hat, little rocky hill of cats. Craggan Chaat (I), Craeg'n-chat (R 14). North of Invercauld.

**Creag a' Chait** (OS, 080885), usually Creagan Chait (3, C), ˌkregən'hatʃ, little rocky hill of the cat. Creagan chait (Gr) agrees with this, but Creag a' Chait also heard (3), ˌkrekɐ'hatʃ (WG), (kreg'hatʃ (A)), rocky hill of the cat. Also the Hill o' Cat (Crom). Near Inverey.

**Creagach Bhealdair** See the Pass of Ballater.

**Creag a' Chlamhain** (OS, 267956), rocky hill of the buzzard. Behind Crathie.

**Creag a' Chleirich** (OS, 3, C, 141934), kreg'çlirɪç, rocky hill of the clergyman. Craig Chlerich (Gr), Craig Chlerach (I), Craeg Clerach (R 14). North of Braemar.

**Creag a' Choire Dhirich** (OS, 3, U, 123777), ˌkreg̩ˌkɒr'jirəç, rocky hill of the perpendicular corrie. The cliffs are all in Perthshire, but the top of this little hill comes up to Aberdeenshire. Craig-corr-Yirach (Ro), Creag Cor-eirach, Creag Corierach (R 14, 16). West of the Cairnwell.

**Creag a' Gheoidh Bheag** See Creag na Gaoithe.

**Creag a' Gheòidh Mhór\*** (3, 268954), kreg'jui (F), big rock of the goose. Craig Buie More (I, with the B in Buie probably an error), Craig an Iui (Mg), Craig Youie, yoi, goose (D), Craig Yoo-ie (A). See Creag na Gaoithe. Also the Muckle Craig (C), ðɪ'mʌkəl'kreg. A broken crag behind Crathie, formerly used as a quarry.

**Creag a' Ghlas-uillt** (OS, 252840), rocky hill of the green burn. South of Lochnagar.

**Creag a' Ghobhainn** (OS, 3, 251939), rocky hill of the smith. The Croft (formerly the Smiddy Croft) lies below the hill to the west. See Craig Gowan. At Balmoral.

**The Creag a' Ghobhainn Wuid\*** (F, 250940), ðɪˌkreg'ʌu.ən'wɪd. At Balmoral.

**Creagaidh Làrach** (4, C, 421028), ˌkregi'larɐχ, ˌkregi'lerɐχ to younger people, possibly from Creagan, or Scots borrowing Craigie, both mean little rock of ruined sites. Craigilarach (G 15), Craggielerach (Aj 8). A former farm on a rocky place west of Logie Coldstone.

**The Creagaidh Larach Park\*** (U, 421029), ðɪˌkregi'lerɐχ'park. A field at the above place.

**Creag a' Mhadaidh** (OS, 3, C, 123846, wrong location on a smooth hill, should be at rocks at 138848), kreg'mate, (kreg 'vat (A)), rocky hill of the fox or dog. Craig mattie (Roy), Craig Matte (I), Crek vat (D). In upper Glen Clunie.

**The Creag a' Mhadaidh Face\*** (F, 135845), ˌðɪˌkreg'mate'fes. A long stony hill-face in upper Glen Clunie.

**Creag a' Mhortair** See Lion's Face.

**An Creagan** (OS, 3, F, 246995), ðɪ'kragən, the little rocky hill. North-west of Crathie.

**An Creagan\*** (3, 113904), as above, the little rock. Cragan (Fa), the Craggan (Cr 4), Craggan (Roy). A former farm east of Mar Lodge, named after a rocky ridge to the west. The present house of Cragan lies to the west of the ridge, nearer the site of the former farm of Druim a' Chreagain.

**An Creagan\*** (3, U, 357972), as above, the little rock. A steep little wall of rock near the Bridge of Gairn.

**An Creagan** (3, U, 143905), as above, n'grɛken (Sch), the little rock. The Craggan (Mp). A rock outcrop above Braemar.

**Creagan a' Choire Etchachan** (OS, 015999), from Creagan a' Choire Éiteachan (6, F), ˌkrɛkɐnˌkɒr'ɛtʃɐχen, cliffs of the corrie of ? expansive place (see Coire Etchachan). The name also includes the rocks on the south side of the corrie, south of the Hutchison Memorial Hut. At the top of Glen Derry.

**Na Creaganan** or **Na Creagain\*** (3, 230939), classic Gaelic for the Craggans (I), the little rocks. A field at the Inver.

**Na Creaganan** See Craggans.

**Creagan Briste-amhaich\*** (3, 196812, including rocks on both sides of waterfall), rocks of broken neck. Craigs of Priesh auich (I), Crags of Priesh-auch (R 14). At the head of Glen Callater.

**Creag an Dail Bheag** (OS, 146980), should be Creagan Dail Beag (3, C), ˌkregənˌdal'beg, little clifflet at haugh. The OS form has a grammatical error as Dail is a feminine noun and was feminine in Braemar Gaelic also; Creag an Dail can only be an erroneous attempt at a genitive, whereas the genitive here would have to be Creag na Dalach. Diack's evidence is also important here as he recorded the name as N grekan (i.e. An Creagan), or 'the little craig'. Alexander correctly noted that part of the name must be Creagan Dail, but ignored Diack's key evidence and decided mistakenly that it must be Creagan = craigs and not Creagan = little craig. 'There are two Craigendalls, the Big and the Little' (D), but more often they are called the Muckle and the Little (A). Craignan dale beg (I), Craeagan Dal Bheg (R 14). The old map (I) shows both names as referring to the hilltops behind the two cliffs that face each other across a haugh on the upper Gairn, and this still applies in local use but the names more commonly refer to the cliffs. Also Little Creag an Dail (C), 'lɛtəlˌkregən'da·l.

**Creag an Dail Mhór** (OS, 140983), should be Creagan Dail Mór (3, C), ˌkregənˌdal'mo·r, big clifflet at haugh. Craignan dale more (I), Craeg-an-Dal More (R 14). See above name. Also Muckle Creag an Dail (C), 'mʌkəlˌkregən'da·l. South of Ben Avon.

**The Creag an Dails** (F), ðɪˌkregən'da·lz. Craigendalls (D). A collective anglicised name for Creag an Dail Bheag and Mhor.

**Creagan Deimh\*** (3, 291837), dark little rock. Craigenday (Am). A rock outcrop above Loch Muick.

**Creag an Diuchd** (OS, 2, F, 057916), ˌkregən'dju·χk, cliff of the duke. Craignaduich (R 10). In Glen Lui.

**Creagan Doimhneachd\*** (4, 378030), little rocky hill of depth. A little hill Craigindonich, Craigindonnich (Io 20). Craigindonich or Sundays croft (Io) would suggest Creit an Domhnaich, but this was probably an error as Gaelic died out; there is no croft but there is a little rocky hillock. South of Morven.

**An Creagan Domhain** (3, 213924), the deep little rock. Craggan Down (I), the Craggandoun (Mi 225), N grekan tong (D) probably referred to this place. A rock outcrop south-west of the Inver.

**Creagan Domhain Pool**. Craigendune (Ly). A pool in Dee, probably the same as the Split Stane Puil.

**Creag an Dubh-loch** (OS, 3, 233826), locally the Craigs o the Dubh-loch (C), ðɪˌkregzɪðɪˈduˌlɔχ, cliffs of the black loch. This local name includes the cliff on the Eagle's Rock side as well as the bigger one west of the Dubh Loch. Craigs of the Duloch (I) referred to the big cliff, but that map did not include the other side of the Loch. Craig of the Duloch (In) is shown twice, one for each cliff. The Craigs of the Duloch (Mg 267). West of Loch Muick.

**Creag an Fhir-Shaighde** (OS, 197830), should be Creag an Fhleisdeir (3, C), ˌkregənˈliʃtər, cliff of the arrowmaker, after an arrowmaker in mid 1600s. Craign Leshter (I), Craig Leshter, Crag'n Leshter (R 13, 14), Creag an Leasdair (Mg 148), Creag an Leisdhair (McC 1891). In upper Glen Callater.

**Creag an Fhithich** (OS, 2, C, 096890, should be cliff at 104893), kregˈniːç, cliff of the raven. Craigenonich (Me 15) suggests Creagan an Fhithich, rocks or little rock of the raven. Also the Raven's Crag (Crom). East of Inverey.

**The Creag an Fhithich Wuid*** (C, 104894), ðɪˌkregˈniːçˈwɪd. Craigneich Wood (Ra 14). A wood beside the above cliff.

**Creag an Fhleisdeir** See Creag an Fhir-Shaighde.

**Creag an Fhuathais** (OS, 3, C, 098838), kregˈnuˑɪʃ, cliff of the spectre. Craignuash (Roy), Craig nuish (Io 79), Crek nuash (D in A). Creag-an-aibhse, rock of the ghost (Gr 41) was probably the same place. In upper Glen Ey.

**The Creag an Fhuathais Burn** See Allt a' Mhoir Grianach.

**Creag an Loch** (OS, 2, C, 192848), ˌkregənˈlɔχ, rocky hill of the loch. Craign Loch (I, R 13), Creag'n Loch (R 14). Above Loch Callater.

**Creag an Lochain** (OS, 2, C, 082839), ˌkregənˈlɔχən, rocky hill of the tarn. Craiginlochin (Roy). This name refers to the whole big hill-mass on which Carn Creagach is a small top; it includes the hill rising above Altanour Lodge. The tarn referred to is probably the one just east of Carn Creagach, high on the hill. In upper Glen Ey.

**Creagan Lochan na Gàire** (3, 248856), cliffs of tarn of the noisy sound. Creacan lochan-a-ghar (Mg 60). The big cliffs in the Corrie of Lochnagar.

**Creag an Lurachain** (OS, 259933), should be Creag Lurgainn (3), rocky hill with a shin. Craiglurakin (B), Craig Luraghain (V), Creag Lùrachan (M), Crek luriking 'shin' (D) clearly indicates a *nn* ending to the name. Current pronunciation is usually kregˈlurɐχən (C), similar to that recorded by Alexander as kregˈlurəçən and kregˈlʌurəçən and possibly influenced by the map spelling, but older people gave it to us as kregˈlurɐkɪn (F). A hill sending out a long ridge towards the distillery at Balmoral.

**The Creag an Lurachain Prop*** See Prince Albert's Cairn.

**The Creag an Lurachain Wuid*** (F, 260930), ðɪˌkregˈlurɐχən ˈwɪd. At Balmoral.

**Creagan Mor*** See Little Craig.

**Creagan nan Gabhar** (OS, 2, C, 999923), ˌkrɪkɐnɐnˈgʌu̇ɛr, rocks of the goats. Also the Goat's Craig (McC 1932). A hilltop with several small rocky outcrops, in Glen Dee.

**Creagan nan Gabhar*** (2, U, 074876), as above, rocks of the goats. South-west of Inverey.

**Creagan Riabhach** (OS, 3, U, 371990), ˌkragənˈriˑəç, brindled little rock. A hilltop with little rocks, north of Ballater.

**Creagan Ruairidh*** (3, 304008), Rory's little rock. Craggan Ruarie, fine limestone quarry (I). A small rock and quarry in the wood near Gairnshiel.

**An Creagan Seileach** (3, 124895), the willow little rock, with willow used in an adjectival sense. N greagan shellach, 'willow' (D). A little cliff east of Corriemulzie.

**Creagan Seileach*** (3, 138870), willow rocks. Craggan Shellach (I). Slabby wet rocks in mid Glen Clunie.

**Creag an Sglèait** (3, 209813), cliff of the slate. Creag an Sgliat (A), kregənˈskletʃ, but this pronunciation fits Creag an Sgleait better. See Creag Leachdach. A broken cliff south-east of Loch Callater.

**Creag Anthoin** (OS 1869, 099881), from Creag Eanntoin (3), krɛkˈjʌuntən (A), Anton's rock. The hillock is Tom Anthon and the hollow below is Glac Anthon. The legend is that Anton or Anthony murdered a man at Corriemulzie in the early 18th century but was followed and killed, and his head buried here (Gr). South-east of Inverey.

**Creagan Tobair*** (3, 342978), little rocky hill of a well. Craigen Douper (I). North-west of the Bridge of Gairn.

**Creag an t-Seabhaig** (OS, 3, U, 367971), ˌkregənˈdʒuɐk, cliff of the hawk. Craigenshoak (G 19), Creag ant-sheobhaig (Mg), pronunciation tyùag (M), Crek an jauag 'Hawk' (D). Also Sgòr an t-Seabhaig (3), skɔrnˈdʒʌuk (A), rock of the hawk. Sgor n djau-ag (D in A). The cliff at the Pass of Ballater.

**Creag an t-Sean Ruigh** (OS, 3, U, 149825), ˌkregənˈʃɛnˌrui, classic form Creag an t-Seann-ruighe, rocky hill of the old shiel. Craign-den-rie (I), Crag'n denrie (R 14), pronunciation tean ruie (M), Crek an dshunngrui (D in A). There is an old shiel or house below, at 139831. In upper Glen Clunie.

**Creag Asp** (OS 1869, 300938), rock of adders. A rocky top south-east of Abergeldie.

**Creag Bad an Eas** (OS, 2, A, F, 071888), classic Gaelic form would be Easa, ˌkregˌbɐdˈnjɛs, cliff of clump of the waterfall. Above the Linn of Dee.

**Creag Bad an t-Seabhaig** (OS, 036942), rock of clump of the hawk. Creag an t-Seabhaig (A). North-west of Derry Lodge.

**Creag Bhalg** (OS, 3, 205960), rock of bags. Craig Vallack (I). North-east of Auchtavan in Glen Feardar.

**Creag Bhalg*** (3, 199962), rocky hill of bags. Craig Vallack (I). A hummocky and rocky slope in Glen Feardar.

**Creag Bhalg** (OS, 2, C, 092912), krɛkˈvaləg, cliff of bags. Craig Valloch (Crom), Crek valluk (D in A). Refers to the hill as on OS map but also to the cliff at 106913 above the foot of Quoich. The hill was Benavoulg (R 10), so the original names were probably Beinn a' Bhuilg (3), hill of the bag, and Creag Bhalg for the cliff. The Bag in such names refers to the shape of the hill or cliff (A). The Foxes Craig Hill (Ra 14), is an inaccurate translation, probably mistaking Bhalg for Bhalgair. North of Mar Lodge.

**The Creag Bhalg Wuid*** (C, 105915), ðɪˌkregˈvaləgˈwɪd. A wood in lower Glen Quoich.

**Creag Bheag*** (3, 158903), little rocky hill. Craig Veck (I). South of Braemar.

**Creag Bheag*** (3, 251959), little rocky hill. Craig-veg (R 3). Also Little Creag Mhor. Little Craig More (R 8). Forms a pair with Creag Mhor (OS) nearby. North-west of Crathie.

**Creag Bheag*** (3, 211942), little rocky hill. Craig Beg (I). West of the Inver.

**Creag Bheag** (OS, 223944), from A' Chreag Bheag (3, U), ðɪ ˌkregˈbɛg, (krɐkˈvɛk (A)), little rocky hill. Craig Beg (I). A chrek vek (D in A) refers probably to this name but possibly to the above one. North-west of the Inver.

**Creag Bheag** (OS, 333910), little rocky hill. In mid Glen Muick.

**Creag Bheag** (3, OS 1869, McC, 094891), little rocky hill. The whole hill from Ey to Corriemulzie (McC), with the cliff of Creag an Fhithich at its east end; Creag an Fhithich (OS) is in the wrong place.

**Creag Bheag*** (3, 142923), little rocky hill. Craig Veck (I). North-west of Braemar, beside Allanmore.

**Creag Bhiorach** (OS, 295826), locally Creag Firich (3, C), kreg 'fɪrɪç, (krəg'fɪrəç (A)), rock of high ground. Above Loch Muick.

**Creag Bhiorach Gleann Giubhasachain** See the Devil's Point.

**Creag Chàis*** (3, U, 265812), kreg'ha·ʃ, rock of the difficulty. See Corrie Chash. Slabby broken rocks on a steep hillside above Loch Muick.

**Creag Chàis*** (3, 196960), rock of the difficulty. Craig Chaash (I). A rock in Glen Feardar.

**Creag Choinnich** (OS, 4, C, 160919), kreg'koinəç, crag with the moss. Kenneth's Craig (A), kreg'kʊnjɐχ, kreg'kɔnjɐχ (Sch). Craighinnich (Io 63), Craig Kynich, Creag Kienach (R 7, 14). At Braemar.

**The Creag Choinnich Mast*** (C, 160919), ðɪˌkreg'koinəç'mast. A radio mast near Braemar.

**Creag Chrithich** See Creag na Creiche.

**Creag Clunie** (OS, C, 174910), kreg'kluni, kreg'çlueni (Sch), from Creag Chluainidh (3), cliff of the Clunie (Cluainidh = at a plain). Locally, the name more often refers to the cliff at 178914 above the main road near Invercauld Bridge, and this is also where old maps put it. Craig Clunie, Creag of the Clunie (R 7, 14), Craig Chliny two times (Gr) and note spelling Clinny under Clunie Cottage.

**Creag Coire Bhàthaich** (3, 156773), rocky hill of corrie of the shelter. Craig Cor Vaich (I), Craig-Corr-Vaich (Ro). Mostly the broken rocks on the Perthshire side, but comes up to the top on the Aberdeenshire side, Meall Odhar being the entire hill. East of the Cairnwell.

**Creag Coire na h-Oisinn*** (3, U, 276906), ˌkregˌkọrnɐ'họʃən, rocky hill of corrie of the nook. Also the Craig o Coire na h-Oisinn (F). Craig of Cornyhoshan (Am). In upper Girnock.

**Creag Curraigh*** (4, U, 336968), kreg'kɔre, Creag (3) = rocky hill, Curraigh from Currach = marsh place, possibly Coire = corrie. Also the Little Craig (I). West of the Bridge of Gairn.

**Creag Dearg** (OS, 3, F, 360876), classic Gaelic form would be Creag Dhearg, kreg'ʤerg, red rocky hill. Craig Derg (I). Also Carn Dearg (3, U), kerṇ'ʤerg, red hill. South-east of Linn of Muick.

**Creag Dhearg*** (3, 188918), red rock. Craig Derg (R 7). Near Invercauld Bridge.

**Creag Dhearg*** (3, 125906), red rock. Craigderg (Im 3, Opr 21b). Former habitation at roadside west of Braemar.

**Creag Doin** (OS, 038924), should be Creag Daimh (3, A, U), krẹk'ḍae, (krək'tɛɪ (A)), rock of stag. Slabby rocks south of Derry Lodge.

**Creag Drochaide** (3, ? 092932, but map too vague to give location for certain), rock of bridge. Craigdroicht (R 10), Craig Drochit (Crom). Up Glen Quoich.

**Creag Dubh-ghleann*** (3, C, 072963), ˌkreg'duˌglən, rock of dark glen. A slope with broken rocks above the Dubh-Ghleann.

**Creag Gaoithe*** (2, U, 085906), krẹ'gɯi (JB), rocky hill of wind. An exposed spur on the corner of the hill above Mar Lodge.

**Creag Gheallaig** (3, 310980), rocky hill of Geallaig or bright one. Crek yallik (D). This is the location of Creag na Creiche (OS) but Creag na Creiche should be much further south, in sight of the main road below. North-west of Coilacriech.

**(A') C(h)reag Ghiubhais** (OS, 312955), from A' Chreag Ghiubhas (2, C), ðɪˌkreg'ju:z, the fir rock. Crag-gewis (Bla), Craig Ewes (In), Chreag ghiuthais (D in A), the Craig Yews (A). Ghiubhas here is used in an adjectival sense, thus giving the article with Creag. Craig-Uithasach; from its resemblance to Craigendarroch, also called the Sister Hill by the natives (Brow). This prominent hill east of Abergeldie still has an old fir wood on its top.

**The Creag Ghiubhais Camp*** (F, 317959), ðɪˌkreg'ju·z'kamp. A former lumbermen's camp east of Abergeldie.

**The Creag Ghiubhais Puil** (F, south of 311965), ðɪˌkreg'ju·z'pil. Craigews (Sc). A pool in Dee west of Ballater.

**The Creag Ghiubhais Wall*** (U, 312960), ðɪˌkreg'ju·z'wɑ·l. A well with a memorial stone at the roadside east of Abergeldie.

**The Creag Ghiubhais Wuid*** (C, 310956), ðɪˌkreg'ju·z'wɪd. Crag-gewis silva (Go). A fir wood on the above hill.

**Creag Ghlas*** (3, 308014), grey rock. Craig Glass (I), probably an error for Crait, from Creit = croft. A field near Gairnshiel.

**Creag Inse*** (3, 404963), rock of Inch or meadow. Craig Inch (Roy). A rocky spur west of Headinch and Inchmarnoch, near Cambus o' May.

**Creag Leachdach** (OS, 210817), should be Creag Leacach (2, U), kreg'lekɐχ, rocky hill abounding in flat stones. Craig Lekach (I, R 13), Creag Leacach (R14), Creag leagach (Mg 142). Alexander rejected the OS name completely, saying it should be Creag an Sgliat, kregən'skletʃ, see Creag an Sgleait. However this name refers to the broken cliff, whereas the whole hill is Creag Leacach, not far off the OS form. A hill south-east of Loch Callater.

**Creag Liath*** (3, Dms, U, 428947), kreg'li·, grey rocky hill. Craig le (Dms). A ridge south of Cambus o' May.

**Creag Liath** (OS, 3, F, 333939), kreg'liɐ, grey rocky hill. Craiglea (G 5). Also Carn Mhaide (4), hill of sticks. Cairn Vate (In, Am). South-west of Ballater.

**Creag Liath** (OS, 3, C, 244882), as above, grey rocky hill. OS location is too specific. Name at OS location should be Meall Creag Liath (3, U), ˌməlˌkreg'liɐ, lump of grey rocky hill. Maul Craiglia (B). Creag Liath refers (C) to the whole big stony hill from the Prince's Stone south-east to Coire Glas, and includes Stob Liath or Stob of Creag Liath, Meall Creag Liath, Creag Liath Bheag at 238888, and other names as far out as the Black Hillocks of Creag Liath at 240896. North of Lochnagar.

**Creag Liath Bheag*** (3, U, 238888), ˌkregˌliɐ'bɛg, little grey rocky hill. Also the Little Creag Liath (C), ðɪ'lɛtəlˌkreg'liɐ. Little Craiglia (B). A spur north-west of Lochnagar.

**Creag Loisgte** (OS, 3, 177869), burnt rock. Craig Loishk (I, R 7). Refers to the 795 m hilltop as well as the broken cliffs to the north-east. North of Loch Callater.

**Creag Loisgte*** (3, 210923), burnt rock. Craig Loishk (I). An outcrop of rock above the main road south-west of the Inver.

**Creag Mheann*** (3, 339981), rocky hill of kids. Craig Vaun (I), note that the same set of maps elsewhere gives Auchtavaun and Island-na-Vaun for Auchtavan and Eilean nam Meann, two names still in local use, where the y sound in Meann is clear. A group of rocks above lower Glen Gairn.

**(A') C(h)reag Mhór** (OS, 3, 246964), krəg'mor (A), the big rocky hill. A chrek vor (D in A). Also Meikle Creag Mhor. Meikle Craig More (R 8). Also the Queen's Hill (U), ðɪ 'kwinz'hɛl. Muckle Craig (Philip), but this is now used for Creag a' Gheoidh Mhor. North-west of Crathie.

**Creag Mollachdaidh*** (5, north of 351923), rock of cursing. Craig Molachty (I). A field in lower Glen Muick.

**The Creag Mor-thulaich Park*** (F, 415957), ðɪˌkreg'mʌrle'park. An old field south of Cambus o' May. This and the name below are the same name as in the erroneously spelled Creag Mullach (OS), see below.

**The Creag Mor-thulaich Plantin*** (F, 415953), ðɪˌkreg'mʌrle 'plɛntɪn. A wood south of Cambus o' May.

**Creag Mullach** (OS, 413954), should be Creag Mór-thulaich (3), kreg'mʌrle (C), kreg'mọrle from best informants, who say it used to be kreg'mọrlɪç, rock of big hillock. Diack (ms) recorded it as 'Craig Murlich, sometimes reduced to Murley' and the pronunciation later has been kreg'mʌrle (A). A prominent rocky small hill south of Cambus o' May.

**Creag na Creiche** (OS, 309980, should be at 312976; top of hill at 309980 is Creag Gheallaig), should be Creag Chrithich (3, C), kreg'çriç, rocky hill of the aspen or of the shaking (see Coilacriech). Crek chrich 'the shaking craig' (D). North-west of Coilacriech.

**Creag na Dearcaige** (OS, 170876), locally Creag nan Dearcag (3, C), ˌkregnən'dʒërkɐg, rock of the little berries. This name is used locally for the broken cliff at 176876 and for the hilltop behind it. Also, records in old maps show it at the hilltop:—Craig nan derkaig (R 7), Craignan Derkag (I), Craignan Derkag (R 13). Locally, 170876 is An Sleaghach Gorm. A hill above lower Glen Callater.

**Creag na Gaoithe** (OS, 266952), should be Creag a' Gheòidh Bheag (3), little rock of the goose. Craig Buie Beg (I, with the B in Buie probably an error). Other evidence under Creag a' Gheòidh Mhor. Also the Little Craig (F), ðɪ'lëtəl'kreg. A little rocky spur behind Crathie, above the house Craighuie.

**Creag na Glaiseath*** (5, 183787), rocky hill of the green grassy place. Craig na Clasha (I) is shown at the hilltop, but another map in the same set gives the hilltop as Cairn na Clasha. Creag-na-Clasha (R 14). North-east of the Glas Maol.

**Creag na h-Eaglais** (2, U, 306970), kreg'hɛklɪʃ, rocky hill of the church. Craig-Eaglais (S). A spur west of Coilacriech, above the former Chapel Ma-Dheoir.

**Creag na h-Earba*** (3, probably 119932, exact location uncertain from map), rocky hill of the roe. Craig na herb (R 10). In Glen Quoich.

**Creag na h-Iolaire** (3, U, 365893), kreg'hëlër, rock of the eagle. Craig Hillar (Mg 248), rocks at this spot called Cairn-na-Heulre (I) probably in error for Craig-na-Heulre, as the same map gives another Cairn-na-Heulre correctly for the hilltop. In mid Glen Muick.

**Creag na h-Iolaire** See Eagles Rock.

**Creag nam Ban** (OS, 3, C, 299946), ˌkregnɐ'baˑn, rocky hill of the women. Witches were said to have been burned there, and Kitty Rankie's Cairn marks the last one. East of Abergeldie.

**Creag nam Muc** (3, probably 134902), rock of the pigs. Craig na Muc (Gr 151). Note Coire nam Muc is nearby. West of Braemar.

**Creag nan Gabhar** (OS, 3, C, 154841), ˌkregnən'gʌu.ër, rocky hill of the goats. Rocks of Craig-na-Goir (I) shown at 146840. In mid Glen Clunie.

**Creag nan Gall** (OS, 3, C, 262921), ˌkregnɐ'gaˑl, rocky hill of the foreigners. South of Balmoral.

**Creag nan Leachda** (OS, 179887), should be Creag Leacach (3, A, C), kreg'lekɐx, kreg'ljɛçkɐ (Sch), rocky hill abounding in flat stones. Craig Legach (R 7). South-east of Braemar.

**Creag nan Saobhaidhe*** (3, 025874), rocky hill of the fox's den. Craignasuivie (Roy). South-west of the Linn of Dee.

**Creag na Sine** See Craig Moseen.

**Creag na Slabhraidh** (OS, 319851), locally Creagan Slabhraidh (3, F), ˌkregən'slʌuri, little rocky hill of a chain. Craggan Slaurie (I). A hill in upper Glen Muick.

**Creag na Spàine** (OS, 218933), locally Creag Spàine (3, D, A, C), kreg'spanji, rock of spoon (i.e. shape). Pronounced Craig Spàingie or Spàinye (M), Crek spannyi, Spainnidh, spoon (D in A). Craig Spane (Roy). West of the Inver.

**Creag na Sròine** (OS, 3, 210919), rock of the nose. The OS map does not make clear which of the two prominent noses has Creag na Sroine, but an old map (I) shows the Stroin as the northern one. West of the Inver.

**Creag Phàdruig** (OS, 2, C, 175859), kreg'faˑrək, Patrick's rocky hill. In lower Glen Callater.

**Creag Phadruig** (OS, 2, C, 047896), as above, Patrick's rocky hill. Craigpharich (R 10). West of the Linn of Dee.

**Creag Phàdruig*** (2, C, 047894), as above, Patrick's rocky hill. Crag Fadrik (Go), Craigphatrick (Me 3), Cryk pharik (Cr 24), Craigpharick (Opr 25). A former farm west of the Linn of Dee, named from the hill beside it (see above).

**The Creag Phadruig Brig*** (F, 046894), ðɪˌkreg'faˑrək'brɪg. In Glen Dee.

**The Creag Phadruig Burn*** See Allt Creag Phadruig.

**The Creag Phadruig Wuid*** (C, 050896), ðɪˌkreg'faˑrək'wɪd. An old fir wood west of the Linn of Dee.

**Creag Phiobaidh** (OS, 3, C, 327949), kreg'fibi, rocky hill of the piping. In Glen Girnock.

**The Creag Phiobaidh Wuid*** (F, 328952), ðɪˌkreg'fibi'wɪd. A wood west of Ballater.

**Creag Thulaich** See Craig of Tullich.

**The Creel Road*** (U, 403039), ðɪ'kril'rod. Also later the Shepherd's Roadie (U), ðɪ'ʃəpərdz'rodi. A narrow track for carrying creels of peats on horseback from the Roar peat-mosses, west of Logie Coldstone.

**The Creeper's Roadie*** See the Gruer's Road.

**Creit a' Bhothain*** (3, 156931), croft of the bothy. Craitvoan (Fa), Craitivoin (Cr 5), Crecht a von (Im 4), Creitvoan (Rli 19). A former farm near Invercauld.

**Creit an Easaidh*** (3, west of 155883), croft of the waterfall place. Craitn Ese (I). A field in lower Glen Clunie.

**Creit an Lòin*** (3, 186912), croft of the wet meadow. Crait-n-loan (R 7). A piece of farmland beside Invercauld Bridge.

**Creit an Roide*** (3, 220938), croft of the bog myrtle. Cruitinrad (Roy), Creitinroid (Io 33), Craft hroat, Craigrote, Creiteanreothaid, Craganrot (Opr 10, 22, 25a, 31), Craitinroit (I), Croftanroit (Rli 23). A former farm west of the Inver.

**Creit an t-Seapail** (3), croft of the chapel. Creitsh-an-tsehpal (D). Also the Chapel Croft (U), ðɪ'tʃapəl'krɒft. Chapel croft (D). Possibly the same as the Chapel Glebe. At Braemar.

**Creit Beithe*** (3, 343904), croft of birch. Crait Bea (I). A field in mid Glen Muick.

**Creitean Lise*** (3, 364944), little croft of garden. Craitn Lies (I). A former field in lower Glen Muick, now in a wood.

**Creit Ghlas*** (3, 308015), green croft. Crait Glass (I). A field near Gairnshiel.

**Creit Mhór*** (3, 157891), big croft. Crait More (I). A former field in lower Glen Clunie.

**Creit Mhuiceann** See Croft Muickan.

**Creit na Ceardaich*** (3, 158928), croft of the smithy. Craitna Cardich (I). A former field north-east of Braemar.

**Creit na h-Àtha*** (3, 133830), croft of the kiln. Craitnaha (I). A field at the Baddoch.

**Creit nam Meann*** (3, 342905), croft of the kids. Cruitnaman (Rli 2), Crait na nyaun (I). A field in mid Glen Muick.

**Creit nan Clach*** (3, 153905), croft of the stones. Crait na-Clach (I). A former field immediately south-west of the right-angle bend of Clunie, now part of Braemar Golf Course.

**Creit Sgotaidh*** (3, 390972), croft of little piece of land. Crait scottie (R 4). A piece of farmland north-east of Ballater.

**Creit Ruighe Crìon*** (3, 155889), croft of little reach. Crait ri crean (I). A former field in lower Glen Clunie.

**Creit Seasg*** (3), barren croft. Craitshesk (R 4), Crait Shesk (Io 58). Former farmland north-east of Ballater.

**The Cricket Park*** (C, 371961), ðɪ'krëkët'park. Also the Monaltrie Park (Gl, F), ðɪˌmɒn'altri'park. Park used for Ballater Highland Games.

**Crioch Dhubh*** (3, 330002), dark end. Criach Du (I). A field in Glen Gairn, at the east end of woods.

**The Crion*** (U, north of 420962), ðɪ'krin, from Gaelic Crìon (3)

= little. The Creen (Dms). A track at Inchmarnoch, on north side of burn.

**The Crion Stile*** (U, north of 419962), ðɪˈkrinˈstɛil, Scots Stile = gate. The Creen style (Dms). Sometimes the Stile o the Crion, ðɪˈstɛilɪðɪˈkrin. A gate between two fields at Inchmarnoch.

**Cristie Hill.**(McArthur 1982, 044860). The Hill of Cristie (Wy). South-west of Linn of Dee.

**The Cristie Moss Road*** (U, 071870), ðɪˈkriəstjiˈmɒsˈrod. An old track, now bulldozed, to a peat-moss south-west of the Linn of Dee, at top of Allt Cristie Beag.

**An Crò Chlach** (3, 001855), kroˈhlaç (A), the stone fold. Croclach, Crocluch Lodge (Ce 1, 3). N grōhklach, sheepfold of stones, the old name of Bynack shieling (D), Cro-hlach (A). Also the Bynack Shiel, a former shieling beside Bynack Lodge. The lodge was also sometimes called the Bynack Shieling (Cj 7).

**The Croft** (Er, C, 244939), ðɪˈkroft, ðɪˈkraft. Smyddie Croft, Smiddie Croft (Mc 3), Smiddy Croft, Fabrile (i.e. smithy) de Inueryalder (Ca), the Smith's Croft of Inverzaldie (Ri 4a), the Crofts, the Crofts of Balmoral (Ra 7, 9), Crofts of Ballmoral (Opr 29). Note Creag a' Ghobhainn, rocky hill of the smith, rises above this place. A house, formerly a croft, at Balmoral.

**The Croft*** (I, 348912). A field in mid Glen Muick.

**The Croft*** (I, 343902). A field in mid Glen Muick.

**The Croft*** (I, 361942). Now the Wall Park (F), ðɪˈwaˈlˈpark, Scots Wall = well. A field in lower Glen Muick.

**The Croft*** (I, 300015). A field near Gairnshiel.

**Croft Fùcadair** Croftfugater (Ri 17), a pendicle of Balmore in Glen Feardar. Probably original name was Creit Fùcadair (3), fuller's croft.

**Croft Mowatt*** A farm that suggests a translation from Gaelic Creit = croft, and Mowatt (personal name). Croft Mouit (Me 3), Kroft Mowatt (Io 38). A pendicle of Camas na Ciste south of Braemar.

**Croft Muickan** (Er, C, 149903), krɒftˈmëkən, from Creit Mhuiceann (3), krʊtʃˈvuːikɐn (Sch), croft of baldmoneys or spignels. Cruit Vougan (Roy), Creit a Vuigan, Creitvuican (Cr 36, 38), Crait Muickan (I), Creitsh vukyan (D). Micken (as in lowland Scots pronunciation of Muickan) is bald-money, a plant common in these upland pastures (A). Muilceann is baldmoney (Dw) and the genitive Mhuilcinn would fit Diack's and Alexander's notes with the *l* missing. It seems likely that Muiceann was local Braemar Gaelic for baldmoney, and ˈmëkən (CMcH) is still known for this plant. A former croft, now a house at Braemar Golf Course.

**The Croft of Abergeldie** (S 27). Croft of Abergeldie (Ce 5). Former habitation at Easter Balmoral.

**Croft of Bad Charn** See Croit Caluim.

**Croft of Balnalan** (Mc 25). Former place near the Inver.

**Croft of Birkhall*** (G 35). In lower Glen Muick.

**Croft of Bovaglie*** (301919). Croft of Balvagly (In). In upper Glen Girnock.

**The Croft of Brochdhu.** Crofte Bruchdow (Ab 19), the Croft of Broghdow (Ri 24a), the Craft of Broughdou (Io 8–9). In lower Glen Muick, slightly to east of Brochdhu.

**The Croft of Bruach Dhubh** (3, c. 415959). Croft of Broikdowis (Ab 13), the Crofts of Broighdowes (Dms 13). South of Cambus o' May.

**The Croft of Daldownie.** Croftam de Daldouy (Ca), the Croft of Daldunie (Ri 4a). West of Gairnshiel.

**Croft of Etnach** (Dms 3) in 1600. Ethniche with the Croift (Rlh). In upper Glen Tanar.

**Croft of Knockanduie*** (Io 80). A former croft presumably just east of the bridge at the Inver.

**Croft of Milltoun*** Croift of Miltoune (G 4). At Inchmarnoch.

**Croft of Tigh na Criche*** Croft of Tynacreich (Io 80). A former croft west of Balnault.

**The Croft of Tom Bealaidh*** The Croft of Tombelly (Io 42). A former croft west of Bridge of Gairn, probably near Newton.

**Croft of Tullochcoy*** Croft of Tullachcoy (Opr 50). Possibly same as Wester Tullochcoy. Former habitation near the Inver.

**Croft of Upper Ardmeanach*** Croft of upper Ardmenach (G 10). Possibly same as Croft of Wester Ardmeanach. Former farm west of Ballater.

**Croft of Wester Ardmeanach*** Croft of Wester Ardmanach (G 28). A former farm west of Ballater.

**(The) Crofts** (OS, C, 359944), ðɪˈkrofts, ðɪˈkrafts. The Croft (I). Misread Litil Crosat, Meikil Crosat (Ab 9). A farm in lower Glen Muick.

**The Crofts*** (U, 212939), as above. A field west of the Inver.

**The Crofts Brae*** (C, 358942), ðɪˈkraftsˈbreˑ. A hill on the road up Glen Muick.

**The Crofts Brig*** (F, 359943), ðɪˈkraftsˈbrɪg. A bridge in lower Glen Muick.

**(The) Crofts Cottage** (OS, F, 357941), ðɪˈkroftsˈkɒtədʒ, ðɪˈkrafts ˈkɒtədʒ. Crofts Cottages (OS 1904) included what is now Birch Cottage (Er) nearby. Also the Cottar House o the Crofts (U), ðɪˈkɒtërˈhusəiˈkrafts. In lower Glen Muick.

**The Crofts Haugh*** (F, 362946), ðɪˈkraftsˈhaˑχ. Includes two former fields both called the Marcach formerly. A field in lower Glen Muick.

**Croft Shiel*** (C, 238903), krɒftˈʃil. Croft Sheal (B). A ruin at the roadside west of Glen Gelder.

**The Crofts of Aberarder*** (I, U, 211939), ðɪˌkraftsɐˈabërˈardër. Crofts of Balnoe (OS 1869). Balnuadh Croft, Balno Croft (Io 52, 53). Ruins of former crofts west of the Inver.

**The Crofts o Tomintoul** (C, 146906), ðɪˈkroftsɐˌtamənˈtʌuḷ, the Tomintoul Crofts (D). A collective name for several former crofts near Braemar, from Woodhill east to Cluniebank.

**Croft Sutair** (3). Croft Sutar (Ri 17), a pendicle of Balmore in Glen Feardar, probably had been Creit Sutair (3), tanner's croft.

**The Crofts Wall*** (U, north-west of 360943), ðɪˈkraftsˈwaˑl. A well at roadside in lower Glen Muick.

**Croit Caluim*** (3, c. 275003), Malcolm's croft. Crotcallame (G 3), Croitcallume of Badquharn, Croit of Badquharn (Io 14, 16), Croft of Badquharn (Ri 21, Io 14). West of Gairnshiel.

**Croiteach*** (5, c. 219942), possibly croft place. Possibly Crotach = hump-backed, or variant Cruiteach (Dw). Cruitach (Roy). Building, probably a former farm, north-west of the Inver.

**The Cromlins** See Na Crom-raon.

**Crom-raon*** (3, 346938), crooked field or meadow. Cromeran (Am). In lower Glen Muick.

**Na Crom-raon** (3, 153917), the crooked fields. The Croum Runes (I), Na Cromaran (D), the Cromlins (A, C), ðɪ ˈkrɒmlənz. Note that Cromaran in Badenoch 'is possibly for Crom-raon, the crooked field' (Mb), and the evidence from Braemar indicates this. Former fields between Braemar and Creag Choinnich.

**(The) Crooked Grain** (OS, C, 360865), ðɪˈkrukətˈgren, Scots Grain = stream. Runs into mid Glen Muick.

**The Crooked Rigs*** (I, 281953). A former field east of Crathie.

**The Crooked Wreath** See Cuidhe Crom.

**Crookie's Wall*** (F, south-east of 316008), ˈkrukizˈwaˑl. A well east of Gairnshiel.

**Cross Butts*** (I, 352924), now the Cnocan Dubh Park (F), ðɪ
ˌknǫkɐnˈduˑˈpark. A field in lower Glen Muick.

**The Cross Path*** (C, 271840), ðɪˈkrǫsˈpaθ. A path from Glas
Allt to the head of Glen Gelder.

**(The) Cross Stripe** (OS, F, 315837), ðɪˈkrǫsˈstrɛip. A burn in
upper Glen Muick, running at right angles down the hill into
Allt Darrarie, so had probably been an Allt or Alltan
Tarsuinn originally.

**The Croy** (west of 150925), Scots Croy = structure built into a
river. The Croy (Ta). A ford with stepping stones across Dee
(see also Gf 67), near Braemar.

**The Croy*** (3, U, 151913), ðɪˈkrɔi, Scots Croy = mound or quay
built into a river. A place on Clunie Water at Braemar where
the river was once divided artificially to form a lade.

**Cruinn Choire** (OS, 142803), round corrie. Cor Croin (I)
indicates Coire Cruinn (3), same meaning. A corrie of semi-
circular shape north of the Cairnwell. Also the Sean Spittal
Corrie (U), ðɪˈʃanˌspëtəlˈkǫre, after the Sean Spittal Bridge
below it.

**Crystalls** (OS, C, 260953), should be the Chrystal's (D), ðɪ
ˈkrëstəlz. A house named after a person of that name who
lived there, at Crathie. An Alexander Chrystal lived at
'Crathie Cottage' in 1851 (Io).

**Crystall's Burn*** (C, 260952), ˈkrëstəlzˈbʌrn. The lower part of
Crathie Burn, near the above house. Also the Piper Burn (F),
ðɪˈpɛipërˈbʌrn.

**Crystall's Smiddie*** (U, 259952), ˈkrëstəlzˈsmɪdi. Former smithy
below main road at Crathie.

**Cuailean Chlach*** (3, 290992), wreath of stones. Cualin Clach
(I), Coullan clach (R 14). On a hill spur south of Gairnshiel.

**(The) Cuidhe Crom** (OS, C, 260849), ðɪˌkuiˈkrǫm, from A'
Chuithe Chrom (2), the crooked wreath. Locally, the name is
understood to refer to a prominent crooked snow wreath at
261852 that usually persists into July. However, it is also
used for the whole hill between the OS location and the cliff
edge to the north-west. A better spelling would be A' Chuithe
Chrom as Cuithe is a snow wreath but Cuidhe a cattle fold.
Cuidhe Crom probably a mistake for Cuithe Chrom the bent
snow wreath (Erskine 1912). The Cuithe Crom (Gordon
1912). Also the Crooked Wreath (U), ðɪˈkrukətˈvreθ, Scots
vreθ = wreath. The Crookit Vrythe (A). Note that there is
another Cuithe Chrom at the top of Coire Cas on the Spey
side of Cairn Gorm, where a crooked wreath also lasts far
into the summer. On Lochnagar.

**Cùil a' Phuirneidh*** (5, F, 302936), ˌkɐləˈfǫrnjə, nook of the
hunter. Given to us as if California. A little hollow south-east
of Abergeldie.

**Cuir ? Bhuig Gnòdh*** (5, 234907), turns (i.e. stream bends) of
the gloomy bog. Cuirvygnaw or Cor-buie burn (Io 78). West
of Balmoral, in an area with a boggy, slow-running burn.

**The Cuithe Iomlan Burn*** See Feardar Burn.

**An Cùl*** (5, 344978), the back. The Coul (I). A field in lower
Glen Gairn.

**An Cùl*** (5, 303014), the back. The Cul (I). A field north-east of
Gairnshiel.

**Cùl** (5, 143906), back. Cul (D). A field south-west of Braemar.

**Cula Burn** (OS, 182994), locally the Coire na Culath Burn (U),
ðɪˌkǫrnəˈkulɐˈbʌrn. Also Allt na Cùlath (5), burn of the back
place. Ault na Cula (I), Allt na Cula (D, A 283). South-east
of Ben Avon.

**Culardoch** (OS, C, 193988), kəlˈaˑrdǫç, from Cùl Ardach Mór
(3, U), kəlˈardǫçˈmoˑr, big back high place. Coulardochie
(Roy), Cullardachy (R 5), Culardach More (I), Culardoch
Mhoir (R 7, 14) (but the latter map often gives Mhoir and
Bheg even in cases where the noun is definitely masculine,
such as Creagan, Mullach, and Socach), Culardach (R 17).

Roy's Coulardochie suggests Cùl Ardachaidh Mór originally.
A hill south of Loch Builg. Note Culardoch Bheag below.

**Culardoch Bheag** (OS, 192008 is wrong location, should be at
194999 (I, U)), from Cùl Ardach Beag (3, U), kəlˈardǫçˈbeg,
little back place. Culardach Beg (I). Also Little Culardoch
(OS). The old OS 1-inch maps give Little Culardoch at about
192002, much nearer the correct location.

**The Culardoch Burn** See Allt nan Sgalan.

**The Culardoch Deer Fence*** (U, 202994), ðɪˌkəlˈardǫçˈdirˈfɛns.
North-west of the Inver.

**The Culardoch Stable*** (C, 180981), ðɪˌkəlˈardǫçˈstebəl. A hut
north of Invercauld.

**The Culath Ridge*** (U, 115771), ðɪˈkulɐˈrɪdʒ. A broad ridge west
of the Cairnwell.

**Culblean Cottage*** See Trochietroddles.

**Culblean Hill** (OS, 412010), locally usually Culblean (C) with
no Hill, kəlˈbliˑn, from Coille ? Bhliann (5), wood of
? possibly the sun-basking. Cül-vlīūn, cül-vlĭŭn, cül na vlĭŭn,
kyl-ya-vlīun; the first syllable is known to be *coille*, 'wood';
coill' bhlīunng, coill' bhlīunn, final *nn* broad (D), D in A
transcription probably has errors by A. Hill of Colblean
(R 1), the hill of Colblaine (Io 20). Several old records show
Kil as the first part of the name (A). Alexander noted the old
saying 'Cushnie for cauld, Culblean for heat'. A hill north of
Cambus o' May.

**The Culblean Road*** See the Auld Ballater Road.

**Cùl Cheardaich*** (5, F, 412969), kəlˈçjardǫç, back of the smithy,
possibly first word is Coille = wood. Kilchardach (Dms).
Near Inchmarnoch.

**The Cul Cheardaich Park*** (F, 414967), ðɪˌkəlˈçjardǫçˈpark. A
little field south of Cambus o' May.

**The Cul Cheardaich Wuid*** (C, 413968), ðɪˌkəlˈçjardǫçˈwɪd. A
wood south of Cambus o' May.

**The Cul Dorch Corrie*** See Coire Cul Dorch.

**Cùl Fearn*** (5, 152905), alder back. Coul Fyarn (I). A field by
Clunie, south of Braemar.

**Cùl Garaidh*** (3, F, 146914), kəlˈgaˑre, back of dyke. A small
piece of land and former house at Braemar, whose last
inhabitant is still remembered as Auld Cul Garaidh's, ˈaˑlˌkəl
ˈgaˑrez. The land is now part of the west end of the garden at
Lilybank, and is marked by an old gean tree (MC).

**Cùl Leasachaidh** (F, north of 347953), kəˈlɛsɐxe, Cùl (5)
= back, or Cùil = nook, Leasachaidh (3) = of improving,
manuring. Cullesachie (Io 33), Collesachy (Ap), Colesachy
(Am). A former farm west of Ballater.

**The Cul Leasachaidh Park*** (U, 344951), ðɪˌkəˈlɛsɐxeˈpark. A
field beside above farm.

**Cùl nan Gad** (5, A, 328888), back of the withes. Culnagad (I). A
stretch of rough moor running down to the river in upper
Glen Muick, with boggy patches.

**(An) Cùl Riabhach** (OS, 5, C, 178798), ðɪˌkəlˈriǫç, the brindled
back. Cul Riabhach is a general name for a big area north of
the Glas Maol, and the OS location is Cul Riabhach Beag
(see below).

**An Cúl Riabhach** (5, C, 332996), as above, the brindled back
Culriach (I), Culreach (OS 1869). A former farm in Glen
Gairn.

**Cùl Riabhach Beag*** (5, U, 175797), ˌkəlˌriǫçˈbeg, little brindled
back. This is approximately the place given the name Cul
Riabhach on the OS map. The name refers not to the ridge as
on the OS map, but to the corrie below, as in the nearby Cul
Riabhach Mor. North-east of the Glas Maol.

**The Cul Riabhach Brae** (C, 331998), ðɪˌkəlˈriǫçˈbreˑ. The
Culreoch Brae (Af). A hill on the road in Glen Gairn.

**The Cul Riabhach Haugh*** (F, 334995), ðɪˌkəlˈriǫçˈhaˑχ. A field
in lower Glen Gairn.

**Cùl Riabhach Mór*** (5, 178789), big brindled back. Culriach more (I). A corrie north-east of the Glas Maol.

**(The) Culsh** (OS, C, 345978), ðɪˈkʌlʃ, from A' Chùilt (3), the nook (note W 140). The Culltes (Io 8), Cuillt (Cr 15), Coults (R 14), Cults (Gr 240), Chūiltsh (D). A farm near Bridge of Gairn. A Culsh said to be in Braemar parish (M) on the basis of an old spelling Quiltis (Ca) was probably confused with the Gairn one.

**(The) Culsten Burn** (OS, C, 394994), ðɪˈkolstənˈbʌrn, from ? Còmhdail = meeting (3, W 492) and English Stone, as in Logie Coldstone Burn, for early forms of Coldstone see Barrow (1981). Also the Burn of Glen Colstane. The Burn of Glencoldstane (Ra 2a). West of Cambus o' May.

**The Currie** (M), Braemar parish, no other evidence. Probably from Curra (4) = a marsh, or Curraigh from Currach = marsh place.

**Cuttie's Croft*** (Am, 346937), a former croft, now in a wood, in lower Glen Muick.

**Dail** See Dail Ruighe an Fhliuch-choille-shlat.

**Dail a' Bhaird*** (3, 348920), haugh of the park. Dailevard (I). A field in lower Glen Muick.

**Dail a' Bhoididh** (OS, 3, A, U, 999825), a better spelling would be Bhoitidh, dalˈvoitʃi, haugh of the sow or of the pig-calling (i.e. people calling to pigs). Dal-vaotshi (D in A). A haugh on the march north of Glen Tilt.

**Dail a' Bhreac-achaidh** (3, C, 148910), ˌdalˈvrɛgˌɐxe, dalˈvreːgçi (Sch), haugh of the speckled field. Dalvrakachy (Im 5), Dellavreikkichi (Cr 3), Dalvreckachy (Gr), Dal-vrehki, Dal-vryk-achy (D in A). A farm at Braemar, now called the Easter Manse; the ruins of the old steading are still visible.

**Dail a' Bhreac-achaidh*** (F, 149910), as above. A field at Braemar.

**The Dail a' Bhreac-achaidh Wuid*** (F, 147909), ðɪˌdalˈvrɛgˌɐxe ˈwɪd. Usually now the Manse Wuid (C), ðɪˈmansˈwɪd. A birch wood near Braemar.

**Dail a' Chata*** (5, 146863), haugh of the sheep-cot, possibly Dail a' Chait = haugh of the cat. Dallachat (Ra 6), Delachat (Rli 23). A former farm in mid Glen Clunie, above Fraser's Brig.

**Dail a' Chata Bheag*** (5, U, south-west of 148864), ˌdalˌxatˈbɛg, little haugh of the sheep-cot, see above. A small haugh in mid Clunie, forms a pair with the name below.

**Dail a' Chata Mhór*** (5, 145861), big haugh of the sheep-cot, see above. Dalchat Mor (Roy). A fuller name for Dail a' Chata above.

**An Dail a' Choirce** (3, F, 173917), ðɪˌdalˈxork, dalˈfork (U), the oats haugh. Dellfork (Pb), Delchork (Fa), Dellachork, Dellachoirk (Cr 8, 34), Dalchoirk (Rli 23), Dalchork (Ri 17), Haugh of Dalechork (R 7). The Della-chork, the Dellchoirk (Cr) and Burn of the Dalechork (R 7) indicate the article, i.e. An Dail a' Choirce with Choirce used in an adjectival sense (see Caochan Bheithe for further explanation). A former farm near Invercauld, now known as a field, see Dail a' Choirce Park.

**The Dail a' Choirce Park*** (F, 173917), ðɪˌdalˈxorkˈpark. Formerly was called Dail a' Choirce. Dale Chork (I). A field at Invercauld.

**The Dail a' Choirce Puil*** See Poll Dail a' Choirce.

**Dail Aitinn** (3), haugh of juniper. Dalaben misread for Dalaten (S 8), Dallaitin (Me 20), Dalleatin, Dallaiton (Io 14, 74). A former grazing that went with Braeneach north of Crathie.

**Dail a' Mhorair** (3, Cj 1, 314, 034933), haugh of the nobleman. West of Derry Lodge.

**Dail a' Mhorair Bheag** (3, OS 1869, McC, 044892), little haugh of the nobleman. Also Easter Delvorar (M1), Easter

Dellvorar (Mc 21). Part of Dalvorar, refers to a former farm and also to the haugh beside it. West of the Linn of Dee.

**Dail a' Mhorair Mhór** (3, OS 1869, McC, 039893), big haugh of the nobleman. Another former farm and haugh, as above.

**Dail an Sgeich*** (3), haugh of the thorn. Delnaskainch, Delinskainch (Cr 36, 37). A former habitation in the Braemar area, possibly near Ach an Sgeich.

**Dail an t-Suidhe** (3, A, U, 150874), dalˈdui, haugh of the seat. Dallindui (Roy), Dellnidui, Dellnadui (Cr 25, 29), Dallantuigh (Opr 26), Daldooie (I), tal n dui (D in A). A former farm in mid Glen Clunie.

**The Dail Baitidh Moss*** (U, 320959), ðɪˌdalˈbeʤiˈmos, Dail Bàitidh (3) = haugh of marshy ground, Scots Moss = peat-moss. A bog at the foot of Glen Girnock.

**Dail Bheag*** (3, 304012), little haugh. Dale Beg (I). A field east of Gairnshiel.

**Dail Bhreac*** (3, U, 350936), dalˈbrɛk, speckled haugh. Delbreck (Am). Also the Birkhall Haugh (U), ðɪˌbërkˈhaˈˈhaˑχ. A field in lower Glen Muick.

**Dail Bhreac*** (3, 169922), speckled haugh. Dalbreachk (R 7). A former field beside Dee, at Invercauld.

**Dail Bhùirn** (3, U, 179916), dalˈvurn, haugh of the water, i.e. liable to flood (D). Dal-vūrn (D). A flat haugh near Poll Bhuirn on Dee, at Invercauld.

**Dail Chapall*** (3, C, north-east of 370953), dɐlˈhapəl, haugh of horses. Dalhapple known as former name of one of Ballater's older houses, but possibly it was named after a piece of ground there; a former smithy stood close by, not far from the ford over Dee.

**Dail Choirce** (3, U, 218946), dɐlˈxork, haugh of the oats. Dalfork (Roy), Dalchork (Rli 19), Dale Chork (I), Dalchork (OS 1869). Also Derleks (U), ˈdërlëks, ? a nickname for someone there, or from the English word derelicts. A former farm north-west of the Inver.

**Dail Choirce*** (3, 219946). Dale Chork (I). A field near above farm.

**Dail Chòis*** (3, probably 132830), haugh of the hollow. Dallchosh (Ra 3). At the Baddoch.

**An Dail Cnapach*** (3, 341904), the hillocky haugh. The Delcnapack (Rli 2), Dale Knappach (I). A hillocky former field in mid Glen Muick.

**Dail Cnoc Dubh*** (3, 138835), haugh of black hillock. Dale Knock Du (I). A former field on the east side of the river in upper Glen Clunie.

**Dail Gainimh** (5, 054921), haugh of sand or Ghaineamhach = sandy. Dalgirmich (Roy) might suggest Gairmeich = of calling, but numerous errors in Roy. Dalgennie, Dalgenie (Me 15), Dalgwnich (Ar). A former farm in Glen Lui.

**Dail Iaruinn** (3, U, 292957), dalˈiərən, haugh of iron. Dal-iarun (D). A hard field below Greystone east of Crathie, also the former name of the farm now called Greystone, the original Greystone being further west (WD).

**Dail Laoigh*** (3, 214019), haugh of calf. Dail Bhuie (R 3) indicates Bhuidhe = yellow, but Dalluie (Io 22), Sheals of Daluie (I) and Rie Dalluie (R 12) indicate Laoigh. By Gairn side, west of Corndavon Lodge.

**Dail Léigidh*** (396974), Dail (3) = haugh, Léigidh (5) from Léig = marshy pool, possibly Dail Eugaidh = spectral haugh. Dalaigies (R 4, Io 58), a plural. On the farmland at Tullich east of Ballater.

**Dail Lìn** (3, 299008), haugh of flax. Dal-yean, lint-haugh (D). A field near Gairnshiel.

**Dail Mallachaidh** (3, U, two fields at 358945 and 359947), dal ˈmalɐχe, haugh of cursing. Dalmalochy (Ap), Dalmallochy (Am), Delmalochy (Vr 2). Also Haugh of Dalmulachy (Ap), Haugh of Delmulachie (Rli 17). Also the Haugh of Aucholzie

(Ri 10), Haugh of Auchoillie commonly called the Haugh of
Dalmulachy (G 35). In lower Glen Muick, far below
Aucholzie but formerly at the edge of the former estate of
Aucholzie. Field 359947 later the Little Squarie (U), ðɪˈlɛ̈təl
ˈskwere, Scots Squarie = little square.

**An Dail Mhór** (2, Gr 34, C, 096899), ðɪˌdalˈmoˑr, the big haugh.
N dal mor, N dal vor (D). The big haugh at Mar Lodge.

**An Dail Mhor** See Mar Lodge.

**Dail Mhór** (3, 337995), big haugh. Dalmore (A 362). A haugh
at Lary in Glen Gairn.

**Dail Mhorair\*** (3, U, 270820), dalˈvɔrër, haugh of the
nobleman. Flat moor called Dale vorar (I), Dalvorar Muir
(Am). At the top of Loch Muick.

**The Dail Mhor Park\*** (F, 335997), ðɪˌdalˈmoˑrˈpark. A field at
Lary (see two names up).

**Dail na Cachaileithe\*** (3, C, 028889), ˌdalnɐˈkaχḻa, haugh of the
field gate. The evidence here, together with the final *a* in
Dalnacochla (I) in the name below, suggests a local spelling
of Cachalaith, and Cachalath was said (Dro) to be a gate in
Braemar Gaelic. A big haugh west of the Linn of Dee.

**Dail na Cachaileithe\*** (3, U, west of 026887), as above, haugh of
the field gate. A former house in Glen Dee.

**Dail na Cachaileithe\*** (3, 136834), haugh of the field gate.
Dalnacochla (I). A former field at the Baddoch.

**Dail na Croise\*** (3, 132828), haugh of the cross. Dalna-croish
(I), Dallnicross (Ra 3). A former farm at the Baddoch.

**Dail na h-Eagarrath\*** (5, south of 329003), haugh of ? the place
in rows, or possibly from Eagar = notched, from Eag
= notch. Dalenahekra (I). A field at Torbeg in Glen Gairn.

**Dail na Lacha\*** (3, 359945), haugh of the wild duck. Dalnalach
(I). A field in lower Glen Muick.

**Dail nam Bó\*** (3, 305011), haugh of the cows. Dalnabo (I). A
field with no farm (1807–9), so the farm Dalnabo is more
recent. East of Gairnshiel.

**Dail nam Bòrd\*** (3, U, 079898), ˌdalnɐˈbɔrd, haugh of the
planks. Dal nam bord (Da). A former field east of the Linn
of Dee.

**Dail nam Bòrd** (3, 076898). Dailnabord (Opr 25), Dellnabord,
Dalnamboord (Cr 5, 38), Dalnabord (Opr 9, Gr), Dal nam
bord (Da). A former farm at the above place.

**Dail nam Breac\*** (3, probably 092859), haugh of the ? speckled
places, see Sron nam Breac. Delnabrock (Io 21), Delnabreak,
Delnabreck (Me 13, 18). A former farm in Glen Ey.

**Dail nam Fiadh** (3, F, 100854), ˌdalnɐˈfeː, haugh of the deer.
Dalnafia (Roy, Ar), Dalnafeu (Io 79), Dalnafae (Ra 6, Mpj),
Delnafea, Dalnafae (Me 13, 21). A former farm in mid Glen
Ey.

**Dail nan Crodh\*** (5, 387972), haugh of the cattle, or possibly
Dail nan Crò = haugh of the folds. Dalnagro (Io 58). On
farmland at Tullich.

**Dail nan Gamhainn\*** (4, U, 131912), dalɡʌu.ən, haugh of the
stirks. West of Braemar. See Dalgowan.

**Dail nan Sleac\*** (3, U, 076897), ˌdalnɐˈsleçk, haugh of the rock
slabs. Sleac is an eastern form of Leac. East of the Linn of
Dee, beside slabby rocks at the river.

**Dail Nighinne\*** (3, 343903), maiden's haugh. Delnene (Rli 2). A
former field in mid Glen Muick, on east side of burn.

**Dail Riabhach\*** (3, 093834), brindled haugh. Dalreach,
Dulreoch (Io 79). In upper Glen Ey.

**Dail Roibidh** (3, F, 337999), dalˈrɔbi, Robbie's haugh. Dalrobie
(A 362). A field at Lary in Glen Gairn.

**Dail Rosaigh** (3, C, 048925), dalˈrɔse, haugh at wooded place
(note W 497). Dail an rosaich (D), Dail n-rosaich (Drc) with
phonetics that we would give as dalṇˈrosiç, but Diack
elsewhere gave Dail rossi (D), Dail arasaidh (Dro). A former
farm in Glen Lui.

**The Dail Rosaigh Burn\*** (U, 048924), ðɪˌdalˈrɔseˈbʌrn. In Glen
Lui.

**Dail Ruighe an Fhliuch-choille-shlat\*** (3, 095859), haugh of shiel
at the wet wattle-wood. See Ruighe an Fhliuch-choille-shlat.
Dell Riin Luchulit clearly written (Cr 30), with the *u*
elsewhere indicating an *oo* sound in well-known names.
Delrienlucherit (Fa), Dalrienduchlat (Ra 6), Dalruchlait,
Dal-ruie duchach (Io 21, 79), Delrielughlach (Opr 22),
Delruchlait, Dalrinduchlat (Me 13, 15), Dail (OS 1869). A
former farm in Glen Ey.

**Dail Sheasaimh\*** (3, 275948), haugh of the firmness. Dalehessie
(I). A former field on a stony plain east of Crathie.

**Dail Sheasaimh\*** (3, 274946), all as above. A former field
adjacent to above.

**Dailthean Teannta\*** (3, 096786), compact haughs. Daln tent (I).
A grassy patch by the burnside at the top of the
Baddoch.

**Dail Tom nam Meann\*** (3, 128817), haugh of hillock of the kids.
Dale-Toum-na-maun (I). Also the Haugh of Tom nam
Meann. The Haugh of Tomnamoan (Io 23). Formerly an
island (I), now land on east side of Baddoch Burn.

**Dairbhreadh** (3, 058906 and 080910), grove. Dereray silva (Go),
Darrarey, Woods of Derrerey, fir trees of Dararay (Me 2, 3,
3), Wood of Dereray (Fa), the fir wood of Dirrirai (Vd),
Dereraie (Im 3), Dereray (Io 25a). Dairbhreach = of an oak-
grove in Irish Gaelic (Od), and in Irish names Dairbhre
generally means a place of oaks and is pronounced Darrery
(J). Doire or the anglicised Derry usually refer to oak woods
in Ireland, but Doire, Derry and Dairbhreadh on Mar were
all fir woods, and still are. A wood shown (Fa) as stretching
from Luibeg to the Linn of Dee down the west side of Glen
Lui, but now mostly gone. Other maps (Go, Im) and papers
(Io) referred to it as the big fir woods on the east side of
lower Glen Lui, and Doire Bhraghad (OS) may have been a
mistaken attempt to represent Dairbhreadh.

**The Dairy Dip\*** (U, 261945), ðɪˈdereˈdëp. A little hollow near
Balmoral.

**Dalbagie** (OS, C, 340965), from Dail Bàitidh (3), dalˈbeʤi,
flooded haugh. Dalpadie (Ca), Dalbattie (Vr 1), Dalbàdgie
(M), Dal-pāji (D). A farm west of the Bridge of Gairn, beside
a boggy flat that fills up with water after much rain.

**Daldownie** (OS, C, 246009), dalˈduni, from Dail Dùnaidh (3),
haugh of little knoll. Daldoonie (Opr 40), Daldùnie (M), Dal-
dūni (D). A former farm south-east of Corndavon Lodge,
beside the prominent knoll of Tom an t-Sidhein.

**The Daldownie Burn\*** (F, 244008), ðɪˌdalˈduniˈbʌrn. Burn of
Daldownie (R 6a). Beside Daldownie.

**The Daldownie Corrie\*** (U, 240004), ðɪˌdalˈduniˈkɔre. The
whole basin to the south and south-west of Daldownie,
including the Corrie o the Bittie and the Black Corrie.

**The Daldownie Puil\*** (C, north-west of 245001), ðɪˌdalˈduniˈpil.
A pool in Gairn at Daldownie.

**Dalfad** (OS, C, 316007), dalˈfad, from An Dail Fhada (3), the
long haugh. Dellfad (Cr 7), Dalfat, N dal-àt (D), Dailfhad (D
in A). A former farm east of Gairnshiel, above a long haugh
at 315005.

**Dalgowan** (OS, C, 132911), dalˈɡʌu.ən, from Dail nan
Gamhainn (4), haugh of the stirks. Dellnagowin (Cr 1, 6, 6,
27), Dallgowine (Opr 16), Dalagowan (Ra 7), Dalnagowan
(Io 79). A house west of Braemar.

**The Dalgowan Brae\*** (C, 132910), ðɪˌdalˈɡʌu.ənˈbreˑ. A hill on
the road west of Braemar.

**The Dalgowan Burn\*** (Md, C, 133910), ðɪˌdalˈɡʌu.ənˈbʌrn. Burn
at Dalgowan.

**The Dalliefour Haughs\*** (U, 355957), ðɪˌdaleˈfuṛˈhaˑχs. Flat
fields by Dee, west of Ballater.

**(The) Dalliefour Wood** (OS, C, 343958, should be further east at 353960), ðɪˌdaleˈfuɾˈwɪd. A wood near Dallyfour, west of Ballater.

**Dallyfour** (OS, C, 359950), ˌdaleˈfuɾ, often called Scurriestone locally, from Dail a' Phùir (3), haugh of the pasture, as in Balfour, Pitfour etc (note W 377). Dillyfour (Rli 23), Delafhuar (I, Ro), Dal-fur and Dailidh Phuir (D in A). The oldest spellings in 1599 and 1622 are Dalfour and Delfour (A). A farm south-west of Ballater, was originally on site of present Dallyfour Cottage.

**Dallyfour Cottage** (OS, C, 356957), ˌdaleˈfuɾˈkɔtədʒ. West of Ballater.

**Dalmochie** (OS, C, 379961), dalˈmʌχe, from Dail Muc-achaidh (3) haugh of pig field. Dalmuchachie (Io 6), Dalmuckachie (G 4), Dalmuickeachie (Bal), Dalmuckachye (Hr), Dalmuckty (Roy), pronounced Dalmuckie (A) but this was incorrect. Pananich Cottage (OS 1869). A house east of Ballater.

**(The) Dalmochie Burn** (OS, C, 386954), ðɪˌdalˈmʌχeˈbʌrn. A burn east of Ballater.

**(The) Dalmochie Camp** (OS, C, 379960), ðɪˌdalˈmʌχeˈkamp. A camp for lumbermen during the 1939–45 war, east of Ballater.

**The Dalmochie Roadie*** (C, 376958), ðɪˌdalˈmʌχeˈrodi. A footpath through the wood to Dalmochie.

**Dalnabo** (OS, C, 303011), ˌdalnɐˈboː, sometimes ˌdɛlnɐˈboː, from Dail nam Bó (3), haugh of the cows. A farm east of Gairnshiel.

**The Dalnabo Brae*** (F, 309008), ðɪˌdalnɐˈboˑˈbreˑ. A hill on the road in Glen Gairn.

**The Dalnabo Wuid*** (F, 303008), ðɪˌdalnɐˈboˑˈwɪd. A wood east of Gairnshiel.

**Dalphuil** (OS, C, 299009), dalˈful, older speakers used the Gaelic palatal *l* (A), from Dail a' Phuill (3), haugh of the pool. Delfuill (Io 53a), Dalefuil (I). Also the name of a school later (which was marked as a school on the Invercauld map), subsequently used as a house. Also the Auld Schoolhouse (C), ðɪˈaˑlˈskulˌhus. The Old Schoolhouse, or Teapot Cottage (Evening Express, Sept. 10, 1983). East of Gairnshiel.

**Dalraddie** (OS, C, 303958), dalˈradi, from Dail Radaidh (3), dark red haugh, as in Dalraddy in Badenoch (Mb). Dal-rati (D). A house east of Abergeldie, beside a haugh which is now wooded.

**The Dalraddie Puil** (C, 302958), ðɪˌdalˈradiˈpil. Dalraddie (A, Sc). In Dee, near above house.

**Dalvorar** (OS, C, 044892), dalˈvɔrër, from Dail a' Mhorair (3), haugh of the nobleman. Della-voirrar, Della vorrar (Cr 33, 34), Dalavorror (Ra 11), Dalmorear (Opr 39), Delavorar (K). A former farm (Dail a' Mhorair Mhor), and haugh, west of the Linn of Dee. See Dail a' Mhoraire Bheag and Mhor.

**(The) Dalvorar Burn** (OS, F, 047889), ðɪˌdalˈvɔrërˈbʌrn, locally usually Allt Leth-allt (3, C), ˌaltˈljeɐlt, burn of half burn or half slope (i.e. with a steeper slope on one side than on the other, as is the case here). Here Allt possibly retains its old meaning of a steep slope or bank (note Mb 264, Robertson 1929). Some informants gave it as the Leth-allt, but the most knowledgeable ones as Allt Leth-allt. This is confirmed by the anglicised name of the pool in Dee below, the Allt Leth-allt Pool. Lealt (Go), Allt Leth (OS 1869), Allt leth, allt lye (D), Leth-Allt, ljealt, half-burn (A), nearby hill Carn an Leth-allt (OS). South-west of the Linn of Dee.

**Dalvorar Corrie** (OS, 040876), locally Coire Allt Leth-allt (3, C), ˌkɔrˌaltˈljeɐlt, corrie of burn of half burn (i.e. with a steeper slope on one side). See above name.

**The Dalvorar Pool** (C, 039894), ðɪˌdalˈvɔrërˈpul. Dalvorar Pool (Ly). In Dee, west of the Linn of Dee.

**The Dalvorars*** (U) ðɪˌdalˈvɔrërz. Dalavorars (Im 3). A composite name for Dail a' Mhorair Bheag and Mhor, two former farms west of Linn of Dee.

**The Damhaidh Pass*** (F, 965908), ðɪˈdaviˈpas. A pass on Beinn Bhrotain, named after the nearby Allt Dhaidh Beag.

**The Damhaidh Pool*** (U, 969873), ðɪˈdaviˈpul. A pool on Geldie, named after the nearby Allt Dhaidh Mor.

**The Dam Park*** (U, 416041), ðɪˈdamˈpark. A field west of Logie Coldstone.

**The Dam Road*** (U, 256956), ðɪˈdamˈrod. An old track west of Crathie.

**The Danzig Shiel** See the Garbh Allt Shiel.

**The Danzig Shiel Bridge** See the Suspension Brig.

**The Darach** (C, 361963), ðɪˈdarɐχ. The Darrach (Afr). The hill where the Braemar road from Ballater climbs below Craigendarroch.

**The Darach Road** (A, C, 360965), ðɪˈdarɐχˈrod. Road out of Ballater towards Braemar, below Craigendarroch.

**Darach Well*** (R 4, 379973), Darach (3) = oak. A well at the east end of the Pass of Ballater, below the former Oak Wood of Tullich, on north side of road.

**The Darling Way*** See the Moss Road.

**Na Da Shidhean** (3, Sg, U, 060919), ˌnəˈdaˑˈhiˑən, the two hillocks. Also the Sidheans (U), ðɪˈʃiənz. Also the Fairy Hillocks (F), ðɪˈfereˈhëlëks. Two symmetrical hillocks in Glen Lui.

**Dawan** See Loch Davan.

**An Deamhas** (3, 076824), the shears. N djensh, deamhas, sheep-shears (D). A spot that looks like a sheep shears (D). The grooves on the hillside are conspicuous from Glen Ey above Altanour Lodge, and look remarkably like sheep shears.

**The Dee** See River Dee.

**Deecastle** (OS, C, 438967), diˈkasəl, diˈkaˑstəl (F). Formerly Ceann na Coille (3), end of the wood. Also Hunthall in 1638 (Dms 6), Keanakyll (Go), Castle of Kean-na-kyll (Mf), Candakyle or Hunthall called Dee Castle (Asr) in 1815, Cean-na-coil (Milne), Cyanng a coill (D). A former castle of the Earls of Aboyne, now a farm, south-west of Dinnet.

**The Deecastle Brig*** (C, 438969), ðɪˌdɪˈkasəlˈbrɪg. A former bridge near Inchmarnoch.

**The Deecastle Burn*** (C, 437960), ðɪˌdiˈkasəlˈbʌrn. Above Deecastle. Lower part below the farm is the High Burn.

**Deecastle Cottage** (C), diˈkasəlˈkɔtədʒ. Lower (Er, C, 437967), Upper (Vr, C, 438968). Beside above farm.

**The Deecastle Hill*** (C, 440950), ðɪˌdiˈkasəlˈhël. A general name for the hill grazing above Deecastle, south-west of Dinnet.

**Dee Cot** See Ruighe na Culath.

**Dee Ford*** (Im 3, 021885). The Foord called Dee ford (Im). West of Linn of Dee.

**The Deer Gate*** (U, 276932), ðɪˈdiɾˈget. A gate in a deer fence, now a cattle grid, south-west of Abergeldie.

**The Deer Park*** (F, 073898), ðɪˈdiɾˈpark. A former enclosure near Mar Lodge, for keeping captive red deer before releasing them.

**The Deer Park*** (C, 235934), as above. A field where deer were once kept, south-west of Balmoral.

**The Deer Park*** (F, 110900), as above. Near Mar Lodge.

**The Deer Parkie*** (U, 371943), ðɪˈdiɾˈparki. A field used for feeding deer in lower Glen Muick.

**Deers Well*** (In, south-east of 316951). In lower Glen Girnock.

**Deeside** (A, C), diˈsɛid. A general name for anywhere in the Dee valley. In Gaelic was Oir Dhé (3, D), orr-yē (D), side of Dee.

**The Deil's Needle*** See the Kelpie's Needle.

**The Deil's Needle Park*** (U, 429965), ðɪˈdilzˈnidl̩ˈpark, Scots

Deil = devil. A field named after a stone with a hole in it, in the river below, south-east of Cambus o' May.

**Demesne of Invercauld** See the Mains of Invercauld.

**(The) Den Burn** (OS, C, 290940), ðɪˈdɛnˈbʌrn. A burn in the Den o Abergeldie.

**The Den o Abergeldie\*** (C, 291945), ðɪˈdɛnɐˌɛbërˈgɛ̣ldi. A defile.

**The Den Road\*** (U, 288947), ðɪˈdɛnˈrod. A track near Abergeldie.

**Derleks\*** See Dail a' Choirce.

**The Derry** (Roy, C, 042934), ðɪˈdɛre, from An Doire (2), an dürr (Da), n dör with front *r* (A), the grove. The Diry, the Dairy (Fi), Derry (R 10). Further details in A. A general name for the area at the junction of Derry and Luibeg.

**(The) Derry Burn** (OS, C, 035958), ðɪˈdɛreˈbʌrn. B. of the Dirr (Crom). Also Uisge an Doire (2, U), ˌuʃkɐnˈdo̩r, water of the grove, or An Doire. An doir, uisg an doir (D). Also Water of Derie (Fa). In Glen Derry.

**(The) Derry Cairngorm** (OS, C, 017980), ðɪˈdɛreˌkernˈgo̩rɔm, from An Carn Gorm (2, U), nˌgarnˈgo̩rɔm, the blue hill, later called Carn Gorm an Doire, or Cairn Gorm of Derry (A), to distinguish it from the Cairn Gorm on Strath Spey, and later the Derry Cairngorm, also formerly the Eastern or Lesser Cairngorm (McC in Cj). Carn Gorum, the Cairngorum (Fi), Carn gorm n doir (D). A striking hill from Inverey, looking much higher than Ben Macdui. From Inverey it often has a dark blue colour, though less so from Glen Derry; similarly the Strath Spey Cairn Gorm often has a dark blue colour from Nethy Bridge though less often from Aviemore. West of Glen Derry.

**(The) Derry Dam** (OS, C, 034961, should be at 039958), ðɪˈdɛreˈdam. Remnants of the wooden foundations were clearly visible in the early 1950s, and no dam could have worked in the location shown on the OS map. Ruins of Dam shown on an 1826 map (R 10). In Glen Derry.

**The Derry Dam Brig\*** (C, 040958), ðɪˈdɛreˈdamˈbrig. A bridge beside the above dam.

**The Derry Dam Fuird\*** (F, just west of 040958), ðɪˈdɛreˈdamˈfjurd. A ford for horses, just west of a footbridge over Derry Burn.

**The Derry Dam Lochie\*** (C, 038956), ðɪˈdɛreˈdamˈlo̩χe. A small loch near the above dam.

**The Derry Falls\*** See Easan Doire.

**The Derry Fit Brig\*** (F, 040935), ðɪˈdɛreˈfëtˈbrɪg. A foot bridge at Derry Lodge.

**The Derry Gate\*** (C, 068898), ðɪˈdɛreˈget. A gate at the foot of Glen Lui.

**The Derry Haughs\*** (C, 035960), ðɪˈdɛreˈhaˑχs. Grassy valley floor in Glen Derry. Sometimes the Derry Flats.

**The Derry Lochan Uaine\*** See Lochan Uaine.

**The Derry Lochie\*** (U, 044935), ðɪˈdɛreˈlo̩χe. A pond near Derry Lodge.

**(The) Derry Lodge** (OS, C, 041934), ðɪˈdɛreˈlo̩ʤ. A former shooting lodge at the top of Glen Lui.

**The Derry Plantin\*** (F, 045930), ðɪˈdɛreˈplantɪn. Plantation near Derry Lodge.

**Derry Pool** See Poll Inbhir Laoigh.

**The Derry Road\*** (C, 050927), ðɪˈdɛreˈrod. Glenluie Road (R 10), lower part at 067899 was Luieside Road (R 10). Road to Derry Lodge, up Glen Lui.

**The Derry Shiel\*** See Auld Derry Lodge.

**The Derry Wuid\*** (C, 042936), ðɪˈdɛreˈwɪd. Wood of Derie (Fa). Wood in Glen Derry. A repetitive anglicisation, as Derry means a wood.

**(The) Deuchrie Burn** (OS, 240947), from the nearby Dubh-chatharaigh (see below). There is no corrie here, so Dubh-

choire is unlikely. The lower part of the Coldrach Burn. North-east of the Inver.

**The Devil's Cave** See Geusachan Cave.

**The Devil's Glen** See Gleann Garbh-choire.

**The Devil's Kitchen** (Wa, C, 196832), ðɪˈdɪvəlzˈkëtʃën. The whole big face of broken cliffs and steep slopes on the east side of Glen Callater from the loch upwards.

**The Devil's Point** (OS, C, 976951), ðɪˈdɪvəlzˈpoint, ðɪˈdɪvəlz ˈpɛint, from Bod an Deamhain (2, F), ˌbo̩ḍɐnˈdjo̩n, penis of the demon. Potindeon (Go), Potenjohn (Fi), huge rocks of Poten Duon (K). Other old spellings (see A) confirm this, but none of the writers gave the translation, either leaving it as 'the deivells —', or saying it is a 'literal translation' (A). From the Lairig Ghru path the hill rears up steeply, and no doubt the view from here gave the hill its name. Also Bod an Diabhail (3, IG), ˌbo̩ḍɐnˈdjiəl, penis of the devil. Bodindeweill (Bal), Potters Dioul (Ros), Bod-an-diaouil (Mg), Bod an Diabhoil (Bu). Also Stob nan Deamhain (3, Grigor Grant of Speyside, heard by IG), ˌsto̩ḅnɐnˌdjo̩n, point of the demons. Also Creag Bhiorach Gleann Giubhasachain (3), sharp rock of Glen Geusachan or glen of little fir wood. Creag Bhiorach Gleann Giuthsachain (Bu). Also Pioc an Donais (3, Bu), pick-axe of the devil. South-east of Cairn Toul.

**(The) Devil's Point Burn** (OS, U, 965945), ðɪˈdɪvəlzˈpointˈbʌrn. On the above hill.

**The Devil's Punch Bowl** See the Punch Bowl.

**The Diagonal Path** (Wa, C, 271816), ðɪˌdaeˈagənəlˈpaθ. South-west from the top of Loch Muick.

**Dikehead Cottage** (OS 1904, 352979). A former house at the top of field dykes north of Bridge of Gairn.

**The Dining Room\*** (F, 022967), ðɪˈdɛinənˌrum, sometimes the Duke o Fife's Dining Room, ðɪˈdjukɐˈfɛifsˈdɛinənˌrum. A gentle slope on Derry Cairngorm.

**The Dining Room Butts\*** (U, 227015), ðɪˈdɛinənˌrumˈbʌts. Two sets of grouse butts, Upper and Lower, south of Corndavon Lodge.

**The Dining Room Corrie\*** (F, 963821), ðɪˈdɛinənˌrumˈko̩re. A little corrie near the top of Bynack Burn.

**The Dining Room Pass\*** (F, 020967), ðɪˈdɛinənˌrumˈpas. A pass offering an easy way from Carn Crom through to Coire Sputan Dearg.

**Dinnet** (OS, C, 460988), ˈdënët. Earlier forms were Dunnatye, Dunnatie, Dunatye, later Dinnatie, then Dinnet (see A). Dunatie (G) in 1639, Dinetie (Go). In Gaelic Duinidh, Donnaidh (D), earlier sound presumably Duineadaidh or Donnaididh (5), from Donn = brown (note W 1904, 179 for Inverinate and Coire Dhuinnid in Ross). Brown would fit, as the Dinnet area is the most heathery part of the Dee valley east of Crathie. Michie (1877) wrote 'the upward traveller by the old Deeside coach, on crossing the burn of Dinnet, was apt to fancy himself as entering some vast wilderness of brown heath, where no human habitation had ever stood'. A village and former railway station ten km east of Ballater.

**(The) Dinnet Bridge** (OS, C, 461982), ðɪˈdënëtˈbrig, formerly the Brig o Dinnet (U). Bridge of Dinnet (Gf). Across Dee.

**(The) Dinnet Burn** (OS, F, 466992), ðɪˈdënëtˈbʌrn is the burn from the Clarack Loch along the north side of the village to the burn junction, then down to the bridge carrying the main road. Below the bridge is the Mill o Dinnet Burn, and above the junction the Goc Stane Burn. Formerly the Burn of Dinnet (Gf).

**Dinnet House** (OS, C, 449979), ˈdënëtˈhus. A big house near Dinnet.

**The Dinnet Lochs** (Nw, F), ðɪˈdënëtˈlo̩χs. A collective name for Loch Davan and Loch Kinord.

The Gairnshiel Brig, built in the 1750s as part of the military road from Braemar to Grantown.

After a May snowstorm on the Sron Ghearraig road from Gairnshiel to Crathie, looking south to the Balmoral woods and Lochnagar.

**The Dinnet Reserve*** See Muir of Dinnet National Nature Reserve.

**An Dìollaid** (OS, 2, U, 076970, should be at col at 075968), ðɪ 'dʒɪʌltʃ, the saddle. Also the Saddle o Beinn a' Bhuird (F), ðɪ ‚sɛdlɐ‚bɛnɐ'boˑrd. A saddle-like ridge.

**An Dìollaid** (3, Bu, 970954), the saddle. At the top of Coire Odhar, between Cairn Toul and the Devil's Point.

**Dìollaid Sgeire*** (3, U, 293968), ‚dʒɪəl'sker, saddle of rock, or Dìollaid Sgair (3), ‚dʒɪəl'skar, saddle of a seam. A saddle north-east of Crathie, with a rocky ridge on its north side.

**The Dipper House*** (U, north-west of 416960), ðɪ'dëpër‚hus. A building for heating former dipping liquid for sheep, near Inchmarnoch.

**The Dipper Park*** (F, 417960), ðɪ'dëpër'park. A field with a sheep dipper, south of Cambus o' May.

**The Dipper Park*** (U, 214944), as above. As above, west of the Inver.

**Distillery Burn** (OS, 265939), locally the Still Burn (C), ðɪ'stël 'bʌrn. Also formerly March Burn (Im 3) on the Balmoral–Abergeldie boundary. At the distillery at Balmoral.

**The Doctor Puil*** See Poll Bhuirn.

**The Doctor's Brig*** (C, 421961), ðɪ'dɔktërz'brɪg. A bridge at Inchmarnoch. This and the next two names are after a doctor who once lived at Ballaterach.

**The Doctor's Park*** (C, 416961), ðɪ'dɔktërz'park. A field at Inchmarnoch.

**The Doctor's Wall*** (C, 422962), ðɪ'dɔktërz'waˑl. A well at Inchmarnoch.

**Dod's Croft** (G 28), Scots Dod = George. Doues Croft, Dowes Croft (Ab 19). Former farm probably in Balhennie–Cnoc Dubh area west of Logie Coldstone.

**Dog Hillock** (OS, A, 286794). A low hill rising from the plateau south of Loch Muick, but big and steep on the Angus side.

**The Dog's Cairn** (Ri 29, 392903). Dog Cairn (I). A march cairn in upper Glen Tanar.

**An Doire** See the Derry.

**Doire Bhraghad** (OS, 075908), grove of the upper part, locally Preas na Bràidich (3, D), copse of the upland place. A big old fir wood on a high slope north-west of Mar Lodge.

**Doldencha** (W). An ancient name for Braemar village, 8th century. The first part is obviously Dol = a haugh, later to become the modern Gaelic Dail. The rest is obscure.

**The Domhnullach Road*** (2, C, south-east of 144914), ðɪ'dɔnlɐχ 'rod, means the MacDonald's road. A track at Braemar, between the Linn of Dee road and Chapel Brae.

**The Dominie's Puil*** (F, 300008), ðɪ'dɔmɪnɪz'pil, Scots = schoolmaster's pool. East of Gairnshiel.

**Donal** See Big Donal and Little Donal, a pair of fields south of the Muir of Dinnet.

**Donald Dinnie's Stane*** See the Liftin Stane.

**Donal Reid's Wall*** (F, north of 008938), 'dɔnəl'ridz'waˑl, now often the Wall (C). A well on north side of path from Derry Lodge to the Lairig Ghru.

**Doocot*** (c. 110894), Scots = dovecot. Ducat, Ducket (Ce 3, 5). Former habitation at Corriemulzie.

**The Doocot Park*** (F, 110894), ðɪ'du‚kɔt'park. A former field at Corriemulzie, on north side of road.

**The Dooker*** (C), ðɪ'dukër, Scots Dook = bathe in water. A former sandy pool on an inlet of Dee at Ballater Golf Course, used as a children's paddling pool, but river has changed course and it is now mainly dry, hence commonly referred to now as the Auld Dooker, ðɪ'aˑl'dukër. A collective name for two pools, the Little Dooker for small children, north-west of 370951 (now mostly shingle), and further up the inlet a deeper pool (now shallow) called the Big Dooker for bigger children, at 369951.

**The Dooker*** (U, 248948), as above. Bathing pool on west bank of Dee east of Balnault, formerly with diving board.

**The Dooker*** (C, 283941), as above. A paddling pool in the Geldie Burn near Abergeldie.

**The Dookin Hole*** See The Lui Brig Puil.

**The Doon Half*** (U, north of 326002), ðɪ'dun'haˑf. Scots Doon = down. A field forming the downstream half of the farmland at Torbeg in lower Glen Gairn, includes the former fields of the Meikle Rig and Dail na h-Eagarrath.

**Dorsincilly** (OS, C, 354942), ‚dɔrsən'sële, from Dorus an t-Silidh (3), passageway of the shedding or dripping, i.e. a wet place. Dorsin tshillidh (D), Dorsantshilli (D in A). A farm in lower Glen Muick.

**The Dorsincilly Brig*** (F, 355942), ðɪ‚dɔrsən'sële'brɪg. A former footbridge over Muick.

**The Dorsincilly Burn*** (U, 354942), ðɪ‚dɔrsən'sële'bʌrn. In lower Glen Muick.

**Dorsincilly Cottage** (Vr, C, 353942), ‚dɔrsən'sële'kɔtədʒ. A former house in lower Glen Muick, demolished to make way for a forestry office.

**The Dorsincilly Haugh*** See the Aller Island.

**The Double Corners*** (C, 119898), ðɪ'dʌbəl'kɔrnërz. Double corners, now straightened out, on the road west of Braemar.

**The Double Drive Butts*** (U, 325048), ðɪ'dʌbəl'draev'bʌts. At the top of Glen Fenzie.

**The Double Fords*** (F, 098852), ðɪ'dʌbəl'fɔrdz, ðɪ'dʌbəl'fjurdz. A ford via an island, in mid Glen Ey.

**The Double Fords Brig*** (F, 100850), ðɪ'dʌbəl'fɔrdz'brɪg. In mid Glen Ey.

**The Double Skies*** (C, 270907 and 270903), ðɪ'dʌbəl'skaez. Two hillocks east of Glen Gelder. Sky in Upper Deeside is often used for a skyline.

**Dougie's Brae*** (C, 099901), 'dʌgiz'breˑ. A steep hill on a road at Mar Lodge, named after a resident, Douglas Dempster.

**(The) Doulich Burn** (OS, 371021), 'A relic of Allt an Tulaich, Gael. for the Tullich burn itself' (A). However, this was probably only an interpretation by Alexander. In fact, the Gaelic name for Tullich Burn was Allt Dobharaidh. The names of the burns in this area were discussed in detail by many witnesses during a legal case involving a dispute over land boundaries. Some witnesses said that the burn at 371021 was the Burn of the Branndair. The Burn of the Brander, the Burn of Brander (Io 20), Burn of Brander (G 19). Also the Stripe of Branndair. The Strype of Brander (G 19). Also the Dry Stripe, the Dry Stripe of Blar nam Marbh, the Dry Stripe of the Branndair, the Dry Burn. The Dry Stripe, the Dry Stripe of Blarnamarra, the Dry Stripe of the Brander, the Dry Burn (Io 20), 'a little strype mostly dry in summer' (Io 20). Doulich Burn was probably an attempt to represent the nearby Duibh-leathad Burn, and one witness at the legal case said the Duibh-leathad Burn was what is now Doulich Burn on the map. A burn south of Morven.

**Downie's*** (U, 305962), 'dʌuniz, 'duniz. A stretch of land with caravans and huts east of Crathie, named after former farmers who rented this area as part of the Lebhall farm.

**The Drag Path*** (C, 206901), ðɪ'drag'paθ. In Ballochbuie Forest, named after shot deer were dragged down it.

**Drochaid an Léim** (2, U, 086884), ‚drɔχtən'lem, bridge of the leap. Drochaid an Leum (Gr, A). A former bridge where the Black Colonel once jumped the river in lower Glen Ey.

**Drochaid an t-Seann-spideil** (3, 149800), bridge of the old hospice. Drochaid an t-sean Spideal (Alexander 1942). Also now the Auld Sean Spittal Brig (C), ðɪ'aˑl'ʃan‚spëtəl'brɪg. Carries the old military road north of the Cairnwell. Formerly was called the Sean Spittal Brig, but this now refers (see Sean Spittal Bridge) to the bridge carrying the main road further downstream.

**Drochaid Bhicteoiriath\*** See the Victoria Bridge.

**An Drochaid Dhubh\*** (2, U, 064915), ðɪˌdrɔχt'du·, the black bridge. Also the Black Brig (C), ðɪ'blak'brɪg. The Black Bridge (Ky). A bridge in Glen Lui, formerly tarred black.

**Drochaid Eidh\*** (6, U, 086891), ˌdrɔχt'ɛi·, bridge of Ey. Also the Brig o Ey (C), ðɪ'brɪgɐ'ɛi·, often now the Ey Brig. At Inverey.

**An Drochaid Gheal** See White Bridge.

**Drochaid Laoigh\*** See Lui Bridge.

**Drochaid Linne\*** See the Linn of Dee Brig.

**Drochaid na Laoigh\*** (3, 395973), bridge of the calf. Drochatnaloi (R 4). On farmland at Tullich.

**An Druim\*** (3, 355920), the ridge. The Drum (I). A field in lower Glen Muick.

**An Druim\*** (3, 366012), the ridge. The Druim (G 30). A former cornfield within the South Park of Ach Chadha, up Tullich Burn.

**An Druim\*** (3, 395977), the ridge. Cornland called the Drum (Io 58), Druim (R 4). At Tullich.

**Druim a' Chreagain\*** (3, 113901), ridge of the little rock. Drumcragan (Fa), Drimma-craggan (Cr 7), Dream a Chraggan (Cr in 1703–57), Drumcraggan (Ra 11), Drumachraggan (Opr 9). A former farm east of Mar Lodge, named after the ridge in the name below.

**Druim a' Chreagain\*** (3, U, 113902), ˌdruəm'çragən, ridge of the little rock. A rocky ridge east of Mar Lodge.

**The Druim a' Chreagain Park\*** (115902). The Drumcraggan Park (Ra 11). Now the Cragan Park (F), ðɪ'kragən'park. A former field, made boggy since the big Quoich flood in 1829.

**Druim a' Mhaigh** (3, 392975), ridge of the plain. Drumavay (R 4), Drumavey (D). On farmland at Tullich north-east of Ballater.

**Druim an t-Seilich\*** (3, 166926), ridge of the willow. Drum Dellich (I). A ridge beside boggy ground near Invercauld.

**Druim Choille\*** (3, 346908), ridge of woods. Drumquhulie (I). A field in mid Glen Muick. Drum Cholzie on the hill 3 km to the south is another example of this name.

**Druim Coire an Loch\*** (3, 981836), ridge of corrie of the loch, possibly Druim Carn Loch but more likely Druim Coire an Loch as Coire an Loch lies below it in Perthshire. Drumcairn-loch (At), Drumcairnloch (Ath). South of Bynack Lodge.

**Druim Dearg\*** (3, 152897), red ridge. Druim Derg (I). A former farm, now part of Braemar Golf Course.

**Druim Dubh\*** (3, 298018), dark ridge. Druim Du (I). A heathery ridge north-east of Gairnshiel.

**Druim Gorm\*** (3, 250874), blue ridge. Drum Gorm (B, Bs). A ridge north of Lochnagar, often with a grey-blue colour because of its many stones. Druim Gorm, a summit south-east of Creag a Ghlas-uillt (M, notes in OSn) probably mistaken for 250874.

**Druim Mór\*** (3, 156891), big ridge. Druim More (I). A field in lower Glen Clunie.

**Druim nam Fiadh\*** (3, 956913), ridge of the deer. Druim nan Fiadh (Mm). On Beinn Bhrotain.

**Druim nam Fiann\*** (3, 270967), ridge of the crowberries. Druim nan fionn (R 3), Dreim-na-fian (I), Dreim na-bian (R 14). On the hill north-east of Crathie.

**Druim nan Saobhaidh** (OS, 3, F, 974861), ˌdruəmnɐ'so·vi, ridge of the foxes' dens. Drumnasavay (Me 7). In Glen Geldie.

**Druim na Pairce** (3, F, 289946), ˌdrʌmnɐ'park, ridge of the park. Dremnapark (Ri 4a), Drumna Park (Am), Drumnapark (M). Also the Lower Druims Park (F), ðɪ'loɐr 'drʌmz'park. A field south of Abergeldie.

**Druim na Pairce\*** (3), ridge of the park. Drumnaperk (Opr 3). A former habitation, probably at the above place.

**(An) Druim Odhar** (OS, 3, F, 247898), ðɪˌdrʌm'ʌur, sometimes ðɪˌdrʌm'ʌurz (suggests a plural), the dun ridge. Drumour (B). West of Glen Gelder.

**(An) Druim Odhar** (OS, 3, C, 209876), as above, the dun ridge. Druim Our (R 7). Above Ballochbuie Forest.

**Druim of Morven\*** See An Druim.

**The Druim Parks of Ach Chadha\*** (370015). The Druim Parks of Achaw (G 33). Also Park of Ach Chadha. Park of Achaw (Io 50). A collective name for a group of fields all enclosed by a stone dyke. Up Tullich Burn.

**Druim Ruighe nan Smeur\*** (3, 338883), ridge of shiel of the blackberries. Drum rie na smair (G 5). A ridge south of Linn of Muick.

**The Druims\*** (F), ðɪ'drʌmz. A collective name for the Upper and Lower Druims Parks at Abergeldie.

**Druim Sgarsoich** (OS, 948832), from Druim Sgarsaich (5), Sgarsaich possibly from Sgar = knot. The ridge extends up north along the Aberdeenshire boundary as well as in Perthshire. South of Glen Geldie.

**Drum Cholzie** (OS, C, 345876, should be ridge at 345880, hilltop at 345876 is Sgor Dearg), drʌm'hwɛili, but drʌm'çwɪli, drʌm'χɔili from best informants; from Druim Ach Choille (3), ridge of Aucholzie or field of woods, note Drum of Aucholzie, drʌma'hʌljɛ (A). A broad hill ridge south-east of the Linn of Muick.

**Drum Cholzie Burn\*** (F, 350880), ðɪˌdrʌm'hwɛili'bʌrn and variants as in name above. The upper part of Allt Cholzie above the old fields and dykes.

**The Drum Hill\*** (F, 235959), ðɪ'drʌm'hël, the hill ground up from Drummargettie.

**Drummargettie** (OS, F, 241956), drʌm'argəte, from Druim Airgididh (3), ridge of silver or money. Drumargadie (R 3). A former farm west of Crathie, also now usually called the Drums (C), ðɪ'drʌmz.

**The Drums** See Drummargettie.

**The Drums Burn\*** (F, 244955), ðɪ'drʌms'bʌrn, sometimes the Drummargettie Burn (U), ðɪˌdrʌm'argəte'bʌrn. Drumargadie Burn (R 3). West of Crathie.

**The Drums Park\*** (U, 242956), ðɪ'drʌmz'park. A field west of Crathie.

**The Dry Burn\*** See Doulich Burn.

**Dryburn\*** See Rashy Burn.

**The Dry Grain\*** See West Grain o Allt Deas.

**Dry Lea** (OS, C, 395975), drae'lɛi·, to older people drɛi'lɛi·. Also Newton of Tullich (OS). A house north-east of Ballater.

**Drymill** (OS, C, 268942), drae'mël. Milltown of Abergeldie (I), Mill of Balmurrel (Lp 4), Miln of Balmoral (Crg 17), Mill of Balmoral (Je). Also the West mill of Abergeldie (Aj) in 1666. A former mill at Balmoral.

**Drymills** See Jock Robertson Puil.

**The Dry Stripe\*** See Doulich Burn.

**The Dry Stripe of Blar nam Marbh\*** See Doulich Burn.

**The Dry Stripe of the Branndair\*** See Doulich Burn.

**Dubby Toun\*** See Ruighe an Loin.

**Dubhag** (3, probably 152910). Duack (Mpj). A former farm near Braemar, named after the nearby Allt Dubhag.

**The Dubhag Burn\*** See Allt Dubhag.

**(An) Dubh Alltan Beag** (OS, 3, F, 008830), ðɪ'duɐltɐn'bɛg, ðɪ 'doultɐn'bɛg, the little black burnie. Forms a pair with (An) Dubh Alltan just over the Perthshire boundary at the head of Glen Tilt. Dualdton (Roy).

**An Dubh-bhruach** (3, C, 351921), ðɪ'duˌbrɐχ, the black bank. Dubrach (Ri 29, I). A former farm in lower Glen Muick.

**An Dubh-bhruach\*** (3, U, 155904), as above, the black bank. A
heathery bank beside the road south of Braemar.

**An Dubh-bhruach\*** (3, 352918), the black bank. The Dubrach
(I). A field in Glen Muick.

**The Dubh-bhruach Brae\*** (C, 155905), ðɪˈduˌbrɐχˈbreˑ. A hill on
the Perth road south of Braemar.

**The Dubh-bhruach Pool** (F), ðɪˈduˌbrɐχˈpul. Dubrach Pool (Ly).
In Dee, beside the former farm of Dubrach, west of the Linn
of Dee. A collective name for two pools, Upper and
Lower.

**The Dubh-bhruach Stane\*** (U, 155903), ðɪˈduˌbrɐχˈstin. A
boulder beside the road to Perth, south of Braemar.

**The Dubh-bhruach Wuid** See Coille na Dubh-bhruaich.

**The Dubh-chails** (C, 325966), ˈduçəlz, from the Dubh-chail (3),
the black flat, as in Duchall at Kilmacolm (W 201), but the
Dubh-chails suggests an original plural name. Dubh Choille
suggested (A), but does not fit local pronunciation of Coille
or Choille. The Duchalls (A). A pool in Dee below
Coilacriech, beside a flat area of heather.

**An Dubh-chàtharaigh\*** (3, U, 238948), ðɪˈduçri, the black place
of broken moor (note W 1904, 255 for Douchary in Ross,
with the Gaelic form shortened to Duchairidh). An area of
rough ground with many rocks, on a hillside north-east of
the Inver.

**Dubh-chàtharaigh Mór\*** (3, 181916), big black place of broken
ground. Duchriemore (R 7). See above name. Dubh-choire
does not apply, as it is on the broad haughs at Invercauld.

**(An) Dubh-chlais** (OS, 3, C, 258936), ðɪˈduˌçlɐʃ, the black
hollow. Also the Muckle Dubh-chlais (F), ðɪˌmʌkəlˈduˌçlɐʃ,
forming a pair with the Little Dubh-chlais. A rocky hollow
near Balmoral.

**An Dubh-chlais** (3, D, C, 263005), as above, the black hollow.
Duchlash (R 12). A former farm, named after the hollow
beside it (see below). West of Gairnshiel.

**An Dubh-chlais\*** (3, U, 261007), as above, the black hollow.
West of Gairnshiel.

**An Dubh-chlais** (2, F, 164915), as above, the black hollow.
Dubh-chlais (OS 1869), Dachlash (Sim). A former
gamekeeper's house near Braemar.

**Dubh Chlais** (OS, 165917), classic form An Dubh-chlais (2, C),
as above, ðɪˈduˌχlaʃ (Sch), the dark hollow. N du-hlas, duchlash (D). A gap east of Braemar, dark with heather and
rocks.

**An Dubh-choire\*** (3, U, 330922), ðɪˈduçr̩e, the black corrie. A
corrie in lower Glen Muick, formerly heathery but now
under trees. Note Burn of Dubh-choire in this corrie.

**An Dubh-choire\*** (3, U, 209947), ðɪˈduçr̩i, the black corrie.
Duchory (Ra 6). A former farm in Glen Feardar, named
after the corrie above it (see Duchrie).

**An Dubh-choire\*** (3, U, 241001), as above, the black corrie.
Also the Black Corrie (F), ðɪˈblakˈkọre. South-east of
Corndavon Lodge.

**An Dubh-choire** (3, C, 239000), as above, the black corrie.
Duchory (Ano), Duchory, Duchrie, Douchrie, Duchorie
(R 3, 5, 12, 14), Duchory (Ro), Duchorie (Cr 55). A former
farm south-east of Corndavon Lodge, named after the above
corrie.

**Dubh-choire** (OS, 139803 is wrong location on a ridge, should
be upper corrie at 133795), from An Dubh-choire (3, U), as
above, the black corrie. Dhu Cor (I) at 133795. See Coire
Chronaidh, which is lower corrie further north. North of the
Cairnwell.

**An Dubh-choire** See Duchrie.

**The Dubh-choire Burn\*** See Allt an Dubh-choire.

**The Dubh-choire Burn\*** (U, 205945), ðɪˈduçr̩iˈbʌrn. In the
Dubh-choire west of the Inver.

**Dubh-ghlais\*** (3, 218945), dark stream. Du Glash (I). A little
burn in lower Glen Feardar.

**Dubh-Ghleann** (OS, 070960), from An Dubh-ghleann (2, Sg, C),
ðɪˈduˑˌglɐn, the dark glen. Duglennen (Me 7), Dugleanan
(Io 19), Dow Glennan (Roy) suggest Dubh-ghleannan =
little dark glen. Also An Du-ghleannan, translated the dark
wee glen (Sin), the Dark Wee Glen (McC 1923). A steep,
dark, heathery glen north-east of Glen Derry.

**The Dubh-Ghleann Bothy\*** See Bothan Dubh-Ghleann.

**The Dubh-Ghleann Burn\*** See Allt an Dubh-ghlinne.

**The Dubh-Ghleann Face\*** (F, 070980), ðɪˈduˌglɐnˈfes. A steep
stony face above the Dubh-Ghleann.

**The Dubh-Ghleann Ford\*** (C, 080947), ðɪˈduˌglɐnˈfọrd. A ford
on Allt an Dubh-ghlinne.

**The Dubh-Ghleann Moss\*** (Fi). Probably the peat-moss north of
the Dubh-Ghleann, on the eastern part of Moine Bhealaidh.

**The Dubh-Ghleann Plantin\*** (F, 075947), ðɪˈduˌglɐnˈplantɪn. A
new conifer plantation.

**The Dubh-Ghleann Water** See Allt an Dubh-ghlinne.

**The Dubh-Ghleann Wuid\*** (C, 073956), ðɪˈduˌglɐnˈwɪd. Old fir
wood.

**Dubh Loch** (OS, 240826), classic form An Dubh-loch (2, C), ðɪ
ˈduˌlọχ, the black loch. West of Loch Muick.

**Dubh Lochain** (OS, 101995), classic form Dubh-lochain, black
tarns. Small tarns on Beinn a' Bhuird, downhill from the
much bigger Dubh Lochan.

**Dubh Lochan** (OS, 096991), classic form An Dubh-lochan (2,
Sg, F), dɪˈduˌlọχɐn, the black tarn. Also L. Caich (Mg), L.
Quoich (Crom). On Beinn a' Bhuird.

**The Dubh-loch Burn\*** See Allt an Dubh-loch.

**The Dubh-loch Corrie\*** See Coire an Dubh-loch.

**(The) Dubrach** (OS, C, 030888), ðɪˈduˌbrɐχ, from An Dubh-
bhruach (2, C), the black bank. Dubrech (Fa), the Dupprach
(Cr), N dūprich (D), Dubh-bhruach (OS 1869). West of the
Linn of Dee.

**Duchess of Kent's Cairn** (OS, 300938), locally the Duchess's
Prop (C), ðɪˈdʌtʃ̃ɛsɪzˈprọp. A big cairn on a hilltop south-east
of Abergeldie.

**The Duchess's Pool\*** See Poll na Claraig.

**The Duchess's Prop\*** See Duchess of Kent's Cairn.

**(The) Duchrie** (OS, 207947), from An Dubh-choire (3, U), ðɪ
ˈduçr̩i, ˈduçr̩i (Sch), the black corrie. Duchorry, hollow (I).
A corrie in Glen Feardar.

**(The) Duchrie Burn** (OS, C, 241003), ðɪˈduçr̩iˈbʌrn. Also Allt
Dubh-choire (3), burn of black corrie. Ault Duchory (Ro),
Alt Duchorie (R 14). Flows through An Dubh-choire, also
called the Black Corrie, south-east of Corndavon Lodge. Due
to the emphasis on the Dubh, the *o* sound in Choire has
disappeared. However, the early maps and the name the
Black Corrie, plus the facts that the place is in a corrie, and
that the nearby former farm there was once spelled Duchory,
show that this was Dubh-choire and not Dubh-chatharaigh.

**An Duibh-leathad\*** (3, 385031), the dark slope, possibly An
Dubh-leathad, same meaning. The Duileat, the Douliet, the
Diulot, the Dowleit, mostly the first of these (Io 20). A slope
south of Morven, which featured in a legal controversy over
land in the 18th century (G 19, Io, Me 13). One side claimed
it was south of Little Burn (365020), but most evidence put it
on the north slope.

**The Duibh-leathad Burn\*** See Allt Duibh-leathad.

**The Duibh-leathad Stripe\*** See Allt Duibh-leathad.

**The Duke o Fife's Dining Room\*** See the Dining Room.

**(The) Duke's Chair** (OS, F, 972884), ðɪˈdjuksˈtʃer. A name from
the Duke of Leeds' Chair (A). A little rocky top with a good
view of the deer-stalking grounds of Glen Geldie. Also
Cnapan Damhaidh (5, F), ˌkrapɐnˈdavi, little knob of

Damhaidh or stag stream (i.e. referring to the Allt Dhaidh (should be Damhaidh) Mor and A.D. Beag on either side of the hill. Cnapan Dhaidh (Mm).

**The Duke's Moss*** (F, 075923), ðɪ'djuks'mǫs. North of Mar Lodge.

**The Duke's Seat*** (U, 096941), ðɪ'djuks'sit. On a hill on the east side of Quoich.

**Dùnaidh Beag** (3, F, 116895), ˌduni'bɛg, little hillocklet. Dunibeg Cottage (Ha). A former house on north side of the road at Corriemulzie.

**Dùn Bheathagan** (5, 355971), hillock of ? birch place. Dunvegan (A), in Gaelic Tūn-fecan (D). A knolly field near Bridge of Gairn.

**Dùn Bheathagan*** (5). Dunveggan (Crg 9). A former habitation near Bridge of Gairn.

**Duncan Gray's Burn** (OS, C, 024882), 'dʌŋkən'grez'bʌrn. Near the White Bridge in lower Glen Dee.

**Duncan Shaw's Mill Lade*** (205994). Duncan Shaw's Mill Led (R 9). A diversion of a burn north-west of Crathie.

**Duncan Shaw's Old Lime-Kiln*** (R 5, 238974). North-west of Crathie.

**Duncan's Stile*** (U, 344950), 'dʌŋkənz'stɛil, Scots Stile = gate. A gate west of Ballater.

**The Dyke Butts*** (U, 295012), ðɪ'dɛik'bʌts. Butts beside an old stone dyke at Gairnshiel.

**The Dyke Park*** (U, 346914), ðɪ'dɛik'park. A field in Glen Muick.

**The Dynamo Dam*** See the Corriemulzie Dam.

**The Dynamo Pool*** See Poll Coire Mhuillidh.

**The Dynamo Pool*** (F, 104896), ðɪ'dɛinəmo'pul. Formerly the Dynamo Pool was named after a former dynamo where Corriemulzie Burn enters Dee (see Poll Coire Mhuillidh), but the name is now used for a seldom-used, different pool upstream.

**Eadar Allt** (3, 280990), between burns. Ederauld (Io 14), Edderauld (Mc 5), Edderallt (D). A stretch of hill grazing between two burns south-west of Gairnshiel.

**Eag Dhubh** (OS, 3, 302051), ɛk and ɛk'tu (A), black notch. A gully at the top of the road from Gairnshiel to Strath Don.

**Eag Dhubh** (OS, 3, 134970, extends right to the top at 121969), as above (A), black notch. Eig Du (I), Eigh-dhu (R 14). Shown at 121969 (I, R 14), with Carn Eag Dhubh at the location of Carn na Craoibhe Seileich (OS). In other words, Eag Dhubh includes the steep banks on both sides, forming a major long notch at the source of Gairn.

**Eaglais Ceann na Dalach** (3), church of head of the haugh. Eclis-Ceann-na-dallach, or the church at the head of the haugh (E), Eglish-kian-na-dalach (Mf), Eaglais ceann-dallach (D in A). Near the upper end of the plain at Mar Lodge (E).

**The Eagle's House** (McC, c. 110894). Former building at Corriemulzie.

**The Eagle's Nest Path*** (F, 194889), ðɪ'igəlz'nɛst'paθ. Near a former eyrie in Ballochbuie Forest.

**Eagles Rock** (OS, 238835), locally Eagle's Rock (C), 'igəlz'rɒk, from Creag na h-Iolaire (3, McC 1891), rock of the eagle. This referred to the highest point at the top of the cliff, not to the cliff itself which is Creag an Dubh-loch, the same name as the bigger cliff on the other side of the Dubh Loch (McC).

**The Eagle's Stone*** (R 3, 228019). South of Corndavon Lodge.

**Eagles' Well*** (R 9, 210029). West of Corndavon Lodge.

**? Eang an Eilein*** (3), point of the riverside-field or island. Ainenelan (G 5). In lower Glen Muick, in Birkhall–Dorsincilly area.

**Ear-allt a' Challtuinn** See East Allt Coultain.

**Ear-choire Sneachdach** (OS, 095976), locally Ear-choire an

t-Sneachda (2, U), 'ɛr,χǫrn̩'drɛçk, east corrie of the snow. Pairs with Iar-choire an t-Sneachda. On Beinn a' Bhuird.

**Earl Mar's Hill** (O, 428006). Also the Earl of Marr's Board (Stu). A hillock named after the Earl of Mar, west of Loch Davan.

**The Earl of Marr's Board** See Earl Mar's Hill.

**The Earl of Mar's Breakfast Stone** (O, 428005), a big flat stone on Culblean on the above hillock. Refers to an incident in 1431 (Mil), not to 1715 as stated by Ogston. Also the Table Stane (U), ðɪ'tebəl'stin.

**The Easaidh Path*** (F, 148001), ðɪ'ǫse'paθ. Beside Allt an Eas Mhoir on Ben Avon.

**The Easaidhs*** (C), ðɪ'ǫsez. The Essies (R 14). A big area of gentle slopes draining into the burns Allt an Eas Bhig and Mhoir (should be Easaidh, not Eas), on Ben Avon. Probably named after the burns, which are now called the Little Easaidh and the Muckle Easaidh.

**Eas Allt a' Chlair** (OS, 3, U, 118897), ˌǫs.alt'χlaːr, waterfall of burn of the board. Also the Linn of Allt a' Chlair (F), ðɪ'lënɐ ˌalt'χlaːr. The Linn of Altchlar (Cromb). Near Corriemulzie.

**Eas Allt Briste-amhaich** (3, 197812), waterfall of burn of broken neck. Eas auillt brist amhach, fall of breakneck brook (Mg). Also Falls of Prieshauich (I), the Break-Neck Waterfall (Crom), and the Breakneck Falls (Cj 14, C), ðɪ'brek'nɛk'faˑlz. A high waterfall on cliffs south-east of Loch Callater.

**Easan De*** See the Falls of Dee.

**Easan Doire*** (3, U, 044952), ˌǫsɐn'dǫr, falls of Derry. Also formerly the Falls o the Derry (U), ðɪ'faˑlzɪðɪ'dɛre, now the Derry Falls (C). Waterfalls north of Derry Lodge.

**Easan Laoigh*** (3, U, 066903), ˌǫsɐn'lui, linn of Lui or calf-one (see Glen Lui). Also the Falls o Lui (F), ðɪ'faˑlzɐ'lui, usually now the Lui Falls (C). The Falls of Lui (McC 1885). Also the Linn of Lui (Br). Waterfalls in lower Glen Lui.

**Easan Ruighe nan Àiridh** (3), waterfalls of reach of the pastures. Easan Ruidh-nan-àiridh (T 33, 17). An interesting name, as it is the only case we have come across with the word Àiridh in Upper Deeside. In an old Braemar poem, a place south-east of Culardoch, probably in Glen Feardar.

**Eas Coire Mhuillidh*** See Linn of Corriemulzie.

**Eas De** See Linn of Dee.

**Eas Eidh** or **Easan Eidh*** (6, JB, 088863), ǫs'ɛiˑ or ˌǫsɐn'ɛiˑ, linn of Ey. (For meaning see Ey Burn).

**Easg Chapall*** (3, U, 185833), ǫsk'hapəl, now sometimes ðɪ 'skafəl, bog of mares. Eisk Chapel (I), Eisk Chaple (R 14). Note the Mares' Brae at 183836. South of Loch Callater.

**The Easg Chapall Face*** (U, 187821), ðɪ,ǫsk'hapəl'fes. A steep rocky face extending from the Mares' Brae at 183836 to where it turns south-west into Coire Loch Kander.

**Easg Chrogan*** (5, 261042), bog of old sheep, with Chrogan probably a variant genitive plural. Easg Chroganach would be shrunk or scraggy bog. Esk-Chroggan (I). A piece of pasture north-west of Gairnshiel.

**An Easg Leathan*** (3, 165792), the broad bog. Nesk Lean (I). A wet grassy hillside north of the Glas Maol.

**Eas nam Mèirleach*** (3, 132785), local form Meàrlach, waterfall of the thieves. Ess-na-myarlach (I). A small fall north of the Cairnwell.

**East Allt Clacharraidh*** (391027). East Auldclachrie (G 19). A burn south-east of Morven.

**East Allt Coultain** (OS, 136923), from Ear Allt a' Challtuinn (OS 1869), classic form Ear-allt etc, east burn of the hazel. Easter Ault Chaldin (I). North-west of Braemar, pairs with West Allt Coultain.

**The East and West Park*** (U, 300957), ðɪ'istən'wɛst'park. The only field at the Lebhall where one ploughed east and west (WD). East of Crathie.

**East Auchendryne\*** See Lower Auchendryne.

**East Bridge** See Fraser's Brig.

**East Croft\*** (Io 58, 248948). Two former pieces of land at Balnault.

**The East Drive\*** (C, 194894), ðɪˈistˈdraev. A road in Ballochbuie Forest, pairs with the Mid and West Drives.

**Easter Abergairn**. Easter Abergarden (Pb), Easter and Wester Aber Gardynes (Ab 12), Abergairn Wester and Easter (Gr). A former farm north-west of Ballater, possibly the same as the Castletoun.

**Easter Ach a' Mhaigh\*** See Wester Ach a' Mhaigh. Easter and Wester Auchavay (Me 15). Former farmland near Mar Lodge.

**Easter Allanaquoich** See Allanaquoich.

**Easter Allt a' Chlaiginn\*** (192838). Easter Ault chlaggan (I). A burn near Loch Callater.

**Easter Allt an Droighinn\*** See Allt an Droighnean.

**Easter Allt Bealach Buidhe\*** See Allt a' Bhealaich Bhuidhe.

**Easter Ardmeanach** See Ardmeanach.

**Easter Auchallater** (OS, C, 157893), ˈistɛrˌaˈχalɐtɛr. A house south of Braemar. It is north of Auchallater, not east of it. This is another of several relics of Braemar Gaelic. Sios or down usually meant east down Deeside, but in this case it did mean downstream. However it has presumably been translated as East, hence the apparently incongruous name. Lower Achalater (Opr 41). Also Little Auchallater (F), ˈlɛtəl ˌaˈχalɐtɛr.

**Easter Auchtavan\*** (208956). Easter Auchtavaun (Io 66). A former farm in Glen Feardar.

**Easter Balhalloch\*** Easter Balchalloch (Ce 5). Probably same as present Balchalloch, with original Balchalloch west of 330961. Former habitation west of Ballater.

**Easter Ballater**. Ballater Easter (Mc 20), Bellater easter (Asr), Easter Ballader (Io 46). The form Ballater Easter rather than Easter Ballater possibly was an early translation of Gaelic Bealadair Shios. A former farm about the east end of the Pass of Ballater.

**Easter Balmoral** (OS, S 25, C, 266942), ˈistɛrˌbəlˈmọrəl. Originally Baile a' Mhorair Shìos (3), east farm-town of the nobleman. Bail-mhoir (Mp), Balvorar ias (D). A hamlet south of Crathie, pairs with Wester Balmoral.

**Easter Balmore** See Balmore.

**Easter Claignean\*** (344972). Easter Claggans (I). See Na Claignean. A field near Bridge of Gairn.

**Easter Coire Allt a' Chlaiginn\*** (3, 196842), downstream corrie of burn of the rounded hillock. Easter Cor Ault chlaggan (I). Easter here means downstream, as the burn runs into Loch Callater further west than the exit of Wester Allt a' Chlaiginn (for explanation see Allt a' Chlaiginn).

**Easter Coire Gorm\*** (167883), Easter Corry Goram (I). Easter here means downstream, as the corrie is if anything west of Wester Coire Gorm (for explanation of this, see Allt a' Chlaiginn). A corrie in lower Glen Callater.

**Easter Corn Eilean Park\*** (379971). Easter Conellan Park (Io 64). Also Conellan (R 4). A field near Ballater.

**Easter Dalvorar** See Dail a' Mhorair Bheag.

**Easter Feuragach\*** Easter Fergach (Opr 28). Probably same as the Feuragach. Former habitation near Crathie.

**Easter Garbh Allt**. Easter Garvall Burn (Ri 27). Almost certainly the same as the Ballochbuie Burn, to judge from the description. In Ballochbuie Forest.

**The Easter Garbh-leathad\*** (3, 437960), the easter rough slope. The Easter Garlet (Dms). A hillside south-west of Dinnet, pairs with the Wester Garbh-leathad.

**Easter Grain of Allt Darrarie\*** (322793), Scots Grain = small branch-stream. Easter Grain of Ault Darrarie (I). South of Loch Muick, pairs with Mid Grain of Allt Darrarie.

**Easter Grain of Glas Allt\*** (255845). Easter Grain of Glassauld (G 35). A burn on Lochnagar.

**Easter Inverey\*** Easter Invereye (Me 13). A former name probably for Meikle Inverey.

**(The) Easter Kirn** (OS, F, 212018), ðɪˈistɛrˈkɛrn̩, often the East Kirn, or the Big Caorainn (U), ðɪˈbɪgˈkʌrɛn. Burn of the Easter Courn (I). Also Allt a' Chaorainn (3), burn of the rowan (see also the Wester Kirn). Ald a' Chaorin, Alt churn (R 3, 14), Aldcairn Easter (Io 1800s). See Kirn. A burn west of Corndavon Lodge.

**Easter Micras** (Ri 36, C, 303964), ˈistɛrˈmikrəs. Now a general name for an area east of Crathie, but originally (I) referred to a settlement at about the present location of Rinabaich. Eʳ Mickerys (Roy), L. Micrass (Ro) presumably for Lower Micras, Easter Micrass (I). From Miagra Shìos (6), downstream Micras. Miagra hios (D). For meaning see Micras. Pairs with Mid and Wester Micras.

**Easter Micras Burn** (OS, 302968), locally Allt na h-Eaglais (2, F), altˈhẹklɪʃ, burn of the church. Allt Eaglais (A 221). Allt Coire na h-Eaglais higher up. East of Crathie.

**Easter Morven** (Gf, C, 372008), ˈistɛrˈmọrˌvən. Farmland and former farm up the Tullich Burn, pairs with Wester Morven.

**The Eastern Cairngorm** See Derry Cairngorm.

**Easter Pannanich** See Pannanich Village.

**Easter Rann na Bruaich\*** (330999). Easter Rienabroich (Io 65). A former farm in Glen Gairn.

**(The) Easter Shenalt** (OS, C, 217033), ðɪˈistɛrˈʃɛnəlt, often the East Shenalt. Easter shan Ault (I), Easter Shen-ald, Easter Shinault (R 3, 12). A burn west of Corndavon Lodge, pairs with the Wester Shenalt.

**Easter Shenval\*** See Wester Shenval.

**Easter Sleach** (OS, F, 263020), locally is now usually the Sleach (C); it is many decades since Wester Sleach was occupied. See the Sleach. A former farm north-west of Gairnshiel.

**Easter Strathgirnock** (Vr 2). A farm, probably former name for Strathgirnock farm.

**Eastertoun\*** (U, 418980), ˈiˈstɛrtən. Farmland at Cambus o' May, probably also a former farm, pairs with Wastertoun, now part of the Cambus Parks.

**Easter Tulach Chocaire\*** (U, 277934), ˈistɛrˌtəlˈfogɛr. Pairs with Wester Tulach Chocaire. Easter Dalfouger (In). A former farm, later fields, south-east of Balmoral.

**Easter Tulloch** (F, north-east of 280011), ˈistɛrˈtʌləç, or Tulloch (F). Tulloch minister (Io 77), Easter Tullichmacarrick (Afr). A former manse west of Gairnshiel.

**The Eastfield Brig\*** (C, west of 384971), ðɪˈistˌfildˈbrɪg. A bridge north-east of Ballater.

**Eastfield of Monaltrie** (OS, C, 384971), locally just Eastfield (C), ˈist, fild, as in OS 1869. Formerly a moor, Muir of Tullich. Muir of Tullich, now Eastfield (Io in 1818), Eastfield of Ballater (Opr 44). A farm north-east of Ballater.

**The East Golf Course\*** (F, 105900), ðɪˈistˈgọlfˌkors. A field at Mar Lodge, on a former golf course.

**(The) East Grain** (OS, U, 390873), locally is usually the East Grain o Allt Deas (F), ðɪˈistˈgrenɐˌaltˈdẹs. Scots Grain = small branch-stream. The East Grain of the burn of Aldess (Ri 29), the East Grain of Aldess (G 32). A burn at the top of Glen Tanar, pairs with the Mid and West Grains.

**The East Grain o Allt an t-Sneachdaidh\*** (F, 344866), ðɪˈist ˈgrenɐˌaltənˈdrẹcte. A burn south-east of Linn of Muick, pairs with Mid and West Grains.

**The East Grain o Allt Fileachaidh\*** (F, 328850), ðɪˈistˈgrenɐˌalt ˈfiləçi. A burn north-east of Loch Muick, pairs with Mid and West Grains.

**The East Grain of Luibeg\*** (Fi, 011958). A burn in Glen Luibeg, running up towards Coire Sputan Dearg, pairs with the West Grain of Luibeg.

**The East Haugh\*** (F, 165924), ðɪˈistˈhaˑχ. A field at Invercauld.

**East Haugh\*** (R 4, 395974). On farmland at Tullich.

**East Island\*** (Io 58, south of 395970). A former island in Dee near Tullich.

**The East Lairig** See Lairig an Laoigh.

**The East Lodge Park\*** See Tom na Seilg.

**East Milton Burn** (OS, 320995), locally the Torbeg Burn (F), ðɪ ˌtɔrˈbɛgˈbʌrn. Also Burn of Preas Dubh. Burn of Press Du (I). See Coire Preas Dubh. South-east of Gairnshiel, pairs with West Milton Burn.

**East Park\*** (Io 58, 348970). A field on Newton of Gairn.

**The East Park\*** (U, 375008), ðɪˈistˈpark. A former field at Easter Morven, including the unfenced ground. Pairs with the West Park.

**East Park\*** See Corby Hall.

**East Park Dalbagie\*** (342965). East Park Dalbadie (Io 58). A field west of Bridge of Gairn.

**East Park of Ach an Daimh\*** (367002). East Park of Auchindow (G 30). Part of what was collectively called the West Park this century. A former field up Tullich Burn.

**The East Park of Ach Chadha\*** (370016). The East Park of Auchaw (G 30). A former field up Tullich Burn.

**The East Pass\*** (U, possibly 960924), ðɪˈistˈpas. Pairs with West Pass. On Beinn Bhrotain.

**The East Point o the Lair\*** (U, 319781), ðɪˈistˈpointɪðɪˈleṛ. The eastern end of the hill called the Lair of Aldararie, south of Loch Muick.

**East Rhebreck** (c. 262940). East Relrick (Vr 2 with many spelling or printing errors). A former habitation at Balmoral, ruins probably used for foundations of later buildings or roads.

**East Street\*** (Im 8, Io 58, 245947 or 246949). A former farm comprising two current fields near Balnault.

**The East Top\*** (U, 099806), ðɪˈistˈtɔp. On An Socach north-west of the Cairnwell.

**East Toun.** Eastoun in the Barony of Abergeldie (Mc 2). Probably a former farm.

**Eas Tuilidh\*** (3, U, south of 087889), ɛsˈtuli, waterfall of little torrent. A little fall on Ey near Inverey.

**Edmond's Brig\*** (F, 101922), ˈɛdməndzˈbrɪg. Former footbridge in Glen Quoich, washed away by a spate in 1982.

**An t-Eilean\*** See Eilean Gaineamhach.

**An t-Eilean\*** (3, 140836), the riverside-field. The Island (I). A flat field near the upper Clunie, shown as some distance from the river on the early map (I), so obviously is the usual Upper Deeside Eilean or riverside-field, not an island.

**An t-Eilean\*** (3, 348924), the riverside-field. The Island (I). On this old map, most of the field was separated from the river by a strip of trees. Obviously a flat field, not an island. In lower Glen Muick.

**An t-Eilean\*** (U, 347968), ðɪˈɛlən, the island. Also the Island (F), ðɪˈɛilənd, formerly Upper Island (Io 58). A stretch of rough grass and trees beside Dee west of Ballater, may have been an island.

**An t-Eilean\*** (3, U, 348922), as above, the riverside-field. On west side of Muick, at Alltcailleach.

**An t-Eilean\*** (3, U, 297959), as above, the riverside-field. A narrow wet field on north side of road. East of Crathie.

**An t-Eilean\*** (3, F, 333997), as above, the riverside-field. Below Lary in Glen Gairn.

**Eilean Aitinn\*** (3, 153880), riverside-field of juniper. Ellan Aiten (I). A former field ('poor land'), in lower Glen Clunie, has now reverted to moor.

**The Eilean Burn\*** (3, U, 426027), ðɪˈɛlənˈbʌrn. Eilean in Deeside

often refers to a stream-side field, and there is one nearby here, at a former farm called Eilean Burn (Ellenburn, OS 1869) just outside our area. A burn north-west of Loch Davan.

**An t-Eilean Dearg\*** (3, 348915), the red riverside-field. The Ellindarge (Rli 13). Also Eilean Dearg Allt an Ruighe (3), the red riverside-field of Aultonrea. Island Dearg Altonrie (Ri 29), Eandarghaugh of Achollie (Ab 19) misread as if one name, not two. Was formerly on 'north' (i.e. west) side of lower Muick.

**Eilean Dearg Allt an Ruighe** See An t-Eilean Dearg.

**Eilean Dearg Toll Dubh\*** (3, 348915), red riverside-field of Toldhu. Island Derg Toldow (Ri 29) was formerly on 'south' (i.e. east) side of lower Muick. Also Allt an Ruighe (3), see Allt an Ruighe, a nearby burn. Aultan Rie (I). A field.

**Eilean Dubh\*** (3, 150908), black riverside-field. Island Du (I). Formerly an island, now part of east bank of Clunie at Braemar.

**An t-Eilean Fearn** (3, U, 149908), ðɪˌɛlənˈfjaˑrn, the alder island. N jellan fyarn (D) indicates the article (for further explanation see Caochan Bheithe). A former island on Clunie at Braemar, but now part of the west bank as the river has changed course.

**Eilean Fearn\*** (3, U, 298956), ˌɛlənˈfjaˑrn, riverside-field of alder. A field east of Crathie, still with alders at one end.

**Eilean Gaineamhach\*** (3, 307011), sandy riverside-field. Ellan Gannich (I). Also An t-Eilean (3, F), ðɪˈɛlən, the riverside-field, and the Torran Eilean (F), ðɪˈtɔrɛnˈɛlən, distinguishing it from Eilean on other farms. A gravelly former field east of Gairnshiel.

**Eilean Giubhas\*** (3), island with fir wood. Elinguise (Me 18), Elanguis (Cr 37a). A former habitation and area of farmland on north side of Dee, west of the mouth of Quoich, probably was near, but not on, the island in the name below.

**Eilean Giubhas\*** (3), island with fir wood. Island Guise (Io 24). Note the habitation Eilean Giubhas, but there is no evidence that it was on this island. This was a small island in Dee, with most water on the south side of it (Io). It seems unlikely that such an island would have had people living on it. An island west of Braemar, between Cragan and Arderg.

**Eilean Gréine\*** (3, U, 439006), ˈɛiləndˈgrin, but ˌɛlənˈgrin from best informant, waterside-ground of sun, or Grein, of lake bottom. A promontory on Loch Davan.

**Eilean Mór\*** (3, 155894), big island. Ellan More (I). An island in lower Clunie.

**Eilean na Fiodhaige\*** (2, U, 063908), ˌɛlɛnɛˈvjohɪk, island of the hagberry or bird-cherry. An island in lower Glen Lui, with no bird-cherry there now.

**Eilean nam Meann** (2, C, 149919), ˌɛlɛnɛˈmjʌŋ, riverside-field of the kids. Island-na-Vaun (I), Ellen na VYANG (A 1954) suggest an original Eilean Mheann, riverside-field of kids. Formerly on the east side of Clunie (I), but now on the west side due to the river changing its course.

**Eilean na Strì\*** (3, 149923), riverside-ground of the strife, possibly referring to a dispute over land. Island-na-stree (I). A narrow patch of ground where Clunie enters Dee, on the west side.

**The Eilean of Baile Nodha** (near 347911), Eilean (3) = riverside-field. Island of Balnoe (Ri 29). Formerly on 'north' (i.e. west) side of lower Muick. The Island Derg Altonrie, the Island Derg Toldow, the Island of Balnoe, and Eland Euowan (below) were all mentioned in the same document (Ri 29).

**Eilean of Cragan\*** Eilean (3) = riverside-field. Ellen of Craggan (Me 15). A former field near Mar Lodge.

**The Eilean Park\*** (3, U, 334997), ðɪˈɛlənˈpark. A name referring

to the whole field, whereas An t-Eilean is the flat, west end of
it by the river. Below Lary in Glen Gairn.

**Eilean Uan** (3), island of lambs. Eland Euowan or Lamb Island
(Ri 29). A piece of ground in lower Glen Muick (see the
Eilean of Balnoe above).

**The Eilean Yard*** (U, north-east of 320946), ðɪˈe̞lənˈjaˑrd, Eilean
(3) = streamside-field. Often the Eilean Yardie, Scots Yardie
= little yard. The bottom of this old field in lower Girnock is
flat, by the burnside.

**Eileirig Bheag*** See Little Elrick.

**Eileirig Mhor*** See Meikle Elrick.

**(The) Einich Cairn** (OS, 937993), from the Eanaich Cairn (3,
U), ðɪˈɛˑnɪçˈkærn, referring to Gleann Einich or Loch Einich
(or rather Eanaich) below, in Inverness-shire. Gleann
Eanaich is glen of marsh. A cairn on the plateau of
Braeriach. We heard the name from Strath Spey people only.

**The Elrigs*** (F, 095940), ðɪˈe̞lrɪks. A collective name for the area
around Carn Elrig Beag and Mor in Glen Quoich.

**The Enclosures of Invercauld*** (170930). The Inclosures of
Invercauld (Io 30). Several areas enclosed by stone dykes for
former afforestation, behind Inverchandlick, Alltdourie, on
Meall Alvie and round Invercauld.

**The End of the Land*** (Io 18). A piece of farmland on the
former Mill Croft of Inver.

**The End o Megen*** (U, 316906), ðɪˈɛndɐˈmɛgən. The north end
of the steep stony hill of Craig Megen, in Glen Girnock.

**The End o the Easg Chapall*** (U, 191817), ðɪˈɛndɪɒɪˌɛskˈhapəl.
Where the Easg Chapall Face ends in a corner at the north
side of Coire Loch Kander. South of Loch Callater.

**Erskine's Stane** See the Clunie Stane.

**The Etchachan Brig*** (C, 032995), ðɪˈɛtʃəçɑnˈbrɪg. A footbridge
on the Coire Etchachan Burn.

**The Etchachan Hut*** See Hutchison Memorial Hut.

**(The) Etnach** (OS, C, 416915), ðɪˈe̞tnɐχ, ðɪˈetnɐχ (U), from An
Aitionnach (3), the place abounding in juniper. Junipers are
still common there. Attanich (Po), the Attnich (Cr 30),
Atnach (R 1) are interesting, in showing an original *a* sound
rather than *e*, as is nearer the Gaelic pronunciation of
Aitionnach. A former few farms, and more recently a former
keeper's house also called New Etnach (Gler), in upper Glen
Tanar.

**The Etnach Brig*** (C, 419916), ðɪˈe̞tnɐχˈbrɪg. A bridge near the
above place.

**The Etnach Burn*** (C, 415915), ðɪˈe̞tnɐχˈbʌrn. The lower part of
the Burn of Coire Meacan in upper Glen Tanar.

**The Etnach Parks*** (C, 414914), ðɪˈe̞tnɐχˈparks. Former fields in
upper Glen Tanar.

**The Etnach Red Craig*** See Red Craig.

**The Etnach Sand Hole*** (U, 419920), ðɪˈe̞tnɐχˈsanˈhol. A sand
pit in Glen Tanar.

**Ettrick Croft** (OS, C, 426959), ˈe̞trɛ̈çˈkrɑft. A fairly modern
name, was known formerly to local people as Torr Dubh (C),
tɔrˈduˑ, after a nearby former farm of that name. Toredoo
Cottage (Ce 5). A former farm, now a house, near
Inchmarnoch.

**Ewe-boucht of Crathienaird*** (245991), Scots Boucht = pen.
Ewebught of Crathienaird (R 3). A former sheep pen north-
west of Crathie.

**Ewen's Pot*** See Poll Chais.

**The Ey Brig Puil*** (U, 086891), ðɪˈeiˈbrɪgˈpil. A pool at Inverey.

**(The) Ey Burn** (OS, F, 085893), locally now usually the Ey (C),
ðɪˈɛiˑ. Formerly Water of Ey (Fa, A), in Gaelic Uisge Eidh (6,
D), uisg ɛi, nearly e-i (D), uʃkˈɛiˑ (U), Eidh (Sto). Old forms
of the name (in A and elsewhere) add no extra evidence.
Diack speculated that Eidh is from Ag, meaning to go or
drive. Joins Dee west of Braemar.

**Ey Pool** See Poll Eidh.

**The Factor's Boat** See the Alltdourie Cottage Boat.

**The Faen Trees*** (F, 029934), ðɪˈfaˑn̩ˈtriz, Scots Faen = fallen.
A group of fallen old firs in Glen Luibeg; a gale blew them
down in November 1893.

**The Faen Trees Hillock*** (F, 029933), ðɪˈfaˑn̩ˈtrizˈhe̞lëk. A
hillock in Glen Luibeg.

**Fafernie** (OS, C, 215823), fəˈfe̞rnie, from Féith Fearnaidh (3),
bog-stream of alder place. Fe-ferni open *e* (D). The solution
to the derivation of the name of this hill south-east of Loch
Callater comes from the Burn of Fafernie in Angus to the
south-east, which rises near the top of Fafernie. It is recorded
as Fea Fearnie on two old maps (I, R 13).

**Faiche na Muin*** (3, 402980), field of the back. Faichnamuin
(R 4). A little field west of Cambus o' May.

**The Fairies' Hillock** See Tom na Feoraich.

**The Fair Well*** (U, 414917), ðɪˈfe̞r̩ˈwe̞l. A well in upper Glen
Tanar, with an inscribed stone which says the Fair Well.

**The Fairy Glen** (Ms, 124949). The steep little defile with a
grassy floor at the top of Gleann an t-Slugain. Not a local
name.

**The Fairy Hillock Park*** (U, 262955), ðɪˈfereˈhe̞lëkˈpark. A field
north of Crathie, with a prominent hillock at the top of it.

**The Fairy Hillocks*** See Na Da Shidhean.

**The Falls o Connie** (C, 085882), ðɪˈfaˑlzeˈkɔne, usually now the
Connie Falls (C). The Falls of Connie (Gf), the Connie Falls
(Br). Waterfalls near Inverey.

**(The) Falls of Dee** (OS, C, 944991), ðɪˈfaˑlzeˈdiˑ. Also Easan Dé
(3, JB), ˌe̞sɐnˈdjeˑ, falls of Dee (see Dee for meaning). Big
waterfalls near the source of Dee.

**The Falls of Dinnet** (Bg 1969, 450978), not known locally. On
Dee.

**The Falls o Feith Ord*** (F, 230890), ðɪˈfaˑlzeˌfeˈhɔrt. A steep
part of a burn north-west of Lochnagar.

**(The) Falls of (the) Garbh Allt** (OS, F, 199896), ðɪˈfaˑlzɪðɪ
ˈgarəwe̞lt, now usually the Garbh Allt Falls (C). The Falls of
the Garrawalt (Ke), the Falls of the Garbh Allt (V). The Lower
Falls of the Garr-valt (Wilson), but he named the Lower and
Upper Falls the wrong way round. A waterfall in Ballochbuie
Forest.

**(The) Falls of the Glasallt** (OS, F, 271831), ðɪˈfaˑlzɪðɪˈglasəlt,
now usually the Glasallt Falls (C). A waterfall near Loch
Muick.

**The Falls o Lui** See Easan Laoigh.

**The Falls o Muick** (C, 332895), ðɪˈfaˑlzeˈmëk. The big waterfall
at the Linn of Muick.

**The Falls o Piper*** (F, 253966), ðɪˈfaˑlzeˈpɛipër. A small fall on a
burn near Piper Hole, north-west of Crathie.

**The Falls o Quoich** (F, 113914), ðɪˈfaˑlzeˈkoɪç. The Falls of the
Quoich (Brow). Waterfalls in Glen Quoich.

**The Falls o the Derry Lochan Uaine*** (U, 024987), ðɪˈfaˑlzɪðɪ
ˈde̞rɪˌlɔχɐnˈuɐn. A tall waterfall on Derry Cairngorm.

**Farley's Cast** (Wav, C, 342961), ˈfarlezˈkast. A pool in Dee,
west of Ballater.

**Farm of Ballater*** (Io 58, 376966). Also Ballater House Farm
(Io). A former farm north-east of Ballater village, comprising
the fields of Corn Eilean, Mid Park and Cobletoun Park.

**The Farquharson Monument** See Monaltrie Monument.

**Farquharson's Cave** See the Colonel's Cave.

**Fas Ailleach** (5), stance of rough, steep place. Fasálloch (D). In
a list of names about Wester Morven–Glen Fenzie.

**Fàs-choille*** (5, U, 338951), ˈfaskəle, ? empty wood. A spot with
a well west of Ballater, in a fairly open wood.

**Fasheilach** (OS, 342858), locally the Hill o Fasheilach (F), ðɪ
ˈhe̞lɐˌfəˈʃilɪç, (feˈʃɛlɑç (A)). From Carn na Féithe Seilich (3),
hill of the willow bog-stream. Cairne of Feashelach (G 5),

Carn-a Fea-Shalloch (R 16), shown also at 364863, Cairn of Feashelloch (I), Cairn of Feasheloch (Io 43a). The burn Feith Seilich is on the Angus side (A), now Burn of Fasheilach (OS). Burn of Feashelloch (I). Fasheilach 'properly the name of the burn on the south side' of the hill (A). A hill in upper Glen Muick.

**Father Farquharson's Seat*** See the Priest's Chair.

**The Faulds*** (U, 427958), ðɪˈfɑːlz, Scots = folds. A field near Inchmarnoch.

**The Faulds*** (F, 414961), as above. A field near Inchmarnoch.

**The Faulds*** (U, 343974), as above. Small former enclosures north-west of Bridge of Gairn.

**Na Feadan** (3, D, U, 103876), ðɪˈfedɐnz, the whistles or chanters, referring to rocks 'where the wind whistles' (U). Also the Whistles (C), ðɪˈhwɛsəlz. Feadan in place names usually refers to small whistling streams, gullies, or narrow valleys, but in all cases below to runnels in rocks. A gully through which the wind moans and howls (MacKinnon, Argyll). Rocks south-west of Corriemulzie.

**Na Feadan*** (2, F), ðɪˈfedənz, ðɪˈfetənz, the whistles. A collective name for the Little Feadan and the Muckle Feadan. Rocks on Conachcraig in upper Girnock.

**Feadan Dubh** (3, Mg 148, 158861), black whistles or chanters. Fadandow (Io 25a). Rocks in lower Glen Callater.

**Am Feadan Mór*** (3, U, 329914), ðɪˌfedanˈmoˑr, the big whistle. Also the Muckle Whistle (U), ðɪˈmʌkəlˈhwɛsəl. A rock on the Coyle in Glen Muick.

**Feadan Odhar*** (3, 284883), dun whistle. Fedenaur (In, Am). Also the Muckle Feadan (F), ðɪˈmʌkəlˈfedən. A rocky depression in upper Glen Girnock.

**(The) Feardar Burn** (OS, 220940), locally now the Feardar (C), ðɪˈfjardɐr, fjaːrdər (Sch), from Féith Ardair (3), bog of high water, Gaelic pronunciation Fĕàrdour (M). The Feardar Burn is a big, fast stream and does not fit the word Feith. However, Aberarder lies about 2 km up from the mouth of the Burn, up the little Felagie Burn which is a typical Feith-type of slow stream or bog. A possible explanation is that (a) Feith Ardair was the lower part of the Felagie Burn or bog, with Aberarder at the mouth where it joins the latter-day Feardar Burn, (b) the main glen-stream later took its name from this smaller stream, as did the main glen, and (c) the Inver was named as the mouth of the latter-day Feardar Burn. The points (a) and (c) seem obvious. The key point is that there is good evidence for (b), as the upper part of the Feardar Burn at 193957 was Ault chley (I) in 1807–09 (i.e. Allt Chlì (3), left burn), and the Feardar Burn below that was marked Ault Guish (i.e. Allt Giubhais) at 200952 and right down at 210947. Robertson's map agrees with this, as does the MacGillivray map with Ault Guish and Ault Chlie. Diack gave a different explanation based on arguing that the Aber in Aberarder was from Abar = a marsh, but he did not mention the key evidence about our point (b). Also Allt Féith Ardair (3), burn of bog of high water. Allt feith ardar (D). Note Uisge Féith Ardair (3), water of bog of high water. Uisg fyarter (D in A). Ferder Water (Fa). Abhainn Féith Ardair (3), river of bog of high water. Avon Fairdour (Bla MS). The forms Allt Feith Ardair and Uisge Feith Ardair corroborate the above argument; it seems unlikely that there would have been an Abar = bog here as well as a Feith. A small water called Arder (Wi). The upper part at 193957, formerly Allt Chli, is now the Cuithe Iomlan Burn (C), ðɪ ˈgwimlənˈbʌrn, after the nearby Ach nan Cuithe Iomlan. North-west of the Inver.

**Feardar Water*** See Feardar Burn.

**The Fearns** (A, F, 275942), ðɪˈfjaˑrnz, from Fearn (3) = alder. A wood east of Balmoral.

**Feindallacher Burn** (OS, 198858), from Féith an t-Salachair (5), fenˌdaləçër, bog of the willow place (note W 1904, 8). Macdonald suggested 'Marshy burn of the filth or mud' and wrote that the Gaelic natives understood the name to mean the muddy burn. Feintallacher (Roy), Burn of Feandalachar (Ro, R 7), Fē-in-dallacher broad *l* (D). Also Allt Féith an t-Salachair (5), burn of bog of the willow place. Ault Feandalacher (Mg). South of Ballochbuie Forest.

**Féith an Laoigh** (OS, 233898), locally Féith Laoigh (3, A, C), fe 'lui, bog-stream of calf. Fea Lui (Ro), Fea Luie (R 7), Faeluie Burn (B), Feithluie (V). Also Allt Laoigh (3, A), alt'lui, burn of calf. In Glen Gelder.

**Féith an t-Searraich*** (3, F, 919872), ˌfeɐnˈdʒariç, bog-stream of the colt. Feith deorich (Mm). At the top of Glen Geldie.

**Féith Badan Buidhe*** (3, 253913), bog-stream of yellow little clump of trees. Faepattenbuie (B). In Glen Gelder.

**Féith Bheag Bhàn** (2, A, F, 975850), ˈfeˌvɛgˈvaˑn, little white bog-stream, or An Fhéith Bheag Bhàn (U), ˈneˌvɛgˈvaˑn, the little white bog-stream. Up the Bynack Burn, forms a pair with Feith Mhor Bhan.

**Féith Bheal Luachrach*** (3, 233980), bog-stream of passage of rushes, from Bealach. Fevalluachrich (R 9). Also Rushy Mire (R 3). North-west of Crathie.

**Féith Chaorach*** (3, 295805), bog-stream of sheep. Fe Chirach (R 6), Burn of Faechurrach (I). South of Loch Muick.

**Féith Eag Dhubh*** (3, 124967), bog of black notch. Fegodow (Im 3), Fego Dow (Io 63). South of Ben Avon.

**Na Féithean Rod** (3, 276813), classic Gaelic for the Feith Rods (C), ðɪˌfɛˑˈrodz, the ruddy bogs. The Ferods (In, Am), the Fir Roads (McC 1891) and the current pronunciation indicate a plural (i.e. bogs). A big boggy plateau south of Loch Muick. See Ferrowie, a similar name less than 3 km to the east.

**The Feith Fiogaidh Burn*** (U, 309949), ðɪˌfeˈfɪgiˈbʌrn. Féith Fiogaidh (5), rushy bog. Fiag = rushes (Dw). Magherafelt in Ireland was pronounced Magherafiggy and was from Fiogaidh = rushy (J 3, 495). Fighidh = of braiding, is possible, referring to the watery network of this peat-bog. East of Abergeldie.

**Féith Ghille*** (3, U, 232875), fe'hil, bog of the lad. Feidhe Gheal (Bs). The stream from it is Allt Gille Geal, presumably named after the same lad; lower down it is the Blacksheil Burn. North-west of Lochnagar.

**Féith Luid*** (3, 245924), bog-stream of the marsh. Faelutch (B). In Glen Gelder.

**Féith Mhór Bhàn** (OS, 2, C, 964840), 'feˌvor'vaˑn, big white bog-stream, or An Fhéith Mhór Bhàn (U), 'neˌvor'vaˑn, the big white bog-stream. Up the Bynack Burn, forms a pair with Feith Bheag Bhan.

**Féith nam Madadh*** (4, 160935), bog of the dogs or wolves, or nam Maide, of the sticks. Fae na Matt (I). A boggy patch north-west of Invercauld.

**Féith nan Caorach*** (3, 399932), bog-stream of the sheep. Fena Cirach (R 6). South-east of Ballater.

**Féith nan Sgòr*** (2, C, 020920), ˌfɐnɐ'skọr, bog-stream of the rocky hills. A group of hills north-west of the Linn of Dee, see name below.

**Féith na Sgòr** (OS, 028909), classic Gaelic form would be Féith nan Sgòr (3), bog-stream of the rocky hills. The original name of the bog-stream has now been forgotten, and locally the name means the group of hills between the Linn of Dee and Glen Luibeg, including Sgor Dubh and Sgor Mor. It was also used by Gaelic speakers in this sense (D, A).

**Féith Ord** (3, F, 231889), fe'họrt, bog-stream of round hills. Faichort (B), Feithort (V). North-west of Lochnagar.

**Féith Preasan a' Chuilinn*** (3, 230993), bog-stream of little copse of the holly, or Chuilein = of the cub. Fepresnichoulan (R 9). North-west of Crathie.

**Féith Preas an Eich Bhlàir\*** (3, 228989), bog-stream of copse of the white-faced horse. Faepresneighplair or well of the tree of the ? hauched (writing indistinct) horse (Im 9), Fepresnichovlar (R 9). Note also Well Called Bush of the Bald Horse (R 5). Also Bald Horse Strype (R 3). North-west of Crathie.

**Féith Ruighe na Coille\*** (3, 244001), bog-stream of cattle-run of the wood. Fearnoch-chaol, Ferinachoil twice, and the mire of the rive of the wood (R 3, 5 & 9, 9). South-east of Corndavon Lodge.

**Féith Salach** See Allt Salach.

**Féith Seileach** (OS, 150809), willow bog-stream. North of the Cairnwell.

**Féith Shearrach\*** (3, F, 995853), feˈharəç, bog-stream of colts. West of Bynack Lodge.

**Felagie** (OS, C, 193922), fəˈlegi, from Féith (2) = bog-stream, Léigidh (5) from Léig = marshy pool. Feith leaghaidh, 'slow burn' (D in A), Leugach = slow (Dw). A house beside a flat bog north-east of Invercauld Bridge.

**(The) Felagie Burn** (OS, C, 199928), ðɪˌfəˈlegiˈbʌrn. At the above bog.

**The Felagie Moor\*** (U, 195925), ðɪˌfəˈlegiˈmu̩r. The flat bog at Felagie.

**The Felagie Rocks\*** See Am Mir Dubh.

**Felagie Village\*** (195924). Fealeagie Village (Opr 48). A former group of houses east of Invercauld.

**The Fence End Puil** (F, 275946), ðɪˈfɛnsˈɛndˈpil. Fence (Wav). A strainer post nearby shows where there had been a fence. A pool in Dee.

**Na Feòrachan\*** (317944), now the Feorachans (C), ðɪˈfjurəçənz, the grassy places, from Feòran (3) = a green. A grassy hill-nose in lower Glen Girnock.

**The Feorachans Brae\*** (F, 318944), ðɪˈfjurəçənzˈbre·. A hill on a road in Glen Girnock.

**The Feorachans Corner\*** (F, 319947), ðɪˈfjurəçənzˈkᴐrnër. Sharp bend on above road.

**The Feorachans Plantin\*** (F, 318947), ðɪˈfjurəçənzˈplantɪn. A plantation beside above hill.

**The Feoraich Brae\*** (C, 337998), ðɪˈfjᴐrɪçˈbre·. A hill on the road at Lary in Glen Gairn, named after the nearby Tom na Feoraich.

**The Fergie Burn\*** See Allt Gheallain.

**(The) Ferny Howe\*** (U, 307925), ðɪˌfɛrneˈhʌu·. A hollow with bracken in Glen Girnock.

**Ferrowie** (OS, F, 303795), fɛˈrʌu.i. 'Locally interpreted as from Feith ruadh, red moss-burn; if so the triphthongal sound is unusual' (A). The explanation comes from an early map (I), where the name is Hill of Fea-roy. This would give a genitive for Ruadh, probably from Carn na Féithe Ruaidhe (3), hill of the red bog-stream. Probably the original Féith Ruadh = red bog-stream was the little burn to the east, now the Burn o Ferrowie. 'The Gaelic natives say feith ruadh, "red marsh or marshy burn," and that this is descriptive of the marsh and the burn flowing out of it' (M). A hill south of Loch Muick, pairs with Little Ferrowie.

**The Ferry Inn** (Pj, 420978). A former inn at an old ferry over Dee near Cambus o' May, later called Railway Cottage and more recently Cut-away Cottage (Er) as a corner of it had to be removed to make way for the Deeside railway.

**The Feuragach** (3, F, 277954), ðɪˈfɛrgɐχ, likely to have been An Fheuragach originally, the grassy place. Fergach (I, R 14), Fergachs (R 12). In Gaelic Fergach or sometimes Fer-ig-ach (D in A). Note Little Fergachs. A former farm east of Crathie. OS 1869 shows Fergach at the present Wester Micras, with Wester Micras nearby at 282955 (now ruins).

**The Feuragach\*** (3, U), as above. A general name for the fields between Tomidhu and Wester Micras near Crathie, sometimes the Feuragachs (anglicised plural).

**The Feuragaidh** (3, U, 278954), ðɪˈfɛrgi, at grassy place. Feragie (Vr 4), the Fergie (A). A field east of Crathie.

**An Fhéith Chrom\*** (3, 158888), the crooked bog-stream. Nea Chroum (I). South of Braemar.

**An Fhéith Dhubh** (2, U, 077895), ðɪˌfeˈdu·, neˈdu·, the dark bog-stream. Fae Goo (A 1954). Also the Black Burn (U), ðɪˈblak ˈbʌrn. East of the Linn of Dee.

**An Fheith Ghlas\*** See Allt Glas.

**An Fhéith Seileach\*** (3, 179972), the willow bog, with Seileach used in an adjectival sense. Nea Shellach, 'moss' (I). North of Invercauld.

**The Fhionnaidh Burn\*** See Glenfenzie Burn.

**The Fife Brae** (Er, C, east of 150915), ðɪˈfɛifˈbre·. A hill on a road beside the Fife Arms Hotel in Braemar.

**Finlay's Croft** (Ab 19). Findlaycroft (G 28). A former farm probably in Balhennie–Cnoc Dubh area west of Logie Coldstone.

**Am Fionn-choire** See Coire Fionn.

**The Fionn-choire Burn** See Allt Coire Fionn.

**(The) Fir Bog** (OS, F, 415896), ðɪˈfɛrˈbᴑg. A peat bog with fir roots. In upper Glen Tanar.

**The Fir Bog Burn\*** See Fir Burn.

**Fir Burn** (OS, 416899), locally the Fir Bog Burn (F), ðɪˈfɛrˈbᴑg ˈbʌrn. In upper Glen Tanar.

**The Fir Hillock** (OS, F, 432918), ðɪˈfɛrˈhɛlëk. In upper Glen Tanar.

**The Fir Park\*** (Me, 066894). A planted wood east of Linn of Dee.

**The Fir Park\*** (F, 282950), ðɪˈfɛrˈpark. A planted wood at Abergeldie.

**The Fir Park Puil** (F, 281951), ðɪˈfɛrˈparkˈpil. Fir Park (Sc). A pool in Dee above Abergeldie Castle, includes Great and Little.

**The Fir Tree Puil** (F, south-west of 358967), ðɪˈfɛrˈtriˈpil. Fir Tree (Sc). A pool in Dee, east of Gairn junction.

**The Fishermen's Roadie\*** (U, 423970), ðɪˈfɛʃërmənzˈrodi. A track south-east of Cambus o' May.

**The Fit o Gairn** (C, 350970), ðɪˈfɛtɐˈgern̩, Scots Fit = foot. Foot o' Gairn (Gr), Fit of Gairn (V 4), Foot of Gairn (A 136). The area around the Bridge of Gairn.

**The Fit o Girnock\*** (C, 326958), ðɪˈfɛtɐˈgernɐk. Foot of Girnuck (Opr 51). The general area around Littlemill at the foot of Glen Girnock.

**The Fit o the Baddoch\*** (F, 136832), ðɪˈfɛtɪðɪˈbadəç. A general name for ground at the foot of Baddoch.

**The Fit o the Toun\*** (C, 419030), ðɪˈfɛtəiˈtun, ðɪˈfɛtɪðɪˈtun, Scots = foot of the town (i.e. farm-town). Also Auchnerran Cottage (U), aχˈnerɛnˈkᴑtədʒ. A former cottage south-west of Logie Coldstone.

**The Five Cairns\*** (C, 137895), ðɪˈfaevˈkern̩z. A group of cairns on the skyline of Morrone as seen from Braemar.

**The Flats\*** (U, 345025), ðɪˈflats. A flattish area in the glen west of Morven.

**The Flats o Monelpie\*** (F, 272835), ðɪˈflatsɐˌmᴑnˈɛlpi. A flat plateau north-west of Loch Muick.

**Fleming's Moss\*** See Moine Taibhseach.

**The Floating Bank Puil** (F, 356966), ðɪˈflotɛnˈbaŋkˈpil. Floating Bank (Sc). A pool in Dee, at mouth of Gairn.

**The Flood Stane\*** (C, 176919), ðɪˈflʌdˈstin. Flood mark (OS 1869). A stone near Invercauld, marking the point reached by the exceptional 1829 flood.

**The Flood Stane Park*** (F, 186912), ðɪˈflʌdˈstinˈpark. A field at Invercauld, including Creit an Loin and other former fields.

**Foggo's Fence** (Anony, C, 155913), ˈfɒgozˈfɛns. A fence erected by a Mr Foggo, a former factor, who tried unsuccessfully to stop Braemar people going up Creag Choinnich.

**The Fog House*** (F, 258945), ðɪˈfɒgˌhus, Scots = moss house. Fog houses are small stone summer-houses in shady, damp spots with much moss. This one was at Balmoral (no longer exists). There was one or more at each of the main estates from Ballater upwards, with a prepared, broad, smooth path leading to it.

**The Fog House** (C, 371971), as above. Fog-house (Gf). In Pass of Ballater near Monaltrie House.

**The Fog House*** (U, 338951), as above. Near Strathgirnock.

**The Fog House*** (C, 104894), as above. South-east of Mar Lodge.

**The Fog House*** (C, 112893), as above. On east side of burn at Corriemulzie.

**The Fog House*** (F, 178925), as above. Near Invercauld House.

**The Fog House Brae*** (F, 372971), ðɪˈfɒgˌhusˈbreˑ. A hill on the road in the Pass of Ballater, beside a Fog House.

**The Fog House Brig*** (F, 373971), ðɪˈfɒgˌhusˈbrɪg. In Pass of Ballater.

**The Fog House Brig*** (U, north-east of 198898), as above. In Ballochbuie Forest.

**The Fog House o the Garbh Allt** (U, 199896), ðɪˈfɒgˌhusəi ˈgarəwɛlt. The Garrawalt, the Bridge, and Fog-house thereof (Brown 1). A former fog house in Ballochbuie Forest; only the site is now visible.

**The Fog House Path*** (U, east of 198897), ðɪˈfɒgˌhusˈpaθ. Along east bank of Garbh Allt in Ballochbuie Forest.

**The Folds of Ruighe an t-Sagairt*** (374007). The folds of Rientaggart (Io 20). Former farmland up Tullich Burn.

**Forbes' Corrie*** See Coire Chrid.

**Forbes' Moss*** (Am, 337930). A peat-moss in lower Glen Muick, now under planted trees.

**Ford Cottage** (OS, C, 137912), ˈfɒrdˈkɒtədʒ. West of Braemar, near a former ford on Dee.

**Ford House** (Vr 1899, C, 371955), ˈfɒrdˈhus. At Ballater, beside a former ford over Dee.

**Fordmouth*** (Opr 47, Io 77, Ce 2, north-east of 289955 on south side of road, beside the ford Athan Phuill (see Mi 258)). Possibly from an original Beul an Àtha = mouth of the ford, as Fordmouth is not a usual term in English or in Aberdeenshire Scots. A former farm near Micras east of Crathie.

**The Ford of Dinnet** (Gf, 469985). A former ford over Dee.

**The Ford of the Coinlach Burn*** (G 25, 395032). Where a path crosses a burn south-east of Morven.

**Ford of the Slugan*** (221962). Ford of the Sluggan (I). A crossing place on the Coldrach Burn north-west of the Inver.

**The Ford of the Tree** (Di1), said to be in the Glack o' Morven, but there is only a tiny stream there. Possibly south-west of 319024.

**Ford Pool** (Ly, 157926). Former pool in Dee west of Invercauld.

**The Fore Coire Buidhe*** See Coire Buidhe air Bheul.

**The Fore Coire Buidhe Burn*** (U, 293877), ðɪˈforˌkɒrˈbuiˈbʌrn. On Conachcraig in upper Glen Muick.

**The Forest*** (C), ðɪˈfɒrëst. Open moor and hill forming the deer forest between Balmoral and Lochnagar, distinguished from the grouse moors of Girnock and upper Glen Muick.

**Forester Haugh*** (I, C, 316868), ˈfɒrëstɐrˈhaˑχ. Ruins of former houses, different from the ruins at Bealachodhar. Forrester Haugh (Io 53). A former farm in upper Glen Muick.

**Forester Haugh*** (U, 318867), as above. A flattish grassy area in upper Glen Muick.

**The Foresters Shiel** (Cj 1, 098952). A former hut once used by deer-stalkers on Mar. At mouth of Allt an t-Sneachda in upper Glen Quoich.

**The Forest of Beinn a' Bhuird*** (100970). The Forrest of Bennibord (Io 29). A former name for a deer forest, comprising 'the Glens of Caich, Beachan, Sluggan, Aultwrotachan, Glassault and Aultdowry'.

**The Forest of Beinn nan Ciochan*** (220880). The Forrest of Beinichichness (Io 63). Beinichichness suggests a plural Beinn Chiochans, or Beinn Chioch. A former deer forest extending from Invercauld Bridge to the top of Lochnagar and Carn an t-Sagairt Mor.

**Forest of Beitheachan** (093957). Forrest of Beachan (Bla), Forrest of Beachan or Caich (Im 3). A former name of a deer forest in upper Glen Quoich.

**Forest of Breacach**, from Breacach (3) = speckled place. Forest of Breckach, Forest of Braceo (Ri 13, 29), Forest of Bracach (R 1), Forrest of Bracach and Kirn (Io 31), Forest of Brecach (Cj 11). Forest of Brechahill (Roy) might be Breacach Hill but possibly Breac-choille = speckled wood. Roy shows it at Hunt Hill south of the Linn of Muick. A former deer forest stretching from Linn of Muick round the south side of Loch Muick to Carn an t-Sagairt (boundaries described in Ri, 35).

**The Forest of Bynack and Coire Bhronn*** (010850). The Forrest of Bainack and Corry Wran (Io 25a). A former name of the deer forest south-west and south of Bynack Lodge.

**Forest of Culblean** (400000). Forrest of Colblean (G 24), forrestis de Morvein et Coblein (Ab 19). An old name for the hill ground north of Cambus o' May.

**The Forest of Derry*** (040930). The Forrest of Derie (Io 25a). A former name for the deer forest in Glen Derry and Glen Luibeg.

**The Forest of Dubh-Ghleann*** (071965). The Forrest of Duglennan (Io 25a). A former name of the deer forest in the Dubh-Ghleann north-west of Glen Quoich.

**Forest of Etnach** (M). Former deer forest in Glen Tanar.

**The Forest of Geldie** (990870). The Forrest of Gaulaig (Hi), Forrests of Gaullie (Im 5). A former name of the deer forest in Glen Geldie.

**Forest of Glen Callater*** (170860). Forrest of Glencallater (Io 29). A former deer forest.

**The Forest of Glen Ey*** (OSn, 060820). A former deer forest, now part of Mar.

**(The) Forest of Glen Tanar** (OS, C), ðɪˈfɒrëstɐˌglənˈtaˑnɐr. Refers to the deer forest on open hill ground in Glen Tanar as well as to the old woods.

**The Forest of Invercauld*** (I, 166916). Deer forest, which extends over many hills near Braemar.

**(The) Forest of Mar** (OS, F), ðɪˈfɒrëstɐˈmaːr, now Mar Forest (C). Also Frith Mharr (6), forest of Mar. Fridh mhàrr (D). Formerly all ground in Aberdeenshire west of Braemar, but split up in the early 1960s. A deer forest.

**Forest of Morven.** For-rest of Morvin (Bla), Forrest of Morvine (G 24). An old name for the hills around Morven.

**The Forest Road*** (Gler, 408899). Road from Glen Tanar House up the former deer forest to the Shiel of Glentanar.

**The Forestry Cottages*** (C, 347924), ðɪˈfɒrëstreˈkɒtədʒiz. Cottages that were built by the Forestry Commission. In Glen Muick.

**The Forkings*** (Io 20, 377016). Where a burn divides south of Morven.

**The Forkings*** (R 3, 250031). Where a burn forks, north-east of Corndavon.

**The Forkings of Alltan Odhar*** (079819). The Forkins of

Aultanour (Io 79). A junction of two burns near Altanour Lodge in Glen Ey.

**The Forkins*** (U, 287966), ðɪˈfɔrkënz. A place where two burns meet, north-east of Crathie.

**The Forkins o the Glas Allt*** (U, 257843), ðɪˈfɔrkënzɪðɪˈglasəlt. As above on Lochnagar.

**The Forkins o the Luibeg*** (U, 010957), ðɪˈfɔrkënzɪðɪˌluiˈbeg. As above in Glen Luibeg.

**The Foul Gutter*** (F, 303807), ðɪˈfulˈgʌtër. A burn that crosses the Capel Road south-east of Loch Muick.

**The Foul Gutter*** (F, 342940), as above. A boggy burn in lower Glen Muick.

**The Fountain Burn** See Corrie Burn.

**The Four Lords' Stones** See the Mary Stanes.

**Fox Cairn** (OS, 285020, should be the cairn at 284018), locally Cairn Fox (C), kernˈfɔks. Fox Monument (R 12). A cairn north-west of Gairnshiel, said to have been erected to commemorate Fox the statesman (A), but locally said to have been to the memory of Major Fox who built the Gairnshiel Bridge.

**Fox Cairn*** (OSn), rough stones around Fox Cairn Well on Lochnagar.

**(The) Fox Cairn Well** (OS, 263857), locally the Fox's Well (C), ðɪˈfɔksɪzˈwel. 'Now called Fox's Well' (McC 1891). A fox cairn in Aberdeenshire Scots means a stony patch where a fox can make a den in the holes amongst the stones. On Lochnagar.

**The Foxes' Well*** See the Well o Morven.

**The Fox's Cairn*** (U, 423985), ðɪˈfɔksɪzˈkern. A rocky hillock above the Muir of Dinnet.

**Francis Stone*** (B, north-west of 230921). On the hill south of the Inver.

**Fraser's Brig** (C, 148865), ˈfrezërzˈbrɪg. Fraser's Bridge (I, Gf). Formerly East Bridge (Tay) in 1776. In Glen Clunie.

**Fraser's Pot*** (U, 393971), ˈfrezërzˈpɔt, Scots Pot = deep pool. A deep pool on the Tullich Burn near where it enters Dee.

**Frith Bhealaich Bhuidhe** See Ballochbuie Forest.

**Frith Mharr** See Forest of Mar.

**The Front o the House Park*** (U, west of 416037), ðɪˈfrʌntəiˈhusˈpark. A field west of Logie Coldstone.

**Na Fuaireachan** (259973), from Fuaireach (3), cold place. The Furriachs, a lot of small burns (D). North of Crathie.

**Fuaran an t-Sagairt*** See Priest's Well.

**Fuaran Dhe** See Wells of Dee.

**Fuaran Fearn** (3, D, 142907), well of alder. At Woodhill above Braemar.

**Fuaran Lag nan Laogh*** (3, 243005), well of hollow of the calves. Fuaran Lag na Laodh (R 3). South-east of Corndavon Lodge.

**Fuaran Mhic Coinnich na Gruaig** (2, U, 115907), ˌfuɐrɐnˌviç ˌꞔɔnjɐꭓnɐˈgruig, (fuərənəkˈhonjəꭓnanˈgruək (A)), well of Mackenzie of the long hair. Fuaran mhic coinneach gruaic (D), Fuaran 'Ic Choinnich nan Gruaig (A). Named after an incident where two men died in a clan fight. Near the mouth of Quoich.

**Fuaran 'Ic Fhearghais** (3, east of 004893), Ferguson's well. Fuaran mhic Fheargas, ik erash (D). In Glen Dee.

**Fuaran Mhonaidh*** (3, U, 181810), ˌfuɐrɐnˈvɔne, well of the hill. South of Loch Callater.

**Fuaran Mhungo** See St Mungo's Well.

**Fuaran na Claise Challtuinn*** (3, north-east of 261994), well of the hollow of hazels. Furan-na-clash-chauldin (I). South-west of Gairnshiel.

**Fuaran nan Aighean** (OS, 331905), well of the hinds. In mid Glen Muick.

**Fuaran nan Sgòr** (3, 150903), well of the peaks. Fuaran na Sgor (D). Beside the Braemar Golf Course.

**Fuaran na Sgeire** (3, 144904), well of the rock. Sgeir is unusual inland, but see other cases under Sgeir. Fuaran na sgeir (D). Beside a rock on Morrone above Braemar.

**Fuaran Nigheanaig** (3, 261982 at east side of road), little girl's well. Fuaran-yirnach, lassie's well (D). At the roadside north of Crathie.

**Fuaran Phananaich** See Pannanich Wells.

**Fuaran Phollath** (3, north of 144914), well of the pool place (see Am Pollath). Fuaran Pholla (D). Beside a pool in Dee called Am Pollath, west of Braemar.

**Fuaran Roibidh** (3, south-east of 303965), Robbie's well. Fuaran Ropie, fuaran Robaidh, Robbie's well (D). East of Crathie.

**Fuaran Ruighe Bhùirn** (3, D, south of 985914), well of shiel of the water. In Glen Dee below Beinn Bhrotain.

**Fuaran Ruighe Ealasaid** (3, D, north-west of 002869), well of Elizabeth's shiel. In lower Glen Geldie.

**Fuaran Toll Bhalgair** (3, D, north of 244859), well of hole of foxes. Fuaran nam Balgair (Cj 16). Also Queen's Well (D), and the Poachers' Well (Cj 1, 71; McC 1891) after a poacher who died there in a snowstorm in the 1790s. Near the top of Lochnagar.

**Am Fuar Garbh-choire** See Garbh Choire Dhaidh.

**The Fuird of Candacraig*** (342994), Scots Fuird = ford. The Foord of Candacraig (Io 47). Over Gairn.

**The Fuird of Clacharraidh*** (388022). The Foord of Clachrie (G 19). At Allt Clacharraidh south-east of Morven.

**The Fuird o Inchnabobart** (F, 313877), ðɪˈfjurdɐˌɪnʃˈbɔbërt. The Ford of Inchnabobart (McC 1891). A ford on the upper Muick.

**The Fuird o the Glas Allt*** (F, 267835), ðɪˈfjurdɪðɪˈglasəlt. A ford on the burn above Glas-allt-Shiel at Loch Muick.

**The Fuird o the Lairig Ghru** See Beul-ath na Lairige Ghru.

**The Fuird Park*** (U, 315005), ðɪˈfjurdˈpark. A field beside a ford on Gairn.

**The Fuird Puil** (F, north-east of 213920), ðɪˈfjurdˈpil. Ford (Wav). In Dee, at a former ford south-west of the Inver.

**The Fuird Road*** (U, 290954), ðɪˈfjurdˈrod. Ford Road (Cp, Am). A road to a ford over Dee at Abergeldie.

**The Fuird Road*** (F, 315876), as above. A road to a ford on the upper Muick.

**The Fuird Road*** (C, 136912), as above. A track to a ford on Dee west of Braemar.

**The Fuird Road*** (U, 342990), as above. A former road to a ford over Gairn, north-west of Bridge of Gairn.

**The Fuird Road*** (U, south of 152922), as above. Also the Boat Road (U), ðɪˈbotˈrod. Boat Road (S 20). Track to a former ford north of Braemar.

**The Fuirds o Geldie** (U, 005868), ðɪˈfjurdzɐˈgeldi. The Fords of Geldie (Cj 7). Over Geldie Burn.

**Gain Dhearg** (5, c. 405981), red sand, Gain from Gaineamh, or Gàinne Dhearg = red shaft. Ganjarg a road or bank (D). West of Cambus o' May.

**The Gairbheach*** (3, 281964), likely to have been A' Ghairbheach originally, the place of roughness. The Gariach (I). A rough patch that had been worked before 1807–9 (I), and was reseeded in the 1960s. North-east of Crathie.

**The Gairdener's Brae*** (C, 257948), ðɪˈgerdꞏnërzˈbreꞏ, Scots = gardener's hill. A little hill on a road near Balmoral Castle.

**The Gairden Park*** (U, 428045), ðɪˈgerdənˈpark. A field near Logie Coldstone.

**The Gairden Park*** (U, 438968), as above. The gairden parkie (Dms 6). Also the Orchard Yaird, Scots Yaird = yard. Formerly the orchard yeard (Dms 6). A field at Inchmarnoch.

82

**The Gairden Puil** (C, 385965), ðɪ'gɛrdən'pil. Garden Pool (Sc). In Dee below Ballater.

**The Gairn** See River Gairn.

**The Gairney Burn** See Water of Gairney.

**Gairnsdale** (Ri), Scots Dale = a portion of land, or English Dale = valley. Also Gardensdale (Io 61). A name for the former Rineten estate west of Gairnshiel.

**Gairnshiel** See Gairnshiel Lodge.

**The Gairnshiel Brig** (C, 295008), ðɪˌgɛrn̩'ʃil'brɪg. Upper Bridge of Garden (Im 3), Gairnshiel Brig (Wy). Carries the old military road across River Gairn.

**Gairnshiel Lodge** (OS, 294007), locally Gairnshiel, gɛrn̩'ʃil (C). Garden Shiel (K). Named Garden Shiel or Gairden Shiel, not after the river but after Mr Garden of Troup (near Banff), who built it (Io 64, Mg, Ri). A house in Glen Gairn.

**The Gairnshiel Puil*** (F, 294008), ðɪˌgɛrn̩'ʃil'pil. A pool in Gairn, at Gairnshiel.

**Gairnside** (Cg, A, C), gɛrn̩'sɛid. Gardenside (Fi). A name for any place along the River Gairn.

**The Gala Hill*** (F, 358029), ðɪˌgalɐ'hël. A grassy top south-west of Morven. Gallowhill (G 33). Also used now for the ridge to north-east up to the top at 367039. Probably Geal (3) = white; in north-east Scotland, the words 'a black hill' are often used for a heathery hill, and 'a white hill' for a hill with rough grass. Too high up to be a gallows place.

**The Gallow Hill** See Tom Mallachd Mathair.

**(The) Gallow Hill** (OS, C, 424030), ðɪ'galɐ'hël. A low rise covered with rough grass and heather, with some boggy ground around it, south-west of Logie Coldstone. Near enough to human habitations to have been a gallows place, but possibly from Scots Gall = bog myrtle, or Gaelic Geal = white.

**Gallow Hillock** (OS, I, C, 298799), ˌgalɐ'hëlɐk. The galloa hill (G 5), Gala Hillock (Bs). A grassy hillock near the top of where the Capel Road dips into Angus, probably from Geal = white, too high up to be a gallows place.

**The Gallow Hill Park*** (U, 423032), ðɪˌgalɐ'hël'park. A field near a low hill (see two names up).

**Gallows Hill** See Tom na Croiche.

**The Gallows Tree** See Craoibh na Croiche.

**Gall's Wall*** (U, 302815), 'gaːlz'waːl, possibly Gauld's. Gall's Well (Bs). A well named after a shepherd, on east side of the Capel Road south-east of Loch Muick.

**Gamhann Dearg** (5), red ditch. Gavinderg, a holding in 18th century (D). Location not stated, but near Cambus o' May implied.

**An Garadh*** (3, F), n'garɐ, ðɪ'garɐ, the dyke. An old road from Catanellan to the corner of a road at 286936, beside an old dyke running south up the hillside south of Abergeldie.

**Garadh Madaidh*** (3, 231932), wolf's den. Garmaddie (B). A boggy patch on south side of Dee, opposite the Inver Inn.

**Garaidhean Móra** (4, C, 371954), ˌgarən'moːr, big dykes; Garan Mór, big grove, less likely as Ballater was built on a bare moor. Garranmore (Vr 1899), now Garranmhor, is known as the name of one of Ballater's older houses, but possibly was named after a place nearby; the house stands near the former ford over Dee, and there are dykes and bulwarks on the river bank.

**(An) Garbh Allt** (OS, 2, C, 199906), ðɪ'garəwɛlt, from An Garbh-allt, the rough burn. Also formerly Burn of Garbh Allt. Burn of Garval (Im 2), Garvel Burn (Fa), Garvel (Ri 23b), Garvault Burn (R 7), Garavalt (Mg), N garualt (D in A). In Ballochbuie Forest.

**An Garbh-allt*** (2, C, 077905), as above, the rough burn. A little burn west of Mar Lodge.

**Garbh-allt*** (3, 213956), rough burn. Garraw ault (I). A little burn north-west of the Inver.

**The Garbh-allt Birk Wuid*** (U, 075906), ðɪ'garəwɛlt'bërk'wɪd, often just the Birk Wuid (C). A birch wood north-west of Mar Lodge.

**The Garbh Allt Brae*** (C, 198897), ðɪ'garəwɛlt'breˑ. A hill on a road in Ballochbuie Forest.

**The Garbh Allt Brig*** (C, 200901), ðɪ'garəwɛlt'brɪg. A bridge above Garbh Allt Shiel.

**The Garbh Allt Falls Brig*** (C, 199895), ðɪ'garəwɛlt'faˑlz'brɪg. Bridge at Falls of Garbh Allt.

**(The) Garbh Allt Shiel** (OS, C, 200904), ðɪ'garəwɛlt'ʃil. A house in Ballochbuie Forest, formerly called (the) Danzig Shiel (OS 1961, C) till around the first world war, ðɪ'danzɪg'ʃil, often just the Danzig, after the proprietors of a former sawmill nearby who also had a business in Danzig (McC).

**The Garbh Allt Shiel Brig** (C, 197908), ðɪ'garəwɛlt'ʃil'brɪg. The Garrawalt Shiel Bridge (Gf). Also the Suspension Brig (F), ðɪˌsəs'pɛnʃən'brɪg. Formerly the Danzig Shiel Bridge or Danzig Bridge (Gf). East of Invercauld Bridge.

**The Garbh Allt Wuid*** (F, 200895), ðɪ'garəwɛlt'wɪd. Garrow Alt Silva (Go). Part of Ballochbuie Forest.

**The Garbhanach Haugh*** (351938), from Garbhanach (3), rough place. The Garnich Haugh (Am). In lower Glen Muick.

**Garbh-chlais*** (3, 181949), rough hollow. Garraw Chlash (I). A rough defile north of Invercauld.

**An Garbh Choire** (OS, 2, C, 953985), classic form An Garbh-choire, ðɪ'garçəre (in Gaelic 'garahər (A)), the rough corrie. Garrachory (Fi, Mg), Garchory (Mg). The vast stony corrie between Cairn Toul and Braeriach. Sir James Balfour's Collection (quoted in Robertson 1843) gave 'The river Dee springes out of Corredee, on the confynes of Badenocht, at a place caled by the barbarous inhabitants Pittindawin and Bodindeweill (that is the deivell's . . .); so speakes these wylde scurrilous people, amongst wych there is bot small feare and knowledge of God'. This has been incorrectly interpreted as meaning that Pittindawin and Bodindeweill (i.e. Bod an Deamhain and Bod an Diabhail) are Garbh Choire Dhaidh, whereas they are undoubtedly the Devil's Point (see Devil's Point). Seton Gordon (1925) wrote 'one looks west into the grand Garbh Choire that in the fifteenth century was called "Pit an Deamhain"', and Perry (1948) added 'this Hollow of the She-Devil, as the shieling folk had referred to the Garbh Coire three centuries before my day'. These errors, and the mistake about the sex of the demon, later led to a rock climb on Garbh Choire Mor being named She-Devil's Buttress (Ms). Sir James Balfour's Corredee presumably came from Coire Dé or possibly from Garbh Choire Dhaidh.

**An Garbh-choire*** (3, U, 353010), as above, the rough corrie. South-west of Morven. See name below.

**An Garbh-choire*** (3, U, 353018), as above, the rough corrie. This and the above form a pair.

**(An) Garbh-choire** (OS, 174788, 3, C, should be at 173783), as above, the rough corrie. Garbchory (V). A stony corrie north-east of the Glas Maol.

**An Garbh-choire** (3, F, 262927), as above, the rough corrie. Garcorrie (B). A stony corrie south of Balmoral.

**Garbh-choire*** (3, 268983), rough corrie. Garra Chorry (I). A stony corrie south-west of Gairnshiel.

**Na Garbh-choireachan Dhé** (3), the rough corries of the Dee or goddess. No'n Garbh-choireachan Dhe, or the rough corries of Dee (Sin). Also the Garbh-choires (U), ðɪ'garçərez. A collective name for Garbh Choire Dhaidh and Garbh Choire Mor on Braeriach.

**The Garbh-choire Burn** (F, 262929), ðɪ'garçəre'bʌrn. South of Balmoral.

**Garbh Choire Dhàidh** (OS, 947988), should be Garbh-choire

Dhé (3, Gr, Sg, Al, A, F), 'garɐ'χɔr'jeː, (garçɔr'ye (A)), rough corrie of the Dee or goddess. Garra Chory Iea (Roy). The Falls of Dee are in this corrie on Braeriach. 'The River Dee springes out of Corredee, on the confynes of Badenocht' (Bal). Also Fuar Garbh Choire (OS 1869), from Am Fuar Garbh-choire (3), m'fuɔr'garɐˌχɔr (SGo), the cold rough corrie (Cj 2 and 4, McC, Sg), but Sg earlier (1912) described it in more detail as the innermost high recess of Garbh Choire Mor (at 942979), which holds the most permanent snow patches in the British Isles.

**Garbh-choire Hill** See Braigh nan Garbh-choire.

**The Garbh-choire Hill\*** (U, 350017), ðɪ'garçɔre'hël. A rough hill south-west of Morven.

**The Garbh-choire Linn** (F, 157803), ðɪ'garçɔre'lën. The Linn of Allt a' Gharbh Choire (Wa). A gorge north of the Glas Maol.

**(An) Garbh Choire Mór** (OS, 2, F, 946979), classic form An Garbh-choire Mór, ðɪ'garɐˌχɔr'moːr, the big rough corrie. An Garbh Choire Mór (Gordon 1951). On Braeriach.

**The Garbh-choires\*** See Na Garbh-choireachan Dhe.

**Garbh-chutach\*** (3, U, 339997), 'garɐˌχutɐχ, rough short place. Rough stony spot at Candacraig in Glen Gairn.

**Garbh Coire** (OS, 397909), from An Garbh-choire (3, F), ðɪ 'garçɔre, the rough corrie. Garrochrie (Dms 9). In upper Glen Tanar.

**Garbhlach\*** (3, 266978), rough place. Garlach (R 3). A little hill north of Crathie.

**Garbh-mheall\*** (3, 203895), rough lump. Garmault (R 7, 14), R 7 gives Garvault for the nearby Garbh Allt. A stony little top in Ballochbuie Forest.

**Na Garbh-phòcan\*** (3, U, 337001), ðɪ'garɐˌpɔkɐn, the rough pockets. Stony patches in Glen Gairn.

**(The) Garchory Burn** (OS, F, 349021), ðɪ'garçɔre'bʌrn. Also Allt a' Gharbh Choire (3, A), alt'garhɔre (A), burn of the rough corrie. South-west of Morven.

**Gardiebane** (444990), Scots Gardie-bane = arm bone. A peninsula on south side of Loch Kinord, formerly separated from land by an old rampart and ditch (see A).

**Garlot** (OS, 355933), from An Garbh-leathad (3, U), ðɪ'garˌlët, the rough slope. The Garlet (I, Mg, A). A hill in lower Glen Muick.

**Garmaddie** (Er, C, 238937), gar'madi. Garmadie (Cr 28), Garamadish, Garrowmadies (Me 20, 22) suggest a plural. Named from nearby Garadh Madaidh, in Gaelic Garumattie (A). A house south-west of Balmoral.

**The Garmaddie Park\*** (U, 237937), ðɪˌgar'madi'park. A field at Invergelder.

**Garrachorry Hill** See Braigh nan Garbh-choire.

**The Garranmhor Puil\*** (U, 372954), ðɪˌgarən'mor'pil. A pool in Dee at Ballater, named after a nearby house (see Garaidhean Mora).

**Gate Keeper's Croft\*** (Io 64). A former croft north of Dalmochie and south of Dee, east of Ballater.

**Gate of Balmoral\*** See Stile of Balmoral.

**Gateside** (I, 235939), Scots Gate = road. Gate side (Ri 32), Gateside of Tullochcoy (Io 25a). A former farm near the Inver, near the Old Deeside Road.

**(The) Gathering Cairn** (OS, F, 423886), ðɪ'gɪðërən'kern. Supposed to mean a hill to which cattle or sheep were gathered (A). Probably translated from Carn Tionail = hill of gathering (see A). In upper Glen Tanar.

**Geal-charn\*** (3, 271979), white hill. Geal Cairn (I), Geal Charn (R 14). A little stony top with short vegetation, north of Crathie.

**Geal Charn** (OS, 032833), from An Geal-charn (2, F), ðɪ'gjel 'χɐrn or ðɪ'jelˌχɐrn (gɛl'harn and gɛlə'harn (A) have stress in wrong position), the white hill. Gelly Cairn (T), Gelly Hill

(Ro, Mg), Gailcharn (Scr). South-west of the Linn of Dee.

**Geal-charn Mor\*** See Meikle Geal Charn.

**Geallaig Bheag** (3, 286980), little white one. Gyallik vek (D). Also Little Geallaig (F), 'lëtəl'gjalək. Pairs with Geallaig Mhor or Geallaig Hill. A little top north-east of Crathie.

**Geallaig Dubh\*** See Geallaig Hill.

**Geallaig Hill** (OS, 298982), locally simply Geallaig (3, D, A, C), 'gjalək, 'galək, white one, but recently the 'Hill' is beginning to be added among younger people, probably influenced by the map spelling. Mountains of Gallag (R) in 1725. Also Geallaig Dubh (3), black Geallaig. Gyallick Du (I), Black Geallaig (Mi). Also Geallaig Mhór (3), Gyallik vōr (D), big white one. Also Muckle Geallaig (D, A, F), 'mʌkəl'gjalək. A hill north-east of Crathie.

**Geallaig Mhor** See Geallaig Hill.

**An Gearr-lom\*** (3, U, 201908), ðɪ'gjarˌlʌm, the short bare plain. Gyarlum, 'moor, been laboured' (R 7). A rough piece of moor north of Ballochbuie Forest.

**The Gearr-lom Puil** (F, 200908), ðɪ'gjarˌlʌm'pil. Garlum (Wav). In Dee, beside the above place.

**An Geinn Dearg** (5, 343901), the red wedge. Gainderg (Ri 14), the Gainderge (Rli 2), Ganderg (Io 53, I). Also Little Aucholzie (Gr, U), 'lëtəlˌa'χɔlji. A former farm in mid Glen Muick.

**The Gelder Brig\*** (F, 251909), ðɪ'gɛldër'brɪg. In Glen Gelder.

**(The) Gelder Burn** (OS, F, 250921), ðɪ'gɛldër'bʌrn, often now the Gelder (C), from Gealldair (3), gyalter (D, A) = clear water. Gaelic pronunciation Geauldour (M). The burn was Allt Ghealldair (3), burn of the clear water. Yallder (Go), Yaldyr (Bla), Gealder (Fa), Allt yallder (D in A). Joins Dee west of Balmoral.

**(The) Gelder Shiel** (OS, C, 257900), ðɪ'gɛldër'ʃil, to old people the House i the Glen (F), ðɪ'husəi'glɛn, Scots o = of, or i = in. The Glen Gelder Shiel (Vi). Also Ruighe na Ban-rìgh (3), shiel of the queen, named after Queen Victoria. Ruidh na Bhan Righ (McC 1891). A former shooting lodge in Glen Gelder, now a bothy.

**(The) Geldie Burn** (OS, F, 013880), ðɪ'gɛldi'bʌrn, usually now the Geldie (C), from Geallaidh (3, Sto, U), 'gjʌuli, clear one. Geaullie (K, Gr), Giuly (V), Gyowly (A). The stream was Uisge Ghealllaidh (3), water of the clear one, uisg yeolli (D), with short close o, also guilli, gaoli, and gūlli (D). Water of Geauley (Ro). Also Allt Geallaidh (3), burn of clear one. Alt Galdy (Bla), Ault Galby (Ro) shown as the top branch at the Black Bothy, Auld Galdie (Stob). Joins Dee west of Linn of Dee.

**(The) Geldie Burn** (OS, C, 286951), as above, from Allt Ghealllaidh, a name still known recently for the top part of the burn. Near Abergeldie.

**The Geldie Gate\*** (C, 061897), ðɪ'gɛldi'get. Beside the Linn of Dee.

**(The) Geldie Lodge** (OS, C, 955867), ðɪ'gɛldi'lɔʤ. Also the Tap House (U), ðɪ'tap'hus, Scots = top house, pairs with Middle and Bottom. A ruin in upper Glen Geldie.

**The Geldie Road\*** (C, 016883), ðɪ'gɛldi'rod. In Glen Geldie.

**Geldieside\*** (U), ˌgɛldi'sɛid. Gealdie Side (Fi). A name for any place up the side of Geldie Burn, below Geldie Lodge.

**The Geldie Suspension Brig\*** (F, 019883), ðɪ'gɛldiˌsəs'pɛnʃən 'brɪg. Also the Tom Bhodaich Brig (U), ðɪˌtam'vɔtəç'brɪg. Near where Geldie meets Dee.

**Gelly Hill** See Geal Charn.

**(The) Genechal** (OS, C, 290930), ðɪ'ʤɛnəçəl. Teanchal (Opr 65), Geannachoil (V). Ruin of a house, named after Sean-choille, south of Abergeldie.

**(The) Genechal Burn** (OS, C, 290939), ðɪ'ʤɛnəçəl'bʌrn. South of Abergeldie.

Craoibh na Croiche, the Hangman's Tree or Gallows Tree, of Mar.

On Dee above Dinnet Bridge, the Lucky Holies Puil lies above the rapids of the Logie Puil.

*The Place Names of Upper Deeside*

**The Geordie Mitchell Puil** (F), ðɪˈdʒɔrdiˈmɛtʃəlˈpil. Geordie Mitchell (A, Sc). A pool in Dee, beside Balmoral Castle. See under Upper and Lower.

**Geordie's Brae*** (U, 436005), ˈdʒɔrdizˈbreˑ. A hill on the road near Loch Davan, after George Stewart who formerly lived at Lochhead.

**Geordie's Hillock*** (U, south-west of 292963), ˈdʒɔrdizˈhɛlɛk, named after George Symon, once a farmer at Greystone east of Crathie.

**Geordie's Wall*** (U, 438003), ˈdʒɔrdizˈwɑˑl, Scots Wall = well. A well between Loch Davan and Loch Kinord, see Geordie's Brae.

**(The) Gerach** (OS, C, 294959), ðɪˈgirəç, ˈgɛrəç, ? from the Gairbheach (5), the place of roughness, or An Geur-achadh (5), the short field. See the Gairbheach. The Gerrick (A). A former farm, now houses, east of Crathie.

**The Gerach*** (295958). The Gearach (I). A field beside the above houses, now part of the Black Wood Park.

**(The) Geusachan Burn** (OS, Ro, C, 970943), ðɪˈgjusəçɛnˈbʌrn. Also Allt Giubhasachain (3, U), altˈgjusɐχɛn, burn of little fir wood. Alt Gousachan (Bla). In Glen Geusachan.

**Geusachan Cave*** (U, 972948), ˈgjusəçɛnˈkeˑv. The Devil's Cave (Ms). On the slabs of the Devil's Point.

**The Ghillie Hall*** (F, 276824), ðɪˈgiliˈhaˑl. An out-building at Glas-allt-Shiel near Loch Muick.

**The Ghillies' Hall*** (F, 299858), ðɪˈgilizˈhaˑl. The Gillies' Hall (Hu). An outhouse at Allt-na-giubhsaich near Loch Muick, now a bothy.

**A' Ghlac*** (3, U, 332022), ðɪˈglak, the hollow. Note Allt na Glaic nearby. Also the Glack o' Morven (Dil). North-east of Gairnshiel.

**A' Ghlais Liath*** (4), the grey stream. The Glashlee, the Glashlie (Io 44, 46). The shielings of the Croft of Tom Bealaidh were there (Io), probably high on the hill above Glen Gairn.

**Gilderoy's Cave** See the Vat.

**Gillanders' Still*** (F, 338003), gəlˈandɛrzˈstɛl. Mrs Jane Forbes (nee Gillanders) told us the Gillanders family farmed Lary in Glen Gairn from 1809–1949, and the still was up the burn there. Gillanders' Quaich was the name of a Gaelic poem from Glen Gairn (D 152).

**The Girnel o Groddie*** (C, 396045), ðɪˈgɛrnɐlɐˈgrɒdi. Sheep were driven there in snowstorms as it was a sheltered corrie (EMcD). Scots Girnel = meal chest, and Groddie is a nearby farm just outside the area covered in this book. Groddie from Grod (3) = rotten, local Gaelic given as Grotaig (Da). East of Morven.

**Girnock*** (C, 325958), ˈgɛrnɛk. A general name for the group of houses where the south Deeside road crosses Girnock Burn.

**(The) Girnock Burn** (OS, C, 317929), ðɪˈgɛrnɛkˈbʌrn, often now the Girnock (C), from Goirneag (3), Gaelic pronunciation gaornag, goirnag (D), the little crier (W 449). Girnack (R 6). Water-girnack (Cpb 3) suggests a translation from Uisge Goirneag. West of Ballater.

**Giubhsach** (3), place abounding in firs. Guastoch (Mf), Giusach (Mp). A former church in Ballochbuie four miles below the Braemar parish church (Mp), five miles below (Mf), near Danzig Shiel or Garbh Allt Shiel (E).

**The Glac** See Glac Anthon.

**Glacach*** (3, 398977), place of hollows. Glackach (Io 58) clear three times, Clachack (R 4) but with two letters overwritten and not clear. On farmland at Tullich.

**The Glacaidhs*** (U, 436006), ðɪˈglakez, from Glacaidh (3) = little hollow. A hollow on the road west of Loch Davan.

**Na Glacain*** (3, 391977), the little hollows. Glackings (R 4). On farmland at Tullich.

**Glac Aitinn** (3, 331938), hollow of juniper. Glac Aiten (Mg). On the Coyles of Muick south-west of Ballater.

**Glac a' Mhinn*** (3, 251983), hollow of the kid. Glachd 'a Mhinn (R 3). North-west of Crathie.

**Glac an ? Airthir*** (5, 268962), hollow of the ? edge, and other possibilities. Glachd 'n-airair (R 3). North of Crathie.

**An Glacan Odhar*** (3, F, 303929), ˌglaχɛnˈʌur, ðɪˌglakɛnˈʌur, the dun little hollow. South-east of Abergeldie.

**The Glacan Odhar Road*** (U, 299928), ðɪˌglakɛnˈʌurˈrod. A path from the Genechal over the hill to the Camlet in Glen Girnock.

**Glacan Poll Smioraich** (3, D), little hollow of hole of sheep-dipping. Smior, sheep-dipping (D). Smeur (Dw) = anoint, smear (as sheep). On east side of Glen Ey, between Allt an Tuim Bhain and Allt a' Mhoir Ghrianaich.

**Glac an Rathaid*** (3, JS, 329933), ˌglaχɛnˈratʃ, hollow of the road. A hollow where an old track crossed the hill from Glen Girnock to lower Glen Muick.

**The Glac an Rathaid Road*** (U, 337926), ðɪˌglaχɛnˈratʃˈrod. The above track, east part now a forest road.

**Glacan Rinneidh*** (3, U, 327940), ˌglakɛnˈrini, little hollow of the ? from Rinneach = pointed, or abounding in promontories. In lower Glen Girnock.

**Glac an Ruighe** (3, north of 261023), hollow of the shieling. Glahcan rui (D). Near the Sleach north-west of Gairnshiel.

**Glac Anthon** (OS, 098878), from Glaic Eanntoin (3, U), glaik ˈjʌuntən, Anthony's hollow; for legend see Creag Anthoin. Glaic Anton (D). Also the Glac (Gl, C), ðɪˈglak. A hollow with an old track from Glen Ey to Corriemulzie.

**Glac an t-Sabhail** (3, U, 334031), ˌglaχɛnˈtʌul, hollow of the barn. Glachantoul (OS 1869), Glackentoul (D). A former farm west of Morven.

**Glac Buidhe*** (3, 341886), yellow hollow. Glack Buie (I). In mid Glen Muick.

**The Glac Burn** See Allt na Glaic.

**Glac Carn an t-Sagairt*** (3, U, 211848), ˌglakˌkɛrn̩ˈtagɛrt, hollow of hill of the priest. East of Loch Callater.

**The Glack o' Morven** See A' Ghlac.

**The Glac of Ach Uanan*** (328916), Glac (3) = hollow, or borrowing into Scots. The Glack of Auchuanan (G 5). Between Girnock and lower Glen Muick.

**(The) Glac of (the) Bunzeach** (OS, F, 357048), ðɪˈglakɪðɪˈbunjeχ, Glac (3) = hollow, Bunzeach is from Buidheannach (3), yellow place. Vunjach, bunjach (D). The Bunzeach is a big grassy area (now mostly under trees) on the Don side of Morven.

**The Glac Road*** (F, 333024), ðɪˈglakˈrod. An old track from Wester Morven past A' Ghlac to Glen Fenzie.

**Glac Ruighe Ruairidh*** (3, 198939), hollow of Rory's shiel. Glack-ri-Ruary (I). A shiel is nearby at 197936. North-east of Invercauld.

**Glac Tom Sgonnach*** (3, 242971), hollow of lumpish hillock. Glack Tom sconnach (R 3). North-west of Crathie.

**Glaic an Àgaidh*** (3, 194944), hollow of the ox. Glaichk-n-Akie (I). North-east of Invercauld.

**Glaicean*** (3, 200921), little hollow. Glaichkein (I). On Meall Alvie east of Invercauld.

**An Glaicean*** (3, U, 009865), ðɪˈglaiçkɛn, the little hollow. North-east of Bynack Lodge.

**The Glasach*** (3, 220943), the green place. The Glassich (I). Grassy braes north-west of the Inver.

**An Glas Allt** (OS, 3, C, 273827), ðɪˈglasəlt, the green burn. All the Glas-allts are green burns, referring to the green, grassy places that they cross. In this case, the corrie above Loch Muick has big grassy patches on otherwise dark heathery slopes, and there is a fine green where the burn joins the loch.

86

**An Glas-allt** See Glas Allt Beag.

**Glas Allt Beag** (OS, 152950), should be An Glas-allt (3, F), as above, the green burn. Glasalt (Fa), the Glassault (Io 63), Glass Ault (I), Glassalt (V). In lower Gleann an t-Slugain.

**An Glas-allt Beag*** (3, U, 114000), ðɪˌglasəltˈbȩg, the little green burn. East of Beinn a' Bhuird, pairs with Glas Allt Mor.

**An Glas-allt Beag*** (2, F, 037999), as above, the little green burn. Comes down a grassy hollow on a heathery hillside at the top of Glen Derry. Pairs with Glas Allt Mor.

**The Glas Allt Boat House*** (C, 277824), ðɪˈglasəltˈbotˌhus. At Loch Muick.

**The Glas Allt Brig*** (C, 277824), ðɪˈglasəltˈbrɪg. A bridge at Loch Muick.

**The Glas Allt Brig*** (C, 036987), as above. A former footbridge in Glen Derry, damaged by spate and now removed.

**The Glas Allt Brig*** (F, 151942), as above. In Gleann an t-Slugain.

**The Glas Allt Corrie*** (3, F, 158973), ðɪˈglasəltˈkȯre. Glass-alt Corie (R 14). North-west of Invercauld.

**The Glas Allt Corrie*** (U, 044993), as above. In upper Glen Derry.

**The Glas Allt Island*** (F, 275822), ðɪˈglasəltˈɛilənd. In Loch Muick.

**(An) Glas Allt Mór** (OS, 2, F, 040990), ðɪˈglasəltˈmoːr, the big green burn, usually now the Glas Allt (C). Anns a' Ghlasallt, in the Glassalt (Sin). Also the Green Burn, the Green Burn of Dairy (Fi), i.e. Derry, a name not used in recent decades. In Glen Derry.

**(An) Glas Allt Mór** (OS, 3, U, 114991), as above, the big green burn. Glass Ault more (I). At the top of Quoich.

**Glas-allt-Shiel** (OS, C, 276824), ˈglasəltˈʃil. A lodge built by Queen Victoria as at Loch Muick.

**The Glas Allt Wuid*** (C, 275824), ðɪˈglasəltˈwɪd. Wood around the above lodge.

**(A') G(h)las-choille** (OS, 2, C, 309033), ðɪˈglasçəl, the green wood. Glaschell, Glasschyle (Ri 21, 37), Glass Choil (I), Glas-choile (R 14). In Gaelic was pronounced Glass-hill with no article (D), but always now has the article. A name for the bottom of a little glen north-east of Gairnshiel.

**The Glas-choille Brae*** (F, 310040), ðɪˈglasçəlˈbreˑ. A hill on the road north-east of Gairnshiel.

**The Glas-choille Brig*** (C, 312027), ðɪˈglasçəlˈbrɪg, to oldest people the Brig o the Glas-choille (U). Bridge of the Glasschoil (I). North-east of Gairnshiel.

**The Glas-choille Burn** See Allt Glas-choille.

**The Glas-choille Hill** (F), ðɪˈglasçəlˈhël. The Glascoille Hill (Ne). Refers to the crossing of the hill by the Glas-choille Road from Glen Gairn to Corgarff, often just called the Glas-choille (C).

**The Glas-choille Road** (C, 313032), ðɪˈglasçəlˈrod. Road from Gairnshiel to Don.

**Glas Choire** (OS, 163778), classic form Glas-choire, green corrie. A green, grassy corrie north of the Glas Maol.

**An Glas-choire** (3, C, 396961), ˈglasˈkȯre to a few old folk, glas ˈkȯre otherwise, (ˈglaskȯre (A) probably indicates an earlier pronunciation), the grey corrie. Not a green, grassy corrie, so probably Glas = grey here. The aspiration in Choire has now been dropped, as has the usual article in front of this type of name, and the emphasis is no longer on the adjective although Alexander recorded it as such. Glass Chorry (I), The Glaschory (Dms). A corrie above Pannanich Inn.

**Glascorrie** (OS, C, 400970), as above. An old farm east of Pannanich, named after the corrie near it (see above name).

**An Glas-doire*** (3, 175935), the green wood. The Glaster, birch wood (R 7). North of Invercauld, now under planted conifers.

**An Glas-leathad*** (3, U, 007836), ðɪˈglasˌlët, the green slope. A grassy hillside south-east of Bynack Lodge.

**Glas Maol** (OS, 167766), should be A' Ghlas-mheall (3, D, A), in Gaelic ˈhlasvjal (A), the green lump. Glass Mhiel (I), the Glas-mheal (Mg), the Glassmeal (E), Ghlasvyaull, Ghlasvyal (D), An Glas-mheall, now Glass Meel (A). Now usually ðɪˈglasˌmil (C). A big green lump of a hill where Aberdeenshire, Perthshire and Angus meet.

**Glas-thulach*** (3, 322001), green hillock. Glasstulloch (I). A former field with a hillock, east of Gairnshiel, now a wood.

**Gleann an t-Slugain** (OS, 145944), locally was Gleann Slugain (2, F), glanng slukan (D), glənˈslugən, Gaelic glauŋˈslugən (U), glen of a gullet. The glen is now usually called the Slugain (C), ðɪˈslʌgən. Formerly it was Gleann Chanlaig, glunng chanlic (D), from Gleann Ceann-bhuilg (3), glen of head-bag, or Cheann-bhuilg, of the head-bag. Allt Chanlaig or Cheann-bhuilg was the main headwater at the top of the glen. Inverchandlick north of Braemar preserves the Chanlaig part of the name (i.e. Inbhir Chanlaig or mouth of the Canlaig stream). Glencanlig (Fa), Glen Callanich (Roy), Glenchanleck, Glencanloch, Glen Canlick (Ri 17, 22, 40), Glen Chanlig (Cr 32), Glencandluig (R 1), Glen Candlic (Mg), the Black Sloggan of the Candlic (Gr), Gleann an t-Slugain Chandlic (McC), Glen Sluggan but formerly Glen Candlic (McC 1896). Roy's Callanich suggests Calanach or calling one, but this was probably an error, as all other records are of a different word. Glencanvuloge, Glencanbuloge in 1699 (Me) suggest Ceann-bhuilg, as do Glencanbulge (Io 12), and Glencoubulge (Ri 17, same document as Io but misread). On a map in 1828 (R 14), the glen also appears as Glen Fhionlaidh, i.e. glen of Finlay, probably named after Fionnlagh or Finla Mor, early ancestor of the Clan Farquharson. North of Braemar.

**Gleann Badaich** (3, 125814), glen of place of clumps. Glenabaddoch, Glen of Baddoch (Ri 22), Glen Baddoch (Io 78, Mg). Branches off south-west from Glen Clunie.

**Gleann Beidhneig** (6, 002860), glen of Bynack. Glen Bynack (Sm), Glenboynach, Glenbaynoch (Vr 1, 2). The glen at Bynack Lodge.

**Gleann Beidhneig Lodge** See Bynack Lodge.

**Gleann Beitheich*** (3, 090953), glen of birch place. Glen Baich (Ra 14). Referred to the top part of Quoich or Am Beitheachan.

**Gleann Bruthainn** (3, 140820), glen of heat or boiling (note W 469, N 178). Glenbruine (Ra 3), Glenbrowine (Ri 17, Me 3). Water of Bruin (Ra 3), see Allt Bhruid. Probably was the same sound as in Glenbrown and Bridge of Brown (pronounced ˈbruən (CN)) between Tomintoul and Grantown (note T 41, 229). The glen north of the Cairnwell, joins with the glen at Baddoch to form Glen Clunie.

**Gleann Cheann-bhuilg** See Gleann an t-Slugain.

**Gleann Chriosdaidh** (4, 060868), glen of swift one, or of Christie, or of a Christian. Glenchristin (Po), Glen Chrisdaidh (MacRae), Glen Cristie (Gr). South of the Linn of Dee.

**Gleann Coireach na Mòine*** (3, 083818), glen of corries of the peat-moss. Glen Corrachnamoin (I 33), Glen of Corrachnamoin (Io 34, Rli 19). In upper Glen Ey.

**Gleann Connaidh** (5, U, 080876), glənˈkȯne, Gaelic glauŋˈkȯne, glen of firewood or of dog-stream. Glenconnigh (Po), Glen Connie (Ro), Glen-co-na-feidh (Gr) suggests 'of the deer' but this attempt to explain the name does not fit the pronunciation. South-west of Inverey.

**Gleann Cùlachain*** (5, U, 262992), glənˈkuləçɐn, glen of Coulachan or little back place. North of Crathie.

**Gleann Fhionnlaigh** See Gleann an t-Slugain.

**Gleann Garbh-choire** (3, 969985), glen of rough corrie. Glen Garrachory (Mg), Glen Garchory (Sm), Shepherds called it the Devil's Glen (Ke), Glen Garbh-choire (Cj 3). Referred to the glen running west of the confluence of Allt na Lairig Ghru, north of Cairn Toul.

**Gleann Gheallaidh\*** (3, U, 980870), glauŋˈjʌuli, glen of the clear one, referring to Geldie Burn. Now usually Glen Geldie (A1, C), glənˈgɛldi. West of the Linn of Dee.

**Gleann Giubhasach** (3, 285857), glen abounding in fir. Glen Gusach (R 6). Glengusachin (Ri 13) suggests Gleann Giubhasachain (3), glen of little fir wood. Glen running up from Allt-na-giubhsaich towards Lochnagar, north of Loch Muick.

**Gleann Mór-bheinn** (3, 346010), glen of Morven or big hill. Glen Morven (Mg), Glen of Morven (Crg 2, Gr), the Glen of Morven (Ne). Glen leading from Lary in Glen Gairn up to the basin west of Morven.

**The Glebe** (OS, C, 365948), ðiˈglib. A modern house at the foot of Muick, named after the nearby Glebe of Glenmuick.

**The Glebe\*** (U, 315007), as above. Patch of ground behind the old manse, east of Gairnshiel.

**The Glebe of Braemar** (S 20, south-west of 153922). A former glebe by the former St Andrews Chapel north of Braemar.

**(The) Glebe of Crathie\*** (I, U, 266945), ðiˈglibɐˈkraˑθe, usually now just the Glebe (F). At the manse at Crathie.

**Glebe of Glenmuick\*** (I, 367949). A former patch at the old manse of Glenmuick, now part of a field. Much of it has been washed away by Dee since the early map (I) in 1807-9. Note the Glebe above. At the foot of Glen Muick.

**The Glebe Park\*** (U, 358945), ðiˈglibˈpark. A field in lower Glen Muick.

**Glen Bardy** (OS, C, 352994), glənˈbardi, from Gleann Bardaidh (3), glen of little enclosed meadow. There is a former farm (below) up this little glen north of the Bridge of Gairn.

**Glenbardy** (OS, C, 351998), as above. A former farm in the above glen.

**The Glen Bardy Brae\*** (U, 346985), ðiˌglənˈbardiˈbreˑ. A hill on an old road north of Gairnshiel.

**The Glen Bardy Brig\*** (F, 343990), ðiˌglənˈbardiˈbrɪg. In lower Glen Gairn.

**(The) Glen Bardy Burn** (OS, C, 351995), ðiˌglənˈbardiˈbʌrn. Also Allt Bhardaidh (3, U), altˈvardi, burn of the little enclosed meadow. Ault Vardie (I). North of the Bridge of Gairn.

**The Glen Bardy Fuird\*** (U, 349994), ðiˌglənˈbardiˈfjurd. An old ford with stepping stones north of Bridge of Gairn.

**The Glen Bardy Village\*** (U, 349981), ðiˌglənˈbardiˈvɪlədʒ. Former houses in Glen Gairn.

**Glen Beg** (OS, F, 321045), glənˈbɛg, from Gleann Beag (3), little glen. Pairs with Glen More, north-east of Gairnshiel. Diack has them the wrong way round.

**(The) Glen Beg** (OS, C, 187879), ðiˌglənˈbɛg, from An Gleann Beag (2), the little glen. The article is used by older people and also appears in Burn of the Glen Beg (third name below). A glen in Ballochbuie Forest.

**The Glen Beg Brae\*** (F, 193898), ðiˌglənˈbɛgˈbreˑ. A hill on a road in above glen.

**The Glen Beg Brig\*** (C, 190889), ðiˌglənˈbɛgˈbrɪg. In Ballochbuie Forest.

**(The) Glenbeg Burn** (OS, C, 190888), ðiˌglənˈbɛgˈbʌrn. Burn of the Glen Beg (R 7). In the above glen.

**The Glen Beg Wuid\*** (F, 190895), ðiˌglənˈbɛgˈwɪd. Part of Ballochbuie Forest.

**The Glen Builg Pass** (Gf, 190030). A pass from the Bealach

Dearg and Corndavon past Loch Builg to Glen Avon in Banffshire.

**Glen Callater** (OS, C, 175843), glənˈkalətër, from Gleann Chaladair (3), glen of the hard water. Glencaleter (Fa), Glen Callader (Hi), Gleann challater (D). South-east of Braemar.

**Glen Carn a' Mhaim** (Cj 2, 78, 000963). North-west of Derry Lodge.

**Glen Clunie** (OS, Fa, C, 147861), glənˈkluni, from Gleann Cluainidh (3), glen at a plain. This glen south of Braemar contains two plains, probably referred to south one (see Milltoun of Glen Clunie).

**Glen Clunie Lodge** (OS, C, 138832), glənˈkluniˈlɔdʒ. A ruin south of Braemar, only the foundations left.

**The Glen Clunie Lodge Brig\*** (F, 137832), ðiˌglənˈkluniˈlɔdʒ ˈbrɪg. Bridge in Glen Clunie.

**Glen Colstane** (A, C, 393995), glənˈkolstən, from Gleann ? Còmhdail = glen of meeting (3, W 492) and English Stone, as in Logie Coldstone Burn. See Culsten Burn. West of Cambus o' May.

**The Glen Colstane Brig\*** (U, 404980), ðiˌglənˈkolstənˈbrɪg. West of Cambus o' May.

**The Glen Colstane Moss Road\*** (U, 390999), ðiˌglənˈkolstən ˈmɔsˈrod. Track to peat mosses south-east of Morven.

**The Glendavan Brig\*** (C, south of 438012), ðiˌglənˈdavɐnˈbrɪg. To older people the Cleikumin Brig (U), ðiˌklikəmˈɛnˈbrɪg. The Cleikum Muir Bridge (O). Near Loch Davan, carries public road.

**The Glendavan Burn\*** (F, 438012), ðiˌglənˈdavɐnˈbʌrn. Lower part of the Red Burn, beside Glendavan House which is outside the area covered in this book. Glendavan is an invented modern name for this house, as there is no glen called Glen Davan. Beside Loch Davan.

**The Glendavan Fit Brig\*** (U, 438012), ðiˌglənˈdavɐnˈfɛtˈbrɪg. Footbridge near Loch Davan.

**The Glendavan Sand Hole\*** (U, west of 438012), ðiˌglənˈdavɐn ˈsanˈhol. Beside Loch Davan.

**The Glendavan Wuid\*** (C, 438013), ðiˌglənˈdavɐnˈwɪd, often plural wɪdz. Glendavan Wood (O). Glendavan Wood (OS) is shown only on the east side of the boundary burn, in Logie Coldstone parish, but locally applies to both sides of the burn. Formerly the Grip Muir (O), Scots Gruip = ditch, narrow groove. Near Loch Davan.

**Glen Dee** (OS, C, 008891), glənˈdiˑ, from Gleann Dhé (3, D, A), glauŋˈjeː (JB), glen of the Dee or goddess. Gleann De (Sin). The glen of Dee from the Linn of Dee up to Glen Geusachan. Beyond this point it has been called Gleann Carbh-choire, and the Lairig Glen.

**The Glen Dee Lochies\*** (U, 985926), ðiˌglənˈdiˈlɔχez. A composite name for two tarns at 985926 and others at about 986933 on both sides of Dee.

**Glen Derry** (OS, C, 036966), glənˈdɛre, from Gleann Doire (3), glauŋˈdɔr (JB), glen of grove. Gleann doir (D). North-west of Inverey.

**The Glen Doll Road** See Jock's Road.

**Glen Dui** (OS, C, 426939), glənˈdui, from Gleann Duibhe (4), glen of blackness, or Dubhaidh (Nic) from Dubh = black. Glendowy (Po). A dark, heather-covered glen in Glen Tanar.

**The Glen Dui Burn** See Burn of Glendui.

**Glen Ey** (OS, C, 090863), glənˈɛiˑ, from Gleann Eidh (6), glauŋ ˈɛiˑ (JB), glen of Ey (see Ey Burn for meaning). Glen ey (Fa), Glen of Ey (Lp), Gleaneye (Opr 39), Gleann-eidh (Gr), Gleann Eigh (Sin), Glunng ei, ɛi (D). South of Inverey.

**The Glen Ey Road\*** (C, 087882), ðiˌglənˈɛiˈrod. South of Inverey.

**Glen Feardar** (OS, C, 205950), glənˈfjardër, from Gleann Féith

Ardair (3), glen of bog of high water. North-west of the Inver Inn.

**Glen Fenzie** (OS, C, 320024), glənˈfɪŋi, from Gleann Fionnaidh (3), glen of white one (referring to the stream). Glenfinzie (Crg 1), Glenfigny (Cr 42), Glung fing-yie (D). North-east of Gairnshiel.

**Glenfenzie** (OS, C, 316029), as above. Also Loinn Liath (3), grey land-portion. Loynley (Im 3), Lone Ley (I), Linleigh (Ar). A ruined farm at the above glen.

**(The) Glenfenzie Burn** (OS, C, 320022), ðɪˌglənˈfɪŋiˈbʌrn. Also Allt Fhionnaidh (3, WD), altˈɪnji, burn of the white one. Allt inyi, eenyee (D in A). Also the Fhionnaidh Burn (U), ðɪˈɪŋi ˈbʌrn, written the Engie Burn (MFr). Note also Inverenzie which is Inbhir Fhionnaidh. North-east of Gairnshiel.

**The Glen Feshie–Geldie Pass** (Gf, 924877). An old drove road from Dee over the top of Glen Geldie to Spey.

**Glen Gairn** (OS, C, 303012), glənˈgern̩, from Gleann Ghàrain (5), glen of the crying one, referring to the stream (see River Gairn). Gleanngarain (Iop), Gleann-Gharain (Mg), Gleann garan (D). Often Glen Garden in earlier writings (see under River Gairn). North-west of Ballater.

**Glen Gelder** (OS, C, 247913), glənˈgɛldër, from Gleann Ghealdair (3), glen of the clear water. Invergelder was pronounced Innir-yalldar in Gaelic (D). Glenyelder (Me 5). South-west of Balmoral.

**The Glen Gelder Shiel** See Gelder Shiel.

**Glen Geldie** See Gleann Gheallaidh.

**Glen Geusachan** (OS, C, 965943), glənˈgjusəçɛn, from Gleann Giubhasachain (3), glauŋˈgjusɐχɐn (JB), glen of little fir wood. Glengusachin (Fa, Fi), Glenguissich (Hi), Glen guishchan (Me 11), Glen Eusechan (Ros). Many fir roots are in the peat. South of Cairn Toul.

**Glen Girnock** (OS, C, 315928), glənˈgërnɐk, from Gleann Ghoirneag (3), glen of the little crier. Strathgirnock was Straghaornak, Stra-ghoirnag (D). Gurnock (Am). West of Ballater.

**Glen Lui** (OS, C, 063918), glənˈlui, from Gleann Laoigh (3, Sin), glauŋˈlui (JB), glen of Lui or calf-one, referring to the stream of Lui Water. It does not mean glen of a calf, as the stream name is Lui. Another Gleann Laoigh in Lochaber has the stream Laogh, or calf (W 453). Glenlie (Fa), Glenluie (Fi). Glen Lui is a wide glen north-west of Inverey.

**Glen Luibeg** (OS, C, 023938), ˌglənˌluiˈbɛg, from Gleann Laoigh Beag (3), ˌglauŋˌluiˈb̩ɛg (JB), glen of little Lui or little calf-one, referring to the stream now called Luibeg Burn. West of Derry Lodge.

**Glen Lui Road*** See Derry Road.

**Glen More** (OS, F, 329046), glənˈmoˑr, from Gleann Mór (3), big glen. Pairs with Glen Beg nearby. North-east of Gairnshiel.

**Glen Muick** (OS, C, 350920), glənˈmëk, from Gleann Muice (3), glənˈmuiçk (Sch), glen of Muick or pig-one, referring to the River Muick. Gleannmuic (Gr), Glenmuke, Glenmyk (Ab 2, 7), Glung mūchk or muichk, same sound as genitive of sow (D). South-west of Ballater.

**The Glen Muick and Lochnagar Wildlife Reserve** (Pj), locally the Glen Muick Reserve (F), ðɪˌglənˈmëkˌrɪˈzɛrv.

**Glen Muick Forest*** (C), glənˈmëkˈfǫrɛst. Deer forest on open hill on east side of Muick.

**Glenmuick House** (C, 358938), ˌglənˈmëkˈhus. A big house now demolished. The present House of Glenmuick (OS, 372945) was formerly called Braichlie House when Glenmuick House existed. South of Ballater.

**The Glen of Aberarder** (Ke, U, 215938), ðɪˈglɛnɐˌabërˈardër. West of the Inver.

**The Glen of Ballochbuie*** The Glen of Ballochbuy (Io 63). In Ballochbuie Forest, either the glen leading up to Allt Lochan nan Eun, or the one to the north-east with Ballochbuie Burn.

**The Glen of Clais Mhor*** (178906). The Glen of Clashmore (Io 63). South-west of Invercauld Bridge.

**The Glen of Coire Bhronn*** (007852). The Glen of Coriewran (Me 15). Near the Bynack.

**The Glen of Coirebhruach** (406900). The Glen of Corrie Vruach (V). The top part of Glen Tanar where the Mounth Road crosses from the Ballater side of the hill down to Coirebhruach and then up towards Mount Keen.

**The Glen of Coire Buidhe*** (230910). The Glen of Corrybuie (Ra 14). The glen with the Connachat Burn, south-west of Balmoral.

**The Glen of Corriemulzie*** (Fi, 112888). The glen up from Corriemulzie, east of Inverey.

**The Glen of Easter Morven*** (Io 20). Valley up the Tullich Burn.

**The Glen of Etnach*** (413918). The Glen of Etnich (Rli 21). The little side-glen containing the former farms at Etnach in upper Glen Tanar.

**The Glen of Feindallacher*** (202873). The Glen of Feantallacher (Io 63). West of Lochnagar.

**The Glen of Ruighe Raibeirt*** (3, 123811). The Glen of Rirebart (Me 15). At the Baddoch.

**The Glen o' the Spittal** (Dil). Beside the Spittal of Glenmuick.

**Glen Quoich** (OS, C, 085930), glənˈkoɪç, from Gleann Coich (6), glauŋˈkoɪç (U), glen of Quoich, referring to Quoich Water (see under Caich). Glenaquhoiche (Dms 10), Glen Coich (R 1), Gleann cōich (D). North-west of Braemar.

**Glenshee Chairlift** (Er, 139781), locally the Cairnwell Chairlift (C), ðɪˈkernˌwɛlˈtʃerˌlëft, or simply the Chairlift. The 'Glenshee' is a misnomer, as Glen Shee is in Perthshire, but this name came from the fact that the Glenshee Chairlift Company runs the chairlift.

**The Glens of Allt Phouple** (175008). The Glens of Altefugle (Hi). South of Ben Avon.

**Glen Tanar** (OS, C, 426923), glənˈtɑˑnɐr, with *a* longer and further back than in English tanner. Tannar, the *nn* sounds *ung*, tangir, uisg thangir, the *nn* sounds like *ang* (D), from Gleann Tannar (6), glen of ?. Tanaros was a Gaulish and British thunder-god and this origin was suggested for Tanar and for the Tanner in Selkirkshire (W 431), i.e. a noisy or thundering stream. Another suggestion links it with Tay, Tain, Teviot and Tyne, from an Indo-European root Ta = to melt or to flow (N 190). South of Dinnet.

**The Glen Tanar Deer Fence*** (U, 398936), ðɪˌglənˈtɑˑnɐrˈdir ˈfɛns.

**The Glide** (C, 436971), ðɪˈglɛid. Glide (Wav). A glide is a word used locally by salmon fishers for the tail of a pool, but in this case is almost a separate pool from Poll Ba above it. In Dee west of Dinnet.

**Goat Cot Bush*** (R 4, 382972). Probably translated from Preas, which can mean a tree-copse or a bush; it usually means copse in place names, but bush is the commoner meaning of the word in conversation. So, as Gaelic died, it was presumably often translated to give an inappropriate meaning. On farmland at Tullich.

**The Goats' Cot*** (U, south-west of 433998), ðɪˈgotsˈkǫt. Near Loch Kinord.

**The Goats' Cot Road*** (U, 434998), ðɪˈgotsˈkǫtˈrod. A track near Loch Kinord.

**The Goat's Craig** See Creagan nan Gabhar.

**The Goats' Park*** (F, 292945), ðɪˈgotsˈpark. A rough grazing south of Abergeldie.

**The Goat Stones*** (U, 411963), ðɪˈgotˈstonz. Boulders on a hillside south-east of Pannanich, beside a sheepfold.

**Goban Stair** (3, 413984), little point with a path. Goupinstair (D). The brae behind Turnerhall at Cambus o' May.

**Gobhal Breac*** (3, 360924), speckled fork. Goal Breack (I). A former field in lower Glen Muick, divided into a fork by a long hollow.

**An Goc** (3, 112873), the pipe. The Koke (D). A Goc (gok) in Braemar is still known (CMcH) to mean a smooth eddy behind a stone, in a place between rocks or stones where the water rushes through quickly. A narrow, fast place on the Corriemulzie Burn.

**An Gocan*** (3, U, north-east of 155897), ðɪˈgokɐn, the little pipe. See above. A fast part of Clunie Water south of Braemar.

**The Gocan Stane*** (F, 150909), ðɪˈgokɐnˈstin. A Gocan stone (see above) was a poaching stone where one could stand in the river beside a rapid stretch where fish were easily gaffed. South of Braemar.

**The Gocan Turn*** (U, 150909), ðɪˈgokɐnˈtʌrn. A bend in the road near Braemar, beside An Gocan in Clunie.

**Goc Gob nan Gobhal*** (4, 392974), narrow place of point of the forks. Cockupnagowl (R 4), Cockupnagoul (Io 58). On the fields at Tullich east of Ballater, near where Tullich Burn runs into Dee.

**The Goc Puil** See Poll Goc.

**The Goc Stane Brig*** (C, 455005), ðɪˈgokˈstinˈbrɪg, ðɪˈgokˈsten ˈbrɪg from best informants, the Goc Stane Briggie (U), ðɪˈgok ˈstinˈbrɪgi. A bridge on the road north of Dinnet, beside the former house (just outside our area) of Goukstone (OS 1869). Several informants said ˈgʌukˈstin, as if from Scots Gowk = a stupid person or a cuckoo. Alexander also noted this and found it difficult to see how this meaning applied in this place name. However, informants who knew the area best gave it as ˈgokˈstin, which suggests Goc Stane, see Gocan Stane above. Note Gowk Stane sometimes a standing stone (Gm).

**The Goc Stane Burn*** See Monandavan Burn.

**The Gold —*** (U, 063918), ðɪˈgold—. Informant could not remember second part of name. A formerly boggy open patch in an old plantation in Glen Lui, named possibly because it had much of the grass *Molinia caerulea* which turns golden in autumn.

**The Gold Loch** See Lochan Oir.

**The Golds*** (F), ðɪˈgoldz. A hill ridge from 107867 to 112870, south of Corriemulzie, named after the yellowish gravel in water on the hillside.

**The Gordon Bridge** See the Cambus Brig.

**Gordon's Clarag** (C, north-west of 417979), ˈgɔrdənzˈklarɐk, Clàrag (3) = little flat place. Gordon's Cleireach (P, Sc) is not the sound. Gordon's Clarack (A), Clarach (Wav). A pool in Dee beside a flat stretch of ground near Cambus o' May.

**The Goring Hut** See Radio Relay Hut.

**The Grains*** (In, Am, C, 275852), ðɪˈgreːnz. A big area south-west of Allt-na-giubhsaich in upper Glen Muick, between Clais Rathadan and the Monelpie Moss and including the slope down towards the old shielings on Allt na Giubhsaich; has a number of Grains (Scots = small burns) on it.

**The Grains** (OS, 342865), from the Grains o Allt an t-Sneachdaidh (F), ðɪˈgrenzɐˈaltənˈdrҿte. A group of little burns south-east of the Linn of Muick. See East, Mid and West Grain o Allt an t-Sneachdaidh.

**The Grains o Allt Darrarie*** (F), ðɪˈgrenzɐˈaltˈdarəre. A collective name for two burns south of Loch Muick. See Easter Grain of Allt Darrarie, and Mid Grain.

**The Grains o Allt Deas*** (F), ðɪˈgrenzɐˌaltˈdҿs. A collective name for three burns in upper Glen Tanar. See East, Mid, and West Grain o Allt Deas.

**The Grains o Allt Fileachaidh*** (F), ðɪˈgrenzɐˌaltˈfiləҫi. A collective name for three burns north-east of Loch Muick. See East, Mid, and West Grain o Allt Fileachaidh.

**(The) Grains of Tanar** (OS, F, 386898), ðɪˈgrenzeˈtɑˑnɐr. Three little burns running into Allt na Conair in upper Glen Tanar.

**Grampian Cottage*** (C, 063918), ˈgrampianˈkǫtədȝ. Site of a former house in Glen Lui, beside some spruces which have now blown down.

**The Grampians** (C), ðɪˈgrampiənz. A vague name for the hill-ranges from the Central Highlands along the Mounth and also often including the Cairngorms and hills north of the Dee valley. Now even vaguer, as it has recently been used to describe the entire north-east of Scotland as a regional area of local government. A name seen in maps and books, and learned at school, but not in local use in Upper Deeside to describe any of these hills. For further details see A.

**The Granary*** (C, 151913), ðɪˈgranəre. A building at Mill o Auchendryne at Braemar.

**The Granary*** (F, 111892), as above. A former building at Corriemulzie, now a shed.

**Grant's Henhouse*** (U, 133822), ˈgrantsˈhҽnˌhus. A former pen or shieling, later used by a farmer at the Baddoch who kept poultry high on the hill so that they would be disease-free. Above the Baddoch.

**The Graves*** (F, 307787), ðɪˈgrevz. A broad hill ridge south of Loch Muick.

**The Great Fir Park Puil*** (F, 281951), ðɪˈgretˈfҽrˈparkˈpil. A pool in Dee at Abergeldie, pairs with the Little Fir Park Puil.

**The Green** (Cj 1, 318; Cm, 008962). Also the Green Foot (Cj 2, 244). The lower grassy part of the broad ridge leading up to the Sron Riach in upper Glen Luibeg.

**The Green*** (Am, 287952). A patch of ground at Abergeldie Castle.

**Green Bank*** (F, 162932), grinˈbaŋk. Greenhill Cottage (OS 1869). A former house near Invercauld.

**Green Bank** See the Bankie Puil.

**The Green Bank** (Afr, F, 317008), ðɪˌgrinˈbaŋk. Greenbank (Afr). A former house and shop east of Gairnshiel.

**The Green Bank*** (F, north of 214919), ðɪˈgrinˈbaŋk. A grassy bank south-west of the Inver.

**The Green Bank Puil** See the Woodlands Puil.

**Greenbrae*** (F, north-east of 144905), grinˈbreˑ. A former house just north of the Mains of Tomintoul near Braemar.

**The Green Brig*** (F, 346935), ðɪˈgrinˈbrɪg. A green-painted bridge in lower Glen Muick.

**The Green Burn*** (Fi, 988950). Probably a translation of An Glas-allt, as the same writer used this translation for the Glas Allt in Glen Derry. Runs off Carn a' Mhaim into Glen Dee.

**The Green Burn*** See Glas Allt Mor.

**(The) Green Craig** (OS, C, 297873), ðɪˈgrinˈkreg. A crag with some grassy patches, in upper Glen Muick.

**The Green Face*** (F, 973835), ðɪˈgrinˈfes. Green Face (Mm). A grassy hillside up the Bynack Burn.

**The Green Face*** (U, 061966), as above. A grassy slope above Dubh-Ghleann.

**Greenfield** See Ailean nan Cearc.

**The Green Field*** See Ailean nan Cearc.

**The Green Fold*** (I, 345982). A field in lower Glen Gairn.

**The Green Foot** See the Green.

**The Green Gate*** (U, 130910), ðɪˈgrinˈget. An opening in a dry-stone dyke, on an old track from Dalgowan to Carr Cottage, west of Braemar.

**Greenhill Cottage** See Green Bank.

**The Green Howes*** (079937), Scots Howe = hollow. The Green Hows (Fi). Grassy hollows in Glen Quoich.

**The Green Road*** (U, 350027), ðɪˈgrinˈrod. A path through grassy ground, running east from Morven Lodge.

**The Green Road\*** (U, 412982), as above. Part of the old Deeside road south of the railway near Cambus o May.

**The Green Roadie\*** (U, 447998), ðı'grin'rodi. A track along the north side of Loch Kinord.

**The Green Roadie\*** See the Old Ford Road.

**The Greens\*** (U, 232985), ðı'grinz. Grassy places on a ridge rising out of peat-mosses north-west of Crathie.

**Greens of Creag Liath\*** (252883). Greens of Craiglia (B). Green spots in upper Glen Gelder.

**The Greens of Roinn a' Bhathaich\*** (365025). The Greens of Rinavaich (Io 20). South-west of Morven.

**The Greens of the Branndair\*** (370026). The Greens of the Brander (Io 20), the Greens of Brander (G 19). South of Morven.

**Grewar's Leap** (Aj 10, probably c. 140835). A place where a Grewar from Glen Isla once jumped the Allt a' Mhaide in spate, to avoid being caught by caterans. In Glen Clunie.

**The Grey Moss\*** (U, 135906), ðı'gre'mǫs. Grey Moss (Md 12). A peat-moss west of Braemar.

**(The) Greystone** (OS, C, 292958), ðı͵gre'ston. Formerly A' Chlach Ghlas (3), the grey stone. Chlach glas (D), also Cloch without glas (Da). The original Greystone lay further west, north of 288957 (I, WD), and the present Greystone used to be called Dail Iaruinn. Daliorn (Ce 1). A former farm at Micras.

**Greystone** (OS, C, 431962), gre'stin. Formerly Nether Greystone (U, G 22, Dms), 'nęðėr͵gre'stin. Inferiorem Grystone (Ab 19), Nether Grystone (Ab). A farm east of Inchmarnoch.

**The Greystone Burn\*** (F, 433956), ðı͵gre'stin'bʌrn. Also the Stane Burn (U), ðı'stin'bʌrn, Scots Stane = stone. Beside the above farm.

**The Greystone Burn\*** (F, 292958), as above. At Micras.

**The Greystone Hill\*** (F, 433950), ðı͵gre'stin'hël. The hill grazing above Greystone, near Inchmarnoch.

**The Grip Muir** See the Glendavan Wood.

**The Groat Puil\*** (F, south of 215925), ðı'grot'pil. A little pool on north side of Dee, south-west of the Inver.

**The Grocer's Park\*** (F, 080898), ðı'grosërz'park, after a Mr MacGregor who once farmed it and had a grocer's shop in Braemar. Subsequently called Mitchell's Park (C), 'mėtʃəlz 'park, after another who farmed it. A field at Inverey.

**(The) Groddie Burn** (OS, C, 403047), ðı'grǫdi'bʌrn. A burn near Groddie, for meaning see the Girnel o Groddie. West of Logie Coldstone.

**The Groddie Park\*** (U, 416045), ðı'grǫdi'park. A field by the Groddie Burn near Logie Coldstone.

**The Groddie Ruighe na Beinne\*** (U, 408045), ðı'grǫdi͵rʌne'bęn. Pairs with the Balhennie Ruighe na Beinne. A field west of Logie Coldstone.

**The Gruer's Bothy\*** (U, 143789), ðı'gruėrz'bǫθe. Gruer's Bothie (Md 1). A former bothy beside the Cairnwell road.

**Gruer's Road\*** (Md 1, 153913). At Braemar.

**The Gruer's Road\*** (U, 146908), ðı'gruėrz'rod. Also later the Creeper's Roadie (U), ðı'kripërz'rodi, after James McGregor, nicknamed Creeper, a former resident of Tomintoul. A track from the back of the manse at Braemar up to Tomintoul.

**The Gunner\*** (U, 435965), ðı'gʌnër, ? Gaelic An Conair = the path. A field south-west of Dinnet.

**Half Bad Charn** (probably north-east of 274017). Half Badaquharn (Io 34), Half Badquharine (Mc 5). A former farm on east side of Gairn, later became part of Tullochmacarrick. West of Gairnshiel.

**The Half Dabhach** See An Leth-taobhach.

**(The) Half Way Hut** (OS, C, 436931), ðı'haf'we'hʌt, ðı'haf'wae 'hʌt. In Glen Tanar.

**The Half Wey Butts\*** See the Wire Fence Butts.

**The Ham\*** (U, 148919), ðı'ham. A ham-shaped field at Braemar.

**The Hame Ferm\*** See Alltdourie.

**The Hame Ferm\*** (C, 120914), ðı'hem'fęrm. Home farm for Mar Lodge.

**The Hame Ferm Parks\*** (F, 120910), ðı'hem'fęrm'parks. Fields at Allanaquoich west of Braemar.

**The Hangman's Hillock\*** See Tom na Croiche.

**The Hangman's Tree\*** See Craoibh na Croiche.

**The Hangman's Tree\*** (JE, 216943), ðı'haŋmənz'tri. An old larch tree with graves nearby, at Balmore west of the Inver.

**The Hard Park\*** (I, 156917). A field on gravelly ground by Dee, beside Braemar Castle.

**The Hard Park\*** (U, 418966), ðı'hard'park. A field near Inchmarnoch.

**Hard Waird\*** (R 6a, 255960), Scots Waird = piece of land enclosed by a dyke. A hard former field, now under trees, north-west of Crathie.

**(The) Hare Cairn** (OS, C, 378880), ðı'her'kern, possibly Scots Hair = hoary. Hill called the Hare Cairn (I). A hill in upper Glen Tanar.

**The Hare Hill** See Carn Dubh and Carn na Greine.

**Harper's Burn\*** (C, east of 150917), 'harpërz'bʌrn. A stream at Braemar, named after a former resident; the upper part below the Games Park is now piped underground.

**Harper's Gairden\*** (C, east of 372955), 'harpërz'gęrdən. A former market garden, now a field, beside the Brig o Ballater.

**Haugh\*** (R 4, 392972), Scots Haugh = riverside meadow. On farmland at Tullich.

**The Haugh\*** (U, 247010), ðı'ha·χ. A field south-east of Corndavon Lodge.

**(The) Haugh** (OS, C, 432970), as above. Hach (Ri 11), Haugh of Cambus o' May (Di). A former farm by Dee, west of Dinnet.

**The Haugh\*** (F, 432967), as above. A riverside field beside the former farm of Haugh west of Dinnet.

**The Haugh\*** (U, 291956), as above. A field east of Crathie.

**The Haugh\*** (F, two fields 274948 and 275949), as above. East of Crathie.

**The Haugh\*** (I, 154905). A former field, now part of Braemar Golf Course.

**The Haughie\*** (U, 414039), ðı'haχe. Also the Little Haugh (U), ðı'lëtəl'ha·χ. A little field west of Logie Coldstone.

**The Haughie\*** (U, 302010), as above. A little field by Gairn, west of Dalnabo near Gairnshiel.

**The Haughie\*** (U, 359957), as above. Flat ground by Dee near Ballater.

**The Haugh o Bridgefoot\*** (U, 414041), ðı'ha·χę͵brıg'fët. A field west of Logie Coldstone.

**Haugh of Allt a' Mhaide\*** (312876). Haugh of Aultavaid (Rli 19). Former farmland by Muick, at Inchnabobart.

**The Haugh of Allt a' Mhaide\*** (258011). The Haugh of Ault Matt (I). Rough pasture by Gairn, at the Sleach west of Gairnshiel.

**The Haugh of Aucholzie** See Dail Mallachaidh.

**The Haugh of Dail a' Choirce\*** See An Dail a' Choirce.

**The Haugh of Dail Mallachaidh** See Dail Mallachaidh.

**The Haugh of Dubh-bhruach\*** (154902). The Haugh of Dubroch (Io 43a). South of Braemar, now part of golf course.

**Haugh of Easter Micras\*** (I, 302960), now the Three-cornered Park (U), ðı'θri'kǫrnërd'park. A field near the river, east of Crathie.

**Haugh of Milltown\*** (Io, 160927). A former field beside Dee, at Invercauld.

**The Haugh of Tom nam Meann\*** See Dail Tom nam Meann.

**The Haugh Puil** (C, 434969), ðɪˈhaˑχˈpil. The Haugh (Sc), Holly-Haugh (Ly) probably same. In Dee near former farm called the Haugh.

**The Haughs o Allanmore\*** (U, 143917), ðɪˈhaˑχsɐˌalɐnˈmoˑr, usually now the Allanmore Haughs (F). Flat land by Dee, near Braemar.

**The Haughs o Callater\*** (F, 190834), ðɪˈhaˑχsɐˈkalətër. Haughs of Glen Callater (I). Above Loch Callater.

**The Haughs o Creag an Dail** (F, 146984), ðɪˈhaˑχsɐˌkregənˈdaˑl. Rough pasture by Gairn, south-east of Ben Avon.

**Haughs of Torgalter\*** (I, 286954). Flat field near Dee, on north side of road east of Crathie.

**The Haughs o Geusachan\*** (U, 971943), ðɪˈhaˑχsɐˈgjusɔçɐn, more often now the Geusachan Haughs (U). Grassy flat land by the burn in Glen Geusachan.

**The Haughs o Glen Ey\*** (F, 090830), ðɪˈhaˑχsɐˌglɐnˈɛiˑ, now sometimes the Glen Ey Haughs (F) or the Altanour Haughs (U). Extensive rough pasture by Ey Burn, in upper Glen Ey.

**The Haughs o Invercauld\*** (F, 172920), ðɪˈhaˑχsɐˌɪnvërˈkaˑld, usually now the Invercauld Haughs (C). Flat farmland and rough grazing between Invercauld Bridge and Invercauld Monument.

**The Haughs o the Baddoch\*** (U, 129820), ðɪˈhaˑχsɪðɪˈbadəç, usually now the Baddoch Haughs (F). Haughs of the Baddach (G 10), Haughs of Baddach (Io 33). Flat grassland for 2 km up Baddoch Burn from the house at Baddoch.

**The Haughs o the Bynack\*** (U, 003859), ðɪˈhaˑχsɪðɪˈbɛinək, more often now the Bynack Haughs (F). Grassy flat ground near Bynack Lodge.

**The Hazels\*** (C, south-east of 416037), ðɪˈhezəlz. A former garden beside hazel trees west of Logie Coldstone.

**Headinch** (OS, C, 413969), hɛdˈɪnʃ, hidˈɪnʃ. Heide of the Insch in 1665 (Dms 10). The Inch referred to is Inchmarnoch. A farm east of Pannanich.

**The Headinch Hill\*** (F, 407965), ðɪˌhɛdˈɪnʃˈhël. A hill grazing for the above farm.

**The Head o Allt Deas\*** (F, 389867 and ridge to west-north-west), ðɪˈhɛdɐˌaltˈɛs. Head of Ault-dess (Io 70). Part of the Hill of Doune to Glen Esk people. At top of Glen Tanar.

**The Head o Cowie\*** (F, 417873), ðɪˈhɛdɐˈkʌu.i. A big corrie north-east of Mount Keen.

**The Head o Dubh-Loch** (F, 212846), ðɪˈhɛdɐˈduˌloχ. The Head of Dow Loch (Ri 29). Ground at top of watershed of Allt an Dubh-Loch west of Lochnagar.

**(The) Head of Black Burn** (OS, F, 394871), ðɪˈhɛdɐˈblakˈbʌrn. A hill in upper Glen Tanar.

**(The) Head of Garbh Choire** (OS, F, 392907), ðɪˈhɛdɐˈgarçɔre. A little top in upper Glen Tanar.

**The Head of Gleann Cheann-bhuilg** (119952). The Head of Glenchanleck (Ri 17). At top of Gleann an t-Slugain.

**Head of Knock\*** (Opr 56). Former habitation, probably 351952 near Knock west of Ballater.

**The Head of Preas Bealaich\*** (probably 336849), Preas Bealaich (3) = copse of a pass. The Head of Pressbaylich (G 5). Bealaich might seem unlikely from the spelling Baylich, but one local pronunciation of Bealach is ˈbeiləç (see Am Bealach). The Burn of Presney runs off the Angus side of this top east of the Spittal of Glenmuick.

**Head of Slochd an Airich\*** (116011), Slochd an Àirich (4) = pit of the ? grazier. Head of Sloch-garich (R 2b) suggests Slochd Garbhaich = pit of rough place, but Muckle Slochd (i.e. Slochd Mor) used to be Slochd an Araich or Sloch Garich (Cj 1), Slochd an Araich (OS 1869). The Slochd referred to lies to the north in Banffshire, but the head-ridge marches with Aberdeenshire. West of Ben Avon.

**Head of the Bad Leathan\*** (395918). Head of the Badlean (I). A little top south of Pannanich.

**The Head o Gairn\*** (C), ðɪˈhidɐˈgern̩. Head of Gairn (Opr 8). Formerly inhabited part up to Daldownie west of Gairnshiel.

**The Head o Garbh-choire\*** (U, 175778), ðɪˈhɛdɐˈgarçore. North-east of the Glas Maol.

**The Head o Muick\*** (F), ðɪˈhɛdɐˈmëk. Head of Muick (Fa). A name for the hilly ground around Loch Muick.

**The Head o the Leg o Moss\*** (U, 441873), ðɪˈhɛdɪðɪˈlegɐˈmɔs. Scots Leg of a plough = a measure of land (Gm). The top of the Invermark grouse beat the Leg o Moss, a big area of peat-moss.

**The Head Ridge\*** (R 4, 389971). On farmland at Tullich.

**The Heather Butts\*** (U, 250994), ðɪˈhɛðërˈbʌts. Grouse butts with heather turves, north of Crathie.

**The Hedge Park\*** See Rainies Stack.

**The Heich Muir\*** (F, 338964), ðɪˈhiçˈmir̩, ðɪˈhiçˈmjur̩. Scots = the high moor. Pairs with the Low Muir. An enclosed area of rough ground west of Ballater.

**The Heid o Gelder\*** (F, 270860), ðɪˈhidɐˈgɛldër. Head of Gelder (B). Ridge at top of Glen Gelder.

**The Heid o Glen Beg\*** (F, 184870), ðɪˈhidɐˌglənˈbɛg. Head of Glenbeg (I). The last flattish ground at the top of Glen Beg in Ballochbuie Forest.

**The Heid o Glen Geusachan\*** (F, 947957), ðɪˈhidɐˌglənˈgjusɔçɐn. The Head of Glengusachan (Fi). Steep slopes at top of Glen Geusachan.

**The Heid o the Baddoch\*** (F, 096783), ðɪˈhidɪðɪˈbadəç. The Head of Baddach (Me 15). Top part of the Baddoch glen.

**The Heid o the Dubh-Ghleann\*** (U, 065985), ðɪˈhidɪðɪˈduˌglən. Refers to the last flattish ground at the top of the glen, enclosed by steep slopes.

**The Heid o the White Mounth\*** See Carn a' Choire Bhoidheach.

**Hen Field\*** See Ailean nan Cearc.

**The Hens' Croft\*** (F, 289953), ðɪˈhɛnzˈkrɔft. Hen's Croft (Am). A field at Abergeldie Castle.

**The Hens' Park\*** (U, 240937), ðɪˈhɛnzˈpark. A field at Invergelder.

**The High Approach\*** (U, 349946), ðɪˈhaeˌaˈprotʃ. A high road leading towards Birkhall in lower Glen Muick.

**High Broo** See the High Burn Peel.

**The High Burn\*** (F, 439972), ðɪˈhaeˈbʌrn. The lower part of Deecastle Burn.

**The High Burn Puil** (C, 439972), ðɪˈhaeˈbʌrnˈpil or High Burn (F, Sc). Also Highbroo (A). In Dee beside the above burn.

**The Highland Boundary Stone** (Wy, 466991). A stone erected in 1965 by the Deeside Field Club along the main road east of Dinnet. It announces 'You are now entering the Highlands'.

**High Torr an Fhraoich\*** (169929). High Tonrich (Im 4). A former field at Invercauld.

**High Waird\*** See the Wairds.

**The Hillock\*** (U, 422046), ðɪˈhëlëk. A hillock near Logie Coldstone.

**Hillockhead\*** (C, 435006), ˌhëlëkˈhɛd. A house west of Loch Davan.

**Hillocks of the Croft\*** (I, 355939). In lower Glen Muick.

**The Hill o Cuidhe Crom\*** (U, 258851), ðɪˈhëlɐˌkuiˈkrɔm, now usually just the Cuidhe Crom, see under that name.

**Hill of Ais an Tulaich\*** See Ais an Tulaich.

**Hill of Allt an Aitinn** See Carn Eag Dhubh.

**The Hill o Fasheilach\*** See Fasheilach.

**Hill of Aucholzie\*** See Auchnacraig Hill.

**The Hill of Bad a' Chairr\*** (398008). Hill of Badaquhar (Io 20). South-east of Morven.

**(The) Hill of Candacraig** (OS, C, 346000), ðɪˈhëlɐˌkandiˈkreg. A hill in Glen Gairn.

**The Hill of Coire Bhraineich\*** (098888). The Hill of Corrievranoch (Me 15). Near Inverey.

**Hill of Coire Mor\*** (364993). Hill of Corrymore (Io 20). North of Ballater.

**(The) Hill of Doune** (OS, C, 390867), ðɪ'hᴇlɐ'dun, from Dùn (3), a hillock. South of Glen Tanar in Glen Mark, Angus, but the name covers a long hill stretching to the Aberdeenshire boundary.

**The Hill of Feith Ruaidhe\*** See Ferrowie.

**(The) Hill of Gairney** (OS, C, 448875), ðɪ'hᴇlɐ'gjarne, usually now ðɪ'hᴇlɐ'gerne. For meaning see Water of Gairney, which runs below this hill in upper Glen Tanar.

**Hill of Inchnabobart** See Craig of Inchnabobart.

**Hill of Liath-choire Beag** See Carn Liath.

**The Hill of Lochnagar\*** See Lochnagar.

**Hill of Loinn Muaidh\*** Hill of Lenmoui (Roy) shown as the Coyles of Muick south-west of Ballater.

**Hill of Loinn nam Muileann\*** (382981). Hill of Loinamulian (R 4). North-east of Ballater.

**The Hill of the Branndair\*** See Peter's Hill.

**Hill of the Camlet\*** (In, 309934). In Glen Girnock.

**Hill of the Slugain\*** See Meall an t-Slugain.

**The Hill Park\*** (I, 327968). A rough area of former pasture, now a wood, beside Coilacriech.

**The Hill Park\*** (U, 412030), ðɪ'hᴇl'park. A field next the hill, west of Logie Coldstone.

**The Hill Park\*** (U, 274953), as above. A field next the hill, at Crathie.

**The Hill Park\*** (U, 281955), as above. A field next the hill, east of Crathie.

**Hills of Cadhach Dubh\*** (073783 east to the 855 m top). Hills of Caach-du (Ma), Caach-du (Ro). At the top of Glen Ey on the south side.

**The Hollow of the She-Devil** See An Garbh Choire.

**The Holly Buss\*** (F, 418978), ðɪ'hole'bᴧs, Scots Buss = bush. A holly bush at Cambus o' May.

**The Holly Buss Puil** (C, 415981), ðɪ'hole'bᴧs'pil. Holly Buss (A), Holly Bush (Sc) the anglicised version. A pool in Dee beside a holly bush, at Cambus o' May.

**Holly-Haugh** See the Haugh Puil.

**Holmesdale\*** (JE, 209978), 'homz,del, after Viscount Holmesdale who rented Corndavon in 1866 (OSn). A place on the deer fence south-east of Culardoch where deer could get through a one-way gate.

**The Holmesdale Path\*** (F, 209012), ðɪ'homz,del'paθ. Path from Gairn, west of Corndavon Lodge, towards Culardoch.

**Homehead** (OS, C, 432044), ,hom'hᴇd, from Scots Howm = a hollow, which fits this place well. Holmhead (Er). A house at Logie Coldstone.

**Homehead Cottage** (OS, C, 432045), ,hom'hᴇd'kɒtədʒ. Beside above place.

**The Homehead Wuid\*** (C, 430044), ðɪ,hom'hᴇd'wɪd. A wood at Logie Coldstone.

**The Horses' Burn\*** (U, 138906), ðɪ'hɒrsəz'bᴧrn. On Morrone west of Braemar.

**The Horseshoe\*** (F, 333859), ðɪ'hɒrs'ʃuˑ. A horseshoe-shaped patch that looks as if cut out of the hill, south of the Linn of Muick.

**The Horseshoe Butts\*** (F, 344021), ðɪ'hɒrs'ʃu'bᴧts. A curved line of grouse butts, south-west of Morven.

**The Horseshoe Corrie\*** See Coire Fionn.

**Horseshoe Gully** (Sd, 161773). A ski-run on the Glas Maol, named after the horseshoe-shaped snow patch in Fionn-choire.

**(The) Horseshoe of the Lair** (OS, U, 313786), ðɪ'hɒrs'ʃuɪðɪ'ler. The Horseshoe (F), ðɪ'hɒrs'ʃuˑ. A horseshoe-shaped, convex slope south of Loch Muick, on Lair of Aldararie.

**Hospital Haugh** See Spittal Haugh.

**The Hotel Ferm\*** See Corn Eilean.

**The Hotel Parks\*** (F, 372963), ðɪ,hə'tᴇl'parks. Fields north-east of Ballater.

**The House i the Glen\*** See Gelder Shiel.

**House of Crathienaird\*** (on the site of Newton (OS)). Crathienaird House (R 3), House of Crathienard (R 5). A former estate house west of Crathie.

**(The) House of Glenmuick** (OS, C, 372946), ðɪ'husᴇˌglən'mëk. Formerly this house was Braichlie House, and at that time Glenmuick House (now demolished) was at 358938. South of Ballater.

**The House Park\*** (U, 239939), ðɪ'hus'park. A field at Invergelder.

**The Houses of Glen Lui\*** The Houses of Glenluie (Fi). Collective name for the former habitations in Glen Lui.

**Houston's Stane\*** (C, 204866), 'hustənz'stin. An upright, 19th century stone with a metal plaque and inscription, after a shooter who collapsed on a hot day and died west of Lochnagar.

**The Howe Burn\*** (C, 424040), ðɪ'hᴧu'bᴧrn, often the Big Howe Burn (F). Lower part of Coinlach Burn and its lower continuation west of Logie Coldstone, where it comes into the low ground or Howe of Cromar.

**The Howe o Corn Arn\*** (U, 398946), ðɪ'hᴧu.ᴇ,kɒrn̩'ern̩. Flattish part at the bottom of the Coire of Corn Arn south-east of Ballater. See Corrienearn.

**The Howe o Cromar** (C), ðɪ'hᴧu.ᴇkrə'maːr. The Howe of Cromar (A). The low ground around Logie Coldstone and Tarland, mostly outside our study area.

**The Howe o Culardoch\*** (U, 198974), ðɪ'hᴧu.ᴇ,kəl'ardəç. A big basin at the top of Glen Feardar, including the area around Stable Burn.

**The Howe o Moine Taimhseich\*** (U, 313025), ðɪ'hᴧu.ᴇ,mɒn'dᴧusəç. Flat area beside Allt Glas-choille north-east of Gairnshiel.

**The Howe o the Cailleach** (370950). The Howe o' the Kyloch (A 235). A dip in the road beside Ballater. See Craig Coillich.

**The Howe o the Pots\*** (U, 435998), ðɪ'hᴧu.əi'pɒts, Scots Pot = deep pool. Near Loch Kinord.

**The Howf** (U) ðɪ'hᴧuf, Scots = the shelter. The Howff (Smith 1980). Also Freddie and Sticker's Howf (U), 'frᴇdi.ən'stëkᴇrz 'hᴧuf, after the nicknames of its two originators. Not local names, except to a few who picked them up from climbers. A rough shelter for climbers among rocks in the Braemar area, location not divulged here for security reasons.

**Howmies\*** (F, 415036), 'homiz, 'homez, probably from Scots Howm = a hollow, which would fit this field well. South-west of Logie Coldstone.

**The Hummel Corrie\*** See Coire an Daimh Mhoile.

**Humphrey's Folly** (Crom). Humphrey Cottage (Ce 3). A former cottage by roadside near Craigendarroch Hotel at Ballater.

**The Hungry Howe\*** (U, 294931), ðɪ'hᴧŋri'hᴧuˑ. A hollow between Khantore and the Camlet, south of Abergeldie.

**Hunthall** See Deecastle.

**(The) Hunt Hill** (OS, 336864), ðɪ'hᴧnt'hël. The Black Lump of the Hunt Hill (I). In upper Glen Muick.

**The Hut** See Allt-na-giubhsaich.

**Hutchison Memorial Hut** (OS, 023998). A hut in Coire Etchachan, built in memory of an Aberdeen climber. Is called the Etchachan Hut (C) in local use, ðɪ'ᴇtʃəçən'hᴧt.

**Ian Grant's Park\*** (F, 083897), ,iən'grants'park, after one who once farmed it. A field at Inverey.

**Iar-allt a' Challtuinn** See West Allt Coultain.

**Iar-choire Sneachdach** (OS, 094971), locally Iar-choire an t-Sneachda (2, U), 'iər‚χɔrn̩'dreçk, west corrie of the snow. Pairs with Ear-choire an t-Sneachda on Beinn a' Bhuird.

**Iar-sliabhach\*** See Wester Sleach.

**Imir an t-Sneachdaidh** (3, 147906), ridge of the snow. Imir n drechky, the snowy rig (D). On Tomintoul above Braemar.

**Inbhir Allt Shlat\*** (3, probably 099854), mouth of burn of wands. Inveraltalat, Inveraltlat (Me 6, 9). A former grazing, probably in Glen Ey.

**Inbhir Ardair** See Inver.

**Inbhir Choich\*** (6, U, 122907), ‚ɛnër'χɔıç, mouth of the Quoich, for meaning see Quoich Water. Usually now the Mouth o Quoich (C), ðı'mu‚ɐ'kɔıç. Mouth of Quoich (Fi). Flat land where Quoich meets Dee.

**Inbhir Feallta\*** (4, 047891), treacherous mouth. Grassings called Innerffzeald beside the Lin of Die (G 2). Possibly Inbhir Leth-allt, mouth of half burn. Grazings near Linn of Dee.

**Inbhir Geallaidh\*** (3, 018884), mouth of Geldie or clear one. Invergeallie (Cr 35). A former habitation near where Geldie meets Dee, most of ruins used for road metal.

**Inbhir Goirneig** (3, 330961), mouth of Girnock or little crier. Innir-garnak (D). Flat ground where Girnock joins Dee.

**Inbhir Laoigh\*** (3, U, 071897), ‚ınvër'lui, in Gaelic ‚ıŋër'lui, mouth of Lui or calf-one. Note Poll Inbhir Laoigh. Flat ground where Lui meets Dee.

**Inbhir nan Easach** (3, 154993), mouth of the rapidly-falling burns (see Allt an Eas Bhig). Enernaneshah (Hi). South of Ben Avon.

**Inbhir na Sròine\*** (3, probably 136832), mouth of the nose (referring to Strone Baddoch). Invernastroin (Ra 3). A former farm at the Baddoch.

**The Inbhir of Allt Beag\*** (360026), Inbhir (3) = mouth, or borrowing into Scots. The Inver of Aldbeg (G 19). Up Tullich Burn.

**The Inbhir of Allt Clacharraidh\*** (377016). The Inver of Auldclachrie (G 19). Where Allt Clacharraidh joins Allt Blar nam Marbh to form the larger Allt Dobharaidh. Up Tullich Burn.

**The Inbhir of Allt Deas** (388890). The Inver of the Burn of Aldess (Ri 29). Stream junction in upper Glen Tanar.

**The Inbhir of Allt Dobharaidh\*** (375006). The Inver of the Burn of Altdourie (G 33). Stream junction up Tullich Burn.

**The Inbhir of Bynack\*** (006867). The Inver of Bynack (Fi). Stream junction near Bynack Lodge.

**The Inbhir of Coinneachaig** (220926). The Invar of Kynachack (Ri 17). Where Connachat Burn meets Dee, south-west of Balmoral.

**The Inbhir of Ey** (087897). The Inver of Eye (Mc 18, Io 21). Where Ey meets Dee.

**The Inbhir of Geldie** (021884). The Inver of Geoldie (Mc 18, Io 21). Where Geldie meets Dee.

**The Inbhir of the Burn of Glen Colstane\*** (407979). The Inver of the Burn of Glencoldstane (Io 20). Where Culsten Burn enters Dee.

**The Inbhir of the March Burn\*** (399973). The Inver of the March Burn (G 22). Where this burn meets Dee, near Pannanich.

**The Inbhir of the Wheel Burn\*** (368021). The Inver of the Quilburn (Io 20). South of Morven.

**Inbhir Uisge\*** (3, south-east of 155883), mouth of waters. Inver Uishk (I). A field where Callater Burn meets Clunie Water.

**Inchmarnoch** (OS, C, 424963), ınʃ'marnɐχ, from Inis Mheàrnaig (3), island of St Marnock or Mo-Eàrn-oc. Insh-viarnaik, Insh-vyarnag (D). There was a former chapel on an island in Dee here. Annual games were held near there, and old people told Diack (ms) that they called this 'haudan (holding) their Marnan'. It was also referred to as 'the Marnoch shooting'

(McC). Inchmarnoch is now a group of houses east of Pannanich, but locally it is also commonly used for the area round about, including all the flat farmland.

**Inchnabobart** (OS, C, 310876), ‚ınʃnɐ'bɔbërt, from Inis nam Bó-bard (3), river-meadow of the cow enclosures. Often Inchbobart (C), ınʃ'bɔbërt, always in older records (M) and among older people who know the area best, from Inis Bó-bard (3), river-meadow of cow enclosure. Inshbobard (R 1), Inchbobart (Ri 24b, In, Am), Inchbobbart (Io 33), Inshnabobart, innsh-bobart, -pobart (D). Now a house in upper Glen Muick, beside a grassy haugh.

**The Inchnabobart Brig\*** (C, 311876), ðı‚ınʃnɐ'bɔbërt'brıg. A bridge in Glen Muick.

**The Inchnabobart Wuid\*** (C, 310877), ðı‚ınʃnɐ'bɔbërt'wıd. A planted wood in upper Glen Muick.

**The Inis Gheal Puil** (C, 371953), ðı‚ınʃ'gel'pil, from Inis Gheal (3), white riverside meadow. Inchgale (A), Inchgael (Sc). In Dee beside Ballater. Presumably was originally the name of the ground there, beside the river.

**(The) Inver** (OS, C, 233938), ðı'ınvër, from An t-Inbhir (3, D), 'ıŋër or ɛnër (JB), the mouth. N jenner (D), n'jɛnər (Sch). Inver (I), Inver is from Inbhir (Mp). Originally referred to a farm (D); an old map (I) shows that this was on the site of the present Inver Inn. However the name is used more generally for the flattish ground around where the Feardar Burn meets Dee. Diack noted that An t-Inbhir was a shortened name, the full name being Inverarder, i.e. Inbhir Ardair (3), mouth of high water, referring to the Feardar Burn. Inver of Arder (G 27), the Inver of Ferder (Io 18), Inner-arder (D). South-west of Crathie.

**The Inver Brae\*** (F, 234938), ðı'ınvër'brae·. A hill on a road at the Inver.

**The Inver Burn\*** (C, 231937), ðı'ınvër'bʌrn. Lowest part of Feardar Burn.

**Invercauld** (C), ‚ınvër'ka·ld or ‚ınvër'ka·l, but to the oldest people ‚ınër'ka·l, in Gaelic ‚ıŋër'ka·l, or ɛnër'ka·l (JB), from Inbhir Chala (5), mouth of the hard one, referring to a stream. Two spellings from 1481 and 1611 Innercaddill, Innerchall (A), Inuercald (Ca), Innercauld (Anon 4), Invercald (Fa), Innercald (R 1), Inverchalla (Gr). Other old spellings (D) were Endercauld, Innercall, and Morchalla, the last one perhaps from Mothar, 'a stone fort in ruins'. In Gaelic Inbhir-call (Drc). Gaelic speakers said Enner-call, pronounced Ear cala, 'but some say the proper Gaelic is inbhir-cala. Braemar Gaelic says er-caull; laird of Invercauld, tshuirn er-call' (D), i.e. Tighearn. The local Gaelic was also noted as Inbhir-chall, probably from old Gaelic Call = hazel (Mp). Miss J Macdonald gave ɛr'kal (Sch). Invercauld is a name for the land on Invercauld estate in general, and the flattish ground around Invercauld House in particular. Originally it referred to a small area near the house, where there is a tiny, slow-running burn Allt Chala (Alt Challa (Gr), Allt chall (D)). The well where this burn rises is Tobar Chalaig or Well of Calaig (Tobar chall (D), Tobar Challag, genitive (D in A)). Presumably Invercauld had therefore been the area at the mouth of this burn, i.e. Inbhir Chala. An early suggested meaning for Allt Challa was burn of the loss or defeat, referring to the defeat of Fionnlagh Mor's enemies in a fight here (Gr), but local folk would have called this a victory, not a loss. However, this can be rejected as it does not fit Invercauld in any case; the mouth of the loss makes no sense, and it is fairly obvious that the Cauld part of the name must refer to a stream. Call = hazel has also been suggested (Mp). Cala = hard, as in Caladair = hard water, seems a likely possibility, or Cala = a wet meadow or hollow (note W 1904, 68).

**Invercauld Bridge** (OS, 185910), locally the Brig o Dee (C), ðɪ 'brɪgɐ'diˑ. The Bridge of Dee, sometimes the Bridge of Invercauld (Brown). East of Braemar, pairs with the hump-backed Auld Brig o Dee further downstream.

**Invercauld House** (OS, C, 174924), ˌɪnvёr'kald'hus, formerly the House of Invercauld (Ri), ðɪ'husɐˌɪnёr'kaˑl (U). Sometimes the Castle of Invercauld, but not in the common speech of people brought up in the Braemar area. A big house north-east of Braemar.

**Invercauld House Boat** (Gf, 168922). Also the Ladies' Boat (Gf). Former ferry over Dee.

**Invercauld's Stables** See Clach Choutsaich.

**Invercauld Monument** (OS, 158929), locally the Needle (C), ðɪ 'nidəl. A stone monument north-east of Braemar.

**The Inverchandlick Boat** (U, 150925), ðɪˌɪnvёr'χanlёk'bot. Inverchandlick boat (Gf). Former ferry over Dee at Braemar.

**Inverchandlick Boat Pool** See the Inverchandlick Puil.

**Inverchandlick Cottage** (OS, 149926), locally just Inverchandlick, ˌɪnvёr'χanlёk (C), (ˌɪnər'hanlək (A)), from Inbhir Chanlaig, ˌɪɲər'χanlɪç (Sch), ˌɪɲёr'χanlёk or ˌёnёr 'χanlёk (JB), mouth of the Canlaig (the old name for the stream in Gleann an t-Slugain). Chanlaig comes from Cheann-bhuilg (3), of the head-bag (see Gleann an t-Slugain). Inner-chanlik (D), Inverchanlick (Fa), Inverchannalick (Roy), Inverchanlig, Inverchainlig (Cr 2, 30), Innerchanlick (Io 45), Ferryman's House and Ferry (I). A name also used for the flat area further east to about 160930, north of Braemar.

**The Inverchandlick Fuird\*** (U, west of 149925), ðɪˌɪnvёr'χanlёk 'fjurd. Former ford over Dee at Braemar.

**The Inverchandlick Island\*** (U, 154927), ðɪˌɪnvёr'χanlёk'ɛilənd. An island in Dee north of Braemar.

**The Inverchandlick Park\*** (F, 149925), ðɪˌɪnvёr'χanlёk'park. A field north of Braemar, including Creit na Ceardaich and other former fields.

**The Inverchandlick Puil\*** (F, 152926), ðɪˌɪnvёr'χanlёk'pil. Inverchandlich Boat Pool (Ly). In Dee, north of Braemar.

**The Inverchandlick Wuid\*** (C, 145924), ðɪˌɪnvёr'χanlёk'wɪd. A plantation near Braemar.

**Inverenzie** (OS, C, 330006), ˌɪnvёr'ɪɲi, from Inbhir Fhionnaidh (3), mouth of the white one, referring to the Glenfenzie Burn. Inuerenze (Ca), Innaringie (Io 8), Inveringy (R 1), Inverenyie (Mg), Inverinzie (OS 1869), Inver-ingyie (D). The OS location is a house, locally called the Laggan (C), ðɪ'lagən, from An Lagan (3), the little hollow. The Lakkan (D). Inverenzie is usually a more general name for the area at the foot of Fenzie, and Inverenzie as applied to the farm is a recent change within living memory. The name of the Laggan still appears in the map, in the nearby Laggan Cottage.

**Inverey** (OS, 087895), ˌɪnvёr'ɛiˑ, in Gaelic ˌɪɲər'ei (Sch), ˌɪɲёr'ɛiˑ or ˌёnёr'ɛiˑ (JB), from Inbhir Eidh (6), mouth of Ey, for meaning see Ey Burn. Innerey (Anon 7), Inerey (R 1), Enverey (Me 8). The OS name, and the name locally, originally referred to the flat ground around where Ey meets Dee, but now it is used just for the village, west of Braemar. See Little Inverey and Meikle Inverey.

**Inverey Castle** (OS, C, 088893), ˌɪnvёr'ɛi'kasəl. Also Caisteal Inbhir Eidh (6, JB), ˌkastjəlˌɪɲёr'ɛiˑ, castle of Inverey. Formerly the Castle of Inverey (Brow 1835). Remains of a castle.

**Inverey Cottage** See the Knock.

**Invergairn\*** (Cr 41), from Inbhir Ghàrain (5), mouth of the Gairn or the crying one. The area around Bridge of Gairn.

**Invergairn** (Vr 4, U, west of 353970), ˌɪnvёr'gern̩, as above. A former house beside kirkyard at Bridge of Gairn.

**Invergelder** (OS, C, 241938), ˌɪnvёr'gɛldёr, from Inbhir Ghealdair (3), mouth of the Gelder or the clear water. Inueryalder (Ca), Inverhalder (Tayl), Innir-yālldar, long *a* (D). Abergelder (Mc 11). A farm south-west of Balmoral, and the flat ground nearby where Gelder meets Dee.

**The Invergelder Brig\*** (C, 241939), ðɪˌɪnvёr'gɛldёr'brɪg. Formerly Bridge of Invergalder (Io 51). Near above farm.

**The Invermark Deer Fence\*** (F, 441873), ðɪˌɪnvёr'mark'dir'fɛns. At top of Glen Tanar, bordering the Invermark ground in Angus.

**Inver Mill Cottage** (OS, 233938). Locally the Mill of Inver is used for this house and the nearby former mill itself.

**Invermuick** (OS, C, 365949), ˌɪnvёr'mёk, from Inbhir Muice (3), mouth of Muick or pig-one. Innermuck (Ri) in 1746. A house which was the former old parish manse, now uninhabited because of river erosion of the bank. Earlier (I), the manse was beside the graveyard on the south side of the road at 365948. Where Muick meets Dee.

**The Inver Quarry\*** (C, 225931), ðɪ'ɪnvёr'kware. Disused, west of the Inver.

**The Inver Straucht\*** (C, 225930), ðɪ'ɪnvёr'streçt, Scots Straucht = straight. Also formerly the Lang Mile (U), ðɪ'laŋ'mɛil. A straight road near the Inver.

**Iochdar Ghlinne Ghàrain\*** (5), lowest part of the glen of the Gairn or the crying one. Iochdar Ghlinngarain (Iop). Probably same as the Fit o Gairn.

**The Iron Gate\*** (F, south of 179919), ðɪ'ɛirən'get. Near Invercauld House.

**The Iron Hillock\*** See Tom Bad Phut.

**The Island\*** See An t-Eilean.

**The Island\*** (C, 367950), ðɪ'ɛilənd. A flat stretch beside Dee covered with trees and scrub, possibly formerly an Eilean or riverside flat. Near Ballater.

**The Island Cast** (C, 419968), ðɪ'ɛilənd'kast. Island Cast (Sc). A pool in Dee beside an island south of Cambus o' May.

**The Island Puil\*** See Anthony's Cast.

**The Island Puil** (C, 469986), ðɪ'ɛilənd'pil. Island Pool (P). In Dee, east of Dinnet.

**The Island Puil\*** (F, 327965), as above. In Dee, beside a big wooded island west of Ballater.

**Ivertown Aucholzie\*** See Upper Aucholzie.

**James Coull's Cairn\*** (I, 212982). A cairn north-west of Crathie.

**James Downie's Shiel\*** (236977). James Dunie's Sheal (R 5). North-west of Crathie.

**James Ley's Croft\*** (I, 351922). A field in lower Glen Muick.

**James MacDhomhnuill's Shieling\*** (north of 388020). James McKoil's Shealling (Io 20). South-east of Morven.

**Jane's Firs** (OS, F, 299940), 'ʤinz'fёrz. A group of firs high on the hill south-east of Abergeldie, named after a woman who threw fir seeds away there, after failing to get the price agreed by the estate for them.

**Janet's Yard\*** (F, 362974), 'ʤanёts'jard. A field beside the former farm of Allt Mor, north of the Pass of Ballater, named after Janet Ritchie (Ce 1), the last person who lived there.

**Jean Miller's Park\*** (C, 084896), ʤin'mёlёrz'park, after one who formerly farmed it. A field at Inverey.

**Jebb's Brae\*** (U, 384974), 'ʤɛbz'breˑ. An old name for the steep drive up to the Tullich Lodge Hotel, north-east of Ballater; Jebb was the original owner of Tullich Lodge.

**The Jerrie Brig\*** (C, 435010), ðɪ'ʤere'brɪg. Carries public road near Loch Davan, see Marchnear.

**The Jerrie Burn\*** (C, 437010), ðɪ'ʤere'bʌrn. A burn running into the west side of Loch Davan, see Marchnear. Also Marchnear Burn (Wy), but Marchnear is a modern name for a house and this name is not used locally for the burn.

**The Jerrie Inn\*** See Marchnear.

**The Jetty Puil\*** (F), ðɪˈʤɛteˈpil. A collective name for two pools, Upper and Lower. In Dee above Invercauld Bridge.

**The Jetty Puil\*** (F, north-east of 359955), as above. A pool in Dee west of Ballater.

**Jimmy's Housie\*** (C, north-east of 109916), ˈʤɪmizˈhusi. A former hut for a deer watcher in Glen Quoich.

**Jimmy Smith's\*** (U, west of 239941), ˈʤɪmiˈsmɛθs. A former house near the Inver, the western of the two houses at Lower Carnaquheen.

**Jimmy Stewart's Park\*** (U, 366944), ˈʤɪmiˈstjuərtsˈpark, after a former inhabitant of nearby Balintober. A field in lower Glen Muick.

**Jock Dubh's Hole\*** (3, U, north-east of 305927), ˈʤɔkˈduzˈhol. Jock Dubh was presumably dark John. A hole in rocks in lower Glen Girnock.

**The Jock Robertson Puil** (F, 269943), ðɪˈʤɔkˈrɔbɛrtsənˈpil. Jock Robertson (P, Sc), Drymills (A). A pool in Dee at Easter Balmoral.

**Jock's Cast** (Sc, F, 333963), ˈʤɔksˈkast. A pool in Dee, west of Ballater.

**Jock's Road** (OS, C, 215807), ˈʤɔksˈrod. Old path from Glen Callater to Glen Doll, named after a John Winter who took refuge at the top of Glen Doll after a dispute with Lord Aberdeen (more details in Cj 12). Also the Glen Doll Road (A, F), ðɪˈɡlənˈdɔlˈrod.

**The John Brown Junior Puil\*** (F, 322966), ðɪˈʤɔnˈbrʌunˈʤunjərˈpil. A pool in Dee west of Ballater.

**The John Brown Puil** (C, 317967), ðɪˈʤɔnˈbrʌunˈpil. John Brown (Sc). A pool in Dee, west of Coilacriech.

**John Fleming's Croft\*** (I, 152879). A former croft in lower Glen Clunie.

**J. Symon's Goat Cot\*** (229020). J. Symon's Goat Cott (R 5). John Symon and James Symon mentioned several times in estate lists (Io, Ri). A former goat cot opposite Corndavon Lodge.

**The Jubilee Prop Drive\*** (F, 337055), ðɪˈʤubəliˈprɔpˈdraev. A grouse drive west of Morven, beside the Jubilee Prop (Jubilee Cairn (OS)), a cairn just outside the area covered in this book.

**The Jungle Park\*** (U, 414033), ðɪˈʤʌŋɡəlˈpark. Named after small patches of trees and scrub beside it. A field west of Logie Coldstone.

**The Juniper Butts\*** (U, 259025), ðɪˈʤunəpɛrˈbʌts. Grouse butts north-west of Gairnshiel, on a hillside with many juniper bushes.

**Juniper Cairn** (OS, 216825). A cairn east of Loch Callater, above Allt an Aitinn or burn of the juniper.

**The Juniper Hill\*** See Cnocan Aitinn.

**The Kate Puil** (C, west of 401974), ðɪˈketˈpil, or Kate's Puil (U). Kate's Peel (A), Kate (Sc). A pool in Dee, beside Pannanich.

**Kate's Stripe** (OS, Bs, F, 325825), ˈketsˈstrɛip, Scots Stripe = small burn. East of Loch Muick.

**Kaurry's Croft\*** (R 4, 393976). On farmland at Tullich.

**The Keeper's Park\*** (F, 448986), ðɪˈkipɛrzˈpark. A field next a gamekeeper's house west of Dinnet.

**(The) Keiloch** (OS, C, 187915), ðɪˈkiləç, from An Caolach (3), the narrow place. Killoch (Fa), the Cullach, the Caoilach (Cr 26, 47), Kulach (Roy), Kilach, Kiloch (R 1, 7), n gaolach, n gulach (D). Formerly a farm, now a group of houses near Invercauld Bridge.

**The Keiloch Puil\*** (F), ðɪˈkiləçˈpil. A composite name, includes Upper and Lower. In Dee near Invercauld.

**The Kelpie's Needle** (M, C, 429965), ðɪˈkɛlpizˈnidəl, Scots Kelpie = water spirit. A stone in Dee with a big hole in it,

also called the Deil's (i.e. Devil's) Needle, ðɪˈdilzˈnidəl, or the Needle. East of Pannanich.

**The Kennel Burn\*** (U, 228022), ðɪˈkɛnəlˈbʌrn. The bottom part of the Corndavon Burn, beside former kennels at Corndavon Lodge.

**The Kennel Burn\*** (F, 173931), as above. Lower part of Allt Dourie at Invercauld, next the kennels.

**The Kennels Wuid\*** (F, 175934), ðɪˈkɛnəlzˈwɪd. Near Invercauld House.

**The Key Pool** See Poll na h-Iuchrach.

**Khantore** (OS, 287939), from Ceann Torr (3, C), kɪnˈtor, end of hillock. Kintore (Am), Kyantor (D in A). A group of houses south of Abergeldie Castle.

**The Khantore Brae\*** (F, 287941), ðɪˌkɪnˈtorˈbreˑ. A hill on a road near Abergeldie.

**The Khantore Burn\*** (U, 286937), ðɪˌkɪnˈtorˈbʌrn. South of Abergeldie.

**The Khantore Park\*** (F, 289941), ðɪˌkɪnˈtorˈpark. Kintore Park (Am). A field south of Abergeldie, near the former farm of Khantore.

**The Khantore Wuid\*** (U, 286940), ðɪˌkɪnˈtorˈwɪd. A wood near Abergeldie.

**Kidd's Rock\*** (F, 062896), ˈkɪdsˈrɔk. A rock at Linn of Dee, above the widest pool.

**The Killing House\*** (C), ðɪˈkɛlɛnˌhus. A building formerly used for killing farm livestock locally, a job now done outside Upper Deeside. There were two near Ballater, one at 380962 at Dalmochie (now demolished), and another at 377965 near Aberdeen Cottage, now used as pony sheds.

**Kiln Croft\*** (I, 364943). Also the Paddock (F), ðɪˈpadək. A former field in lower Glen Muick, now partly overgrown with trees.

**The Kiln Know\*** (I, 145854), Scots Know = knoll. A hillock at Newbigging in Glen Clunie.

**The Kiln Park\*** (U, 416035), ðɪˈkɛlˈpark. A field west of Logie Coldstone.

**Kindrochit** (C, 152913), kɪnˈdrɔχët, from Cinn Drochaide (3), at end of bridge. In Gaelic Kindrotsh (A). Kindrocht alias Castletoun (Ca), Kindrocht (M) in 1564, the castell of Kindrocht (Rg) in 1634, Kindrocht (Pb). Also Bridgend of Castletown or Auchindryne (Me 15). Former name of Castleton of Braemar.

**Kindrochit**, as above. Former name of Braemar parish.

**The King's Butts\*** (U, 270987), ðɪˈkɪŋzˈbʌts. Grouse butts north of Crathie, named after a former king who used them. Also the Royal Butt (Af).

**The King's Butts\*** (U, 215997), as above. South of Corndavon Lodge.

**The King's Road** (Rt, 323888). Private road up west side of Muick, used by royal family.

**The King's Road\*** (154922), ðɪˈkɪŋzˈrod (F, heard at Corgarff on Don). King's Road (Blm 2). The old military road from Braemar to the Lecht. We have not heard this name on Deeside, though the old map shows it at Braemar Castle, but it is still well known at Corgarff as the right of way track from 296064 north-west to Don.

**Kingston of Monaltrie\*** Kingston of Menaltry (Opr 17). Former habitation at Monaltrie west of Crathie.

**The Kirk Burn\*** (I, JS, 396921), ðɪˈkɛrkˈbʌrn, Scots Kirk = church. Runs into Pollagach Burn south-east of Ballater, named after the Kirk Road there.

**The Kirkie Brae\*** (C, south-east of 152914), ðɪˈkɛrkiˈbreˑ. A hill in Braemar, past Episcopal Church to the school.

**The Kirk Park\*** (U, 264952), ðɪˈkɛrkˈpark. A field at Crathie.

**The Kirk Park\*** (U, 266947), as above. A field beside the church at Crathie.

**The Kirk Road** (Gf, U, c. 398924), ðɪ'kërk'rod. A path formerly used by people at Etnach in upper Glen Tanar to walk over the hills to church in Ballater (JS).

**The Kirk Road*** (U, 424979), as above. An old path from A97 road south-west to Cambus o' May Hotel.

**The Kirk Road*** (F, 358970), as above. A path from the east side of Gairn past Craggan and below the Craigendarroch Hotel to the old free church at Ballater.

**The Kirk Road** (Gf, U, 273953 and 268952), as above. A track beside Wester Micras, from Micras to Crathie church.

**The Kirk Road*** (F, 412968), as above. A path formerly used by people at Bellamore and Ballaterach walking past Pannanich to church at Ballater.

**The Kirk Road** (Gf, F, 373968), as above. An old right of way from Easter Morven to the church at Ballater, crossing the Pass of Ballater near Monaltrie House and then to Ballater by the Cinder Path.

**The Kirk Road*** (U, 286941), as above. Near Khantore at Abergeldie, along west side of stone dyke.

**Kirkstyle** (OS, F, 298011), kërk'stɛil, Scots Style = gate. A former house near the church at Gairnshiel.

**The Kirkstyle Brig*** (F, 299011), ðɪ₍kërk'stɛil'brɪg. A bridge near Gairnshiel.

**Kirkton.** Kirktoune of Glengairne (Io 9), Kirktoune (Pb), Kirktoun, Kirktown (Ab 8, Ra). A former farm at the foot of Gairn, on east side of river; Kirkton probably referred to the settlement beside the former church on east side of bridge.

**The Kirkton Wuidie*** See Tom Glady Wood.

**Kirktoun of Braemar*** Kirktown of Braemar (Opr 13).

**Kirktoun of Crathie** (Ri, S, probably 264947). Kirktoun de Crathye (Ca).

**Kirn**, also called Burn of the Kirn or Kirn Burn (A). See Easter Kirn and Wester Kirn.

**The Kirn** (Ri 13, I, F, 302842), ðɪ'kërn, Scots Kirn = churn, also used for ravines or washed-out hollows (A). A stretch of moor at the bottom end of Loch Muick, also the hill nose above at 309833 (JR). Kairn (Bs) refers to this nose.

**The Kirn Burn*** (F, 306833), ðɪ'kërn'bʌrn. Also the Rough Burn (I). Beside the above place.

**The Kist*** (U, 50 metres south-east of 247946), ðɪ'këst, Scots = box or chest, possibly Gaelic A' Chiste (3), the chest. A little pool on the Balmoral side of Dee.

**The Kist*** See Chest of Dee.

**Kitty Rankie's Cairn** See Caitir Fhrangach's Cairn.

**Kitty's Bog*** (U, 354032), 'këtez'bog. West of Morven.

**(The) Knaps of Fafernie** (OS, F, 219809), ðɪ'napsɐ₍fə'fɛrne, from Cnap (3) = a knob, or borrowing into Scots. Rocky hillocks on the county boundary south-east of Loch Callater.

**The Knobbies*** (F, 360023, on site of Tom Garchory OS which should be at 357015), ðɪ'nobiz. Hillocks south-west of Morven.

**Knock** (OS, 351952), locally the Knocks (C), ðɪ'knoks, often now ðɪ'noks, named from the nearby hill of the Knock and other knolls, from Cnoc (3) = a knoll. Cnocke (G 4), Knock (Io 33), Knocks (Opr 45) in 1822. A farm west of Ballater.

**The Knock** (OS, C, 348957), ðɪ'nok, from An Cnoc (3), the knoll. A low hill west of Ballater.

**The Knock** (OS, C, 088890), ðɪ'nok, from An Cnoc (2, JB), n'grok. Knock of Inverey (Me 21), Inverey Cottage (OS 1869). A house on a low knoll at Inverey, formerly a farm.

**Knockan** (OS, I, U, 221937), 'knokɐn, from Cnocan (3), little knoll. Knockan of Aberarder (Opr 16). A former farm west of the Inver.

**Knockanduie** (OS, U, 235939), ₍knokɐn'dui, from Cnoc an t-Suidhe (3̇), knoll of the level shelf. Cnoctuie (Ce 1),

Knockandowie (Cpb 10). Also (the) Toll Cottage (Er), locally the Toll House (C), ðɪ'tol₍hus. A house beside the Inver.

**The Knockan Kirk*** (U, 221937), ðɪ'knokɐn'kërk. Also the Mission Church (Gf). A former church and school just east of Knockan, west of the Inver.

**The Knockan Parkie*** (U, 216938), ðɪ'knokɐn'parki, Scots Parkie = little field. A small narrow field west of the Inver.

**Knock Castle** (OS, C, 352952), 'knok'kasəl, often now 'nok or 'noks'kasəl. Also Caisteal Cnoc (3), castle at knoll. Castyal Crochk (D). Remains of a castle west of Ballater.

**Knockie Branar** (OS, 401928), from Cnocaidh Branndair (3, C), ₍knokɐ'brandër, little hill of place of tangled roots (note D 202). Knock Brander (Ri 29), Knockiebrander (Gler), Knockie Branders (Io 43a). Fir roots are in the peat around this hill south of Pannanich.

**Knock of Aberarder*** See Cnoc.

**(The) Knock of Lawsie** (OS, F, 261965), ðɪ'knokɐ'la·zi. Cnochd Lawsie (R 3) indicates an original Cnoc ? Lamhsaich (5), knoll of Lawsie (see Lawsie). North of Crathie.

**The Knock of the Branndair*** See Peter's Hill.

**The Knock Park*** (U, 338953), ðɪ'nok'park. A field west of Ballater.

**The Knocks Brae*** (C, 353949), ðɪ'noks'bre·. A hill on the road west of Ballater.

**(The) Knocks Cottages** (OS, C, 352749), ðɪ'noks'kotədʒɪz. West of Ballater.

**(The) Knocks House** (OS, C, 340953), ðɪ'noks'hus. West of Ballater.

**The Knocks Wuid*** (F, 349949), ðɪ'noks'wɪd. A wood west of Ballater.

**The Knock Wuid*** (C, 090890), ðɪ'nok'wɪd. A wood at Inverey.

**The Know of Garbh-choire*** See Tom Dubh Garbh-choire.

**Lach na Gualainn** (OS, 397918), from Lag na Gualainn (3), hollow of the shoulder. A hollow below a long shoulder in upper Glen Tanar.

**Lachy's Wood** (Dil, probably 318006). Named after Lachlan McIntosh, a former Catholic priest in Glen Gairn.

**The Ladder*** (C, 259856), ðɪ'ladër, probably from An Leitir (3), the slope. A steep slope on Lochnagar.

**The Ladder** (Al, C, 258855), as above. A zig-zag path, originally made for deer stalkers, up the above slope.

**The Ladies' Boat** See Invercauld House Boat.

**Lady McQuarrie's Chair*** (U, 292962), 'ledimə'kworez'tʃer, 'ledimə'korez'tʃer. No local story, so first two words possibly from Gaelic. Two boulders forming a huge seat, at Micras.

**Lady's Boat Pool** See Lower Boat Pool.

**The Lafts*** (Am, 348937), ? Scots Laft = loft, upper floor. A field opposite Birkhall Cottage in lower Glen Muick.

**Lag a' Bhagaiste** (3, 081885), hollow of the baggage. Lag-a-bhagaiste, a deep gully (Gr) south-west of Inverey. Stolen booty was said to have been stored there (Gr 169).

**An Lagan** (3, U, 150905), ðɪ'lagən, the little hollow. Laggan (A). On Braemar Golf Course.

**The Lagan Pool*** (F, 150905), ðɪ'lagən'pul. On Clunie near Braemar.

**Lag an Amair*** (3, 161915), hollow of the channel. Lack-n-amer (I). In Corrie Feragie east of Braemar.

**Lag an Daimh*** (3, 228005), hollow of the stag or ox. Lag n Daibh, Lackindae or ox how, Laighn-Daoidh (R 3, 5, 14). A hollow south of Corndavon Lodge.

**Lag an Làmhaich** (4, U, 148905), ₍lagən'lae.əç, hollow of the gleaning. N d lagan lly-ach, corn was always laid on it (D), Lagan Laimhach (A). A field south of Braemar.

**Lag an t-Searraich** (3, D, 143901), hollow of the colt. On

Morrone above Braemar. Diack noted there were several places of this name in Braemar, but unfortunately did not say exactly where.

**Lag Chairr*** (3, 346974), hollow of the rough ground. Lagharr (I). A field on rough ground near the Bridge of Gairn, now partly taken over by trees.

**The Laggan** See Inverenzie.

**The Laggan Brig*** (C, 330007), ðɪˈlagənˈbrɪg. In Glen Fenzie.

**The Laggan Burn** (C, 329008), ðɪˈlagənˈbʌrn. Laggan Burn (Afr). The lower part of Glenfenzie Burn.

**Laggan Cottage** (OS, C, 329007), ˈlagənˈkɔtədʒ. Laggan (OS 1869). At the bottom of Glen Fenzie in Glen Gairn, named after the Laggan.

**Lag Garbh*** (3, 187891), rough hollow. Lack Garraw (R 7). In Glen Beg, Ballochbuie Forest.

**Lag Geal*** (OSn, probably north-east of 273928), white hollow, after its many white stones. South of Balmoral.

**Lag Luachrach*** (3, 162852), rushy hollow. Lack Luachrach (R 13). A damp hollow in lower Glen Callater.

**Lag na Coille*** (3, U, west of 209907), ˌlagnəˈkɛil, hollow of the wood. A hollow low down in the eastern part of Ballochbuie Forest.

**The Lag na Coille Path*** (C, 211904), ðɪˌlagnɐˈkɛilˈpaθ. In Ballochbuie Forest.

**Lag na Creige*** (3, 177928), hollow of the rock. Lag na Craig (R 7). Above Invercauld House.

**Lag nam Buachaillean*** (3, 273970), hollow of the herdsmen, with Buachaillean probably a variant genitive plural. Lag-na-buachaillean (R 3). East of an old stone dyke north-east of Crathie.

**Laich Yards*** (387975), Scots Laich = low. Laigh Yards (R 4). On farmland at Tullich.

**The Laird and his Lady** (U, 373967), ðɪˈlerdənɪzˈledi. Twin larch trees near Monaltrie House at Ballater, both now blown down (1984).

**The Laird of Cluny's Charter Chest** See Charter's Chest.

**The Laird's Bed** (McC 1891, Wy, U, 331913), ðɪˈlerdzˈbɛd. A shelf of rock on the Coyle in lower Glen Muick, used after the 1745 rising by Joseph Gordon of Birkhall (McC, Wy).

**The Laird's Moss*** (U, 305954), ðɪˈlerdzˈmɔs. A peat-moss east of Abergeldie.

**The Laird's Park*** (F, 117895), ðɪˈlerdzˈpark. A rough field east of Corriemulzie.

**The Laird's Seat** (Nei, 318005). A mound near a former chapel in Glen Gairn, named after a former laird at Dalfad.

**The Laird's Tablecloth** (Afr, F, 093979), ðɪˈlerdzˈtebəlˌklɔθ. The small patch of snow in late summer in Ear-choire Sneachdach on Beinn a' Bhuird, prominent from Invercauld. The local legend is that if the snow disappears the Farquharsons will lose Invercauld. In fact it melts completely in most summers, but the most the lairds have been said to admit was that the tablecloth might be very dirty but was still there!

**The Laird's Well** (Nei, north of 318005). Near a former chapel (see the Laird's Seat) in Glen Gairn.

**The Lairig*** (C), ðɪˈlaˑrɪg. Often used for short for Lairig Ghru or Lairig an Laoigh, especially for Lairig Ghru.

**Lairig an Laoigh** (OS, 033004), should be Làirig Laoigh (3, C), ˌlaˑrɪgˈlui, often ðɪˌlaˑrɪgˈlui (in Gaelic la.rɪkˈlui (A)), the pass of Lui or calf-one, referring to Lui Water. A pass Larig Lui (Roy). Also An Làirig Shìos (3, U), nˌlaˑrɪgˈhiˑs, the east pass, an Lairig shios (D). Now often the East Lairig (D, C), ðɪˈist ˈlaˑrɪg. From Glen Lui to Abernethy on Spey.

**Làirig Bheag*** (3, 229997), little pass. Little Larig (R 3, 9), Larigh Bheig (R 14). Also shown (R), at 216011 and 221006, so obviously started approximately where Wester Shenalt

joins Gairn and reached its highest point at 229997. South-west of Corndavon Lodge, pairs with Lairig Mhor.

**Làirig Bheàrraidh** (3, F, 254958), ˌlaˑrɪgˈvjaˑre, short pass. Larig vyarri (D). A short road from the Gairnshiel road to the Braemar road west of Crathie.

**Làirig Bhràighdean** (3, 218804), pass of pack-saddles, presumably meaning fit for horses with a pack-saddle. Larig vrachtan, braghdan was a kind of pack-saddle (D in A). Note Camas-bhrachdain in Glen Lyon (T 35, 290). The pass from Callater over to Glen Doll.

**Lairig Ghru** (OS, C, 973012), ˌlaˑrɪgˈgru, often ðɪˌlaˑrɪgˈgruˑ (in Gaelic la.rɪkˈhru (A)), ˌlaˑrɪgˈruː (Sch), should be Làirig Dhrù (3), pass of Dru or Druie, referring to Allt Dhrù which becomes River Druie lower down on the Rothiemurchus side of the pass. Tullochgrue and Inverdruie in Rothiemurchus are other examples of the word, which is probably from Drù = flow (Mb), or Drùthaidh = oozing. Largrue (Fa), Larig Grue (Roy), the Larig Ru (Gr), Larig Ru, in Gaelic Larig Dhru from Druie (Mp in 1906, from Gaelic spoken in the Braemar district), Lairig Dhru (Mb, W, D, A). Also An Làirig Shuas (3, U), ðɪˌlaˑrɪgˈhuəs, the west or upstream pass. Laraig shuas (D). Formerly was sometimes the West Lairig (D) but this name has died out, though the East Lairig is still frequently used for Lairig an Laoigh.

**The Lairig Glen** (982962). The Larig Glen, a continuation of Glen Dee (Gi). See Glen Dee.

**The Lairig Lochans*** (U, 994935), ðɪˈlaˑrɪgˈlɔχɛnz. A composite name for this tarn and Lochan Feith nan Sgor slightly to the north, below the path from Luibeg to the Lairig Ghru.

**Làirig Mhór*** (3, 225998), big pass. Larig, Larigh Mhoir (R 9, 14), an Lairig (T 33). Further west and higher up than the nearby Lairig Bheag. Also Muckle Lairig. Meikle Larig (R 3). The name still lives on in the names the North Lairig and the South Lairig (U), referring to the parts of it north of the pass summit on Tom Breac, and south of the summit. South of Corndavon Lodge.

**Làirig nam Bràidean** (3, U, 124852), ˌlaˑrɪgnɐˈbraˑtɐn, pass of the mountains, or of the horse-collars (see also Lairig Bhraighdean). From upper Glen Clunie to Glen Ey via Coire na Lairige. Also the Pass o the Salmon (U), ðɪˈpasɪðɪˈsaˑmən, but this was obviously a mistake in translation, Bradan = salmon being a more common word than Bhràighdean, or Bràidean.

**The Lairig Path*** (U, 132839), ðɪˈlaˑrɪgˈpaθ, up the east side of Coire na Lairige in upper Glen Clunie.

**Lairig Shios** See Lairig an Laoigh.

**Lairig Shuas** See Lairig Ghru.

**Lair of Aldararie** (OS, 312780), from the Lair of Allt Darrarie (C), ðɪˈlerɐˌaltˈdarəre, Scots Lair = boggy area. The Lair of Ault Darrarie (I), Lair Aldararie (Sm). A hilltop south of Loch Muick, at the head of a peaty basin.

**The Lamb Corrie*** (U, 254007), ðɪˈlamˈkɔre. West of Gairnshiel.

**Lamont's Seat** (Cj 1, 090978). A circle of low stones near the South Top of Beinn a' Bhuird, once used by deer watchers on Mar Forest.

**The Land*** (C), ðɪˈlaˑnd. A collective name for the farmland on the west side of Clunie between Braemar village and Dee.

**The Land*** (C), as above. A collective name for farmland between Inverey and Dee.

**The Land*** (U), as above. A collective name for farmland at Tomintoul above Braemar.

**Landseer's Mound** (Wy, north-west of 083893). A knoll in Little Inverey where Landseer 'painted the background to one of his most famous pictures' (Wy).

**The Lang Back*** (U, 297958), ðɪˈlaŋˈbak, Scots Lang = long. A field that could formerly be ploughed only in a long narrow section because of piles of stones on either side; these piles eventually disappeared in the 1920s when roadmen used them for road metal, thus allowing the whole field to be ploughed (WD). The name goes back to the period before the 1920s. East of Crathie.

**The Lang Bend** (C, 411981), ðɪˈlaŋˈbɛnd. The Bog (Ly). Long Bend (P). A pool in Dee at Cambus o' May.

**The Lang Cast** (C, 451979), ðɪˈlaŋˈkast. Long Cast (Sc). A pool in Dee, south-west of Dinnet.

**The Lang Fuird** (U, 129912), ðɪˈlaŋˈfjurd. The Long Ford (Gf). A former ford west of Braemar, long because it crossed Dee at an angle from south-east to north-west.

**The Lang Haugh*** (U, 436968), ðɪˈlaŋˈhaˑχ. A field by Dee, east of Pannanich.

**The Lang Haugh*** (U, 423041), as above. A field west of Logie Coldstone.

**The Lang Haugh*** (U, 355944), as above. The Long Haugh (Am). A field in lower Glen Muick.

**The Lang Lot*** (U, 147917), ðɪˈlaŋˈlɔt. A long field at Braemar.

**The Lang Mile*** See the Inver Straucht.

**The Lang Park*** See Burnside.

**The Lang Park*** See An Roinn Mhor.

**The Lang Puil** (C, 361952), ðɪˈlaŋˈpil. Long Pool (Sc). In Dee at Ballater.

**The Lang Puil*** See Poll Churraich.

**The Lang Puil** See Poll Choinnich.

**The Lang Straucht*** (F, 309965), ðɪˈlaŋˈstraχt. Usually now the Coillies Straight (C), ðɪˈkeiliz'streçt, after the nearby Coilacriech. A long straight road west of Ballater.

**The Lang Straucht*** (F, 316004), as above. A road east of Gairnshiel.

**The Lang Straucht*** (U, 351917), as above. A road in Glen Muick.

**The Lang Straucht*** (F, 357950), as above. A road south of Ballater.

**The Lang Straucht*** (U, 418046), as above. A long, straight-sided field west of Logie Coldstone.

**The Lang Straucht** (Gf, U, 464990), as above. A road near Dinnet.

**The Lang Straucht*** (U, 394977), as above. A road at Tullich.

**Lang Toman a' Bhothain*** (F, 413032), 'laŋˌtamnəˈvon. A field south-west of Logie Coldstone.

**The Lanie*** (F, 423962), ðɪˈlene, Scots = little lane. A path west of the houses at Inchmarnoch, on the north side of the burn.

**Na Lanndaichen*** (3, 366935), the enclosures. The Launtikins, moor and mark of ridges (I). An area showing regular ridges as if it had been enclosed and some attempt made at cultivation. On the hill south of Ballater.

**The Lantern*** (F, 409997), ðɪˈlantɛrn. A lantern-shaped point on a hillside north-west of Cambus o' May.

**Larach Mhór*** (3, 349917), big site or farm. Larach Mhor (I). A field in Glen Muick.

**The Larch Tree*** (F, 430925), ðɪˈlartʃˈtri. A gnarled old larch in Glen Tanar, prominent in a wood of Old Caledonian firs.

**The Larch Tree Puil** (F, north of 360958), ðɪˈlartʃˈtriˈpil. Larch Tree (Sc). A pool in Dee above Ballater.

**Lary** (OS, C, 336002), 'leˑre, ? from Làraigh, a locative from Làrach (5) = site of a building (Aldlarie, Badenoch was 'Gaelic Allt-Làirigh, the stream of the làrach or gorge' (Mb 1890)), Gaelic Lāri (D). Lairie (G 8, Ro). Also Lower Lary (F), 'loërˈleˑre. A farm in Glen Gairn.

**(The) Lary Burn** (OS, C, 340005), ðɪˈleˑreˈbʌrn. Burn of Lairie (I). Beside the above place.

**(The) Lary Hill** (OS, C, 332015), ðɪˈleˑreˈhël. East of Gairnshiel.

**The Latch of Dubh-loch*** See Allt an Dubh-loch.

**The Latch of the Dubh-loch** See Caochan Tarsuinn.

**The Laundry Puil** (C, 257953), ðɪˈlandriˈpil. Laundry Pool (P). In Dee beside Balmoral Castle.

**The Laundry Wuid*** (C, 115892), ðɪˈlandriˈwɪd. At Corriemulzie, named after a former laundry for Mar Lodge.

**Lawsie** (OS, C, 261960), 'laːzi, ? from An Lamhsaich (5), meaning uncertain, Gaelic Lausich, nasal, n lausich (D in A). Lausie (Ri 18), Lausich (Cr 54), Laazie (A). The *lasie* in Birselasie north of Torphins has the same pronunciation. A former farm near Crathie.

**The Lawsie Burn*** (F, 262960), ðɪˈlaˑziˈbʌrn. Lower part of Rintarsin Burn.

**The Lawsie Corrie*** (F, 268972), ðɪˈlaˑziˈkǫre. North of Crathie.

**Lawsie Moss*** (R 3, 238987). An area on the peat-mosses north-west of Crathie, not near Lawsie but refers to the area of peat formerly worked by people from Lawsie.

**The Lawsie Rig*** (U, 265980), ðɪˈlaˑziˈrɪg, Scots Rig = ridge. To Gairnside folk this was the skyline on a short-cut route over the hill to Lawsie and Crathie.

**Laws Rock*** See Cadha Shiorram.

**Leabaidh an Daimh Bhuidhe** (OS, 132018), bed of the yellow stag. Marked at the summit of Ben Avon, presumably referring to the ground below the summit rock. The summit rock is Stob Dubh Easaidh Mor.

**Leabaidh Choirneil*** See the Colonel's Bed.

**Leac an Uidhear** See Carn an 'Ic Duibhe.

**Leac Chruaidh*** (4, 310011), hard slope. Lea Cruie (I). A field east of Gairnshiel.

**An Leac Dhubh*** (3, U, 188873), ðɪˈliɐχˈdu, the black slope. A slope with slabby rocks in Glen Beg, Ballochbuie Forest.

**Leac Ghorm** (OS, 222954), should be An Sglèat Gorm (3), the blue slate. Scleat-ghorm, Scliach-gorm (R 3, 14). The second name shows a stage towards the present pronunciation ðɪˌsliɐχˈgɔrɔm (C), Slioch gorm (D). A hill with flat, slate-like rocks, north-west of the Inver.

**Leac Ghorm** (OS, 943932), blue slope. Lieachk Gorm (Mg). A gentle grassy slope with some greyish-blue screes at the south end of the Monadh Mor, above Glen Geusachan.

**The Leachd Roadie*** (U, 261006), ðɪˈlɛçtˈrodi, Gaelic Leachd (3) = declivity. An old track west of Gairnshiel.

**The Lead Mines** (F, 371973), ðɪˈlɛdˈmɛinz. Old Lead Mine (OS 1904). Former mines near the Pass of Ballater.

**Leathad Gheallaidh** (3, U, 022892), ˌlɛɐtˈjole, slope of the Geldie or clear one, referring to the stream. Leadyolly, Lead-yeolley, three miles up from Inverey (Mf), Gaelic speech Gheaully (M), Lyet yollidh (D in A). The slope where Geldie joins Dee.

**Leathad Grianain*** (3, 147814), slope of sunny spot. Leat Grianan (I). North of the Cairnwell.

**Leathad nan Saighdear*** (3, 128819), slope of the soldiers. Leytt ni Saydir a glen room in the baddoch, Letnansoidar (Cr 30, 41), Leadnasaider (Io 53), Letnasoider (I), Lednasoidher (R 14). Lytnasydarin and Leitnaseidarin (Io 16, 33) indicate Saighdearan, a variant genitive plural. A former farm up the Baddoch.

**(The) Lebhall** (OS, C, 299961), ðɪˈlɛvəl, from An Leth-bhaile (2, Sg, ED, WD), the half farm-town. Midtown Micras (Opr 21), Midd Micras, Middle Micras (Im 3), the Leaval or Mid Micrass (I), Mid Micras (Leval) (Ri 34a), Gaelic speech Lével (M), N lyēvəl (D), 'ljɛvɐl (Sch). A farm east of Crathie.

**The Lebhall Burn*** See Burn of Lebhall.

**Leisean Dubh-choille*** (3, WR, 339998), ˌleiʃɐnˈduçəl, little thigh of black wood. A little enclosed patch in a wood in Glen Gairn.

**Leitir Aitinn** (3, 185015), slope of juniper. Lettrettyne, Lettretine (Ri 17), Leater Aiten (I). A former shieling south of Loch Builg.

**Leitir an t-Suidhe** (3), slope of the level shelf. Letterendowie (Mc 3), Letterindowie (Io 25a, Me 3), Ladderindowie (Io 74). A former shieling in Glen Callater.

**An Leitir Bheag\*** (3, U, 074875), ðɪˌliʃtjërˈvɐg, the little slope. A grazing on a slope in lower Glen Ey, now mostly inside a plantation, stretches as far north as the dyke south of Colonel's Cave. Pairs with the name below.

**An Leitir Mhór\*** (3, U, 090875), ðɪˌliʃtjërˈvoːr, the big slope. As above, stretches from Alltan Imire southwards to the dyke on the Carn Dearg. Cristie vor and C. vek were grazings (D), but this was probably an error for An Leitir Mhor and Bheag.

**Leitir Mhór\*** (3, 235024), big slope. Lettermhore, Leder Mhoir (R 3, 14). A long slope near Corndavon Lodge.

**Leitir Mhór\*** (3, 117920), big slope. Lettermor silva (Go). A slope at the mouth of Glen Quoich.

**The Lesser Cairngorm** See Derry Cairngorm.

**Leth-allt Pool** See Poll Leth-allt.

**The Leth-allt Wuid\*** (F, 053890), ðɪˈljɐɐltˈwɪd. A wood near the Linn of Dee.

**An Leth-taobhach** (3), half side. 'All one side of Glengairn, or anywhere else, was called n lyetach; suas an letach, up the glen side' (D). Also the Half Dabhach (F), ðɪˈhafˈdaˑχ, referring to one side of Glen Gairn from Kirkstyle to Balno. The Half Dauch (Gr). This suggests An Leth-dabhach but Diack's evidence goes against this, though it may be correct in other cases of the name Lettoch or Leddach. The Half Dabhach may therefore be an incorrect translation, the terms Dabhach and Half Dabhach being well known but Taobhach being less well known. A Dabhach or Davoch was a former Scots measure of agricultural production (Ja, MacQueen 1979).

**Leth-taobhach Fhreumh** (3, 363043), lɛdaˈhre (A), half side (i.e. slope on one side of a hill) of roots. Leadach Reave (I), the Lettach Rae (A). North-east of Morven Lodge.

**Leth-taobh Cathaidh** (3, U, 097873), ˌleçteˈkai, half side (see above) of snow drifting. Lethtaobh Cathaidh, lyeti ca-i (D in A), Lyeti-ky, leth-taobh ky, the last word uncertainly thought to be Mackay, any hill slope being called leacainn, or lyeti (D). An exposed hillside above lower Glen Ey.

**The Letter Box Park\*** (F, 335000), ðɪˈlɛtërˌbɒksˈpark. A field at Lary in Glen Gairn, on west side of road.

**Leum na Gaoithe** (3, WD, 329965), ˌlemnɐˈgui, leap of the wind. Luimnaghui (Gr). Also the Windy Turn (A, C), ðɪˈwɪmiˈtʌrn. A windy corner west of Gairnshiel.

**Leyhead** (H, Ro, U, 419049), lɛiˈhẹd. Leyheade (Pb). A former farm west of Logie Coldstone.

**The Leys\*** (Gler, 412918). The enclosed former farmland at Etnach in Glen Tanar.

**Leys of Ballater\*** (Opr 36). A former habitation, presumably on farmland, near Ballater.

**Liath-choire** See Carn Liath.

**An Liath-choire Beag\*** (3, F, 170972), ðɪˈliɐçareˈbẹg, the little grey corrie. Lia Chorry Beg (I), Lia chorie Bheg (R 14). On south-east side of Carn Liath north of Invercauld, pairs with the corrie below.

**(An) Liath-choire Mhór\*** (OS, 3, 163982), the big grey corrie, An Liath-choire Mór would be classic form. Lia Chorry more (I), Lia chorie Mhoir (R 14). Also the Muckle Liath-choire (F), ðɪˈmʌkəlˈliɐçare. Muckle Licherie, Liath-choire (A 283). On north side of Carn Liath, north of Invercauld, pairs with the corrie above.

**The Liftin Stane** (F, 230934), ðɪˈlëftënˌstin, usually now Donald Dinnie's Stane (C), ˈdɒnəlˈdënezˈstin, after the athlete who lifted it. Lifting Stone (A). Opposite Inver Inn.

**The Lime Kiln Butts\*** (U, 278037), ðɪˈlɛimˌkël'bʌts. Grouse butts north-west of Gairnshiel.

**The Lime Kiln Park\*** (F, 288946), ðɪˈlɛimˌkël'park. Lime Kiln Park (Am). A field south of Abergeldie.

**The Lime Kiln Park\*** (U, 347915), as above. A field in Glen Muick.

**The Lime Kiln Park\*** (U, 334960), as above. A field on lower Girnock.

**Lime Kiln Park\*** (175923). Lime Kill Park (Im 4). A former field at Invercauld.

**The Lime Kiln Puil\*** (U, 140837), ðɪˈlɛimˌkël'pil. A pool in Glen Clunie.

**The Lime Kiln Road\*** (U, 380976), ðɪˈlɛimˌkël'rod. A road to a lime kiln near Tullich, now mostly bulldozed into a wider road to a radio mast.

**Lindsay's Burn** (OS, F, 278828), ˈlɪnzizˈbʌrn. Runs into Loch Muick.

**The Linn Brae\*** (F, 062896, north of bridge), ðɪˈlënˈbreˑ. Scots Linn = rocky gorge with pools. A hill on the road at Linn of Dee.

**The Linn Brae\*** (C, 336898), as above. A hill on the road at Linn of Muick.

**Linn Cottage** See Muir.

**The Linn o Allt Fileachaidh\*** (F, 323848), ðɪˈlënɐˌaltˈfiləçi. A waterfall with rocks, in upper Glen Muick.

**The Linn o Callater\*** (U, 159880), ðɪˈlënɐˈkalətër, more often now the Callater Linn (F). A small rocky gorge on lower Callater.

**The Linn o Clunie\*** (F, 151914), ðɪˈlënɐˈkluni. At Braemar.

**The Linn of Allt a' Chlair** See Eas Allt a' Chlair.

**The Linn of Allt Dobharaidh\*** (377012), The Linn of Auldowrie (G 19). A narrow channel in a burn south of Morven.

**(The) Linn of Corriemulzie** (OS, C, 112894), ðɪˈlënɐˌkɒreˈmulzi. Also Eas Coire Mhuillidh (3, U), ˌesˌkɒrˈmulji, linn of corrie fit for driving a mill. Below the road at Corriemulzie, east of Inverey.

**(The) Linn of Dee** (OS, C, 062896), ðɪˈlënɐˈdiˑ, often just the Linn (C). Also Eas Dé (2, D, A), ess De (D), ɛsˈdje (A), waterfall of Dee or goddess (see River Dee). Also An Linne (3, D), the linn. The Lin of Die (G 2), Yelin (Go). West of Inverey.

**The Linn of Dee Brig** (C, 062896), ðɪˈlënɐˈdiˈbrɪg. The Linn of Dee Bridge (Gf). Also Drochaid Linne (3, U), drɒχtˈlɪn, bridge of linn. Bridge at the Linn of Dee.

**Linn of Dee Pool**. Linn o' Dee Pool (Ly). Pools in Dee, locally called the Linn of Dee.

**The Linn of Lui** See Easan Laoigh.

**(The) Linn of Muick** (OS, C, 332895), ðɪˈlënɐˈmëk. In mid Glen Muick.

**Linn of Muick Cottage** (OS, 335897), locally usually the Linn (C), ðɪˈlën, or the Linn of Muick (C) as above.

**(The) Linn of Quoich** (OS, C, 115913), ðɪˈlënɐˈkɔɪç. Near the foot of Glen Quoich.

**The Linn of Quoich\*** (118912), as above. Lin of Queich (Crg 9). A house, now usually called simply the Quoich (Er, C), ðɪˈkɔɪç.

**(The) Linn of Tanar** (OS, C, 387890), ðɪˈlënɐˈtɑˑnɐr. In upper Glen Tanar.

**The Linn Park\*** (U, 346910), ðɪˈlënˈpark. A field downstream from the Linn of Muick.

**The Linn Wuid\*** (C, 062895), ðɪˈlënˈwɪd. A wood above the Linn of Dee.

**The Linn Wuid** (C, 339898), as above. The Linn Wood (McC). Near the Linn of Muick.

**Lint Mill\*** Lint Miln (Io 55), Lint Milln (Rli 23). At Castleton of Braemar or Glen Clunie.

**Lint Mill Croft\*** Lint Miln Croft (Io 55). At Castleton of Braemar or Glen Clunie.

**(The) Lion's Face** (OS, C, 166917), ðɪˈlae.ənzˈfes. Also Creag a'

Ballater, the largest settlement in Upper Deeside, from the woods of Craig Coillich, looking north-west to the Knock (left) and Geallaig Hill (right).

Sklaichie Brae, the north end of Dee Street, Ballater, with the oakwood and rocks of Craigendarroch behind.

Mhortair (3), rock of the murderer. Cregg-a' mhurdair (Mg). East of Braemar.

**The Lion's Face Quarry*** (C, 167920), ðɪ'lae.ənz'fes'kware. East of Braemar.

**Lion's Face Road*** See the Queen's Drive.

**Lios Mór*** (3, south of 153897), big garden. Lessmore (I). A former field, now part of Braemar Golf Course.

**Little Allanaquoich** (117910). Little Allanquoiche (Anon 8), Little Alenchoich (Fa), Little Allanaquoich (Cr 34). Also Wester Allanaquoich. Wester or Little Allanquoich (Cr in 1703–57), Wester Allanquoich (Ri 23). A former farm on west side of Quoich.

**Little Ardmeanach*** Little Armenach, Little Ardmanach (G 10, 28). A former farm west of Ballater, different from Wester Ardmeanach and probably different from Easter Ardmeanach.

**Little Athan Phuill** (F, 290955), 'lëtəl,aˑn'ful, often just Little Athan. See Athan Phuill. A pool in Dee near Abergeldie.

**Little Auchallater** See Easter Auchallater.

**Little Aucholzie** See An Geinn Dearg.

**The Little Back Latch** See Allt Coire Uilleim Mhoir.

**Little Balintober*** See Littleton.

**Little Bealach Dearg*** (179995). Little Balloch Derg (I). A subsidiary summit on the Bealach Dearg road south of Loch Builg.

**The Little Beinn a' Chaorainn** See Beinn a' Chaorainn Bheag.

**The Little Beinn Iutharn** See Beinn Iutharn Bheag.

**Little Brochdhu*** Little Brochdoie (G 36). A former farm in lower Glen Muick.

**The Little Bruach Ruadh Puil** (F, 277950), ðɪ'lëtəl,broɣ'roi'pil. Little Broch Roy (P). Also the Upper Bruach Ruadh Puil (F), ðɪ'ʌpër,broɣ'roi'pil. Pairs with Big, and with Lower and Middle. A pool in Dee east of Crathie.

**Little Burn** (OS, 367022, should be at 361031, 367022 is Allt Roinn a' Bhathaich). Also 361031 was Allt Beag (3), little burn. Auld Begg, Auldbeg or Little Burn (Io 20), Aldbeg (G 19). Also now the Back Burn (U), ðɪ'bak'bʌrn. South-west of Morven.

**The Little Cadha Chuirn** See Cac Carn Beag.

**(The) Little Cairn** (OS, I, F, 389043), ðɪ'lëtəl'kern̩. A cairn on a stony little top called the Blue Cairn of Morven.

**The Little Cairn*** (I, 293017). A low stony hill north of Gairnshiel.

**(The) Little Cairngorm** (OS, C, 020972), ðɪ'lëtəl,kern̩'gǫrəm, from An Carn Gorm Beag (3, U), the little blue hill. Carn Gorm Beag an Doire (3), now Little Cairn Gorm of Derry (Bu). A subsidiary top on Derry Cairngorm, above Glen Derry.

**Little Caochan Duird*** See Caochan Duird Beag.

**The Little Caochan Ruadh*** See Caochan Ruadh Beag.

**Little Caochan Tachaidh*** See Caochan Tachaidh Beag.

**The Little Caorainn*** See Wester Kirn.

**Little Carn an t-Sagairt** See Carn an t-Sagairt Beag.

**Little Carn an Tuirc** See Carn an Tuirc Beag.

**The Little Ceannair** (C, 450994), ðɪ'lëtəl'kënër, from Ceannair or Ceanndair (3), head water, referring to the former name of nearby Loch Kinord. Parvas Keandore (Ab 19), Mickle and Little Candors (G 9), Little Kinner (A). A house and former farm near Dinnet, pairs with Muckle Ceannair (see Meikle Kinord).

**The Little Cluain*** (356928), Cluain (3) = meadow. The Little Cluhan (I). A former field in lower Glen Muick.

**Little Cnap a' Choire Bhuidhe*** (U, 233903), 'lëtəl'knapɐ,kǫr 'bui. Knap of Little Cor buie (Io 78), Little Knap of Corbuie (B). Probably Scots form Little Knap o Coire Buidhe. A little rocky knob west of Glen Gelder.

**Little Cnapan Nathraichean*** (231882), from Little Cnapan Fhearchair, see Cnapan Nathraichean. Little Knapan erachar (B). A hilltop north-west of Lochnagar.

**The Little Coire Buidhe** See An Coire Buidhe Beag.

**Little Coire Dubh*** (222864). Little Corry Du (R 7). Pairs with Muckle Coire Dubh, west of Lochnagar.

**Little Conachcraig** (OS, C, 272891), 'lëtəl'kǫnɐχrek. A rocky little hill in upper Glen Gelder.

**The Little Corrie*** (F, 191878), ðɪ'lëtəl'kǫre. Little Corrie (Bs). Pairs with the Big Corrie. In Glenbeg, Ballochbuie Forest.

**(The) Little Corrie of Lochnagar** (OS, B, C, 256869), ðɪ'lëtəl 'kǫrɐ,lǫχnə'gaˑr. A subsidiary small corrie below the main Corrie of Lochnagar.

**Little Craig** (OS, 302872). Above Inchnabobart in upper Glen Muick.

**(The) Little Craig** (OS, U, 294011), ðɪ'lëtəl'kreg. Also Creagan Mór (3), big rocklet. Craggan More (I). A low rocky top above Gairnshiel.

**(The) Little Craig** (OS, I, F, 248815), as above. Also A' Chreag Bheag (3), the little rocky hill. Craig Beg (R 16). Note the Little Craig o the Dubh-loch just to the north. West of Loch Muick.

**The Little Craig*** (F, 263938), as above. Little Craig (B). Little Craig Cottage (Er) lies below. A small rocky hillock above the distillery at Balmoral, part of the larger Creag an Lurachain.

**The Little Craig*** See Creag Corraidh.

**The Little Craig o the Dubh-loch*** (U, 248818), ðɪ'lëtəl'kregɪðɪ 'du,lǫχ, Little Craig of the Dulloch (I). A cliff west of Loch Muick, much smaller than the massive wall of Creag an Dubh-loch further up the valley. The flat little top to the south is the Little Craig, obviously taking its name from the nearby cliff.

**Little Creag an Dail** See Creag an Dail Beag.

**Little Creagan Reamhar*** (180926), pairs with Craggan Rour higher up the same hill. Little Craggan Rour (R7). A rocky hillock near Invercauld.

**The Little Creag Liath*** See Creag Liath Bheag.

**Little Creag Mhor*** See Creag Bheag.

**Little Creag nan Gall*** (F, 267926), 'lëtəl,kregnɐ'gaˑl. A low top north-east of Creag nan Gall, south of Easter Balmoral.

**Little Croft*** (R 4, 391976). Also Little Croft North (Io 58). On farmland at Tullich.

**Little Croft** See the Crofts.

**Little Croft*** (R 4, 385973). On farmland at Tullich.

**Little Croft North*** See Little Croft.

**Little Croft South of Kirk*** (R 4, 391975). Little Croft South of the Kirk (Io 58). On farmland beside the Tullich Kirk.

**Little Culardoch** See Culardoch Bheag.

**The Little Dam*** (F, 267938), ðɪ'lëtəl'dam. A water reservoir at the distillery at Balmoral.

**Little Donal*** (U, 439972), 'lëtəl'dǫnəl, as in Scots pronunciation of Donald. Pairs with Big Donal. A former little triangular field south of the Muir of Dinnet.

**The Little Dooker*** See the Dooker.

**Little Druim*** (B, 245921), Druim (3) = a ridge. A small ridge in lower Glen Gelder.

**The Little Dubh-chlais*** (B, F, 258938), ðɪ'lëtəl'du,çlaʃ. A small dark hollow that pairs with the bigger Dubh-chlais or Muckle Dubh-chlais at Balmoral.

**The Little Dubh-chlais Burn*** (F, 260940), ðɪ'lëtəl'du,çlʃ'bʌrn. In the above hollow.

**Little Elrick** (OS, C, 163945), 'lëtəl'ɛlrɪk. Also Eileirig Bheag (3), little deer-trap. Elrick Veck (Im 4), Eldrick Beg (I), Eldrick Bheg (R 14). Pairs with Meikle Elrick north-west of Invercauld.

**The Little Feadan\*** (U, 289883), ðɪˈlɛtəlˈfedən. A small rocky furrow on Conachcraig in upper Girnock. See Na Feadan.

**Little Feuragachs\*** (I, 274953), see Feuragach. A former farm, further west and nearer Crathie than the Feuragach.

**Little Ferrowie\*** (F, 303800), ˈlɛtəlˌfɛˈrʌu.i. A low top north of Ferrowie, south of Loch Muick.

**The Little Fir Park Puil\*** (F, 280951), ðɪˈlɛtəlˈfɛrˈparkˈpil. A pool in Dee at Abergeldie, pairs with the Great Fir Park Puil.

**Little Geallaig** See Geallaig Bheag.

**The Little Glen** See Clais Fhearnaig.

**The Little Haugh\*** See the Haughie.

**The Little Hill\*** See the Tom o Loinn Mhor.

**The Little Hillie\*** (U, 416959), ðɪˈlɛtəlˈhɛle, a double diminutive. A hillock near Inchmarnoch, east of Pannanich.

**Little Inverey** (OS, C, 082894), ˈlɛtəlˌɪnvɛrˈɛiˑ. Also Inbhir Eidh Bheag (6, D), ˌɛnɛrˈɛiˑˈbɛg (JB), little Inverey (see Ey Burn). Invereybeg (Roy). See also Wester Inverey. Pairs with Meikle Inverey, the two forming the village of Inverey west of Braemar.

**The Little Island\*** (U, 443995), ðɪˈlɛtəlˈɛilənd. A crannog (artificial island) on Loch Kinord. Also the Crannog Island (Mi 1877), from Crannag (3) = a fortified island in a lake, partly natural and partly artificial (Dw).

**Littlejohn's Brig\*** (F, 299859), ˈlɛtəlˌʤɔnzˈbrɪg. A former bridge at Allt-na-giubhsaich, above the present road bridge, named after its builder (McC 1891); the piers are still visible.

**The Little Kate Puil\*** (F, north-east of 401974), ðɪˈlɛtəlˈketˈpil. A pool in Dee, beside Pannanich.

**Little Khantore\*** (290938). Little Kintore (In). A former farm near Khantore, south of Abergeldie.

**The Little Knock\*** (Io 7, south of 353953). Also Nether Knock (Ab 19), paired with Muckle Knock. A former farm west of Ballater.

**The Little Liath-choire Burn** See Allt Liath-choire Bheag.

**Little Loch Etchachan** (OS, F, 012004), ˈlɛtəlˌlɔχˈɛʧɛχɛn. Also Loch Éiteachan Bheag (6), little loch of ? expansive place (see Coire Etchachan). Loch Etchachan Beag (Sg). A tarn beside Loch Etchachan, north-east of Ben Macdui.

**Little Loch Vrotachan\*** See Loch Coire Direach.

**The Little Luibeg\*** (Fi, 013943). The upper part of Glen Luibeg, north-west of Derry Lodge.

**The Little Mains\*** (F, 284947), ðɪˈlɛtəlˈmenz. Also West Mains (Am). A field, formerly a farm, near Abergeldie.

**The Little Mains Wuid\*** (U, 283948), ðɪˈlɛtəlˈmenzˈwɪd. A wood at Abergeldie.

**The Little Meedow\*** (F, 308817), ðɪˈlɛtəlˈmidə, Scots = meadow. A grassy stretch next to the Muckle Meedow, south of Loch Muick, also shown (I) at 310796.

**Little Micras\*** See Wester Micras.

**Littlemill** (OS, C, 325957), ˌlɛtəlˈmɛl. Also Muileann Beag (3), little mill. Milnebeg (Ap). Also Waulkmill. Wauk Mill (In, Am). At the foot of Glen Girnock west of Ballater.

**The Littlemill Brig\*** See the Brig o Girnock.

**(The) Little Ord\*** (OS, F, 445000), ðɪˈlɛtəlˈɔrd, Ord (3) = round hill. Between Loch Davan and Loch Kinord, pairs with the Ord (Ord Hill OS), south of Loch Kinord.

**The Little Ord\*** (F, 430003), as above, Ord (3) = round hill. Pairs with the Big Ord, west of Loch Davan.

**(The) Little Pap** (OS, C, 265844), ðɪˈlɛtəlˈpap. Also Cioch Bheag (3), little pap. Ciche Beag (McC 1891), KEECH-vek (A 1954). Pairs with Meikle Pap on Lochnagar.

**Little Park\*** (R 6a, 254957). A birch wood in 1809 and now, north of Balmoral Castle.

**The Little Park\*** (U, 303921), ðɪˈlɛtəlˈpark. A field in Glen Girnock.

**Little Park\*** (Io 53a). An area of farmland once separately tenanted. Near Braemar, between Castleton and Braemar Castle.

**Little Poll a' Bhior** (F, north-east of 358966), ˈlɛtəlˌpɔlˈvir. Little Polveir (Sc). A pool in Dee above Ballater, pairs with Big Poll a' Bhior.

**The Little Red Brae Puil** See the March Puil.

**The Little Sauchs Hill\*** (U, 405013), ðɪˈlɛtəlˈsaχsˈhɛl, Scots Sauchs = willows. West of Loch Davan.

**The Little Scarsoch\*** See Scarsoch Bheag.

**The Little Sean-bhaile Puil** (F, 336962), ðɪˈlɛtəlˈʃɛnˌvɛlˈpil. Little Shenval (Wav). Pairs with the Big Sean-bhaile Puil. See the Sean-bhaile Puil. In Dee east of Coilacriech.

**The Little Slack** (A 144, 351057), ðɪˈlɛtəlˈslɔks (U), Scots Slack = gap. A notch on the hill ridge north-east of Morven Lodge, east of the much bigger notch of Slacks of Glencarvie.

**The Little Socach** See An Socach Beag.

**The Little Squarie\*** See Dail Mallachaidh.

**Little Srathan\*** See An Srathan Beag.

**The Little Taggart Burn\*** See Caochan Beith.

**The Little Thorny Buss Puil** (C, 389966), ðɪˈlɛtəlˌθɔrneˈbʌsˈpil. Little Thorny Bush (Sc). A pool in Dee north-east of Ballater, pairs with Big. Often just Little Thorny (C).

**Little Tom Sgonnach** See Tom Sgonnach Beag.

**(The) Littleton** (OS, C, 363944), ðɪˈlɛtəltən. Also Little Balintober. Little Ballentober (I). Also Nether Balintober. Nether Bellintober (Io 9). A former farm in lower Glen Muick, now a house.

**The Little Torr\*** (351926), Torr (3) = hillock. The Brae called the Little Tor (Rli 15). In lower Glen Muick.

**The Little Tulloch Road\*** (F, 440966), ðɪˈlɛtəlˈtʌləçˈrod, Tulach (3) = hillock. A track to the house of Little Tulloch which is outside our study area. East of Inchmarnoch.

**Little Woodhill\*** (F, 142907), ˈlɛtəlˌwudˈhɛl. Also the Woodhill Barns (F), ðɪˌwudˈhɛlˈbarnz. Woodhill sometimes wɪdˈhɛl. A former house just south-west of Woodhill near Braemar.

**The Loan\*** (C, 150915), ðɪˈloˑn, see name below. Ground behind Braemar Post Office.

**The Loans\*** (U, east of 282942), ðɪˈloˑnz. Scots Loan = a paddock for milking cows, near a farm. A patch of open dry grassy ground on north side of public road at Tornauran, Abergeldie. Too dry for Gaelic Lòn = damp meadow.

**An Lochan\*** (3, U, 408040), ðɪˈlɔχɛn, the tarn. A marshy patch west of Logie Coldstone.

**An Lochan\*** (3, C, 407040), as above. A former farm near the above place.

**Lochan a' Chreagain** (OS, 2, U, 116907), ˌlɔχɛnɐˈχrɛkən, tarn of the Cragan or little rock. Near the mouth of Quoich, formed after the big flood of 1829.

**Lochan Allt Sgreuchaig** (3, 140892), tarn of burn of screeching one (e.g. an owl). Lochan allt sgreuchag (D). A tiny tarn high on Morrone south of Braemar.

**Lochan an Tàrmachain** (3, 225855), tarn of the ptarmigan. Lochan an Tarmachan (McC 1891, M). West of Lochnagar.

**An Lochan Beag\*** (2, U, 093839), ðɪˌlɔχɛnˈbɛg, the little tarn. In upper Glen Ey.

**Lochan Dubh** (OS, 3, F, 270865), ˌlɔχɛnˈduˑ, black tarn. Loch Gelder (Roy), Lochandu (B). On peaty ground at the top of Glen Gelder.

**Lochan Dubh Dùn Ard\*** (3, 193027), black tarn of high hillock. Lochan-du dunard (I). One of a group of tarns beside Loch Builg, below a steep little hillock on the north side.

**Lochan Dubh Mòine Chraichidh\*** (6, 214990), black tarn of Crathie peat-moss (see Crathie). Lochan Dhu Moin Chrachie (I). A peaty pool north-west of Crathie.

**Lochan Dubh na Lairige** See the Pools of Dee.

**Lochan Fear Mhuil*** (3, 177921), tarn of man of the mill, from Muileann. Lochan fer mhuil (R 7). Near Invercauld House.

**Lochan Féith nan Sgòr** (3, Sg, 995937), ˌlɔχɐnˌfenɐˈskɔr (SGo), tarn of bog-stream of the rocky hills. The bog-stream of Feith na Sgor (OS) is on the Linn of Dee side of the hill, but this name was later used for the entire hill-range between Luibeg and Glen Dee, so the Feith nan Sgor in Lochan Feith nan Sgor applies to this range.

**Lochan Feurach** (OS, 190027), from Lochan Feòrach (3), lɔχan ˈfjoraç (A), grassy tarn. Also Lochan Fheòir (3), tarn of the grass. Lochan Nyore (I, Io 71). A tarn beside grassy patches south of Loch Builg.

**An Lochan Mór*** (2, U, 095842), ðɪˌlɔχɐnˈmoːr, the big tarn. In upper Glen Ey.

**An Lochan Mór*** (3, U, south-east of 341971), as above, the big tarn. West of Bridge of Gairn, bigger than the pools nearby.

**Lochan Muine Eanruig*** (3, 227953), tarn of Henry's hill-ridge. Loch muine Eanruig (R 3), Lochan Munaric (I). A pool north-west of the Inver.

**Lochan na Circe** (2, U, north-west of 304963), ˌlɔχɐnɐˈkirk, little loch of the hen. Lochanakirk (D). A former house at Micras, above a wet place.

**Lochan na Feadaige** (OS, 3, McC 1891, 226856), tarn of the golden plover. West of Lochnagar.

**Lochan nam Ban*** (3, 179919), tarn of the women. Lochan-na-bann (R 7). A small pool near Invercauld, now a wet patch.

**Lochan nan Corra*** (4, 173891), tarn of the herons, or nan Curra, of the bogs. Lochan na gurr (I, R 13). On a boggy hill south-east of Braemar.

**The Lochan nan Eun Burn*** See Allt Lochan nan Eun.

**Lochan nan Gabhar*** (3, 177889), tarn of the goats. Lochan na Gour (I, R 13). On a hilltop south-east of Braemar, near the above tarn.

**Lochan Oir** (OS, 3, 191028), lɔχanˈor (A), tarn of gold. Lochan Ore (I). Also the Gold Loch (A). The biggest of the group of tarns near Loch Builg.

**Lochan Poll Mhuilinn** (3, D, 139908), tarn of pool of the mill. Lochan poll vulnn (D). On lower slopes of Morrone above the Mill of Coull.

**Lochan Seilich*** (3, 395978), tarn of willow. Lochin Shelach (R 4). A boggy part of a field at Tullich, still becomes a tarn in winter or after heavy rain.

**Lochan Seilich*** (3, 381971), tarn of willow. Lochnshelach (R 4). A former boggy patch on farmland at Tullich.

**Lochan Seilich*** (3, north-west of 397978), tarn of willow. Lochinshelach (R 4). A former boggy patch on farmland at Tullich.

**Lochan Seilich*** (3, U, 342972), ˌlɔχn̩ˈʃiləç, tarn of willow. West of Bridge of Gairn.

**Lochan Teinntidh*** (5, 190024), fiery, hot tarn. Lochan Tainsh (I), Loch Tainsh (Io 34). The southernmost of the group of tarns near Loch Builg.

**Lochan Uaine*** (3, 281046), green tarn. Lochan Uan (I). On the march with Strathdon, north-west of Gairnshiel.

**Lochan Uaine** (OS, C, 001980), ˌlɔχɐnˈuɐn, green tarn. Also the Ben Macdui Lochan Uaine (F), ðɪˌbɛnˌmɐçˈduiˌlɔχɐnˈuɐn. On Ben Macdui.

**Lochan Uaine** (OS, C, 026986), as above, green tarn. Also the Derry Lochan Uaine (F), ðɪˈdɛreˌlɔχɐnˈuɐn. Above upper Glen Derry.

**(An) Lochan Uaine** (OS, C, 960980), as above, the green tarn. An Lochan Uaine (Gordon 1920). On Cairn Toul.

**Loch Buidhe** (OS, 253827), locally Lochan Buidhe (F), ˌlɔχɐn ˈbui, yellow tarn, but Loch buy (R 6), Lochbuy (In), lɔχˈbui (A). West of Loch Muick.

**Lochbuilg Lodge** (OS, C, 188027), lɔχˈbuləgˈlɔʤ. A ruin beside Loch Builg, east of Ben Avon. Loch Builg (OS, 3, R 14, C), means loch of bag, referring to the loch's shape; it lies just outside the area covered in this book.

**The Loch Builg Path*** (F, 182026), ðɪˌlɔχˈbuləgˈpaθ. A path on to Ben Avon.

**Loch Callater** (OS, C, 184840), lɔχˈkalətɛr, from Loch Caladair (3), loch of Callater or hard water. Pronounced by Gaelic people Callter and Callater (M). South-east of Braemar.

**Loch Callater Shieling*** See the Shiel.

**Loch Coire Dìreach*** (3, 120776), loch of perpendicular corrie, or Loch a' Choire Dhìrich, loch of the perpendicular corrie. Loch Cor Yirach (I). An Coire Dìreach is a short distance to the east, in Perthshire. Also Little Loch Vrotachan (U), ˈlɛtəl ˌlɔχˈvrɔtəçən. West of the Cairnwell.

**The Loch Corrie*** See Coire an Loch.

**Loch Davan** (OS, C, 440010), locally lɔχˈdaˑwən (C), or lɔχ ˈdaˑvɪn (F). Dawan (Go), Loch Dawan (R) in 1725, Loch Dawin (Opr) in 1770, Loch Da-win (Sm), Da-wen (A), in Gaelic Loch an dāvan (D) from Loch an Dabhan (6), in lowland Scots Daawan (D). We came across only one person (AG, who did know the names in the area better than any other informant) who agreed with Alexander's note that the local pronunciation was Da-wen, with no Loch. The farm of Davan (locally pronounced ðɪˈdaˑwən) is on dry ground almost 1 km north-east of the loch, and the farm of Monandavan (locally ˌmɪnənˈdaˑwən) is 1 km to the east, so the name applies to a much bigger area than the loch. Note Daan, Dawane and Dawin, Ross-shire (M). Meikle and Little Daan (W 1904) were in Gaelic Dathan Mhor and Dathan Bhig, with old forms Dachynbeg and Little Dovane. This suggested (W 1904) a possible diminutive of Dabhach, an old measure of land. However, as Daan lies at the confluence of two streams and there is an Old Irish word An, water, 'the name may really be da-an two waters' (W). Two burns enter Loch Davan too, but as the name here refers to a farm also, the idea of Dabhach is possible.

**Loch Dubh*** (OSn, 222856 by elimination), black loch. West of Lochnagar.

**Loch Dubh Creag Doimhne*** (3, 226896), black loch of rock of depth. Craig Doin (OS) rises to the north. Loch du Craig Doyne (R 7). East of Ballochbuie Forest.

**Lochend** (Wa, C, 302838), lɔχˈend. Also Loch-head (Di). A former bothy near the end of Loch Muick, now demolished; was a keeper's house last century.

**Lochend*** (F, 302839), as above. The area at the north end of Loch Muick.

**The Lochend Boat House*** (C, 300836), ðɪˌlɔχˈendˈbotˌhus. At Loch Muick.

**The Lochend Wuid*** (C, 303837), ðɪˌlɔχˈendˈwɪd. Wood at Lochend near Loch Muick.

**Loch Etchachan** (OS, C, 005003), from Loch Éiteachan (6), lɔχ ˈɛˑtʃɐχɐn (F), lɔχˈɛtʃəçən (C), loch of ? expansive place (see Coire Etchachan). Loch Eitachan (R 2a). North-east of Ben Macdui.

**Loch Etchachan Beag** See Little Loch Etchachan.

**The Loch Etchachan Burn*** (U, 006999), ðɪˌlɔχˈɛtʃɐχɐnˈbʌrn. Runs into Loch Etchachan.

**Loch Gelder*** See Lochan Dubh.

**Lochhead** (OS, C, 435008), lɔχˈhɛd. A house at the head of Loch Davan.

**Loch-head** See Lochend.

**The Lochhead Craft*** (F, 435008), ðɪˌlɔχˈhɛdˈkraft, Scots Craft = croft. Several small fields west of Loch Davan.

**The Lochie*** (F, 414966), ðɪˈlɔχe, Scots = small loch. A pool in a wood, on west side of the road, east of Pannanich.

**The Lochie\*** (U, 281027), as above. A tiny tarn north-west of Gairnshiel.

**Loch Kander** (OS, 190809), from Loch Ceanndair or Ceanndobhair (3), lǫχ'kjandër, loch of head-water. Loch Khaunter (I, R 13), Loch ceanndoir, Kyander, high water (Mp), Kyaunder, cyanner (D). South of Loch Callater.

**Loch Kinord** (OS, C, 440995), ˌlǫχˌkɪn'ǫrd, from Loch Ceanndair (3), or Ceannair, loch of head-water, ˌlǫχ'kɪnër (U). Canmore & Lough thereof (G 1), Loch Keanders (Bla), Loch Kanders (Roy), Loch Canore (R 1), Loch Ceannor (Mg), L. of Keanore (Io 20), Keandore (Io 20), Loch Kennor (Milne). Diack (in Mi 1877, 1910 edition) explained how the name changed to Kinord, and Alexander gave a summary. The loch was Kinner or Kenner (A, anglicised spellings). This name still lives in local speech in the Muckle Ceannair (erroneously Meikle Kinord (OS)) south of the loch, and the Little Ceannair east of the loch. Old Kinord was a settlement at the west end of the Little Ord, which is the ridge between the two lochs Kinord and Davan (Kinord said to be from ceann nan ord, end of the ords (A) but Ceann Ord, end of round hill, seems more likely as there is only one Ord there). Cainord (G 9). West of Dinnet village.

**Loch Muick** (OS, C, 290830), lǫχ'mëk, from Loch Muice (3), loch of pig-one, referring to the stream. The Loch of Muck (G 10), Loch muic (D). South-west of Ballater.

**Lochnagar** (OS, C, 247855), ˌlǫχnə'ga:r, a hill named after a tarn (name below). Loch-na Garr (Roy) in 1747, Laghin y gair (Pe) in 1769, Lochnagar (Simps) in 1776, and Lochnagarbh (R) in 1828 referred to the hill. Nevertheless, much later records use it for the loch only. For instance, a special map of Balmoral estate after it was bought by Queen Victoria (B, in 1857) uses Lochnagar for the loch and gives the various tops their individual names. A map in 1867 (R 16) also uses it for the loch, giving Ca-Ciorn for the hilltop. The Top of Lochnygaar (Rli) in 1721, Top of Lochnagar (Io) in 1806, and the Hill of Lochnagar (Ra) in 1848 show the way in which the name for the tarn became the name of the hill, through an intermediate stage involving the Top of or the Hill of . . . . The original name for the hill was Beinn nan Ciochan (see under that heading), with different names for the individual tops, such as Ca Chuirn Mor, Carn nan Gabhar and A' Chioch Mhor. A note with a poem by Byron (born 1788, died 1824) refers to the hill as 'Lachin y Gair, or, as it is pronounced in the Erse, Lochna Garr' (Ri). As his poem became a well known song when set to music, this may have helped increase the use of the name Lochnagar for the hill. Abbreviated by some climbers to the Gar.

**Lochnagar** (OS, C, 252860), as above, from Lochan na Gàire (4, W in Cj), tarn of the noisy sound. Loch Garr (Bla), Lochangar (Roy). In Gaelic Lochěn i gyàr (M), Lochan a' ghair, the noisy little loch (Mp), Lochan-a-gharr, lochan gharr (D), Lochan ghàir (Dro). The loch on the hill of Lochnagar (see above name).

**(The) Lochnagar Burn** (OS, C, 257869), ðɪˌlǫχnə'ga·r'bʌrn. B. of Lochnagar (Ro). Runs out of the loch of Lochnagar, into Glen Gelder.

**The Lochnagar Gîte** (Ms, 252864). Not a local name. A climbers' shelter in boulders.

**Lochnalair** (OS, C, 253953), ˌlǫχnɐ'le·r̩, from Lochan na Làire (3), little loch of the mare. Lochan na Lar, Lochannalar (Cr 44), Locnalar (R 6a), Lochnalar (R 6a, Crg 10). A house beside a wet place, west of Crathie.

**Loch nan Cearc\*** (3, 169925), loch of the hens, Cearc can mean grouse hens and not necessarily poultry (J). Lochnakairk (R 7). A former tarn near Invercauld, now wet only after much rain.

**Loch nan Eun** (OS, 2, C, 230853), ˌlǫχnən'je·n, loch of the birds. Common gulls have nested there since at least the late 1800s. Loch nan ean, Loch na nean (R 7, 14). West of Lochnagar.

**Loch nan Sìdhean** (3, 192026, by elimination), loch of the fairy hillocks. Lochnashien (Hi). South of Loch Builg.

**Loch nan Stuirteag** (OS, 3, A, C, 941957), ˌlǫχnɐ'stjurtək, loch of the black-headed gulls. Loch na Stirtag (Ro), Loch na surtaig, stuirdag, saordag (D). South-west of Cairn Toul.

**Loch Phàdruig** (OS, 3, C, 176861), lǫχ'fa·rək, Patrick's loch, after a priest also referred to in the Priest's Well (McC 1891). Loch Patrick (I, R 7), Loch pharig (D in A). Above lower Glen Callater.

**Loch Quoich** See Dubh Lochan.

**Loch Ullachie** (OS, 340949), from Loch Iolachaidh (3, C), lǫχ 'juləçi, (lǫχ'juləçi (A)), loch of shouting. Lochyulachy (Ap), Lake Yulachy (In), Loch Yullachy (Am), Loch Yeùllachie (M). West of Ballater.

**The Loch Ullachie Brae\*** (U, 340952), ðɪˌlǫχ'juləçi'bre·. A hill on a road west of Ballater.

**The Loch Ullachie Burn\*** (F, 338951), ðɪˌlǫχ'juləçi'bʌrn. West of Ballater.

**Loch Vrotachan** (OS, I, C, 123785), lǫχ'vrǫtəçən, from Loch Bhrot-choin (3), loch of the mastiff. Loch vrottchan, Vrottachan (D). North-west of the Cairnwell.

**The Lodge Park\*** (U, 243941), ðɪ'lʌʤ'park. A field at Invergelder.

**The Lodge Puil** (C, 378964), ðɪ'lǫʤ'pil. Lodge Pool (Sc). A pool in Dee, near the site of old Pannanich Lodge on the south bank.

**The Log Cabin\*** (C, 190889), ðɪ'lǫg'kabən. A picnic house in Ballochbuie Forest.

**The Logie Coldstone Burn\*** (U, 431045), ðɪˌlogi'kolstən'bʌrn. Logie from Gaelic Logaigh (3), later Lagaigh, locative of Logach = place in the hollow (W 147), Coldstone from ? Còmhdail = meeting (3, W 492) and English Stone, for early forms see Barrow (1981). Part of Burn of Mosstown.

**The Logie Puil** (C, slightly west of 460982), ðɪ'logi'pil, from Logaigh (3) = at hollow place (see name above). Logie (P). A pool in Dee above the bridge at Dinnet.

**(The) Loin** (OS, F, 214957), ðɪ'lɛin, from An Loinn (3), the enclosure. The Loin (Ri 32), the Line (Opr 1), Loinn (Io 52), Loynacoy (Opr 16), Line of Tullochcoy (I), Loighn (R 14). A former farm north-west of the Inver. See the Loin Park.

**Loinahaun** (OS, C, 277010), ˌlɔnɐ'hʌun, lɔnɐ'ha·n, from Loinn na h-Aibhne (3), enclosure of the river. Loinahabhen (R 14), Loinnahavin, Loinahaimhn (Io 75, 77). Occasionally héavan (M) in speech and writing. Loinn may mean cornyard in Braemar; aun, river (D). A former farm beside River Gairn, west of Gairnshiel.

**Loin-a-veaich** (OS, C, 086888), from Loinn na Fiodhaige (3), ˌlɔinɐ'vjohɪk (U), ˌlɔnɐ'vi·ɐk (C), ˌlaɲɐ'vi:ɐk (Sch), enclosure of the bird-cherry. Loinafhighac (Crg 8), Loinnafioghag (Cr 44), Loinn na vyughag, hagberry meadow (D), but Diack also gave it as Lon or meadow (W). A house near Inverey.

**(The) Loin Burn** (OS, U, 364982), ðɪ'lɛin'bʌrn. Also An t-Allt Mór (3), the big burn. Altmore (G 19), the Aultmore (Io 20). At the Pass of Ballater.

**An Loinn** (3, F, 363979), ðɪ'lɛin, the enclosure. The Loin of Abergairn (Pr). A former farm north of the Pass of Ballater.

**Loinn a' Choirce** (3, C, 266003), lɪn'χǫrk, lɪn'fǫrk (U), ˌlɪnɐ'χǫrk (U), enclosure of the oats. Lynfork, Lyne-a-chork (R 3, 13), Loinchork (D, A). A former farm west of Gairnshiel.

**Loinn a' Choirce** (3, F, 322936), lɪn'χǫrk, enclosure of the oats. Lynefork otherwise called Overpleuche of Strathgirnok (Bul), Scots Overpleuch = upper ploughing. Lynewhork (Aj 1),

Lynachork (Opr 27), Linquork (Am), Loinchork (D). A former farm in lower Glen Girnock.

**The Loinn a' Choirce Brig*** (U, 321937, ðɪˌlɪnˈχọrkˈbrɪg. A bridge in Glen Girnock.

**Loinn Aitionn** (3, 258001), enclosure of junipers. Linyatun (D). An enclosure on east side of the road at Blairglass, west of Gairnshiel.

**Loinn an Arbhair*** (3), enclosure of the corn. Lyninarar, Lynnynnarrow, Lynarar (Me 2, 6, 9). A former grazing in the Glen Dee–Quoich area of Mar.

**Loinn Bheag*** (3, 341023), little enclosure. Lingbegh (Roy). Building, probably a former farm, west of Morven, pairs with Loinn Mhor.

**An Loinn Bheag*** (3, F, 300920), ðɪˌlɪnˈveg, the little enclosure, or the Loinn Bheag Park (F), Scots Park = field. Also the Newton (U), ðɪˈnjutən, had been a separate farm once. In Glen Girnock.

**Loinn Bhealaich** (3, probably in OS section NO 19 SE), enclosure of the pass. Lynvallich, Lendvellich (G 3), Loinvellick, Lainvalluk (Ri 17, 40), Loinvalich (Io 63). A former grazing near Invercauld, possibly near Am Bealach.

**Loinn ? Ceatharnaich*** (5), enclosure of a soldier, note Allt Chernie is near here. Possibly Cairnie (personal name), or Caorann = rowan. Lyncirnie (Rli 2). A former farm near Aucholzie in mid Glen Muick.

**Loinn Chronaidh** (5, probably 323022), enclosure of the little hollow, for other possible meanings see Coire Chronaidh. Loinn-chronie (Gr). In Glen Fenzie.

**Loinn Fhuar** (3, 145858), cold enclosure. Loinnfhuair (Io 52), Loinuir (Rli 23), Loinfhuar (I), Loinn nu-ir (D). A former farm in upper Glen Clunie.

**Loinn Ghorm*** (3, 301852), green enclosure. Lingorum (In, Am), Lingorm Meadow (OSn). A green patch immediately below the peat-bog north of Loch Muick.

**Loinn Iodhlaidh** (4), enclosure of ? Iodhlach = corn-handling. Linynyoley, Lynyullie, Lynyullie of Altduald (Io 12, 29, 32), Loyneayollrie (Io 2) might suggest Loinn Iolaire, but not clearly written and an unlikely place for an eagle to be. In Glen Gairn, probably about Glen Fenzie.

**Loinn Liath** See Glenfenzie.

**An Loinn Mhór** (3, 320032), the big enclosure. Lynemore (Io 32), the Lynmore (G 17), Lenmore (Crg 1), Lynmore (D). A former farm in Glen Fenzie.

**Loinn Mhór*** (3), big enclosure. Lynemoir, a pendicle of Easter Allanaquoich (G 3), Loynemoir (Me 5). East of Mar Lodge.

**An Loinn Mhór** (3, U, 362925), ðɪˌlọnˈmoˑr, (ˌlɛinˈmor (A)), the big enclosure. Loinmore (I, A). A former farm in lower Glen Muick.

**Loinn Mhór** (3, U, 341032), lɛinˈmoˑr, big enclosure. Loignemore (OS 1869), Loinmore (A). A former farm west of Morven, pairs with Loinn Bheag.

**The Loinn Mhor Burn** (U, 340031), ðɪˌlɛinˈmoˑrˈbʌrn. Loinmore burn (D). The lower part of Allt Coire nan Imireachan west of Morven.

**Loinn Muighe** (3, C, 340925), lɪnˈmui, lọnˈmui to oldest people, enclosure of field. Line-moo-ie (A), note Craig of Loinmuie (OS) nearby. A former farm in lower Glen Muick, now afforested.

**Loinn na Guail** (3, C, 269004), ˌlənɐˈguəl, (laŋnəˈgel (A)), enclosure of the coal (i.e. hard dark peat). Lyne-a-Goul (R 12), Lynagale (Cg), Loin na guail (D in A). A former farm west of Gairnshiel.

**Loinn nam Muileann*** (3, 376980), enclosure of the mills. Loinamulian (R 4). A stretch of ground inside an old stone dyke on the hillside above Milton of Tullich.

**Loinn na Mòine*** (3), enclosure of the peat-moss. Loinnamoin

(Cr 41). A former habitation probably in Glen Clunie.

**Loinn nan Gabhar** (3), enclosure of the goats. Lynagour, a pendicle of Bellemoir (Ri 17), Loynnagour (Io 60, Me 3). Near Balmore west of the Inver.

**Loinn Odhar*** (3), dun enclosure. Lyneowar (Ra 6), probably about Abearder, possibly same as Loin (OS). A former farm.

**The Loinn Park*** (F, 362979), ðɪˈlɛinˈpark. A field north of the Pass of Ballater.

**The Loin Park*** (U, 215957), as above. The field at the Loin, north-west of the Inver.

**Loinveg** (OS, C, 316935), lɪnˈveg, from Loinn Bheag (3), little enclosure. Linghabheag (S 25), Linveg (In), Lonibeg, loinn beag or Loinveg (A). A former farm in lower Glen Girnock.

**The Loinveg Birks*** (U, 318933), ðɪˌlɪnˈvẹgˈbërks. Birch wood in Glen Girnock.

**The Loinveg Burn*** (F, 316934), ðɪˌlɪnˈvẹgˈbʌrn. In Glen Girnock.

**The Loinveg Wuid*** (U, 316934), ðɪˌlɪnˈvẹgˈwɪd. A wood in Glen Girnock.

**An Lòn*** (3, 281953), the damp meadow, possibly Scots Loan = paddock. The Lone (I). A field east of Crathie.

**Lón Gaothach*** (3, 145855), windy damp meadow. Lone Gaich (I). A field in upper Glen Clunie.

**(The) Long Bank** (OS, U, 392892), ðɪˈlaŋˈbaŋk. A steep hillside in upper Glen Tanar.

**The Long Goit*** (337886), Scots Goit = channel. Gwight, Goyt, Gyte on the Aberdeenshire coast is a cleft (A). The Long Goyt (I). A hollow on the hill in mid Glen Muick.

**Long Hill*** (Roy). Shown as a hill range about the Glas Maol.

**Long Land*** (R 4, 391971). On farmland at Tullich.

**Long Runs*** (Am, 287950 and 290950), 287950 now the Mains Park (F), ðɪˈmenzˈpark, and 290950 now the Stackyard Park (F), ðɪˈstakˈjardˈpark. Fields at Abergeldie.

**The Lon Parks*** (G 22). Two fields in Glen Gairn, probably near Bridgend, from Lòn (3) = damp meadow, or Scots Loan = paddock.

**Lord Elphinstone's Butts*** (U, 254995), lọrdˈɛlfənztənzˈbʌts. Grouse butts north of Crathie.

**Lord Fife's Dyke*** (U, 145920), lọrdˈfɛifsˈdɛik. Embankments on Clunie and Dee near Braemar.

**Lord Frederick's Walk*** (F, 451906), lọrdˈfredrəksˈwaˑk. A path in Glen Tanar, named after a friend of former laird Cunliffe Brooks.

**Lorgaidh*** (3, 391974), little track. Lorgy (R 4). On farmland at Tullich.

**Losaid Beag*** (3, 186914), little kneading trough or little hip. Losit Beg (R 7). A small piece of land near Invercauld.

**Loudon's Hillock*** See Tom Fhreumhaigh.

**Lovers' Walk** See the Auld Line.

**Low Castleton*** (152921). Low Castelltown (R 1a). Flat haughs on east side of Clunie near church, north of Braemar.

**Lower Auchallater*** See Easter Auchallater.

**Lower Auchendryne*** (F, 147919), ˈloërˌaχənˈdrɛin. Also the Auchendryne Land (F), ðɪˌaχənˈdrɛinˈland. Also East Auchendryne. E. Auchindryne (Im 3). Farmland between Braemar and Dee, on west side of Clunie.

**Lower Ballabeg*** See Ballabeg.

**The Lower Boat Puil*** (F, 248947), ðɪˈloërˈbotˈpil. In Dee above Balmoral Castle.

**The Lower Boat Puil*** (F, 167923), as above. Lady's Boat Pool (Ly). A pool in Dee above Invercauld, pairs with Upper.

**The Lower Bobbie Puil*** (C, 447978), ðɪˈloërˈbọbiˈpil. A pool in Dee south-west of Dinnet, pairs with Upper and Middle.

**Lower Braehead*** (F, 422963), ˈloërˌbreˈhẹd. A field at Inchmarnoch.

**The Lower Bruach Ruadh Puil\*** See the Big Bruach Ruadh Puil.

**The Lower Cabrach\*** See under the Cabrach.

**Lower Carnaqueen** (OS 1903, F, 239941), 'loɐrˌkɛrnɐ'çwin. Ruined houses east of the Inver.

**The Lower Ceapaich Puil** (F, 178919), ðɪ'loɐr'kɛpɐç'pil. Lower Keppoch (A). For meaning see Poll Cheapaich. Roger's Pool (Ly). In Dee at Invercauld.

**The Lower Clachanturn Puil\*** (F, 276948), ðɪ'loɐrˌklaχɐn'tʌrn 'pil. A pool in Dee west of Abergeldie.

**Lower Coire Beag** (F, 353978), 'loɐrˌkǫre'bɛg. Lower Corrybeg (OS 1904). A former farm near Bridge of Gairn, pairs with Upper Coire Beag.

**Lower Creit Seasg\*** (385974 on north side of road). Lower Craitshesk (R 4). A former piece of farmland north-east of Ballater.

**Lower Deecastle Cottage** See under Deecastle Cottage.

**The Lower Druims Park\*** See Druim na Pairce.

**The Lower Dubh-bhruach Pool\*** (F, 028888), ðɪ'loɐr'duˌbrɐχ 'pul. Also the Wee Dubh-bhruach Pool (U), ðɪ'wi'duˌbrɐχ 'pul, Scots Wee = little. In Dee, west of Linn of Dee, pairs with Upper.

**The Lower Falls\*** (U, 064901), ðɪ'loɐr'falz. On Lui, pairing with Upper.

**The Lower Falls of the Garbh Allt** See Falls of Garbh Allt.

**The Lower Geldie\*** (C, 004869), ðɪ'loɐr'geldi. The area at and around Ruighe Ealasaid where Bynack meets Geldie.

**The Lower Geordie Mitchell Puil\*** (F, 252952), ðɪ'loɐrˌdʒǫrdi 'mɛtʃɐl'pil, often just Lower Geordie. A pool in Dee, at Balmoral, pairs with Upper.

**The Lower Haugh\*** See Corby Hall

**The Lower Jetty\*** (F, below 184915), ðɪ'loɐr'dʒɛte. Above Invercauld Bridge.

**The Lower Jetty Puil\*** See Poll Bhuirn.

**The Lower Keiloch Puil** (F, 185913), ðɪ'loɐr'kiləç'pil. Lower Keiloch Pool (Ly). Pairs with Upper. In Dee, near Invercauld.

**Lower Lary\*** See Lary.

**Lower Moine Fhearn\*** (U, 290972), 'loɐrˌmɔin'ja·rn. A peat-moss north-east of Crathie, pairs with Upper Moine Fhearn.

**Lower Rintarsin\*** (U, 263953), 'loɐrˌrən'tarsən. A former house north of Crathie.

**The Lower Sleac Puil** (C, 431965), ðɪ'loɐr'slak'pil. Lower Slachd (Wav). A pool in Dee south-east of Cambus o' May.

**Lower Tom Bhadaidh\*** See under Tom Bhadaidh.

**Lower Tornauran\*** (U, 282945), 'loɐrˌtǫr'nuɐrən. A field south-west of Abergeldie, pairs with Upper and Middle.

**Lower Torr Dubh\*** (U, 424958), 'loɐrˌtǫr'du·. A hillock at Inchmarnoch.

**The Low Muir\*** (F, 339966), ðɪ'lo'miɾ, ðɪ'lo'mjuɾ, Scots Muir = moor. Pairs with the Heich Muir. An enclosed area of rough boggy ground west of Ballater.

**The Lowpin Stane** (U, 308850), ðɪ'lʌupən'stin, Scots Lowpin = jumping. Loupin Stane (McC 1891). A stone at the Spittal of Glenmuick, once used for jumping on to a pony.

**The Low Road\*** See Old Ford Road.

**Low Road** (Gf). A former track from Ballater village over a former moor to the Braemar road, joining it roughly where the former Free Church now stands.

**Low Torr an Fhraoich\*** (168928). Low Tonrich (Im 4). A former field at Invercauld.

**Low Wester Park\*** (Im 4, 170925). A former field at Invercauld.

**An Lùb\*** (3, U, 440977), ðɪ'lup, the bend. A bend in Dee south-west of Dinnet.

**Lùb Ghealtaidh\*** (6, 144856), bend of the ? white place. Loop Yaltie (I). A field at a bend on upper Clunie Water.

**Lùb nam Mèirleach\*** (3, 115972), bend of the thieves. Loup-na-myrlack (I). A bend in upper Quoich Water.

**The Lub of Poll Choinnich\*** (421967), Lùb (3) = bend. The Loup of Pollchynnich or Kenneth's pool (Rli 16), on north side of river. A big bend in Dee south-east of Cambus o' May.

**The Lucky Holies** (P, C, 459982), ðɪ'lʌke'holez, Scots Holies = small holes. 1, 2, 3 Lucky Holies (Ly), Lucky Hole (A). A pool in Dee, west of the bridge at Dinnet.

**Lùib Àiteach** (4, west of 345949), bend of ? from Àite = part, region, or Fhàdach a variant of Fhòideach = turfy, peaty. Leepaittach (G 35). Leep Cúttach (M) with no other evidence, and Leep Cultach (Ap, read by M, but Macdonald made many errors in transcribing from old records) might possibly suggest Cuilteach = with corners. A boggy hollow with an old cairn marking a former march between two estates, west of Ballater.

**Lùib an Fheòir\*** (3, 151879), bend of the grass. Luib an fheor (Cr 45), Loupnore (I), Luibneor, Loipnoir (Io 53, 75). A former farm in Glen Clunie, near a bend in Clunie Water.

**Luibeg** (OS, C, 037933), lui'bɛg. For meaning see Luibeg Burn below. A cottage beside the Luibeg Burn near Derry Lodge, often called Luibeg Cottage.

**The Luibeg Bog\*** (C, 038934), ðɪˌlui'bɛg'bǫg. Peat-bog north of Luibeg.

**The Luibeg Bothy** (Wa, C, 036933), ðɪˌlui'bɛg'bǫθe. A well-known bothy used by many walkers and climbers, often Scott's Bothy (C) or Bob Scott's Bothy, 'bǫb'skǫts'bǫθe, after a former deer-stalker there.

**Luibeg Bridge** (OS, 013942), locally was formerly the New Brig (C), ðɪ'nju'brɪg, later the Luibeg Fit Brig, ðɪˌlui'bɛg'fɛt'brɪg, Scots Fit brig = footbridge.

**The Luibeg Brig\*** (C, south of 041933), ðɪˌlui'bɛg'brɪg. Bridge at Luibeg.

**(The) Luibeg Burn** (OS, Ro, C, 010955), ðɪˌlui'bɛg'bʌrn, from Laoigh Beag (3), little calf-one. Pairs with Lui or calf-one in Glen Lui. Burn of Luibeg (R 10), Burn of Luiebeg (Im 5). Also Uisge Laoigh Bhig (3), ˌuʃkˌlui'bɛg (JB), water of little calf-one. Uisge Lui beg, Lui bheag or beg (D in A). Water of Lie Fig (Fa) with Fig from Bhig.

**The Luibeg Fit Brig\*** See Luibeg Bridge.

**The Luibeg Haughs\*** (F, 039933), ðɪˌlui'bɛg'ha·χs. Grassy flats by the burn near Luibeg.

**The Luibeg Park\*** (F, 036933), ðɪˌlui'bɛg'park. A field near Derry Lodge.

**The Luibeg Wuid\*** (C, 035932), ðɪˌlui'bɛg'wɪd. Old fir wood above Luibeg.

**(The) Lui Bridge** (OS, C, 070899), ðɪ'lui'brɪg. Also the Brig o Lui (F), ðɪ'brɪgɐ'lui. Also Drochaid Laoigh (3, JB), drɔχt'lui, bridge of Lui or calf-one. On Lui Water near where it joins Dee.

**The Lui Brig Brae\*** (F, 069898), ðɪ'lui'brɪg'bre·. A hill on the road west of Mar Lodge.

**The Lui Brig Puil\*** (U, 070898), ðɪ'lui'brɪg'pil. Also the Dookin Hole (U), ðɪ'dukɪn'hol, Scots Dook = bathe in water. A pool west of Mar Lodge.

**The Luibs\*** (380972), anglicisation of Na Lùibean (3), the bends. The Loibs (R 4). On farmland north-east of Ballater, beside a former big horn or bend of Dee mentioned under Corn Eilean.

**Luibs\*** (3). Loops (Opr 36). A former habitation in the parish that includes Ballater, probably at the above place.

**The Lui Falls Brae\*** (U, 065902), ðɪ'lui'fa·lz'bre·, sometimes the Lui Brae (U). A hill on the road up Glen Lui.

**Luig\*** (3), at a hollow. Loig (Io 55). A former farm near Newbigging in Glen Clunie.

**The Lui Haughs*** (F, 050924), ðɪ'luiˈhaˑχs. Grassy flat ground between Derry Lodge and the Black Brig in Glen Lui.

**Lui Side Road*** See the Derry Road.

**Lui Water** (OS, 058921), locally the Lui (C), ðɪ'lui, from Laoigh (3), calf-one (see Glen Lui). Water of Luie (R 10), Laoighe (Gle). In Gaelic n lūi, or lūi (D). Lui Burn (Ro), A. Luy (Bla MS) for Avon from Abhainn (3) = river, or possibly Allt (3) = burn. A river north-west of Inverey.

**The Lui Wuid*** (C, 070900), ðɪ'luiˈwɪd. Old fir and birch wood in lower Glen Lui.

**The Lump o Culblean** (C, 422014), ðɪ'lʌmpɐˌkəl'bliˑn, often just the Lump (C). The Lump of Culblean (Mi 1877). A rocky lump sticking out from the slope of Culblean north-west of Loch Davan. A little gap lies behind it, and a local story (JK) is that the Devil once drove through it with a pair of horses.

**The Lunndaidh Moss*** (F, 318882), ðɪ'lʌndi'mọs, 'lʌndiz'mọs (U), Lunndaidh (3) = marshy place, as in the hill Maoile Lunndaidh above Loch Monar in Ross-shire (W 1904). One informant said it might be after Lundie, a Birkhall keeper who was one of several who cut peats there. A peat-moss in upper Glen Muick.

**Lurg Dubh*** (3, 187933), black ridge. Luruck Du (I). A little top above a rocky ridge extending down to the glen. North-east of Invercauld.

**MacDonald's Aisle** See the Aisle.

**Macdonald's Brig*** (F, 422039), mək'dọnəldz'brɪg. West of Logie Coldstone.

**The MacDuff Road*** (C, 114907), ðɪˌmək'dʌf'rod. A road up to the bottom of Glen Quoich.

**MacIntosh Bend** (Ly, 160924). A pool in Dee west of Invercauld.

**Mackie's Butts*** (F, 440939), 'makez'bʌts. Grouse butts in mid Glen Tanar, built by a former keeper at Etnach.

**The Maclaren Puil** See the Clagganghoul Puil.

**Màgaidh Boireann** (3, D in Crev 39, 165, 117897), Diack's phonetics suggest our ˌmaki'bọrn, little rocky field. Boireann, as in the Burren, is a rocky district in Irish (J 1). Magh-a-Buirn in 1819 (Bg 1) suggests Bùirn, of water. A small field and former croft at Corriemulzie, near Allt a' Chlair.

**Maighdean Mhonaidh** (3, D, 037969), maiden of the hill. Maighdean Monadh (Cj 2). A spring in Glen Derry.

**The Maim** (OS, C, 279968), ðɪ'mɛim, from A' Mhàim (3), the round hill. Maim (I), Vyim, a mhaim (3). North-east of Crathie. Another west of Braemar (see A' Mhaim).

**The Mains*** (U, 146906), ðɪ'meˑnz. The former main farm at Tomintoul south-west of Braemar.

**The Mains Brig*** (U, 286951), ðɪ'menz'brɪg. A bridge at Abergeldie.

**The Mains Burn*** (F, 240951), ðɪ'menz'bʌrn. Part of a burn west of Crathie.

**The Mains Cairn*** See Carn Moine an Tighearn.

**(The) Mains of Abergeldie** (OS, C, 289952), ðɪ'menzɐ,abër 'gẹldi, usually the Mains (C). Mains (Am). Farm at Abergeldie.

**Mains of Aucholzie** See Aucholzie.

**The Mains of Balmoral*** (Io 50). A former farm at Balmoral.

**The Mains of Bellamore*** See Bellamore.

**Mains of Braichlie** (Mg, 372946). Mains of Braichly (Io 69), Maines de Braichlie (Ab 19). Also formerly just Braichlie. Breachlie (I). A former farm in lower Glen Muick, on the site of the present House of Glenmuick.

**Mains of Crathie*** (Io 43, Rli 23). A former farm.

**The Mains of Dail Mhor*** Mains of Delmore (Me 15). Former farm near Mar Lodge.

**The Mains of Invercauld*** (Rli 19, R 7). A former name for farmland beside Invercauld House. Keiloch Farm . . . at one time the Home Farm or Demesne of Invercauld (All).

**The Mains of Inverey** (C, 088892), ðɪ'menzɐ,ɪnvër'ɛiˑ, usually the Mains (C). Mains of Inverey (Er). A former farm, now a house.

**(The) Mains of Monaltrie** (OS, C, 243953), ðɪ'menzɐ,mọn'altri, usually the Mains (C). Monaltrie House (R 3), the house of the original Monaltrie estate, was on this site. House of Monaltrie (Crom). A former farm west of Crathie, was at 241953 when Monaltrie House was at 243953.

**The Mains of Monaltrie Cairn*** See Carn Moine an Tighearn.

**The Mains of Monaltrie Moss Road*** (D, 237968). A road to the peat-mosses north-west of Crathie.

**Mains of the Coldrach*** (I, 153883). A former farm in lower Glen Clunie.

**Mains of Tullochcoy** See Tullochcoy.

**Mains of Tullochmacarrick*** Mains of Tullichmacarig (Opr 45). Probably same as Tullochmacarrick.

**The Mains o Tomintoul** See Tomintoul.

**The Mains Park*** See Long Runs.

**The Mains Stackyard*** (F, 290951), ðɪ'menz'stak'jard. A long narrow field, formerly a stackyard, at Abergeldie.

**Malcolm Canmor's Island** See the Muckle Island.

**(The) Mammie** (OS, C, 316019), ðɪ'mame, from the Màimidh (3), likely to have been A' Mhàimidh originally, the rounded hill. Maimidh (D). East of Gairnshiel.

**The Mammie Road*** (F, 312018), ðɪ'mame'rod. A road north-east of Gairnshiel.

**Mam nan Carn** (OS, 3, C, 050781), ˌmɛimnɐ'gaːrn, (maəmnan 'garn (A)), round hill of the cairns (i.e. screes). Mam-na-garn (Io 79). Maim nan garn (D). Mym nan garn, maim carn (D in A). The evidence suggests Màim, variant of Màm. A green round hill with big patches of grey screes, at the very top of Glen Ey; the actual summit is in Perthshire.

**The Mantlets*** (F, 416017), ðɪ'mantləts, ? anglicised plural from Meanbh = small and Leathad = slope. Note also the Mantlet Butts, ðɪ'mantlət'bʌts at 417018 on this slope north-west of Loch Davan.

**The Manse Brae** (Afr, C, 316006), ðɪ'mans'breˑ. A hill on a road beside a former manse, on a short cut from Ballater to Corgarff avoiding Gairnshiel to the west.

**The Manse Glebe*** (U, 425041), ðɪ'mans'glib, or the Glebe (U). A field west of Logie Coldstone.

**Manse of Glenmuick** (I, 365948). Former manse at the foot of Glen Muick.

**The Manse o Glen Gairn** (C, 316006), ðɪ'mansɐˌglən'gern̩. Former manse west of Balno in Glen Gairn.

**The Manse Puil** See the Minister's Puil.

**The Manse Puil*** See Poll na Trid.

**The Manse Wuid*** (U, 300011), ðɪ'mans'wɪd. Larch wood beside the manse at Gairnshiel.

**The Manse Wuid*** See the Dail a' Bhreac-achaidh Wuid.

**Mar** (C), maːr, from Marr (6), a district name that once covered much of Deeside and Donside. Now means the area around Braemar and all of Aberdeenshire west of Braemar. 'The name of Mar is not in local use, except in the compound names Braemar, Cromar, Midmar' (A), but this was incorrect. The name is well known as a reference to any place in Aberdeenshire west of Braemar. Officially this is Mar Estate and Mar Lodge Estate, but locally the word Mar is generally used. It also appears in Forest of Mar or Mar Forest, the Braes o Mar at Braemar, and near Logie Coldstone in the Braes o Cromar or the Braes o Mar. Alexander gives old historical details on this name, as do Jackson, and Robertson (1798).

**The Marcach\*** (3, north of 363946), likely to have been A' Mharcach originally, the horse place. The Markach (I). A field in lower Glen Muick.

**The Marcach\*** (3, 361945), the horse place. The Markach (I). A field in lower Glen Muick, part of what is now the Crofts Haugh.

**March Burn\*** See Distillery Burn.

**The March Burn\*** (G 22, 399970). On a former boundary between two estates, near Pannanich.

**(The) March Burn\*** (OS, F, 447931), ðɪˈmɛɾtʃˈbʌrn. In mid Glen Tanar, on the march or boundary of two parishes.

**(The) March Burn\*** (OS, F, 977011), as above. Also Allt na Criche (3, Sg, U), ˌaltnɐˈkriç, burn of the boundary. In the Lairig Ghru near the Inverness-shire boundary.

**The March Burn\*** See Stang Raibeirt.

**March Burn of Coinneachaig\*** See Connachat Burn.

**The March Butts\*** (U, 254036), ðɪˈmɛɾtʃˈbʌts. Grouse butts north-west of Gairnshiel, near the march between Corndavon and the Sleach beats.

**The March Cairn** See Carn na Criche.

**The March Cairn\*** (Me 24, U, 128938), ðɪˈmɛɾtʃˈkern. Can be seen on the skyline from the Dee valley below. North-west of Braemar.

**The March Cairn\*** See Carn na Criche.

**The March Dyke\*** (U, 207918), ðɪˈmɛɾtʃˈdɛik. A high stone dyke along a former boundary of Invercauld estate, from Clagganghoul beside Dee over Meall Alvie and Craig Leek east of Invercauld to Carn Liath.

**The March Dyke\*** (F, 363967), as above. Stone dyke on boundary of the former Monaltrie and Morven estates.

**The March Fence\*** (U, 435952), ðɪˈmɛɾtʃˈfɛns. A boundary fence on hill ground between two farms at Inchmarnoch.

**The March Fence\*** (U, west of 132919), as above. A former boundary fence between Mar and Invercauld estates, now largely disappeared.

**The March Fence\*** (F, 297887), as above. Between Abergeldie and Balmoral estates.

**The March Haugh\*** (U, 133917), ðɪˈmɛɾtʃˈhaˑχ. Flat ground by the march between Mar and Invercauld, west of Braemar.

**March Haugh\*** (132919). March Hall (Io 77, Ce 2). A former house at the above haugh.

**Marchnear** (OS, C, 435010), mɛɾtʃˈniɾ, i.e. near the (parish) boundary. An invented modern name, locally is the Jerrie Inn (C), ðɪˈdʒɛreˈɛn, often just the Jerrie (C), meaning of Jerrie unknown, but not Gerrie = German, which is pronounced dʒɛˑre. Possibly from Deireadh = end; Tigh Deiridh means house of end (i.e. last house). This would fit as the Jerrie was and is the last house in the inhabited Loch Davan area before a long stretch of moorland on the road north to Logie Coldstone. Formerly an inn, now a house, near Loch Davan.

**Marchnear Burn** See the Jerrie Burn.

**The March Park\*** (U, 347918), ðɪˈmɛɾtʃˈpark. A field in lower Glen Muick, at the north edge of the Toldhu fields.

**The March Path\*** (F, 181900), ðɪˈmɛɾtʃˈpaθ. A path near the edge of Balmoral estate, west of Ballochbuie Forest,

**The March Puil** (F, north-west of 133912), ðɪˈmɛɾtʃˈpil. March Pool (Ly). In Dee on the Mar–Invercauld boundary west of Braemar.

**The March Puil\*** (F, south-west of 398972), as above. A pool in Dee beside the march of Glenmuick and Glentanar estates. Also the Little Red Brae Puil (F), ðɪˈlɛtəlˈrɛdˈbreˈpil, after a gravelly bank there. Little Red Brae (Wav). North-east of Ballater.

**The March Road\*** (F, 132916), ðɪˈmɛɾtʃˈrod. A track along the march between Mar and Invercauld estates, runs north from Dee opposite Dalgowan, west of Braemar.

**March Stone\*** (I, east of 141775). A former stone marking the county boundary at the top of the Cairnwell road.

**The Mares' Brae\*** (F, 183836), ðɪˈmerzˈbreˑ. Easg Chapall, bog of mares, is nearby. South of Loch Callater.

**Mar Forest Cottage** (OS, 075900), locally just Mar Forest (C), ˈmarˈfɔrɛst. A cottage west of Mar Lodge.

**Margaret McKenzie's Cairn\*** (354057). Margᵗ. McKenzie's Cairn (R 14a). On a hilltop north-west of Morven.

**Market Cross\*** (R 4, 390976). Note 'the Market at Tullich' (Ri). On north side of the road opposite Tullich Kirk.

**The Market Ford\*** (Cp). Presumably a ford over Dee, at Crathie.

**The Market Park\*** (I, 153916). A field at Braemar, see name below.

**The Market Stance\*** (C, 153915), ðɪˈmarkëtˈstans. Market Stance (Ce 4). At the stable yard behind the Invercauld Arms at Braemar.

**Mar Lodge** (OS, C, 096899), ˈmarˈlɔdʒ, ˈmarˈlʌdʒ (F). A hotel west of Braemar. Formerly was called Old Mar Lodge to distinguish it from New Mar Lodge (now gone) or Corriemulzie Cottage (Sm), locally the Cottage (F), ðɪˈkɔtədʒ, which stood on the west side of the burn at the Corriemulzie Brig (McC). Also An Dail Mhór (3, C), ðɪˌdalˈmoˑr, the big haugh, after the haugh there. Dalmore (Re), Dalmoir (Rg), Del Mor (Fa), Delmore (R 2).

**The Mar Lodge Brae\*** (C, 107895), ðɪˈmarˈlɔdʒˈbreˑ. To old people the Cottage Brae (F), ðɪˈkɔtədʒˈbreˑ, after the name of a former Mar Lodge there. A hill on the road east of Inverey.

**Marlodge Bridge** See Victoria Bridge.

**The Mar Lodge Fuird\*** (U, 094894), ðɪˈmarˈlʌdʒˈfjurd. A former ford over Dee, now much altered.

**The Mar Lodge Masts\*** (C, 108909), ðɪˈmarˈlɔdʒˈmasts. Television masts.

**The Mar Lodge Park\*** (C, 098898), ðɪˈmarˈlɔdʒˈpark, English park is meant here. The Park of Mar Lodge (Ra 14). The big park, now farmland, beside Mar Lodge.

**The Marmalade Puil\*** (F, south-east of 359964), ðɪˈmarml̩ədˈpil. A pool in Dee below the Craigendarroch Hotel at Ballater, named after Keiller the marmalade manufacturer who once owned this beat.

**(The) Marquis of Huntly's Well** (OS, U, 374025), ðɪˈmarkwɪɐˈhʌntlizˈwɛl. A spring by the path south of Morven.

**Mar's Hill** (Crom, 100905). Hillside of Beinn a' Bhuilg north of Mar Lodge, 'christened Mar's Hill by tourists to avoid breaking their delicate Saxon jaws with the guttural Gaelic name' (Crom).

**Mar's Road** See the Auld Ballater Road.

**Mary Jean's Brae\*** (C, west of 368957), ˈmereˈdʒinzˈbreˑ. Officially Viewfield Place. In Ballater.

**Mary's Cottage\*** (C, 276947), ˈmerezˈkɔtədʒ. A cottage at Clachanturn east of Crathie, named after a former inhabitant.

**Mary's Cottage Park\*** (U, 274945), ˈmerezˈkɔtədʒˈpark. A field west of Abergeldie.

**Mary's Cottage Puil** (F, east of 275947), ˈmerezˈkɔtədʒˈpil. Mary Cottage (Wav). Also the Back o the House Puil (F), ðɪˈbakɪðɪˈhusˈpil. A pool in Dee east of Crathie.

**The Mary Stanes\*** (F, 424002), ðɪˈmereˈstinz. Often the Four Marys (F), ðɪˈfoɾˈmerez after the old Scots ballad of Mary Hamilton. Also the Four Lords' Stones (O). Four stones in close contact in a row, on north side of track from Loch Davan to Cambus o' May.

**The Mast Road\*** (C, 382985), ðɪˈmastˈrod. A road to a mast near Ballater.

**The Maut Steeps\*** (JS, 335922), ðɪˈmaːtˈstips, Scots Maut = malt. A place on the Craig of Loinmuie in lower Glen Muick where the malt was steeped for making illicit whisky.

**The McAndrew Brig*** (F, 348907), ðɪˌməkˈandrəˈbrɪg. A bridge in Glen Muick.

**The McAndrew Burn*** (C, 350906), ðɪˌməkˈandrəˈbʌrn. The lower part of Allt Chernie in mid Glen Muick.

**McDougall's Boat*** (F, 134912), məkˈdugəlzˈbot. MacDougall's Boat (Gf). Former ferry over Dee west of Braemar.

**McDougall's Boat Puil*** (F, 134912), məkˈdugəlzˈbotˈpil. Boat Pool (Ly). A pool in Dee, west of Braemar.

**McDougall's Nose*** See Sron na Corra.

**McHardy's Corrie*** See Coire na Lairige.

**McKenzie's Cairn*** (F, 271840), məkˈënzezˈkern̩. A cairn about the highest part of the Cross Path from Glas Allt below the Little Pap of Lochnagar.

**McPeder's Causeway*** (238940). Peter's Causeway (I), Mcpeder's casway (R 9). A former crossing place on Dee east of the Inver.

**Meadow Butts*** (R 4, 384973). On farmland at Tullich.

**Meadowland*** (Io 58, 384974). A former section of farmland at Tullich.

**Meadow of Baile an Loin*** Meadow of Balinloan (Io 53). A former farm beside Baile an Loin south of Braemar.

**The Meadow of Glen Ey*** (probably 102845). The Meadow of Gleney (Io 21). Also Meadow of Ruighe Dubh. Ridow and Meadow thereof (Io 21). A former pasture.

**Meadow of Ruighe Dubh*** See the Meadow of Glen Ey.

**Meall a' Challain*** (3, 333972), lump of the noise. Maulachallan (I). A little hill west of Bridge of Gairn.

**Meall Ainmeil Tàine** (4, 010827), special lump of cattle. Meal Animaltan (At), Mealanimaltan (Ath), Meal Animaldan (Th). A prominent hill south-east of Bynack Lodge.

**Meall Alvie** (OS, C, 204919), məlˈalvi, from Meall Ailmhaigh (3), lump of stony plain. Maul Alvie (I), Meall allivi (D in A), Mil-yalvie (A). A hill north-east of Invercauld Bridge.

**The Meall Alvie Wuid*** (C, 205915), ðɪˌməlˈalviˈwɪd. A wood east of Invercauld Bridge.

**Meallan Clach Dhubh*** (3, 206984), little lump of black stone. Meal-an Clach-dhu (R 16). Cnoc na Cloiche Duibhe was probably at this location on map R 14, but was certainly at 211976 on map R 3, so the two names obviously refer to two different adjoining tops. A little top north-west of Crathie.

**Meall an Fheòir*** (3, 128879), lump of the grass. Maul Nyore (I), Maul Noir, Meal Nieor (R 14, 16). The next top on the hill ridge south of Morrone in Glen Clunie.

**Meall an Lundain** (OS, 062948), locally Meall Lunndan (3, C), məˈluntən or mjeˈlʌuntən, (mjalˈuŋtan (A)), lump at marshy ground or at green place, or at green marshy place. A hill north-east of Derry Lodge, a favourite place for deer because of its damp grassy spots.

**The Meall an Lundain Moss*** (F, 052952), ðɪˌməˈluntɛnˈmɔs. A peat-bog north-east of Derry Lodge.

**Meall an Tionail** (OS, 224877), locally Meall Tionail (3, A, C), məlˈtʃenəl, (məlˈtjɛnəl (A)), lump of gathering. Maul Tchenal (R 14), Meall tshunal, tshenal (D). A hill north-west of Lochnagar. Local people often call it the Meall Tionails, which suggests that there may have been a big and a little Meall Tionail, but when asked about this they know only the one hill. This name of the Meall Tionails is used not for the one hill specifically but for the general area of the hill and its surroundings.

**Meall an t-Slugain** (OS, 3, U, 126958), ˌmələnˈslʌgən, (mjɛlən ˈlukan and mjalanˈljukan (A)), lump of the gullet. Maul Sluggan (R 14), Hill of the Sluggan (I). A hill at the top of Gleann an t-Slugain.

**Meall an t-Slugain** (OS, 3, F, 185863), ˌmələnˈlugən, (as above for A), lump of the gullet. Mauln lugan, Maul Luggan (R 7,

14). Also Black Hill (Roy), which he possibly meant for Carn Dubh south-west of Loch Callater. North of Loch Callater.

**Meall Bad an Eachrann*** (3, 321918), lump of clump of the place where brambles grow. Malbadnechrew (In), Malbadnechraw (Am), with the w possibly an error for n, especially as the same person made both maps. Ben Nathraichean (Bs). Now bədˈnjaχrɛn (U), or bənˈjaχrɛn (F). A hilltop in Glen Girnock.

**Meall Bheachdaich*** (3, 168896), lump of the watching. Maul Vechkich (I). A small rocky bump offering a very good view down Clais Mhor towards Invercauld Bridge.

**Meall Bheag Ailmhaigh*** (3, 199921), little lump of stony plain. Maul Beg Alvie (I). A little top north-east of Invercauld Bridge, beside Meall Alvie.

**Meall Chaol-bhaid** (4, C, 325924), mɛlˈçɛlvət, məlˈçɪlˌbɛt, lump of the narrow spot. Milchilbad (In, Am), Meal Chelvat (Mg). A hilltop in Glen Girnock.

**Meall Coire Buidhe*** (3, Bs, U, 229900), ˌməlˌkɔrˈbui, lump of yellow corrie. Maul Cor Buie (I). On the location of Cnap a' Choire Bhuidhe (OS), but it is incorrect and should be at 230902. A hill west of Glen Gelder.

**Meall Coire na Saobhaidhe** (OS, 3, 242873), ˌməlˌkɔrn̩ˈsɪvi (F), kɔrnˈsɪvi (C), lump of corrie of the fox's den. Mealcornasaoghnacak (Ra 15) suggests Meall Coire na Saobhaidhe ? nan Cadha = of the steep hills, see Cac Carn Beag. Maul Carnasuvie (R 7), Maul Cornasaughie (B). A hill north of Lochnagar.

**Meall Creagan Dearcaig*** (3, 191853), lump of little rock of little berry. Maul Gracan Jinccan (R 16, not reliable as many printers' errors). A hill north-east of Loch Callater.

**Meall Creag Liath*** See Creag Liath.

**Meall Cula** (OS, 184998), from Meall Cùlath (5), lump of back place. On Culardoch south-east of Ben Avon.

**Mealldarroch Cottage** (OS, 095894), from Mile Dhorch (2, C), milˈdɔrɐχ, (milˈdorəç (A)), dark mile. Mieldorrach (1922 gravestone at Braemar). The cottage is at the west end of A' Mhile Dhorch, the dark mile east of Inverey.

**Meall Dorch** (OS, 134958), from Meall Dhorch, dark lump. A hilltop above Gleann an t-Slugain.

**Meall Dubh** (OS, 325920), from Meall Dhubh (3, C), məlˈduˑ, black lump. Maldieu (In, Am). A dark heathery hill, the right-most of the three Coyles of Muick when seen from Ballater.

**Meall Dhubh Coire Buidhe*** (3, 155855), black lump of yellow corrie. Maul Du Cor Buie (I). On the location of Sron nan Gabhar (OS), which should be the rocky nose much lower down to the west. A hilltop between Clunie and Callater.

**Meall Ghall*** (3, 191931), lump of foreigners. Maul Gall (I). A little top on Craig Leek north-east of Invercauld Bridge.

**Meall Ghorm*** (3, 268916), blue lump. Maul Gorm (B), Meall Gorm (OSn). A hill south of the distillery at Balmoral, with many greyish-blue boulders and stones.

**Meall Ghrianach*** (3, F, 111842), məlˈgriɛnəç, sunny lump. A prominent hill in Glen Ey, above Allt a' Mhoir Ghrianaich.

**Meall Glasail Beag** (OS, A, U, 147963), from Meall Glas-allt Bheag (3), ˌməlˈglasəlˈbɛg, little lump of green burn. Little hill of the Glas Allt (A), glasalt bheag (D in A). Glas Allt Beag (OS) to the east should be Glas-allt, and in this case there is only one Glas-allt, not a big one and a little one as in two other cases. Hence the two hills (see name below) refer to the one burn below them. Meall Glasail Beag is slightly higher than Meall Glasail Mor, but is a less prominent hill. A pair of hills north of Gleann an t-Slugain.

**Meall Glasail Mór** (OS, 145958), from Meall Glas-allt Mhór (3, U), ˌməlˈglasəlˈmoˑr, big lump of green burn. See above name. Alexander incorrectly wrote 'The Meall Glasail Mor is at the west end of Ben Avon'. Above lower Gleann an t-Slugain.

**Meall Gorm** (OS, 185946), from Meall Ghorm (3, C), məl 'gɔrəm, blue lump. Maul Goram (I, R 14). A heathery hill north-east of Invercauld, with greyish-blue rock-outcrops and stones.

**Meall Gorm** (OS, 299890), from Meall Ghorm (3, C), as above, blue lump. A heathery hill in upper Glen Girnock, with numerous greyish-blue boulders and stones.

**Meall gun Aon** (3, U, 125861, Carn na Drochaide (OS) is on this location but should be at 132868), ˌmjal ˌkənˈʌun, literally lump without one. Meall gun aun, hill without an owner (D), and certainly the hilltop does lie on the boundary between Mar and Invercauld. Maul-kin-aun (I, R 14), Meal Kin Ann (R 16). A hill between Clunie and Ey.

**Meall Liath Clach Dhubh*** (3, 211976), grey lump of black stone. Maul-lia-Clach du (I). A little top north-west of the Inver, same location as Cnochd na-clach-dhuth (R 3).

**Meall Mheadhonach*** (3, 232948), middle lump. Maul Mainach (I). A little top north of the Inver, the middle one in a series of three hills, Meall Mhor (Craig Nordie (OS)), Meall Mheadhonach and Meall Otrach.

**Meall Mhór*** (3, 201941), big lump. Maul More (I), Maul Mhoir (R 14). A little top west of the Inver, looks prominent from below.

**Meall Mhór*** (3, 235945), big lump. On the location of Craig Nordie (OS), but Craig Nordie should be at 239943. Meall-more (R 3), Maul More (I, R 14). A hill north of the Inver.

**Meall na Bà*** (3, F, 395041), ˌmɑlnɐˈbaˑ, lump of the cow. A top east of Morven.

**Meall na Broighlich*** (4, 329930), lump of the noise, possibly Meall nam Broilleach, lump of the breasts. Malnybrylach (In Am). A little top south-west of Ballater.

**Meall nam Bò** (3, 259006), lump of the cows. Mulnabo (D). A little top west of Gairnshiel.

**Meall nan Caorach** (OS, 3, A, U, 144949), ˌmɑlnɐˈgirɐχ, (mɑlnə ˈgöraç (A)), lump of the sheep. In Gleann an t-Slugain.

**Meall nan Uan** (OS, 3, C, 054931), ˌmjalnənˈuɐn, lump of the lambs. Malnanuan (R 10), Meall-nan-uan (Sin). Meall uaine, either green hill or lamb's hill (D in A), but Diack probably noted the pronunciation incorrectly. Alexander noted it correctly as Myal nan oo-an, mjɛlnanˈuən with final *n* nasal, hill of the lambs. A hill in Glen Lui.

**Meall Odhar** (OS, 249000), dun lump. A small top west of Gairnshiel.

**Meall Odhar** (OS, 156773), from A' Mheall Odhar Mhór (3, Bu, F), ðiˌmɑlˌʌuˈrˈmoˑr, the big dun lump. Maul Our More (I). Also the Big Meall Odhar (F), ðiˈbɪgˌmɑlˈọ̈ër. Pairs with Mheall Odhar Bheag, east of the Cairnwell.

**(The) Meall Odhar Hut** (OS, F, 149776), ðiˌmɑlˈʌuˌˈhʌt. A ski hut east of the Cairnwell.

**The Meall Odhar Lochie*** (F, 149776), ðiˌmɑlˈʌuˌˈlọχe. An artificial tarn east of the Cairnwell.

**The Meall Odhars*** (F), ðiˌmɑlˈọ̈ërz. A collective name for the Big and the Little Meall Odhar (see Meall Odhar).

**Meall Òtraich*** (3, 230950), lump of dung, dirt. Maul Utrach (I). A small top north of the Inver.

**Meall Sgalan*** (3, F, 062814), məlˈskalɐn, lump at sheltered place. Sgalan is used sometimes in the sense of a sheltered place, for instance An Sgalan on Culardoch, which is a big sheltered corrie. A small top in upper Glen Ey.

**Meall Tionail** (OS, 3, C, 012847), məlˈtʃenəl, lump of gathering (probably sheep gathering). Melteanel (Roy). A hill south-east of Bynack Lodge.

**Meall Tionail** (3, 108010), lump of gathering. Meal teanail (Mg), Meall Tionail, one near Invercauld (A). It is clear from

MacGillivray's description that Meall Tionail is the big hill east of the North Top of Beinn a' Bhuird, on which Cnap a' Chleirich is a small top.

**The Meal Mill Dam*** (F, 298012), ðiˈmilˈmëlˈdam. A pond for a former mill near Gairnshiel.

**Meal Mill of Tom Bealaidh*** See Mill of Tom Bealaidh.

**The Meal Mill o Torgalter*** (U, 288955), ðiˈmilˈmëlɐˌtọrˈgaltër. Former mill east of Crathie.

**The Meal Mill o Tullich*** See the Mill o Tullich.

**Megen*** (C, 321905), ˈmɛgən, from Migein (3, W), bog place. Megan (R 6). Mig is a bog or quagmire in Welsh, and many names in the Highlands have this term (W). Megen is a general name for a big boggy area between Glen Girnock and the Linn of Muick.

**(The) Megen Burn** (OS, 308912, should be at 316911), burn at 308912 is Allt Coire na Cloiche (3, A), altkɔrnəˈkloɐç (A), burn of corrie of the stone. Also the Burn of Coire na Cloiche (C), ðiˈbʌrnɐˌkọrnɐˈklɔiç. Burn of Cornycloich (In, Am). Now usually the Coire na Cloiche Burn (C). The Megen Burn is sometimes the Burn o Megen (U), ðiˈbʌrnɐ ˈmɛgən, but usually the Megen Burn (F). Also Allt na Megein (3), burn of the bog place. Allt na Meggen (OS 1869). In Glen Girnock.

**Meggie McAndrew's Cairn** (Wa, C, 272994), ˈmɛgiˌmɐkˈandrəz ˈkern̩. Cairn erected after the death of Meggie McAndrew, who died in a snowstorm while walking back to the Newton of Crathie from Corgarff, probably mid 1800s. Near the road from Gairnshiel to Crathie, on north side.

**Meggie's*** (U, south of 310013), ˈmɛgiz. A field east of Gairnshiel, named after a former inhabitant who lived in a house uphill.

**Meg Gow's Howe** (D 198), Scots Howe = hollow. Up the Tullich Burn.

**Meg Wright's Hole*** (F, 039934), ˈmɛgˈrëçtsˈhol. A boggy pool near Derry Lodge, where one of the servants at the Lodge once fell in.

**Meikle Elrick** (OS, 159955), locally Muckle Elrick (C), ˈmʌkəl ˈɛlrɪk. Also Eileirig Mhór (3), big deer-trap (i.e. where deer were driven in). Eldrick More (I), Eldrick Mhoir (R 14). Also Carn na h-Eileirige (3), hill of the deer-trap. Carn nyillrig, carn na h-elrig (D), karnˈɛlrək, (karnˈjɛlrək (A)). Pairs with Little Elrick, north-west of Invercauld.

**(The) Meikle Geal Charn** (OS, U, 200053), ðiˈmʌkəlˈgɛləhɐrn. Also Geal-charn Mór (3), big white hill. Gelcharn More (R 2b), Geal charn (R 14), Gyall Charn (Io 43a). Pairs with Little Geal Charn to the north-west, outside the area covered in this book. A hill north-east of Loch Builg.

**Meikle Inverey** (OS, 090893), locally Muckle Inverey (C), ˈmʌkəlˌɪnvër'ɛiˑ. Big Inverey, Mucle Inverey (Cr 47, 49), Muckle Inver-ey (Sm). Also Inbhir Eidh Mhór (6, D), ˌ̈ënër ˈɛiˈmoˑr (JB), big Inverey (see Ey Burn for meaning). Invereymor (Roy). See also Easter Inverey. The bigger part of Inverey village, west of Braemar, pairs with Little Inverey further west.

**Meikle Kinord** (OS, 441989), locally the Muckle Ceannair (C), ðiˈmʌkəlˈkënër, pairing with Little Ceannair. Cainmore or Canmore in 1535, Candmoir, Meikle and Little Chandmoiris in 1639, Mickle and Little Candors (G 1, 7, 8, 9), Magnas Keandore (Ab 19). See Loch Kinord. A former farm, now a house, west of Dinnet.

**(The) Meikle Pap** (OS, 260861), locally the Muckle Pap (A, C), ðiˈmʌkəlˈpap. Muckle Pap (B, OSn). Also A' Chìoch Mhór (3), a hi.ç vor (A), the big pap. Ciche Mhor (McC 1891), Chioch vōr (D), A' Chioch mhor (Dro). A conical hill on Lochnagar.

**Memorial Cairn** (OS, 372953), locally the Monument (C), ðɪ 'mǫnjəmɪnt. Not a cairn. A granite monument near Ballater, in memory of a former owner of Glenmuick Estate.

**Menzies' Grave*** (U, north-west of 304831), 'mɛŋiz'grev. Near the Capel Road above Loch Muick, where a young man looking for cattle died in a snowstorm last century; a flattish stone 15 m north-west of bottom butt.

**Meòir Ghrianaich** (3, U, 107822), mjur'griɛnəç, of sunny stream-branch, possibly Meòir Ghrianach = sunny stream-branches, but see Allt a' Mhoir Ghrianaich. Myor Grianich (I), Meoir ghrianaich (D). A little burn starting on the watershed between Clunie and Ey, runs northwards into Glen Ey and becomes Allt a' Mhoir Ghrianaich (OS) lower down.

**The Metal Bulwark*** (F, south of 379966), ðɪ'mɛtəl'bulwɔrk. On Dee north-east of Ballater.

**A' Mhàim** (3, F, 133900), ðɪ'mɛim, the round hill. Maim (Mp), the Mime (D). On Morrone west of Braemar.

**A' Mheall Odhar Bheag** (3, U, 146777), ðɪˌməl'ʌur'bɛg, the little dun lump. Maul Our Beg (I). Also the Little Meall Odhar (F), ðɪ'lɛtəlˌməl'ǫ̈ër. East of the Cairnwell.

**A' Mheall Odhar Mhor** See Meall Odhar.

**A' Mhìle Dhorch** (3, C, 100895), ðɪˌmil'dǫrɛχ, the dark mile. Mile dorcha (Mp), the Mil dorach, dark mile (A). A dark stretch of the Braemar–Inverey road under tall trees.

**A' Mhòine Mhairrneach** (3, 067810), the peat-moss of the Mar men. A mhoine Mharnyach, the Mar men's moss, where the Glenshee people used to come to dig for fir candles (D). A peat-moss in upper Glen Ey.

**A' Mhòine Mhór*** (3, 156906), the big peat-moss. The Moinmore (I). Also Cavan's Park, 'kavənz'park, after Lord Cavan who once had a house nearby. A wet field just outside Braemar on the Perth road.

**Am Miadan*** (3, U, 076897), ðɪ'miɛdɐn, the green. A grassy stretch west of Muir cottage at Inverey.

**Am Miadan** (3, D, 042818), the green. A flat grassy spot on the Perthshire boundary at the very top of Glen Ey.

**Micheil's Road*** (3, U, 072911), 'mɪçəlz'rod, Michael's road (Micheil is the Gaelic form). A track from Glen Lui on to the hill north-west of Mar Lodge.

**The Micras** (C), ðɪ'mikrəs, from Miagra (6). A general name for the farms between Rinabaich (west of Coilacriech) and Wester Micras east of Crathie. Note Easter, Mid and Wester Micras, and Miagra Shìos and Shuas. Alexander suggested that the *s* in Micras is an English plural, to cover Easter Micra and Wester Micra. Old spellings give the evidence, with Mecra in 1438 (Re), Mekra in 1451 (Cro), Mecraw (Ca), and the Gaelic Miagra (D) or Miacra (D in A). Other old spellings are Westir Mecraw and Eister Mecraw in 1564 (Ca), Mickerys (Roy), and Micaras (Cg). The meaning is unknown, but may possibly come from Mig = bog, as in many other names beginning with Mig or Meg (W 374–6), and Ràth = fort. Diack (Rc) suggested Miog, smile, hence Miogradh or cheerful, sunny place, but this is doubtful.

**Micras Hill*** (C), 'mikrəs'hël. A name for the hill ground between Dee and Gairnshiel, including Geallaig Hill as its highest point.

**Micrasses*** (Io in 1749). A collective name for Easter, Wester and Mid Micras east of Crathie.

**The Mid Cairn** (OS, U, 382042), ðɪ'mɪd'kerṇ. The Meikle Cairn (I). A stony little top east of Morven.

**Mid Corrie Burn*** (Md 10, 135908). The middle of three burns running out of Coire nam Muc west of Braemar.

**The Middle Allt Giuthas*** (170870), Allt Giuthas (3) = burn with fir. The Middle Altguise (Io 43a). A burn in lower Glen Callater.

**The Middle Bobbie Puil** (C, 446978), ðɪ'mɪdəl'bǫbi'pil. A pool in Dee south-west of Dinnet, pairs with Lower and Upper.

**Middle Braehead*** (F, 419963), 'mɪdəlˌbre'hḙd. A field at Inchmarnoch.

**The Middle Bruach Ruadh Puil*** (F, 278951), ðɪ'mɪdəlˌbrǫχ'roi 'pil. Pairs with Upper and Lower. A pool in Dee east of Crathie.

**The Middle Cast** (F, 355966), ðɪ'mɪdəl'kast. Middle Cast (Sc). A pool in Dee, below the junction with Gairn.

**Middle Grain** (OS, 355868), locally the Mid Grain o Allt Cholzie (F), ðɪ'mɪd'grenɐˌalt'χǫili. Mid Grain of Ault Chulzie (I). A burn south-east of the Linn of Muick.

**The Middle House*** See Ruighe Ealasaid.

**The Middle Park*** (U, 414034), ðɪ'mɪdəl'park. A field west of Logie Coldstone.

**Middleton of Aberarder** (OS, C, 205935), 'mɪdəltənɐˌabër'ardër. A group of former crofts west of the Inver.

**Middleton's Brig** (C, 334896), 'mɪdəltənz'brɪg. A former footbridge below Linn of Muick, named after a family who lived formerly at Linn Cottage. Middleton's Bridge (Rt).

**Middle Tornauran*** (U, 281944), 'mɪdəlˌtǫr'nuərən. A field south-west of Abergeldie, pairs with Lower and Upper.

**Middletown*** (Opr 34, east of 336003). Former habitation beside Lary in Glen Gairn.

**Middpark*** See the Athan Phuill Park,

**The Mid Drive*** (C, 193898), ðɪ'mɪd'draev. A road in Ballochbuie Forest, pairs with East and West Drive.

**Mid Grain*** (I, 318786). Pairs with Easter Grain of Allt Darrarie. A burn south of Loch Muick.

**The Mid Grain o Allt an t-Sneachdaidh*** (F, 343863), ðɪ'mɪd 'grenɐˌaltən'drɛçte. A burn south-east of Linn of Muick, pairs with East and West Grains.

**The Mid Grain o Allt Deas*** (F, 385873), ðɪ'mɪd'grenɐ,alt'dɛs. Pairs with East and West Grain o Allt Deas. A burn in upper Glen Tanar.

**The Mid Grain o Allt Fileachaidh*** (F, 328847), ðɪ'mɪd'grenɐˌalt 'filəçi. Pairs with East and West Grain o Allt Fileachaidh. A burn in upper Glen Muick.

**Midhouse Inverey*** (Ce 3). Former habitation.

**Mid Island*** (390968). Midd Island (Io 58). A former island in Dee near Tullich.

**Mid Micras** See Lebhall.

**Mid Park*** (R 4, 375967). Also Middlefield (Io 68). A field north-east of Ballater.

**Mid Rintarsin*** (U, 264960), 'mɪdˌrən'tarsən. A former house north of Crathie.

**The Mid Stile Park*** (F, 335999), ðɪ'mɪd'stɛil'park, Scots Stile = gate. A field on Lary in Glen Gairn.

**Midtown Micras*** See the Lebhall.

**The Mile Stone*** (I, 206006). Large stone called the Mile Stone (I). On the Holmesdale Path south-west of Corndavon Lodge.

**The Mill Brae*** (F, 415966), ðɪ'mël'bre·. A hill on the road to the Mill of Bellamore, east of Pannanich.

**The Mill Course Park*** (U, 420048), ðɪ'mël'kurs'park. A field near Logie Coldstone.

**The Mill Craft** See Renatton.

**Mill Croft*** (I, 153882). A field in lower Glen Clunie, beside the former Mill of Coldrach.

**Mill Croft*** (I, 349925). A field in lower Glen Muick.

**Mill Croft*** (I, 362947). A field west of Bridge of Muick.

**Mill Croft*** (R 15, 388976). Buildings at Tullich, later Tullich Mill erroneously on the current OS map, and locally called the Mill House, ðɪ'mël'hus, or the Milton of Tullich along with other houses to the west.

**Mill Croft** (I, 227936). Mylecroft (Ri 17). A former field west of the Inver.

**Mill Croft*** (G 15). Formerly at Bellamore near Inchmarnoch.

**Mill Croft\*** (probably c. 159928). Miln Croft (Rli 19). About Milltoun of Invercauld.

**The Mill Croft\*** (U, 269943), ðɪˈmɛlˈkrɔft. A field at Easter Balmoral.

**The Mill Croft\*** (I, 347977). Former croft in lower Glen Gairn.

**Mill Croft\*** (R 6a, 262951, on north side of road). At Crathie.

**Mill Croft** (S, probably near 268943). Milnecroft (Io 41). Former croft east of Balmoral.

**The Mill Croft\*** The Miln Croft, Mill Croft at the Inver (Io 18). A former croft near the Inver Inn.

**Mill Croft of Aberarder \*** (Io 76). Near Ballachlaggan. Possibly same as Mill Croft at 227936 west of the Inver.

**Mill Croft of Prony\*** Miln Croft of Prony (G 20). Former croft on east side of lower Glen Gairn.

**Mill Croft of Richarkarie\*** Miln Croft of Riecharkry (Io), Riecharkry Miln Croft (Rli 19). A former croft near Gairnshiel.

**The Miller's Birks\*** (U, 320950), ðɪˈmɛlɛrzˈbɛrks. A birch wood in lower Glen Girnock.

**The Miller's Burn\*** (I, 220965). A burn north-west of the Inver.

**Miller's Cairn\*** (Md 1, 144791). A former cairn beside the Cairnwell road. It marked the grave of a Captain Miller, nicknamed Muckle Miller (Gr).

**The Miller's Corrie\*** (F, 308942), ðɪˈmɛlɛrzˈkɔre. In lower Glen Girnock.

**The Miller's Dam\*** (F, 321949), ðɪˈmɛlɛrzˈdam. In lower Glen Girnock.

**The Miller's Gate\*** (U, 319946), ðɪˈmɛlɛrzˈget. In lower Glen Girnock.

**The Miller's Park\*** (U, 269942), ðɪˈmɛlɛrzˈpark. A former field at Easter Balmoral, now a wood.

**Millford\*** (Ce 1, probably south-east of 288956). Former habitation at Micras east of Crathie.

**The Mill House\*** See Tullich Mill.

**Mill Loch of Aucholzie\*** Miln Loch of Aucholzie (Io 43a). In Glen Muick.

**The Mill Loch of the Croft\*** (357939 or 362943). The Miln Loch of the Croft (Io 43a). Near the Crofts in lower Glen Muick.

**The Mill o Auchendryne\*** (F, 151913), ðɪˈmɛlɛˌaχənˈdrɛin, usually now the Auchendryne Mill (C). The mill of Achyndryne (Ra 7). At Braemar, on the west side of Clunie, with a former meal mill and sawmill.

**Mill o Chritheannaich** See Muileann Chritheannaich.

**The Mill o Dinnet Brig\*** (C, 468991), ðɪˈmɛlɛˈdɛnɛtˈbrɪg. East of Dinnet.

**The Mill o Dinnet Burn\*** (C, 469990), ðɪˈmɛlɛˈdɛnɛtˈbʌrn. Lower part of Dinnet Burn.

**The Mill o Dinnet Parks\*** (F, 468988 and 467985), ðɪˈmɛlɛ ˈdɛnɛtˈparks. Two fields east of Dinnet.

**Mill of Aberarder\*** (Io 25a). A former mill in lower Glen Fearder, near Ballachlaggan.

**Mill of Abergairn.** Mill of Abergarden (Ab 8). A former farm near the foot of Glen Gairn.

**Mill of Abergeldie\*** (Opr 21). Former habitation, probably same as Drymill.

**Mill of Allanaquoich\*** (R 2, 117912). On the site of the house now called the Quoich, west of Braemar. The mill lade is to the west .

**The Mill of Arderg\*** (121904). Milne of Ardarg (Me 3), the Mill of Arndarg (Me 19, Lp 5). A former mill near Arderg west of Braemar.

**Mill of Aucholzie** (I, OS 1904, 350923). See the Milltoun of Aucholzie. A former mill in Glen Muick.

**Mill of Balmoral** See Drymill.

**(The) Mill of Bellamore** (OS, D, C, 415962), ðɪˈmɛlɛˌbɛlɛˈmoˑr, ðɪ ˈmɛlɛˌbalɛˈmoˑr (U). A house and former mill near Inchmarnoch.

**Mill of Birkhall** See Mill of Sterin.

**Mill of Braichlie\*** Miln of Braichley (G 10). Former mill south-west of Ballater.

**The Mill of Castleton\*** (Ra 5, 151915). At Braemar, on east side of Clunie, where a house called the Mill House still preserves the name.

**Mill of Coldrach\*** (I, 152882). Mill of Cordillach (Cr 23). In lower Glen Clunie.

**Mill of Cosh** (OS, C, 321953), ˌmɛlɛˈhɔʃ, ˌmɛlɛˈkɔʃ. Quhoise (Rg), Mill of Quoch (In). Also Muileann a' Chòis (4), mill of the hollow. Mulnchois (Opr 5), Miln Chosh (Crg 9), Miln hosh (D in A). Under Mill of Quoise (mistakenly said to be in Braemar parish), Diack noted mul an hōsh, mulin a hōsh. In lower Glen Girnock.

**Mill of Coull** (OS, C, 138912), ˌmɛlɛˈkul. Also Muileann na Cùile (5, U) ˌmulənɛˈkul, mill of the corner. Milnacoule (Me 15), Mulnn na cul (D). On a corner of land sticking out, west of Braemar.

**The Mill of Coull Burn\*** (Md 1, C, 138910), ðɪˌmɛlɛˈkulˈbʌrn. West of Braemar.

**The Mill of Coull Haugh\*** (U, 140914), ðɪˌmɛlɛˈkulˈhaˑχ. West of Braemar.

**Mill of Coull Pool** (137913). Mull o' Coull Pool (Ly). In Dee west of Braemar.

**Mill of Crathie** (Gf, south-west of 262951). Also Mill of Lawsie (Ra 7). Miln of Lawsie (R 3). A former mill at Milltoun of Crathie.

**Mill of Crathienaird\*** Miln of Crathynaird (R 5). A former mill near Crathie, possibly same as Mill of Lawsie and Mill of Crathie.

**The Mill of Culsh.** The Mill of Cults (Io 45, Ri 34), Milne of Cults (G 17). Possibly same as Muileann Chritheannaich, but may well have been further upstream (Io).

**Mill of Dail Mhor\*** (117911). Mill of Dellmore (Cr 9), Mill of Delmore (R 2). Mil delmore (Fa) suggests Gaelic Muileann Dail Mhór, mill of big haugh. On west side of lower Quoich, with Mill of Allanaquoich on east side at same place.

**Mill of Dinnet Farm** (Gf). Farmland on both sides of Dinnet Burn below the North Deeside Road, part of a former farm.

**(The) Mill of Gairn** (OS, C, 352973). ðɪˈmɛlɛˈgern̩. A former woollen mill, now a house, on west bank of river near Bridge of Gairn.

**Mill of Glen Clunie\*** Miln of Glencluny (Rli 19). Probably was near Coireyaltie.

**The Mill of Glen Muick** The Milne of Glenmuick (Io 7, Ri 14). Probably near the Milltoun of Aucholzie.

**(The) Mill of Inver** (OS, C, 233937), ðɪˈmɛlɛˈmvˑer. At the Inver west of Crathie, now a house.

**Mill of Invercauld** (Ri 38). Miln of Invercauld (Io 28). Presumably near Milltoun of Invercauld.

**Mill of Inverenzie\*** See the Mill o the Laggan.

**Mill of Inverey** (087887). Miln of Inverey (S 12). Former mill.

**Mill of Lary** See Muileann Lairidh.

**Mill of Lawsie\*** See Mill of Crathie.

**The Mill of Monaltrie** (Ri 17). Mill of Minaltrie (Ga). West of Crathie.

**Mill of Prony** See name below.

**Mill of Prony Cottage** (OS, C, 351974), locally Mill of Prony (C, Er), ˈmɛlɛˈprone. Mill of Pronie (H). On east bank of Gairn near Bridge of Gairn.

**Mill of Richarkarie\*** See Muileann Deire.

**Mill of Rineten*** (probably near 269017). Miln of Rineten (R 5). West of Gairnshiel.

**The Mill of Srath an Aitinn*** The Miln of Straaneaton (G 6), Miln of Stranetten (Io 37). Probably same place as Baile a' Mhuilinn in Glen Gairn.

**Mill of Sron*** (136833). Mill of Stroin (I). At the Baddoch, below Strone Baddoch.

**Mill of Sterin** (OS, C, 349929), 'mɛlɐ'stɛrn. Sterin (Dms 5) in 1636, Sterryne, Stering (Ap), Sterrein (Pb), Mill of Stern, clattering mill (McC 1891), Stern (A). In Gaelic Muileann Stairein (3), mill of path or stepping stones. Miln stirn (D). Clattering mill suggested (McC 1891), from Stairn, but the name of a former croft, Stairean Beag, makes this a less likely meaning. Sterin, the old name of Birkhall (A), has survived in the mill name even though the mill was Mill of Birkhall for some time: Miln of Birkhall (Ri) in 1743, and Mill of Birchhall (I) in 1807–9 shown on the same site as Mill of Sterin. A house in lower Glen Muick.

**The Mill of Sterin Brae*** See the Cock's Neck.

**The Mill of Sterin Brig*** (C, 349930), ðɪ'mɛlɐ'stɛrn̩'brɪg. A bridge in Glen Muick.

**The Mill of Sterin Park*** (U, 350927), ðɪ'mɛlɐ'stɛrn̩'park. A field in lower Glen Muick.

**Mill of Stranlea** (Ri 39). East of Gairnshiel.

**Mill of the Braes of Cromar*** (c. 417041). Miln of the Braes of Cromar (Io 20). Also Whitehouse Miln (G19). A former mill at Milton of Whitehouse west of Logie Coldstone.

**Mill of Tom Bealaidh*** (352973). Mill of Tombelly, Meal Miln of Tombelly (Io 42), Old Mill of Toumbyallie (I). A former meal mill near Bridge of Gairn, later the woollen Mill of Gairn.

**The Mill o Ruighe an Luig*** (U, south-west of 131825), ðɪ'mɛlɐ ˌrɪn'luəg. A former mill in the Baddoch.

**The Mill o the Laggan** (F, 330008), ðɪ'mɛlɪðɪ'lagən. Milne of Laggan (Crg 16), Mill of Laggan (Cg), Mill of the Laggan (Bl). Mill of Inverenzie or Waulkmill of Inverenzie were probably other names for Mill o the Laggan; Inverenzie and the Laggan are in the same small area, and a Janet was recorded at both (Crg). Milne of Inverenzie (Crg 4). Miln of Inverinzie or Waulkmilne of Inverinzie (Crg 5). Near the foot of Glen Fenzie.

**The Mill o Tullich*** (F, 387976), ðɪ'mɛlɐ'tʌləç, or the Meal Mill o Tullich (U), ðɪ'mil'mɛlɐ'tʌləç. Mill of Tullich (R 15). North-east of Ballater.

**The Mill Park*** (U, 415034), ðɪ'mɛl'park. Named after a former mill dam. A field west of Logie Coldstone.

**The Mill Puil** (C, north of 407979), ðɪ'mɛl'pil. Mill Pool (Sc). Turner's Pool (Ly). A pool in Dee beside former bobbin mill west of Cambus o' May.

**Mills of Gairn Cottage*** (Ce 5). House beside Bridge of Gairn, probably site of one of houses now on west bank.

**Millstone Burn** (OS, 170885). Also Burn of Easter Coire Gorm. Burn of Easter Corry Goram (I). In lower Glen Callater, beside the Millstone Cairn (below).

**Millstone Cairn** (OS, M, 169890), locally the Millstone Hill (A, U), ðɪ'mɛlˌstɔn'hɛl. Also Carn nan Clach-mhuilinn (3), hill of the millstones. Carn na Clach Mulin (I). A hill at the mouth of Glen Callater, formerly used for making millstones (CMcI).

**Millstone Cairn** (OS, 286879). A stony little top in upper Glen Girnock.

**The Millstone Cairn*** (U, 279865), ðɪ'mɛlˌstɔn'kern̩. Millstone Cairn (B). Highest point of the hill of Conachcraig in upper Glen Muick.

**The Millstone Cairn** See Carn Clach-mhuilinn.

**The Millstone Hill** See Carn Cloich-mhuilinn.

**The Milltoun*** The Millton (In). At Mill of Sterin in Glen Muick.

**The Milltoun*** (C, 426964), ðɪ'mɛltən. Was also called Milltoun of Inchmarnoch or Milltoun of Ballaterach. Milltoune Inchmarnot (G 4). Millhouse (Roy), Milton of Ballaterach (Opr 53). The Milton and Newton Parks formed the arable land for this former farm east of Pannanich (Dms).

**The Milltoun*** See Baile a' Mhuilinn.

**The Milltoun Brig** (C, 319002), ðɪ'mɛltən'brɪg. Milton Brig (Afr). In Glen Gairn.

**The Milltoun Brig*** (C, 425963), as above. Also the Newton Brig (F), ðɪ'njutən'brɪg; the Pollach Brig (U), ðɪ'puləç'brɪg. Bridge carrying the public road at Inchmarnoch.

**The Milltoun Brig Park*** (F, 320003), ðɪ'mɛltən'brɪg'park. A field in lower Glen Gairn.

**The Milltoun Burn*** (C, 426964), ðɪ'mɛltən'bʌrn, or the Burn of the Milton (Dms). Lower part of Pollagach Burn at Inchmarnoch.

**The Milltoun Burn** (U, 160931), as above. The Milton Burn (Brown). Lower part of Allt an t-Slugain near Invercauld.

**Milltoun Cottage*** Milton Cottage (Opr 63). Former habitation beside Milltoun of Invercauld.

**Milltoun of Abererder*** Milntown of abererder (Cr 38a). Also Milltown of Ballchlaghan (Io 66). Near Ballachlaggan west of the Inver.

**Milltoun of Abergeldie*** See Drymill.

**Milltoun of Auchendryne*** Miltoune of Achendrain (Cr 38a). At Braemar.

**The Milltoun of Aucholzie** (F, 350923), ðɪ'mɛltənɐˌa'hwɛili, but ðɪ'mɛltənɐˌaχ'ɔlji from oldest informant. Milne and Milnetown of Glenmuick (Ri 14) probably here. Milntown in Acholie, Milton of Acholie (Rli 18, 20). Often the Milltoun (F). A former farm in lower Glen Muick.

**Milltoun of Ballachlaggan** See Milltoun of Abererder.

**Milltoun of Ballaterach*** See the Milltoun.

**Milltoun of Chritheannaich*** (350975). Milltown of Crinach (Im 7). A former house near Bridge of Gairn. Note Muileann Chritheannaich or Mill o Chritheannaich near here.

**Milltoun of Coldrach*** (c. 152882). Milltoune of Cordillach (Cr 16). Former habitation in Glen Clunie.

**Milltoun of Crathie** (Ri 22, 262951). A ferry and ford over Dee were here. By 1801 the name still remained though the mill had gone and the ferry and ford were no longer used (Ri). Also the Milltoun of Lawsie (R 3, 6 a), the milltun of Lausie (Ri 18). A former farm.

**Milltoun of Dinnet*** (469990). Milntoun of Dinnat (Io 39). Former name of buildings on both sides of Dinnet Burn at Mill o Dinnet; the Mill o Dinnet was on east bank, just outside our study area.

**Milltoun of Glen Clunie*** Milntown of Glencluny (Rli 23), Milntown of Glenclunie (Io 53). Probably was near Coireyaltie.

**The Milltoun of Glen Muick** The Milnetoune of Glenmuick (Io 7). Probably the same as the Milltoun of Aucholzie.

**Milltoun of Inchmarnoch** See the Milltoun.

**Milltoun of Inver** Miltown of Inver (Opr 29). Former habitation.

**The Milltoun of Invercauld** (F, 159928), ðɪ'mɛltənɐˌɪnvɛr'ka·ld, often just the Milltoun. Miltowne (Fa), Milton of Invercauld (Mc 23), Milltown of Invercauld (R 7). North-west of Invercauld House.

**The Milltoun of Lawsie** See Milltoun of Crathie.

**Milltoun of Prony*** (350975). Milltown of Pronie (Im 7), Milltown of Pronnie (Rli 10). Former mill house on east side of lower Gairn.

114

Scurriestone, a standing stone near Ballater, with the ruin of Knock Castle above it.

The Clunie Stane or Erskine's Stane lies beside the main road near Invercauld Bridge.

**Milltoun of Tom Bealaidh\*** (352972). Milltown of Tombelly (Im 7). Former mill house near Bridge of Gairn.

**The Milltoun o Inverey\*** See Baile a' Mhuilinn.

**The Milltoun Park\*** (F, 425964), ðɪˈmɛltən'park. Also the Tassack Park (U), ðɪˈtasɐk'park. A field between the public road and Dee, at Inchmarnoch.

**The Milltoun Parks\*** (U, 163930 and 160928), ðɪˈmɛltən'parks. Fields north-west of Invercauld, including Ach an Sgeich Park.

**Milne's Brae\*** (C, south-east of 152915), 'mɛlzˈbreˑ. Officially Castleton Place. In Braemar.

**The Milton Burn** (C, 319003), ðɪˈmɛltənˈbʌrn. Milton Burn (OS 1869). The lower part of West Milton Burn (OS) and also the main burn below the junction of East and West Milton Burns east of Gairnshiel.

**The Milton Cottage\*** (F, 384975), ðɪˈmɛltənˈkɔtədʒ. The northern one of a pair of houses near Tullich.

**The Milton Hill\*** (U, 381985), ðɪˈmɛltənˈhɛl. The hill grazing for Milton of Tullich farm near Ballater.

**Milton of Brackley** (OS, C, 362947), 'mɛltənɐˈbreçle. Milntown of Breachly (Ri 24a). A farm at the foot of Glen Muick.

**(The) Milton of Tullich** (OS, C, 386975), ðɪˈmɛltənɐˈtʌləç, often just the Milltoun (F). A farm north-east of Ballater.

**Milton of Whitehouse** (OS, F, 417041), 'mɛltənɐˈhwɛitˈhus, or the Milton o the Braes (F), ðɪˈmɛltənɪðɪˈbrez, i.e. the Braes o Cromar, or simply the Milton (C). Milltoune of Whithouse (Pb). A farm west of Logie Coldstone.

**The Milton Plantins\*** (F, 417039), ðɪˈmɛltənˈplantɪnz. A pair of hillocks with trees, in a field near Logie Coldstone.

**The Miners' Hut** (McC 1896, 142004). A former hut used by people digging for gemstones last century, by Allt an Eas Mhoir on Ben Avon.

**The Mines o' Abergairn** (Dil, south of 355975). Former mines near Ballater.

**Minister's Ford\*** (R 3, 239976). A ford on the Crathie Burn, north-west of Crathie.

**The Minister's Puil** (C, 417978), ðɪˈmɪnɪstɛrzˈpil. Minister's (Sc). In Dee, above the bridge at Cambus o' May. This and the other Minister Puils below are often called the Minister's, or just Minister.

**The Minister's Puil** (C, 461982), as above. Minister's (P). In Dee, beside the manse at Dinnet.

**The Minister's Puil** (F, 264947), as above. Minister (A). Also the Manse Puil (U), ðɪˈmansˈpil. Manse Pool (Sc). In Dee, near the old manse at Crathie.

**The Minister's Puil** (C, east of 365950), as above, or the Minister's Pot (F), ðɪˈmɪnɪstɛrzˈpɔt, Scots Pot = deep pool. Minister's Pool (Sc). In Dee, near the old manse at the foot of Glen Muick.

**Am Mìr Dubh\*** (3, 186925), the black bit or top. The Meer Du (I), Mheer Dhu (R 14). Also the Felagie Rocks (U), ðɪˌfəˈlegiˈrɔks. The cliffs on Craig Leek east of Invercauld.

**The Mission Church** See the Knockan Kirk.

**The Mitchell Puil** See Poll na h-Iuchrach.

**Mitchell's Park\*** See the Grocer's Park.

**Mitchel's Croft\*** (I, west of 355949). A field near the foot of Glen Muick.

**M'Kenzies Tree** (Brown, probably 15-91-). A tree formerly used for hanging, on Creag Choinnich at Braemar.

**Mòine a' Chaochain Odhair** (OS, 257902), peat-moss of the dun streamlet. In Glen Gelder.

**Mòine a' Chuir** (3, F, 270939), ˌmɔnɐˈχur, peat-moss of the turn. Monachur (In, OS 1903). A house south of Easter Balmoral, a place where the aspect of the ground takes a big turn in direction.

**Mòine Allt Duisgan** (OS, 315048), from Mòine Allt Dubh-easgainne (3, U), ˌmɔinˌaltˈduəskən, peat-moss of burn of black little bog. Also the Allt Duisgan Moss (F), ðɪˌalt 'duəskənˈmɔs. On the hills at the top of Glen Fenzie.

**Mòine an Eich\*** (3, 227976), peat-moss of the horse. Moin'n Eich, Moss of Moninaich, Horse moss (R 3, 5, 9). North-west of Crathie.

**The Moine an Tighearn road** (Wyness 1971, 222969), Mòine an Tighearn (3) = peat-moss of the laird. North of the Inver.

**Mòine an t-Sagairt** (3, near 139907), peat-moss of the priest. Moine dakart (D), Mon dakartsh (D in A). West of Braemar, between Woodhill and An Car.

**Mòine Bad a' Chabair** (OS, 3, U, 287894), ˌmɔinˌbadˈhabɛr, peat-moss of clump of the pole. Also the Moss o Bad a' Chabair (F), ðɪˈmɔsɐˌbadˈhabɛr, now usually the Bad a' Chabair Moss (C). The Moss of Badhabber, the Badhabber Moss (A 159). In upper Glen Girnock.

**Mòine Bhealaich Bhuidhe** (OS, 167831), peat-moss of the yellow pass. South-west of Loch Callater.

**Mòine Bhealaidh** (OS, 4, CG, 054992), mɔnˈvjal, peat-moss of the broom, locally now ðɪˈjalɐˈmɔs (C), 'jalɐ being possibly from Bhealaidh. Muneveall (Io 19, Me 6). Several authors writing about place names (e.g. Sg, A) referred to it as the Yellow Moss on the assumption that 'jalɐˈmɔs represented Scots for Yellow Moss. The name is known to many people, and we have discussed it with over twenty. We have found that 'jɛloˈmɔs or 'jɛloˈmɔs is never used by locally-reared folk, except when telling people from outside north-east Scotland about the name. A rough grassland and peat-moss east of Glen Derry.

**Mòine Bhuidhe** (OS, 3, U, 298035), ˌmɔinəˈbui, yellow moss. North of Gairnshiel.

**Mòine Bhuidhe** (OS, 230919), yellow moss. South of the Inver.

**Mòine Chair** (3, U, 126903), mɔnˈχaˑr, peat-moss of the bend. Mon charr (D). Named from the nearby little top of An Car south-west of Braemar.

**Mòine Chraichidh\*** (6, 215985, on the location of Monaltrie Moss (OS), which should be at 228975), peat-moss of the Crathie or ? shaking place (for meaning see Crathie). Moine Chrathie (R 3). North-west of Crathie.

**Mòine Chreagain\*** (3, 363882), peat-moss of the little rock. Moin Chraggan (I). South-east of the Linn of Muick.

**Mòine Chruinn** (OS, 223916), should be A' Chruinn-mhòine (3, F), 'χrunɐˈmon, almost 'mun, the round peat-moss. Note A chruinne mhoine in Kintyre (T 27, 37). Cruinavean (B). Also Moss of Connachat. Moss of Coinachaig (R 7). Also Bowman's Moss (Io 78, A, C), 'bumənzˈmɔs, after a man of surname Bowman, who accidentally hanged himself on a fence (CW). In the woods west of Glen Gelder.

**Mòine Dhubh\*** (3, 313878), black peat-moss. Mindoue (Io 1), Mondu (R 6). Also Muir Dhubh, a semi-anglicised form. Muirdoue (Io 1). A peat-moss below Inchnabobart in upper Glen Muick.

**Mòine Eun\*** (3, 366924), peat-moss of birds. Munain (R 6), Moin Ain (I). South of Ballater.

**Mòine Fhearn\*** (3, U), mɔinˈjaˑrn, peat-moss of alders. A collective name for Lower and Upper Moine Fhearn north-east of Crathie.

**Mòine Ghrod** (3, A, near 139907), rotten moss. West of Braemar, between Woodhill and An Car.

**Mòine Lic\*** (3, 165005), peat-moss at a slope. Moin Leek (I), Moin Loich (R 16, but many misprints in this map). Up on the south-east slope of Ben Avon.

**Mòine na Cloiche** (OS, 305901), peat-moss of the stone. Also the Moss of Coire na Cloiche (A, F), ðɪˈmɔsɐˌkɔrnɐˈklɔiç. Moss of Cornycloich (In). In upper Glen Girnock.

**Mòine na Cloiche*** (3, 293972), peat-moss of the stone. Moin-na-cloich (I). North-east of Crathie.

**Mòine nam Bó*** (3, 260006), peat-moss of the cows. Mon-na-bo, Moin-a' bho (R 3, 14). Beside the hillock of Meall nam Bo, west of Gairnshiel.

**Mòine nan Ceap*** (3, F, 272912), ˌmo̯nɐˈgep, peat-moss of the stumps. Mooniegape (B). Moine a' chat (Bs) is on this site, and Alexander gave Monaget, 'presumably for moss of the cats', but we think these are errors for Moine nan Ceap. Also the Moss o Moine nan Ceap (F), ðɪˈmo̯sɐˌmo̯nɐˈgep. South-west of Abergeldie.

**Mòine nan Con** (3, A, U, 068906), ˌmoɪnɐˈgon, peat-moss of the dogs. In lower Glen Lui.

**Mòine nan Con** (3, 290925), peat-moss of the dogs. Monagon (A). Also the Moss o Moine nan Con (U), ðɪˈmo̯sɐˌmo̯nɐˈgon. South of Abergeldie.

**Mòine nan Gall** (3, A, U, 147912), ˌmo̯nɐˈgaˑl, peat-moss of the foreigners. Moine na gall, the lowlanders moss (D). Also the Princess Royal and Duke of Fife Memorial Park, but this official name for the Braemar games park never became used in local speech. Locally the Games Park (C), ðɪˈgemzˈpark.

**The Moine-na-vey Loch*** See the Balanreich Loch.

**Moine Ranntaich** (3, probably 246053), divided moss. See Coire Poll Randaidh. Moun Grauntich (Dil). One interpretation of Poll Randaidh was 'Pol Ghrantaich, Grant's pool' (A). A peat-moss in Glen Gairn, probably in Coire Poll Randaidh.

**Mòine Rumaich*** (3, U, 290970), moɪnˈrumɪç, peat-moss of marsh. North-east of Crathie.

**Mòine Taibhseach** (4, U, 313026), mo̯nˈdʌusəç, (mʌnˈdausəç with nasal diphthong (A)), ghostly peat-moss, or Taimhseich = Tawse's. Moine Dausich (A). Also Fleming's Moss (F), ˈflimənzˈmo̯s. Flemings were former residents in this area. North-east of Gairnshiel.

**Am Monadh** (3), the hill-range. For early references see A. Also the Mòunth (C), ðɪˈmʌnθ. The Munth (Gler). The hill range on the south side of Deeside; it runs from Drumochter to just south of Aberdeen.

**Am Monadh Geal** See White Mounth.

**Monadh Gheallaig** (3, 297981), hill-range of the white one. Mon yallik (D). Old name for the whole hill mass centred on Geallaig Hill, now Micras Hill.

**Mona Gowan** (OS, C, 336058), ˌmo̯nɐˈgʌu.ən, from Monadh Ghobhainn (4), hill of the smith. Moine = peat-moss suggested (A), as there is a peat-moss on the Don side of the hill, which is still worked. This is possible, but all our informants who knew the place said the name refers to the whole hill, and pronounced the Mona part as in Am Monadh Mor (see name below). Minagowen (R 14a). The highest point of the hill is just on the Don side, but the Mona Gowan Butts are well down on the Dee side at 340047 (WGi). A hill north of Morven Lodge.

**Monadh Mór** (OS, 939942), from Am Monadh Mór (2, D, C), ðɪˌmo̯nɐˈmoːr, the big hill. At the west end of Glen Geusachan.

**Am Monadh Ruadh** (2, F), ðɪˈmo̯nɐˈruɐ, the red hill-range. Old name for the Cairngorms. The Monadhruadh (Gr), Na monadh ruadh = the red mountains, given in a list of names whose Gaelic forms were given as spoken in the Braemar district (Mp). The local name Monadh Ruadh has died out in Deeside but is still known on the Spey side of the Cairngorms. Mountains of Monroy (Roy).

**Monaltrie** (C), mo̯nˈaltri, from Mòine Ailtridh (6), peat-moss of ? stony place. Mon-naltrich, mon-altrin, the latter from old people (D). Monaltrie, Monaltarie (Io 11, 41). A former estate that stretched from Brown Cow Hill south to Dee at Balnault. Still known locally for the general area of Balnault.

The estate house stood on the site later used for the farm of Mains of Monaltrie, and the family later moved (carrying the place name with them) to Monaltrie House at Ballater. An old map (R 3, 1788) shows the burn nearby (the present Coldrach Burn OS), as the Altrie Burn. There was formerly a place called Altrie near Old Deer (A), mentioned in the Book of Deer as Alteri (dative) and Alterin (accusative), from a nominative Ailtere, with a contraction used for *er*, thus Ailtri or Ailtrin (Ja 46). The meaning is unknown but may be based on Ail = rock or stone. Thus Altrie Burn had probably been Allt Ailtridh = burn at stony place, and Monaltrie had been Mòine Ailtridh or Mòine Ailtrin = peat-moss at stony place. Note spelling Altran also, see under Bridgend of Altrie. Probably the peat-moss had been the one on the hill near the house, and it is a stony area. The well-known name of the Monaltrie Moss, referring to a peat-moss several miles away out of sight beyond the hill to the north, was probably a later name referring to the biggest peat-moss on the Monaltrie estate.

**The Monaltrie Brig*** (U, 374971), ðɪˌmo̯nˈaltriˈbrɪg. North-east of Ballater.

**Monaltrie Burn** See Balnault Burn.

**The Monaltrie Ford** (Wy). A former ford over Dee, probably near Balnault west of Crathie.

**Monaltrie House** See Mains of Monaltrie, and the name below.

**Monaltrie House** (OS, C, 372967), mo̯nˈaltriˈhus. A house near Ballater, originally called Ballater House in 1790 (R 4). The original owner was Francis Farquharson of Monaltrie who had to give up his estate at Monaltrie west of Crathie after the 1745 Jacobite rising, but later owned an area at Ballater which thus came also be to called Monaltrie because of his courtesy title. Sometimes was called Tullich Lodge (Brown 1835).

**(The) Monaltrie Monument** (OS, C, 400977), ðɪˌmo̯nˈaltri ˈmo̯njəmɪnt. A monument east of Ballater to William Farquharson of Monaltrie, (i.e. the Ballater Monaltrie), who developed the rectangular planned layout of Ballater village. Also the Farquharson Monument (Rt).

**(The) Monaltrie Moss** (OS, C, 215985, should be at 228975, 215985 is Moine Chraichidh), ðɪˌmo̯nˈaltriˈmo̯s. Moss of Monaltrie (R 3 in 1788) at a time when other mosses nearby had Gaelic names. North-west of Crathie.

**The Monaltrie Park** See the Cricket Park.

**Monandavan Burn** (OS, 450004, should be at 456010), ˌmɪnən ˈdaˑwənˈbʌrn, from Mòine an Dabhan (6), peat-moss of ?, (see also Loch Davan). Monandavan is a farm just outside the area covered in this book. The burn running out of Loch Davan near Dinnet, but locally this is the Goc Stane Burn. The Monandavan Burn is locally used for the small burn to the north-east, outside the area covered in this book.

**The Monega** (F, 169779), ðɪˌmo̯nˈegə, possibly from Am Monadh Eagach (4), the notched mounth; but Gaelic pronunciation was mon-ŭgh (D), suggesting possibly Aghaidh = face (Dro). Mon-agh (Dro). Moneygy (Po, Go), Minegy (Roy), Month Eigie (V), the Monega (A and other references). The Monega reaches a higher altitude and crosses a more exposed plateau than any other Mounth road in the Highlands. Note Monega Hill (OS) on the Angus side of this mounth road over the Glas Maol from upper Clunie to upper Glen Isla. Often described in books (Al, Moi) as the Monega Pass, but the local name is simply the Monega.

**The Monega Pass** See the Monega.

**The Monega Road*** (F, 169779), ðɪˌmo̯nˈegəˈrod. Footpath over the Monega from upper Glen Clunie to upper Glen Isla.

**(The) Monelpie Moss** (OS, C, 275837), ðɪˌmo̯nˈɛlpiˈmo̯s, from Mòine Ealpaidh (3), notched moss. Said to mean jagged moss (McC 1891), Mon ēlpi (D), The Moss of Monelpie (A). Same sound as in Glen Eilpy on the Don side of Morven. This moss has one notable long notch for over ½ km on the west side of An t-Sron, along the upper part of Alltan Dearg, and several smaller ones due to shorter furrows and peat hags. On the plateau on the Lochnagar side of Loch Muick.

**The Monument Park*** (F, 155928), ðɪˈmɒnjəmɪntˈpark. A field at Invercauld including Uchdach and other fields.

**The Monument Puil** (F, 157927), ðɪˈmɒnjəmɪntˈpil. Monument (A). In Dee beside the Invercauld Monument north of Braemar.

**The Moor of Ach Eich an Easa*** (202907). The Moor of Auchichnes (Im 6). A former moor, now a wood, east of Invercauld Bridge.

**Moor of the Baddoch*** (I, 130812). Moorland hillsides beyond the former farmlands at the Baddoch.

**Moor of the Inver** (I, 225930). A former moor south-west of Inver Inn, now a wood.

**Na Móra-lannan*** (3, C, 402972), ðɪˈmurlənz, the big enclosures. Unlikely to be Moorlands, as there is no moorland here or at the similar-named place nearby (see the name below), and in any case the word moorland is not used in local Scots speech. A former house at Glascorrie east of Pannanich Hotel, stones recently dumped in Dee by gamekeepers.

**The Mora-lannan Puil*** (C, 409981), ðɪˈmurlənzˈpil. A pool in Dee, west of Cambus o' May.

**Morgan's Brig*** See the Rinabaich Brig.

**Morrone** or **Morven** (OS, C, 132886), mɒˈron. Diack noted that all in Braemar called it Mōr-vinn, the same sound as in Morven (but later wrote 'approximate sound, Mor-Rone') and he criticised the OS for calling it Mor-Shron = big nose on their first map. Macpherson also stated this, with Morbhinn, morving, big hill. Furthermore, note ˈmoːrɪŋ, ˈmoːrvɪŋ with indistinct *v* (Sch). However, an early map (I, in 1807–9) gives More Roin at about 138890. A map R 16 in 1867, with many misprints, gives Moir Buin, which might be Beinn or Roinn. MacGillivray wrote 'a large hill, named Morrone,—Mor-sthroine'. Thus the name might have been Mór-roinn = big point, or Mór-shròin = at big nose. However, Mór-bheinn pronounced with a svarabhakti vowel as ˈmorovɪn would give a stress less emphatically on the first syllable than in ˈmorvɪn. If the *v* sound dropped out (as in Sch above) and the stress became even less pronounced or wandered to the right, as could happen in such a case, then this would give the present mɒˈron from an original Mór-bheinn, and yet would not conflict with the spellings More Roin and Mor-sthroine. A similar case with an adjective before a noun, where the stress has certainly moved to the right in recent decades is Glas-choire and Glascorrie at Pannanich near Ballater. A big hill at Braemar, sticks out into the Dee valley in a point forming the north end of the hill range on the west side of Glen Clunie.

**Morrone Birkwood National Nature Reserve** (Pj, 140905), locally the Morrone Reserve (C), ðɪˌmɒˈronˌrɪˈzɛrv. A nature reserve in the birch-juniper wood west of Braemar.

**The Morrone Hut*** See Radio Relay Hut.

**The Morrone Mast*** (C, 132886), ðɪˌmɒˈronˈmast. A radio mast south-west of Braemar.

**The Morrone Road*** (C, 140880), ðɪˌmɒˈronˈrod. A former peat road up towards Morrone from lower Glen Clunie, now a Land Rover track to the radio relay hut at the top of Morrone.

**Morven** (OS, C, 377040), ˈmɒrˌvən, but Murr-vin (A), ˈmʌrˌvən to people who live beside the hill (C), from Mór-bheinn (3), big hill. Morvine (Io 50), Morevene (Ab 7a), Mons de

Morving (Rg), Morven or Morveen—Mor-bhein, the great mountain (Mg). A big hill west of Logie Coldstone, looks the biggest hill in Deeside when seen from Cromar or east of the Muir of Dinnet. Note Easter and Wester Morven, two extinct farming communities.

**(The) Morven Burn** (OS, C, 345029), ðɪˈmɒrˌvənˈbʌrn. West of Morven.

**Morven Cottages** (OS, C, 338996), ˈmɒrˌvənˈkɒtədʒɪz. In Glen Gairn.

**Morven Lodge** (OS, C, 339030), ˈmɒrˌvənˈlɒdʒ. The site of a former shooting lodge in the big basin west of Morven.

**The Morven Lodge Wuid*** (C, 338030), ðɪˈmɒrˌvənˈlɒdʒˈwɪd. A wood west of Morven.

**The Morven Mosses*** (F, 342039), ðɪˈmɒrˌvənˈmɒsɪz. A peat-moss north of Morven Lodge.

**The Morven Parks*** (U, 335032), ðɪˈmɒrˌvənˈparks. Former fields beside Morven Lodge.

**The Morvens*** The Morvins (G 19). A collective name for the two sets of farmlands at Wester and Easter Morven.

**The Morven View Brig*** (F, south-east of 409045), ðɪˈmʌrvən ˈvjuˈbrɪg. A bridge over Groddie Burn west of Logie Coldstone, beside a house called Morven View (outside our study area), and formerly called Auld Groddie. Formerly the Auld Groddie Brig (U), ðɪˈalˈgrɒdiˈbrɪg.

**Moses' Cairn*** See Carn Aosda.

**The Moss Butts*** (U, 261040), ðɪˈmɒsˈbʌts. Grouse butts north-west of Gairnshiel, made of sods from a peat-moss.

**The Mosses o Megen** (F, 325896), ðɪˈmɒsɪzeˈmɛgən. Moss of Megan (In), the Moss of Meggen (A). A peat-moss in upper Glen Muick, now under planted conifers.

**The Mosses o Tuirc*** (F, 177817), ðɪˈmɒsɪzeˈtʌrk. Peat-mosses high on Carn an Tuirc south of Loch Callater.

**The Moss o Eilean Greine*** (U, north-east of 439006), ðɪˈmɒseˌɛlənˈgrin. A peat-moss at Loch Davan.

**The Moss of Ach Chadha*** (363015). The Moss of Acha (G 19). A peat-moss south-west of Morven.

**The Moss of Allanaquoich*** (Fi, 103938). In Glen Quoich.

**The Moss of Bad a' Chairr*** (388015). The Moss of Badaquhar, Badechur, Badicurr (G 19). A peat-moss south-east of Morven.

**Moss of Bad Fiantaige*** (248986). Moss of Bad feandaig (R 3). North-west of Crathie.

**Moss of Bad nan Cuileag*** (218968). Moss of Badnaculack (I). North-west of the Inver.

**Moss of Blairglass*** (262003). Moss of Blarglass (R 3). West of Gairnshiel.

**Moss of Bogingore*** (Io 20, 435995). A peat-moss at Loch Kinord.

**The Moss of Branndair*** (361014). The Moss of Brander (Io 20). A peat-moss south-west of Morven.

**The Moss of Clais Mhor*** (166893). The Moss of Clashmoir (Io 25a). A peat-moss south-east of Braemar.

**Moss of Coire Chuilinn** (283987, by elimination). Moss of Corryquholdin (Ri). South-west of Gairnshiel.

**Moss of Coire na Cloiche** See Moine na Cloiche.

**The Moss of Coirenalarig** (124853). The Moss of Corielairick (Ri). A peat-moss high on the hills west of Glen Clunie.

**Moss of Connachat*** See Moine Chruinn.

**Moss of Coulachan*** (236988). Moss of Culachan (R 9). North-west of Crathie.

**The Moss of Crathienaird** (Io 16, Ri 21). A peat-moss north-west of Crathie.

**Moss of Dubh-choire*** (240005). Moss of Duchory (R 3). South-east of Corndavon Lodge.

**Moss of Felagie*** (193926). Moss of Filegie (Im 4). A peat-moss east of Invercauld.

**Moss of Kinord\*** Moss of Keandore (Io 20), from Ceanndair. Possibly same as the Moss o Old Kinord.

**Moss of Moine Odhar\*** (310915). Mòine Odhar (3) = dun moss. Moss of Monour (Am). In Glen Girnock.

**The Moss of Morven\*** See the Moss of Tullich.

**Moss of Ruighe Chreichidh\*** (265995). Moss of Rie Crathie (I). South-west of Gairnshiel.

**Moss of the Bad Fearn\*** (298026). Am Bad Fearn (3) = the alder clump. Moss of the Bat-fyarn (I). This is another case like An t-Eilean Fearn where the article is retained, presumably with Fearn in an adjectival sense. North of Gairnshiel.

**Moss of the Glas-allt\*** (158970). Moss of the Glass Ault (I). North-west of Invercauld.

**The Moss of Tillyhip** (Gf, U), ðɪ'mɔsɐˌtɪle'çɛp, from Tulach Cheap (3), hillock of blocks. A peat-moss probably east of Dinnet, near if not the same as the Peat Hillock Bog.

**The Moss of Tullich\*** (G 19, 370021). Tullich Moss (Io 68). Also the Moss of Morven (Io 68). A peat-moss near Morven.

**Moss o Moine nan Ceap\*** See Moine nan Ceap.

**The Moss o Moine nan Con\*** See Moine nan Con.

**The Moss o Old Kinord\*** (U, 438000), ðɪ'mɔsɐ'aˑlˌkɪn'ɔrd, usually now the Old Kinord Moss (F). A peat-moss at Loch Kinord.

**The Moss o the Haugh\*** (F, 432982), ðɪ'mɔsɪðɪ'haˑχ, ðɪ'mɔsəi 'haˑχ. A hollow on the Muir of Dinnet, formerly a peat-moss for the farm of the Haugh.

**The Moss o the Haugh Brae\*** (U, 428978), ðɪ'mɔsəi'haˑx'breˑ. A hill on the road at Muir of Dinnet.

**The Moss o the Haugh Road\*** (U, 430985), ðɪ'mɔsəi'haˑχ'rod. An old track from Wisdomhow south-east to the North Deeside Road, on Muir of Dinnet.

**The Moss o the Pollach\*** See the Pollach Moss.

**The Moss Park\*** (U, 424034), ðɪ'mɔs'park. A wet field beside a peat-moss near Logie Coldstone.

**The Moss Road\*** (C, 425953), ðɪ'mɔs'rod. Also the Darling Way (JO), ðɪ'darlɪŋ'weˑ, named after Dr Frank Fraser Darling who once used it. Old track to the peat-mosses south-east of Pannanich.

**The Moss Road\*** (Io 58, U, 392982), as above. A track to a peat-moss north-east of Tullich.

**The Moss Road\*** (U, 331904), as above. A former peat road from Loinn Muighe to Megen, now overgrown with trees.

**The Moss Road\*** (U, 309917), as above. Old track to peat-mosses in Glen Girnock.

**The Moss Road\*** (Fi, 086905). An old track above Mar Lodge, to peat-mosses.

**(The) Mosstown** (OS, C, 423048), ðɪ'mɔstən, often the Mosstown o the Braes (F), ðɪ'mɔstənɪðɪ'brez, to distinguish it from another Mosstown east of Logie Coldstone (outside our area), called the Mosstown o Blelack. A farm on the edge of a peat-moss west of Logie Coldstone.

**The Mosstown Brig\*** (C, 426050), ðɪ'mɔstən'brɪg. A bridge near Logie Coldstone.

**The Mosstown Brig Park\*** (U, 423050), ðɪ'mɔstən'brɪg'park, or just the Brig Park. A field near Logie Coldstone.

**The Mosstown Burn Park\*** (U, 50 metres west of 428046), ðɪ 'mɔstən'bʌrn'park. A field near Logie Coldstone.

**The Mosstown Haugh\*** (F, 426048), ðɪ'mɔstən'haˑχ. Also the Smiddie Park (U), ðɪ'smɪdi'park. A field west of Logie Coldstone.

**(The) Mosstown Plantation** (OS, C, 422043), ðɪ'mɔstən'plantɪn, Scots Plantin = plantation. West of Logie Coldstone.

**The Mounth** See Am Monadh.

**(The) Mounth Road** (OS, Gler, C, 392918), ðɪ'mʌnθ'rod. An old track from Ballater to Glen Mark in Angus.

**Mount Keen** (OS, C, 409869), mʌn'kin, often now mʌunt'kin,

from Monadh ? Choinn (5), hill of ? (see below). Month Kyin (Po), Month Kein (Bla), Monadh chuimhne, Mona-Chuine, Mona-chween or Month Keen (Mg). In Gaelic Mon kīng, mon Chaoin, mon cīn, mon ə chounn (D). Commonly thought to be Monadh Caoin, beautiful hill (A). However, Diack's and MacGillivray's notes suggest a noun in the genitive case, possibly Choinneamh = of meetings, as in Carnaquheen, or Chuing = of difficulties. A hill at the top of Glen Tanar.

**The Mount Keen** (U, 392918), ðɪˌmʌnθ'kin. The Month Keen (Gr), Munth Keen (A), the Mounth Keen Pass (Gf). Often just the Mounth (Gf, C). One of the passes over the Mounth, from Ballater to Glen Mark.

**The Mouth o Gairn\*** (F, 353966), ðɪ'mu.ɐ'gern̩. Where Gairn meets Dee.

**The Mouth o Girnock\*** (F, 332963), ðɪ'mu.ɐ'gërnɐk. Where Girnock meets Dee.

**The Mouth o Muick\*** (U, 367949), ðɪ'mu.ɐ'mëk. The mouth of Muick.

**The Mouth o Quoich\*** See Inbhir Choich.

**Mrs Middleton's Puil\*** (F, 154891), 'mɪsɪz'mɪdəltənz'pil, after a former inhabitant of nearby Balintuim. In Clunie south of Braemar.

**Mrs Shepherd's Park\*** (U, south of 358969), 'mɪsɪz'ʃëpërdz 'park. A field east of Bridge of Gairn, named after a former inhabitant of a house on the site of the Craigendarroch Hotel.

**Muckle Allanaquoich\*** See Allanaquoich.

**The Muckle Back Latch\*** (220831), Scots Latch = stream. The Meikle Black Latch (I). Pairs with the Little Back Latch. See the Back Latch. A burn west of Loch Muick.

**Muckle Balintober\*** See Balintober.

**Muckle Beinn Iutharn\*** See Beinn Iutharn Mor.

**The Muckle Birks\*** (U, south of 147909), ðɪ'mʌkəl'bërks. A place in the Manse Wuid at Braemar where birch trees are of great thickness.

**Muckle Brochdhu\*** Meikle Brochdoie (G 36). A former farm in lower Glen Muick.

**Muckle Broom Know\*** (229984, on site of Tom a' Bhealaidh OS but it should be at 228980), Scots = big broom knoll. Mickle broom know, Muckle broom (R 5, 9). Muckle Broom Know had probably come from Tom Bealaidh Mór = big hillock of broom. On the peat-mosses north-west of Crathie.

**The Muckle Buidheannach** See Buidheanach of Cairntoul.

**The Muckle Cadha Chuirn\*** See Cac Carn Mor.

**The Muckle Cairn\*** (F, 377040), ðɪ'mʌkəl'kern̩. The Meikle Cairn (I). Also the Cairn o' Morven (Dil). On the top of Morven.

**Muckle Cairn\*** (350958). Meikle Cairn (I). A little top on the Knock west of Ballater.

**Muckle Cairn\*** (096942). Meikle Cairn (Ra 4). A cairn on the top of Carn Suilean Dubha east of Glen Quoich.

**Muckle Carn an t-Sagairt** See Carn an t-Sagairt Mor.

**The Muckle Ceannair** See Meikle Kinord.

**Muckle Coire Dubh\*** (213858). Meikle Corry Du (R 7). Pairs with Little Coire Dubh, west of Lochnagar.

**Muckle Corrie o Lochnagar** See Corrie of Lochnagar.

**The Muckle Craig\*** See Creag a' Gheoidh Mhor.

**Muckle Creag an Dail** See Creag an Dail Mhor.

**Muckle Creag Mhor\*** See (A') C(h)reag Mhor.

**The Muckle Croft\*** (233937). The Meikle Croft (I). A field at the Inver.

**Muckle Croft** See the Crofts.

**Muckle Croft\*** (391972). Meikle Croft (R 4). On farmland at Tullich.

**The Muckle Dubh-chlais** See Dubh-chlais.

**The Muckle Dubh-chlais Burn*** (F, 262940), ðɪˈmʌkəlˈduˌçɫɐʃ ˈbʌrn. At Balmoral.

**Muckle Feadan** See Feadan Odhar.

**Muckle Geallaig** See Geallaig Hill.

**The Muckle Hillock*** (335886). The Meikle Hillock (I). A hillock south-east of the Linn of Muick.

**The Muckle Island*** (U, 440996), ðɪˈmʌkəlˈɛilənd. Malcolm Canmor's Island (Mg). Also the Castle Island (O). The biggest island on Loch Kinord.

**Muckle Knock*** (Opr 27, 349950). Meikle Knock (In, Io 33), Superiorum et inferiorum Knocks (Ab 19), Over and Nether Knocks (Ab). A former farm west of Ballater.

**Muckle Knock*** (348952). Meikle Knock (Am). A field west of Ballater.

**Muckle Lairig** See Lairig Mhor.

**The Muckle Liath-choire** See Liath-choire Mhor.

**The Muckle Liath-choire Burn** See Allt Liath-choire Mhor.

**The Muckle Meedow** (F), ðɪˈmʌkəlˈmidə, Scots = big meadow. The face of Black Hill from 318822 to 313815. Meikle Meadow (I). A grassy slope east of Loch Muick, pairs with the Little Meedow.

**Muckle Micras** See Wester Micras.

**The Muckle Moss*** (Md 12, U, 131905), ðɪˈmʌkəlˈmɔs. A peat-moss west of Braemar.

**The Muckle Moss*** (F, 433986), as above. A peat-moss on the Muir of Dinnet.

**The Muckle Ord** See the Ord.

**The Muckle Rig*** (south of 327003). The Meikle Rig (I). A field on the south of the river Gairn, east of Gairnshiel.

**Muckle Srathan*** (230937 on north side of burn). Muckle Strans, Mickle Strahans (Io 43, 53). Part of Na Srathanan, two grassy areas near the Inver.

**The Muckle Stane o the Clunie** See Clunie Stane.

**The Muckle Stane o Bad a' Chabair** See Clach Mhor Bad a' Chabair.

**Muckle Willie's Corrie** See Coire Uilleim Mhoir.

**The Muick** See River Muick.

**The Muickan Burn*** (U, 149903), ðɪˈmëkənˈbʌrn. At Croft Muickan and from there into Clunie; is Allt Beag higher up.

**Muileann Chritheannaich** (3), mill of aspen place. Muln chrunngich (D in A). Now Mill o Chritheannaich (F, 350976), ˌmëlɐˈçrinɪç. Chrinic (Io 75), Miln of Crinack, Mill of Crinach (Im 3, 7), Mill of Chrienach (R 14). A former mill near Bridge of Gairn, on west side of river.

**Muileann Deire** (4, 301015), mill of ? end (place), from Deireadh. Mulajyre (D). Also Miln of Richarkery (Io 45), Riecharkry Miln (Rli 19). Former mill of Richarkarie near Gairnshiel.

**Muileann Làraigh*** (5, north-west of 337000), mill of Lary, from Làrach = site of a building. Milne Larie (Io 8). Mill of Lary (Ab 8), Milne of Larie (G 12). In Glen Gairn, on east side of Lary Burn.

**Muileann Shàibh** (3, Cj 16), sawmill. A former keeper's house at a former sawmill near the Lui Bridge. Also the Saw Mill of Glen Lui. The Saw Milne of Glen Luy (Io). R 10 shows a Saw Mill north-west of 075897.

**The Muir** (C, 290005), ðɪˈmir, Scots Muir = moor. Achintowl about The Meer (R 1), Muir (Rli 23), Muir of Reinloan (Io 75), that is, Rinloan. A former house near Gairnshiel, incorrectly marked 'Grouse Butt' on the recent OS 1 : 25000 map.

**Muir** (OS, 065895). At Linn Cottage east of the Linn of Dee. Muir also (OS 1869) at c. 070896. Local informants say these are errors for Muir Cottage below.

**Muir Cottage** (OS, 077897), locally the Muir (C), ðɪˈmur.

Residenters at the Muir of Dee (Cr 55) probably here. A house at Inverey, now a climbing club hut.

**Muir Dhubh*** See Moine Dhubh.

**Muirend*** (Ce 3). Former habitation in Burnside-Braes area of Cromar.

**The Muir Kirk** See the Centrical Kirk.

**Muir of Cnoc nan Uan*** (probably 365018), Cnoc nan Uan (3) = hill of the lambs, probably 364017. Muir of Knocknenouan (G 30). In the basin about the upper Tullich Burn.

**The Muir of Dee*** See Muir Cottage.

**(The) Muir of Dinnet** (OS, C, 445983), ðɪˈmirɐˈdënët. Also Sliabh Muileann Duinidh (5), moor of mill of Dinnet. Sliu mulin Dunie (D). West of Dinnet.

**Muir of Dinnet National Nature Reserve** (Pj), locally the Dinnet Reserve (F), ðɪˈdënëtˌrɪˈzɛrv. North-west of Dinnet, mostly within the triangle of roads A 93, A 97 and B 9119.

**Muir-of-Gairnshiel** (OS, 291007). Flat moor near Gairnshiel.

**Muir of Richarkarie*** Muir of Richarkrie (Opr 30). Former habitation near Gairnshiel.

**Muir of Ruighe Riabhach*** (362017). Muir of Ree Riach (G 30). See Shiels of Ruighe Riabhach. In the basin about the upper Tullich Burn.

**Muir of Tullich*** (R 4, 381969). A former moor, now sandy fields, north-east of Ballater.

**Muir o Milton** (U, 42-03-), ˈmirɐˈmëltən. Muir Milton (Vr 3), Muir, Milton (Vr 4). A former house west of Logie Coldstone, different from South Milton which was also in these lists (Vr).

**The Muir o Milton*** (U, 424039), ðɪˈmirɐˈmëltən. A former moor, now a wood, west of Logie Coldstone.

**The Muir Pool*** See Poll nan Sleac.

**The Muirtoun** (U, 361950), ðɪˈmirtən. The Muirtown (Roy, I, Ri 2), Muirtown of Braichly (Opr 4), Moorton (Io 77), the Meerton (Dug). A former farm at the foot of Glen Muick, on site of present house Woodstock.

**Muirtown of Ach Eich an Easa** (209910). Muirtown of Auchichness (Io 44). Also Calder's Croft (Im 3, Ri 27). Also Calder's Cottary (Ri 27). A former farm east of Invercauld Bridge.

**Muirtown of Tullich** (Mc 9, 384968). Also the Muir of Tullich (Cr 24, R 4, Mc 7), and Muir (Go), Muir of Tulloch (Roy). A former farm north-east of Ballater.

**Am Mullach** (OS, 3, U, 375904), ðɪˈmuləç, the top. Also the Easter Mullach. The Easter Mulloch (I). There is no record of a Wester Mullach, but it was probably at 373903, as Am Mullach has a pair of tops on an east–west line. Note Am Mullach Dubh to the south-west. A hilltop on east side of Glen Muick.

**(The) Mullach** (OS, Cr 33, C, 323011), from Am Mullach (3), as above, the top. Mulloch (H). Also Mullach Ardach (3), top of Ardach or high place. Mulachardoch (Io 20). A former farm east of Gairnshiel, high on the hill.

**Mullach Ardach*** See Mullach.

**Am Mullach Beag** (3, D, 085821), the little top. In upper Glen Ey, below Mullach Cruinn.

**Am Mullach Beag*** (3, U, 204026), ðɪˌmuləçˈbeg, the little top. Below Am Mullach Mor, east of Loch Builg.

**Am Mullach Beag*** (3, U, 284019), as above, the little top. Below Am Mullach Mor, north-west of Gairnshiel. The cairn called Fox Cairn (OS) is just below the top.

**Mullach Cruinn** See Carn Cruinn.

**(The) Mullachdubh** (OS, C, 354057), ðɪˌmuləçˈduˑ, ðɪˌmʌləçˈduˑ, from Am Mullach Dubh (3), the black top. Marked on the map on the Don side of the hill, but also includes the top to the south-west, which goes to the Dee side. A hilltop north-west of Morven.

**Am Mullach Dubh** (3, 370899), the black top. The Mulloch Du (I). A hilltop east of Glen Muick.

**Mullach Lochan nan Gabhar** (OS, Rob, 143025), top of tarn of the goats. On the Banffshire side of Ben Avon, but comes up to the Aberdeenshire side at the top (Rob).

**Mullach Màimidh** (3, 316019), top of Mammie or rounded hill. Mullach Màimidh (D). Hilltop east of Gairnshiel.

**Am Mullach Mór*** (3, 201033), the big top. The Mullach (F), ðɪ 'muləç, now refers to the whole ridge from here to the south-east, including Am Mullach Beag. The Mulloch More (I), Mulloch Mhoir (R 14). A hilltop east of Loch Builg.

**Am Mullach Mór*** (3, U, 287028), ðɪ,muləç'moˑr, the big top. Mulloch More (I). A hilltop that pairs with Am Mullach Beag, north-west of Gairnshiel.

**Murdoch's Cairn** (Lindsay 1902, F, 316959), 'mʌrdəz'kern. Former cairn where a tramp was murdered last century on south side of road east of Abergeldie, removed for road widening in early 1940s.

**Murley** (OS, C, 325802), 'mʌrle, from Mór-thulaidh (3), big hillock, see Creag Mullach. A little hilltop south-east of Loch Muick.

**Murray's Drive*** (R 7, 180927). An old track on the hill above Invercauld House.

**(The) Naked Hill** (OS, C, 441873), ðɪ'nekəd'hël. South of Water of Gairney in Glen Tanar.

**The Nameless Corrie*** (Bs, C, 243847), ðɪ'nemlës'kọre. On south side of Lochnagar.

**The Narrow Gruip*** (U, 325003), ðɪ'narɐ'grëp, Scots Gruip = groove. A place on a track from Inverenzie to Balno in Glen Gairn, where a birch wood comes steeply towards the river, leaving only a narrow strip of flat ground by the waterside.

**Narrow Pool** See Am Pollath Caol.

**The Near Half*** (U, 324002), ðɪ'nir'haˑf. The west half of the farmland at Torbeg in lower Glen Gairn, and the nearer half to Delnabo from which it is now farmed.

**The Needle*** See Invercauld Monument.

**The Needle*** See the Kelpie's Needle.

**The Needle Park*** (U, 433966), ðɪ'nidəl'park. A field near the above, east of Pannanich.

**Neil's Quarry*** (F, 305964), 'nilz'kware, after a former resident of Rinabaich. West of Coilacriech.

**Nell McIntosh's Cairn*** (F, 052926), nẹl'makəntọʃiz'kern. Beside a corner of the road in Glen Lui, where a gale blew Nell McIntosh off her bicycle, before 1912. Now destroyed by quarrying.

**The Nelly Puil** (F, 219926), ðɪ'nẹle'pil. Nellie (Wav). In Dee, south-west of the Inver, named after Nelly's Bush (see below).

**Nelly's Bothy*** (U, 219925), 'nẹlez'bọθe. Ruin at Aberdeen Haugh, south-west of the Inver.

**Nelly's Bush** (V, C, north-east of 218925), 'nẹlez'buʃ. Now said to be a big birch tree on south bank of Dee, south-west of the Inver. However, local people do not use the word Bush for a tree, so the Bush in this name suggests a Gaelic translation from Preas = a copse (see Bush Crathie), possibly Preas an Ealaidh = copse of the crouching (to get within reach of game), or an Eunlaith, of the birds, as in Pitnellies in Ross-shire (W 1904).

**Nether Ach Chadha** (371015), Scots Nether = lower. Achas Upper and Nether (Mc). Part of the former farm of Ach Chadha up Tullich Burn.

**Nether Aucholzie** See Aucholzie.

**Nether Balintober*** See the Littleton.

**Nether Beal*** (388971), from Bealach (3) = passage. Nether Byall (R 4). A piece of former farmland at Tullich, paired with Upper Beal.

**Nether Bealach*** (193933). Nether Ballach (Fa), Lower Balloch (I). One map (I) notes 'the Cyards' (presumably tinkers) as being at this former farm north-east of Invercauld. Pairs with Upper Bealach.

**Nether Ceann na Creige*** (north of 242945). Nether Canacraig (Io 58). A former farm north-east of the Inver.

**Nether Ceann na h-Innse*** (386971), Ceann na h-Innse (3) = end of the streamside meadow. Nether Kinnahinch (Io 58), Nether Kyannahinch (R 4). A field at Tullich.

**Nether Ceann na h-Innse*** (3, 385970), references as above. A field at Tullich.

**Nether Claigionn Dubh** See Na Claignean.

**Nether Greystone** See under Greystone.

**Nether Island*** (Io 58, 351967). An island in Dee near where Gairn runs in.

**Nether Knock** See the Little Knock.

**The Nether Way** (O 123). An old route used by soldiers at the Battle of Culblean, between Culblean and the lochs Davan and Kinord.

**The Neuk Park*** (U, north-east of 346914), ðɪ'njuk'park, sometimes just the Neuk, Scots = corner. A triangular field in Glen Muick.

**Newbigging** (OS, C, 144853), nju'bɪgən, Scots = new building or farmstead. Newbigging of Glencluny (Ml). Also Coire Laoigh (3, D), after the corrie above it (see Coire an Laoigh). Coire laoigh, calves' (D), corr laoigh, calves' corrie (D in A 342). A former farm in Glen Clunie.

**The Newbigging Birks*** (F, 146856), ðɪ,nju'bɪgən'bẹrks. A group of birch trees in Glen Clunie.

**The Newbigging Brae*** (C, 146856), ðɪ,nju'bɪgən'breˑ. A hill on a road in Glen Clunie.

**The Newbigging Brig*** (C, 144853), ðɪ,nju'bɪgən'brɪg. A footbridge in Glen Clunie.

**The Newbigging Corrie** See Coire an Laoigh.

**Newbigging of Abergeldie*** (Cpb 5). A former habitation.

**The Newbigging Puil*** (U, 144853), ðɪ,nju'bɪgən'pil. A former fishing pool in Clunie, now spoiled by spates.

**The New Bridge of Dee** See Invercauld Bridge.

**The New Brig*** See Luibeg Bridge.

**New Etnach*** See Etnach.

**New Kinord** (OS, C, 448999), 'nju,kɪn'ọrd. A house north-west of Dinnet, near Loch Kinord. Pairs with Old Kinord.

**New Mar Lodge** See Mar Lodge.

**New Park** (S 21). A former school in Glen Gairn.

**The New Road*** (U, 205877), ðɪ'nju'rod. A bulldozed track west of Lochnagar.

**New Stile** See Newton of Tullich.

**The Newton*** See An Loinn Bheag.

**(The) Newton** (OS, C, 256955), ðɪ'njutən, often the Newton o Crathie (C), ðɪ'njutənɐ'kraˑθe. A farm. On the site of the former Crathienaird House (R 3).

**The Newton** (C, 318939), as above. Newtown Girnack (Opr 30). A former farm in lower Glen Girnock.

**Newton** (Tay, 201909). Newtown (Im 3). A former farm east of Invercauld Bridge.

**Newton Aberarder*** See Balnoe.

**The Newton Birks*** (U, 319937), ðɪ'njutən'bẹrks. Sometimes the Newton Wuid (U), ðɪ'njutən'wɪd. A former field in Glen Girnock, now a birch wood.

**The Newton Brig*** See the Milltoun Brig.

**The Newton Burn*** (C, west of 257953), ðɪ'njutən'bʌrn. Near Crathie.

**The Newton Cottage** See the Cottar House o the Newton.

**Newton Cottage** (OS, 396980), locally Tomnakeist Cottage (C), ,tamnə'kist'kọtədʒ. North-east of Ballater.

**(The) Newton of Gairn** (OS, C, 346970), ðɪ'njutənɐ'gern.

Newton of Balgairn (Opr 46a). Formerly Newton of Tom Bealaidh. Newtown of Tombelly in 1778 (Io). Was the new town of Tombally (A 343), note the Old Town nearby. A farm west of Bridge of Gairn.

**Newton of Tom Bealaidh** See Newton of Gairn.

**(The) Newton of Tullich** (OS, C, 395975), ðɪ'njutənɐ'tʌləç, often just the Newton (F). Locally is usually Dry Lea (OS). Newton Tullich (Io 64), a former farm. Formerly Newstyle (Vr 1, 2), Newton or Newstyle (Vr 3), New Style (Io 69). Note also the Stile of Tullich. A house north-east of Ballater.

**The Newton Park*** (F, 427964), ðɪ'njutən'park. A field at Inchmarnoch, presumably named after a former farm called the Newton.

**The Newton Park*** (U, 319939), as above. Field at a former farm in lower Glen Girnock.

**The Newton Puil** (F, 348967), ðɪ'njutən'pil. Newton (Sc). In Dee, below the Newton of Gairn north-west of Ballater.

**The Newton Quarry*** (F, 344969), ðɪ'njutən'kware. West of Bridge of Gairn.

**The Newton Redd*** (F, east of 350967), ðɪ'njutən'rɛd, Scots Redd = salmon spawning ground. A pool in Dee west of Ballater.

**Nine Maidens' Well** (S, probably 087894). Names with Seven or Nine Maidens occur in other parts of Scotland, associated with daughters of St Donald (Fo). Former well at Inverey.

**No Man's Land*** See the Tinkers' Parkie.

**The Nora Puil*** (F, 380965), ðɪ'norɐ'pil. A pool in Dee, named after a woman who often fished there. North-east of Ballater.

**North Auchnerran** (OS, C, 423037), 'norθ,aχ'nerën. Pairs with South Auchnerran. Also now Auchnerran Cottage (C). Also to older people Back Rashes (F), 'bak'raʃɪz, Scots Rashes = rushes. A house near Logie Coldstone.

**North Coirenalarig** (137838). North Cornlarich (Vr 2). A former habitation in Glen Clunie.

**The North Deeside Road** (Gf, C), ðɪ'norθ'di'sɛid'rod. Public road from Aberdeen to Invercauld Bridge along north side of Dee.

**The North Gate*** (F, 243918), ðɪ'norθ'get. A former gate into a planted wood in lower Glen Gelder.

**North Gully** (Sd, 167780). A ski-run on the Glas Maol.

**The North Lairig*** (U, 222001), ðɪ'norθ'la·rɪg. The northern part of Lairig Mhor, a way over the hills south of Corndavon Lodge. Pairs with the South Lairig.

**North Lary*** See Upper Lary.

**The North Nib*** (C, 249830), ðɪ'norθ'nɪb. A rocky spur north-east of the Dubh Loch, west of Loch Muick.

**The North Park of Ach Chadha*** (364016). The North Park of Auchaw (G 30). A former field up Tullich Burn.

**North Roinn a' Bhathaich*** (367024), Roinn a' Bhàthaich (3) = land-portion of the sheltered place. North Rinnavaich (G 19). A stretch of ground south-west of Morven.

**(The) North Top** (OS, Ro, C, 092006), ðɪ'norθ'top. Summit of Beinn a' Bhuird, pairs with the South Top. Also top of Coire Ruairidh. Top of Corryrury (R 2a).

**The North Top** (Rob, Wa, F, 991995), as above. On Ben Macdui.

**The North Top** (Sg, 963972), as above (SGo). Summit of Cairn Toul, with the South Top nearby.

**North Top*** See Beinn a' Chaorainn.

**The Nursery Park*** (F, 264945), ðɪ'nʌrsəre'park. A field near a former tree nursery at Balmoral.

**The Nursery Puil** (F, 179917), ðɪ'nʌrsəre'pil. Nursery Pool (Ly). In Dee above Invercauld Bridge.

**The Oak Brae*** (F, 424962), ðɪ'ok'bre·. A bank with oak trees, east of Pannanich.

**Oakwood Cottage** (OS, C, 384975), 'ok'wɪd'kotədʒ. Was there in 1832 (Io). The southern one of a pair of houses in an old oak wood at Tullich.

**Oak Wood of Tullich*** (R 4, 378974). Now a fir plantation, but still oaks nearby beside the Tullich Lodge Hotel and east of it, a part locally called the Oak Wuid (U), ðɪ'ok'wɪd. North-east of Ballater.

**The Oak Wuid*** (U, 345974), as above. North-west of Bridge of Gairn.

**Oir Dhe** See Deeside.

**Old Etnach*** See the Auld House o the Etnach.

**The Old Ford Road** (Gf, 416974). A track from Pannanich to a former ford at Cambus o' May.

**The Old Ford Road** (Gf, west of 372956). At Ballater.

**The Old Ford Road** (Gf, 389965), sometimes locally the Green Roadie (U), ðɪ'grin'rodi. A track on the former route of the South Deeside Road west of Pannanich, near a former ford over Dee. Also the Low Road (U), ðɪ'lo'rod.

**Old Hospital** See the Sean Spittal.

**Old Kinord** (OS, C, 441001), 'a·l,kin'ord. Cainord (G 9). Was formerly called Ceann nan Ord (3, A), end of the ords or round hills, but only one Ord there, so Ceann Ord, end of round hill, more likely. A former farming community north of Loch Kinord.

**Old Mar Lodge** See Mar Lodge.

**Old Military Road** (OS, 139824, 223929, and 263985). Old road built by the army in the mid 1700s from Perth to Fort George at Inverness via the Cairnwell, Braemar, Gairnshiel and the Lecht.

**Old Mill of Abergeldie*** (Opr 41e). Former habitation.

**Old Mill of Tom Bealaidh*** See Mill of Tom Bealaidh.

**Old Shelter Cairn*** (Me 24, 112944). On top of Carn Suilean Dubha east of Glen Quoich.

**Old Toll House*** See Bridge Cottage.

**The Old Town*** (I, 348971). A field west of Bridge of Gairn, beside Newton of Gairn. Probably had been a separate farm before the Newton was formed.

**The Orchard Yaird*** See the Gairden Park.

**The Ord**, from An t-Ord (3), the round hill. There are two pairs of them near Dinnet. One pair (the Big and the Little Ord) is west of Loch Davan, and the other (the Little Ord and the Ord or the Muckle Ord) is north and south of Loch Kinord; see under these names.

**Ord Hill** (OS, 440985), locally the Ord (A 311, C), ðɪ'ord, from An t-Ord (3), the round hill. Also the Muckle Ord (U), ðɪ'mʌkəl'ord. The Mickle Ord (Mi 1877). A low hill west of Dinnet.

**The Ord Park*** (F, 443987), ðɪ'ord'park. A field west of Dinnet.

**The Ord Wuid*** (F, 440985), ðɪ'ord'wɪd. A birch wood on Ord Hill west of Dinnet.

**Over Aucholzie** See Upper Aucholzie.

**Over Claigionn Dubh** See Na Claignean.

**Over Corndavon*** (Io 71). A former farm in upper Gairn.

**Over Croft** or **Upper Croft of Ardmeanach**. Crofte superiori Ardmenach crofte Bruchdow (Ab 19) misread as Overcroft, Ardemenach Croft, Bruckdow, instead of Overcroft of Ardmenach, Croft of Bruchdow. A former croft in lower Glen Muick.

**The Overflow Puil** (C, 416980), ðɪ'over,flo'pil. Overflow (Sc). In Dee at Cambus o' May.

**Over Greystone** See Upper Greystone.

**Over Knock** See Muckle Knock.

**Overpleuch of Strathgirnock** See Loinn a' Choirce.

**The Paddock\*** See Kiln Croft.

**The Painter Puil\*** (F, 230932), ðɪ'pɛntër'pil. In Dee, beside the Inver Inn, named after a big stone with an iron bolt for attaching to the painter of a boat.

**Painter's Corrie\*** (U, 303925), 'pɛntërz'kǫre. Behind Bovaglie in Glen Girnock.

**The Painter Stane\*** (U), ðɪ'pɛntër'stin. Beside the Painter Puil at Inver.

**Pannanich** (C, 408973), 'panɐnɪç, sometimes ðɪ'panɐnɪç. From the Pananaich (3), possibly at the place of hollow, from the old British or Welsh Pant = a hollow, with the *t* dropped as it often is elsewhere (W 373–4). Same pronunciation in Gaelic and English (D). Pananich in 1769 (Pe), and Pannanich, Panninich, Pananich in 1790, 1801 and 1806 (Ri). An area by the South Deeside Road, east of Pannanich Hotel (Dms), now used more generally for the area between Dalmochie in the west and Headinch in the east.

**The Pannanich Brae\*** (C, 389965), ðɪ'panɐnɪç'bre·. A hill on the road from Ballater to Pannanich.

**The Pannanich Burn\*** (C, west of 394968), ðɪ'panɐnɪç'bʌrn. Near Ballater.

**Pannanich Cottage** See Dalmochie.

**Pannanich Hill** (OS, C, 392944, should be 390958, 392944 is Carn Coire an Eirbhein (see Corrienearn), 'panɐnɪç'hël. A wooded, rocky hill that can be seen well from Ballater, whereas the OS location is out of sight to the south.

**Pannanich Lodge** (F, 378963), 'panɐnɪç'lǫʤ. Pananich Lodge (Ri 39a), the Lodge of Pannanich (Gf). A former lodge on south side of Dee below Ballater.

**Pannanich Lodge Farm\*** Pananich Lodge Farm (Io 64). A former farm north of Dalmochie and south of Dee, east of Ballater.

**Pannanich Village\*** (Be, U, 400971), 'panɐnɪç'viləʤ. Also Easter Pannanich (Vr 1, Be). The group of former crofts east of Pannanich.

**Pannanich Wells** (OS, C, 395967), 'panɐnɪç'wɛlz. Formerly the Wells of Pannanich (Gf), the Pannanich Springs (Ri). Also Fuaran Phananaich (3), wells of the Pannanich, for meaning of Pannanich see Pannanich above. Fuaran fananich (D). Mineral wells east of Ballater.

**The Pannanich Wuid\*** (C, 410972), ðɪ'panɐnɪç'wɪd. The Wood of Pannanich (Dms). East of Ballater.

**The Pap**. There is a pair of them on Lochnagar, see the Little and the Meikle Pap.

**The Paps of Lochnagar\*** The Paups of Lochnagar (G 5). A composite name for the Little Pap and the Meikle Pap, two hills on Lochnagar.

**Parish of Braemar, Parish of Crathie** (now Parish of Crathie and Braemar); **Parish of Glen Muick, Parish of Tullich**, and **Parish of Glen Gairn** (now Parish of Glenmuick, Tullich and Glen Gairn).

**Park of Ach Chadha** See the Druim Parks of Ach Chadha.

**The Park of Allanmore\*** (Ra 5, 133918), Scots Park = field. Flat, grassy ground west of Braemar, now boggy due to flooding.

**Park of Braichlie\*** (370947). Park of Breachlie (I). Included two fields now called the Clay Hole Park and the Braichlie Park. Arable land south of Ballater.

**The Park of Ceann na Coille\*** See the Castle Park.

**Park of Dalphuil\*** (299010). Park of Dalefuil (I). A former moor, now a wood east of Gairnshiel.

**Park of Inis Lagaigh\*** (267945), Inis Lagaigh (3) = meadow at hollow, from Lagach = place in the hollow (W 147). Park of Inchlagie (I). A flat field by Dee, at Crathie.

**Park of the Ceapach\*** See the Ceapach.

**Park of the Ceapach\*** (173919), Ceapach (3) = tillage plot,

likely to have been A' Cheapach originally. Park of the Cabich (R 7). A former field at Invercauld.

**Parks of Ballochbuie\*** (R 7, 199905). Grassy ground, formerly farmed, at Garbh Allt Shiel in Ballochbuie Forest.

**Parliament Knowe** (OS, 247958). Parliament Hillock (R 3, 9), Hillock of Parliment (R 5). Also the Tynabaich Hill (U), ðɪ ˌtɛinɐ'beç'hël. North-west of Crathie.

**Pass Cadha nam Fiann**. Probably a variant of Cadha nam Fiann in Glen Geusachan. Pas cadha nam Fionn (Drc). Diack speculated with little evidence that this came from Gaelic Pas = a way.

**The Pass o Broad Cairn\*** (C, 236818), ðɪ'pasɐ'brǫd'kern̩. West of Loch Muick.

**(The) Pass of Ballater** (OS, C, 367970), ðɪ'pasɐ'balətër. The Pass of Tullich or of Ballater (Mg). Also Creagach Bhealdair (5), craigs of the ? (see Ballater). Creagach Bhyalter (D), Crekich Vyalter (A). Also Craigs of Ballater (G 19). Also still called the Craigs in Diack's time. North of Ballater.

**The Pass o Little Craig\*** (C, 248819), ðɪ'pasɐ'lëtəl'kreg. West of Loch Muick.

**The Pass o the Salmon\*** See Lairig nam Braidean.

**The Pass Road\*** (C, 370970), ðɪ'pas'rod. In the Pass of Ballater.

**The Peat Ford\*** (I, 223928). Over Dee, south-west of the Inver.

**Peat Hillock** (OS 1869, C, 469990), pit'hëlëk. A former house on a hillock above a peaty hollow east of Dinnet.

**The Peat Hillock Bog\*** (C, 466988), ðɪˌpit'hëlëk'bǫg. Near the above house.

**The Peel of Kinord**, English and Scots Peel = fortified stockade or tower. The Peel or Castle of Kinnord (Mi 1877), the Pele of Kinnord (Ab), Castle Caenmore (Di). Former wooden castle on the Castle Island at Loch Kinord, at 440996.

**The Peep o Dee** See the Queen's View.

**The Pend Door\*** (F, 255951), ðɪ'pɛnd'dor, Scots Pend = arch. At Balmoral Castle.

**The Perth Ski Club Hut** (C, 150775), a skiers' name. East of the Cairnwell.

**Peter Benton's Craft\*** (F, 251953), 'pitër'bɛntənz'kraft. A former croft, now a house, west of Crathie.

**The Peter Ogg Puil** (C, 414981), ðɪ'pitër'ǫg'pil. Peter Ogg (Sc). Pool in Dee, at Cambus o' May.

**Peter's Hill** (OS, F, 363008), 'pitërz'hël. Also Cnoc a' Bhranndair (3), hill of the place of tangled roots. The Knock of Brander, Croak a vrainter (G 19, 30), the Knock of the Brander (Io 20). Also the Hill of the Brander (Io 20). South-west of Morven.

**Peter's Pouch** See Peter's Stripes.

**Peter's Stripes** (Sc, C, 421971), 'pitërz'strɛips, Scots Stripes = small streams. Peter's Pouch (Ly) probably same. A pool in Dee, below Cambus o' May Bridge.

**The Picts' Housie\*** (F, 393974), ðɪ'pëkts'husi. A souterrain north-east of Ballater.

**The Picts' Park\*** (U, 417044), ðɪ'pëkts'park. A field around the Picts' Ring.

**The Picts' Ring\*** (U, 417043), ðɪ'pëkts'rɪŋ. Also the Picts' House (F), ðɪ'pëkts'hus. A souterrain in Cromar.

**The Pinkie Brae\*** (U, 419968), ðɪ'pɪŋki'bre·, Scots = primrose slope. Above Dee, on Inchmarnoch side.

**Pioc an Donais** See the Devil's Point.

**The Piper Brig\*** (C, 254964), ðɪ'pɛipër'brɪg. Also formerly the Brig o Bush (U), ðɪ'brɪgɐ'buʃ, or the Bush Brig (F). Bridge of Bush (Opr 55). North of Crathie.

**The Piper Burn\*** (C, 254965), ðɪ'pɛipër'bʌrn. The part of Crathie Burn at Piper Hole, north-west of Crathie.

**Piper Hole** See Toll Phiobair.

**The Piperhole Brae\*** (C, 259959), ðɪ'pɛipër'hol'bre·. A hill on the A 939 road, from Crystalls up to Bush. Near Crathie.

**The Piper's Stane\*** (F, 368991), ðɪ'pɛipĕrz'stin, Scots Stane = stone. On the hill north of the Pass of Ballater.

**The Piper's Wuid** See Coille Phiobair.

**The Piss o the Coire Boidheach\*** (U, 231835), ðɪ'pɛ̈sɪðɪˌkɒr 'buˑəç. A waterfall on Allt a' Choire Bhoidheach, above the Dubh Loch west of Loch Muick.

**Pistol Fearnach\*** (U, 418969), ˌpĕstəl'fɛrnɐχ, Pistol doubtful, possibly Beiseil (5) = shelf, or by metathesis from Bad = clump and ? Sabhal = barn or Sàil = heel; Fearnach (3) = alder place. In a wood at Inchmarnoch.

**Pistols Neuk\*** (C, 417969), 'pĕstəlz'njuk, Scots Neuk = corner, see name above. A corner on the road at Inchmarnoch.

**Pistols Tree\*** (C, north of 417969), 'pĕstəlz'tri. An old crab-apple tree on east side of road near Inchmarnoch.

**Na Plaidean\*** (3, F, 307018), ðɪ'pladənz, the plots of ground. Former arable fields north-east of Gairnshiel.

**The Plantin\*** (C, south-east of 371957), ðɪ'plantɪn. A grassy patch planted with trees in front of the Invercauld Arms Hotel at Ballater, now a traffic roundabout.

**The Plantins Park\*** (U, 418039), ðɪ'plantɪnz'park. Named after two plantations of firs on hillocks in this field. West of Logie Coldstone.

**The Play Cock\*** (303832), meaning doubtful, could be from Gaelic or Scots. Green called the Play Cock (I). A grassy area above Loch Muick.

**The Pleasant Walk\*** (U, 442976), ðɪ'plɛzənt'wak. A path through trees by the south bank of Dee west of Dinnet.

**The Pleasant Walk Puil** (C, 442977), ðɪ'plɛzənt'wak'pil. Pleasant Walk (P). A pool beside the above path.

**The Ploughboy Puil\*** (F, 233936), ðɪ'plʌuˌboi'pil. Called the Black Shed Puil (F), ðɪ'blak'ʃɛd'pil on the Balmoral side, after a former shed there. In Dee, below the Inver Inn.

**Poacher's Cave** (McC 1896, 142005). By Allt an Eas Mhoir, 'capable of sheltering half a dozen men'. On Ben Avon.

**Poachers' Well** See Fuaran Toll Bhalgair.

**Pòc an t-Saighdeir\*** (3), pocket of the soldier. Pockentyter (Io 20), Pockentiter (Lp 1). About Easter Morven, up the Tullich Burn.

**Poind Fold\*** (R 7, 183912), Scots Poindfold = enclosure for keeping forfeit animals (Gm). A formerly farmed patch beside Invercauld Bridge.

**The Point Park\*** (U, south of 357968), ðɪ'point'park. A field with a sharp point to the east, south-east of Bridge of Gairn.

**The Poles' Road\*** (F, 278014), ðɪ'polz'rod. A road built by Polish soldiers during the second world war near Gairnshiel.

**Polhollick** (OS, C, 344965), pəl'hɒlək. Polchollaik (Opr 18). A former farm, now a house, beside the pool Poll Chollaig, west of Ballater.

**The Polhollick Brig\*** (C, 344965), ðɪˌpəl'hɒlək'brɪg. A bridge over Dee at the above house.

**The Polhollick Park\*** (F, 343967), ðɪˌpəl'hɒlək'park. A field west of Ballater.

**The Polhollick Road\*** (U, 338958), ðɪˌpəl'hɒlək'rod. From the North Deeside Road to the South one via the above bridge.

**Am Poll\*** (3, U, 008869), ðɪ'pol, the pool. In Geldie.

**Poll a' Bhior** (C, 359966), pɒl'viɾ, to fishers Big Poll a' Bhior, pool of the sharp point. Powlaveer (G 17), Poul Veer (I), Poll Vear, vir, r very sharp, Poll Bhir (D in A). Pairs with Little Poll a' Bhior. In Dee at a sharp bend above Ballater.

**The Pollach**, ðɪ'pulɐχ (U), ðɪ'puləç (C). This and the other Pollach names below are from the same word as in the erroneously-spelled Pollagach Burn (OS). Padlachye, Padlochie (Io 13), and Podlochy (Io 1, Ri 29, Dms 17) suggest an early Bad Lachaidh (5) clump of wild ducks, or Bad Lòchaidh (5), dark clump, for Lòchaidh = dark, see

W 50. A general name for the boggy upper basin of Pollagach Burn (OS), south-east of Ballater.

**The Pollach Brig\*** See the Milltoun Brig.

**The Pollach Moss** (F, 395931), ðɪ'puləç'mɒs. The Pulloch Moss (Av), Moss of the Poulach (I), the Moss o the Pollach (U), ðɪ 'mɒsɪðɪ'pulɐχ. A peat-moss south of Pannanich.

**Poll a' Chòrr\*** (3, 143848), pool of the horn. Poula Chor (I). A former field in Glen Clunie, beside a long, narrow pool which is on a river horn or bend.

**The Pollach Plantin\*** (C, 410956), ðɪ'puləç'plantɪn. A wood near Inchmarnoch.

**The Pollach Road\*** (C, 368931), ðɪ'puləç'rod. A track from Glen Muick to the Pollagach.

**(The) Pollagach Burn** (OS, 410953), should be the Pollach (F), or the Pollach Burn (C), ðɪ'puləç'bʌrn. Pollach River (R 1), Burn of the Poulach (I, R 17), B. of Poulach (Ro), Poulach Burn (Mg), Poulach Burn (Sm). See the Pollach for meaning. South-east of Ballater.

**Na Pollagan** (3, C, 302013), ðɪ'puləks, the little pools. Pollag, na pollakin (D in A). Marshy pools north-east of Gairnshiel, formerly deeper.

**Pollagan** (3, 301012), little pools. Pollocks (OS 1869). Former house near above place.

**Poll Allanmore** (east of 140915, by elimination), from Poll Àilean Mór (3), pool of big green. Pol Allanmore (A). In Dee near Braemar.

**Poll Allt a' Chlàir** (3, U, 116901), ˌpɒlˌalt'χlaːr, pool of burn of the board (i.e. plank bridge (J)). Pol allt chlar (D), Pol Alltachlair (A). Also the Allt a' Chlair Pool (U), ðɪˌalt'χlaˑr 'pul. In Dee, east of Mar Lodge.

**Poll Allt Dearg** (3, 121905), pool of red burn. Pol allt dearg (D). Also the Allt Dearg Pool (U), ðɪˌalt'dʒɛrək'pul. Arderg Pool (Ly). In Dee east of Mar Lodge.

**Poll an Àgaidh** (3, 129902), pəl'naki (A), pool of the ox. Poll 'n-agi (Mp). West of Braemar.

**Poll an Àgaidh** (3, 093897, by elimination), pool of the ox. Poll nakich, naki, a work stot is akich, a 2-year old bullock is aku (D in A). Pol Nackie (A). Also the Bulwark Pool (F), ðɪ 'bulwɒrk'pul. In Dee near Inverey.

**Poll an Àilein** (3, U, 144919), pɒl'naIən, pool of the green. Pol n'allan (D). West of Braemar.

**Poll an Doimhne\*** (3, F, 150909), ˌpɒlɐn'dɛin, pool of the depth. In Clunie south of Braemar.

**Poll an Éisg** (3, C, 983933), usually pɒl'niʃ, but best informants ˌpɒlɐn'eiʃk (CG, WG), pool of the fish. Poll Iasg, the fish pool (Sg). In Dee, below the entry of Geusachan Burn.

**Poll Annaidh\*** (3, U, 071869), pɒl'ane, Annie's pool. Up the Cristie, south-west of Inverey.

**Poll an Rathaid** (3, U, south-east of 094894), ˌpɒlɐn'ratʃ, pool of the road. Pol an ratsh, road pool (D). In Dee, beside the road east of Inverey.

**Am Pollath** (4, C, 142914), ðɪ'pulɐ, ('pɒla (A)), the pool. Am Polla (Bolla) (D), Am Pollath (D in Rc). Possibly a variant of Poll = pool, or Am Poll-àth = the pool ford or the mud ford. A pool in Dee west of Braemar.

**Am Pollath Caol** (3, F, 144915), ðɪˌpulɐ'kul, the narrow pool. Am Polla caol, the narrow Polla (D in A). See name above. Narrow Pool (Ly). A pool in Dee west of Braemar.

**The Pollath Island\*** (F, 144915), ðɪ'pulɐ'ɛilənd. An island in Dee near Braemar.

**Poll Bà** (4, C, 435971), pɒl'baː, pool of a cow. Pol Ba, cows' pool (A). Pol Balhadh (P, Sc) is incorrect, but Bàthadh = drowning is possible (Dms), thus Pol Bàthaidh, pool of drowning. In Dee west of Dinnet.

**Poll Bhantraich** (3, north-west of 421975), pool of the widower. Pol Phanterich (Mi 1877). Also the Ruighe Bhantraich Puil

(U), ðɪˌrɪˈfantrɪçˈpil. Rifantrach (A). Lower end of the Brig Puil at Cambus o' May.

**Poll Bhat** (OS, 060957), should be Poll Bhàthaidh (4, C), pọl 'vaː, (pɔlˈva (A)), pool of the drowning. In the Dubh-Ghleann.

**Poll Bhùirn** (3, M, A, F, below 184915), pọlˈvurn, pool of the water, i.e. liable to flood. Also the Lower Jetty Puil (F), ðɪ 'loɐrˈʤɐteˈpil. Also the Doctor Puil (F), ðɪˈdọktɐrˈpil. In Dee above Invercauld Bridge.

**Poll Bruaich** (3, C, 449977), pọlˈbruɐç, pool of bank. Pol Bruaich (A, Sc). In Dee, south-west of Dinnet.

**Am Poll Buidhe** (3, M, C, 067897), ðɪˌpọlˈbui, the yellow pool. Pol bhuidhe (D). In Dee, east of the Linn of Dee.

**Poll Chàis** (5, D, A, F, 151915), pọlˈhaˑʃ, pool of the difficulty or Chaise = of streams of water. Now often called the Pot (C), or Ewen's Pot (U), ˈjuɐnzˈpọt, Scots Pot = deep pool, after a Ewen family at the mill there. In Clunie, in a gorge below the bridge at Braemar.

**Poll Cheapaich** (3, F), pọlˈkẹpɐç, pool of the tillage plot. Poll chapich (D). Pool of the Cabich (R 7), Keppoch (A). Also the Ceapaich Puil (C), ðɪˈkẹpɐçˈpil, includes Upper and Lower Ceapaich Puils. In Dee at Invercauld.

**Poll Chòcaire** (3, south of 154926), Cook's pool, probably Mr Cook (see Cook's Park). Pol chogar, the cook's pool (D). In Dee near Braemar Castle.

**Poll Choich** (6, south-east of 122907, by elimination), pool of the Quoich, for meaning see Quoich Water. Pol Choich (D). In Dee east of Mar Lodge.

**Poll Choinnich*** (4, 419967), Kenneth's pool, or Poll Chòinneach = pool of mosses. Pollchynnich or Kenneth's pool (Rli 16, Dms 23). Also the Lang Puil (A, C), ðɪˈlaŋˈpil, Scots = long pool. In Dee, south of Cambus o' May.

**Poll Chollaig** (5, C, 343964), pɐlˈhọlɐk, pool of the ? hazel place, with Coll = old Gaelic for hazel. Said to be little Coll, a saint who did baptising there (AT). Cholg = of fierce looks is also a possibility. The ferry is Bat poll-chollaik, poll chollig (D), Polhollick (A, Sc). In Dee, just above the suspension bridge at Polhollick west of Bridge of Gairn.

**Poll Churraich** (4, U, 183915), ˌpọlˈhurɐç, (pɔlˈhurɐç with short *u* (A)), pool of the bog. Chuirich Pool (Ly). Pol Hurrich, possibly from a method of salmon-fishing called curroch fishing which involved the use of a raw hide boat (A). Also the Lang Puil (F), ðɪˈlaŋˈpil. In Dee at Invercauld.

**Poll Coire Mhuillidh** (3, east of 111898), pool of corrie fit for driving a mill. Pol Coir' mhuillidh (D). Also the Dynamo Pool (U), ðɪˈdɛinɐmoˈpul, after a former hydro-electric dynamo. In Dee, east of Mar Lodge.

**Poll Dail a' Choirce*** (3, U, 173918), ˌpọlˌdalˈχɔrk, pool of haugh of the oats. Also the Dail a' Choirce Puil (F), ðɪˌdalˈχɔrkˈpil. Not fished now, spoiled by flooding. In Dee, beside Invercauld House.

**Poll Dail nam Bòrd*** (3, F, 078898), ˌpọlˌdalnɐˈbọrd, pool of haugh of the planks. In Dee, east of the Linn of Dee.

**Poll Dail nan Gamhainn** (4, 131913, by elimination), pool of haugh of the stirks. Pol Dal-ghobhainn (D). In Dee, west of Braemar. See Dalgowan.

**Am Poll Dearg** (2, F, 091898), ðɪˌpọlˈʤɛrɐk, the red pool. Pol dearg (D). Beside red rocks. Also the Suspension Brig Pool (F), ðɪˌsɐsˈpɛnʃɐnˈbrɪgˈpul. In Dee, west of Mar Lodge.

**Poll De** See Chest of Dee.

**Poll Eachainn** (3, south of 083893), pɔlˈɛhan (A), Hector's pool. Pol Eachainn (A). A small pool behind a hillock at Inverey.

**Poll Eidh** (6, east of 087897, by elimination), pool of Ey, for meaning see Ey Burn. Pol Ey (A). Eye Pool (Ly). In Dee, west of Mar Lodge.

**Poll Glaisean** (4, C, north-east of 406978), pọlˈglaʃën, pool of

little stream or of Glashan, a person's name. Pol Glashen (A), Pol Glashan (Sc). Often just Glaisean (F). In Dee, west of Cambus o' May.

**Poll Goc** (3, U, 342994), pọlˈkok, pool with a Goc or pipe (see the Gocan Stane), supposed to mean a narrow place (WR). Also the Goc Puil or the Goc (C), ðɪˈkokˈpil. The Coke (D), Poll koke (D in A). In Gairn, below Candacraig, where the river runs through a narrow, rushing stretch.

**Poll Inbhir Laoigh** (3, U, 072896), ˌpọlˌɪnvɐrˈlui, pool at mouth of Lui or calf-one. Pol Inverlui (D). Derry Pool (Ly). In Dee west of Mar Lodge.

**Poll Leth-allt*** (3, U, 048892), pọlˈljeɐlt, pool of half burn (i.e. with a steeper slope on one side than the other, see under Dalvorar Burn). Also the Allt Leth-allt Pool (F), ðɪˈaltˈljeltˈpul. Jeahalt Pool (Ly). In Dee west of the Linn of Dee.

**Poll Ma-Chalmaig** (3, F, 301957), ˌpọlˌmɐˈχalmɐk, pool of St Colm. Poll ma chalmag (D), Polmahalmick (A). Note Chapel Ma-Chalmaig nearby. In Dee east of Abergeldie.

**Poll Màiri** (2, A, C, 334001), pọlˈmere, but ˈmaˑri from best informants, Mary's pool. Poll Mary, a Mary was drowned there (D), Pol Mairi (A). In Gairn, beside Lary.

**The Poll Mairi Brae*** (U, 334003), ðɪˌpọlˈmereˈbreˑ. A steep hillside near Lary in Glen Gairn.

**The Poll Mairi Brae Park*** (U, 335002), ðɪˌpọlˈmereˈbreˈpark. A field on the above hillside.

**Poll Ma-Naoimhir** (3, C, west of 259952), ˌpọlˌmɐˈnir̥, pool of St Manirus, an early saint in the parish of Crathie. Poll ma nuier (D), Polmanear (A), Polmonier (Sc). In Dee beside Balmoral Castle.

**Poll Mhaide*** (4, 193910), pool of the stick. Poulvait (R 7). A boggy pool east of Invercauld Bridge.

**Poll Mhire*** (5, F, south of 322003), pọlˈvir̥, pool ? of the vehemence or (Mhir) of the top. Unlikely to be Bhior = sharp place, as one informant (WL) gave the unaspirated sound Poll Mir, pọlˈmir̥. A fast pool in Gairn east of Gairnshiel.

**Poll Mhuilinn*** (3, U, 138908), pọlˈvulən, pool of the mill. South of Mill of Coull, west of Braemar.

**Poll Mór*** (3, 300960), big pool. Poulmore (I). A boggy spot west of Coilacriech.

**Poll na Bruaich Ruaidhe*** (3, U, 154889), ˌpọlnɐˌbruɐχˈruɐ, pool of the red bank. Also the Red Brae Pool (F), ðɪˈrẹdˈbreˈpul. In Clunie south of Braemar.

**Poll na Bruaich Ruaidhe** (3, U, 082899), as above, pool of the red bank. Pol na bruach ruadh (D). In Dee west of Mar Lodge, beside a gravelly bank.

**Poll na Bruaich Ruaidhe*** (U, north of 074896), as above, pool of the red bank. Also the Canadian Camp Pool (F), ðɪˌkə ˈnedjənˈkampˈpul. Smiddy Pool (Ly) probably here. In Dee west of Inverey.

**Poll na Buitsich*** (3, U, south of 341970), ˌpọlnɐˈpʌtʃɐç, pool of the witch. One informant (WD) said his grandmother told him stories about a witch in that area. West of Bridge of Gairn.

**Poll na Céire** (3, C, 143910), ˌpọlnɐˈkir̥, ˌpọlnɐˈker̥, pool of the wax. Pol-na-ceire, the pool of wax, because of a scum of iron phosphate (Mp). A shallow tarn at the top of Chapel Brae in Braemar.

**Poll na Clàraig*** (4, F, 046892), ˌpọlnɐˈklaˑrɪg, pool of the little flat place. Also the Duchess's Pool (F), ðɪˈdʌtʃësɪzˈpul. Also the Princess's Pool (U), ðɪˈprɪnsəsɪzˈpul. In Dee west of the Linn of Dee.

**Poll na Drochaide** (3, 102896, east of bridge), pool of the bridge. Pol na troycht, bridge pool (D). Also the Victoria Brig Pool (F), ðɪˌvɪkˈtoreɐˈbrɪgˈpul. In Dee east of Inverey.

**Poll na h-Iuchrach** (3, 394969), pool of the key. Polniuchrach

(A). Also the Key Pool (A, F), ðɪˈkiˈpul. Also the Mitchell Puil (A, C), ðɪˈmɛ̈ʧəlˈpil. In Dee below Tullich Kirk northeast of Ballater. The old legend is that St Nathalan flung his key into the river and retrieved it again miraculously later during his pilgrimage to Rome.

**Poll na Mìle Duirche** (3, 097895), pool of the dark mile. Pol na mil dorach, dark mile pool (D). Also the Stuffer's Pool (F), ðɪ ˈstʌfɛ̈rzˈpul, after a former taxidermist at Mar Lodge. Stuffer's Pool (Ly). In Dee east of Inverey.

**Poll nam Mult** (3, probably 112900), pool of the wethers. Pol nam mult (D). In Dee east of Mar Lodge.

**Poll nan Clachan Garbha*** (3, C, 025885), ˌpɒlnɐˌklaχɐnˈgaro, pool of the rough stones, Clachan probably a variant genitive plural. A rough, shallow pool in Dee east of the White Bridge.

**Poll nan Sleac** (3, C, 077898), ˌpɒlnɐˈsleçk, pool of the slabs, Sleac an eastern form of Leac. Slyehk, a slab, genitive same as nominative (D in A), but Roinn na Slice goes against this. Pol na Slake (Ly), Pol Slake (A). Also the Muir Pool (F), ðɪ ˈmurˈpul, after Muir Cottage nearby. In Dee, beside rocky slabs west of Inverey.

**Poll nan Sleac** (3, F, 309963), pɒlˈslak, (pɒlnəˈslek (A)), pool of the slabs. Poll na sleac, na slehk (D in A), Polslake (A, Sc). In Dee north-east of Abergeldie.

**Poll na Poite*** (3, probably c. 079819), pool of the pot. Poll-na-Pot (Io 79). On the lower Allt Beinn Iutharn.

**Poll na Sgeire** (3, 095894), pool of the rock. Pol na sgeir, rock pool (D). In Dee east of Inverey.

**Poll na Trid** (3, 334999), pɒlnəˈtriʧ (A), pool of the rag. Poll ma tritsh or na tritsh (D), Pol na Tritsh (A). Also the Manse Puil (F), ðɪˈmansˈpil. In Gairn near Lary.

**Poll Ranntaich*** (3, U, 247051), pɒlˈrandi, divided pool. See Coire Poll Randaidh for old spellings. The pools are high on the hill on a flat part near the Strathdon march, north-east of Corndavon Lodge.

**Poll Seicheidh*** (2, F, 149912), pɒlˈʃeçe, pool of hide place. Hides were said to have been washed there (CMcI). A boggy hole behind Broom Bank at Braemar.

**Poll Sgeir Dhearg*** (3, F, 988916), ˌpɒlˌskərˈjɛrək, pool of red rock. In Dee east of Beinn Bhrotain.

**Poll Sleac** (3, C, 429965), pɒlˈslak, (pɒlˈslek (A)), probably from Poll nan Sleac, pool of the slabs, with the article dropping out, as has now happened with the Abergeldie Poll nan Sleac. Pol Slake (A). Pol Slachd (P, Sc) is incorrect sound. In Dee south-east of Cambus o' May.

**Poll Sleac*** (3, U, 431965), as above, pool of the slabs (see above). Polslake (Ce 3). A former little house near the above pool.

**Poll Sleac** (3, F, 225929), as above, pool of the slabs (see name two up). Polslake (A, Sc). In Dee south-west of the Inver.

**Poll Tearlaich** (3, C, 422973), pɒlˈʃirləs, Charles' pool. Pol Sheerless, Charles' Pool (A). In Dee below the bridge at Cambus o' May.

**The Pollution Hut*** (U, 343966), ðɪˌpɒlˈuʃənˈhʌt. Immediately below the Polhollick Brig, on Dee west of Ballater.

**(The) Pools of Dee** (OS, C, 974006 and 974008), ðɪˈpulzɐˈdiˑ. Also Lochan Dubh na Làirige (2, JB), ˌlɒχɐnˈduˌnɐˈlaˑrɪg, black tarn or tarns of the hill pass. Lochan dubh na lairig (D). Near the top of the Lairig Ghru.

**Postie Allan's*** (U, south-east of 351979, on south side of track), ˈposteˈalɐnz. A former house occupied by a postwoman, north of Bridge of Gairn.

**Postie Bell's*** (U, 216926), ˈposteˈbɛlz. Earlier was the Wuid Cutters' House (U), ðɪˈwɪdˌkʌtɛrzˈhus. A former house west of Inver, made for those who cut the wood that was there

before the present plantation, and last occupied by a postman named Bell.

**The Postie's Leap** (Gl, C, 359966), ðɪˈpostezˈlip. A place with rocks above Dee at the Auld Line at Ballater, where a man once committed suicide by jumping into Dee.

**The Postie's Leap Brig*** (F, 359966), ðɪˈpostezˈlipˈbrɪg. A bridge carrying the Auld Line near Ballater.

**The Post Office Park*** (U, 264949), ðɪˈpostˌɒfəsˈpark. A field at Crathie.

**The Pot*** (U, 186909), ðɪˈpɒt, Scots Pot = deep pool. A small pool on south side of Dee, part of the larger pool the Brig Pot or the Auld Brig Puil. East of Invercauld.

**The Pot*** (U, 434998), as above. A tarn near Loch Kinord.

**The Pot*** See Poll Chais.

**The Pot** See Brig Puil.

**Pot Side*** (F, 434998), pɒtˈsɛid. Potside (Ce 3). A former house beside a pool, near north-west corner of Loch Kinord.

**Preas an Tolmain*** (3, U, 121902), ˌprɛsɐnˈdɒlmən, copse of the little knoll. East of Corriemulzie.

**Preas Bad nan Coileach-dubha*** (3, 195888), copse of clump of the blackcocks. Pres Pat na Coilleach Dubh (Bs). Also the Blackcocks' Howe (C), ðɪˈblakˌkɒksˈhʌuˑ. In Glen Beg, Ballochbuie Forest.

**Preas Bad Smeòraich*** (3, U, 263819), ˌprɛsˌpatˈsmjɒrɐç, copse of clump of a thrush. Also the Bush of Bad Smorack (I), now the Birk Bush (Bs, F), ðɪˈbɛ̈rkˈbuʃ. A copse of old birches west of the top of Loch Muick.

**Preas Bhreac** (4), speckled copse, with Bhreac possibly indicating a locative or dative form, i.e. A' Phreas Bhreac, at the speckled copse. Preas vrachk (D in A). At Inverey.

**Preas Coll** (3, 443986), copse of hazel. Presscow (A 311), see also W 378. A former croft south of Loch Kinord.

**Preas Doirneach*** (3, 250944), copse of stony place. Press Dornoch (Io 50). A low hill near Balmoral.

**Preas Lag nan Con*** (3, F), ˌprɛsˌlagnɐˈgɒn, copse of hollow of the dogs. In Ballochbuie Forest, exact location now unknown (but see name below).

**The Preas Lag nan Con Path*** (C, 214895), ðɪˌprɛsˌlagnɐˈgɒnˈpaθ. A footpath in Ballochbuie Forest.

**Preas na Braidich** See Doire Braghad.

**Preas na Làire*** (3, 145942), copse of the mare. Press-na-laar (I). A birch copse in Gleann an t-Slugain.

**Preas nam Mèirleach*** (2, F, 015938), locally Meàrlach, ˌprɛsnɐˈmjaˑrlɐχ, copse of the robbers. Also the Robbers' Copse (C), ðɪˈrɒbɛrzˈkɒps. Also 'called in English the thieves' wood' (A). A copse of old firs in Glen Luibeg.

**Preas Ruighe*** (3, probably 09-92-), copse of shieling. Pressrie (R 1). A former building in Glen Quoich, on south side of Quoich Water.

**The Priest's Chair*** (C, south of 121904), ðɪˈpristsˈʧer. Also Father Farquharson's Seat (C), ˌfaðɛrˈfarçɛrsənzˈsit. A stone-built seat, with inscribed slab placed there in 1783 in memory of a Braemar priest who retired to nearby Arderg in 1781 (Bl). North-east of Corriemulzie.

**The Priest's Croft*** (U, 340995), ðɪˈpristsˈkrɒft. Consisted of the Chapel Parks and the ground down to the Glen Bardy exit, in Glen Gairn.

**(The) Priest's Well** (OS, Crom, F, south-west of 180844), ðɪ ˈpristsˈwɛl. Also Fuaran an t-Sagairt (3, U), ˌfuɐrɐnˈtagɛrt, well of the priest. Fueran Tackart (I). At Loch Callater.

**Prince Albert's Cairn** (OS, 260934). A big pyramid-shaped cairn at the top of Creag an Lurachain at Balmoral. Locally the Creag an Lurachain Prop (F), ðɪˌkregˈlurəçɐnˈprɒp. This, along with various other cairns, obelisks and monuments below, was erected by Queen Victoria near Balmoral. Most of the names are not locally used.

The cliffs of Coire Bhrochain, encrusted with rime on an April day, plunge from Braeriach's summit, with Sgor an Lochain Uaine beyond.

Loch Etchachan in early June, with Cairn Gorm (right) beyond the trough of Loch Avon in Banffshire.

**Prince Albert's Obelisk** (OS, 262946).

**Prince Arthur's Cairn** (OS, 254943).

**Prince Consort's Statue** (OS, 262947).

**Prince Leopold's Cairn** (OS, 255945).

**Prince of Wales's Cairn** (OS, 334910). In mid Glen Muick.

**The Prince o Wales Butts*** (U, 270033), ðɪ'prɪnsᴇ'welz'bʌts. Grouse butts north-west of Gairnshiel.

**The Prince's Cairn** (Mp, C, 133899), ðɪ'prɪnsɪz'kern̩. A cairn west of Braemar, erected to commemorate the marriage of Prince Edward and Alexandra.

**The Prince's Cairn Road*** (C, 137903), ðɪ'prɪnsɪz'kern̩'rod. A track west of Braemar.

**The Prince's Drive** (McC 1891, 300860). A road in Glen Muick.

**The Princess Alice Park*** (F, 249948), ðɪ'prɪnsəs'aləs'park. A field beside Princess Alice's Monument, near Balmoral.

**Princess Alice's Cairn** (OS, 248937).

**Princess Alice's Monument** (OS, 250948).

**Princess Beatrice's Cairn** (OS, 263938).

**Princess Helena's Cairn** (OS, 256938).

**Princess Louise's Cairn** (OS, 256941).

**Princess Royal's Cairn** (OS, 239929).

**The Princess's Pool*** See Poll na Claraig.

**The Princess's Tea Room*** See Queen Victoria's Tea Room.

**The Prince's Stone** (OS, F, 229891), ðɪ'prɪnsɪz'stin. A stone north-west of Lochnagar.

**Princess Walk** See the Craig Walk.

**Prince's Well** (OS, 251902). In Glen Gelder.

**The Private Water*** (C), ðɪ'praevət'watër. Also the Clunie Water, ðɪ'kluni'watër. Cluny Water (A). Invercauld fishings from Bridge of Dee to west of Braemar.

**(The) Prony** (OS, C, 347979), ðɪ'prone, from A' Phronnaich (3, D), frunngich (D), the dross or thing broken in small fragments, probably referring to the screes on the hill above this farm in lower Glen Gairn. Prannie (Anon 2), Proniche (Ab 8).

**The Prony Bank*** (F, 348981, 348980, 350979, and 352978), ðɪ'prone'baŋk. A collective name for four fields on a steep hillside in lower Glen Gairn.

**The Prony Brae*** (C, 346984), ðɪ'prone'bre·. A hill on a road in lower Glen Gairn.

**The Prony Cairns*** (U, 350984), ðɪ'prone'kern̩z. Screes in lower Glen Gairn.

**The Prop o Fasheilach*** (F, 342858), ðɪ'prɒpᴇfə'ʃiliç. A cairn on a hilltop in Glen Muick.

**The Prop o the Buailteach*** (C, 276937), ðɪ'prɒpðɪ'bultʃəç. A big cairn on Tom Buailteach south-west of Abergeldie.

**The Prop o the Camlet*** (C, 303933), ðɪ'prɒpðɪ'kamlët. A cairn on the hilltop north-west of the Camlet in Glen Girnock.

**The Prop o the Witter*** (F, 320789), ðɪ'prɒpðɪ'wëtër. See the Witter. A cairn on a prominent little top south of Loch Muick.

**The Ptarmigan Brae*** (U, 174800), ðɪ'tarmɪgən'bre·. A good hillside for ptarmigan shooting, north of the Glas Maol.

**The Ptarmigan Brae Burn*** See Allt a' Chuil Riabhaich.

**The Ptarmigan Lochs*** (F), ðɪ'tarmɪgən'lɒχs. A collective name for Lochan na Feadaige and Lochan an Tarmachain west of Lochnagar.

**The Puil Park*** (U, 245010), ðɪ'pil'park, Scots Puil = pool. A field west of Gairnshiel.

**The Puirs' House** See Braehead Cottages.

**The Pulpit*** (F, west of 299873), ðɪ'pul‚pɪt. A pulpit-like rock on the Green Craig in upper Glen Muick.

**The Punch Bowl** (OS, C, 114913), ðɪ'pʌnʃ‚bol. A hole in the rock in lower Glen Quoich, said to be where the Earl of Mar made punch when holding his meeting for planning the 1715 Jacobite rising. Sometimes the Earl of Mar's Punch Bowl in the past (Mp). The Earl o' Mar's Punch Bowl (Br). Also the Devil's Punch Bowl (F), ðɪ'dɪvəlz'pʌnʃ‚bol.

**Am Punnd*** (3, F, 246016), ðɪ'pɒnd, the pound (i.e. for holding cattle). The lower part of the hill north of Daldownie, south-east of Corndavon Lodge.

**The Punt Puil** (F, 217925), ðɪ'pʌnt'pil. Punt (Wav). In Dee, south-west of the Inver.

**Purchase Cairn** (OS, 256943). Near Balmoral, to commemorate Queen Victoria's purchase of the estate.

**The Quarry Butts*** (U, 399021), ðɪ'kware'bʌts. Grouse butts south-east of Morven.

**The Quarry Road*** (U, 140911), ðɪ'kware'rod. A track west of Braemar.

**The Quarter Cake*** (C, 405025), ðɪ'kwartër'kek. A triangular area shaped like the quarter of a cake or bannock, between two burns south-west of Logie Coldstone.

**Quartz Cliff** (OS, 388883), should be the Slate Quarry (C), ðɪ 'slet'kware. Slatequarry (OSn). A steep little cliff in upper Glen Tanar.

**(The) Queel Burn** (OS, C, 402994), ðɪ'kwil'bʌrn, sometimes just the Queel (F), probably from Allt na Cùlaidh (5), burn of the back place, possibly from Caoil = of narrow place. Allt na culy (D) for the similarly-pronounced Wheel Burn south-west of Morven. Quiel burn (G 33). South-east of Morven.

**The Queen's Drive** (Ad, 230921). A track through the Woods of Garmaddie, south-west of Balmoral.

**The Queen's Drive** (Ky, C, 160909), ðɪ'kwinz'draev. Was formerly called the Lion's Face Road (R 7) at east end. 'Pleasure road by the Lion's Face to Invercauld' (I). A track near Braemar.

**The Queen's Hill*** See Creag Mhor.

**The Queen's Puil** (F, 214924), ðɪ'kwinz'pil. Queen (Wav). In Dee, south-west of the Inver.

**The Queen's View** (Mp, C, 122903), ðɪ'kwinz'vju·. Also 'colloquially . . . the Peep o' Dee' (Smith 1911). A favourite viewpoint for Queen Victoria, west of Braemar.

**The Queen's Well*** (F, 258946), ðɪ'kwinz'wel. Near Balmoral Castle, named after Queen Victoria.

**The Queen's Well** See Tobar Chuirn.

**Queen Victoria's Roadie*** (U, 264956), ‚kwin‚vɪk'toreᴇz'rodi. A track built for Victoria to go by horse and gig to a viewpoint above Crathie.

**Queen Victoria's Statue** (OS, 261948). Near the bridge at Balmoral.

**Queen Victoria's Tea Room*** (F, 115913), ‚kwin‚vɪk'toreᴇz'ti ‚rum. Also subsequently called the Princess's Tea Room (F), ðɪ'prɪnsəsɪz'ti‚rum, after Victoria's grand-daughter the Princess Royal who married the Duke of Fife, former owner of Mar Lodge. A building by Linn of Quoich.

**The Quoich*** (C, 118911), ðɪ'koɪç. Area around the house called the Quoich and nearby bridge.

**The Quoich** See the Linn of Quoich.

**The Quoich Brig*** (C, 118911), ðɪ'koɪç'brɪg. A bridge over Quoich beside the above house.

**The Quoich Flats*** (F, 117909), ðɪ'koɪç'flats, or the Flats (F). Flat land with heather, rough grass and bog on west side of Quoich.

**The Quoich Forkins*** (F, 082946), ðɪ'koɪç'fɒrkënz. Where Quoich forks at the foot of the Dubh-Ghleann.

**The Quoich Haughs*** (C, 122908), ðɪ'koɪç'ha·χs, formerly the Haughs of Quoich (Ra 13). Flat lands where Quoich meets Dee.

**The Quoich Quarry*** (U, 116909), ðɪ'koɪç'kware. Near mouth of Quoich.

**Quoich Water** (OS, 082948), locally now the Quoich (C), ðɪ 'koɪç, from Uisge Choich (6, U), uʃk'çoɪç, water of the

Quoich. Uisg choich (D), Co-ich, with long *o* (D), *o* front long (D in A). Coich (Go, Sto), Ushkcaich (Im 2), Uskaich, Usquikaich (Ri 22, 27), River Queich (Roy), Burn of Caich (I) for top part, Water of Quoich (Fa, R 10), Water of Quich (Im 2). Quoich, Gaelic Cothaich—labour, work (Mp), ˌɛkən ˈɡoˑɪç (Sch) from aig an Coich. These spellings show that Caich and Coich were both used, and one map (Ro) gives Burn of Caich for the top part and R. Quich for the bottom. Also Abhainn Coich (6), river of Quoich. Avon Coich (Bla MS). See Caich. Possibly from Cuthach = madness, infuriated. Cothaich = strive and Cathach = warrior, from Cath = battle, struggle, are also likely possibilities. A small river north-west of Braemar.

**The Quoich Wuid*** (C, 095922), ðɪˈkoɪçˈwɪd. Old wood of fir and birch in Glen Quoich.

**Rachaish** (OS, B, 249923), from Ruighe Chòis (4, C), rɪˈχoʃ, cattle-run of the hollow. Richoish, Riechoies (Me 5, 22), Ruiechosh (Ra 10), Re-hosh (A). A former farm in Glen Gelder.

**Rachie's Stile*** (U, 415960), ˈreçɪzˈstɛil, Scots Stile = gate, Auld (old) Rachie or Rachel once lived near there (U). A gate between fields near Inchmarnoch.

**Radach*** (3), red place. Ratach (Cr 58). A former habitation at Abergeldie.

**Radio Relay Hut** (OS, 132886), locally the Morrone Hut (C), ðɪ ˌmoˈronˈhʌt or the Goring Hut (Du, C), ðɪˈɡorɪŋˈhʌt, after a Brian Goring who died in the Cairngorms and whose relatives gave money towards the hut. On top of Morrone near Braemar.

**Radlaich Beag*** (3, 208948), little dark red place. Rattlich Beg (I). Pairs with Radlaich Mor below. A field north-west of the Inver.

**Radlaich Mór*** (3, 211947), big dark red place. Rattlich More (I). Pairs with Radlaich Beag. A field north-west of the Inver.

**Raebush** (OS, 430022), rɪˈbʌs (C), as in Scots Buss = bush. The Bush in the name suggests a Gaelic Preas originally, and Rae from Ruighe = cattle-run or Rèidh = meadow, but possibly Scots Rae = roe. A former farm south of Logie Coldstone.

**Rainies Stack*** (Am, 292952), ? from Rennie's Tack (personal name) with Deeside pronunciation ˈrɛne. Now the Hedge Park (F), ðɪˈhɛʤˈpark, with a hawthorn hedge on one side. A field beside Abergeldie Castle.

**The Ram Park*** (Md 1, F, 138830), ðɪˈramˈpark. A former rough field in Glen Clunie.

**The Rams Park*** See the Crafts o Bridgefoot.

**Rann*** (3, 391976), land-portion. Ran (R 4). On farmland at Tullich.

**Rann a' Chroisg*** (3, 392977), land-portion of the crossing. Rannachrosk (R 4). On farmland at Tullich.

**Rann na Bruaich** (3, F), a collective name for two farms, see under Wester and Easter, ˌrɛneˈbroiç, land-portion of the bank. Rannabroith (Ca), Rannabrocht (Rg), Rinabruach (Cr 42), Rhinabroth, Rienabroigh, Rinabroich (Ri 4, 21, 39), Ruinabroich (Im 3), Rinabrugh (R 1), Rienabroich (I, Ro, R 14), Rinebruich (Crg 5), Renabroich (OS 1869). Alexander decided it was Ruigh na Bruaich, brae sheiling, but it was a farm, so Ruighe here would mean cattle-run or slope. The early spellings indicate Rann, though the latest ones could be interpreted as Ruighe. Rui na vroych or vro-ich (Da) suggest an ungrammatical Ruighe na Bhruaich. A former pair of farms close together beside a steep bank above River Gairn.

**An Raon*** (3, U, 300966), ðɪˈreˑn, the field. A former little field east of Crathie.

**The Rashie Bog*** (389023). The Rashy Bogg, the Bog of the Rashes (Io 20), the Rashes Bog (G 19). Beside Rashy Burn south-east of Morven.

**(The) Rashy Burn** (OS, F, 388022), ðɪˈraʃeˈbʌrn, Scots Rashie = with rushes. Formerly Dryburn, or Burn of Rashes (G 33). See also Allt Bad na h-Earba. The Burn of Rashes (G 19), the Burn of Badnaharb (Io 20). Said to be the Burn of Rashes to Cromar folk but the Burn of Badinyearb to Tullich folk (G 19). Also the Blind Burn (Io 20) above the ford. South-east of Morven.

**An Rathadan Meadhonach** (3, 134900), the middle little road. Ra-adan Meanach, the middle path (Mp). Near Braemar.

**Rathad Bealach Dearg*** (2, JB, 178999), ˌraɐɖˌbjalɐχˈʤɛrəɡ, road of red pass. Also the Bealach Dearg Road (C), ðɪˌbeiləç ˈʤɛrgˈrod, ðɪˌbalɐχˈʤɛrgˈrod. A track over the pass of Bealach Dearg between Invercauld and Loch Builg.

**An Rathad Crìon*** (2, U, 344993), ðɪˌraɖˈkriən, the little road. A footpath from Candacraig in Glen Gairn slanting up the wood to Glen Bardy.

**? Rathad Dairirich*** (2, U, south of 308965), ? raˈtarərɪç, first word uncertain, ? road of loud rattling noise. Informant said it meant a place where one could often hear a loud rattling sound formed as an echo from horses' hooves, from the rocks under the road surface; people could tell from the ringing sound that distant horses were approaching. West of Coilacriech.

**An Rathad Geal** (3, U, 296960), ðɪˌratˈgjal, the white road. The Rathad Geal (Gf). An old track east of Crathie.

**Rathad Geal** (3, east of 296960). Rat-yal (D). Former farm beside above road.

**Ratlich** (OS, Fa, C, 212947), ˈratˌlëç, from Radlaich (3), dark red place. Rottiloch (Ri 17), Rattalich, Ratalich (Cr 13, 17), Ratlich (Rli 19), Ratlich (D). Ra-at-lich (D) suggests a disyllable as in Rathad = road, but many old spellings and many informants gave one syllable for the Rat part of the name, as did Diack himself as an alternative. A former farm north-west of the Inver.

**The Ratlich Brig*** (F, west of 212947), ðɪˈratˌlëçˈbrɪg. In Glen Feardar.

**The Ratlich Burn*** (F, 212949), ðɪˈratˌlëçˈbʌrn. In Glen Feardar.

**The Ratlich Corrie*** (U, 212955), ðɪˈratˌlëçˈkọre. North of Ratlich.

**Ratlich Croft*** Ratilloch Croft (Io 2). A former croft in Glen Feardar.

**The Raven's Crag** See Creag an Fhithich.

**The Rebel's Cave** See the Colonel's Cave.

**The Red Brae*** (F, 398972), ðɪˈrɛdˈbreˑ. A steep gravelly bank on Dee north-east of Ballater.

**The Red Brae*** (F, 294956), as above. A sandy bank on Dee near Abergeldie.

**The Red Brae*** (F, 360959), as above. A sandy bank on west side of Dee, west of Ballater.

**The Red Brae*** See A' Bhruach Ruadh.

**The Red Brae*** See A' Bhruach Ruadh.

**The Red Brae Pool*** See Poll na Bruaich Ruaidhe.

**The Red Brae Puil** (F, 294956), ðɪˈrɛdˈbreˈpil. Red Brae (Sc). In Dee near Abergeldie.

**The Red Brae Puil** (C, 360953), as above. Red Brae (Sc). In Dee west of Ballater.

**(The) Red Burn** (OS, C, 425026), ðɪˌrɛdˈbʌrn. Formerly the Burn of Logie (Mf), from Alltan Lagaigh (3), burnie at hollow (see W 147), note nearby house Allalogie (OS), ˌalɐ ˈlaˑgi (C). North-west of Loch Davan.

**(The) Redburn** (OS, C, 420026), as above. A former farm beside the above burn.

**The Red Burn Brig*** (U, 432024), ðɪˌrɛdˈbʌrnˈbrɪg. A bridge south of Logie Coldstone.

**The Red Cairn** See Carn Dearg.

**The Red Craig** See the Black Craig.

**(The) Red Craig** (OS, F, 423907), ðɪˈrɛdˈkreg, locally often called the Etnach Red Craig (F). A hill in upper Glen Tanar.

**The Red Croft** (Gr, U, west of 355975), ðɪˈridˈkrɑft. A triangular field north of Bridge of Gairn.

**The Redd** (3, F, south-east of 349967), ðɪˈreˑd, Scots Redd = salmon spawning ground. Rade (Sc). A narrow pool at north side of Dee, above Gairn entry.

**The Red Lumps\*** (I, U, 327981), ðɪˈrɛdˈlʌmps. Hillocks north of Coilacriech Inn, with reddish rocks.

**(The) Red Spout** (OS, C, 254853), ðɪˈridˈsput. A wide gully filled with reddish-coloured granite gravel, on Lochnagar.

**The Red Stile\*** (U, 286930), ðɪˈrɛdˈstɛil, Scots Stile = gate. A gap in a dyke south of Abergeldie, where a track passes through; formerly there was a red gate. Now a deer fence and gate there.

**(The) Red Stripe** (OS, U, 405891), ðɪˈridˈstrɛip, Scots Stripe = small burn. In upper Glen Tanar.

**The Redy Way** (Wy 73), ? Reedy Way. A former path round the north side of Loch Davan used at the Battle of Culblean.

**The Red Well\*** (U, 999869), ðɪˈrɛdˈwɛl. In lower Glen Geldie.

**Red Well\*** (I, 214957). At the Loin north-west of the Inver.

**Red Well of Allt Chernie\*** (371890). Red Well of Ault Churnie (I). Source of Allt Chernie, east of the Linn of Muick.

**Red Well of the Cairnwell\*** See Tobar Chuirn.

**The Red Wells\*** (U, 980874), ðɪˈrɛdˈwɛlz. Springs on south side of Geldie Burn in mid Glen Geldie.

**Reeves of Back Coire Buidhe\*** (270872), Scots Reeve = pen or enclosure. Rives of Back Corbuie (B). Note Rhives (Ross-shire) from Gaelic Na Ruigheannan = the slopes (Watson 1904–5). Old shiels in upper Glen Gelder.

**The Reid Brae\*** (F, 440978), ðɪˈridˈbreˑ. A reddish-coloured gravelly bank west of Dinnet.

**The Reid Brae Puil** (C, 440977), ðɪˈridˈbreˈpil. Red Brae (P). A pool in Dee, beside the above bank.

**An Réidhlean Geal\*** (3, C, 122903), ðɪˌrelɐnˈjaˑl, the white (i.e. grassy) green. A small green area formerly above the Braemar–Corriemulzie road but now covered by road widening.

**Réidhlean na Cnadaig** or **Cnèadaig** (3, U, 108877), ˌrelɐnɐ ˈkraχtəg, green of the ball game. In Perthshire (Dw), Cnèadag = shinty, Cneutag = football. Reidhlean na crahtaig, cnataig (D). A green up the Corriemulzie Burn.

**The Reid House\*** See Ruighe Ealasaid.

**Reid Jimmie’s** (F, 343027), ˈridˈdʒɪmiz. Red Jimmie’s (Dil). A former house near Morven Lodge.

**The Reid Peth Brae** (C, 428963), ðɪˈridˈpaeˈbreˑ, ðɪˈrɛdˈpaeˈbreˑ, Scots Peth = path. The Red Pey (A 349). A hill on the road east of Inchmarnoch.

**The Reid Scaurs\*** (U, 004955), ðɪˈridˈskaˑrz, Scots Scaur = bare patch on a hillside. Gravelly slopes on Carn a’ Mhaim in Glen Luibeg.

**The Reid Shank\*** (U, 449896), ðɪˌridˈʃaŋk, the red ridge. A hill ridge south of Glen Tanar.

**The Reid Shank Burn** See Burn of Redshank.

**The Reive** (OS, F, 406915), ðɪˈriv. A lowland Scots version of An Ruighe (3), the slope (note W 1904–5, 64 for Rhives in Ross-shire). A hill slope in upper Glen Tanar.

**Remicras** (OS, C, 267000), rɪˈmicrəs, from Ruighe Mhiagras (6), shiel of the Micras, for meaning see Micras. Gaelic speech Ruigh-vicras (M). Riemicras (R 14, Io 77), Rivicras (Crg 15). A former farm west of Gairnshiel.

**The Remicras Burn\*** (F, 267000), ðɪˌrɪˈmicrəsˈbʌrn. Lower part of Cossack Burn, beside above place.

**Remicras Cottage\*** (Ce 6). Former habitation beside Remicras west of Gairnshiel.

**Renatton** (OS, 269017). Millcroft of Renatton (OS 1869), now the Mill Craft (U), ðɪˈmɛlˈkrɑft. Formerly Bad Charn (4), clump of cairns. Badquharn (Ri 7), Badwharn was the mill croft of Rineaton (D). Renatton is merely another spelling of Rineten. Old Mill (Ce 4). A former croft west of Gairnshiel.

**Rhebreck** (OS, C, 260939), rɪˈbrɛk, from Ruighe Breac (3), speckled cattle-run. Rumbrick, Readbreak (Ra 10), Rubrek (S 25), Rebreck (B), Robrech (V), Ridhebreac (OS 1903). A former farm at Balmoral, now a house.

**The Rhebreck Brae\*** (C, 262939), ðɪˌrɪˈbrɛkˈbreˑ. A hill on a road at Balmoral.

**The Rhebreck Park\*** (F, 261940), ðɪˌrɪˈbrɛkˈpark. A field at Balmoral.

**Ricardo’s Brig\*** (F, 087883), rɪˈkardozˈbrɪg. A bridge over Ey Burn, south of Inverey. No local story, so Ricardo may be from Gaelic.

**Richarkarie** (OS, C, 301015), rɪˈχarçəre, riˈχarχɐre (JB) from Ruighe Charcairidh (3), cattle-run of the little road. Racharchry (Anon 12), Richarcharie, Recharcharie (Ande), Riecharcarie (Ri 21), Richarcrie (Rli 23), Richarkry, Riecharkarie (R 1, 14). Rui-charkri, rucharchari, ‘greep’, the Gaelic for a greep or runnel in a byre is cachkri, carcari (D), but Diack preferred Carcair, a narrow road. A former farm north-east of Gairnshiel. Diack mistakenly gave Richrachrie for Ruighe Chreichidh, and Alexander further added an error by giving it as a Recharchrie 5 km from the Gairnshiel one.

**The Richarkarie Burn\*** (C, 303015), ðɪˌrɪˈχarçəreˈbʌrn. Lower part of Allt Coire an t-Slugain beside above place.

**Rideach\*** (5), ? place of bog myrtle. Riddach (Io 54). A former farm in Glen Gelder, different from Rotaig.

**The Riggin** (Wa, C), ðɪˈrɪgən, Scots = the ridge, skyline. A common term in Glen Esk and Deeside for the hills on the Aberdeenshire–Angus boundary, such as Braid Cairn, Naked Hill etc, or hills on the Dee–Don, Dee–Avon, etc boundaries.

**The Riggin o Lochnagar\*** (F), ðɪˈrɪgənɐˌloχnəˈgaˑr. The skyline of Lochnagar as seen from the Dee valley.

**Rinabaich** (OS, C, 302964), ˌrɐnɐˈbeç, ˌrɪnɐˈbaˑɪç and ˌrɪnɐˈvaˑɪç from two old folk, from Roinn a’ Bhàthaich (3), land-portion of the byre. Rinnavā-ich, byre (D). Usual sound Rin-a-vech but old people still say Rin-a-va-ich (A), rɪnɐˈvaˑɪç. Obviously the aspiration in the original *bh* sound has now dropped to *b*. A former farm west of Coilacriech, now a house.

**The Rinabaich Brig\*** (F, 302962), ðɪˌrɐnɐˈbeçˈbrɪg. Also Morgan’s Brig (U), ˈmɔrgənzˈbrɪg, after a former Rinabaich resident. Road bridge at Micras.

**Rinasluick** (OS, 357932), from Ruighe nan Sleac (3, C), ˌrɐnɐ ˈslek, cattle-run of the slabs. Rinislacke (Io 7), Runslaught (Rli 23), Rie-na-Sleachd (I). A former farm in lower Glen Muick.

**Rineten** (OS, C, 275003), rɪnˈitən, rɪnˈɛtən (U) to some old folk, from Roinn Aitinn (5), land-portion of juniper. Rui-natshing (Da) suggests Ruighe an Aitinn, cattle-run of the juniper. Rhuneiten (I), Rhinetten, Rienetan (R 12, 14), Rienetton (Io 77), Rynatang, Rynatange (Io prob. late 1700s–early 1800s), Rinatang, Rynettan (Me 3, 20). A house west of Gairnshiel, formerly the house for a small estate there.

**The Rineten Brig\*** (C, 276002), ðɪˌrɪnˈitənˈbrɪg. West of Gairnshiel.

**The Rineten Burn\*** (F, 280004), ðɪˌrɪnˈitənˈbʌrn. Burn of Rineten (I). Lowest part of Coulachan Burn west of Gairnshiel.

**The Rineten Park\*** (U, 277002), ðɪˌrɪnˈɛtənˈpark. A former field of rough grazing, now partly overgrown with trees, west of Gairnshiel.

**The Rineten Wuid*** (F, 270003), ðɪˌrɪnˈitənˈwɪd. The Wuid o Rineten (U). A wood at Rineten.

**Rinfold*** (R 4, 398979), ? from Roinn (3) = land-portion and English Fold. On farmland at Tullich.

**The Ring*** (U, north-west of 245010), ðɪˈrɪŋ. A vegetation ring about 30 cm wide and 6 m in diameter, forming a circle in a field west of Gairnshiel and plainly visible when the field was in short grass or oats (RB), but now indistinct.

**The Ringing Stane*** (C, 300016), ðɪˈrɪŋənˈstin, Scots Stane = stone. A stone north-east of Gairnshiel which makes a ringing sound when small stones are rolled down it.

**Rinloan** (OS, C, 293006), rənˈloˑn, in Gaelic ˌriənˈloˑn (JB). Roinn lōn (D) suggests Roinn Lòin (3), land-portion of wet meadow, but some old people said Ree-lone (A), and other spellings also indicate Ruighe an Lòin (3), cattle-run of the wet meadow. Rianloin (Opr 5), Ruinloin (Im 3), Rienloin (Cr 43), Ruidh-an Loin (Iop), Rienlone Inn (I), Rienloan (R 14, Io 77), Reinloan (Io 77). The first four spellings probably refer to the former farm nearby, see Ruighe an Loin. A house at Gairnshiel, formerly an inn.

**(The) Rinloan Burn** (OS, C, 297001), ðɪˌrənˈlonˈbʌrn. At Gairnshiel.

**Rintarsin** (OS, C, 264965), rənˈtarsən, in Gaelic riənˈdarsɪn (JB), from Roinn Tarsuinn (4), cross portion, or Ruighean Tarsuinn, cross cattle-runs. Runtassen (S 22), Rintarsuin (Opr 25), Rie na n taoishen, Reintarsen (R 3, 14), Rin tarshin (Da). Also Upper Rintarsin (U). A former farm north of Crathie.

**Rintarsin*** (U, 263966), as above. A field near the above place.

**(The) Rintarsin Burn** (OS, F, 266967), ðɪˌrənˈtarsənˈbʌrn. Allt nan Deanntag (3, F), altˈdʒandi, (altənˈdʒandi (A)), burn of the nettles. Allt nan Eanntag (OS 1869). North of Crathie.

**Ripe Hill** (OS, F, 240911), ˈrɛipˈhël, locally usually the Ripe (A, C), ðɪˈrɛip, from Sreap (4), climb, see A' Choire Shreap. Ripe (B, OS 1869). On west side of Glen Gelder.

**The Ripe Wuid*** (C, 240910), ðɪˈrɛipˈwɪd. A wood on above hill.

**River Dee** (OS, 340960), locally the Dee (C), ðɪˈdiˑ, in Gaelic ˌdʒeː (Sch). Uisge Dé (3, A), uʃkˈdje: (JB), water of Dee or goddess (i.e. a river deity). Yskaw Jea (Roy) suggests Dhé, of the Dee. The Water of Dee (Fa, A). The word was masculine (D, A) in local speech and place names (Fuaran Dhe, Gleann Dhe, and several others), and was the same in form as the genitive of Dia, the Gaelic for God (A), tshē (D). Diack and Alexander discuss the matter in more detail, and Jackson offers criticism of their discussions, with a useful summary. He states that the word comes from a Pictish Dewa, as also in the Cheshire Dee, meaning goddess. Rises in and flows right through the area covered in this book.

**River Gairn** (OS, 342989), locally the Gairn (C), ðɪˈgern̩, from Uisge Ghàrain (5, T 33, 17; Mg), or Ghairein, water of the Gairn or ? crying one. Uisg gharran (D). Water of Gairdin (Fa), Water of Gairn (Blm), Gairn Water (Jo). Early spellings give Gardene, Gardin, Gardyn, Garden (A) suggesting an earlier Gartain sound in Gaelic, as in Gartain = of a little enclosure. The sound *a* changes to *e* readily in Scots. Gair is an old form of Goir = cry (W 449). The diminutive Goirneag = little crier, gives Garnock and Girnock. The smaller burn of Girnock enters Dee close to the bigger Gairn. Macpherson suggested gar = rough. Avon Garden (Bla MS) from Abhainn Gàrain (5) = river of Gairn. North-west of Ballater.

**River Muick** (OS, 354940), locally the Muick (C), ðɪˈmëk. In Gaelic Uisge Muice or Muc (3), water of Muick or pig-one, referring to the stream (see Glen Muick). Uisg muic, muchk (D). South-west of Ballater.

**River Quoich** See Quoich Water.

**Roadside*** (Ce 3). Former habitation in Glenmuick parish.

**Roadside*** (Opr 43). Former habitation in Crathie parish.

**The Roadside Park*** (U, west of 259959), ðɪˈrodˈsɛidˈpark. A field north-west of Crathie.

**The Roar Burn*** See the Coinlach Burn.

**(The) Roar Hill** (OS, C, 396030), ðɪˈrorˈhël, often just the Roar (C), ðɪˈroˑr̩. The Hill of Rore (Mf). Possibly from Cnoc Reamhar (3), thick hill, 'which somewhat describes it' (A). South-east of Morven.

**The Roaring Stag*** (C, north of 116894), ðɪˈrorĕnˈstag. A house at Corriemulzie.

**(The) Roar Moss** (OS, C, 390025), ðɪˈrorˈmọs, to a few old folk the Moss o the Roar (F), ðɪˈmọsiðɪˈroˑr̩, ðɪˈmọsəiˈroˑr̩. A peat-moss near the above hill.

**The Roar Road*** (C, 399026), ðɪˈrorˈrod. A track to the above peat-moss.

**Robertson's Puil** (C, 368950), ˈrọbërtsənzˈpil, or the Robertson Puil. Robertson's Pool (Sc). In Dee, near mouth of Muick, after a gardener who formerly lived at Bridgefoot nearby.

**Rob Roy's Cave** See the Vat.

**The Rockies Puil** (C, 403975), ðɪˈrọkezˈpil, ðɪˈrọkeˈpil. Rockies (A, Sc). In Dee, north-east of Ballater.

**(The) Rocking Stone** (OS, 409943, should be at 405965, stone at 409943 does not rock). This name is on OS 1 : 50000, but OS 1 : 10000 gives Big Stane o' Carn Beag. Notwithstanding its name . . . it does not rock (Brem). Locally the Rockin Stane (F), ðɪˈrọkĕnˈstin, is an erratic boulder that rocks almost at the push of a fingertip, at 405965 on a hillside east of Pannanich.

**The Rock of Bod an Deamhain*** The Rock of Potenjone (Fi). Rock Pot John (Fi) suggests a translation from a probable Creag Bod an Deamhain. The cliffs of the Devil's Point in Glen Dee.

**Rock of the Tod Holes*** (I, 316842), Scots Tod = fox. Broken rocks south-east of Spittal of Glenmuick.

**The Rocks o Auchtavan*** (U, 199961), ðɪˈrọksɐˌaχtəˈvjan. Rocky hillside near Auchtavan in Glen Feardar.

**The Rocks o Carn Crom*** (U, 023949), ðɪˈrọksɐˌkarnˈkrọm. Small crags north-west of Derry Lodge.

**The Rocks o Clais Fhearnaig*** (U, 069935), ðɪˈrọksɐˌklaʃ ˈjaˑrnək. Small broken cliffs east of Glen Lui.

**The Rocks o Duchrie*** (C, 238995), ðɪˈrọksɐˈduçri. Rocks of Duchry (D). A narrow rocky place on the Duchrie Burn south-east of Cordavon Lodge.

**The Rocks o Maim*** (U, 134901), ðɪˈrọksɐˈmɛim. The rocks of Maim (Mp). Small broken cliffs west of Braemar.

**The Rocks o the Roar*** (U, north-east of 400033), ðɪˈrọksəiˈror̩. A rocky gully east of Morven.

**The Rocky Corner*** (F, 163924), ðɪˈrọkeˈkọrnër. On the Aberdeen road east of Braemar.

**The Rocky Hill*** (F, 950896), ðɪˈrọkeˈhël. Rocky Hill (Mm). A little top in upper Glen Geldie.

**The Rocky Pool*** (U, 059896), ðɪˈrọkeˈpul, ðɪˈrọkez. A pool in Dee with rocky slabs above the Linn of Dee.

**Rodaig** (3, F, 248931), ˈrọdək, ruddy place. Roddack (Io 54), Rodack (B), Roddick (OS 1903), Rotag (D). A former farm in lower Glen Gelder.

**The Rodden Den*** (F, 381964), ðɪˈrọdənˈden, Scots Rodden = rowan. A hollow with rowan trees west of Pannanich.

**Roger's Pool** See the Lower Ceapaich Puil.

**Roinn a' Bhàthaich*** (3, 273000), land-portion of the byre. Runavach (Roy). Buildings, probably a former farm, west of Gairnshiel.

**Roinn a' Chaibeil** (3, 339996), rɪnaˈhapəl (A), land-portion of the chapel. Rinnahapple (A). A field near a former chapel in Glen Gairn.

**Roinn a' Chata** (5, F, 253957), ˌrënɐˈhat, land-portion of the sheep-cot, possibly a' Chait, of the cat. Re na chat, Rhinachat (R 3, 6a), Rinachat (OS 1869), Rhinnachat (A). A former farm north-west of Crathie.

**Roinn a' Chroisg*** (3, 357949), land-portion of the crossing. Rhun na Chroisk (I). A former field in lower Glen Muick.

**Roinn a' Chuir*** (3, 342903), land-portion of the turn. Rhun-na-Chur (I). A former field near a river bend in mid Glen Muick.

**Roinn an Fhùcadair** (3, probably 319028, by elimination), land-portion of the fuller. Ryn-an-ockater (D). Rinnavocater (A) suggests Roinn nan Fucadair = land-portion of the fullers. A former farm in Glen Fenzie.

**Roinn Choirce*** (3, U, 337997), rën'χɔrk, land-portion of oats. A pointed field at Lary in Glen Gairn, so might be Rinn = a point.

**An Roinn Chruaidh*** (3, U, 297960), ðɪˌrën'χrui, the hard portion. A pointed piece of hard ground sticking into a wood slightly south-west of the grid reference given, east of Crathie, so might be Rinn = point.

**Roinn Chruaidh*** (3, 227939), hard portion. Rhun cruie (I). A former field west of the Inver.

**Roinn Chruaidh*** (3, 221942), hard portion. Rhun cruie (I). A former field west of the Inver.

**Roinn Daimh*** (4, 225941), land-portion of ox. Rhun-dye (I). A former field west of the Inver.

**Roinn Doirse*** (3, U, 284957), rën'dorz, land-portion of door. A pointed field east of Crathie, projecting high on to the hill, so might be Rinn = point. It had a 2 m wide rock underneath at one place, where the plough had to be raised to get into the field (WD).

**Roinn Each** (3, 444997), land-portion of horses. Rinyach, horse pasture (A). Flat grassy ground on north side of Loch Kinord.

**Roinn Feadaidh*** (3, 393978), land-portion of whistling. Rinfaitie (R 4, Io 58). A piece of former farmland at Tullich.

**Roinn Fhada*** (3, 312011), long portion. Run-fat (I). A field east of Gairnshiel.

**Roinn Ghlas** (3, south-east of 291031), green portion. Reny Glass (Ande), Corriebeg alias Ryneglas (Ri 21), Ryneglas a shealing in Corybeg (Io 11). Also the Smugglers' Bothy (U), ðɪ'smʌglërz'bɔθe. A former shiel and bothy in Coire Beag north of Gairnshiel.

**An Roinn Mhór*** (3, 224933), the big portion. The Rhun More (I). A former field north-west of the Inver.

**An Roinn Mhór*** (3, C, 425962), ðɪˌrɪn'moˑr, the big portion. Often the Roinn Mhor Park (F). Rinnmore (Dms). A pointed field, so might be Rinn = point. Also the Lang Park (U), ðɪ 'laŋ'park. At Inchmarnoch.

**An Roinn Mhór*** (3, 225942), the big portion. The Rhun More (I). A field north-west of the Inver.

**Roinn Mutaig*** (4), land-portion of ? fright, possibly Mutach = short. Rinnmutack (Dms). Near Creag Mullach south-west of Inchmarnoch.

**Roinn na Min** (3, D, U, 144905), ˌrënɐ'min, land-portion of the meal, locally said to mean ridge of meal (D), so maybe Rinn = point. A field at Tomintoul above Braemar.

**Roinn na Min** (3, F, 144904), as above. A former house beside the above field. Rhin-a-mhin (Mp).

**Roinn na Mòine*** (3, U, 253958), ˌrënɐ'mun, land-portion of the peat-moss. A former farm north-west of Crathie.

**Roinn na Slice*** (3, 220941), land-portion of the rocky slab. Rhun na Slichk (I). A former field west of the Inver.

**Roinn Tàilleir** (3, U, 317026), rën'daˑljër, tailor's land-portion. Ryndalyer or Rintalyer (D). A former farm in Glen Fenzie.

**Roinn Taitneach** (3), pleasant land-portion. Rentatetnich, Reintatenach (Io 14, 60), Rientatnach (Ri 21). Probably a

pasturage, in the Easter Sleach–Braenaloin area west of Gairnshiel.

**The Romans' Cave*** (U, 280945), ðɪ'romənz'kev. A hollow among stones, south-west of Abergeldie.

**The Roof of Mar** (Simpso). A name in a book for the high Cairngorms within Mar.

**Rotten Haugh*** (Opr 1a). Former habitation in Crathie–Braemar parish.

**The Rotten Rocks*** (U, 280931), ðɪ'rɔtən'rɔks. Rotten rocks south-west of Abergeldie.

**The Rough Bank*** See the Rough Craig.

**Rough Burn*** See the Kirn Burn.

**(The) Rough Craig** (OS, F, 354871), ðɪ'rɔχ'kreg, pronunciation Scots Ruch = rough. The Rough Bank (I). A steep rough slope south-east of the Linn of Muick.

**The Round Hill*** (F, 961828), ðɪ'rʌund'hël. Round Hill (Mm). A little round hill at the top of Bynack Burn.

**(The) Rowantree Stripe** (OS, U, 391889), ðɪ'rɔdən'tri'strɛip, Scots Rodden = rowan. A little burn in upper Glen Tanar.

**The Royal Bridge** See the Brig o Ballater.

**The Royal Butt** See the King's Butts.

**The Ruch Burn*** (C, 295862), ðɪ'rɔχ'bʌrn, Scots Ruch = rough. Near Allt-na-giubhsaich in upper Glen Muick.

**The Ruch Grund*** (U, 357942 and partly wooded ground to south-west), ðɪ'rɔχ'grʌn, Scots = rough ground. Rough grazing in lower Glen Muick.

**The Ruch Moss*** (U, 336017), ðɪ'rɔχ'mɔs. A peaty area of moor south of Morven Lodge.

**The Ruch Park*** (U, 070895), ðɪ'rɔχ'park. A field east of the Linn of Dee.

**The Ruch Park** (U, 460983), as above. The Rough Park (Gf). A piece of former farmland at Dinnet.

**The Ruch Stanes*** (C, 255865), ðɪ'rɔχ'stinz, Scots = rough stones. Rough Stones (B). Area of boulders north of the Corrie of Lochnagar.

**The Ruch Stanes*** (Dms, south-east of 431959), see above. A rough area south of Greystone, east of Inchmarnoch.

**Ruighachail** (OS, C, 250914), rɪ'χaˑl, from Ruighe a' Chail (3), cattle-run of the kale. Riechald (Me 5), Richall (Roy), Rochaule (Mc 25), Riachall (Ra 10), Righchaill (S 25), Rachald (B). A former farm in Glen Gelder.

**Ruighe a' Chalbhairigh*** (5), cattle-run of ? from Calbh = tree shoot. Rieachalaveir, Riachalaveire, Reachvayrie, Riachavarie, Riachalvare, Riachalaverie (Me 2, 2, 6, 9, 9, 11). A former grazing in the Glen Dee–Quoich area of Mar.

**Ruighe Aimrid** (4), unproductive cattle-run. Possibly Àmraidh = of a cupboard. Riamri (Ab 19), Rieamry (G 28). A former farm probably near Bridge of Gairn on east side.

**Ruighe Allt a' Mhaide*** (3), shiel of burn of the stick. Riealdivaid, Reialvaid (Io 17, 74). Probably beside Allt a' Mhaide near the Sleach, possibly same as Shiels of the Feuragachs at 253023.

**Ruighe Allt an Aitinn*** (3, 117978), shiel of burn of the juniper. Rie Aultn Aiten (I). At the foot of Allt an Aitinn air Chul in upper Glen Quoich.

**Ruighe an Droma** (3, probably 32-88- on south side of Muick), shiel of the ridge. Rendrum (Asr), Rindrom (Ap, Io 33). Rinedrom (R 6) suggests Roinn, but Riendroum (I) suggests Ruighe an, and the place was a shieling. Shielings in upper Glen Muick.

**Ruighean Dubh-chroite** (5), shiels of black croft. Riendoe Crot, Riendou Crot, Riendou Crout, Reindou Crout (Io 2, 3, 60, 60). A shiel or pasturage probably on north side of upper Gairn.

**Ruighe an Dùnain*** (4), cattle-run of the little hillock. Possibly Roinn Dùnain = land-portion of little hillock. Park of

Achaw and Rindunan, Achdaw and Rindunan (Io 46). Former farmland up Tullich Burn.

**Ruighe an Fhliuch-choille-shlat*** (3, probably 095860), shiel at the wet wattle-wood. Coille-shlat = wood where wattles may be cut (Dw). Note Allt Shlat is nearby. See also Dail Ruighe an Fhliuch-choille-shlat. Rifleuchwood, Rufluchwode, Rifluichwoode, Rienfluichwood or Rienleuchlat (Me 1, 3, 3, 6). A former grazing in Glen Ey.

**Ruighe an Lìn** (3, 358922), cattle-run of the flax. Renlion, Rienlen (Rli 20, 23), Rienlien (I), Rinlian (Opr 44, D). A former farm in lower Glen Muick.

**Ruighe an Lise** (3, 147904), cattle-run of the enclosure. Rui n d lish (D). A piece of former arable land at Tomintoul above Braemar.

**Ruighe an Lòin** (3, 296005), cattle-run of the wet meadow. Rienloyn or Dubytoune (Io 8), Scots Dubby = puddly. See Rinloan. A former farm at Gairnshiel.

**Ruighe an Luig*** (3, U, 130825), rɪn'luəg, cattle-run of the hollow. Ruie inluig (Im 3), Riinluyge (Cr 24), Ruinluig (Ra 2), Ruithanluig (Opr 29), Rie-n-luick (I). A former farm in the lower Baddoch.

**Ruighe an Tighearn*** (3, 179847), cattle-run of the proprietor. Rien diern (I), Rien Diern (R 13). A grassy slope at Loch Callater.

**Ruighe an t-Sagairt** (3, 373011), cattle-run of the priest. Riantagird (R 1), Rintaggart (D). A former farm up the Tullich Burn.

**Ruighe an t-Seilich*** (4, 265880), shiel of the willow. Rynellaick (Fa), Ringeallich (B). In upper Glen Gelder.

**Ruighe an t-Seilich** (3, U, 087867), ˌrui.ɐn'dʒiliç, cattle-run of the willow. Rientellich (Fa), Riindelich (Cr 31), Ruigh an t Seilich (Opr 40), Ruindellich (Me 21), Rui an t-seilich (D). A former farm in lower Glen Ey.

**Ruighe an t-Seilich*** (3, U, north-east of 154913), rën'dʒili, rɪn 'dʒiliç, cattle-run of the willow. A former house at Braemar, at the back of the house now called Dunwoodie.

**Ruighe an t-Sìdhein** (3, 062919), cattle-run of the fairy hillock. Ruie in tian (Im 3), Rintion (Roy, Ar), Rieintiain, Rientien (Me 2, 3). A former farm in Glen Lui beside the hillocks called Na Da Shidhean.

**Ruighe an t-Suidhe** (4), shiel or cattle-run of the level shelf. Rienduy, Rundow (Ri 17), Riendou, Riendow (Io 60), Reindow, Rienduy (Me 3). A shieling or pasturage in Glen Feardar.

**Ruighe an Uillt*** (3), cattle-run of the burn. Reenault (H) in the middle of a list of former farms at Wester Morven.

**Ruighe an Uillt*** (3, 270027), shiel of the burn. Rie-n-Ault (I, R 12). At the junction of two burns north-west of Gairnshiel.

**Ruighean Well** (3, 385977), from Ruighean (3) = cattle-runs. Royan Well (D). Behind Milton of Tullich.

**Ruighe Bad Thomaidh*** (5, 170998), shiel of clump of the little hillock, or of the dipping. Rie Bat Toumie (I) and shiel of Pit-omie (A 283), seem like bad thomaidh, Thomas's clump (A 148). However, Toum elsewhere on the Invercauld maps is Tom = a hillock. South-east of Ben Avon, by Gairn.

**Ruighe Baile a' Chlaiginn** (3, 209019), now the Ruighe Baile (A, C), ðɪ'ruibɐl, often now ðɪ'ribəl, shiel of farm-town of the infield. Rie belchlagan (Fa), Ri-bella-chleughan, Ruibalachlaghan (Cr 28, 35), Ribellachlaggan (Roy), Ribalichlaighan, Rie-Balach-Lagon, Reeballachlagan, Rie-Ballachlagan (R 1, 3, 9, 14), Rie Ballchlaghan (I), the Roo-i-bel (A). A former shiel west of Corndavon Lodge, more recently a building used in summer alongside a pasturage.

**The Ruighe Baile Burn*** See Wester Shenalt.

**The Ruighe Baile Corrie*** (F, 205035), ðɪ'ruibɐl'kǫre. North-west of Corndavon Lodge.

**Ruighe Bàn*** (3, 146876), white shiel. Rie Baan (I). A grassy patch beside a shiel in lower Glen Clunie.

**Ruighe Bhantraich** (3, C, 419974), rɪ'fantrɪç, cattle-run of the widower. Ruffantry (Roy), Rifantrach (Pr), Riefantrach (Rli 19), Trafantrach (R 17), Revàntrach (M). A former farm south of Cambus o' May.

**The Ruighe Bhantraich Puil** See Poll Bhantraich.

**The Ruighe Bhantraich Wuid*** See Torphantrick Wood.

**Ruighe Bhùirn*** (3, U, 986914, by elimination), rui'vurn, shiel of the water. Fuaran ruigh bhuirn (D). In Glen Dee east of Beinn Bhrotain.

**Ruighe Chailleach*** (3, U, 163863), ri'χaləç, cattle-run or shiel of old women. No shiel now, but stones from any former shiel might well have been used for the nearby road or bridge. In Glen Callater.

**Ruighe Cheathraimh*** (5, 199021), shiel of the quarter. Rie herie (I). South-east of Loch Builg.

**Ruighe Chobhain*** (3), shiel of the coffin or hollow. The Shealling of Blaircharidge in Reechovn, Reichovn, Ruchovn (G 14). In Glen Muick.

**Ruighe Choinean*** (3), cattle-run of rabbits. Richonnan (G). A former farm, in 1752 part of the 'six ploughs of Abergarden' (G 20). Near Bridge of Gairn.

**Ruighe Chreagain*** (3, 179011), shiel of the little rock. Rie Chraggan, Rie Chragach (I). By Gairn, south-west of Loch Builg, below a rough rocky hill.

**Ruighe Chreichidh** (6, C, 266992), rɪ'çreçe, rɪ'çriçi, rɪ'çreçi, shiel of the Crathie or ? shaking place, for meaning see Crathie. Riechrache (Mc 4), Riechrathie (R 3), Richrechie (Crg 18), Rie Crathie (I), Reichrechie (Cr 57). Richrachrie (D) and Recharchrie (A) both incorrect (see Richarkarie). Also Crathie Shiel (Crg 2). A former farm north of Crathie.

**The Ruighe Chreichidh Birks*** (U, 268991), ðɪˌrɪ'çreçe'bërks. Birch copse at above place.

**Ruighe Dail Laoigh*** (3, 213019), shiel of haugh of calf. Sheals of Daluie (I), Rie Dalluie (R 12). Also Shiels of Monaltrie (R 5). West of Corndavon Lodge.

**Ruighe Dail na Croise*** (3, 132827), cattle-run of haugh of the cross. Ri Dallnicross (Ra 3), Dalrinacroich (Ra 3) probably same place. At the Baddoch.

**An Ruighe Dubh*** (3, 102846), the black cattle-run. Ridue (Fa), the Ridow (Cr 13), Ridow (R 1). A former farm in mid Glen Ey.

**An Ruighe Dubh*** (3, 360026), the black shiel. Riedou (Io 20). Also the Black Shiel (G 33). Note Tom a' Bhothain Dhuibh nearby, or 'hillock of the black sheill' (Io 20), a shiel probably at the same place as Ruighe Dubh. Also William McKaimis Shealing (Io 20). South-west of Morven.

**Ruighe Ealasaid** (3, A, U, 003869), rui'jalɐsətʃ, (rui'alsətʃ (A)), Elizabeth's shiel. Also the Reid House (C), ðɪ'rid'hus, and the Middle House (U), ðɪ 'mɪdəl'hus. A former house in Glen Geldie, named after a shiel at 002869.

**Ruighe Geal*** (3, 258893), white shiel. Ragyal (B). In Glen Gelder.

**Ruighe Gleann Beag*** (3, 188884), shiel of little glen. Rie Glenbeg (R 7). In Glen Beg, Ballochbuie Forest.

**Ruighe Iomlan Cùldair** (5, F, 246927), 'rʌmlën'kutɐr, full cattle-run of back water, possibly Coltair = of ploughshare, perhaps Scots Rummlin Cooter = rumbling ploughshare. Rumbling Culter (B, A), Rumblingculter (OS 1869). A former farm in Glen Gelder.

**Ruighe Iomlan Culdair** See Bridgend of Bush.

**Ruighe Laoigh*** (3), cattle-run of a calf. Rieluie (Io 53). A former farm near Newbigging in Glen Clunie. Coire Laoigh rises above there.

**Ruighe Leth-allt*** (3), cattle-run of half burn (i.e. with a steeper slope on one side). Rielealt, Relealt (Me 4). Probably near foot of Dalvorar Burn west of Linn of Dee.

**Ruighe Loisgte** (3, M, 408899), burnt shiel. Reilosk (Io 1, Ap), Ruyloisc (Io 1), Rilosck (Im 1). A shieling of Inchmarnoch beside Coirebhruach in upper Glen Tanar.

**Ruighe Loisgte Croft** (405912). Reilosk Croft (Io 1), Riloscroft (Im 1), Corywrauch alias Riloskcroft (Ap 1766). A shieling in upper Glen Tanar.

**Ruighe na Ban-righ** See Gelder Shiel.

**Ruighe na Beinne*** (3, F), ˌrʌneˈbɛn, cattle-run of the hill. Each of two adjoining fields west of Logie Coldstone has this name, but they are sometimes distinguished by being called the Balhennie Ruighe na Beinne and the Groddie Ruighe na Beinne.

**Ruighe na Beinne*** (3), cattle-run of the hill. Ruinabean (Opr 61). Former habitation in Cromar.

**Ruighe na Cailliche*** (3), cattle-run or shiel of the old woman. Riena Calich (Cr 48). A former habitation in Braemar parish.

**Ruighe na Cruinnich*** (4, south-west of 191889), shiel of the mist. Rie na crunich or Picts' sheal (R 7) implies Ruighe nan Cruithneach, shiel of the Picts. In Glen Beg, Ballochbuie Forest.

**Ruighe na Cùlath** (5, U, 003895), ˌruineˈkulɐ, shiel of the back place. Reenacula (Ch). Also Dee Cot (Cj 1). Dee Cote (Fi). Often called the Sheal by the Earl of Fife. In Glen Dee.

**Ruighe na h-Easgainne*** (3, 156801), shiel of the little bog. Wet green called Rie na heskin (I). Note Easgan can be a boggy stream (T 30, 111). North of the Glas Maol.

**Ruighe nam Fiadh*** (3, 225933), cattle-run of the deer. Rinafiach (Io 18), Ruinafey (Im 3), Rinafeadh (Io 52), Rynenfieu (G 6), Run-na-vey (I), Rinafey, Reonavay (Rli 19, 23). A former farm west of Inver Inn.

**Ruighe na Mòine** (4, 258005), slope of the peat-moss. Rinamon, a moss near the Stokach (D). West of Gairnshiel.

**Ruighe nan Caorach** (3, 431939), shiel of the sheep. Rynagirrache (Ab 13), Rennageroch, Rinnagiroch (Dms 6, 9). In Glendui, mid Glen Tanar.

**Ruighe nan Clach*** (3, U, 009872), ˌruineˈglʌχ, shiel of the stones. The nearby ruined keeper's house of Ruigh nan Clach (OS) was named after this shiel.

**Ruighe nan Coire Dubh*** (3, 080818), shiel of the black corries. Ruie-na-Corrie dou (Io 79). Note Coireachan Dubha (OS) above here. Also the Shieling of Coire na Moine. The Shealing of Corrie-na Moan or Corrie dow (Io 79). In upper Glen Ey.

**Ruighe nan Sleac*** (3, 083868), cattle-run of the slabs. Riensleik (Io 21). A former farm in Glen Ey with nearby slabs.

**Ruighe Phris** (3), shiel of the copse. Reyfreish (Ri 17), Ryfreish (Me 3). A shiel in Glen Feardar.

**Ruighe Phris Ghiubhais*** (3), cattle-run of the fir clump. Riefreishyewish, Rieffrishyewish (Me 2). A former grazing for Cragan, on Mar.

**Ruighe Rag-ach*** (4), shiel of stiff field, or Ragach = wrinkled. Rieraagacht (Me 3). Other papers (G 3) suggest Lieragache but handwriting less clear, could be Rieragache. A former shieling, went with Camas na Ciste south of Braemar.

**Ruighe Raibeirt*** (3, 120808), Robert's shiel. Rie Robert (Ra 3), Rirebart (Lp 2). A shiel in the Baddoch.

**Ruighe Tullochcoy*** From Ruighe Tulach Gaoithe (3), shiel of Tullochcoy. Ri Tullachcoy (Cr 42). Probably in Glen Feardar.

**Ruigh nan Clach** (OS, 3, C, 008874), ˌruinaˈglʌχ, shiel of the stones. Also the Ton House (Ros), from Tòn (3) = bottom. Also the Bottom House (U), ðɪˈbɒtʌmˈhus, pairs with Middle and Tap. A ruined house in lower Glen Geldie.

**The Rumbling Burn*** (Gler, 414910). The upper part of Tanar.

**(The) Rumbling Pot** (OS, C, 414910), ðɪˈrʌmlɛnˈpɒt. The Rumbling Pots (A). Scots Rummlin Pot = a deep pool where the water 'rummles aboot', i.e. swirls. A pool on upper Tanar.

**Rumbling Pots*** (Gler, 415911). A former croft beside the Rumbling Pot pool in upper Glen Tanar.

**The Rummlin Brig*** (C, 413908), ðɪˈrʌmlɛnˈbrɪg. The Rumbling Bridge (Gler). A bridge beside the above pool.

**Rummlin Cooter** See Ruighe Iomlan Culdair.

**Rummlin Cooter** See Bridgend of Bush.

**Runing Stock*** (Am, 290952), possibly from Roinn nan Stoc (3), land-portion of the stumps or tree roots. Now the Middle Park (F), ðɪˈmɪdəlˈpark. A field at Abergeldie Castle, the middle one of a set of five.

**The Runs o the Split Stane*** (U, 214923), ðɪˈrʌnzɪðɪˈsplɛtˈstin. A short fishing run on the south side of Dee, just above the Split Stane Puil.

**Rushy Mire*** See Feith Bheal Luachrach.

**Sabhalan Beinn Athfhinn*** (4), barns of Ben Avon. Soulichin Bin Avin a great wilderness rich in Deer (Po, map of Strath Avin), probably referred to the tors on the summit ridge as well as on the Strath Avon side.

**Sabhal Beinn Macduibh*** See Cairn Toul.

**The Saddle*** (U, 212996), ðɪˈsadl̩, ðɪˈsɛdl̩. A saddle between two hills south-west of Corndavon Lodge.

**The Saddle*** (U, 216010), as above, also south-west of Corndavon Lodge.

**The Saddle*** (U, 167815), as above. A saddle between two hills south-west of Loch Callater.

**The Saddle o Beinn a' Bhuird*** See An Diollaid.

**St Bride's** See Cnoc Cheann-bhuilg.

**St Valentine's** (Gr). Former chapel at Abergeldie, same as Chapel Ma-chalmaig. Saint Valentine's Chappell (Vd).

**Salmon Ladder** (OS, 066903), locally the Lui Salmon Ladder (C), ðɪˈluiˈsamənˈladɛr. An unsuccessful ladder built in the 1950s to let salmon get up waterfalls in lower Glen Lui.

**Salmon Ladder** (OS, 332895), locally the Muick Salmon Ladder (C), ðɪˈmɛkˈsamənˈladɛr. At the Linn of Muick.

**The Sanctuary*** (U, 960940), ðɪˈsaŋtjəri. An area with no deer shooting till the mid 1960s, centred on Glen Geusachan.

**The Sanctuary*** (U, 169958), as above. An area that formerly had no deer shooting, north of Invercauld.

**The Sanctuary Burn*** See Allt air Chul.

**The Sand Brae*** (F, 419968), ðɪˈsanˈbreˑ. A hill on a track south of Cambus o' May on a sandy bank above Dee.

**Sand Hillocks*** (B, 263887). In Glen Gelder.

**The Sand Hillocks*** (F, 290899), ðɪˈsanˈhɛlɛks. In upper Glen Girnock.

**The Sand Hole*** (F, west of 248946), ðɪˈsanˈhol. A little pool on the Balmoral side of Dee.

**The Sand Hole*** (F, 432022), as above. A sand quarry south of Logie Coldstone.

**The Sands Fuird*** See Beul-ath na Lairige Ghru.

**The Sands o Lui*** (C, 019937), ðɪˈsandzɐˈlui, ðɪˈsanzɐˈlui. A sandy area in Glen Luibeg, caused by big floods in 1829 and 1956.

**(The) Sandy Hillock(s)** (OS, C, 266805), ðɪˈsandiˈhɛlɛks. Not a single hill as on OS, but a big area with several hillocks, stretching from top of Corrie Chash east to about 281814. South of Loch Muick.

**The Sandy Hillock*** (F, 414032), ðɪˈsaniˈhɛlɛk. South-west of Logie Coldstone.

**The Sandy Hillock*** (I, 349920). An old field in lower Glen Muick.

**The Sandy Hillock Park*** (F, 414031), ðɪˈsaniˈhɛlɛkˈpark. A field south-west of Logie Coldstone.

**The Sandy Hillocks Lochie*** (F, 277812), ðɪˈsandiˈhëlëksˈlo̯χe. A peaty tarn south of Loch Muick.

**(The) Sandy Loch** (OS, C, 228864), ðɪˈsandiˈlo̯χ. Loch nan Eun (R 7, 14), and the same map gives a second Loch nan Eun to the south as in the current OS location. West of Lochnagar.

**The Sandy Loch Burn*** (F, 224866), ðɪˈsandiˈlo̯χˈbʌrn. Part of Allt Lochan nan Eun west of Lochnagar.

**Sandy Tagart's Loch*** (I, west of 358931). Now a boggy pool in lower Glen Muick.

**Sauchen Stripe*** See Allt Seileach.

**(The) Sauchen Stripe** (OS, U, 437898), ðɪˈsaχənˈstrɛip, Scots = willow little burn. In upper Glen Tanar.

**The Sauchs*** (C, 415997), ðɪˈsa·χs, Scots = willows. A boggy area west of Loch Kinord.

**The Sauchs of Creag Liath*** (U, 243887), ðɪˈsa·χsɐˌkregˈliɐ. Saughs of Craiglia (B). A place on a hillside north of Lochnagar.

**The Sauch Valley** (O, 413002). A little hollow north of Cambus o' May.

**Sauchy Burn*** See Allt Seileach.

**The Saw Mill of Glen Beg*** (194896). The Saw Miln of Glenbeg (Io 7), Old Saw Mill (R 7). A former sawmill east of Invercauld Bridge.

**The Saw Mill of Glen Lui*** See Muileann Shaibh.

**The Sawmill Park*** (U, 263952), ðɪˈsa·mëlˈpark. A field north of Crathie.

**Scarsoch Bheag** (OS, 934853), from An Sgarsach Bheag (6), the little Sgarsoch, meaning of Sgarsach unknown. Skersoch beg (Roy), Skaursich veg (D in A), an sgarsaich bheag (D). Also the Little Scarsoch (F), ðɪˈlëtəlˈskarsɐχ. Little Scarsach (Fi). A hill in upper Glen Geldie, pairs with An Sgarsoch.

**The School Brae*** (C, below school), ðɪˈskulˈbre·. A hill on a road in Braemar.

**School Croft*** (R 18, south of 149916). A patch of farmland in 1895 at Braemar, now under houses.

**The School Park*** (U, 267948), ðɪˈskulˈpark. A field at Crathie.

**Scott's Bothy** See the Luibeg Bothy.

**Scott's Face*** (F, 061984), ˈsko̯tsˈfes. A rocky hill face in Dubh-Ghleann, named after the late Bob Scott who often stalked there.

**The Scoube** (OS, 328860), locally the Scob o Bog Allaidh (U), ðɪˈsko̯bɐˌbo̯gˈale, Scots Scob = a splint or rod, Gaelic Sgolb = a splinter, i.e. a point projecting from the hill. A ridge in upper Glen Muick.

**Scraulac** (OS, C, 314056), ˈskrʌulɐk, from Sgrathalag (5), rough place abounding in sods. Scraulack (I, R 14), Sgrabhlag, scraulak (D). An exposed rough hill north of Gairnshiel, with big peat-mosses and many small grassy patches amongst the heather.

**Scurriestone** (OS, A, 358950), ˌskʌreˈstin (C), Scurrie ? from Gaelic Sgòrach = peaked or rugged, or possibly Carragh = erect stone raised as a monument (with prothetic *S* in Scurrie) as a doublet with *stone*. However, Scurvy Stone (I) suggests Sgarbhach = like a cormorant (i.e. pointed), or Sgarbhaidh = of a crossing of a river by a ford. Note Scarry in Ireland from Scairbh, shallow ford (J). Old fords over Dee and Muick were not far away (M), and the field at this stone was Roinn a' Chroisg, land-portion of the crossing. A standing stone south-west of Ballater.

**Scurriestone*** (north-west of 359950), as above (F). Scurvy Stone (I). The former buildings Scurriestone (OS 1869) were south-west of 357952. A former farm beside above stone, on the site of the present farm Dallyfour. This continues in the combined name Dallyfour and Scurriestone used for the farm in modern estate records, or often simply ˌskʌreˈstin (F) in local speech.

**The Scurriestone Park*** (U, 357949), ðɪˌskʌreˈstinˈpark. Includes the former field Roinn a' Chroisg and other ground nearby, beside a standing stone (see above).

**The Scutter Brae*** (F, 253955), ðɪˈskʌtër'bre. Hillside opposite Balmoral Castle.

**Scutter Hole** (C, 254961), ˈskʌtërˈhol, ? from Gaelic Sgotan = a small farm. Scots Scuttle hole, scutter = hole in wall of cowshed, for throwing out dung. A former group of houses north of Crathie, pairs with Piper Hole, often called just Piper and Scutter (A, C).

**The Seal Cave*** (U, 387982), ðɪˈsiəlˈke·v, ? Gaelic Sìtheil, peaceful, fairy-like. The local legend was that if you went in you could come out at Kildrummy Castle on Donside (JH). A cave near Tullich.

**An Sean-allt** (3), the old burn. O'n t-Sean-allt (T 33). Probably same as Easter Shenalt Burn. In upper Glen Gairn.

**An Sean-bhaile** (2, U, c. 096896), ðɪˈʃe̯n,vɐl, the old farm-town. The Shean-bhaile (Gr). A former farm near Mar Lodge.

**An Sean-bhaile** (3, 223932), the old farm-town. Schanvil (Ca), Shanvel (Fa), Shanval (I), N jennval, N junngval, Shannavil (D in A). A former farm west of the Inver.

**An Sean-bhaile*** (3, south of 438966), the old farm-town. The Shannel (Dms). A former house at Deecastle near Inchmarnoch.

**An Sean-bhaile*** (3, U, 337961), ðɪˈʃe̯n,vɐl, the old farm-town, sometimes the Sean-bhaile Park. Now a field near the mouth of Girnock.

**The Sean-bhaile Park*** (U), ðɪˈʃe̯n,vɐlˈpark. See above name.

**The Sean-bhaile Puil** (3, F), ðɪˈʃe̯n,vɐlˈpil. A collective name for two pools, Big and Little. N dshung val (D in A), the Shenval (A). In Dee east of Coilacriech.

**Sean-choille** or **the Genechal** (OS, C, 288934), ðɪˈdʒe̯nəçəl, from An t-Sean-choille (3), the old wood. N jungahyll, old wood (D). The *j* sound (D) in this and other cases below corresponds with the pronunciation of An seo and An sin as ən'dʒɔ and ən'dʒɪn in Braemar Gaelic speech and in that of some other areas in the Highlands including parts of Perthshire. A former wood south of Abergeldie.

**An Seann-ruighe*** (3, 078818), the old shiel. The Shan-ruie (Io 79). In upper Glen Ey.

**Na Seann-ruighean** (3, F, 283899), ðɪˈʃe̯nëriz, the old shiels. The Shenrig, ˈʃe̯nrək (A). In upper Glen Girnock.

**The Sean Spittal** (149800), from An Seann-spideal (3), the old hospice. Shean-Spittal or Old Hospital (Vd), N jung spityal (D). The Spital of Glencluny (Mc 7). Remains of a ruin on east side of an old bridge north of the Cairnwell. There were Spideals or hospices for travellers at both ends of the Cairnwell Pass, one at Spittal of Glenshee and one at An Seann-spideal.

**The Sean Spittal Brae*** (C, 146805), ðɪˈʃan,spëtəlˈbre·. A hill on the road north of the Cairnwell.

**(The) Sean Spittal Bridge** (OS, C, 145806), ðɪˈʃan,spëtəlˈbrɪg, named after the Sean Spittal. Shan Spital Bridge (I), Shan Spittal Bridge (R 14), the Seann Spittal bridge (Gr) refer to Drochaid an t-Seann-spideil at 149800.

**The Sean Spittal Corrie** See Cruinn Choire.

**The Sean Spittal Quarry*** (C, 144811), ðɪˈʃan,spëtəlˈkware. North of the Cairnwell.

**An Seileach*** (3, U, 333962), ðɪˈʃiləç, the willow copse. A narrow field near the mouth of Girnock, beside damp ground where willows grow.

**Seileach Beag*** (3, 393973), little willow copse. Shelach pek (R 4). On farmland at Tullich.

**The Seileach Crom** (4, 999845), the crooked willow-one (see Allt an t-Seilich). Shelochcrom (Roy). A burn south of Bynack

135

Lodge. Silach crom (Go) given, probably in error, as Allt a' Chaorainn west of Geldie Lodge.

**Sergeant Davie's Grave\*** (U, north-east of 034861), 'sardʒənt 'deviz'grev. An upright slabby stone about a foot high, on a small mound, marking the grave of a Sergeant who was stationed with some other English soldiers in Glen Dee after the 1745 Jacobite rising, and who was murdered in 1749. South-west of Inverey.

**The Seven Rigs of the Cluain\*** (357930), Cluain (3) = a meadow. The Seven Rigs of the Cluhan (I). A former field in lower Glen Muick.

**Sgàileag nam Mortair** (3, 166916), arbour of the murderers. Skaillig na mustard (Io 63), Scailloch-na-Moustard (Anonym). Creag a' Mhortair is a nearby cliff in this area. The hill behind Lion's Face, east of Braemar.

**An Sgàirneach\*** (3, C, 296897), ðɪ'skarnjɐχ, the heap of loose stones. A rough stony slope in upper Glen Girnock.

**The Sgairneach Road\*** (C, 293899), ðɪ'skarnjɐχ'rod. On the above slope.

**The Sgairneach Sand Hole\*** (F, 293899), ðɪ'skarnjɐχ'san'hol. A gravel quarry by the above road.

**The Sgairneach Well** (north-west of 294888). The Skarnach Well, from Sgairneach, stony (A). In upper Glen Girnock.

**An Sgalan\*** (3, 203976), literally the hut (i.e. sheltered place). Corry called the Scallan (I). A big sheltered corrie north-west of the Inver.

**Sgallach\*** (4, 255943), bald (place). Sculloch (B). A formerly treeless patch on top of a hill near Balmoral.

**An Sgaoileach\*** (3, F, 303933), ðɪ'skɛiləç, the extending, unfolding (place). The Skylich (Am). A hilltop south-east of Abergeldie.

**Sgarach nam Feadan\*** (3, 213927), severed place of the rocky gullies. Scarrach-ma-fettan (I). A rocky outcrop south-west of Inver Inn.

**An Sgarsoch** (OS, 933837), from An Sgarsach (6, C), ðɪ'skarsɐχ, possibly from Sgar = a knot or fissure. The Scairsoch (Go), Skersoch (Roy), Scarsach (Mg), Skaursich vor, skarsich, n sgarsoch, an sgarsaich (D in A). These notes show that it had been An Sgarsach Mhór, the big sgarsach, pairing with Scarsoch Bheag to the north. A hill in upper Glen Geldie. The tradition is that an old cattle market called Féill Sgarsaich used to be held on the top.

**Sgeir an Deoch** (3, C, 286004), skirṇ'dʒɔχ, best informant skerṇ'dʒɔχ, rock of the drink. Given as Sgor an Deoch, skɔrn 'djɔχ (A), but this is not the sound. In Irish names, Sgeir is generally a sea-rock but sometimes occurs inland (J). A rock in a pool of River Gairn, west of Gairnshiel, covered when the river is high.

**The Sgeir an Deoch Puil\*** (F, 286004), ðɪ,skerṇ'dʒɔχ'pil. A pool in Gairn.

**Sgeir Bheachdaich** (3, south-east of 143907), rock of the watch. Sera-vechty ? printer's error for Sger-vechty (Ta), Sgeir vehtich (D). Said to be the same as Watchmount (A). A little rock at Tomintoul above Braemar.

**An Sgeireach\*** (3, C, 427959), ðɪ'skirəç, the rocky place. A stony knoll near Inchmarnoch.

**The Sgeireach Brae\*** (C, 429960), ðɪ'skirəç'bre·. A hill on a road near Inchmarnoch.

**Na Sgeirean\*** (3), the rocks. Na sgeiran (Da). The cliffs above the loch of Lochnagar.

**Sgeir Fhliuch** (3, C, 993915), skër'luχ, one informant skɔr'ljuχ, wet rock. Given as Sgor Fhliuch, skɔr'ljuχ (A), but this is not the sound, and in any case Sgor would have Fliuch, not Fhliuch, as it is a masculine noun. In Glen Dee east of Beinn Bhrotain.

**Sgeir Fhliuch** (3, 142903), wet rock. Sgeir fluch, wet rock (D). On Morrone south-west of Braemar.

**Sgeir na h-Iolaire** (3), rock of the eagle. Sgeir na h-yuller, Cluny (D), i.e. presumably Glen Clunie.

**Sgeir Thioram\*** (3), dry rock. Skerhirrum, Skirhirrum, Skirhirum (Me 15). A former farm at Corriemulzie.

**Sgìre Craichidh** (6), parish of Crathie. Sgire Craichidh (M).

**The Sgleat Rock\*** (006945), from Sglèat (3), slate. The Sclate Rock (Fi). A slabby cliff in Glen Luibeg.

**The Sgolbach Puil** (F, 260951), ðɪ'skɔlbɐχ'pil, often the Sgolbaidh (F), ðɪ'skɔlbi, from An Sgolbach (3), the place of splinters. An elderly informant said 'Scolbach, that means there's steens or rocks aboot it' (A). The Scolbach (A), Skolpach (Sc). In Dee at Balmoral.

**An Sgòran** (3, U, 141900), ðɪ'skurən, the little peak. The Scurran (I), Sguran (D). A rocky ridge on Morrone south-west of Braemar.

**Sgor an Aingeil** See Sgor an Lochan Uaine.

**Sgòr an Eòin** (OS, 2, A, U, 997912), skɔrṇ'jɔn, peak of the bird. Scor Noin (Roy). A little crag in Glen Dee, north-west of the White Bridge.

**Sgòr an Fhithich** (3, U, 397989), skɔr'niˑɪç, peak of the raven. Scor an fhidhich, the raven's fissure (Mg), Skir-nyiach (D). A little cliff north-east of Tullich.

**Sgòr an Léim\*** (3, 238944), peak of the jump. Scurn leim (I). North-east of the Inver.

**Sgòr an Lochain Uaine** (The Angel's Peak) (OS, F, 954977), ,skɔrṇ,lɔχɐn'uɐn, peak of the green tarn. A rocky peak west of Cairn Toul. The Angel's Peak was a name invented by a Mr Alexander Copland (Al) as a counter-balance to the Devil's Point. Twenty-five years later, the Glen Feshie stalkers called it Sgòr an Aingeil (3), peak of the angel (Gordon 1951).

**Sgòr an Lochain Uaine** (3, Bu, U, 026991), as above, peak of the green tarn. Sgurr an Lochain Uaine (Rob). Above upper Glen Derry.

**Sgor an t-Seabhaig** See Creag an t-Seabhaig.

**Sgòr Bàn\*** (3, 165915), white peak. Scur baan (I). Above the Queen's Drive east of Braemar.

**Sgòr Bhreac-achaidh\*** (3, 145908), skur'vreːgçi (Sch), peak of the speckled field. A rock above Dail a' Bhreac-achaidh near Braemar.

**Sgòr Buidhe\*** (3, 150004), yellow steep hill. Scor Buie (I). A steep stony hillside on Ben Avon.

**(An) Sgòr Buidhe** (OS, C, 377979), ðɪ,skɔr'bui from best informants, often now ðɪ,skër'bui, the yellow peak. Skirbui (D), Skor-booie (A). A small broken crag north-east of Ballater, but locally often refers to the hill there.

**Sgòr Churra\*** (5, 169894), peak of the bog, possibly Chaorach = of sheep. Scur Chora (I), Scur Cora (R 7). A little crag south-east of Braemar.

**An Sgòr Dearg\*** (3, U, 345876), ðɪ,skɔr'dʒerg, red rocky hill. Scor gairig (G 5), Scor Derg (I). On the location of Drum Cholzie (OS) which is incorrectly placed and is the ridge further north. A hilltop south-east of the Linn of Muick.

**An Sgòr Dubh\*** (3, U, 134002), ðɪ,skɔr'du·, the black peak. On location of Stob Dubh an Eas Bhig (OS) but it is in wrong place. Scor Du (I). A dark rocky tor on Ben Avon.

**(An) Sgòr Dubh** (OS, 2, C, 034921), as above, but best informants ðɪ,sgɔr'du·, the black rocky hill. A dark heathery hill south of Luibeg.

**Sgòr Fithich\*** (3, 218935), peak of a raven. Scur Fiach (I). A small broken crag west of the Inver Inn.

**Sgòr Gàinne Dhearg\*** (5, 166909), peak of red shaft. Scur Ganderg (I). A small rock south-east of Braemar.

**Sgòr Gaoithe\*** (3, 309054), peak of wind. Scorguie (I). An exposed little rock on the Strathdon march north-east of Gairnshiel.

**Sgòr Glas\*** (3, 192944), grey peak. Scur Glass (I), Sgur-Glas (R 14). A rocky top above upper Glen Feardar.

**(An) Sgòr Mór** (OS, 2, C, 007914), ðɪˌskǫrˈmoˑr, but best informants ðɪˌsgǫrˈmoːr, the big rocky hill. South-west of Glen Luibeg.

**Sgòr Mór** (OS, 115825, should be rocks at 126825, hilltop at 115825 is Carn Grianach), big peak. Scur More, rocks (I). A rocky steep hill above the Baddoch.

**Sgòr na Cùileige** (OS, 004905), should be Sgòr na Cùlath (5, C), ˌsgɔrnɐˈkulɐ, (skɔrnəˈkula (A)), rocky hill of the back place. Sgor na Cula (D, A). A little top above Coire na Culath north-west of the White Bridge in Glen Dee.

**Sgor na h-Iolaire** (OS, 3, U, 303935), ˌskёrnɐˈhilёr, peak of the eagle. Skor n yuller (D) and skɔrnˈjɪlər (A) suggest Sgòran Iolaire = little peak of eagle. A small crag south-east of Abergeldie, also little top behind at 304934.

**Sgòr na h-Iolaire\*** (3, U, 122952), ˌskǫrnɐˈhilər, peak of the eagle. In upper Gleann an t-Slugain.

**Sgòr Preas Poll\*** (3, 162915), peak of copse at a pool. Scur Pres Pol (I). East of Braemar.

**Na Sgraitean\*** (3, U, 340000), ðɪˈskrǫtɐn, the shreds. Steep screes in Glen Gairn.

**Na Sgraitean Ruadha** (3, 226033), the red shreds. Scrattan Ruadh (R 12), Scratin-rui (D). Bare patches of red gravel on a steep slope caused by water erosion north of Corndavon Lodge.

**The Shank\*** (U, 401917), ðɪˈʃaŋk, Scots = broad descending spur or ridge. West of Etnach in upper Glen Tanar.

**(The) Shank of Corn Arn** (OS, C, 401941), ðɪˈʃaŋkɐˌkǫrn̩ˈern̩, from the Shank of Coire an Eirbhein. OS spelling is not the right sound, see Corrienearn for meaning. South of Pannanich.

**The Shank of Cuidhe Crom\*** (258857). The Shank of Cuicrom (Ra 15). Broad ridge forming east edge of the Corrie of Lochnagar.

**(The) Shank of Fafernie** (OS, F, 218814), ðɪˈʃaŋkɐˌfəˈfɛrne. South-east of Loch Callater.

**The Shank of Feith an t-Salachair\*** (194869), see Feindallacher Burn. Shank of Feandalacher (R 7). South of Ballochbuie Forest.

**The Shank of Ruighe an Droma** (U, 325880), ðɪˈʃaŋkɐˌrɛnˈdrʌm. The Shank of Lyndrum (Ab 2), Shank of Rinedrom (R 6), Shank of Riendrum (I). In upper Glen Muick.

**Shank of Stair nan Gall\*** (252874), see Burn of Stair nan Gall. Shank of Stair na Gall (B). In Glen Gelder.

**The Shank o the Cadha Chuirn\*** (F, 250863), ðɪˈʃaŋkɪðɪˈkaˈχɐrn. Shank of Ca-Cairn (B). The broad ridge forming the west rim of the Corrie of Lochnagar.

**The Shank o the Dubh Loch\*** (C, 242835), ðɪˈʃaŋkɪðɪˈduˌlɔχ. A long, broad ridge north-east of the Dubh Loch.

**The Shank o the Glas Allt\*** (C, 257836), ðɪˈʃaŋkɪðɪˈglasəlt. Shank of the Glashel (In). Broad ridge west of the Glas Allt near Loch Muick.

**The Shank o the Pap\*** (F, 259865), ðɪˈʃaŋkɪðɪˈpap. Shank of the Pap (B). Broad ridge north of the Meikle Pap on Lochnagar.

**The Sheep Bridge\*** Proper access to Ballater Bridge from the County Road on the North side of the Dee at the Sheep Bridge (Io in 1806). Probably this access was about the north end of where the present bridge stands at Ballater.

**The Sheep Fank Park\*** (U, 354976), ðɪˈʃipˈfankˈpark. A field north of Bridge of Gairn.

**The Shelf\*** (U, 304017), ðɪˈʃɛlf. A small enclosed field north-east of Gairnshiel.

**The Shelter Puil\*** (F, south-west of 370951), ðɪˈʃɛltёrˈpil. A pool in Dee at Ballater, near a shelter on the Golf Course.

**The Shenalt\*** (216022). Shan Ald (Roy), Shenald (R 3). A shiel west of Corndavon Lodge.

**The Shenalt Corrie\*** See Coire Sean.

**The Shenalts\*** (F), ðɪˈʃɛnəlts. Shennells (Io 15). A composite name for the two burns Easter Shenalt and Wester Shenalt west of Corndavon Lodge.

**(The) Shenval** (OS, C, 305017), ðɪˈʃɛnˌvɛl, in Gaelic ðɪˈʃauŋˌvɛl (JB), from An Sean-bhaile (2, JB), the old farm-town. Shenaval (Im 3), n jennval, n junngval (D). Note Easter and Wester Shenval. A former farm north-east of Gairnshiel.

**The Shenval Brae\*** (C, 307019), ðɪˈʃɛnˌvɛlˈbreˑ. A steep hill on the road near the above place.

**The Shepherd's Bothy\*** See the Auld House o the Etnach.

**Shepherds Cairn** (OS, 299049). North of Gairnshiel.

**Shepherds Cairn** (OS, 355053). North-west of Morven.

**Shepherds' Cairns** (OS, 260050). North-west of Gairnshiel.

**Shepherd's Croft.** Shepherdscroft (G 28), Shepherd's croft (Ab 19). Former farm probably in Balhennie–Cnoc Dubh area west of Logie Coldstone.

**The Shepherd's Hill\*** (U, 333034), ðɪˈʃёpёrdzˈhёl. An area of hill grazing behind Morven Lodge, including Tom Liath and the hill to the north.

**The Shepherd's House\*** (U, 373011), ðɪˈʃёpёrdzˈhus. Deserted house at Easter Morven.

**The Shepherd's House\*** (U, 395033), as above. A former bothy south-east of Morven.

**The Shepherd's Roadie\*** See the Creel Road.

**Shepherds Shiel\*** Shepherds Sheal (Ce 1). Possibly same as the Shepherd's House at 395033.

**The Shiel\*** (U, 176845), ðɪˈʃil. Lochcallater Shealling (Ce 1). Below Lochcallater Lodge.

**The Shiel\*** See Ruighe na Culath.

**The Shielin\*** (F, 399970), ðɪˈʃilən. The west house at Glascorrie east of Pannanich.

**The Shielin** See Shiel of Glentanar.

**The Shieling of Aultonrea\*** (north-west of 327870 on west side of burn, by elimination). The Shealling of Altonree in Stronnews (G 14), i.e. An t-Sron Ghiubhas. In upper Glen Muick.

**The Shieling of Blar Charraid\*** See Ruighe Chobhain.

**The Shieling of Coire na Moine\*** See Ruighe nan Coire Dubh.

**The Shieling of Dalmochie** (398932). The Shealing of Dalmulachie (misread) alias Dalmuchie (Ri 29), the Shealling of Dalmalachie alias Dalmuchie (Io 60a), Shealling of Delmuckachie (G 22), Old Sheals of Dalmuchie (I). South of Pannanich.

**The Shieling of Glac Mam Caorach\*** Glac Màm Caorach (3) = hollow of round hill of the sheep. The Shealling of Glackmamocurich (Io 12), of Glackmamocusich (Me 4). Uncertain location, possibly in the Crathie–Balmoral area.

**Shieling of Lawsie\*** (229020). Shealing of Lawsie (R 3). On south side of Gairn at Corndavon Lodge.

**The Shieling of Moine Dhubh\*** (313878). The Shealing of Mindoue (Io 13). In upper Glen Muick.

**The Shieling of Ruighe an Luig\*** (118801). The Shealling of Ruinluig (Ra 3). In the Baddoch.

**The Shieling of Sron Fhionn\*** (117803). The Shealling of Stronein (Ra 3). In the Baddoch.

**Shielings of Baddoch and Ruighe Raibeirt\*** Shealings of Baddach and Rirebart (Me 15). A collective name for several shielings in the Baddoch.

**Shielings of Bad nan Laogh\*** See Shiels of Lawsie.

**Shielings of Coire Bhuth\*** (158804). Shealings of Corryvue (I). North of the Glas Maol.

**Shielings of Hospital Haugh\*** Sheallings of Hospitall Haugh (Io 17). Shielings of a former farm on the haugh at Spittal of Glenmuick.

**The Shielings of Milltoun of Invercauld\*** The Sheallings of Milntown of Invercauld (Ra 5). In mid Glen Quoich.

**Shielings of Rioch and Edmondston\*** (231989). Shealings of Rioch and Edmondston (R 5). North-west of Crathie.

**Shielings of Tynabaich and Coldrach\*** (232988). Shealings of Tynabeach and Coldrach (R 5). North-west of Crathie.

**Shiel of Back Coire Buidhe\*** (269877). Sheal of Back Corbuie (B). In upper Glen Gelder.

**Shiel of Crathienaird\*** (249991). Sheal of Crathienaird (R 5). North-west of Crathie.

**Shiel of Glentanar** (OS, 400894), locally the Sheilin (Gler, F), ðɪ 'ʃilən, or the Shiel (Gler, F). A hut in upper Glen Tanar.

**Shiel of the Herds of Lawsie\*** (274981 on west side of burn). 'Found of an old Sheal called Sheal of the Herds of Lawsie' (R 3). Only a difference in vegetation is now visible. North of Crathie.

**The Shiel Puil\*** (U, 176844), ðɪ'ʃil'pil. In Callater, beside the Shiel.

**Shiels of Ach Latharn\*** (186012). Sheals of Achlarn (I). South of Loch Builg.

**Shiels of Allt a' Mhaide\*** (154801). Sheals of Ault Vait (I). North of the Glas Maol, with Allt a' Mhaide referring to the former farm of Alltamhait in upper Glen Clunie.

**Shiels of Allt Chronaidh\*** (141810). Sheals of Aultchronie (I). North of the Cairnwell.

**Shiels of Allt na Meadhonaidh\*** (173994). Sheals of Aultnamainie (I). South-east of Ben Avon.

**Shiels of Allt Phouple\*** (177008). Sheals of Ault Phouple (I). South-west of Loch Builg.

**Shiels of Castleton\*** (124810). The shealling or lair of the Castletoun (Ra 3), Sheals of Castletown (I). Up the Baddoch Burn.

**Shiels of Crasg Binneiche\*** (300050). Sheals of Grasspywnich (I). North-east of Gairnshiel.

**Shiels of Dail Laoigh\*** See Ruighe Dail Laoigh.

**Shiels of Easaidh Beag\*** (150992). Sheals of Essie Beg (I). South-east of Ben Avon.

**Shiels of Easaidh Mor\*** (156996). Sheals of Essie More (I). South-east of Ben Avon.

**Shiels of Glendui** (OS, 436935), locally the Shiel o Glendui (F), ðɪ'ʃilᵊglən'dui. In Glen Tanar.

**Shiels of Lawsie\*** (247019). Shealing of Lawsie, Sheals of Lasi (R 3, 5). Also Sheallings of Badnaloach (G 3). East of Corndavon Lodge.

**Shiels of Monaltrie\*** See Ruighe Dail Laoigh.

**Shiels of Monaltrie\*** (R 5, 231988). North-west of Crathie.

**Shiels of Newbigging\*** (151790). Sheals of Newbigging (I). North-east of the Cairnwell.

**The Shiels of Ruighe Riabhach\*** (363017). The Sheills of Ririach (Io 20). See Carn an Ruighe Riabhaich which indicates an original An Ruighe Riabhach (3), the brindled shiel. South-west of Morven.

**Shiels of the Braes of Whitehouse\*** (388022). Sheals of the Braes of Whitehouse (Io 20). South-east of Morven.

**Shiels of the Feuragachs\*** (253023). Sheals of the Fergachs (R 12), Sheals of the Feregach (I). East of Corndavon Lodge.

**Shiels of the Keiloch\*** (166851). Sheals of the Kiloch (I). In Glen Callater.

**Shiels of the Sron\*** (148794). Sheals of the Stroin (I). North-east of the Cairnwell.

**Shiels of the Tomidhu\*** (254018). Sheals of the Tamiedows (I). East of Corndavon Lodge.

**Shiels of Tom nan Rabhadh\*** (119803). Sheals of Touman Rau (I). Up the Baddoch Burn.

**Shiels of Tomnavey\*** (306041). Sheals of Toumnavey (I). North-east of Gairnshiel.

**The Shiels o the Altanour\*** (F, 076819), ðɪ'ʃilzɪðɪˌaltən'ʌuɾ. The Sheals of the Aultanour (Io 79). In upper Glen Ey.

**The Shiels o the Cristie\*** (U, 056868), ðɪ'ʃilzɪðɪ'kriəstji. A group of shielings south-west of Inverey.

**(The) Shiel Stripe** (OS, F, 308811), ðɪ'ʃil'strɛip. A small burn south-east of Loch Muick.

**Shore\*** (Ce 3). Former habitation beside Meikle Kinord.

**(The) Short Bank** (OS, F, 402892), ðɪ'ʃɔrt'baŋk. A steep bank in upper Glen Tanar.

**Short Butts\*** (R 4, 387972), Scots Butts = small pieces of land. On farmland at Tullich.

**Short Haugh\*** (R 4, 392971). On farmland at Tullich.

**Sìdhean\*** (3, 173847), hillock. Shian (I). Below Loch Callater.

**An Sidhean\*** See Tom an t-Sidhein.

**An t-Sìdhean Chòrr** (3, F, 087881), ðɪˌʃiɐn'χɔˑr, at the great hillock. An t-sithean chorr (D) suggests dative case also. Sithean Corr (A) suggests nominative Sìdhean Còrr. South of Inverey.

**The Sidhean Chorr Brae\*** (C, 087882), ðɪˌʃiɐn'χɔr'breˑ. A hill on the Glen Ey road south of Inverey.

**Sìdhean Dubh\*** (3, 344979), black hillock. Shihan Du (I). North-west of the Bridge of Gairn.

**The Sidhean Haugh\*** (U, 243010), ðɪ'ʃiən'haˑχ. At Daldownie in Glen Gairn.

**Sìdhean Odhar\*** (3, 141969), dun hillock. Shihan Our (I). North of Gleann an t-Slugain.

**An Sidhean Odhar\*** (3, 108959), the dun hillock. Sheanour (Ra 5), the Shianour (Io 43a), the Sheanour (Me 15). In upper Glen Quoich.

**The Sidhean Park\*** (U, 243010), ðɪ'ʃiən'park. A field west of Gairnshiel.

**The Sidheans\*** See Na Da Shidhean.

**The Sileach** See Allt an t-Seilich.

**Sileach Bhronn** See Allt an t-Seilich.

**Sileach Crom** See Allt an t-Seilich.

**The Siller Stane** (O, 434008), Scots silver stone. West of Loch Davan.

**The Silver Springs\*** (U, 316984), ðɪ'sëlvër'spriŋz. A group of springs north of Coilacriech Inn.

**Simpson's Burn** (OS, F, 390893), 'sɪmsənz'bʌrn. In upper Glen Tanar.

**Simpson's Cairn** (OS, 1869, 388894). A cairn in upper Glen Tanar.

**Simpson's Cairns\*** (F, 389893), 'sɪmsənz'kerɳz. Stony patches on a hillside in upper Glen Tanar.

**Sir Allan's Prop** (Gl, U, 369934), usually now Allan's Prop (C), 'alɛnz'prɔp. A cairn south of Ballater, after Sir Allan Mackenzie a former owner of Glenmuick estate.

**Sir Allan's Seat** (And, U), sër'alɛnz'sit. A rocky top on which the above Prop stands.

**The Sister Hill** See Creag Ghiubhais.

**Sir Veitch's Butts\*** (U, 234996), sër'vitʃɪz'bʌts. Grouse butts south of Corndavon Lodge.

**The Skirts of the Forest\*** (080870). The Skirts of the Forrest (Io 43a), the Skerts (Fi). An old name for the hills south of Inverey, which were not regarded as proper deer forest in the 18th century.

**Sklaichie Brae\*** (C, west of 369958), 'skleçi'breˑ, local Scots = gossipy hill. Note Scots Claik = gossip (Gm). Northernmost part of Dee Street in Ballater.

**The Sky of Coire an Eirbhein** See Corrienearn.

**The Sky of Leth-taobh Ainneartaidh\*** (355015), Scots Sky

= skyline, Leth-taobh Ainneartaidh (5) = oppressive side. The Sky Leatianarty, the Sky of Leatiannarty (Io 20). Above Allt Ainneartaidh. South-west of Morven.

**The Sky of the Glack** (Ri 30, 212847). A watershed east of Loch Callater. See Glac Carn an t-Sagairt nearby.

**The Slack of Allt Dobharaidh*** See An Slugan.

**(The) Slacks of Glencarvie** (OS, C, 347055), ðɪˈslaksɐˌɡlənˈkarvi, Scots Slack = gully. Older people said the Sloc o Glencarvie (slɔχ). The Slocks of Glencarvie (A), ðɪˈslɔ̜ksɐˈkarvi (U). A rocky gully beginning on the Dee side of a hill north-west of Morven but mostly on the Don side in Glen Carvie. Glen Carvie from Gleann Charbhaidh (4), glen of the carving, probably referring to the remarkable rocky gully at the top of the glen. Glen caravi, glen caratsh (D), Glen-charvi (D in A), Caratsh suggests Caraid = a pair. Also Sloc na Cailliche (3), pit of the old woman, after the legendary Cailleach Bheàthrach. She was said to have caused this unusual dry rocky gully (in fact cut by a former glacial river) by trying to cut with her teeth a way through the hills so that the water of Don would flow into Dee (Gr). Sloc na Caillich (Gr).

**The Slate Quarries*** (U, 088917), ðɪˈsletˈkwarez. Former quarries in lower Glen Quoich.

**The Slate Quarry*** See Quartz Cliff.

**The Slate Quarry*** (F, 159880), ðɪˈsletˈkware. Former quarry in Glen Callater.

**Sleac Gorm** (OS, 225890), from An Sleaghach Gorm (4, C), ðɪ ˌsliɐχˈɡɔrɔm, the blue spear, as in the peak Slioch in Ross-shire (note W 1904, 233). Sleagh Goram (R 7), Slichorum (Ra 15). A pointed hill with steep bluish-grey slabs of rock. East of Ballochbuie Forest.

**The Sleach** (C), ðɪˈsliəç, from An Sliabhach (3, JB), ðɪˈsliɐχ, the moory place. Slowach (Pb), Aig an t-sliach (D), i.e. at the Sleach. Na slyiach (D) indicates a plural, probably referring to the two places Easter and Wester Sleach. An old map (R 12) calls the single enclosed area inside the dyke around both places Sliachs. The Sleach is now used for Easter Sleach, as it is many decades since people lived at Wester Sleach. It is also used as a general name for a big area around Easter Sleach, north-west of Gairnshiel.

**(The) Sleach Burn** (OS, C, 269024), ðɪˈsliəçˈbʌrn, formerly was Allt Feurglaidh (3, U), altˈfɛrkle, from Feur = grass. Ault Ferklie (Ro, I, R 12), alt fercri (Da), Allt Ferkrie, altˈfɛrkri (A). A burn north-west of Gairnshiel.

**The Sleach Fuird*** (F, 268017), ðɪˈsliəçˈfjurd. A ford over Gairn.

**The Sleach Moss*** (U, 257029), ðɪˈsliəçˈmɔs. A peat-moss east of Corndavon Lodge.

**The Sleach Puil*** (U, 268016), ðɪˈsliəçˈpil. On Gairn, near Easter Sleach.

**An Sleaghach Gorm*** (4, U, 170876), ðɪˌsliɐχˈɡɔrɔm, the blue spear. A cliff in lower Glen Callater.

**The Sleepy Knows*** (U, 403957), ðɪˈslipiˈknʌuz, Scots Knows = knolls. South-west of Inchmarnoch.

**An Sliabhach Gorm*** (4, c. 000945), the blue moory place. The Sleach-gorum (Fi). A hillside with many boulders on south side of Carn a' Mhaim.

**Sliabh Fhearchair** (3, D, F, 073895), sliuˈɛrɐχ̈ër, Farquhar's moor. Sliu erracher (D). A moor between Inverey and the Linn of Dee, named after a story that Fearchar Cam, a legendary progenitor of the Farquharson clan, had been drowned in Dee nearby (Gr). Said to be a sandy flat below where Ey enters Dee (Ta), but this is not a moor and all the local evidence puts it at least half way between Ey and Linn of Dee, at 073895 (JB) which was a moor all of this century until recently, or at 065895 (CG, WG) which was a moor before being planted in the 19th century.

**Sliabh Muileann Duinidh** See Muir of Dinnet.

**An Sliochd** (3, C, 962968), ðɪˈslɪçɪt, ðɪˈslë̈çët, the track, rut, with *d* in *chd* pronounced not χk but χt as in Coire an Leachd and the Strath Don Lecht (An Leachd), note other cases in Carn a' Bhacain and Cnapan Dubh Coire an Leachd. The word slɪçɪt is still used locally (CW) for a narrow hollow or gully. The Slichit (Sg). A wide scree gully on Cairn Toul offering the only easy way up out of Coire an t-Saighdeir.

**An Sliochd*** (3, U, 097886), as above. South-east of Inverey.

**An Sloc** (3, 419984 to 423984), the pit. The Sloc (Mi 1877). A small gully near Cambus o' May.

**Sloc na Cailliche** See Slacks of Glencarvie.

**An Sluaisd Mór** (3, U, 261946), ðɪˈsluəʃˈmoˑr, the big shovelled area. The Sluistmore, Sluarst Moir (Io 50, 54), Sluishmore (D). A former field at Balmoral, now part of the golf course.

**Slugain Lodge** (OS, C, 120952), ˈslʌɡənˈlɔ̜ʤ. Sluggan Cottage (V). Also Ciach Lodge (OS 1869, Cj 1), Cioch Lodge (Ba), possibly from A' Chioch on Beinn a' Bhuird, but quite likely from Caich, as this was in the middle of the big area of hill ground formerly called Caich. Ruin of a former shooting lodge at top of Gleann an t-Slugain.

**Slugain Pool** (157927). Sluggan Pool (Ly). Former pool in Dee west of Invercauld.

**An Slugan** (OS, C, 181867), ðɪˈslʌɡən, the gullet. Sluggan (R 7). A rocky gully at the head of Glen Beg, Ballochbuie Forest.

**An Slugan*** (3, U, 220963), as above, the gullet. A little gully north-west of the Inver.

**An Slugan*** (3, U, 273900), as above, the gullet. A gully in upper Glen Girnock.

**An Slugan** (3, A, C, 120952), as above, the gullet. The Sluggan (I), an lukan (D). Also Slugan Dubh Inbhir Cheann-bhuilg (3), black gullet of Inverchandlick (see Gleann an t-Slugain). Slugain dubh eanar-chanlig (Da). Also the Black Slugan of the Candlick. Black Sloggan of the Candlic (Gr). A big rocky gully at the top of Gleann an t-Slugain.

**An Slugan*** (3, F, 362001), as above. Also the Slugan of Allt Dobharaidh. The Sluggan of Auldaurie (Io 20). Also the Slug of Allt Dobharaidh. The Slugg of Aldourie (Io 20), Gaelic Slug (3) = gulp. Also the Slack of Auldourie (Io 20), Scots Slack = rocky gully. North of Ballater.

**An Slugan*** (3, F, 289031), ðɪˈsluɡən, the gullet. A gully north of Gairnshiel.

**An Slugan*** (3, 426946), the gullet. The Sluggan (Dms). A shallow, steep little gully south of Inchmarnoch.

**The Slugan Burn** See Allt an t-Slugain.

**The Slugan Burn** See Allt Coire an t-Slugain.

**The Slugan Corrie*** See Coire an t-Slugain.

**Slugan Dubh Inbhir Cheann-bhuilg*** See An Slugan.

**The Slugan of Allt Dobharaidh*** See An Slugan.

**The Slugan Wall*** (F, 426950), ðɪˈslʌɡənˈwaˑl. A well south of Inchmarnoch, below An Slugan.

**(The) Sluggan Burn** (OS, A, C, 373998), ðɪˈslʌɡənˈbʌrn. Also Allt an t-Slugain (3, OS 1869, A), burn of the gullet. North of Ballater.

**Sluggan Burn*** Slogan Burn (Ce 1). Former habitation north of Ballater.

**The Slug of Allt Dobharaidh*** See An Slugan.

**Sluievannachie** (Av, A, C, 361959), sləˈvanɐχe, often shortened to ˈsluiz, from Sliabh Fionn-achaidh (3), moor of white field, presumably referring to a grassy stretch. Muir of Slivyonochty (R 4), Sleuvennachie, Sleaveannachie (Opr 56, 59), Slīu viunngachi, sliu vyŭnn-gachi, white-field moor (D), Slui-vyunng-achi (D in A). A former farm, now a house, beside what was once the moor of Ballater (A).

**The Sluievannachie Puil*** (F, north of 360959), ðɪˌsləˈvanɐχeˈpil. In Dee, near above house.

**The Smiddie Croft\*** (F, 280947), ðɪ'smɪdi'krǫft, Scots Smiddie = smithy. A former croft, now a field, west of Abergeldie.

**The Smiddie Croft\*** (U, 354947), ðɪ'smɪdi'krǫft. A series of small fields in lower Glen Muick.

**Smiddiecroft** (Ab 19). Former farm probably, though not certainly, in our study area, in the Mosstown area west of Logie Coldstone. See the Mosstown Haugh.

**The Smiddie Croft** See the Croft.

**The Smiddie Green\*** (U, 300012), ðɪ'smɪdi'grin. A grassy patch beside a former smithy near Gairnshiel.

**The Smiddie Larach\*** (U, 300012), ðɪ'smɪdi'lerɐχ, Scots Larach = a site, from Gaelic Làrach. Ruin of a former smithy near Gairnshiel.

**The Smiddie Park\*** See the Mosstown Haugh.

**The Smiddie Park\*** (U, west of 355949), ðɪ'smɪdi'park. Includes Mitchel's Croft which was the north part. A field in lower Glen Muick.

**Smiddie Pool** See Poll na Bruaich Ruaidhe.

**Smiddie's Brig\*** (F, south of 037895), 'smɪdiz'brɪg, see name below. In Glen Dee.

**Smiddie's Burn\*** (3, F, 037895), 'smɪdiz'bʌrn. A little burn west of the Linn of Dee. Smiddie was a nickname for a local man McDonald who hid behind a boulder there when caught poaching (IG).

**Smiddie's Stane\*** (U, 037895), 'smɪdiz'stin. The above boulder.

**The Smith-Winram Bivouac** (Ms, 097995). A hole under boulders on Beinn a' Bhuird.

**The Smithy Craigs\*** (Io 20), Probably in the basin of upper Tullich Burn.

**The Smugglers' Bothy\*** See Roinn Ghlas.

**The Smugglers' Den\*** (U, 261008), ðɪ'smʌglɛrz'dɛn. A deep hollow west of Gairnshiel.

**The Smugglers' Shank** (McC, C, 207856), ðɪ'smʌglɛrz'ʃank, Scots Shank = broad descending ridge. An old route over Lochnagar from Deeside to Angus (McC). A broad ridge south of Ballochbuie Forest.

**The Sneck\*** (F, 416905), ðɪ'snɛk. Scots = the notch, and Gaelic An Sneag (3) also = the notch. This applies to all the other Sneck names below. A little gully south of Etnach in upper Glen Tanar.

**The Sneck** (OS, F, 118010), as above. Col between Ben Avon and Beinn a' Bhuird.

**The Sneck o Carn a' Mhaim\*** (3, U, 997950), ðɪ'snɛkɐˌkarnɐ 'vɛim. A little col between the two tops of Carn a' Mhaim, south of Ben Macdui.

**The Sneck o Garbh-choire\*** (F, 258928), ðɪ'snɛkɐ'garçǝre. Sneck of Garcorrie (B). A col between Creag an Lurachain and Creag nan Gall south of Balmoral, above the corrie of An Garbh-choire.

**The Sneck o Gourock\*** (F, 283798), ðɪ'snɛkɐ'gurǝk, possibly from Guireach (5) = pimple place. Guarich, Gurach (I). A col south of Loch Muick, above a steep little corrie in Angus called the Gourock (OS).

**The Sneck o Lochnagar** (Wa, F, 241869), ðɪ'snɛkɐˌlǫχnǝ'gaˑr. A col between Meall Coire na Saobhaidhe and the higher part of Lochnagar.

**The Sneck o the Coire Glas\*** (F, 244878), ðɪ'snɛkɪðɪˌkǫr'glas. A col between Creag Liath and Meall Coire na Saobhaidhe north of Lochnagar.

**The Sneck o the Craggan\*** (F, 317856), ðɪ'snɛkɪðɪ'kragǝn. A col between Craggan Hill and Creag na Slabhraidh in upper Glen Muick.

**The Sneck Path\*** (F, 416905), ðɪ'snɛk'paθ. A path in upper Glen Tanar, beside the Sneck south of Etnach.

**The Snipes' Bog\*** (U, north of 999825), ðɪ'snɛips'bǫg. A favourite bog for snipe, south of Bynack Lodge, mostly in Perthshire but partly in Aberdeenshire.

**The Snob\*** (F, 285820), ðɪ'snǫb, Scots = protruding place. A high point south of Loch Muick.

**The Snobs\*** (F, 422925), ðɪ'snǫbz. Rocky bumps in upper Glen Tanar. See above.

**Snout na Loinne\*** (3, 303923), ˌsnutɐ'lɔin, ˌsnutni'lɪŋ, ˌsnutnɪ 'lǫŋ, ˌsnutnǝ'lɛin, snout of the enclosure. A part-Scots, part-Gaelic name, Scots pronunciation 'snut = snout. Pairs with the South Snout. A snout-shaped field in Glen Girnock.

**The Snowy Burn\*** See Allt an t-Sneachda.

**The Snowy Corrie** See Coire an t-Sneachda.

**The Snowy Corrie\*** See Coire an t-Sneachda.

**The Snowy Corrie Burn** See Allt an t-Sneachda.

**An Socach** (OS, 099806), from An Socach Mór (3, C), ðɪˌsǫχkɐχ 'moːr, the big snouted one. Soccach Braemar (Roy), the Sockach more (I), Sochach Mhoir (R 14), n sohkach mǫr (D), the Socach Mor (A). A long hill north-west of the Cairnwell, with several big snouts sticking into Glen Ey and the Baddoch. It consists of the East Top and the West Top, of which the West Top at 080800 is the higher. Pairs with An Socach Beag below.

**An Socach\*** (3, 262009), the snout. The Sockach or hollow (Io 80). West of Gairnshiel.

**An Socach Beag\*** See name below.

**Socach Mór** (OS, 111806, should be at location of An Socach (OS), 111806 is An Socach Beag (3, F)), ðɪˌsǫχkɐχ'bɛg, the little snouted one. Sockach Beg (I), Sochach Bheg (R 14). Also the Little Socach (A, F), ðɪ'lɛtǝl'sǫχkɐχ. Pairs with An Socach Mor north-west of the Cairnwell.

**The Sodger Puil** See the Upper Jetty Puil.

**The Sodger's Grave\*** (U, south-west of 309019), ðɪ'sǫʤɛrz'grev. An upright stone east of Gairnshiel, said to mark the grave of a soldier wounded at Culloden.

**The Sodgers' Park\*** (U, 365946), ðɪ'sǫʤɛrz'park. Named after soldiers who had stables in this field during the 1939–45 war. In lower Glen Muick.

**The Soldier's Cairn\*** See Stob Coire an t-Saighdeir.

**The Soldier's Corrie** See Coire an t-Saighdeir.

**The Soldier's Hillock\*** (I, west of 352932). In lower Glen Muick.

**The Soo's Lug\*** (F, 250020), ðɪ'suz'lʌg, Scots = sow's ear. A grouse drive near the Sleach north-west of Gairnshiel, named because the area covered is in the shape of a sow's ear; it looks greener and grassier than nearby ground.

**The Souter's Cairn** (McC 1891, U, 304826), ðɪ'sutɛrz'kern, Scots Souter = shoemaker. Beside the Capel Road above Loch Muick.

**The Souter's House\*** (F, 415912), ðɪ'sutɛrz'hus. A former house near Etnach in upper Glen Tanar.

**The Souter's Plantin\*** (U, 267941), ðɪ'sutɛrz'plantɪn. A plantation beside a former shoemaker's shop at Balmoral.

**South Auchnerran** See Auchnerran.

**The South Deeside Road** (Gf, C), ðɪ'suθ'di'sɛid'rod. Public road from Aberdeen to Balmoral Bridge along south side of Dee, formerly went further up to the Auld Brig o Dee at Invercauld till this part was closed as a public road by an Act of Parliament in 1855 (Gf).

**The South Lairig\*** (U, 224995), ðɪ'suθ'laˑrɪg. The south part of Lairig Mhor, a way over the hills south of Corndavon Lodge. Pairs with the North Lairig.

**The South Milton** (F, 425039), ðɪ'suθ'mëltǝn. South Milton (Vr 3). A former farm west of Logie Coldstone.

**The South Park\*** (F, 445986), ðɪ'suθ'park. A field west of Dinnet.

**The South Park of Ach Chadha\*** (366012). The South Park of Auchaw (G 30). A former field up Tullich Burn.

Upper Glen Derry in autumn has been a favourite deer-stalking ground for nearly 200 years, with its grassy haughs, Caledonian firs and high corries. The poem 'Allt an Lochain Uaine' (in Appendix 4) was named after the burn coming out of Coire an Lochain Uaine (top left), and the Glas Allt Mor comes from the grassy hillside of Beinn a' Chaorainn (right).

Stags graze by the Old Caledonian firs at Luibeg. Derry Lodge stands in the distant wood and Meall an Lundain beyond.

**The South Road*** (C, 154911), ðɪ'suθ'rod. Main road to the south in Braemar, now given the sign Glenshee Road.

**The South Snout*** (U, 305921), ðɪ'suθ'snut. Pairs with Snout na Loinne. A snout-shaped field in Glen Girnock.

**(The) South Top** (OS, Ro, C, 090979), ðɪ'suθ'tɒp. On Beinn a' Bhuird, pairs with the North Top.

**South Top*** See Beinn a' Chaorainn Bheag.

**South Top** See Stob Coire Etchachan.

**The South Top** (Sg, 964971). Near the summit of Cairn Toul, with the North Top nearby.

**Spinnin Jenny** (C, 372952), 'spënën'dʒene. Spinning Jenny (Gl). A hill on the Glen Muick road near Ballater.

**Spinnin Jenny's Stane*** (C, slightly west of 372952), 'spënën 'dʒenez'stin. A rock formerly at the roadside near Ballater (see above name). The Witch's Stone (A 235) is the same.

**An Spiodagan*** (3, U, 328978), ðɪ'spiḍəkən, the little sharp-topped place. A pointed hillock north-west of the Bridge of Gairn.

**Spiodagan** (3, north-east of 242960), meaning as above. Speedikin (D). North-west of Crathie.

**The Spital of Glen Clunie** See the Sean Spittal.

**The Spittal Burn*** (C, 309855), ðɪ'spëtəl'bʌrn. Lowest part of Allt Darrarie in upper Glen Muick.

**The Spittal Haugh** (C, 303851), ðɪ'spëtəl'haˑχ. The Hospitall hauch, Spittle Haugh (Ri 13, 20), Hospitall Hach (R 6), Spittlehaugh of Glenmuick (Ml). Low-lying valley grassland beside the Spittal of Glenmuick.

**(The) Spittal of Glenmuick** (OS, C, 308850), ðɪ'spëtəlɐˌglən'mëk, from Spideal (3) = a hospice. A house in upper Glen Muick, had formerly been a hospice for travellers coming over the Capel Road from Glen Clova.

**The Spittal Wuid*** (C, 308852), ðɪ'spëtəl'wɪd. A wood at the above place.

**The Splash** (Duf, C, 058924), ðɪ'splaʃ, sometimes the Water Splash (C), ðɪ'watɐr'splaʃ. A place where the road in Glen Lui crosses Allt Mhadaidh-allaidh.

**The Splash Wuid*** (F, 060922), ðɪ'splaʃ'wɪd. A wood in Glen Lui.

**The Split Stane*** (U, 214923), ðɪ'splët'stin. A stone on Balmoral side of Dee, split and still carrying a drill hole.

**The Split Stane Puil** (F, north of 214923), ðɪ'splët'stin'pil, or the Split Rock Puil (U). Split Stone (Wav). In Dee, south-west of the Inver.

**The Spring of Glen Colstane*** (388013). The Spring of Glencoldstone (Io 20). South-east of Morven.

**The Springs of Dee** See Wells of Dee.

**Springs of Moine Eun*** (368922). Springs of Munain (R 6). Springs on a boggy area south of Ballater.

**Sputanan*** See Na Srubanan.

**Na Spùtan Dearga** (3, C, 005991), ðɪˌsputɐn'dʒɛrɐk, the red spouts. Sputan Dearg (A). Wide gullies with reddish-tinged screes on Ben Macdui, widest one is at 005991.

**The Sputan Dearg Brig*** (U, 012961), ðɪˌsputɐn'dʒɛrɐk'brɪg. A footbridge in upper Glen Luibeg.

**The Sputan Dearg Linn*** (U, 012960), ðɪˌsputɐn'dʒɛrɐk'lën. Rocky falls and pools in upper Glen Luibeg.

**Spùt na h-Àtha*** (3, U, 186915), ˌsputnɐ'haˑ, spout of the ford. A little brae beside Dee, north of Invercauld Bridge.

**The Sput na h-Atha Puil** (F, west of 185915, on bend), ðɪˌsputnɐ 'haˑ'pil. Sputnaha (A). In Dee, north of Invercauld Bridge.

**The Spying Hillock*** (I, 195800). South-east of Loch Kander above Glen Callater.

**The Spying Hillock*** (I, 244824). South of the bottom end of the Dubh Loch west of Loch Muick.

**The Spying Hillock*** (U, south-east of 039957), ðɪ'spae.ən'hëlëk.

A good place for stalkers to search for deer, using telescopes. In Glen Derry.

**The Square Park*** (U, 304922), ðɪ'skwer'park. A field in Glen Girnock.

**Square Toman a' Bhothain*** (F, 413033), 'skwerˌtamnə'von. A field south-west of Logie Coldstone.

**The Squarie*** (U, 355946), ðɪ'skwere, Scots = little square. A field in lower Glen Muick.

**An t-Sradag*** (3, F, 284833), ðɪ'stratɐk, the little fast one. A steep burn on north side of Loch Muick.

**The Sradag Face*** (F, 283832), ðɪ'stratɐk'fes. A steep hillside above Loch Muick.

**Sràid Mhòine Ailtridh** (6, 244945), street of Monaltrie. Stratsh vonaltrie (D). Also the Street of Monaltrie (A). Street (R 3). A former row of houses south of Balnault, north-east of the Inver.

**Srath an Aitinn** (3, 319003), river-plain of the juniper. Straenetten (Pb), Straneten (I, Ro), Stranetan (R 14). A former farm east of Gairnshiel.

**Na Srathanan** (3), the little riverside meadows. The Straans (Ri 32), Strahans (Rli 23). A holding divided into two halves with different tenants in 1772 (Ri). Two low grassy areas on either side of the Feardar Burn west of the Inver, see Muckle Srathan and An Srathan Beag.

**An Srathan Beag** (3, 232937, on south side of Feardar Burn), a double diminutive, the little Srathan or small riverside meadow, distinguishing it from Muckle Srathan nearby. The Stran Vig (Ri 32), Little Strahans (Io 53). A former field near the Inver.

**Srathan Riabhach** (3, 238950), strən'riəç (A), brindled little streamside meadow. Strahanriach (Opr 2), Stranriach (Roy), Straanrioch (Im 8), Stronriach (R 3), Stranriach (OS 1869), Stranreach (A). Srathan, not Sron as might be suggested by Stronriach (R), as there is no hill nose there and the ruins are beside grassy flat ground by a burn. A former farm north-east of the Inver.

**Srathan Riabhach** (3, farm probably at Rann na Bruaich), brindled little river-plain. Straenariach (Io 8), Stranreich, Stranriach (Ri 9a, 24). A pendicle of Rann na Bruaich, along with Torbeg. The Srathan was probably at 333000, or at 334995 below Cul Riabhach. A former farm east of Gairnshiel.

**Srath Dhé** (3), river-plain of the Dee. Sra-yē or Strathdee (D). Stradee (Rg). Used formerly for the Dee valley from foot of Gairn to Invercauld (A), and Wade's map showed it as far up as Mar Lodge. Note Church of Crathie or Strathdee (Gf).

**An t-Sròn** (OS, 199938), the nose. A protruding nose north-east of Invercauld Bridge, the little hilltop on it being Carn Dearg.

**An t-Sròn** (OS, 3, C, 285845), ðɪ'stron, the nose. The actual nose is to the east, and locally the name refers to that, not to the hilltop as on the OS map. West of the north end of Loch Muick.

**An t-Sròn** (OS, 3, C, 310842), as above, the nose. Sometimes the Sron o the Spittal (F), ðɪ'stronɪðɪ'spëtəl. The Stroin of the Spittal (I). East of the north end of Loch Muick.

**An t-Sron** (OS, 3, F, 344929), as above, the nose. Often the Sron o Loinn Muighe (U), ðɪ'stronɐˌlɒn'mui, after the name of a former farm there. In lower Glen Muick.

**An t-Sròn*** (3, U, 210919), as above, the nose. The Stroin (I). Also the Big Nose (Crom). South-west of the Inver.

**An t-Sròn*** (3, U, 243996), as above, the nose. South-east of Corndavon Lodge.

**An t-Sròn*** (3, U, 156876), as above, the nose. Old Mrs Kerr at Auchallater called it ðɪ'strɔin (CMcI). Also the Sron o Auchallater (F), ðɪ'stronɐˌa'χalɐtɐr. Stroin of Achalater (I). In lower Glen Clunie.

**An t-Sròn\*** (3, 135831), the nose. The Stroin (I). A former farm at the Baddoch.

**Sròn a' Bhoididh** (OS, 006827), classic form would be Bhoitidh, nose of the sow or of the pig-calling (i.e. people calling to pigs). Stron ya vaotshi (D in A). At the edge of Glen Tilt.

**Sròn a' Bhruic** (OS, 183905), locally Sròn nam Brag (3), strona 'brak (A), nose of the herds of deer, see also Sron nam Breac. Stronabrack (R 7), Sron na brac (D), Stronabrak (A). South of the Invercauld Bridge.

**Sròn an Daimh** (3, Sg, 001004), ˌstrɔnɐn'dai (SGo), nose of the stag. Above Loch Etchachan.

**An t-Sròn Bheag\*** (3), the little nose. The Stronbeg (Io 18). A piece of farmland on north side of Feardar Burn near Tullochcoy at the Inver.

**Sròn Carn a' Mhaim** (3, Sg, U, 008940), ˌstrɔnˌkarnɐ'vɛim, nose of hill of the pass. West of Glen Luibeg.

**Sròn Craobh Chrom\*** (3, 094957), nose of crooked tree. Stroin Cruve Croum (I), Stroin Croubh Croum (R 14). In upper Glen Quoich.

**Sròn Creag a' Chléirich\*** (3, U, 149937), ˌstrɔnˌkreg'çliriç, nose of rocky hill of the clergyman. North of Braemar.

**Sròn Dubh** (OS, 159874), from Sròn Dhubh (3, A), black nose. Strondow (Roy), Sron Dhubh, stron ghu (D in A). Refers to the whole ridge from OS location to above Fraser's Brig. East of Glen Clunie.

**Sròn Dubh** (OS, F, 291964), from Sròn Dhubh (3, A), strɔn'duˑ, black nose. Sron Dhubh, stron ghu (D in A). East of Crathie.

**Sròn Eirbhidh\*** (3, 415956), nose at dyke. Stronervie in 1599 (Dms 2), later the Strone (U), ðɪ'stron. South-west of Inchmarnoch.

**An t-Sron Fhionn** See Strone Baddoch.

**Sròn Fìneige\*** (3, 126806), nose of crowberry. Stroin Feinick (I). Up the Baddoch.

**Sròn Gharbh** (3, 116887), rough nose. Sron gharbh (D). South-east of Corriemulzie.

**Sròn Gharbh** (OS, 326048), should be An Garbh-shròn (3, U), ðɪ'garɐˌrɔn, the rough nose. Garbh Shron (A). At top of Glen Fenzie.

**Sròn Ghearraich** (3), nose of the short one (see name below). Stronyearrich (D). 'This name occurred in Strathgirnock, besides its usage for the Crathie–Glengairn road' (D).

**Sròn Ghearraig** (3, C, 263985), strɔn'jaˑrək (several informants, including the one with most Gaelic, strɔn'jaːrɪç, strɔn'jæˑrɪç, suggesting Gheàrraich), nose of the short one, possibly referring to the road as a short way from Gairnshiel to Crathie. Stron nyarrich (D), Strone Yarrick (A). Sron Dhearg (A) was an incorrect inference, as this would give a Yerrick sound, not Yarrick, and in any case a *d* at the beginning of a word does not aspirate after *n* (T 33, 209). The sound is the same as in the local pronunciation of the Corrieyairack pass from Spey to Fort Augustus, thought to come from Gearrag = short one (Mb), referring to a stream. Gheàrrag = of young hares is also a possibility.

**The Sron Ghearraig Road** (C), ðɪˌstrɔn'jarək'rod. Road from Gairnshiel to Crathie.

**An t-Sròn Ghiubhas\*** (U, 332873), ðɪˌstrɔn'juːz, the fir nose. Stronnews, Stronews (G 14, 16). Stroin Guish (I) suggests Giubhais = of fir. Another case like An Caochan Fearn, where a noun for a plant is used in an adjectival sense, with the article. South of the Linn of Muick.

**An t-Sròn Ghorm\*** (3, U, 317937), ðɪˌstrɔn'gɔrɔm, the green nose. In lower Glen Girnock.

**Sròn Ghrianach** (3, U, 323026), strɔn'griɐnɐx, sunny nose. Stron-rianich (D), Sron Grianach (A). In Glen Fenzie.

**Sron Mhor** See the Strone.

**Sròn ? Mhuilteag** (3, probably 939962), nose of cranberries.

Stromwoldick (Hi):—'through Glenluy and Glenguissich, and at Stromwoldick, and then into the Hills of Badenoch' (Hi). Probably about the head of Glen Geusachan near Loch nan Stuirteag.

**Sròn na Corra\*** (4, U, 050864), ˌstrɔnɐ'cɔr, nose of the heron, possibly nan Curra = of the marshes, or na Cùrra = of the corner. Also McDougall's Nose (U), mək'dugəlz'noz. Between Allt Cristie Beag and Allt Cristie Mor, south-west of the Linn of Dee.

**Sròn na Gaoithe** (OS, F, 157792), ˌstrɔnɐ'gui, nose of the wind. Stron Guie (I). Alexander recorded the sound as strona'kui from Sron na Cuithe (3, F) = nose of the snow wreath, and the most knowledgeable informants independently gave us this sound, ˌstrɔnɐ'kui. A deep drift piles up every winter in a slight hollow north-east of the summit, and lies unusually far into the summer for such a low altitude. North-east of the Cairnwell.

**Sròn na Lairige** (OS, F, 964006), ˌstrɔnɐ'laːrɪk (Speyside folk), nose of the pass. On west side of Lairig Ghru, summit reaches Aberdeenshire but actual nose projects north into Inverness-shire.

**Sròn nam Breac\*** (3, U, 151806), ˌstrɔnɐ'brak, nose of the ? speckled places, note Breac also rarely = badger in Perthshire. Stron-na-brachk (I), Stron a brack (R 14). North-east of the Cairnwell. See Sron a' Bhruic.

**Sròn nam Fiadh** (OS, 119791), nose of the deer. North-west of the Cairnwell.

**Sròn nan Cuithe Iomlan\*** (3, U, 317944), ˌstrɔnɐ'gwimlən, nose of the full snow-drifts. In lower Glen Girnock.

**Sròn nan Cuithe Iomlan\*** (3, 290851), nose of the full snow-drifts. Stronygymalan (In, Am). South-west of Allt-na-giubhsaich in upper Glen Muick.

**Sròn nan Gabhar** (OS, A, 155855, should be rocky nose at 148855, 155855 is Meall Dubh Coire Buidhe), strona'gʌuər (A), nose of the goats. Shown on old map (I) as rocks at 148855. Stron-na-Gour (I). Above Newbigging in Glen Clunie.

**The Sron o Auchallater\*** See An t-Sron.

**The Sron of Coire Chaorach\*** (286821), Sròn (3) = a nose. The Stroin of Cor Churach (I). On south side of Loch Muick.

**Sron of Corrie Chash\*** (264816), Sròn (3) = a nose. Stroin of Corchaash (I). Above the top end of Loch Muick.

**The Sron of Little Beinn Iutharn\*** (071794), Sròn (3) = nose. The Strone or Nose of Little Beinurn (Lp 5). At the top of Glen Ey.

**The Sron o Loinn Muighe\*** See An t-Sron.

**The Sron o the Baddoch\*** See Strone Baddoch.

**The Sron o the Spittal\*** See An t-Sron.

**Sròn Riabhach\*** (3, 175793), brindled nose. Stron Riach (I). North-east of the Glas Maol.

**Sròn Riabhach na Coille\*** (3, 163795), brindled nose of the wood. Stron Riach-na-Kyle (I). North of the Glas Maol, near Sron na Gaoithe.

**(The) Sròn Riach** (OS, C, 000973), ðɪˌstrɔn'riˑəç, ðɪ'strɔn'riˑɐx (JB), from An t-Sròn Riabhach (3), the brindled nose. The Stronruick (Fi). In Ben Macdui, above upper Glen Luibeg.

**Sròn Ruighe Baile a' Chlaiginn\*** (3, 204025), nose of shiel of farm-town of the infield. Stroin Rie Ballchlaghan (I). West of Corndavon Lodge.

**Sròn Shalachar** (3, U, 280907), strɔn'aləçɛr, nose of willow places, note W 1904, 8. Sron Allacher (A). In upper Glen Girnock.

**Na Srùbanan\*** (3, 262924), the little spouts. The Strupans (In). Also Spùtanan (3), little spouts. Spouttans (B). Rocky bits on either side of a little burn south of Balmoral.

**(The) Stable Burn** (OS, C, 186975), ðɪ'stebəl'bʌrn. Also the

West Culardoch Burn (U), ðɪ'wɛst̩ˌkəl'ardəç'bʌrn. Named after the stable on the Bealach Dearg road at the top of this burn.

**The Stackyard Park\*** See Long Runs.

**Stairean** (3). Sterine (Io 9), Sterin (Dms 5), Sterryne, Stering (Ap), Sterrein (Pb). A former farm in lower Glen Muick, different from Mill of Sterin in 1682 (Io). See Mill of Sterin for meaning.

**Stairean** See Birkhall.

**The Stalking Ditch\*** (F, 236921), ðɪ'sta·kën'dëʧ. A ditch for hiding behind while stalking deer, west of lower Glen Gelder.

**St Andrew's Chapel** (OS, 153921). Site of a former chapel. North of Braemar.

**The Stane Brig\*** (F, 170928), ðɪ'stin'brɪg, Scots = stone bridge. Near Invercauld House.

**The Stane Burn\*** See the Greystone Burn.

**The Stane Butt\*** (F, 273045), ðɪ'stin'bʌt. A stone shelter (not a butt) north-west of Gairnshiel.

**The Stane Butts\*** (F, 329014), ðɪ'stin'bʌts. Grouse butts in Glen Fenzie.

**The Stane Hill\*** (C, 419043), ðɪ'stin'hël, ðɪ'sten'hël. A winding bank, stony and gravelly, near Logie Coldstone.

**The Stane Hill Road\*** (C, 418041), ðɪ'stin'hël'rod. A track from the Mosstown to the Milton of Whitehouse near Logie Coldstone.

**The Stane in the Hole Puil** (C, west of 413981), ðɪ'stinɪnðɪ'hol 'pil. Steen wi' the Hole (A), Stone in Hole (Sc). A pool in Dee, at Cambus o' May, beside a big stone on north bank.

**The Stane Park\*** (U, 347913), ðɪ'stin'park. A stony field in Glen Muick.

**Stang Raibeirt\*** (3, 132917), ditch of Robert. Stank Rabart, Stank Robert (Io 43a, 63). A ditch running approximately from Dee north to the hillside west of Allanmore. Also the March Burn (U), ðɪ'mɛrʧ'bʌrn. The march between Invercauld and Mar Lodge.

**The Stanie Howe\*** (U, south-west of 420046), ðɪ'stini'hʌu·, ðɪ 'steni'hʌu· from best informant, Scots = stony hollow. On farmland west of Logie Coldstone.

**Stankry Park\*** (Ra 5, Me 15), Scots Stank = ditch, and Ree = cattle-run, lowland versions of Gaelic Stang and Ruighe, and Scots Park = field. On flat marshy ground with drainage ditches, at Allanmore west of Braemar.

**The Steading\*** See Corn Eilean.

**The Steppin Stanes\*** (C, east of 393971), ðɪ'stɛpën̩ˌstinz. On the lowest part of the Tullich Burn north-east of Ballater.

**Sterinbeg** See Birkhall Cottage.

**The Stile\*** (B, 248945), Scots Stile = gate. A former enclosure in a wood south-west of Balmoral Castle.

**Stile of Balmoral\*** Style of Balmoral (Opr 49). Probably Gate of Balmoral (Cpb 7) was same place. Former habitation.

**Stile of Pannanich\*** Style of Pannanich (Opr 58). See Whitestile of Pannanich.

**The Stile of Tullich** (A, 405978). The Style of Tullich, Style (R 4). A former farm west of Cambus o' May, at the beginning of the Tullich farmlands. The Stile of Tullich was later a public house on the roadside.

**The Still Brae\*** (C, 265941), ðɪ'stël'bre·. A hill on the road to the distillery at Balmoral.

**The Still Burn** See Distillery Burn.

**The Still Park\*** (F, 268936), ðɪ'stël'park. A field near Easter Balmoral.

**The Still Road\*** (U, 273939), ðɪ'stël'rod. Road from Tornauran west to Balmoral.

**The Stirkies' Burn\*** See Allt nan Gamhainn.

**St Manir's Church** (OS, 264947). At Crathie.

**St Morrice Chapel** (D, c. 087894). Near, if not on the site of,

Chapel of the Seven Maidens. Chapel of St Maurice (S). At Inverey.

**St Mungo's Chapel** See Cill Ma-Thatha.

**St Mungo's Well** (OS, 354970). Also Fuaran Mhungo (D), mungidh (D in A). Beside the above chapel.

**St Nachlan's Well** (D, 372968). At Monaltrie House, Ballater.

**St Nathalan's Chapel** See Cill Nachlan.

**St Nathalan's House** (Mac, south-west of 374970). A former building on a grassy mound close by Monaltrie House at Ballater. See also D 198.

**An Stoban Biorach\*** (3, 045987), ðɪˌstouþɛn'þi:rɐχ (WG), ðɪ ˌstupən'pi·rəç (C), the pointed little stake. A pointed little rock east of upper Glen Derry.

**The Stoban Biorach Path\*** (F, 042988), ðɪˌstupən'pi·rəç'paθ. A zig-zag deer-stalkers' path in upper Glen Derry.

**Stob Coire an t-Saighdeir** (3, Rob, 962963), point of corrie of the soldier. A name invented by climbers. Also the Soldier's Cairn (U), ðɪ'soldʒërz'kern̩. A hilltop on Cairn Toul.

**Stob Coire Etchachan** (OS, 025005), point of Coire Etchachan. A name invented by climbers. Also South Top (OS 1869). On Beinn Mheadhoin at the top of Glen Derry.

**Stob Coire Sputan Dearg** (3, Rob, 998985), classic form Spùtan, point of corrie with red spouts. A name invented by climbers. A hilltop on Ben Macdui.

**Stob Dubh** See Stob Dubh Easaidh Mor.

**Stob Dubh an Eas Bhig** (OS, 134002, should be at 129008, 134002 is Sgor Dubh), should be Stob Dubh Easaidh Beag (3), black point of little rapidly-falling burn. A tor on Ben Avon.

**Stob Dubh an t-Slugain\*** (3, west of 134948), black point of the gullet. Stoup-du-n-luckan (I). A hillock in Gleann an t-Slugain.

**Stob Dubh Easaidh Beag\*** See Stob Dubh an Eas Bhig.

**Stob Dubh Easaidh Mór** (3, 132018), black point of big rapidly-falling burn. Stoap-du-Essie more (Ro), Stoup Du (Essie More) (I). Summit tor of Ben Avon, also called Stob Easaidh Mór (3), point of big rapidly-falling burn. R 2a gives Stob Essymore as the summit tor, and R 2b gives it as the summit and also the tor slightly to the east at 134020. Also Stob Dubh (3, A), black point.

**Stob Easaidh Mor\*** See above name.

**An Stob Liath\*** (3, F, 272862), ðɪˌstɔb'liɐ, the grey point. The Stoblia (In), Stoblia (Am). Also Stob Liath Ghealdair (3), of the Gelder. Stob lea zealdir (G 5). A rock at the top of Glen Gelder.

**(An) Stob Liath** (OS, 3, 233893), the grey point. Also Stob of Creag Liath. Stob of Craiglia (B). North-west of Lochnagar.

**Stob Liath Ghealdair\*** See An Stob Liath.

**Stob Loch nan Eun** See the Stuic.

**Stob nan Deamhain** See the Devil's Point.

**Stob of Creag Liath\*** See Stob Liath.

**An Stocach** (3, F, 255005), ðɪ'stɔkɐχ, the root place (i.e. fir roots in the peat). The Stokach (D). A peat-bog west of Gairnshiel.

**The Stocach Brae\*** (F, 250008), ðɪ'stɔkɐχ'bre·. A hill on the road from Daldownie to Blairglass, west of Gairnshiel.

**The Stoitear\*** (6, U, north-west of 352927), ðɪ'stɔtër, ? from Stòite = prominent. A big hillock in lower Glen Muick.

**The Stoitear Brae\*** (U, 352928), ðɪ'stɔtër'bre·. A hill on the road in Glen Muick.

**The Stoitear Croft** (351926), ðɪ'stɔdërt'krɔft (U). The Stodart Croft (Rli 3, G 35), Stoidhird craft (G 4), Stoddert Craft, Stottercroft, Stotherd Croft (Io 7, 33, 56), Stoddart Croft (Rli 23), Stotter (Opr 18), Stodartcroft (Ri 8), Stodartis Croft (Ab 17). A prominent hillock called the Stoitear is nearby. A former farm in lower Glen Muick.

**The Stony Corrie\*** See Coire nan Clach.

**(The) Stotwell Burn** (OS, F, 356039), ðɪˈstɒtwəlˈbʌrn, possibly from Stot Well with Scots Stot = young steer. West of Morven.

**Stranlea** (OS, C, 313006), stranˈliː, sometimes stranˈlɛiˑ (U), from Srathan Liath (3), little grey riverside meadow. Strainlia (Cr 38), Straanlea (I, Ro), Stranlia (R 14), Strathanlia (Ce 1), Stron lia, stran lia (D in A) might suggest An t-Sròn Liath, the grey nose, but 'no *sròn* here' (A). A former farm, now a house, east of Gairnshiel.

**The Stranlea Brae\*** (U, 311007), ðɪˌstranˈliˑˈbreˑ. Also Bremner's Brae (F), ˈbrɛmɛrzˈbreˑ, after a former resident. A hill on the road near above house.

**The Stranlea Burn\*** (C, 314005), ðɪˌstranˈliˑˈbʌrn. East of Gairnshiel.

**The Stranlea Parkie\*** (U, 313007), ðɪˌstranˈliˑˈparki. A field east of Gairnshiel.

**Strath Dee** See Srath Dhe.

**Strathgirnock** (OS, C, 334953), straθˈgɛrnɛk, straˈgɛrnɛk to some old people, from Srath Ghoirneag (3), riverside plain of the Girnock or little crier, referring to the Girnock Burn. Strogarnick (Rg), Stragirnag (R 1), Stra-ghaornak *ao* shortish, stra-ghoirnag (D). A farm west of Ballater.

**The Strathgirnock Burn\*** See Allt na Creige Leith.

**Strawberry Cottage\*** See Burnside.

**The Streak o Lichtnin** (C, 286820), ðɪˈstrikɛˈlɛçtnën. The Streak of Lightning (Gl). Formerly a zig-zag path at Loch Muick, now a rough bulldozed road.

**The Streams o Gairn** (F, 354966), ðɪˈstrimzɛˈgern̩, or now the Gairn Streams (F), Scots Stream = current. Streams of Gairn (Sc). A pool in Dee, below the Gairn–Dee junction.

**The Streams o the Boat Puil\*** (F, south of 247946), ðɪˈstrimzɪðɪ ˈbotˈpil. A pool on north side of Dee south-west of Balmoral Castle, also recently the Buckets Puil (U), ðɪˈbʌkɛtsˈpil, due to the amount of rubbish put into it from nearby houses.

**The Street\*** (U, 277010), ðɪˈstrit. A common term formerly, in Scots and Gaelic (Sràid), for a row of houses or crofts (A). A former row of houses at Loinahaun west of Gairnshiel.

**The Street** (Er, C, 287941), as above. A row of houses south of Abergeldie.

**The Street of Monaltrie** See Sraid Mhoine Ailtridh.

**The Stripe of Bad na h-Earba\*** See Allt Bad na h-Earba.

**The Stripe of Branndair\*** See Doulich Burn.

**The Stripe of Gourock\*** (F, 283804), ðɪˈstrɛipɛˈgurək, Scots Stripe = small burn, for Gourock see Sneck o Gourock. Stripe of Guarich (I). South of Loch Muick.

**Stripe of Rodaig\*** (249932). Stripe of Rodack (B). A tiny burn in lower Glen Gelder.

**The Stripe o Megen\*** (F, 325892), ðɪˈstrɛipɛˈmɛgən. A small burn that runs into Muick above Linn o Muick.

**Stronagoar** (OS, C, 227944), ˌstrɒnɛˈgor, from Sròn nan Corra (4), nose of the herons, but also ˌstrɒnɛˈgʌu.ër (AT) suggests Gabhar or goats. Stronacor (Im 3, Rli 19), Stronachore (Io 28), Stronagour (I, Rli 23), Stronachor (Ra 6), Stronagor (R 14), Stron na gorr (D). A former farm north-west of the Inver.

**The Stronagoar Park\*** (U, 227943), ðɪˌstrɒnɛˈgorˈpark. A field near the Inver.

**The Strone** (OS, A, 272993), from An t-Sròn (3), the nose. Earlier OS had Sron Mhor, and we have heard this name as ðɪˌstrɒnˈmoˑr (U), from An t-Sròn Mhòr (3), the big nose. Stron More (I). South-west of Gairnshiel.

**Strone Baddoch** (OS, 134825), locally the Strone o the Baddoch (C), ðɪˈstronɪðɪˈbadəç, from Sròn (3) = a nose. Also An t-Sròn Fhionn (3), the white nose, probably because it is covered in grass, which stands out clearly against the dark heathery hillsides around. Strone ine (Fa), the Stroin-niin,

Stronigne (Cr 29, 49), Stronyne, Stronein (Ra 2, 3), Stronfinne (G 2), Stroon-een (Ta), Stron Finn, Fingal's nose (Mp). At the Baddoch.

**Stùc Gharbh Bheag** (OS, 3, 145998), little rough projecting hill. Sluch Carrie Beg (I). On south-east slopes of Ben Avon.

**Stùc Gharbh Mhór** (OS, 3, 147013), stukgareˈmor (A), big rough projecting hill. A prominent eastern part of Ben Avon with a pair of big tors.

**An Stùchdan\*** (3, U, 080861), ðɪˈstuɣkən, the little projecting hill. A broad ridge in lower Glen Ey.

**The Stuffers' Pool** See Poll na Mile Duirche.

**The Stuic** (OS, 227852), locally the Stuc o Loch nan Eun (F), ðɪ ˈstjukɛˌlɒɣnanˈjeˑn, from Stùc (3) = a projecting hill. Also Stob Loch nan Eun, stɒplɒɣnanˈyen (A). Often called the Stui (Al), ðɪˈstui, by hill walkers, probably as an attempt to pronounce the OS map name of the Stuic, but neither is used by local people (A and us). Stuc Eoin (McC) suggests Eòin = of a bird, possibly from Loch nan Eun below, which was sometimes incorrectly written Loch an Eoin (Al). West of Lochnagar.

**The Stulan** (OS, C, 257824), ðɪˈstjulən, from An Steallan (3), the little cataract. Also often now the Stulan Falls (F), ðɪ ˈstjulənˈfaˑlz. A waterfall west of Loch Muick.

**The Stulan Burn** (OS, F, 255825), ðɪˈstjulənˈbʌrn. Burn of the Spullan (Spout) (V). West of Loch Muick.

**The Stulan Falls\*** See the Stulan.

**Suckerie's\*** (F, west of bungalow at 433043), ˈsʌkɛrez. A former house at Logie Coldstone, named after a Kennedy whose nickname was Suckerie.

**Sùgh Fhìorag\*** (3, U, 345969), suˈwirɛk, sap of the pure one. A well west of the Bridge of Gairn.

**Summer House Spring** (OS 1869, 257948). Near Balmoral Castle.

**Sunny Brae\*** (U, 434966), ˌsʌneˈbreˑ. A slope east of Inchmarnoch, on north side of road.

**The Sunny Side** (Pj, 144782). A skiers' name for the slope east of the Cairnwell Ski School.

**The Suspension Brig\*** (C, 091898), ðɪˌsəsˈpɛnʃənˈbrig. Also the Swing Brig (F), ðɪˈswiŋˈbrig. A footbridge near Inverey.

**The Suspension Brig\*** See the Auld Brig.

**The Suspension Brig\*** See the Garbh Allt Shiel Brig.

**The Suspension Brig Pool\*** See Am Poll Dearg.

**The Suspension Brig Puil** (F, 198908), ðɪˌsəsˈpɛnʃənˈbrigˈpil. Suspension (Wav). In Dee, east of Invercauld Bridge.

**Swail\*** (243991), Scots Swail = miry place, Well-eye = boggy spring. Swale or Well Eye (R 3). A spring north of Crathie.

**The Swing Brig\*** See the Suspension Brig.

**The Table Stane\*** See the Earl of Mar's Breakfast Stone.

**The Taggart Burn\*** (F, 213845), ðɪˈtagɛrtˈbʌrn. On the Loch Muick side of Carn an t-Sagairt Mor.

**The Taggart Corrie\*** (F, 213845), ðɪˈtagɛrtˈkɒre. Corrie drained by the above burn.

**The Tailors' Burn** See Allt Clach nan Taillear.

**The Tailors' Corrie\*** See Coire Clach nan Taillear.

**The Tailors' Stane** See Clach nan Taillear.

**Talamh Geal\*** (3, 197935), white land, i.e. grassy. Tallowgaill (Rli 19), Talamh Geal, Talamhgeal (Io 52, 53), Tallow Gall (I), Tallowgeal (R 14). A former farm north-east of Invercauld Bridge.

**An Talamh Odhar\*** (3, U, 146905), ðɪˌtɛlˈʌr̩, the dun land. A little field south of Braemar.

**The Tammie Burn\*** (F, 330826), ðɪˈtameˈbʌrn. Was formerly the Burn o Tammie (U), ðɪˈbʌrnɛˈtame. East of Loch Muick.

**The Tanar Burn** See Water of Tanar.

**Tanarside\*** (F), ˌtɑˑnɛrˈsɛid. A name for any place up the side of the Water of Tanar, but not the top part above Etnach,

145

and usually the lowest part in Aboyne parish. Also a house on the lower Tanar, in Aboyne parish.

**The Tanar Valley*** (C, 426922), ðɪ'tɑnɐr'vale. Upper part of Glen Tanar.

**The Tap Braehead*** See Upper Braehead.

**The Tap House*** See Geldie Lodge.

**The Tap o the Slugain*** (F, 118954), ðɪ'tapɪðɪ'slʌɡən. The top of Gleann an t-Slugain.

**The Target*** (F, south of 408036), ðɪ'tarɡət. A metal target for shooting practice, east of Morven.

**The Target*** (F, 281929), as above. A metal deer for shooting practice, south of Abergeldie.

**Tàrr nam Mothar*** (3, 353946), extremity of the parks. Tarnamore (Am). Now the Bog Park (F), ðɪ'bog'park. A field projecting further west into woodland than the main block of farmland at the foot of Glen Muick.

**Tassack Lodge** (Er, U, 424963), 'tasɐk'lɔʤ, often just Tassack (C) with pronunciations as in the Tassack Puil. A former croft, later a house, beside the bridge carrying the South Deeside Road at Inchmarnoch. Formerly was used for the group of houses there. Tassach Lodge (Vr 3), Tassack Cottage (Dms), Tassachd (on house nameplate).

**The Tassack Park*** See the Milton Park.

**The Tassack Puil** (A, C, 427966), ðɪ'tasɐk'pil, but was 'tasɐχ to older folk (F), from An t-Easach (3) = the cataract place, as in Tassagh in Ireland (J). A pool in Dee, near Inchmarnoch.

**The Tattie Pit*** (F, 405995), ðɪ'tate'pët, Scots Tattie = potato. A hillock on Culblean, shaped like a potato pit when seen from the Ballater–Cambus o' May road at Tomnakeist.

**Teapot Cottage** See Dalphuil.

**Teetabootee** (F, 310862), ˌtitɐ'buti, meaning doubtful, might be Scots or Gaelic. Titubooty (Io 60), Titabutie (I, Ro, R 17), Teetaboutie (McC 1891, A). Macdonald wrote 'Look about you', an absurd fanciful name, and Alexander followed more tentatively by saying the usual explanation was Scots Teet aboot ye, meaning look about you. However, the pronunciation of the word and the early forms above are not right for 'teet aboot ye'. Note Scots Teet-about = a nickname for a prying person, snooper (Gm). There is an identically pronounced Titaboutie east of Tarland. A former house in upper Glen Muick.

**The Telegraph Puil** (F, 284953), ðɪ'tëlɘɡraf'pil. Telegraph (Sc). In Dee, above Abergeldie Castle.

**The Thief's Pot** (Brow). The laird formerly had the power of 'Pot and Gallows' over criminals (Brow). Beside the Gallow Hill west of Tomidhu at Crathie.

**The Thorny Puil** (C), ðɪ'θɔrne'pil. Thorny (A). A collective name for two pools in Dee, Big and Little Thorny Buss.

**The Three Bobbies Puil** (C), ðɪ'θri'bobiz'pil. Often just the Bobbies (C). Three Bobbies (A). Bobby's Girnel, not the diminutive of Robert, but Scots bobby 'grandfather', sometimes humorously applied to the Devil (Dms), Scots Girnel = meal chest. A collective name for pools in Dee south-west of Dinnet, Upper, Middle and Lower Bobbie.

**The Three-cornered Park*** See Haugh of Easter Micras.

**The Three Neuk Park*** See Baile Cheothaich.

**The Three Stanes** (Ly, 413981). A former pool in Dee at Cambus o' May; three stones in a group stick out near the middle of Dee.

**The Thunderbowl** (Pj, 134778). A skiers' name for a ski-run on a steep hollow on the Cairnwell.

**The Tiger Run** (Sd, 137777). A steep ski-run on the Cairnwell.

**An Tigh Geal** (3), the white house. The Tigh-Geal (Gr 235). A former lodging house in Castleton, Braemar.

**Tigh Maol*** (5, U, 424963), tɪ'meˑl, bare house, or might be

Meil = of bleating. Former school at Inchmarnoch, now a house.

**Tigh na Cailliche Beathraiche** (3, north of 134897 (U)), house of the wild old woman. Tyna Calich Phurach, Tye na Calich Phurach (I), Tigh na Caillich-byurach, the sharp wifie's house, above the Mime (D). A mythical Cailleach Bheurr, who was a gigantic witch, appears in old legends in several parts of Scotland, and as An Chailleach Bhearach also in Ireland (McKay 1929). She was said to have waded across the Sound of Mull and to have milked the red deer hinds like the deer witch in the Lochaber song Cailleach Beinn a' Bhric (Carmichael 1954; Mackinnon 1970s), and the story of milking hinds appears at Braemar (Gr 62). She was also said to have caused a big rocky gap near Morven, by trying to bite through the hill with her teeth (see Slacks of Glencarvie), and her name also appears in Buailtean na Cailliche Beathraiche in Glen Fenzie. The Scottish examples (McKay) involve Cailleach Bheurr or Bhiurr, interpreted as stingy witch or hag. It is interesting that the Deeside examples are of Cailleach Bheathrach, like the Irish Cailleach Bhearach. Grant called her the Cailleach-Bheathrach the Thunderbolt Carline; this suggests a genitive of Beithir = a serpent, wild beast or thunder-bolt. Diack's note on the sharp wifie's house might suggest Biorach or Beurach = sharp. The old Invercauld map gives the name at the top of Morrone and adds 'highest top of More Roin'. An unusual serrated rocky ridge west of Braemar with vertical blocks of rock almost like gigantic masonry.

**Tigh na Criche** (3, c. 239941), house of the boundary. Teighnachrich, Tynachriech, Tynacreich (Io 64, 69, 80). Tynacriech (M) was based on Tenrich and Tanrich (Pb) which in fact represented Torr an Fhraoich at Invercauld. Probably Tigh na Criche was about the more westerly of the two ruined houses at Lower Carnaqueen. A former farm at the west boundary of the old Monaltrie estate, near Balnault.

**The Tillage*** (U, 286901), ðɪ'tɪlɘʤ. A green patch with a ruin, in upper Glen Girnock.

**The Tilt Road*** (F, 998830), ðɪ'tëlt'rod. Path from Bynack to Glen Tilt.

**The Timber Fuird*** The Timber Foord (Io 24). A former ford on Dee, near Allanmore west of Braemar.

**The Timmer Brig*** (U, 164863), ðɪ'tëmɘr'brɪɡ, Scots Timmer = wooden. A bridge in Glen Callater.

**The Timmer Butts*** (F, 298901), ðɪ'tëmɘr'bʌts. Wooden grouse butts in upper Glen Girnock.

**The Tink*** (C, 372957), ðɪ'tɪŋk. Public bar at Invercauld Hotel, Ballater.

**The Tinker Puil*** (C, 377962), ðɪ'tɪŋkɐr'pil. A pool in Dee north-east of Ballater, near a place where tinkers used to camp.

**The Tinker's Grave*** (U, north-east of 269989 on north side of road), ðɪ'tɪŋkɐrz'grev. Two upright stones about a metre apart, marking an old grave south-west of Gairnshiel.

**The Tinkers' Parkie*** (U, north-west of 351929), ðɪ'tɪŋkɐrz 'parki. Also No Man's Land (U), 'nomɐnz'land. A small area in lower Glen Muick, said to be of uncertain ownership and formerly used by tinkers as a wintering area.

**The Tinkies' Park*** (C, 376962), ðɪ'tɪŋkiz'park. A riverside area east of Ballater where tinkers used to camp in a narrow strip between Dee and North Deeside Road from Ballater to Aberdeen Cottage.

**The Tinks' Green*** (C, 419966), ðɪ'tɪŋks'grin, or the Tinkies' Green (F). A grassy patch near Inchmarnoch, formerly used by camping tinkers.

**? An Tiobair*** (C, 404981), ðɪ'tebër, or Tiobair Cottage, from

Tiobair or Tobair (3) = a well. A former house west of Cambus o' May.

**Tobar Chalaig** (174926), well of ? the hard one, referring to the stream (see Invercauld). Tobar chall (D), Tobar Challag (D in A). Well of Callaick (R 7). A well beside Invercauld House.

**Tobar Chuirn** (3, D, 141775), well of the cairn. Also Red Well of the Cairnwell (I). Also the Queen's Well, where Queen Victoria refreshed herself (Aj 9). Now under the top car park on the Cairnwell pass, but the water seeps out on the east side.

**Tobar Dòmhnaich*** (3, 187913), well of Sunday. Touper Donich (R 7). Note Tobar Domhnaich on Speyside, near a church (Forsyth 1894; T 41, 226). Near Invercauld Bridge.

**An Tobar Dubh** (3, D, U, 092893, by elimination), ðɪˌtǫbɐr'duˑ, the black well. At Inverey.

**Tobar Mhoire** (OS, 3, U, 084892), ˌtobɐr'moˑr, well of Mary, usually now the Tobar (C), ðɪ'tobër. Also the Well of St Mary of Inverey (Gr), or St Mary's Well (F Paul). At Inverey.

**Tobarnaidh*** See name below.

**Tobar nan Cearc** (3, U, 344969), ˌtobɐrnɐ'kërk, well of the hens. Often called Tobarnaidh (3, U), 'tobɐrne, little well. Topernakerak, the hen's well (D). West of the Bridge of Gairn.

**Tod Hillock** (OS, 321804), Scots Tod = fox. South-east of Loch Muick.

**The Tod's House*** (U, 418028), ðɪ'tǫdz'hus. A rocky gully south-west of Logie Coldstone.

**The Tofts*** (C, 416031), ðɪ'tʌfts, ðɪ'tʌfs, ðɪ'tœfs, English Toft = homestead, land with a homestead. A former house beside Auchnerran near Logie Coldstone.

**The Tofts Park*** (U, 415031), ðɪ'tœfs'park. A field beside the above house.

**Toldhu** (OS, C, 346912), tǫl'duˑ, nicknamed 'tǫle (F), from Toll Dubh (3), black hole. Toldow (Ri 14, Rli 19). A farm in mid Glen Muick.

**The Toldhu Brae*** (C, 345913), ðɪˌtol'du'breˑ. A hill on a road in Glen Muick.

**The Toldhu Brig*** (F, 347912), ðɪˌtǫl'du'brɪg. A former bridge over Muick.

**The Toldhu Wuid*** (U, 344912), ðɪˌtǫl'du'wɪd. A wood in lower Glen Muick.

**(The) Toll Cottage** See Knockanduie.

**The Toll House** (Gf, C), ðɪ'tǫlˌhus. Examples west of Braemar Castle, east of Invercauld Bridge, at the house Hamewith (formerly Inver Cottage) west of the Inver, at the Inver (see Knockanduie), at Coilacriech Inn (see Bridge Cottage, demolished), and west of Cambus o' May (see the Auld Toll House, demolished). Former toll houses for travellers on the Deeside road.

**The Tollies Park*** (U, 348914), ðɪ'tǫlez'park. A field on Aultonrea, next to Toldhu but on east side of Muick, includes the former field of Eilean Dearg Toll Dubh. In lower Glen Muick.

**Toll nan Con*** (3, D, 427963), hole of the dogs. Tolnygon (Dms). A hollow in a field at Inchmarnoch.

**The Toll Park*** (U, 405981), ðɪ'tǫl'park. A field next to a former toll house west of Cambus o' May.

**The Toll Park*** (F, 154921), as above. A field opposite the Old Toll House near Braemar.

**Toll Phiobair** (3, 255965), toll fīper (D), hole of pipers, it was once full of pipers, Couttses (D in A). Now Piper Hole (C), 'pɛipër'hol. A former group of houses north-west of Crathie, with Scutter Hole on the other side of the burn, often called just Piper and Scutter (A, C). See also Michie (1922). A

legend about a piper entering a cave and then disappearing is widespread in Britain and Ireland (Buchan 1979).

**(The) Tolmount** (OS, C, 210800), ðɪ'tǫlˌmʌunt, ðɪ'tǫlˌmʌnθ (U), in Gaelic speech n'dulmən (A), from An Dul Monadh (3), the Doll mounth or hill (i.e. leading to Glen Doll), Dul or Dol = a valley. The Toll Mount (I, R 13), referring to the hilltop as in OS. N dullmon, n dulla mon, tuilmean, n dullman (D). In Gaelic called An Dol-mon (Alexander 1942). As Alexander (1952) pointed out, this name is used for the pass from Callater over to Doll as well as for the hilltop as in the OS map (see Glen Doll Road).

**The Tolmount**, (C), as above. A name for the hill pass from Callater to Glen Doll (see above).

**An Tom*** (3, 286955), the hillock. The Toum (I). A field with a hillock, east of Crathie.

**The Tom** (OS, C, 342036), ðɪ'tǫm, from An Tom (3, OS 1869), the hillock. A low hill west of Morven.

**An Tom*** (3, U, 344975), as above, the hillock. Slightly to east of farm below.

**An Tom*** (3, U, west of 344975), as above, the hillock. Toum (I). Also Tom of Culsh, Tomb of Cults (Io 42). A former farm north-west of Bridge of Gairn.

**Tom a' Bhealaidh** (OS, 3, 229984, should be at 228980, 229984 is Muckle Broom Know), hillock of the broom. Tombal (R 5, 9), Tom beal (Da). On peat-mosses north-west of Crathie.

**Tom a' Bhothain Dhuibh*** (3, 358023), hillock of the black shiel. Tomabhoanduie (G 19), Tomavoanduie, Tomanbhoandui or hillock of the black sheill (Io 20). This is about the position of Tom Garchory (OS) which should be at 357015. Tom a' Bhothain Dhuibh, Tom Liath Beag and other hillocks about 360023 are now collectively called the Knobbies. South-west of Morven.

**Tom a' Bhranndair*** (3, probably 363014), hillock of the place of tangled roots. Tomabrander (G 19). South-west of Morven.

**Tom a' Chàirr** (5, F, 239984), tǫm'haˑr, hillock of the bog or rough ground. Tom achar (R 3, 5), toum achar (R 14). Tom-a-Charraigh (T 33), original notes (Iop) Tom-a-Charraidh, suggest Tom Charragh, hillock of rocks. Tomachard (Dil) probably same place. A hillock north-west of Crathie.

**The Tom a' Chairr Deer Fence*** (U, 236989), ðɪˌtǫm'haˑr'dir 'fęns. North-west of Crathie.

**The Tom a' Chairr Moss*** (F, 236987), ðɪˌtǫm'haˑr'mǫs. Moss of Toma har, Moss of Tom a char (R 5, 9). A peat-moss near above hillock.

**Tom a' Chait** (5, U, 155905), tǫm'hat, hillock of the cat, or a' Chata = of the sheep-cot. Toum-a-Chaat (I), Tom Chat (Mp). On Braemar Golf Course.

**Tom a' Chait*** (3, north-east of 155905). Tomachait (Opr 51), Tomchatt (Io 75). A former house beside the above hillock, on east side of road near Braemar. Buildings shown on an early map (I).

**Tom a' Challtuinn*** (3, 196932), hillock of the hazel. Tomachalding (Rli 23), Toum Chaultin (I), Tom chalduinn (R 14). A former farm north-east of Invercauld Bridge.

**Tom a' Channtachain*** (3, 228011), hillock of the little miry place. Tom-Haandachan, Tomachandachan, Toum Haunachan, Toum an dachan (R 3, 5, 12, 14). On peaty ground south of Corndavon Lodge.

**Tom a' Chatha** (OS, 278041), should be Tom a' Chadha (3), tama'ha (A), hillock of the pass. An Cadha is a way over the hills here from Gairn to Don, a route well known as the Ca, note also Cadha Clann Ailein. Tom chā, fight (Da) seems a less likely meaning. North-west of Gairnshiel.

**Tom a' Chuilinn*** (4, U, 112892), tǫm'hulən, hillock of the holly. Tommachullan (Im 3). See name below. A hillock at Corriemulzie.

**Tom a' Chuilinn** (4, 112892), meaning as above. Tomachulan (Me 21), Tom Chullainn, Tom-Chulann (D). Chuilein = of the pup is less likely because of Diack's phonetic tǝm χuLing indicating a double *nn* at the end. A former farm at Corriemulzie beside Baile an Tuim.

**Tom a' Chuir** (OS, 268930), should be Tom a' Chàirr (5, U), tǫmɐ'har, (tǝm'har (A)), hillock of the rough ground. Tom Charr (A). A rocky hill south of the distillery at Balmoral.

**Tom a' Chuir** (OS, 3, 196013), tǝma'hur (A), hillock of the turn. Above where River Gairn takes a sharp turn in direction near Loch Builg.

**Tom a' Ghille Ghoirid\*** (3, 270959), hillock of the short lad. Tom 'a ghille-ghaorid (R 3). North of Crathie.

**Toman a' Bhealaich\*** (3, 233987), little hillock of the pass. Toum-na-bhaillach (R 14). North-west of Crathie.

**Toman a' Bhothain** (3, C, 412033), ˌtamnǝ'von, little hillock of the bothy. Tomavoan (H), Tomnavone (OS 1869). A ruined house south-west of Logie Coldstone.

**Toman a' Bhreac-achaidh** (3, 242957, by elimination), little hillock of the speckled field. Tomnabrekachie (Mc 11). A former farm near Mains of Monaltrie west of Crathie.

**Toman a' Chorda\*** (3, 300828), little hillock of the sedge. Tom-na-chord (I). Above Loch Muick.

**Tom an Àilein** (3, U, 291943), tam'nalǝn, hillock of the meadow. Alexander recorded a Tam-nalan but referred it incorrectly to Tom na h-Ola. In a field south of Abergeldie.

**Toman a' Mhuilinn** (3, U, 416962), ˌtamnǝ'vulǝn, little hillock of the mill. Tomnavoolin (D). Beside the Mill of Bellamore at Inchmarnoch.

**Na Toman Dearga** (2, C, 042943), ðɪˌtoumɐn'djɛrǝks (anglicised plural), the red hillocks. An Toman Dearg (Sg). In lower Glen Derry.

**Na Toman Dearga\*** (3, C, 286892), ðɪˌtǫm'djɛrgs (anglicised plural), the red hillocks. Sandy hillocks in upper Glen Girnock.

**Tom an Fhuarain\*** (3, 246952), hillock of the well. Tomnuarain (R 3), Tomnuaran (Io 58). Tornuaran (Im 8), Tornuran (Io 58), Tornauran (G 25), suggest Torr an Fhuarain, with Torr (3) = hillock. A former farm north-east of the Inver.

**Tom an Imire** (3, C, 437990), ˌtamɐn'ëmër, often now ˌtame 'nëmër, hillock of the ridge. Tom an Iomair, Tammie Nimmer (A). Beside Loch Kinord.

**The Tom an Imire Road\*** (U, 435993), ðɪˌtamɐ'nëmër'rod. A track near Loch Kinord.

**Tom an Lagain** (OS, 3, U, 326943), ˌtamǝn'lakǝn, tam'lakën, hillock of the little hollow. In lower Glen Girnock.

**Tom Anthon** (OS, 099881), toum'jʌuntǝn, from Tom Eanntoin (3, C), Anton's hillock. Tom yaungdan, taum yauntan (D), Tom-Yownten (A). See Creag Anthoin. South-east of Inverey.

**Toman Tioram** (3), dry little hillock. Tommintichran, Tomtirram, Tommentichram (Io 37), Tomtchirom (Io 20). Near the Glas-choille north-east of Gairnshiel.

**Tom an t-Sagairt** (3, Λ, F, 958874), ιoum'dagërtʃ, (tɔmǝn'dagart (A)), hillock of the priest. In upper Glen Geldie.

**Tom an t-Sìdhein\*** (3, 241010), hillock of the fairy hill. Tom'n tiain, Tom dian rising know, Toum tian (R 3, 9, 14). Also An Sìdhean (3, F), ðɪ'ʃiǝn, the fairy hill. At Daldownie south-east of Corndavon Lodge.

**Tom an t-Sìdhein\*** (3, F, 148916), tǫm'tʃiǝn, tǫm'ʤiɐn (Sch), hillock of the fairy hill. Behind the Chapel at Braemar.

**Tom an t-Sùirn** (3, F, 332005), ˌtamǝn'tʌrn, hillock of the kiln. Tomanturn (Cr 42), Tominturn (H, Cg, OS 1869). Former farm near Lary in Glen Gairn.

**Tom an Uird\*** (3, 151932), hillock of the round hill. Tom Nourt (I). North of Braemar.

**Tom an Uird** (OS, 3, F, 270940), tam'nuǝrtʃ, hillock of the round hill. Tom nūrtsh (D), Tam-noortsh (A). At Easter Balmoral.

**Tom a' Phùir** (3, F, 358951), tǫm'fu·r, hillock of the pasture. Tomaphure (Io 20), Tom Fure (I), Tom Fuar, Knock Fuar (Mg). See Dallyfour. South-west of Ballater.

**The Tom a' Phuir Park\*** (U, 356953), ðɪˌtǫm'fu·r'park. A field at above hillock.

**Tom Bac Caorainn\*** (5, 330902), hillock of bank of a rowan tree. Tombacairn (In, Am). North of the Linn of Muick.

**Tom Bad a' Mhonaidh** (OS, 3, C, 287920), ˌtam,pɪt'funi, hillock of clump of the moor. Tombatmunie (In). South of Abergeldie Castle.

**Tom Badan Buidhe\*** (3, 264909), hillock of little yellow clump. Tompattenbuie (B). In Glen Gelder.

**Tom Bad nan Speireag** (3), hillock of clump of the sparrow-hawks. Tom-bad-nan-speireag (Gr). Near the former crofts at Wester Morven.

**Tom Bad Phùt\*** (3, 220921), hillock of clump of young grouse. Tompatfoot (B). Also the Iron Hillock (F), ðɪ'ɛirǝn'hëlëk. South-west of the Inver, formerly moorland but now under planted trees.

**Tombae** (OS, C, 432964), tam'be·, from Tom Beithe (3), hillock of birch. Tombea (H). A former farm, now a house, east of Inchmarnoch.

**The Tombae Brig\*** (U, 431965), ðɪˌtam'be'brɪg. A bridge near Inchmarnoch.

**The Tombae Haugh\*** (Dms, U, 435967), ðɪˌtam'be'ha·χ. Flat ground by Dee below Tombae, including the Needle Park. East of Inchmarnoch.

**The Tombae Road\*** (418928). The Tombay Road (Gler). A former cart track, now bulldozed, in Glen Tanar.

**The Tombae Park\*** (U, 433964), ðɪˌtam'be'park. Field east of Inchmarnoch.

**Tom Baidean\*** See Tom Cholzie.

**An Tom Bàn\*** (3, U, 321969), ðɪˌtǫm'ba·n, the white hillock. A hillock at Coilacriech.

**An Tom Bàn\*** (3, U), as above. A field at the above hillock.

**An Tom Bàn\*** (3, 400979), the white hillock. The Toum Bane (Io 62). On North Deeside Road north-east of Ballater.

**Tom Bàn\*** (3, 282952), white hillock. Toum Baan (I). A field east of Crathie.

**Tom Bàn\*** (3, 280954), white hillock. Toum baan (I). A field east of Crathie, near the above.

**Tom Bealaidh\*** (3, U, 343974), tam'bɛle, hillock of broom. North-west of Bridge of Gairn.

**Tom Bealaidh\*** (3, U, 344974), as above. Tombelly (Roy). A former farm near the above hillock.

**Tom Bealaidh\*** (3, U, 346970), as above, hillock of broom. Beside the former farm of Wester Tom Bealaidh west of Bridge of Gairn.

**Tom Bealaidh\*** (3, U, 351972), as above, hillock of broom. A hillock beside the former farm of Tom Bealaidh near Balgairn, west of Bridge of Gairn.

**Tom Bealaidh** (3, 351972), hillock of broom. Tombelly (Ri 33), Toumbyallie (I), daum-byall, tom-byall, broom hillock (D). A former farm beside the present Balgairn, west of Bridge of Gairn.

**Tom Bealaidh** (3, probably 254031), hillock of broom. Tom beal', broom hillock (D). North-west of Gairnshiel.

**Tom Bealaidh\*** (3, 235032), hillock of broom. Tom-Bell (R 3). North-east of Corndavon Lodge.

**Tom Bealaidh\*** (3, 228980), hillock of broom. Tombal (R 5, 9). Near Tom a' Bhealaidh north-west of Crathie.

**The Tom Bealaidh Park\*** (U, 343974), ðɪˌtamˈbɛ̣leˈpark. A former field, now overgrown with birches, near Bridge of Gairn.

**The Tom Bealaidh Park\*** (U, 351972), as above. A field west of Bridge of Gairn.

**Tom Beithe** (3, 445003), hillock of birch. Tombay (A). South of Loch Davan.

**Tom Beithe\*** (3, 152908), hillock of birch. Toum-Bea (I). South of Braemar.

**Tom Beithe** (3, C, 400977), tǫmˈbeˑ, tamˈbeˑ, hillock of birch. Tombay (A). North-east of Ballater.

**Tom Bhadaidh** (F, 247979), tǫmˈbadi, hillock of the little clump. Tom-Phadie, Tombadie, Toum Phadie (R 3, 5, 14), Tombady (D). Usually now Lower Tom Bhadaidh. Pairs with Upper Tom Bhadaidh, the two often collectively called the Tom Badaidhs, ðɪˌtǫmˈbadiz. North-west of Crathie.

**Tom Bheithe** (OS, 3, U, 298974), tǫmˈveˑ, hillock of birches. Toum Bae (I), Toum Beath (R 14). North-east of Crathie.

**Tom Bhodaich** (3, U, 287948), tamˈvǫtǝç, hillock of the old man. Tamvottach (A). South of Abergeldie.

**Tom Bhodaich\*** (3, F, 019884), toumˈvǫtiç (U), tamˈvǫtǝç (F), hillock of the old man. On the point of land at the junction of Geldie with Dee.

**Tom Bhodaich** (3, D, 263015), hillock of the old man. At the Sleach, north-west of Gairnshiel.

**The Tom Bhodaich Brig\*** See the Geldie Suspension Brig.

**The Tom Bhodaich Pool\*** (U, 019883), ðɪˌtamˈvǫtǝçˈpul. In Geldie.

**Tom Biorach\*** (3, 145847), sharp-pointed hillock. Toum Birrach (I). A pointed hillock beside the road in upper Glen Clunie.

**Tom Bothan\*** (3, 225934), hillock at a bothy. Toum Bohan (I). West of the Inver Inn.

**The Tom Brae\*** (U, 344977), ðɪˈtǫmˈbreˑ. A hill on an old road, now covered with vegetation, near Ballater.

**Tom Breac** (OS, 3, 222998), tamˈbrɛk (A), speckled hillock. South of Corndavon Lodge.

**Tom Breac** (3, F, 346918), tamˈbrɛk, speckled hillock. Tombreck (Ri 29), Tombreak (In, Am). A former farm in lower Glen Muick.

**The Tom Breac Park\*** (U, 347917), ðɪˌtamˈbrɛkˈpark. A field beside above farm.

**(The) Tombreck Burn** (OS, F, 336917), ðɪˌtamˈbrɛkˈbʌrn. Formerly Burn of Tombreck. Burne of tombreack (G 5). Near above places.

**Tom Buailteach** (OS, 3, 276937), classic form Tom Buailteich, hillock of summer hut, locally the Tom o the Buailteach (U), ðɪˈtǫmɪðɪˈbultʃǝç. South-west of Abergeldie.

**An Tom Buidhe\*** (2, C, 062899), ðɪˌtoumˈbui, tǫmˈbui, the yellow hillock. Tombuie (Im 3). North of the Linn of Dee.

**The Tom Buidhe Plantin\*** (F, 060900), ðɪˌtǫmˈbuiˈplantɪn. A plantation near the Linn of Dee.

**Tom Buitsich\*** (3, U, 298954), tǫmˈbutʃǝç, hillock of a witch. Below Creag nam Ban near Abergeldie, where a witch was once burned.

**Tom Cata\*** (5, F, 415966), tamˈkat, hillock of sheep-cot, possibly Cait = of a cat. Near Inchmarnoch.

**The Tom Cata Wuidie\*** (F, 415967), ðɪˌtamˈkatˈwɪdi, Scots Wuidie = little wood. Beside above hillock.

**Tom Cathaig\*** (4, 226937), hillock of jackdaw. Toum Kaick (I). West of the Inver.

**Tom Ceann na Coille\*** (3, 215925), hillock of end of the wood. Toum-Kaun-na-Kyle (I). Beside the road at the west end of a former moor stretching north-east to the Inver.

**Tom Chat\*** (5, 144861), hillock of cats, or a' Chata = of the sheep-cot. Toum Chaat (I). Above Fraser's Brig in Glen Clunie.

**Tom Chluaran\*** (2, U, east of 294963), tǫmˈçluǝrɐn, hillock of thistles. North-east of Crathie.

**Tom Chluig\*** (3, 348974), hillock of the bell. Toum Chloick (I). North-west of Bridge of Gairn.

**Tom Choirce\*** (3, 332000), hillock of oats. Toum Chork (I). East of Gairnshiel.

**Tom Cholzie** (OS, 352896), from Tom Choille (3), hillock of woods. Also Tom Baidein (4), hillock of small flock of sheep, less likely Tom Bad Chon, hillock of clump of dogs. Toum Batchon (I). East of the Linn of Muick.

**Tom Chuilein\*** (4, U, 163838), tǫmˈhulǝn, hillock of the cub. Chuilinn = of the holly is less likely as it is an exposed 740 m top with prostrate arctic-alpine vegetation. Toum Coulin (I). West of Loch Callater.

**Tom Coirce\*** (3, F, 308012), tamˈkǫrk, hillock of oats. A small hillock on a patch that has not been arable since the 1920s but probably had been at one time (WD). East of Gairnshiel.

**Tom Cruaidh** (3, U, probably 324007), tǫmˈkrui, hard hillock. Tomcruidh near Ardoch (D). East of Gairnshiel.

**Tom Cruaidh\*** (3, U, 279933), tamˈkrui, hard hillock. South-west of Abergeldie.

**Tom Cruinn\*** (3, 156935), round hillock. Toum Croin (I). North-west of Invercauld House.

**Tom Cruinn\*** (3, U, 395000), tamˈkrun, round hillock. North-west of Cambus o' May.

**Tom Dà Ghualainn\*** (3, 210996), hillock of two shoulders. Tom-da-Ghualin, Toum da ghaulin (R 3, 14). Between shoulders of two bigger hills east of Culardoch.

**Tom Darach\*** (3, U, 417970), tamˈdarɐχ, hillock at oak wood. North-west of Inchmarnoch.

**Tom Darach** (3, C, 417969), as above, hillock at oak wood. Tomdarroch (R 17, A). Two former houses beside above hillock.

**Tom Dearg\*** (3, 168911), red hillock. Toum Derg (I). East of Braemar.

**Tom Dearg Bad a' Chabair\*** (3), red hillock of clump of the pole. Tom derg bottachabre (G 5). Probably same as Na Toman Dearga. In Glen Girnock.

**Tom Dearg Coire na Cloiche\*** (3, probably 298903), red hillock of corrie of the stone. Tom derg cornacloich (G 5). In Glen Girnock.

**Tom Dubh** (OS, 3, F, 312045), tamˈduˑ, black hillock. Toum Du (I). Toum-dhu (R 14). North-east of Gairnshiel.

**Tom Dubh\*** (3, 289997), black hillock. Toum Du (I), Toum-dhu (R 14). South-west of Gairnshiel.

**Tom Dubh\*** (3, 341902), black hillock. Toumdu (I). A field in mid Glen Muick.

**An Tom Dubh\*** (2, F, 117896), ðɪˌtoumˈduˑ, the black hillock. East of Corriemulzie.

**(An) Tom Dubh** (3, OS 1869, C, 116895), as above, the black hillock. N daum du (D in A). Na tuim ghū (D) indicates Na Tuim Dhubha, the black hillocks. Former houses on north side of road east of Corriemulzie, beside above hillock.

**Tom Dubh Garbh-choire\*** (3, 358017), black hillock of rough corrie. Tom dow Garrochory (Io 20). Also the Black Hillock of Garbh-choire. The Black Hillock of Garrachorie, Blackhill of Garrchorie (G 19). Also the Know of Garbh-choire. The Know of Garrowchorie (Io 20), Scots Know = knoll. South-west of Morven.

**Tom Dubh na Rumaich\*** (4, north-east of 130918), black hillock of the bog. Tomdunaromich (Io 43a). A hillock west of Braemar.

**Tom Dubh Ruighe nan Cuileag\*** (3, 379022), black hillock of shiel of the flies. Tomdowrinagulick, Tomdowrinachulich (G 19), Tomdeurinnguilach, Tomdowrinaculick (Io 20). Also the Black Hillock of the Branndair. The Black Hillock of the Brander (Io 20). South of Morven.

**Tom Fada\*** (3, 148877), long hillock. Toum Fat (I). A long hillock in lower Glen Clunie.

**Tom Fhreumhaigh\*** (3, U, 411958), tam'rivi, hillock of the place with roots, see below. Tomreevie (Dms). South-west of Inchmarnoch.

**Tom Fhreumhaigh** (3, F, north-west of 393988), tǫm'rivi, tam 'rivi, hillock of the place with roots, note Cargacreevy in Ireland (J). Tamreevie (D). Also Loudon's Hillock (F), 'lʌudǝnz'hëlëk, after a former shooter. Up the Culsten Burn north-east of Ballater.

**Tom Fhreumhaigh's Cairn\*** (F, north-west of 393988), tam'riviz 'kjarn. On top of the above hillock.

**Tom Fuar\*** (3, U, north-east of 341010), tǫm'fuǝr, cold hillock. On an exposed corner south of Morven Lodge.

**The Tom Fuar Prop\*** (U, north-east of 341010), ðɪˌtǫm'fuǝr 'prǫp. A cairn on a hillock south of Morven Lodge.

**Tom Gainmheine** (3, 158923, by elimination), hillock of sandy beach. Tom Ghainmheine (Gr). Beside Dee, down from Creag Choinnich (Gr). Tom Ghainmhaine or hill of Peace, behind the Chapel at Braemar (Ta), but this is unreliable as the place is locally well known as Tom an t-Sidhein and in any case this book was largely a work of plagiarism based on Grant.

**Tom Garchory** (OS, F, 360023, should be at 357015, 360023 is the Knobbies), tam'garçǝre, from Tom Garbh-choire (3), hillock of rough corrie. Hillocks south-west of Morven.

**Tom Ghealtaidh\*** (6, 144858), hillock of the ? white place. Toum Yaltie (I). North of the ruined house of Coireyaltie in Glen Clunie.

**Tom Giubhais\*** (3, 167868), hillock of fir. Toum Guish (I). In lower Glen Callater.

**(The) Tom Glady Wood** (OS, F, 432022), ðɪˌtam'gledi'wɪd, from Tom Gleadaidh (below), Glady is the wrong sound. Also the Kirkton Wuidie (C), ðɪ'kërktǝn'wɪdi; the Kirkton is a house to the east, outside the area covered in this book.

**Tom Gleadaidh** (3, F, 432022), tam'gledi, hillock of kite, Scots Gled = kite, so possibly Gleddie = little kite, or else Gleadaidh borrowed into local Gaelic. Meaning not known locally now. A kite in Upper Deeside was a Glead (Sg). Tam Gleddie (A). A sandy hillock south of Logie Coldstone.

**Tomidhu** (OS, 273950), locally the Tomidhus (C), ðɪˌtame'duz, from Na Toman Dhubha or Na Tuim Dhubha (3), the black hillocks. Tomyndow (Mc 4), Tomyadow, Tomidhues, Tomadows, (Ri 3, 23a, 34a), Tommiedows (I), Tomidhu (R 14), Tomandubha (OS 1869), na toman dū, na tuim ghū (D). A farm east of Crathie, beside heathery hillocks with birch trees. One of the hillocks was removed in 1979 to get gravel for road-widening.

**Tomidhu Cottage\*** Tomydoos Cottage (Ce 5). Former habitation beside Tomidhu near Crathie.

**Tomidhu Croft\*** Tomydoos Croft (Ce 5). Former habitation beside Tomidhu near Crathie.

**The Tomidhus Wuid\*** (C, 271947), ðɪˌtame'duz'wɪd. Wood of the Tommie Dows (I). Also the Birks (U), ðɪ'bërks, Scots = birches. A birch wood beside the above farm.

**Tomintoul** (OS, C, 146906), ˌtamǝn'tʌul, from Tom an t-Sabhail (2), tǫm'ḍaul (Sch), hillock of the barn. Tomin toul (Fa), Tomintowill (Ri 3), Tom doul, taum-daul (D). Tomintoul was the highest of a group of crofts on Morrone above Braemar, at 144905, but the name was also used collectively for the whole group. The croft at Tomintoul (OS) was the Mains o Tomintoul (C), ðɪ'menzɐˌtamǝn'tʌul, the biggest of the crofts. Mains of Tomintoul (Ha). The Townland of Tomintoul (S).

**Tom Lèanag** (3, 314034), hillock of little meadows. Toum Lyaunack (I), Toum Lieanack (R 14), Tom Launach (D). Above former farmland at Glenfenzie.

**Tom Leys\*** See Tom Odhar.

**An Tom Liath\*** (2, F, 110895), ðɪˌtoum'liɐ, the grey hillock. A hillock west of the bridge at Corriemulzie.

**(An) Tom Liath** (3, U, 110894), as above, the grey hillock. Tomlea (Me 21, OS 1869), n daum lia (D). Farm of Tomlice at Corriemulzie (Gr) might suggest Tom Lise, hillock of a garden. A former farm beside the above hillock.

**An Tom Liath\*** (2, U, north-west of 083893), as above, the grey hillock. On south side of road at Little Inverey.

**Tom Liath\*** (3, 083893), grey hillock. At Inverey at Tomliath (Cr 45). A former habitation on the above hillock at Little Inverey.

**Tom Liath** (OS, 3, U, 329035), tǫm'liɐ, grey hillock. North-west of Morven Lodge.

**An Tom Liath\*** (3, 366039), the grey hillock. Tomlea (G 33), the Tomlea (Io 20). On Morven, west of the top.

**Tom Liath Beag\*** (3, 363022), the little grey hillock. Tomleabeg (G 19, Io 20). South-west of Morven.

**Tom Liath Mór\*** (3, 365033), the big grey hillock. Tomleamore (Io 20). South-west of Morven.

**Tom Loisgte\*** (3, U, 176872), tǫm'loiʃk, burnt hillock. Above lower Glen Callater, beside Creag Loisgte.

**Tom Mallachd Mathair\*** (3, 272951), hillock of mother's curse. Toum-Malachk-Mahar (I). Also the Gallow Hill (Brow). Beside Tomidhu east of Crathie.

**Tom Meann** (OS, 356974), from Tom nam Meann (3), hillock of the kids, see under that name. Tom-yan (D). Also the Castle-hill (Sm), presumably after the nearby Abergairn Castle. A hillock north-east of Bridge of Gairn.

**The Tom Meann Parks\*** (U, 358971 and 358970), ðɪ'tǫm'min 'parks. Two fields named after the recent house of Tom Meann, north one also the Baile an Lochain Park. East of Bridge of Gairn.

**Tom Mhuilinn\*** (3, 161929), hillock of the mill. Toum Vullun (I). Beside Milltoun of Invercauld, north-west of Invercauld House.

**The Tommie\*** See the Tom o Loinn Mhor.

**Tom Mór** (OS, 3, 280930), big hillock. Tom More (In). South-west of Abergeldie Castle.

**(An) Tom Mór** (OS, 2, F, 318963), ðɪˌtǫm'mo·r, the big hillock. West of the foot of Glen Girnock.

**Tom Muilinn\*** (3, 145860), hillock of a mill. Toum Moulin (I). By the main road south of Fraser's Brig in Glen Clunie.

**Tom na Buaile\*** (3, 268958), hillock of the fold. Tom na Buaile (R 3), Tom-na-puil (I). North of Crathie.

**Tom na Buaile\*** (3, north of 241944), hillock of the fold. Tom 'na buaile (R 3). A former farm north-east of the Inver.

**Tom na Ciste\*** (3, 154890), hillock of the coffin. Tomnikisht, Tomnikist (Cr 18, 27), Tomnakiest (Rli 23). A former house near the Coldrach in lower Glen Clunie.

**Tom na Croiche** (OS, 3, A, F, 280945), ˌtamnɐ'krɔiç, hillock of the gallows. Also the Hangman's Hillock (U), ðɪ'haŋmǝnz 'hëlëk. Also Gallows Hill (S). South-west of Abergeldie Castle.

**Tom na Cùlaige\*** (3, 269961), hillock of the sod. Tom-na-culaig (R 3). North of Crathie.

**Tom na Cùlaige** (3, 145903), hillock of the sod. Toum-na-Cualich (I), Tom na culak, sod hillock (D). On Morrone south of Braemar.

**Tom na Feòraich** (4, F, 335999), ˌtǫmnɐ'fjɔrɪç, hillock of the grassy place. Sometimes Tom na Feòraig, ˌtǫmnɐ'fjɔrɪk (U). Tomnafiorac (Dil). Also the Fairies' Hillock (Ne). At Lary in Glen Gairn.

**Tom na Gaoithe*** (3, U, 143905), ˌtɔmnɐ'gui, hillock of the wind. The hillock with the indicator above Woodhill, south-west of Braemar.

**Tom na h-Aon Chraoibhe** (3, U, 136905), ˌtɔmnɐ'hɛnəçri, hillock of the one tree. Tom na Hennachri (A), Tom na h-aon chraoibh (D in A). South-west of Braemar.

**Tom na h-Eileirige*** (3, 158914), hillock of the deer-trap. Toum-na-helrick (I). East of Braemar.

**Tom na h-Eilrig** (OS, 3, U, 182966), ˌtɔmnɐ'hɛlrɪk, from Tom na h-Eileirige (3), hillock of the deer-trap. Toum-na-elrick (I). North of Invercauld.

**Tom na h-Òighe*** (3, 379947), hillock of the maiden. Tom na hoy (I), Toun-na-noig (R 16) but many spelling errors on this map. A hillock with a cairn south-east of Ballater.

**Tom na h-Ola** (OS, 276927), should be Tom na h-Olla (3, U), ˌtɔmnɐ'houl, hillock of the wool, Ola = of oil. Tomnyhoul (In), Tom na h-Olainn (OS 1869). Diack (in A) recorded a Tom na holnn, wool, suggesting Tom na h-Olainn, and Alexander referred this to Tom na h-Ola, but Alexander also recorded Tam-nalan himself and mistakenly referred it to Tom na h-Ola, whereas there is a Tom an Ailein further east. Diack's pronunciation certainly suggests the original OS spelling, but the current pronunciation suggests that the current OS form is more correct.

**Tomnakeist** (OS, Mc, C, 400981), ˌtamnə'kist, from Tom na Ciste (3), hillock of the coffin. Tomnakeisten (Pb), Tomnakist (R 4). An old graveyard was found here, with stone coffins (M). A farm north-east of Ballater.

**The Tomnakeist Burn** (C, 401981), ðɪˌtamnə'kist'bʌrn. The Burn of Tomnakiest (Cj 2, 250). Lower part of Culsten Burn north-east of Ballater.

**Tomnakeist Cottage*** See Newton Cottage.

**The Tomnakeist Loch*** (F, 394984), ðɪˌtamnə'kist'lɔχ. Formerly the Loch of Tomnakeist (Io 20). North-east of Ballater.

**Tomnakeist Quarries*** See Cambus Quarries.

**Tom na Làirige*** (3), hillock of the hill pass. Tomnalaraig (Opr 24a). Former habitation in Braemar parish, probably near Coirenalarig in Glen Clunie.

**Tom na Loinne*** (3, U, 140909), ˌtɔmnɐ'lɔin, hillock of the enclosure. Tom-na-loine (Md 8, 10). West of Braemar.

**The Tom na Loinne Reservoir*** (140908), Tom-na-loine Reservoir (Md 8, 10). Reservoir for the Braemar water supply.

**Tom nam Buachaillean** (3, F, 357918), ˌtamnə'baχlən, hillock of the herdsmen, with Buachaillean probably a variant genitive plural. Toum na buachlin (I), Tomnabyachlan or byuchlan (D). A former farm in lower Glen Muick.

**Tom nam Fiann*** (5, C, 255919), ˌtɔmnɐ'viɐn, hillock of the crowberries, or of the warriors or Fingalians. Tomnavean (B). In lower Glen Gelder.

**Tom nam Meann*** (3, 128817), hillock of the kids (see Dail Tom nam Meann). Tomnamean (Ra 2). Up the Baddoch.

**Tom nam Meann** (3, 356974), hillock of the kids. Tomnaman (Sh), Tomnamean (Ab 19), Tomean (Io 8), Tomain (G 20, Io 33). A former farm near Bridge of Gairn, named after a nearby hillock Tom Meann (OS).

**Tomnamoine** (OS, C, 034894), ˌtɔmnə'mɔn, ˌtɔmnɐ'mɔn (U), from Tom na Mòine (3), hillock of the peat-moss. Tomnamoun (Io 17), Thomnamoun (Go), Tom moin (Fa), Tomnimuin, Tomnimune (Cr 31, 34). A former farm west of the Linn of Dee.

**Tom na Mòine*** (3, U), as above. Hillock beside above farm, on south side of road.

**Tom na Mòine*** (3, 248016), hillock of the peat-moss. Tom-na-moine, Tom na moin (R 3, 14). East of Corndavon Lodge.

**Tom na Mòine** (3, 253969), hillock of the peat-moss.

Tomnamoun (Io 74), Tom-na-maor (R 3), Tomnamone or Tomnamoss (D). North-west of Crathie.

**The Tomnamoine Plantin*** (F, 030895), ðɪˌtɔmnə'mɔn'plantɪn. A plantation in Glen Dee.

**Tom nan Ceap*** (3, 154901), hillock of the blocks. Tomnakeip, Tomnakep, Tomnakip (Io 43a). A hillock south of Braemar.

**Tom nan Coileach*** (3, F, 301906), ˌtamnɐ'kɔləç, hillock of the cocks (i.e. grouse cocks). South of Bovaglie in upper Glen Girnock.

**Tom nan Critheann*** (3, 183937), hillock of the aspens. Toum na Crian (I). North-east of Invercauld House.

**Tom nan Rabhadh** (3, F, 152907), ˌtamnən'rʌu, hillock of the warnings. Tomnaraw (Rli 19), Tomniraw (Fa), Tomninraw, Tamninraw (Cr 2, 3), Tomnaramh (Io 53), Touman-Rau (I), Toumanramh (R 14), Tomnanrau, warning (D). A former farm near Braemar, on a hillock giving a very good view up Glen Clunie.

**Tom nan Rabhadh** (3, U, 152907), as above. Tom-nan-Rabhadh, warning knoll, pronounced Tom nan-Raoo, on this knoll, an outpost was formerly kept to warn of a hostile force from the south (Mp). At Braemar.

**Tom nan Sealgair*** (3, probably c. 090899), hillock of the hunters. Tom ne shallger (Fa), Tomnishallakar (Cr 20). A former farm a little above Mar Lodge, ruins presumably cleared for road making.

**Tom nan Sealgair*** (3, 142844), hillock of the hunters. Tomna Shallagar (Rli 19), Toum-na-Shalagran (I) suggests Sealgairean, a variant genitive plural. A hillock and the name of a former grazing (presumably at the hillock) in upper Glen Clunie.

**Tom nan Uan*** (3, probably south of 365017), hillock of the lambs. Park of Achaw and Tomnanuan (Io 64). South of Morven.

**Tom na Riabhaig*** (3, 176848), hillock of the lark. Toum-na Riag (R 13). North of Loch Callater.

**Tom na Saobhaidhe*** (3, U, 991861), ˌtoumnɐ'sʊvi, hillock of the fox's den. North-west of Bynack Lodge.

**Tom na Seilg*** (3, 364945), hillock of the hunt. Toum-na-Shallack (I). A former field east of a hillock in lower Glen Muick, now the East Lodge Park (F), ðɪ'ist'lɔʤ'park.

**Tomnavey** (OS, C, 309011), ˌtamnə'vɛiˑ, from Tom nam Fiadh (3), hillock of the deer. Tomnafeu (Pb), Tomnafeadh (Io 52), Tomnanfiagh, Tomnafiagh (Cr 39), Tomnafey (Ri 37), Toumnavey (I), Toum-na-feidh (R 14), tom na vēi (D), tom na biu (D in A). A former farm east of Gairnshiel.

**The Tomnavey Burn*** (C, 309015), ðɪˌtamnə'vɛi'bʌrn. East of Gairnshiel.

**Tom Odhar** (OS, 3, 262036), dun hillock. Toum Our (I, R 14). Also now Tom Leys (U), tam'lɛiz, after a Charlie Leys who once lived at the nearby Easter Sleach. North-west of Gairnshiel.

**Tom Odhar*** (3, 264987), dun hillock. Toum Our (I), Toum Our (R 12). North of Crathie.

**Tom Odhar*** (3, 280027), dun hillock. Toum Our (I, R 14). North-west of Gairnshiel.

**Tom Odhar*** (3, 213970), dun hillock. Toum Our (I). North-west of the Inver.

**Tom Odhar*** (3, 215980), dun hillock. Tom our (R 3). North-west of the Inver.

**Tom Odhar na Seilg*** (3, 221971), dun hillock of the hunt. Tom our na seilg, Tom-our-na-seilg (R 3, 14). North-west of the Inver.

**(The) Tom of Balnoe** (OS, 355907), usually just the Tom locally (F), ðɪ'tɔm, from An Tom (3), the hillock. In mid Glen Muick.

**Tom of Culsh*** See An Tom.

**The Tom o Loinn Mhor** (U, 361925), ðɪˈtǫmɐˌlǫnˈmoˑr, from Tom (3) = hillock. Also was the Tom of Blar Charraid. The Toum of Blacharánge (I). Also the Tommie or An Tomaidh, ðɪˈtǫme, ðɪˈtame (U), the little hillock. Also now the Little Hill (U), ðɪˈlëtəlˈhël. In lower Glen Muick.

**Tom Phìobair** (3, D, 256020), piper's hillock. At the Sleach north-west of Gairnshiel.

**Tom Pighe*** (3, 196957), hillock of jackdaw. Toum Pee (I). In Glen Feardar.

**Tom Reachdan*** (3, C, 149913), tǫmˈrëçtən, hillock of laws, with variant genitive plural, possibly where laws and legal proclamations were made. Tom-richton (Md 6). Tomenrichton (Vr 4) suggests Toman = little hillock. In Braemar. Md 6 and Vr 4 refer to a house.

**The Tom Reachdan Wuid*** (C, 149913), ðɪˌtǫmˈrëçtənˈwɪd. A wood at the above hillock.

**Tom Réite*** (3, 172928), hillock of agreement. Toum Raid (R 7). Near Invercauld.

**An Tom Réite*** (3, 172929), the agreement hillock, with Réite adjectival. Tomraid (Fa), Dumbrytt, Dŭmbrytt (Cr 7, 17–18). A former house beside above hillock.

**Tom Riabhach*** (3, 219941), brindled hillock. Toum Riach (I). In a field west of the Inver.

**Tom Ruighe an Staing*** (3, U, 284925), ˌtǫmɐˌrənˈstɪŋk, hillock of cattle-run of the ditch. Gaelic Staing was pronounced stengk (Da). South-west of Abergeldie.

**Tom Ruighe Chailleach*** (3, 163864), hillock of cattle-run or shiel of old women. Toum-ri-halich (I). In lower Glen Callater.

**Tom Sgalan nan Sasunnach*** (3, 160921), hillock of prop of the Englishmen. Toum Scalan n sasnich (R 7). A cairn stands here, erected by the last of the English garrison at the nearby Braemar Castle.

**Tom Sglèata*** (3, U, 146914), tǫmˈskletʃ, hillock of slate. On Inverey road at Braemar.

**Tom Sgonnach Beag*** (name i) (3, 242970, south one), little lumpish hillock. Little Tom Sconnach, Little Tamsconach, Tom Sconach Bheg (R 3, 5 & 9, 14). Locations for this name and the next one:—R 3499 gives (ii) as the north one, and R 3696 gives (i) as the south one, but R 3647 and 3512 give (ii) as the south one and (i) as the north one. This confusion is understandable, as the south one, though having a summit not so high as the north one, is much bigger in form. Diack noted Tam-seunachs, Little and Muckle, and Alexander gave Tom Shinnich or fox hillock (i.e. Tom Sionnaich). At any rate, the name Tom Sgonnach is still known locally (U), tǫm ˈskǫnɐχ, and obviously fits the old maps. Two hillocks north-west of Crathie.

**Tom Sgonnach Mór*** (name ii) (3, 241972, north one), big lumpish hillock. Meikle Tom Sconnach, Mickle Tamsconach, Muckle Tamsconach, Toum schonach Mhoir (R 3, 5, 9, 14). See above name.

**Tom Sìth*** (3, F, 412964), tamˈʃiˑ, hillock of a fairy. Tom Shee (Dms). West of Inchmarnoch.

**Tom Sròineach*** (3, 251984), projecting hillock (i.e. nose-like, from Sròn = a nose). Tom Stronach (R 3). North of Crathie.

**Tom Tighearn** (3), hillock of a proprietor. Tamtshern (D), in a list of places in the Wester Morven–Gairnshiel area.

**Tom Tioram*** (3, 194893), dry hillock. Toum Tiram (R 7). In Glen Beg, Ballochbuie Forest.

**Tom Ullachie** (OS, 343946), tǫmˈjulǝci, tamˈjulǝçi, from Tom Iolachaidh (3, F), hillock of shouting. Tom ʒeullachie (G 5). South-west of Ballater.

**The Tom Wuid*** (C, 343035), ðɪˈtǫmˈwɪd. A wood at Wester Morven.

**The Tom Wuid*** (U, 344976), as above. A wood north-west of Bridge of Gairn.

**An Tòn Crom*** (3, 157887), the curved bottom-land. Don Croum (I), with Don indicating the definite article. A formerly curved piece of farmland south of Braemar, now part of a bigger field.

**An Tòn Fàil*** (3, 155896), the fold bottom-land, with Fail used in an adjectival sense. Don Fail (I), with Don indicating the definite article. A former field south of Braemar.

**An Tòn Gorm*** (3, 153900), the green bottom-land. Don Goram (I). A former field, now part of Braemar Golf Course.

**The Tongue o the Glas Allt*** (C, 252846), ðɪˈtʌŋɪðɪˈglasəlt. The Tongue (In). A tongue of ground between two burns on Lochnagar.

**The Ton House*** See Ruigh nan Clach.

**Tonnagaoithe** (OS, C, 028892), ˌtǫnɐˈgui, from Tòn na Gaoithe (2), bottom of the wind, probably bottom-land but translated to us as 'winny airse', Scots for windy arse. Note Thundergay in Arran and several other such examples from Gaelic Scotland. Tonna-gow (Cr 33), Tongui (Roy), Tonghaoith (Crg 10). A former farm west of the Linn of Dee.

**Tòn Uillt*** (3, 278952), bottom-land of a burn. Ton Uilt (I). A flat field by a burn east of Crathie.

**The Top Drive*** (U, 346948), ðɪˈtǫpˈdraev. A road west of Ballater.

**The Top Jetty*** (F, west of 379965), ðɪˈtǫpˈdʒete. A former jetty for fishing, now largely washed away. North-east of Ballater.

**The Top Jetty Puil*** (F, 379965), ðɪˈtǫpˈdʒeteˈpil. A pool in Dee, part of the Bumbee Puil. North-east of Ballater.

**Top of Coire Lochan nan Searrach*** (3, 200050), top of corrie of tarn of the colts. Top of Corry Lochan a Sharrach (R 2a). The whole ridge on the watershed from Carn Ulie to Geal Charn Mor east of Loch Builg. Note Coire an Luichan Shalaich (OS) to the north-west, outside the area covered in this book. This OS version seems unlikely, as Luich is only rarely (Dw) a genitive of Loch, and Sharroch appears in other names there (R 2a).

**Top of Coire Ruairidh*** See North Top.

**Top of Liath-choire Mhor*** (162978). Top of Leachorrymore (Io 63). North of Invercauld.

**The Top of Lochnagar*** See Lochnagar.

**Torbeg** (OS, I, R 14, C, 324001), tǫrˈbęg, from An Torr Beag (3), the little hillock. Torrbegg, Toirbegg (Ri 24, 34), n dor peg (D). In lower Glen Gairn.

**The Torbeg Brae** (Afr, C, 322002), ðɪˌtǫrˈbęgˈbreˑ. East of Gairnshiel.

**The Torbeg Burn*** See East Milton Burn.

**Torgalter** (OS, I, C, 286957), tǫrˈgaltër, from Torr a' Ghealtair (4), hillock of the timid fellow, possibly Ghealadair = of the bleacher. Torigalter (Roy), Torghealter (Io 52), Torogalter, Torragalter, Toragalter, Torgalter (Ri 5, 21, 22, 27), Tornagalter (Asr), Torryaltie (Rli 23), Tor-yalter (short *a*, Invergelder, innir-yālter, has long *a* (D)). A former farm east of Crathie, now a house.

**The Torgalter Brig*** (F, 288955), ðɪˌtǫrˈgaltërˈbrɪg. A bridge east of Crathie.

**(The) Torgalter Burn** (OS, F, 286960), ðɪˌtǫrˈgaltërˈbʌrn. Burn of Torgalter (I). Near Torgalter.

**Tornauran** (OS, C, 282942), tǫrˈnuəran, from Torr an Fhuarain (2, JB), tǫrṇˈuɐrən, hillock of the well. Torrenuarn (Crg 18), Tornywarron (In, Am). A house south-west of Abergeldie.

**(The) Torphantrick Wood** (OS, F, 411976), should be the Ruighe Bhantraich Wuid (C), ðɪˌrɪˈfantrɪçˈwɪd. The wood takes its name from the former farm of Ruighe Bhantraich south of Cambus o' May, but a few people incorrectly call the farm trəˈfantrɪç (U), and one old map (R 17) gives it as

Trafantrach. It is therefore not surprising that this incorrect version of the farm name crops up in the name for the wood. However, the most knowledgeable local informants gave the farm as rɪˈfantrɪç (which fits nearly all the old records), and the wood as ðɪˌrɪˈfantrɪçˈwɪd.

**An Torr** (3, 109876), the hillock. An tor (D). A hillock south of Corriemulzie.

**Torraidh Cithe*** (4, F, 415957), ˌtɔreˈkiˑ, little hillock of mist. Torrykee (Dms). South-west of Inchmarnoch.

**Torraidh Sìol*** (4, U, 435969), ˌtɔrəˈʃil, little hillock of seed or spawn. A field north-east of Inchmarnoch, beside Dee.

**(The) Torran** (OS, C, 307015), ðɪˈtɔrɐn, from An Torran (2), the little hillock. The Torrine (Io 8), Torran (Cr 2, I, R 14), n dorran (D). A former farm north-east of Gairnshiel.

**Torr an Àilein*** (3, north-west of 297960, by elimination), hillock of the green. Tornalan (Io 77, Ce 1). A former house at the Micras east of Crathie.

**Torran Beithe*** (3, 394979), little hillock of birch. Turranbay (R 4). At Tullich.

**The Torran Birks*** (F, 309017), ðɪˈtɔrɐnˈbĕrks. A birch wood north-east of Gairnshiel.

**The Torran Burn** (Af, C, 308012), ðɪˈtɔrɐnˈbʌrn. East of Gairnshiel.

**Torran Cruinn*** (3, south-west of 265962), little round hillock. Torancroin (R 6a). A former farm north of Crathie.

**The Torran Eilean*** See Eilean Gaineamhach.

**Torr an Fhraoich** (3, 168930, 170929, and 171929), hillock of the heather. Tornrich (Fa), Torranruich, Torrinruich (Cr 23, 32). A former farm near Invercauld House.

**Torran Uaraig*** (5, north-east of 422958), Torran = little hillock, Uaraig or Uaraich from Uar = water, heavy shower. Tornwarrach (Dms before 1800), Tornawarrack (Dms 15), Torwarrack, Torwarrach (Dms). Former farm on slope south-east of Ballaterach at Inchmarnoch.

**Torr Beag** (3, 252956), little hillock. Torbeg (S 8, R 3, 6a, OS 1869). Alexander gives Torbeg for Braemar parish, which is probably this. A former farm west of Crathie.

**Torr Beag*** (3, F, 259960 and 259961), tɔrˈbeg. Two fields on the farm of Bush north-west of Crathie.

**Torr Darach*** (U, north of 345973), tɔrˈdarɐχ, hillock at oak wood. North-west of Bridge of Gairn.

**Torr Darach** (3, C, 346973), as above. Tordarrach (I), Torandarroch (OS 1904). Alexander gives Tornadarroch for Torr nan darach. A former farm north-west of the Bridge of Gairn.

**The Torr Darach Brae*** (F, south of 347971), ðɪˌtɔrˈdarɐχˈbreˑ. A hill on an old road on north side of main road west of Bridge of Gairn.

**The Torr Darach Park*** (U, 346974), ðɪˌtɔrˈdarɐχˈpark. A field north-west of Bridge of Gairn.

**Torr Dubh*** (3, U, north-east of 424958), tɔrˈduˑ, black hillock. Near Inchmarnoch.

**Torr Dubh*** (3, U, 423958), as above. A former farm near Inchmarnoch (see Ettrick Croft).

**The Torr Dubh Parks*** (U, 424959), ðɪˌtɔrˈduˑparks. Three steep fields at Inchmarnoch including Lower and Upper Torr Dubh.

**Torr na Creige*** (3, 414957), hillock of the rock, often shortened to Torrnaidh (3), Torny (Dms). Tornacraig (Rli 20, Dms). A place with former houses and cultivation, now a wood south-west of Inchmarnoch. The name Tornacraig was recently given to a house renovation at the former steading at Mill of Bellamore.

**Torr na Loinne*** (3, 389971), hillock of the enclosure. Turnaling (R 4). On farmland at Tullich.

**Torr nam Fiann** (5, 127893), hillock of the crowberries, or of the warriors or Fingalians. Tor na viang (D). On Morrone east of Corriemulzie.

**Torr nam Mult*** (3, 300963), hillock of the wethers. Torna-mult (I). East of Crathie.

**Torr nam Preas*** (3, F, 427962), ˌtɔrnɐˈbrĕs, hillock of the copses. A field east of Inchmarnoch.

**Torr nan Caorach*** (3, 247951), hillock of the sheep. Tornankirach (Cr 42), Tornagerach (R 3), Torningurach (Im 8), Tornacaorach (Cpb 6), Tornancaorach (Opr 50), Tornagirroch (OS 1869). A former farm west of Crathie.

**Torr nan Gamhainn** (4, U, probably 347983), ˌtɔrnɐˈgʌu.ən, hillock of the stirks. Tarnagowne (Bul), Torragawane (Ab 8), Tornagawn (G 8). A former farm in lower Glen Gairn.

**The Tothir Way** (Wy 71), Scots Tot, tothir = small. An old route used by soldiers at the Battle of Culblean.

**Tounheid*** (U, 436964), tunˈhid, Scots = town head. A field east of Inchmarnoch.

**Townhead** (B, S 25, Er, C, 264940), as above. A former farm at Balmoral, now houses.

**Townhead** (Gler, A 273, 411915), Townhead of Etnach (Gler). The highest of several former crofts in upper Glen Tanar.

**The Townland of Tomintoul** See Tomintoul.

**The Trap*** (F, 086885), ðɪˈtrap, English translation; informants could not remember the Gaelic. A narrow cascade between rocks on Ey Burn south of Inverey.

**The Trenchin*** (U, 307016), ðɪˈtrɛnʃɪn, Scots = trenching. A field north-east of Gairnshiel.

**The Trenchin*** (U, 347923), as above. A field in mid Glen Muick.

**The Trochie Puil** (P, C, 450978), ðɪˈtroχeˈpil, ? Scots = small trough. Trachie (Sc) is incorrect. A pool in Dee west of the bridge at Dinnet.

**Trochietroddles*** (C, 430023), usually ˌtroχeˈtrɔdəlz, ˌtroχe ˈtɔdəlz from one informant. Scots Trochie = small trough and Troddle, used of a stream, to glide gently, would fit the area nearby. Also Culblean Cottage (U), kəlˈblinˈkɔtədʒ. A former house south-west of Logie Coldstone.

**An Tuil-bhinn** (4, U, 139900), nˈtulˌvin, nˈtuləvin, the melodious torrent. Tuilvien, melodious torrent (Mp), Tuilbhinn (D in Rc 39, 136), n duilivinn (Da). A burn south-west of Braemar.

**Na Tuim Dhubha** See (An) Tom Dubh.

**The Tuips*** (C, 400031), ðɪˈtips, possibly Scots Tuip = ram, teeps were rams to former Glen Gairn folk (Dil), or Gaelic Tioba = heap. Note Tips of Corsemaul (OS), a hilltop west of Huntly, is pronounced ˈtips. A rough slope west of Logie Coldstone.

**Tulach an Tuirc** (3, C, north-east of 318007), ˌtulɐχɐnˈduɐrk, hillock of the boar. Tullichandoorick (A). A former cottage east of Gairnshiel.

**Tulach an Tuirc*** (3, U, south-east of 318008), as above. A hillock east of Gairnshiel.

**Tulach Chòcaire** (3, C), təlˈfogĕr, dalˈfugĕr, hillock of the cook. Gaelic pronunciation Tilhògar (M). Note Easter Tulach Chocaire and Wester Tulach Chocaire. Tullochwhoker (Aj) in 1666, Tulloquhocker, Tulloquhocher (Ap), Tullochogor (Crg 7, Rli 4), Tillyfoker (Io 34), Tulloch Choguir (S 7, separated by a comma but obviously this one name), Dalfouger (In), Tilfogar (A), Tulach chogair (D in A). Diack noted that Tullochagore was a croft in Glen Gelder but we suspect this was an error for Tulach Chocaire. Two former farms south-east of Balmoral.

**The Tulach Chocaire Burn*** (F, 271933), ðɪˌtəlˈfogĕrˈbʌrn. Near Balmoral.

**Tulach Folmaidh*** (6, U, north of 417959), təlˈfolme, təl sound from Tulach (3) = hillock (N 147). Folmaidh ? from Cholmaich of the dove-cot, or Cholm = of Colm, with *cho*

The Place Names of Upper Deeside

becoming *fo* as occurs fairly often in Deeside. Near Inchmarnoch.

**Tullich** (C), 'tʌləç, from Tulach (3), hillock. In Gaelic speech was tullich, not tūllach (D). Old forms Tullach naclethe (Dms 1) in 1284, Tula in marr, Tuluch, Tulynathtlayk, Tulynathelath, Tullinathlak (A), obviously referring to St Nathalan, i.e. Gaelic Tulach Nachlag (3), hillock of Nathalan. A general name for an area north-east of Ballater, between Eastfield of Monaltrie and Tomnakeist, centred on Tullich Kirk.

**The Tullich Arns\*** (U, 390969), ðɪ'tʌləç'arnz, Scots Arn = alder. A wood north-east of Ballater.

**The Tullich Brig** (C, 387975), ðɪ'tʌləç'brɪg. Tullich Bridge (Gf). Formerly the Bridge of Tullich (Io), to old people still the Brig o Tullich (F), ðɪ'brɪgɐ'tʌləç. Over the Tullich Burn, north-east of Ballater.

**(The) Tullich Burn** (OS, C, 386979), ðɪ'tʌləç'bʌrn. The Burn of Tullich (Gf). See Allt Dobharaidh. North-east of Ballater.

**The Tullich Burn Fit Brigs\*** (F, 394971), ðɪ'tʌləç'bʌrn'fɛt,brɪgz. Foot bridges north-east of Ballater.

**Tullich Cottages** See Braehead Cottage.

**Tullich-in-Mar** (McC). A 19th century Post Office at Tullich near Ballater.

**Tullich Inn** (c. 403979). Tulloch Inn (Tay). A former inn west of Cambus o' May.

**The Tullich Islands\*** (F, 396972), ðɪ'tʌləç'ɛiləndz. Islands in Dee north-east of Ballater.

**The Tullich Kirk** See Cill Nachlan.

**Tullich Lodge**. An alternative early name for the more usual Monaltrie House beside Ballater (see Monaltrie House). Tullich Lodge now refers to the Tullich Lodge Hotel nearby (Er).

**The Tullich Mast\*** (C, 378985), ðɪ'tʌləç'mast. A radio and TV mast north-east of Ballater.

**Tullich Mill** (OS, 388976), now regarded locally as part of Milton of Tullich. OS location was Mill Croft in an early map (R 3), the actual Mill o Tullich being at 387976. Locally the Mill House (U), ðɪ'mël'hus. A former mill house north-east of Ballater.

**Tullich Village\*** (R 4, 389977). Former village at Tullich.

**The Tulloch Brig\*** See the Bailey Brig.

**The Tulloch Burn\*** See Allt Coire nam Freumh.

**The Tulloch Butts\*** (F, 275008), ðɪ'tʌləç'bʌts. Grouse butts west of Gairnshiel.

**Tullochcoy** (OS, An, Rli 23, I, C, 230941), ,tʌləç'koi, from Tulach Gaoithe (3), hillock of wind. Tulloquhy (Ca), Tullochquoy, Tullochcoie (R 9, 14), Tulich-gaoi (D). Mains of Tullochcoy (Ri 32, I) is present Tullochcoy. Note Wester Tullochcoy, a different former farm. A farm on a high place above the Inver.

**Tullochmacarrick** (OS, C, 278013), ,tʌləçmə'karək, often just 'tʌləç (C), probably from Tulach na Carraige (4), hillock of the rock, but possibly from a personal name involving Mac. The 1 : 25000 OS location is at some old ruins. Tullochmacarrick locally is at 277014, which is also called Wester Tulloch and was the house occupied most recently, until the 1950s. Tullich McCarrick (Mc 5) in 1634, Tullachnacarig (R) in 1725, Tullochnacarick (Opr) in 1766, Tullachnecarick (Crg 2, 6) in 1786 and 1801, Tullich McCarrich (I) in 1807–9, Tullichnacarrig (Opr) in 1820, Tullich McCarrich (Ro) in 1822, Tullochmacarrock (R) in 1827, Tullichmacaric (R) in 1828, Tullochmacarick (Io) in 1851, Tulloch na carrig (Mg) in 1855. In Gaelic Tulachmathcarraig (Drc), Tulach-maharrig, -makaritsh (D in A). Dalmagarry near Tomatin in Inverness-shire is a similar case, with *ma* in several old forms of the name but with *na* in one

of them:—Tullowch Makcarre, Tullichnagairie, Tullochmakerrie and Tulloch Magarrie (T 30, 111). A former farm north-west of Gairnshiel.

**The Tulloch Mosses\*** (U, 282035), ðɪ'tʌləç'mǫsɪz. Peat-mosses north-west of Gairnshiel.

**The Tulloch Puil\*** (F, 276013), ðɪ'tʌləç'pil. On Gairn near Tullochmacarrick.

**The Turkey Gully** (Sd, 172811), an absurd anglicisation. A ski-run on Carn an Tuirc north of the Glas Maol.

**The Turn\*** (F, 344012), ðɪ'tʌrn. A big bend on the road from Lary up to Wester Morven.

**Turnerhall** (OS, C, 407981), ,tʌrnër'haː, turner haugh. Houses west of Cambus o' May, formerly used by wood-turners, presumably named after the nearby haugh where the bobbin mill still stands.

**Turner Haugh\*** (U, 407980), as above. A haugh near Cambus o' May.

**Turner's Pool** See the Mill Puil.

**The Turn Gate\*** (F, 344012), ðɪ'tʌrn'get. A gate on a road to Morven Lodge.

**Turning Mill\*** See the Bobbin Mill.

**The Twenty Nine Puil** (C, 440973), ðɪ'twənti'nɛin'pil. '29' (P, Sc). A pool in Dee west of Dinnet, formed by a flood in 1829 (Farquhar).

**Tynabaich** (OS, C, 251952), ,tənɐ'beç, but best informants ,teinɐ'beç, possibly from Tigh na Beithich (5), house of the birch place, but Tigh nam Beathach, of the animals, also possible from old spellings. Tyneabeach (Io 64), Tighnabaich (Cr 41), Tynabeach, Teighnabeach (R 3, 14). A former farm west of Crathie, now a house.

**Tynabaich Cottages** (OS, C, 249952), ,tənɐ'beç'kǫtədʒɪz. Empty houses west of Crathie, being renovated as a house.

**The Tynabaich Hill\*** See Parliament Knowe.

**Tynabaich Moss\*** Tynabeach Moss (R 3). A peat-moss north-west of Crathie.

**The Tynabaich Park\*** (U, 250952), ðɪ,teinɐ'beç'park. A field west of Crathie.

**The Tynabaich Wuid\*** (U, 250955), ðɪ,teinɐ'beç'wɪd. A wood west of Crathie.

**An t-Uchd** (3, F, 284945), ðɪ'uχt, the hill brow. In modern Gaelic, Uchd = chest or breast. Sometimes the Uchd Park (U). A field on a hillside south-west of Abergeldie.

**An t-Uchd\*** (3, U, 300962), as above, the hill brow. A field on a steep hillside east of Crathie.

**Uchdach\*** (3, 157929), brae or ascent. Uchkach (I). A former field north-west of Invercauld.

**Uchdan\*** (3, 152907), hillock. Uchkan (I). A piece of former arable land south of Braemar, now part of a larger field.

**Uchdan Corrach\*** (3, 134857), steep hillock. Uchkan Corrach (I). A hillside in upper Glen Clunie.

**Uchd Hill** (210800), Uchd (3) = hill brow. Aught Hill (Ar) shown vaguely as a big stretch of high ground between Glas Maol and Carn an t-Sagairt Mor, around the top of Glen Callater.

**Uisge Bhruidh** (5, 138824), water of ? the raging. Water of Bruie (Fa), the Bruy (Roy), Water of uisk bruie, uisk vruie (Md 1), Uishk Vruie (I), Uisg Vruie (Th), Uishk Bhruie (R 14), Uisg vrui (D). Allt Bhruid or Bhruidh higher up (see it for further details). A burn at the top of Glen Clunie.

**The Uisge Burn** See Allt an Uisge.

**Uisge Chaladair** See Callater Burn.

**Uisge Cheann-bhuilg\*** (4, 160930), water of the head-bag (see Gleann an t-Slugain). Uisg chànlig (Da). Lower part of Allt an t-Slugain west of Invercauld.

**Uisge Chluainidh** See Clunie Water.

**Uisge Choich** See Quoich Water.

154

Decrepit old birches on Cnoc Chadail (knoll of the sleep), Glen Ey. There is a legend that the fairies enticed a man into the hill, and that he slept there for seven years.

Behind the fields of Blair Glass (centre) rises the hill of the Brown Cow and its long-lying snow wreath, the White Calf. A view in May from the two stones marking the Tinker's Grave by the Crathie–Gairnshiel road.

The deserted farmhouse of Tullochmacarrick overlooks the now uninhabited upper Gairnside, with the Sleach fields (centre), Ben Avon (left) and the hill of the Brown Cow (right). In October, a pale band of mat grass (visible above house) shows clearly against the dark heather, marking the location of the White Calf, a snow wreath that usually persists into July each year.

155

**Uisge Chonnaidh** (5, U, 073866), uʃk'χo̯ne, water of the firewood or of the dog stream. Uisg chonni (D). Usually now the Connie (C), ðɪ'ko̯ne. Also Water of Connie; Water Coni (Fa) obviously a semi-Gaelic construction. Lower part of Allt Connie, south-west of Inverey.

**Uisge Chriosdaidh** (5, WG, 070869), uʃk'çriəstji, water of the swift one, or of Christie (a personal name), or of a Christian. Uisg christshi (D). Also Water of Cristie; Water Christie (Fa) obviously a semi-Gaelic construction. The lower part of Allt Cristie Mor south-west of Inverey.

**Uisge De** See River Dee.

**Uisge Eidh** See Ey Burn.

**Uisge Feith Ardair** See Feardar Burn.

**Uisge Gharain** See River Gairn.

**Uisge Gheallaidh** See Geldie Burn.

**Uisge Laoigh Bhig** See Luibeg Burn.

**Uisge Muice** See River Muick.

**Uisge Thanar** See Water of Tanar.

**The Umast Way** (Wy 73), Old Scots Umast = uppermost. A former track used by soldiers at the Battle of Culblean, possibly west of Loch Kinord.

**Upper Ach Chadha** See Ach Chadha.

**Upper Alltcailleach\*** See Alltcailleach.

**Upper Aucholzie** (Ri, I, 347905). Upper Auchoilzie (Ri 29), Upper Achollie (Je). Also Over Aucholzie. Over Achoylie (Rli 2). Also Ivertown Aucholizie (Opr 27), Scots Iver = upper. A former farm in mid Glen Muick.

**Upper Balintober\*** See Balintober.

**Upper Ballabeg\*** (U, 413037), 'ʌpɐrˌbɐlɐ'bɐg. A former farm near Logie Coldstone.

**Upper Balmore\*** (Ce 4). Probably same as Wester Balmore. Former habitation at Aberarder.

**Upper Beal\*** (388972), from Bealach (3) = passage. Upper Byall (R 4). A piece of farmland at Tullich, paired with Nether Beal.

**Upper Bealach\*** (190937). Upper Ballach (Fa), Upper Balloch (I). Pairs with Nether Bealach. A former farm north-east of Invercauld.

**The Upper Boat Puil\*** (F, 165923), ðɪ'ʌpɐr'bot'pil. Auldowrie Pool (Ly). A pool in Dee above Invercauld, pairs with Lower.

**The Upper Boat Puil** (F, 247945), as above. Upper Boat Pool (Sc). In Dee above Balmoral Castle.

**The Upper Bobbie Puil** (C, 445978), ðɪ'ʌpɐr'bo̯bi'pil. A pool in Dee south-west of Dinnet, pairs with Lower and Middle.

**Upper Braehead\*** (F, 415964), 'ʌpɐrˌbre'he̯d. Sometimes the Tap (Scots = top) Braehead or Wester Braehead. A field at Inchmarnoch.

**The Upper Bruach Ruadh Puil\*** See the Little Bruach Ruadh Puil.

**Upper Ceann na Creige\*** See Ceann na Creige.

**Upper Ceann na h-Innse\*** (383973), see Nether Ceann na h-Innse. Upper Kinnahinch (Io 58, R 4). A field at Tullich.

**The Upper Ceapaich Puil** (F, 177917), ðɪ'ʌpɐr'kepəç'pil. Upper Keppoch (A). For meaning see Poll Cheapaich. In Dee at Invercauld.

**Upper Coire Beag** (F, 353979), 'ʌpɐrˌko̯re'bɐg. Corrybeg (OS 1904). A former farm near Bridge of Gairn, pairs with Lower Coire Beag.

**Upper Creit Seasg\*** (385975). Upper Craitshesk (R 4). A former piece of farmland north-east of Ballater.

**Upper Deecastle Cottage** See under Deecastle Cottage.

**Upper Deeside** (C), 'ʌpɐr'di'sɛid. Deeside west of the Dinnet area. Also Bràigh Dhé (3, D), upper part of the Dee or goddess. Pry-yē (D).

**The Upper Druims Park\*** (F, 289943), ðɪ'ʌpɐr'drʌmz'park. A field near Abergeldie.

**The Upper Dubh-bhruach Pool\*** (F, 026886), ðɪ'ʌpɐr'duˌbrɐχ 'pul. Also the Big Dubh-bhruach Pool (U), ðɪ'big'duˌbrɐχ 'pul. In Dee west of Linn of Dee, pairs with Lower.

**The Upper Falls\*** (U, 064903), ðɪ'ʌpɐr'falz. On Lui, pairing with Lower.

**The Upper Falls of the Garbh Allt** (north-east of 198898). The Upper Falls of the Garr-valt; mistakenly named thus by Wilson, these falls are downstream from his Lower Falls. Below a wooden bridge in Ballochbuie Forest.

**The Upper Gairn\*** (C, 188018), ðɪ'ʌpɐr'gern̩. Glen Gairn above the Loch Builg area.

**The Upper Geldie\*** (C), ðɪ'ʌpɐr'ge̯ldi. A big area at and around Geldie Lodge, i.e. upper Glen Geldie.

**The Upper Geordie Mitchell Puil\*** (F, 251951), ðɪ'ʌpɐrˌʤo̯rdi 'me̯tʃəl 'pil, often just Upper Geordie. A pool in Dee, at Balmoral, pairs with Lower.

**Upper Greystone\*** (Dms, U, 430960), 'ʌpɐrˌgre'stin. Superiorem Grystone (Ab 19), Over Grystone (Ab). A former farm east of Inchmarnoch.

**The Upper Haugh\*** (I, north of 294958). A field east of Crathie, on north side of road.

**Upper Island\*** See An t-Eilean.

**The Upper Jetty\*** (F, 184915), ðɪ'ʌpɐr'ʤete. Above Invercauld Bridge.

**The Upper Jetty Puil\*** (F, 184915), ðɪ'ʌpɐr'ʤete'pil. Also the Sodger Puil (F), ðɪ'so̯ʤɐr'pil, Scots Sodger = soldier. Soldier (A). A pool in Dee above Invercauld Bridge, pairs with Lower.

**The Upper Keiloch Puil** (F, 185914), ðɪ'ʌpɐr'kilǝç'pil. Upper Keiloch Pool (Ly). Pairs with Lower. In Dee near Invercauld.

**Upper Lary\*** (F, 336003), 'ʌpɐr'le·re. Also North Lary (Rj). A former farm in Glen Gairn.

**Upper Mar** See Braigh Mharr.

**Upper Moine Fhearn\*** (U, 290975), 'ʌpɐrˌmɔin'ja·rn. A peat-moss north-east of Crathie, pairs with Lower Moine Fhearn.

**The Upper Park\*** (372945). The Uper Parck at Mains of Braichly (Io 69).

**Upper Rintarsin\*** See under Rintarsin.

**Upper Tom Bhadaidh\*** (F, 247982), 'ʌpɐrˌto̯m'badi. A hillock north-west of Crathie.

**Upper Tornauran\*** (U, 280943), 'ʌpɐrˌto̯r'nuərən. A field south-west of Abergeldie, pairs with Lower and Middle.

**Upper Torr Dubh\*** (U, 425956), 'ʌpɐrˌto̯r'du·. A field at Inchmarnoch.

**Uppertown\*** (Opr 38b). Upertown Invergairn (Cr 41). A former farm near Bridge of Gairn.

**Urquhart's Cairn\*** (F, 961887), 'ʌrçɐrts'kern̩. A cairn in upper Glen Geldie.

**The Vat** (OS, C, 425996), ðɪ'vat. The Vatt (Sto). See Vat Burn. The Vat Cave (Gr). Also Gilderoy's Cave (Wy), after Patrick Gilroy MacGregor from the MacGregor clan in west Perthshire, who came thieving in Cromar in the 17th century. Gilderoy is from Gille Ruadh or red-haired lad. Locally sometimes called Rob Roy's Cave (A, C), 'ro̯b'roiz'ke·v, but there are no historical records of his having been there.

**Vat Burn** (OS, 413000), locally the Burn o Vat (Wy, C), ðɪ 'bʌrnɐ'vat, or the Burn o the Vat to older local people, ðɪ 'bʌrnɪðɪ'vat, ðɪ'bʌrne'vat, which is often a rapidly-spoken ðɪ 'bʌrnəi'vat, referring to the Vat or rocky cauldron through which the burn passes. Burn of the Vat (A), Burn o' Vat (Wy). The OS map correctly gives Burn o' Vat as the name of a nearby house, but this name also applies to the stream. Also Alltan Dabhaich (3), burnie of vat or of a vat. Aldondouch, Auldonataich (Io 20), Burn of Auldaindache

(Ap). Allt na dā-ich (D) suggests Allt na Dabhaich (3), burn of the vat. West of Loch Kinord.

**The Verities*** (I, 329865), ? from Feur (3) = grass. Flichity in Strath Nairn, Gaelic Flicheadaidh, is probably the dative of an old noun meaning moisture, derived from Fliuch = wet (W), and other such names are Mussadie and Delgaty (W); similarly, Verities may possibly represent a noun Feuradaidh, with the *s* showing an anglicised plural. Note Vert, in old forest law, meant plants that give cover for deer (Geddie 1959), from French Vert = green. An area of 'good pasture' (I) in upper Glen Muick.

**(The) Victoria Bridge** (OS, C, 102895), ðɪˌvɪkˈtoreɐˈbrɪg. Also Drochaid Bhicteoiriath (2, JB), ˌdrɔχtˌvɪkˈtoreɐ. Also Marlodge Bridge (Gr). Near Mar Lodge.

**(The) Victoria Bridge** (Er, C, 102895), as above. A house at above bridge.

**The Victoria Brig Pool*** See Poll na Drochaide.

**The Victoria Park*** (F, 260948), ðɪˌvɪkˈtoreɐˈpark. A field near a statue of Queen Victoria at Balmoral.

**Victor's Hut*** (C, 195902), ˈvɛktɛrzˈhʌt. A wooden hut in Ballochbuie Forest, named after a Victor McIntosh from Braemar.

**The Viewpoint*** (C, south-east of 145908), ðɪˈvjuˌpoint. A good viewpoint above Braemar.

**Wadlehead*** (311860, by elimination, two adjacent ruins, one to north-east is now inside a plantation), ? from Scots Waggle = bog. Wadlehead, Waddlehead, Titabutie and Wadle Head (Io 45, 52, 55). A former farm in upper Glen Muick.

**The Waggle*** (U, 300850), ðɪˈwagəl, Scots = bog. A wet boggy spot around the west side of a grassy haugh below Loch Muick.

**Waird-Head** (I, 370943), Scots Waird = a piece of land enclosed by a dyke. Wardhead (Rli 19), Wardhead of Braichlie (Opr 50). A former farm south of Ballater.

**The Wairds*** (Dms, 416960), Hiewaird (Dms 2), i.e. high enclosure. Farmland south-west of Inchmarnoch.

**The Wall*** See Donal Reid's Wall.

**The Wallie*** (F, west of 302015, on north side of burn), ðɪ ˈwaˑle, or ðɪˈwɛle, Scots = little well. A well near Gairnshiel.

**The Wallie o the Cairns*** (U, east of 324884, at south side of road), ðɪˈwaleiðɪˈkernz. A well in Glen Muick.

**The Wall of Ruighe Riabhach*** (363016), see Shiels of Ruighe Riabhach. The Wall of Ririach, the Spring or Wall of Ririach (Io 20). A well south-west of Morven.

**The Wall Park*** (U, west of 428047), ðɪˈwaˑlˈpark. A field beside a well, near Logie Coldstone.

**The Wall Park*** (U, 304919), as above. A field in Glen Girnock.

**The Wall Park*** See the Croft.

**The Washin Puil*** (F, 309858), ðɪˈwaʃənˈpil. In River Muick below Spittal of Glenmuick.

**Wastertoun*** (U, 415982), ˈwɑstɛrtən, Scots Waster = wester. Farmland at Cambus o' May, probably also a former farm, pairs with Eastertoun, now part of the Cambus Parks.

**The Wastertoun Burn*** (U, 415983), ðɪˈwɑstɛrtənˈbʌrn. At Cambus o' May.

**The Wast Road*** (U, 307929), ðɪˈwɑstˈrod. In Glen Girnock.

**Watchmount** See Sgeir Bheachdaich.

**The Water Board Hut*** (U, 099895), ðɪˈwatɛrˈbordˈhʌt. A hut used by River Purification Board, east of Inverey.

**The Water Clock*** (C, 435008), ðɪˈwatɛrˈklɔk. Formerly there was a clock run by water in a building at Lochhead near Loch Davan, but local people now use the name to refer to the general area there.

**Water Girnock*** See Girnock Burn.

**Waterhead*** Waterhead and Head of Inch (1826 gravestone at Tullich Kirk). Former habitation, possibly at Inchmarnoch.

**The Waterin Troch*** (F, 123904), ðɪˈwatr̩ənˈtrɔx, Scots = watering trough. A former trough for horses, bulldozed away by Canadian lumbermen during early 1940s, now a stream there.

**The Waterloo Butts*** (F, 303909), ðɪˌwatɛrˈluˈbʌts. Grouse butts in upper Glen Girnock.

**Water Meet** (Ly). Former pool in Dee, probably at the Mouth o Girnock.

**Water of Baddoch*** See Baddoch Burn.

**The Water of Beinn Iutharn*** (072810). The Water of Benurin (Io 79). Lower part of Allt Beinn Iutharn.

**Water of Beitheachan** See the Beitheachan Burn.

**Water of Bruididh*** See Uisge Bhruididh.

**Water of Bynack*** See Bynack Burn.

**Water of Callater*** See Callater Burn.

**Water of Connie*** See Uisge Chonnaidh.

**Water of Coulachan*** See Coulachan Burn.

**Water of Cristie*** See Uisge Chriosdaidh.

**The Water of Dee** See River Dee.

**Water of Derry*** See Derry Burn.

**Water of Ey** See Ey Burn.

**Water of Gairn** See River Gairn.

**Water of Gairney** (OS, 446899), locally the Burn o Gairney (U), ðɪˈbʌrnɐˈgjarne, usually now ðɪˈbʌrnɐˈgerne, the Gairney Burn (F), Gyar-ny (A), from Gàirneidh (4), ? little crier, as in Girnock. The phonetic *j* sound in ˈgjarne may be Aberdeenshire Scots, as in the pronunciation of a Cairn as a kjarn. In upper Glen Tanar.

**Water of Geldie** See Geldie Burn.

**Water of Luibeg*** See Luibeg Burn.

**Water of Quoich** See Quoich Water.

**Water of Tanar** (OS, 450940), locally now the Tanar Burn (F), ðɪˈtaˑnɐrˈbʌrn, for meaning see Glen Tanar. Also Uisge Thanar (6), water of the Tanar. Uisg Tannar, tangir, uisg thangir (D).

**The Water Rigs*** (I, 339902). A former field in mid Glen Muick, near the river.

**The Waterside*** (U, 360946), ðɪˌwatɛrˈseid. A path from Bridge of Muick up west side of Muick past Birkhall.

**The Waterside of Etnach** (Gler, 416915). Waterside (A). A former croft in upper Glen Tanar, on the site of the present Etnach.

**Watery Hill** (OS, F, 309801), ˈwatr̩eˈhɛl. South of Loch Muick.

**Waulkmill*** Walkmiln (Rli 19), Waulkmiln (Io 34). A former farm at Castleton, Braemar.

**Waulkmill*** See Littlemill.

**The Waulkmill.** The Walkmilne (Ri 32), Walkmiln (Io 31). Near Tullochcoy, beside the Inver.

**Waulkmill Croft*** Wauk Mill Croft (In). Beside Little Mill at the foot of Glen Girnock.

**Waulkmill of Inverenzie*** See the Mill o the Laggan.

**The Weaver Puil** (F, 236939), ðɪˈwivɛrˈpil. Weaver (Sc). In Dee, at the Inver.

**The Weaver's Burn*** See Allt a' Bhreabair.

**The Weaver's Cottage*** (U, south of 356975), ðɪˈwivɛrzˈkɔtədʒ. A former house near Abergairn.

**The Wee Dubh-bhruach Pool*** See Lower Dubh-bhruach Pool.

**Wellbrae Cottage*** (U, 436006), ˈwɛlˈbreˈkɔtədʒ, Scots Brae = hill, often on a road. A former cottage west of Loch Davan, on east side of road.

**Well called Bush of the Bald Horse*** (R 5, west of 224992). See Feith Preas an Eich Bhlair. North-west of Crathie.

**Wellhouses of Pannanich** (395967). Wellhouses of Pananach (Ri 39a). Buildings at Pannanich Wells near Ballater.

**The Well of Ardmeanach*** (west of 345949). The Well of Ardminach (G 19). South-west of Ballater.

**Well of Auchlaws** (OS, 412949), Auchlaws possibly from Ach Las (3), field of flame. In OS maps, the spelling Laws or Law in other Aberdeenshire names is an anglicised form of the local sound laːz, or laː, as in Lawsie, the Law and Lawfolds. South-west of Inchmarnoch.

**Well of Calaig*** See Tobar Chalaig.

**Well of St Mary of Inverey** See Tobar Mhoire.

**Well of Tanar*** (I, 372868). Spring of Tanner (R 6). At the head of Water of Tanar.

**Well of the Glas Allt*** (246849). Well of the Glashel (In, Am). On Lochnagar.

**Well of Torran Cruinn*** (264962). Well of Torancroin (R 6a). North of Crathie.

**The Well o Morven*** (U, 378038), ðɪˈwɛlɐˈmʌrˌvən. Also the Foxes' Well (U), ðɪˈfɒksɪzˈwɛl. Near top of Morven.

**(The) Wells of Dee** (OS, C, 937988), ðɪˈwɛlzəˈdiˑ. Also Fuaran Dhé (3, D, JB), ˌfuərɐnˈdjeː (JB), (fuəranˈje (A)), wells of the Dee or goddess. Also the Springs of Dee (Ke). Springis of Dee (Go). Source of River Dee, on Braeriach.

**West Abergairn** See Abergairn.

**West Allt Coultain** (OS, 131927), from Iar Allt a' Challtuinn (OS 1869), classic form Iar-allt etc, west burn of the hazel. Wester Ault Chaldin (I). Pairs with East Allt Coultain, north-west of Braemar.

**West Auchendryne*** (145915). W. Auchindryne (Im 3). Farmland near Braemar.

**West Auchendryne*** West Auchindryne (Cr 47), Wester Achindryne (Cr 50). A former habitation west of Braemar.

**The West Black Burn*** (F, 396886), ðɪˈwɛstˈblakˈbʌrn. In upper Glen Tanar, with Black Burn just to the east.

**West Croft*** (Io 58, 246946). Two former pieces of land at Balnault, north-east of Inver.

**The West Culardoch Burn*** See Stable Burn.

**The West Deer Park*** (U, 233933), ðɪˈwɛstˈdiɾˈpark. A field at Invergelder.

**The West Drive*** (C, 187896), ðɪˈwɛstˈdraev, ðɪˈwɑstˈdraev. A road in Ballochbuie Forest, pairs with the East Drive and Mid Drive.

**Wester Ach a' Mhaigh*** Ach a' Mhaigh (3) = field of the plain. Easter and Wester Auchavay (Me 15). Former farmland near Mar Lodge.

**Wester Allanaquoich** See Little Allanaquoich.

**Wester Croft of Balmoral*** (Opr 41d). Former habitation probably near West Lodge.

**Wester Allt a' Chlaiginn** See Allt a' Chlaiginn.

**Wester Allt an Droighinn*** (208807). Wester Aultn Droin (I). See Allt an Droighnean. Pairs with Easter Allt an Droighinn at the head of Callater.

**Wester Allt Bealach Buidhe*** See Allt Bealach Buidhe.

**Wester Arderg*** Probably on west side of burn at Arderg, presumably ruins on east side had been Easter Arderg. Wester Ardearge (Me 4). A former farm west of Braemar.

**Wester Ardmeanach** See Ardmeanach.

**Wester Ballater**. Ballater Wester (Mc 20), Bellater wester (Asr), Wester Ballader (Io). The form Ballater Wester rather than Wester Ballater possibly was an early translation of Bealadair Shuas. A former farm about Monaltrie House at Ballater.

**Wester Balmoral** (S 25). In the area about Balmoral Castle, pairs with Easter Balmoral.

**Wester Balmore** (Opr 14, Vr 2, 215942). A former habitation in Glen Feardar, paired with Easter.

**Wester Balnoe** (Vr 3, west of 210937). A former habitation in Glen Feardar.

**Wester Braehead*** See Upper Braehead.

**Wester Claignean*** (343972). Wester Claggans (I). A field near Bridge of Gairn.

**Wester Coilacriech*** (west of 319968). Wester Coilacreich (Ce 5). Former habitation west of Ballater.

**Wester Coire Allt a' Chlaiginn*** (200834), wester here means upstream (see Easter Coire Allt a' Chlaiginn). Wester Cor Ault Chlaggan (I). See Allt a' Chlaiginn. East of Loch Callater, pairs with Easter Coire Allt a' Chlaiginn.

**Wester Coire Gorm*** See Coire Gorm.

**Wester Corn Eilean Park*** (377968). Wester Conellan Park (Io 68). Also Conellan Park (R 4). A field near Ballater.

**Wester Garbh-allt*** (205890). Wester Garbell (Im 1). Lower part of Feindallacher Burn (OS).

**The Wester Garbh-leathad*** (430957), for meaning see Easter Garbh-leathad. The Wester Garlet (Dms). A hillside south-west of Dinnet.

**Wester Inverey*** Wester Invereye (Me 13). A former name probably for Little Inverey.

**(The) Wester Kirn** (OS, F, 205013), ðɪˈwastərˈkɛrn, often the West Kirn, or the Little Caorainn (U), ðɪˈlɛtəlˈkʌrɛn. Burn of the Wester Courn (I). From Allt a' Chaorainn (3), burn of the rowan. Aldcairn Wester (Io 1800s). See Allt Bad Creiceal, which is the west branch further up. A burn west of Corndavon Lodge, pairs with the Easter Kirn.

**Wester Land*** (R 4, 389971). On farmland at Tullich.

**Wester Micras** (OS, C, 281954), ˈwɛstərˈmikrəs. Roy's map shows Little Mickerys (presumably Micras) here, and Wᵣ Mickerys about the Lebhall but his locations are not precise. Meikle Micrass (I). From Miagra Shuas (6), upstream Micras. Miagra huas (D). For meaning see Micras. A farm east of Crathie, pairs with Mid and Easter Micras.

**The Wester Micras Brig*** (F, south of 284954), ðɪˈwɛstərˈmikrəsˈbrɪg. Road bridge east of Crathie.

**The Wester Micras Burn*** (F, 283955), ðɪˈwɛstərˈmikrəsˈbʌrn. East of Crathie.

**Wester Morven** (D, C, 340030), ˈwɛstərˈmɒrˌvən. A former group of farms west of Morven, now refers to the area. Pairs with Easter Morven.

**Wester Park*** (Im 4, 171927). A former field at Invercauld.

**Wester Rann na Bruaich*** (329001). Wester Rienabroich (Io 65). A former farm in Glen Gairn.

**(The) Wester Shenalt** (OS, C, 205030), ðɪˈwastərˈʃɛnəlt, often the West Shenalt. Wester Shan Ault (I), Wester Shen-ald (R 3). Also the Ruighe Baile Burn (F), ðɪˈruibəlˈbʌrn. A burn west of Corndavon Lodge, pairs with the Easter Shenalt.

**Wester Shenval*** (I, 305017), further downhill than Easter Shenval which is now Shenval (OS). A former farm north-east of Gairnshiel.

**Wester Sleach*** (F, 258016), ˈwɛstərˈsliəç or ˈwɑstərˈsliəç. Also Iar-sliabhach (3), west Sleach or moory place. Iuslough (Blm 1, 2). A former farming area north-west of Gairnshiel, pairs with Easter Sleach.

**(The) Wester Sleach Burn** (OS, F, 254019), ðɪˈwɛstərˈsliəçˈbʌrn. Also Allt Sliabhach (3), burn of Sleach or moory place. Alt Sliach (R 16). Lowest part used to be Allt a' Mhaide, highest part Burn of Coire Poll Randaidh. North-west of Gairnshiel.

**Wester Tom Bealaidh*** (346970). Wester Tombelly (Roy). A former farm beside the present Newton, west of the Bridge of Gairn, pairs with Easter Tom Bealaidh.

**Westertown Tullochcoy*** See Wester Tullochcoy.

**Wester Tulach Chocaire*** (U, 274935), ˈwɛstərˌtəlˈfogɛr. Pairs with Easter Tulach Chocaire. Wester Dalfouger (In). A former farm, later fields, south-east of Balmoral.

**Wester Tulloch*** (U, 277014), ˈwɛstərˈtʌləç. The most recently occupied farm at Tullochmacarrick north-west of Gairnshiel.

**Wester Tullochcoy** (Ri 32, I, 227941). Westertown Tullochcoy (Opr 25). A former farm west of Tullochcoy, above the Inver.

**Westfield** (Io 68). Westfield Terrace (Vr 1924) east of 368956 in Ballater, and the nearby house of Westfield were presumably named after the former farm of Westfield of Monaltrie. Pairs with Eastfield of Monaltrie.

**The West Golf Course*** (F, 096897), ðɪ'wɛst'gɔlf‚kors. A field at Mar Lodge.

**The West Grain o Allt an t-Sneachdaidh*** (F, 340861), ðɪ'wɛst 'grɛnɐ‚altən'drɛçte, Scots Grain = small branch-stream. South-east of Linn of Muick, pairs with Mid and East Grains.

**The West Grain o Allt Deas*** (F, 381874), ðɪ'wɛst'grɛnɐ‚alt'dɛs. Also the Dry Grain (U), ðɪ'draeˈgren. A burn at the top of Glen Tanar, pairs with the Mid and East Grains.

**The West Grain o Allt Fileachaidh*** (F, 324851), ðɪ'wɛst'grɛnɐ ‚alt'filəçi. A burn north-east of Loch Muick, pairs with Mid and East Grains.

**The West Grain of Luibeg*** See Allt Carn a' Mhaim.

**The West Haugh*** (F, 160926), ðɪ'wɛst'ha·χ. A field at Invercauld, including Haugh of Milltoun and other former fields.

**West Island*** (Io 58, 380966). A former island in Dee, near Tullich.

**West Land*** (Io 64). Former farmland at Ballater, different from Westfield and Wester Land. Westfield and West Land were part of the former Ballater House Farm at Monaltrie.

**West Mains*** See Little Mains.

**The West Mill of Abergeldie** See Drymill.

**West Milton Burn** (OS, 311996). Higher part was Burn of Clais Bhinn. Burn of Clash-vien (I). Lower part is the Milton Burn (C), ðɪ'mëltən'bʌrn. Pairs with East Milton Burn.

**The West Park*** (U, 365003), ðɪ'wɛst'park. A former field at Easter Morven, pairs with the East Park.

**West Park*** (Io 58, 346969). A field on Newton of Gairn.

**West Park Dalbagie*** (Io 58, 340964). A former field west of Bridge of Gairn, later split into a few smaller fields.

**West Park of Ach an Daimh*** (364002). West Park of Auchindow (G 30). This, along with the East Park of Ach an Daimh, was collectively called the West Park this century. A former field up Tullich Burn.

**The West Pass*** (Ros, 947927). Pairs with East Pass. On Beinn Bhrotain.

**The West Point o the Lair*** (F, 309783), ðɪ'wɛst'pointɪðɪ'leᵣ. The western end of the hill called the Lair of Aldararie, south of Loch Muick.

**West Sawmill*** (Opr 34). A former habitation in Braemar parish.

**West Street*** (Im 8, 244947). A former farm near Balnault.

**West Toun.** Westoun in part of Tullich (Mc 16), not same as Westfield which did not exist till the end of 1700s. Probably was in Milton of Tullich–Eastfield–Monaltrie area. Possibly the same as West Land.

**(The) Wheel Burn** (OS, F, 369027), ðɪ'kwil'bʌrn, from Allt na Cùlaidh (5), burn of the back place. Allt na cūly (D). South-west of Morven.

**The Whin Hillock*** (U, 421045), ðɪ'hwën'hëlëk. Near Logie Coldstone.

**The Whin Hillock Park*** (U, 420045), ðɪ'hwën'hëlëk'park. A field near Logie Coldstone.

**The Whisky Burn** See Allt an Uisge.

**The Whisky Road** (Gf, 378900). An old path from Glen Muick to Glen Tanar, started from just west of the former Glenmuick House, rose to the west of Carn Leuchan, crossed Tanar half a mile above the Linn, and joined the Mount Keen pass at the county boundary. A bulldozed road now runs along part of this route, north of Tanar.

**The Whistles*** See Na Feadan.

**(The) White Bridge** (OS, C, 019885), ðɪ'hwɛit'brɪg. Also An Drochaid Gheal (2, JB), ðɪ'drɔχt'jal, the white bridge. Drochaid Geal, drohit GYAL (A 1954). In Glen Dee west of the Linn of Dee.

**The White Bridge Park*** (F, 015885), ðɪ'hwɛit'brɪg'park. A reseeded grassy area in Glen Dee.

**The White Bridge Plantin*** (F, 010880), ðɪ'hwɛit'brɪg'plantɪn. A plantation in Glen Dee.

**The White Brig*** (C, 153904), ðɪ'hwɛit'brɪg. A footbridge across Clunie on Braemar Golf Course.

**The White Brig*** See the Auld Brig.

**The White Calf** (F, 232041), ðɪ'hwɛit'ka·f. Also the Brown Cow's White Calf (Sg) and the Broon Coo and her White Calf (see under Brown Cow Hill). A snow patch on Brown Cow Hill north of Corndavon Lodge.

**(The) White Hill** (OS, F, 398905), ðɪ'hwɛit'hël. In upper Glen Tanar, named after its grassy tracts.

**The White Hillock*** (I, north-east of 326852). In Glen Muick.

**Whitehouse Mill*** See Mill of the Braes of Cromar.

**Whitehouse Shiel*** (369026). Whitehouse Sheal (Io 20). South-west of Morven.

**(The) White Mount** (OS, C, 237838), ðɪ'hwɛit'mʌnθ, from Am Monadh Geal (3), the white hill, probably referring to the big tracts of grass on it, or to the long-lying snow. 'M moni gyall, mon yall (D). The White Moneth (G 32), the Whitemonth (Ri 30), the White Month (In). The OS location is too specific, and the name covers the high plateau south-west of Lochnagar (A, C).

**The White Mounth Pass** (Gf, 257853). An old path from Glen Muick over Lochnagar, via the Ladder.

**The White Muir*** (U, 298001), ðɪ'hwɛit'miᵣ, Scots Muir = moor. A grassy slope above Gairnshiel, beside Rinloan Burn.

**The White Stane Burn*** (U, 101950), ðɪ'hwɛit'stin'bʌrn, Scots Stane = stone. In Glen Quoich.

**The White Stane Burn*** See Allt nan Clach Geala.

**Whitestile of Pannanich*** Scots Stile = gate. Whitestyle, Whitestyle of Pannanich (Opr 46, 52). See Stile of Pannanich. Former habitation.

**The White Water*** (Fi). A stream in upper Geldie, possibly the upper part of Geldie Burn. Note Geldie is from Geallaidh = white or clear one, referring to the stream.

**William McKaimis Shieling*** See An Ruighe Dubh.

**The Windy Turn** See Leum na Gaoithe.

**The Windy Turn Puil** (F, 329964), ðɪ'wɪni'tʌrn'pil. Windy Turn (Wav). Also the Windy Corner Puil (F), ðɪ'wɪni'kɔrnër'pil. A pool in Dee below a windy corner near Coilacriech (see name above).

**The Wire Fence Butts*** (U, 271040), ðɪ'wɛir'fɛns'bʌts. Also the Half Wey Butts (U), ðɪ'haf'wae'bʌts, Scots Wey = way. Grouse butts north-west of Gairnshiel.

**The Wire Fence Butts*** (U, 212027), as above. Butts beside a former fence near Corndavon Lodge.

**Wisdomhow** (OS, C, 428986), wɪsdəm'hʌu·. Wisdom very doubtful, possibly from Uisdean = Hugh, Scots Howe = hollow. Wisdom Cottage (Opr 54), Wisdom (Be). A house south-west of Loch Kinord.

**Wishing Well** (Gl). A former well, now dry, near the top of Craigendarroch at Ballater.

**The Wishin Tree*** (U, 383964), ðɪ'wɪʃən'tri. A large oak tree near Ballater.

**The Witches' Burn*** See Allt Chailleach.

**Witch's Stone** (O, 423005). West of Loch Davan.

**The Witch's Stone** See Spinnin Jenny's Stane.
**The Witch's Well**\* (U, north of 348982), ðɪ'wëtʃɪz'wel. Beside a path north-west of Ballater.
**The Witter** (OS, F, 319791), ðɪ'wetër, Scots = sign, marker, barb of a hook. A hill nose south of Loch Muick.
**The Wolf Burn**\* See Allt a' Mhadaidh-allaidh.
**The Wolf Corner**\* (F, 327887), ðɪ'wulf'kornër. Corner on a road, said to be where the last wolf in Glen Muick was killed.
**Wolf Grain** (OS, 427881), locally the Wolf's Grain (F), ðɪ'wulfs 'gren, Scots Grain = small branch-stream. North-east of Mount Keen.
**Woodcocks Burn**\* See Burn of Bad nan Coileach.
**Woodend** (OS, C, 323957), wɪd'end. Woodend of Craiguish, Woodend of Girnack (Opr 57, 62). House at foot of Girnock.
**Woodhill** (Mp, D, C, 142907), wud'hël, sometimes wɪd'hël. A former farm near Braemar, now a house.
**The Woodhill Barns**\* See Little Woodhill.
**The Woodhill Brae**\* (C, 142907), ðɪ,wud'hël'breˑ. Woodhill sometimes wɪd'hël. A hill on a road near Braemar.
**The Woodlands Puil**\* (F, 214919), ðɪ'wudlɐndz'pil. Also the Green Bank Puil (F), ðɪ'grin'bank'pil. Greenbank (Wav). South-west of the Inver.
**Wood of Bad an Easa**\* See Bad an Easa.
**Wood of the Mill Croft**\* (R 6a, 263951). At Crathie.
**The Wood of Tom nan Rabhadh** (153912). Wood of Tornraw (Ri 27). On south side of Braemar.
**Woodside** (OS, C, 431041), wɪd'seid. A group of houses at Logie Coldstone.
**Woodside** (OS, C, 081896), wud'seid. A house at Inverey.
**Woods of Creag Liath**\* (333944). Woods of Craiglea (G 2a). South-west of Ballater.
**(The) Woods of Garmaddie** (OS, U, 230925), ðɪ'wɪdzɐ,gar'madi. Usually now the Garmaddie Wuid (F). South-west of Balmoral.

**The Wool Mill**\* (U, 353970), ðɪ'wul'mël. A former mill at Bridge of Gairn, on east bank.
**The Wuid Cutters' House**\* See Postie Bell's.
**The Wuiden Bulwark**\* (F, south-east of 380966), ðɪ'wɪdn̩ 'bulwork. Wooden bulwark on Dee north-east of Ballater.
**The Wuid o Ballochbuie** (F, 210900), ðɪ'wɪdɐ,baləç'bui, usually now the Ballochbuie Wuid. The Wood of Ballochbuie (Ri 27), the Woods of Ballachbuie (Me 15). One of the largest tracts of semi-natural Scots fir in Scotland, misleadingly named Ballochbuie Forest (OS) but Forest in the Braemar area always refers to a deer forest, not a wood. South-west of Balmoral.
**The Wuid Road**\* (C, 352942), ðɪ'wɪd'rod. A road in a wood in lower Glen Muick.
**The Wuids o Glen Gairn**\* (F), ðɪ'wɪdzɐ,glən'gern. The Woods of Glengairn (G 22). A composite name for the various, mainly birch, woods in Glen Gairn.
**The Wuids o Mar** (F), ðɪ'wɪdzɐ'maːr, often now the Mar Wuids (C). The Woods of Mar (Ri 32a). A collective name for all woods on Deeside west of Braemar.
**Wright's Cast** (Wav, C, 330963), 'reits'kast. A pool in Dee south-east of Coilacriech, named after a former fishing tenant.
**Wullie Wylie's Well**\* (F, 215916), 'wʌle'weiliz'wel. In Ballochbuie Forest.
**The Y**\* (C, 182889), ðɪ'wae. A Y-shaped gully in Glen Beg, Ballochbuie Forest.
**The Y**\* (U, 222892), as above. A Y-shaped gully with a burn in it, north-west of Lochnagar.
**The Yalla Moss Lochie**\* (U, 059992), ðɪ'jalɐ'mos'loχe. A tarn east of Glen Derry.
**The Yellow Moss** See Moine Bhealaidh.
**The Yowe Corrie**\* See Coire an Turaraidh.

Looking from the Auld Brig Puil past the hump-backed Bridge of Dee to the firs of Ballochbuie and the heights of Lochnagar (left) and White Mounth (right).

# APPENDIX 1

## DOUBTFUL, ERRONEOUS AND BOGUS NAMES

### Doubtful and erroneous names

In old handwritten documents, past writers often gave what look like different spellings of the same name, but in some cases there is doubt as to whether they really differ or whether they are merely variations in handwriting. We checked this by studying the handwriting to find how the doubtful letters had been written in common English words where there was no doubt about the spelling. Secondly, different writers sometimes spelled a name in different ways, but other information given by them usually allowed us to decide whether there was one name or two. Thirdly, the 'Records of Invercauld' and several other old books contain numerous words which might be taken as previously unrecorded place names. However, many are probably misinterpretations of the original handwritten records. Others are probably alternative spellings of known names. Many other distortions and alternative spellings appear in old unpublished maps, but we found these easier to trace as the location was usually fairly clear; we could therefore compare with our more recent records for the same location. In excluding these doubtful and erroneous names from the main list we may have rejected a few genuine place names, but we give them all below so that readers can see what we have done and can search further if they wish.

### Doubtful names

*Left column*—misinterpretation or alternative spelling, as spelled in the book or map mentioned.
*Right column*—name as in our main list.

*Liber Cartarum etc (1228–39), in Thomson (1841), later in Robertson (1847) and Stirton*

| | | |
|---|---|---|
| Auchatendregen | Auchadhendregen ? | Auchendryne |

*Carta Jacobi etc (1564), in Robertson (1804), later in Robertson (1847) and Stirton*

| | | |
|---|---|---|
| Clonye | | Clunie |
| Craigane | | Cragan |
| Dalpadie | | Dalbagie |
| Inverquhanwik, Inverquhanvik | | Inverchandlick |
| Mecraw | | Micras |
| Quiltis | Cuilts ? | Culsh |
| Rannabroith | | Rann na Bruaich |
| Roquhartrie, Roquhartore | | Richarkarie |
| Thoumereauch, Thomenereauch | Thoumenraudh ? | Tom nan Rabhadh (near Kindrochit, so not Torr an Fhraoich) |
| Tulloquhy, Tullochye | | Tullochcoy |

*Poll Book, ed Stuart 1844, original poll book (Anonymous 1696) in parentheses*

| | | |
|---|---|---|
| Achanaran | | Auchnerran |
| Achighouse | | Ach a' Ghiubhais |
| Altanzie (Altanrie) | | Aultonrea |
| Altchaldach | | Alltcailleach |
| Auchinstrine (& Auchendren) | | Auchendryne |
| Ballaver | | Ballater |
| Bellomdoire (Bellendorie) | | Baile an Torraidh |
| Bysantrach (Ryfantrach) | | Ruighe Bhantraich |
| Crost (Croft) | | Crofts |
| Loynchirk | | Loinn a' Choirce |
| Mueress, Muress | Micress ? | Micras |
| Pranie | | Prony |
| Reyenlore (Reyenlone) | | Rinloan |
| Richarbarie (Richarkarie) | | Richarkarie |
| Rinabught | Rinabrugh ? | Rann na Bruaich |
| Sterrein | | Stairean |
| Tanrich | Tornrich ? | Torr an Fhraoich |
| Toldor (Toldou) | | Toldhu |
| Tomindowies | | Tomidhu |
| Tomnafen | | Tomnavey |
| Torron | | Torran |

*View of the Diocese*

| | | |
|---|---|---|
| Granzbin | | Grampian |

*Anonymous (1802), 1755 valuation*

| | | |
|---|---|---|
| Coldraught | | Coldrach |
| Muiras | | Micras |
| Rhynacatten | Rhyneatten ? | Rineten |

*Roy map*

| | | |
|---|---|---|
| Aldennach | | Allt an t-Sionnaich |
| Aldinabeg | Aldinaben ? | Alltan na Beinne |
| Balvirral | Ballinoe ? | Am Baile Nodha |
| Bow Gouln | Bow Gown ? | Brown Cow Hill or Bo Dhonn |
| Carntohich | Carntorich ? | Carn Damhaireach |
| Clachnaspoild | | Caochan nan Spold |
| Corndiarrag | Gaindiarrag ? | An Geinn Dearg |
| Craiginard | Craichinard ? | Crathienaird |
| Craigmadie | | Craig Nordie |
| Dalgirmich | Dalginnich ? | Dail Gainimh |
| Dalinyiouchlat | Dalrinlyiouchlat ? | Dail Ruighe an Fhliuch-choille-shlat |
| Drumagad | Drumargad ? | Drummargettie |
| Garnich | | Girnock |
| Konep | | Canup |
| Mill of Harin | Mill of Starin ? | Mill of Sterin |
| Shelochuren | Shelochvren ? | Allt an t-Seilich or Sileach Bhronn |
| Sherluich | Sgerluich ? | Sgeir Fhliuch |
| Stranloch | | Stranlea |
| Tomnalen | | Tomnavey |
| Torndaroch | | Tom Darach |
| Upper Balachalioch | Upper Alldchalioch ? | Upper Alltcailleach |
| Wood of Claritt | | Clarack Wuid |

*Rental of the Lands and Barrony of Invercauld*

| | | |
|---|---|---|
| Old Townrie, Altounre | | Aultonrea |
| Tallowgrat | | Talamh Geal |

*Robertson 1804*

| | | |
|---|---|---|
| Allantoch | Allankoch ? | Allanaquoich |

*Stockdale*

| | | |
|---|---|---|
| Ben Don | | Ben Avon |
| Cairnmutur | Cairnnelur ? | Carn an Fhidhleir |
| Cmichenard | Crichenard ? | Crathienaird |

*Old Parochial Registers*

| | | |
|---|---|---|
| Tornarave | Tomnaraw ? | Tom nan Rabhadh |

*Invercauld maps*

| | | |
|---|---|---|
| Ballinloan | Ballinalan ? | Balnalan |
| Craig Churach | | Creag Bhiorach |
| Loynafey | Loyneley ? | Loinn Liath |

*Arrowsmith map* (some errors already noted for Roy's map are not repeated here)

| | | |
|---|---|---|
| Aldinilat | | Allt na Slaite |
| Balniall | Possibly misread Roy's Balvirral ? | Am Baile Nodha |

| | | |
|---|---|---|
| Ben Barrow | Ben Garrow ? | Beinn Gharbh |
| Bradniach | | Braeneach |
| Craigfaroy | Craigfarog ? | Creag Phadruig |
| Dalgwnich | Dalginich ? | Dail Gainimh |
| Kinnavey | Kinnacreg ? | Ceann na Creige |
| Linleigh | Shown at Wester Morven, probably confused it with Loinn Liath's correct position in nearby Glen Fenzie. | |
| L Kealter | L Keanter ? | Loch Kander |
| Mill of Dinnant | | Mill of Dinnet |
| Shannoch | Possibly misread Roy's Stranloch (Stranlea) in Glen Gairn and put it in wrong place at Balnault, or meant Shannval (An Sean-bhaile) at the nearby Inver but located it incorrectly. | |
| Tullochnachariet | | Tullochmacarrick |

*RHP 3645*

| | | |
|---|---|---|
| Rhuntashen, Rhintashen | | Rintarsin |

*Seymour*

| | | |
|---|---|---|
| Cairn-trannoch | | Carn Greannach |

*Robertson map*

| | | |
|---|---|---|
| Ault Galbie | Ault Galdie ? | Geldie Burn |
| Ballocks | | Bealachs |
| Burn of Conbreach | Burn of Corbreach ? | Allt Coire Breac |
| Craig-Wall | Cairnwall ? | Cairnwell |
| Dalemore | Balemore ? | Bellamore |
| Delagoral | Delagovan ? | Dalgowan |
| Pothollock | | Polhollick |
| Stopan Fluichk (attributed (A) incorrectly to one of the tors on Ben Avon) | Stopan Tluichk ? | Stob an t-Sluichd |
| Vishk Vruie | Uishk Vruie ? | Uisge Bhruidh |

*Thomson map*

| | | |
|---|---|---|
| Craig Moch | Craigiroch ? | Creag a' Choire Dhirich or Creag Dhireach |
| Dalemore | Balemore ? | Bellamore |
| Delagoval | Delagovan ? | Dalgowan |

*RHP 3596*

| | | |
|---|---|---|
| Knock Halnric | | Cnoc Chalmac |
| Tordien | Tomdien ? | Tom an t-Sidhein |

*Knox map*

| | | |
|---|---|---|
| Cairn Leay | Cairn Yeay ? | Carn a' Gheoidh |

*Lothian's County Atlas*

| | | |
|---|---|---|
| Dalawnich | | Dail Gainimh |

*Census 1841, 1871*

| | | |
|---|---|---|
| Creach Vore | Creacht Vone ? | Creit a' Bhothain |
| Line Veag | Line Veaig ? | Loin-a-veaich |
| Monour | Monachur ? | Moine a' Chuir |

*MacGillivray*

| | | |
|---|---|---|
| Burn of Altarvie | Burn of Altararie ? | Allt Darrarie |
| Creag ant-theombraig | Creag an t-Sheobhaig ? | Creag an t-Seabhaig |
| Creag loithte | | Creag Loisgte |
| Linmuist | | Loinn Muighe |
| Monadh-chuimhue | Monadh-chuimhne ? | Mount Keen |
| Torn-bridge | Tom-buidhe ? | Tom Buidhe |
| Traitor of Muick | Water of Muick ? | River Muick |

*Johnston map* (in MacGillivray)

| | | |
|---|---|---|
| Cairn Brennoch | | Carn Greannach |

*Legal printed papers*

| | | |
|---|---|---|
| Balnagairn | Dalnagowan ? | Dalgowan |
| Dalulangus | Dalvragachy? | Dail a' Bhreac-achaidh |
| Daluragathy | Dalvragachy ? | Dail a' Bhreac-achaidh |
| Mill of Arndarg | | Mill of Arderg |

*Valuation Roll 1860*

| | | |
|---|---|---|
| Cornybreach | Corrybrach ? | Coirebhruach |
| Howhead | | Homehead |

*Grant*

| | | |
|---|---|---|
| Strathlea | | Stranlea |
| Tomlice | | Tom Liath |

*RHP 3330*

| | | |
|---|---|---|
| Blande | Balnoe ? | Am Baile Nodha |
| Bo-cham or Brown Bow | Bo-dhonn or Brown Cow ? | Brown Cow Hill |
| Caea-dach Mon | Culardach Mor ? | Culardoch |
| Cama Goul | Carna Goul ? | Cairn of Gowal |
| Carn-Baen-Ult | | Carn Braigh an Uillt |
| Ceranlac | | Scraulac |
| Cnor Choulter | | Cnoc Choltair |
| Craeg na-clatra | Creag na-clasha ? | Creag na Glaiseath |
| Cragan Berkag | | Creag na Dearcaige |
| Dalemore | Balemore ? | Bellamore |
| Knorie Branders | | Knockie Branar |
| Maul-carna-vuie | Maul-carna-suvie ? | Meall Coire na Saobhaidhe |
| Maul Gracan Jinccan | | Meall Creagan Dearcaig |
| Moir Buin | Moir Bein ? | Morrone or Morven |
| Shochach Nihoir | Socach Mhoir ? | Socach Mor |
| Snacle Hillock | | Sandy Hillock |
| Toldin | | Toldhu |
| Toun-na-noig | Tom-na-hoig ? | Tom na h-Oighe |
| Tourn Bel | Toum Bel ? | Tom a' Bhealaidh |
| Ushr Bruie | Ushk Bruie ? | Uisge Bhruidh |

*Victoria 1868*

| | | |
|---|---|---|
| Aron Ghey | Sron Ghuy ? | Sron na Gaoithe |

*Royal Archives, Ram 2*

| | | |
|---|---|---|
| Balachlachan | | Ballachlaggan |
| Cairn na commholi | Cairn na coimhne ? | Carn na Cuimhne |
| Tullion me barrich | | Tullochmacarrick |

*Map of part of the Grampian Mountains*

| | | |
|---|---|---|
| Cairn Drochel | | Carn na Drochaide |
| Cairn na Cuimnuolt | | Carn na Cuimhne |
| Geldie | | Gelder |
| Tullethroy | | Tullochcoy |

*Valuation Roll 1870*

| | | |
|---|---|---|
| Auchtabaan | | Auchtavan |
| Balcrook | Balcrosk ? | Ballachrosk |
| Ballantruim | | Balintuim |
| Calochy | Palochy ? | Pollach |
| Balminlt | Balnuilt ? | Balnault |
| Boddach | Ballach ? | Am Bealach |
| Cartwellan | | Catanellan |
| Clashbettoch | | Clach a' Bhodaich |
| Cromlet | | Camlet |
| East Relrick | East Rebrick ? | East Rhebreck |
| Gerrachill | Genachill ? | Genechal |
| Kellack | | Keiloch |
| Lochlamar | Lochnalar ? | Lochnalair |
| Loinebeg | Luiebeg ? | Luibeg |
| Rylacreigh | Kylacreigh ? | Coilacriech |
| Tombea | Tomlea ? | Tom Liath |
| Tomran | Tomrau ? | Tom nan Rabhadh |
| Tullochoil | Tullochkoi ? | Tullochcoy |

*Valuation Roll 1880*

| | | |
|---|---|---|
| Dunfeil | Dalfeil ? | Dalphuil |

*Victoria 1884*

| | | |
|---|---|---|
| Cairn-na-Craig | Cainn-na-Craig ? | Ceann na Creige |

*Anderson 1889*

| | | |
|---|---|---|
| Glaschscheill | | Glas-choille |
| Tomnagreen | Tomnaveadh ? | Tomnavey |

*Records of Aboyne*

| | | |
|---|---|---|
| Aldinrie, Aldinruif, Altonrie, Altouries, Auldinrinwe, Auldinruive | | Aultonrea |
| Ardineach, Ardemenach | | Ardmeanach |
| Baldowis, Broikdowis | | Brochdhu |
| Bellaface | Dellafour ? | Dallyfour |
| Bellamonie | Bellamoire ? | Bellamore |
| Bellantuken | Bellanluken ? | Baile an Lochain |
| Bellaren | Bellnien ? | Baile Nighinne |
| Belmachie | | Dalmochie |
| Benasleik | Renasleik ? | Rinasluick |
| Blairquharrach, Blairhargo | | Blar a' Charraid |
| Calochy | Palochy ? | Pollach |
| Camisamari, Cammaseman, Cammosmeyes, Keambus | | Cambus o' May |
| Clavinmore | | Claigionn Mor |
| Craigwalech | | Craig Vallich |
| Crosat, Crosit, Corst | | Crofts |
| Dari | Dori ? | Baile an Torraidh |
| Drome | Pronie | Prony |
| Eandarghaugh of Achollie | Elandarg, haugh of Achollie ? | Eilean Dearg, Haugh of Aucholzie |
| Glendhu | | Glen Dui |
| Handiecraig | | Candacraig |

| | | |
|---|---|---|
| Kanmoris, Kynnoir, Canmore, Keandmoir, Candmoir | | Kinner (see Kinord) |
| Keandores, Theandores, Candord, Candred | | Kinord |
| Knokdelfour | | Knock, Dallyfour |
| Linmure | | Loinn Mhor |
| Niche | | Muick |
| Oldmoir | | Allt Mor |
| Risantrach | Rifantrach ? | Ruighe Bhantraich |
| Steerien | | Stairean |
| Stordherd croft, Stodack Croft | | The Stoitear Croft |
| Tollindul, Toldaire | | Toldhu |
| Tomabuchill | | Tom nam Buachaillean |
| Tomberrie | Tombethie ? | Tombae or Tom Beithe |
| Tomdorack | | Tom Darach |
| Tomnamean | | Tom nam Meann |
| Tornesillie, Tossinsellie | | Dorsincilly |
| Torragawane | | Torr nan Gamhainn |

*Allardyce 1896*

| | | |
|---|---|---|
| Allanabium | Altanabiann ? | Alltan na Beinne |
| Glens of Altefugle | Glens of Altefuple ? | Glens of Allt Phouple |
| Gloshaltmore | | Glas Allt Mor |

*Macdonald 1899*

| | | |
|---|---|---|
| Altanzie | | Aultonrea |
| Balachaileach, parish not known | | Balhalach |
| Ballintorrye, Bellandore | | Baile an Torraidh |
| Bochmoloch | Bachailach ? | Balhalach |
| Carr Mhor | | Carn Mor |
| Crost | | Crofts |
| Lonibeg | Loniveg ? | Loin-a-veaich |
| Mueress | Micress ? | Micras |
| Rannabroith | | Rann na Bruaich |
| Reichul | | Ruighachail |
| Reyenlore | Reyenlone ? | Rinloan |
| Tenrich, Tanrich | Tornrich ? | Torr an Fhraoich |
| Tolachavrych | Tolach chogar ? | Tulach Chocaire |
| Tolyocre | Tolycocer ? | Tulach Chocaire |
| Tomnaharra | Tomnanra ? | Tom nan Rabhadh |
| Tomnaman | | Tom nam Meann |
| Tulloquhy | | Tullochcoy |

Allt Dowrie confused with the dwellings Altourea and Altaurie which obviously stand for Aultonrea.
Auldaindache—did not realise it was Gaelic for Vat Burn.
Croft Muickan and Croft of Muickan in as two names.
Culsh, said to be in Braemar parish, probably confused with Culsh in Glen Gairn.
Loinmore and Lynmuie thought to be the same.
Mill of Cosh and Mill of Quoise in as two names.
Recharchrie and Rycrathie thought to be the same.
Reichul and Ruibal (Ruighe Baile a' Chlaiginn) thought to be the same.

*Michie, Records of Invercauld*

| | | |
|---|---|---|
| Alaveralziane, Altuzealzean | | Allt a' Ghillin |
| Altivaird | Altivaitsh ? | Allt a' Mhaide |
| Ardorchie | | Ard-achaidh |
| Auchidiness | Auchichness ? | Ach Eich an Easa |
| Auchlorkage | Auchoillaye ? | Aucholzie |
| Badquhan | Badquharn ? | Bad Charn |
| Badromeald | Badroneald ? | Bad Ruighe an Uillt |
| Ballindow | Ballindorie ? | Baile an Torraidh |
| Ballingarry | Ballnigarr ? | Baile nan Gabhar |

| | | |
|---|---|---|
| Benouch, Binnich | | Bun Fhiodhaich |
| Bonwin | | Bonn Uaine |
| Bowmach | Bouinnach ? | Buidheannach |
| Breachan | Beachan ? | Am Beitheachan |
| Cansfranvell | | Ceann an t-Sean-bhaile |
| Claskmirick | Clashmuick ? | Clais Muice |
| Cornclarich | Cornalarig ? | Coirenalarig |
| Crort of Badquharn | | Croft of Bad Charn |
| Dalbedie | | Dalbagie |
| Dalimclag | Dalmuchie ? | Dalmochie |
| Dalmulachie | Dalmucachie ? | Dalmochie |
| Glasschony | Glaschory ? | Glas-choire |
| Glenbrownie | Glenbrowine ? | Gleann Bruthainn |
| Glencoubulge | Glencanbulge ? | Gleann Cheann-bhuilg, now Gleann an t-Slugain |
| Inverchanvilk | | Inverchandlick |
| Kuloiss | Ruloisc ? | Ruighe Loisgte |
| Renovocatin | Renovocatir ? | Roinn an Fhucadair |
| Richardline | Richrachie ? | Ruighe Chreichidh |
| Riendonbrout | Riendoucrout ? | Ruighean Dubh-chroite |
| Rienhin | Rienlin ? | Ruighe an Lin |
| Rinabrat | Rinabrach ? | Rann na Bruaich |
| Rynarait | Kynakait ? | Connachat |
| Rynefrew | Rynefey ? | Ruighe nam Fiadh |
| Shank of Lyndrum, Kiendrum | Shank of Ryndrum, Riendrum ? | The Shank of Ruighe an Droma |
| Sterritdie | Sterrinbig ? | Sterinbeg |
| Stotancroft | Stotarcroft ? | The Stoitear Croft |
| Stranvelle | Shanvelle ? | An Sean-bhaile |
| Tainkirach | Fainkirach ? | Feith nan Caorach |
| Tomerhaine | Tomentiram ? | Toman Tioram |
| Torinveck, Tornrich | Torinrech ? | Torr an Fhraoich |
| Tornraw, Tomnavaw | Tomnraw ? | Tom nan Rabhadh |
| Tullochbeg | | Tullochcoy |
| Tynabroich | Rynabroich ? | Rann na Bruaich |

*Sim*

| | | |
|---|---|---|
| Dachlash | | An Dubh-chlais |

*Bulloch 1903*

| | | |
|---|---|---|
| Auldschillauche | Auldchillauch ? | Alltcailleach |
| Lymnoe | Lynmoe ? | Loinn Muighe |
| Tarrinschill | | Dorsincilly |

*Aberdeen Journal Notes & Queries*

| | | |
|---|---|---|
| Bakinloch | Balchioch ? | Baile a' Cheothaich |
| Cordevoch | Corleroch ? | Coldrach |
| Corriedavan | | Corndavon |
| Donebrie | Dorebeic ? | Torr Beag |
| Drumnachraig | Drumachragan ? | Druim a' Chreagain |
| Riedon | Riedou ? | An Ruighe Dubh |
| Straithgruick | Strathgirnick ? | Strathgirnock |
| Tyrabaiek | Tynabaick ? | Tynabaich |

*Mackintosh*

| | | |
|---|---|---|
| Auchdee | Auchdaw ? | Ach an Daimh |
| Aultstrathaig | Aultchrachay ? | Crathie Burn or Allt Chraichidh |
| Balnagoun | Dalnagoun ? | Dalgowan |
| Coble Scatfirth | Coble Seat Ferry ? | Coble Seat of Tullich |
| Craigall | Craigan ? | Cragan |
| Drumwharran | Drumwhallie ? | Drum Cholzie |
| Rieveltaig | Riechalvair ? | Ruighe a' Chalbhairigh |
| Rynataig | Rynatain ? | Rineten |

*Stirton*

| | | |
|---|---|---|
| Balnachochane | Balnachoille? | Baile na Coille |
| Bedal | Bechan ? | Am Beitheachan |
| Bramche | Branech ? | Braeneach |
| Branfatage, Baafantach | Badfantag ? | Bad Fiantaige |
| Chactanturne | Clachanturne ? | Clachanturn |
| Clabochark | Clabochaik ? | Claybokie |
| Corrintavan | | Corndavon |
| Dalaben | Dalaten ? | Dail Aitinn |
| Dorwallie | Domvallie ? | Tom a' Bhealaidh |
| Galbie | Galdie ? | Geldie |
| Garamalldry | Garamaddy or Garawalld ? | Garmaddie or Garbh Allt |
| Inerzaldie, Inverzaldie | Inveryalder ? | Invergelder |
| Innerquhanvit | Innerquhanlik ? | Inverchandlick |
| Oirdearg | | Arderg |
| Runtassen | | Rintarsin |
| Tigh-na-gaoith | | Tonnagaoithe |
| Tullochbeg | | Tullochcoy |
| Tulloch, Choguir | | Tulach Chocaire |

*A & H Tayler*

| | | |
|---|---|---|
| Bonaglie | | Bovaglie |
| Invergeldie | | Invergelder |
| Lynbeg | Lynbheg ? | Loinveg |
| Sinabroch | Rinabroch ? | Rann na Bruaich |
| Straanter | Straneten ? | Srath an Aitinn |
| Strulaie | Stranlie ? | Stranlea |
| Tullich, Choquin | Tullich Choguir ? | Tulach Chocaire |

*Diack*

| | | |
|---|---|---|
| Loinmuic | | Loinn Muighe |

*Alexander*

| | | |
|---|---|---|
| Bochmoloch | Bachailach ? | Balhalach |
| Bullien, a pendicle of Inverenzie | Ballino ?, given as Balline (Io) | Balno |
| Crost | | Crofts |
| Lonibeg | Loniveg ? | Loin-a-veaich |
| Tolachavrych | Tolach chogar ? | Tulach Chocaire |

*Dilworth*

| | | |
|---|---|---|
| Balachroich | Balachloich ? | Baile Cloiche, now Balgairn, or possibly Ballachrosk |

*Scottish Record Office Grants and Deposits*

| | |
|---|---|
| Lochtoune | Probably near Logie Coldstone, possibly the same as An Lochan |

**Erroneous names stated to be in Upper Deeside but in fact outside**

| | *Actual location* |
|---|---|
| *Coire na Craige (M, A)* | *In Perthshire near Loch Tilt* |
| *Pack Merchant's Cairn (McC 1891)* | *In Angus, top of Capel Mounth* |
| *Tornmachie (M)* | *In Aboyne parish (A)* |
| *Tullecarne (M)* | *Tillycairn in Aboyne parish (A)* |

**Bogus Gaelic names**

These appear only on one set of estate maps of Balmoral. We summarise the evidence on this below, comparing names in two different maps. Queen Victoria favoured Gaelic, and the Balmoral estate maps are the only maps in Upper Deeside to include suggested Gaelic derivations. One of them adds these derivations in a list, but also gives the Gaelic names in the writer's own phonetic English, so readers can see the evidence for themselves. A second map, however, gives only the suggested Gaelic derivatives as if they were the real original names. We also noticed that the second map made substitutions for names which appeared in the first one and which may have been considered vulgar; for instance Cor na Keich (Coire na Ciche = corrie of the pap) became Carn a cheatheich (hill of the mist)!

*Left column*—names which we think are phonetically reasonable representations of genuine local names, from an estate map in 1857, with suggested Gaelic spellings (which we think are all incorrect) in parentheses in a list occurring below the map.
*Middle column*—names which we think are bogus, from estate maps in 1856–63 made by the same people using the same layout, type of colouring, and printing.
*Right column*—names as in our main list, where more information can be found.

| 1857 | 1856–63 | Our list |
|---|---|---|
| Back Corbuie (Druim a choire buidhe, the back of the yellow corrie) | Druim a choire bhuidhe | Coire Buidhe air Chul |
| Black Hillocks of Craiglia (Tom dubh na creig leithe) | Tom dubh na creig Leithe | Black Hillocks of Creag Liath |
| Burn of Coinachraig (Allt Creg nan con) | | Connachat Burn |
| Burn of Stair-na-gall | Allt Staire nan gall | Burn of Stair nan Gall |
| Cannape (Ceann nan cnap) | Ceann nan cnap | Canup |
| Clash Cley | Clais nan Cliabh | Clais Cleithe |
| Cor na Keich | Carn a cheatheich | Coire na Ciche |
| Croft Sheal | Buidhe na Cravite, presumably meant Ruidhe | Croft Shiel |
| Cruinavean | Mhoine Chruinn | Moine Chruinn |
| Faeluie Burn | Allt Feithe n Laoigh | Feith an Laoigh |
| Faelutch | Feithe n Luig | Feith Luid |
| Faepattenbuie | Feithe Bhadain Bhuidhe | Feith Badan Buidhe |
| Faichort ('N Fheithe comhnard) | 'N Fheithe comhnard | Feith Ord |
| Fox Cairn | Carn 'n t-Sionnaich | Fox Cairn Well |
| Francis Stone | Clach Fhraing | Francis Stone |
| Garcorrie | 'N Coire Garabh | An Garbh-choire |
| Garmaddie | 'N Garbh Mhada | Garmaddie |
| Gelder | Geal Tir | Gelder |
| Kinacraig | Ceann na creag | Cinn na Creige |
| Little Ca-Cairn | Carn beag a chabhaidh | Cac Carn Beag |
| Knapaneracher | Cnap Fhea . . . | Cnapan Nathraichean |
| Little Conachraik | Creag Bheag nan con | Little Conachcraig |
| Little Craiglia | Chraig Lia bheag | Creag Liath Bheag |
| Little Craignagall | Creag Bheag nan Gall | Little Creag nan Gall |
| Little Knapaneracher | Cnaip Bheag Fhearch . . . | Little Cnapan Nathraichean |
| Maul Corbuie | Maol a choire Bhuidhe | Meall Coire Buidhe |
| Maul Craiglia | Maol na creig leith | Meall Creag Liath |
| Maul Gorm | Maol Gorm | Meall Gorm |
| Muckle Ca-Cairn | Carn mor a chabhaidh | Cac Carn Mor |
| Muckle Corrie of Lochnagar | 'N Coire Mor | Corrie of Lochnagar |
| Muckle Pap | A Chioch | Meikle Pap |
| Muckle Spout | 'M Feadan no t suilag mhor | Black Spout |
| Pattendurna | Bad an Duirn | Bad an Tuairneir |
| Rachaish | Ruidhe Chaise | Rachaish |
| Rachald | Ruidhe chail | Ruighachail |
| Ringeallich | Ruidhe na Cailleich | Ruighe an t-Seilich |
| Ripe | Ribeadh | Ripe Hill |
| Rives of Back Corbuie | Feadanan choire Bhuidhe | Reeves of Back Coire Buidhe |
| Rodack | Grodadh | Rodaig |
| Rumbling Culter | Torman a choltair | Ruighe Iomlan Culdair |
| Sculloch | Sgliatach Leacach | Sgallach |
| Shank of Ca-Cairn | Lurg carn a chabhaidh | The Shank o the Cadha Chuirn |
| Shank of Stair na Gall | Lurg Staire nan gall | Shank of Stair nan Gall |
| Shank of the Pap | Lurg a Chioch | Shank o the Pap |
| Sheal of Back Corbuie | Bothan cul choire Bhuidhe | Shiel of Back Coire Buidhe |
| Sneck of Garcorrie | Glaic a choire Gairbh | The Sneck o Garbh-choire |
| Spouttans | Suithlagan | Na Srubanan |
| Stob of Craiglia | Stob na creig leithe | Stob Liath |
| Tomnavean | Tom nam Bian | Tom nam Fiann |
| Tompatfoot | Tom phutag a Bhada | Tom Bad Phut |
| Tompattenbuie | Tom Bhadain Bhuidhe | Tom Badan Buidhe |

# APPENDIX 2

## FORMER HABITATIONS GROUPED BY AREA

Many people are interested in discovering the names of former habitations in a particular glen or other part of the area that they have visited. To make this easier for them we list these below, separately for each glen and different parts of the Dee valley. These lists exclude names on current OS maps, electoral registers and valuation rolls, house names in villages and hamlets, and shielings and shooting lodges.

These lists should not be taken to represent the sum total of all former habitations. We do not know precise locations for all habitation names found in records, nor do we have names for all the house ruins which can still be seen. It is possible in a few cases that two different names in the lists may be alternative names used by one generation for what was a single habitation. If one location has three ruined houses, it is possible that each was occupied over a different period, and that each had a separate name. On the other hand, all three might have carried the same name in successive periods. In several parts of the area, old folk told us that there used to be so many 'reekin lums' (i.e. smoking chimneys, a term indicating inhabited homes) at one particular time, usually giving an exact figure such as ten or fourteen. This evidence agrees fairly well with what one sees from inspection of the ground. We lack names for most of these, and so our list would tend to underestimate greatly the number of houses formerly occupied there. Thus the number of former habitations listed here should not be taken as an indication of population numbers at any particular time.

**Baddoch**

Ach nan Saighdear
Dail Chois
Dail na Croise
Leathad nan Saighdear
Ruighe an Luig
Sron

**Ballater–Bridge of Gairn**

Alehouse of Abergairn
Allt Mor
Baile an Lochain
Bog Romach
Carn Mor
The Castletoun
Corrach Diubhaidh
Dun Bheathagan
Easter Abergairn
Humphrey's Folly
Invergairn
Kirkton
An Loinn
Mill of Abergairn
Ruighe Choinean
Tom nam Meann
Uppertown

**Ballater–Invergelder (south side)**

Baile a' Cheothaich
Bailean Dabhaich
Baile Meadhonach
Boat Clachanturn
  (Coble Croft possibly same)
Braehead
Braichlie
Burnside of Braichlie
Catanellan Croft
Clais Coinnich

Clais Muice
Clarach
The Creag Ghiubhais Camp
The Croft
The Croft of Abergeldie
Cul Leasachaidh
Druim na Pairce
Easter Balhalach
Easter Tulach Chocaire
East Rhebreck
East Toun
Head of Knock
Little Khantore
The Little Knock
The Little Mains
Mains of Balmoral
Mill Croft
Moine a' Chuir
Muckle Knock
The Muirtoun
Newbigging of Abergeldie
Old Mill of Abergeldie
Radach
Scurriestone
The Smiddy Croft
Stile of Balmoral
Waulkmill Croft
Wester Croft of Balmoral
Wester Tulach Chocaire

**Braemar area**

Baile a' Chlaiginn
Baile an Eilein
Boat of Inverchandlick
Chapel Gate
Cnocan Dubh
Cul Garaidh
Dail a' Bhreac-achaidh
Dail an Sgeich

Dubhag
An Dubh-chlais
Greenbrae
Little Woodhill
The Mains
Milltoun of Auchendryne
Roinn na Min
Ruighe an t-Seilich
School Croft
West Sawmill

## Braemar–Inverey

Baile an Eilein
Baile an Loin
Baile nan Taobhanach
Bridge End
Ceann na Coille
Ceann na Dalach
Cnoc Dubh
An Creagan
Creag Dhearg
Doocot
Druim a' Chreagain
Dunaidh Beag
Eilean Giubhas
Little Allanaquoich
Magaidh Boireann
The Mains of Dail Mhor
March Haugh
An Sean-bhaile
Sgeir Thioram
Tom a' Chuilinn
Tom Liath
West Auchendryne
Wester Arderg

## Bridge of Gairn–Crathie

Baile an Fhraoich
Baile Cloiche
Baile nan Critheach
Boatie's
Bridge Cottage
Burnside of Greystone
Charlie Clais Bhacaidh's
Na Claignean
Clais Thomais
Clinkum's
The Croft of Tom Bealaidh
The Feuragach
Fordmouth
Little Feuragachs
Lochan na Circe
Mill Croft
Millford
Milltoun of Tom Bealaidh
Rathad Geal
An Tom
Tom Bealaidh
Tom Darach
Tomidhu Cottage
Tomidhu Croft

Torr an Ailein
Wester Coilacriech

## Crathie–Inver

Ardoch Cottage
Braeneach Cottage
Braigh Chraichidh
Bridgend
Bridgend of Ailtridh
Burnside
A' Chlais
Cnapach
Cnoc
Coble Croft
Cobletoun of Monaltrie
The Coldrach
Croft of Knockanduie
Croft of Tigh na Criche
East Street
Gateside
Jimmy Smith's
Kingston of Monaltrie
Lower Carnaquheen
Lower Roinn Tarsuinn
Mid Roinn Tarsuinn
Milltoun of Inver
Nether Ceann na Creige
Peter Benton's Craft
Roinn a' Chait
Roinn na Moine
Scutter Hole
Srathan Riabhach
Tigh na Criche
Toll Phiobair
Toman a' Bhreac-achaidh
Tom an Fhuarain
Tom na Buaile
Torran Cruinn
Torr Beag
Torr nan Caorach
Upper Ceann na Creige
Upper Roinn Tarsuinn
West Street

## Cromar

Am Baile Mor
Baile Nighinne
Bourtree Haugh
Cleikumin
The Cnapach
Cnoc Dubh
Creagaidh Larach
The Fit o the Toun
Leyhead
An Lochan
Muirend
Muir o Milton
Ruighe na Beinne
South Milton
Suckerie's
The Tofts
Toman a' Bhothain
Trochietroddles
Upper Ballabeg

**Dee, Dinnet–Ballater (south side)**

Baile Mor
Bruach Dhubh
Ceann a' Gharaidh
Cobletoun of Dalmochie
Cottoune
The Croft of Bruach Dhubh
Croft of Milltoun
Gatekeepers Croft
The Mains of Bellamore
Mill Croft
The Milltoun
Na Mora-lannan
Pannanich Lodge
Pannanich Lodge Farm
Poll Sleac
Ruighe Bhantraich
An Sean-bhaile
Stile of Pannanich
Tom Darach
Torran Uaraig
Torr Dubh
Torr na Creige
Upper Greystone
Whitestile of Pannanich

**Dee, Dinnet–Ballater (north side)**

The Auld Hut
The Auld Toll House
Ballater House Farm
Bogingore Cottage
Brew Croft of Tullich
Brewlands
The Brew Toft
Bridgend
The Castle of Kinord
Cinn a' Gharaidh
Coble Croft
Coble Seat of Tullich
Cobletoun of Ballater
Corn Eilean
Easter Ballater
The Haugh
Leys of Ballater
Luibs
Mill Croft
Milltoun of Dinnet
Muirtown of Tullich
Pot Side
Preas Coll
Shore
The Stile of Tullich
An Tiobair
Wellbrae Cottage
Wester Ballater
Westfield

**Easter Morven**

Ach an Daimh
Easter Morven
Nether Ach Chadha
Ruighe an t-Sagairt
Sluggan Burn
Upper Ach Chadha

**Glen Clunie**

Allt Dearg
Baile an Loin
Baile Meadhonach
Camas na Ciste
Cnoc a' Chuitseich
Cnoc Mharcaich
Croft Mowatt
Dail a' Chata
Dail an t-Suidhe
Druim Dearg
John Fleming's Croft
Lint Mill Croft
Loinn Fhuar
Loinn na Moine
Luib an Fheoir
Luig
Mains of the Coldrach
Meadow of Baile an Loin
Milltoun of Coldrach
Milltoun of Glen Clunie
North Coirenalarig
Ruighe Laoigh
Tom a' Chait
Tom na Ciste
Tom nan Rabhadh
Tom nan Sealgair

**Glen Ey**

Allt Shlat
Baile a' Mhuilinn
Coire nam Fiadh
Dail nam Breac
Dail nam Fiadh
Dail Ruighe an Fhliuch-choille-shlat
Ruighe an t-Seilich
An Ruighe Dubh
Ruighe nan Sleac

**Glen Feardar**

Ach nan Cuithe Iomlan
Baile na Moine
Balnoe Croft
Ceann an t-Sean-bhaile
Clach a' Bhodaich
Clinkamin of Tullochcoy
Cnoc
Creit an Roide
Croft Fucadair
Croft Sutair
The Crofts of Aberarder
Dail Choirce
An Dubh-choire
Easter Auchtavan
Felagie Village
Mill Croft of Aberarder
Milltoun of Aberarder
Nether Bealach
Ratlich Croft
Ruighe nam Fiadh
An Sean-bhaile
Talamh Geal
Tom a' Challtuinn

Upper Bealach
Wester Balmore
Wester Tullochcoy

## Glen Fenzie

Braes of Inverenzie
Loinn Liath
An Loinn Mhor
Roinn an Fhucadair
Roinn Tailleir

## Glen Gairn up to Gairnshiel

Allie Ritchie's Cottage
Annie Bremner's Cottage
Ardach
The Auld Manse
Auld Meggie's
Baile a' Mhuilinn
Balno Cottage
Ceann an t-Sean-bhaile
Chapel House
Clais an Fhraoich
Coire Uchdain
Craig of Prony
An Cul Riabhach
Dykehead
Easter Rann na Bruaich
The Glenbardy Village
Greenbank
Lower Coire Beag
Lower Lary
Middletown
The Mill Croft
Mill Croft of Prony
Mill Croft of Richarkarie
The Mill Croft of Stranlea
The Mill o the Laggan
Milltoun of Chritheannaich
Milltoun of Prony
Muir of Richarkarie
Na Pollagan
Postie Allan's
Ruighe Aimrid
Ruighe an Loin
Srath an Aitinn
Tom an t-Suirn
Torr nan Gamhainn
Tulach an Tuirc
Upper Coire Beag
Upper Lary
The Weaver's Cottage
Wester Rann na Bruaich
Wester Shenval

## Glen Gairn (above Gairnshiel)

Ach an t-Sabhail
Ach Eich
Bad Charn
Bad Fiantaige
The Bittie
Bog Farral
Cata na Cailliche

Cnocan Aitinn
Cnoc Chalmac
Cossack
The Croft of Daldownie
Croit Caluim
An Dubh-chlais
An Dubh-choire
Half Bad Charn
Loinn a' Choirce
Loinn na Guail
The Muir
Nether Corndavon
Over Corndavon
Remicras Cottage
Renatton
Ruighe Baile a' Chlaiginn
Ruighe Chreichidh
Roinn a' Bhathaich
Wester Sleach
Wester Tulloch

## Glen Gelder

Bield
Cinn na Creige
Rideach
Ruighe Iomlan Culdair

## Glen Girnock

Na Cearr-lannan
Clayholes
Cnocan Riabhach
Croft of Bovaglie
Loinn a' Choirce
The Newton

## Glen Lui

Ach a' Mhadaidh
Allt a' Mhadaidh-allaidh
Bad an t-Suidhe
Cnoc na Teididh
Dail Gainimh
Dail Rosaigh
Grampian Cottage
Ruighe an t-Sidhein

## Glen Muick (east side)

Ach na Creige
Allt Chernie
Baile an Torraidh
Baile an Torraidh
Baile Nodha
Blar Charraid
Bog an Roil
The Bog of Baile Nodha
Braeside
Camas Odhar
Chapel Croft of Aucholzie
Clais Muice
Cnocan Dubh
The Croft of Brochdhu
An Dubh-bhruach
Forester Haugh
An Geinn Dearg

Little Brochdhu
Lochend
An Loinn Mhor
The Milltoun of Aucholzie
Muckle Brochdhu
Ruighe an Lin
The Stoitear Croft
Teetabootee
Tom nam Buachaillean
Upper Aucholzie
Wadlehead
Waird-Head

**Glen Muick (west side)**

Allt a' Mhaide
Ardmeanach Croft
Croft of Birkhall
Croft of Wester Ardmeanach
Cuttie's Croft
Dorsincilly Cottage
Little Ardmeanach
Loinn Muighe
Overcroft of Ardmeanach
Stairean
Upper Alltcailleach

**Glen Tanar**

The Auld House o the Etnach
Coirebhruach
Ruighe Loisgte Croft
Rumbling Pots
Townhead
Waterside

**Inver–Invercauld Bridge**

Ach a' Ghiubhais
Ach Eich an Easa
Bridge of Dee Croft
Bun Fhiodhaich
Mill Croft of Inver
Muirtown of Ach Eich an Easa
Newton
Postie Bell's

**Invercauld Bridge–Braemar**

Ach an Sgeich
Ard-achaidh

Baile nan Gabhar
Boat
Creit a' Bhothain
An Carr Odhar
An Dail a' Choirce
Green Bank
Mill Croft
Mains of Invercauld
Milltoun Cottage
Milltoun of Invercauld
An Tom Reite
Torr an Fhraoich

**Inverey–Geldie**

The Canadian Camp
Creag Phadruig
Dail a' Mhorair Bheag
Dail na Cachaileithe
Dail nam Bord
Inbhir Geallaidh
Muileann Shaibh
Ruighe Ealasaid
Tom Liath

**Morven Lodge**

Bog na Muice
Bothan Eitidh
Burnside
Glac an t-Sabhail
Loinn Bheag
Loinn Mhor
Reid Jimmie's
The Shepherd's House

**Uncertain**

Athan Ghiubhais (Crathie–Braemar
    parish)
Roadside (Glenmuick parish)
Roadside (Crathie parish)
Rotten Haugh (Crathie–Braemar
    parish)
Ruighe na Cailliche (parish of
    Braemar)
Tom na Lairige (probably upper
    Glen Clunie)
Waterhead (possibly Inchmarnoch)

# APPENDIX 3

## WHAT ONE CAN LEARN FROM THE NAMES

**Their significance for local people**

Place names are like personal names or any other words in a language in being convenient for communicating precise information easily and quickly. However, they are much more than that. Rathad Bealach Dearg and An Rathad Crion convey more than 42nd Street, as they describe what these places look like. They also give more of a sense of history, tradition and identity even though the story behind the name is not known, just as a person's name is more memorable than a faceless personal number. Many place names are simply brief descriptions of the place or tell of some event that once happened or of some trade that went on there. If a language dies out, as Gaelic has done in our area, the name as a description may mean nothing to local people now. Glen Gairn folk now may not remember that Rineten is an anglicised form from Gaelic words meaning land-portion or cattle-run of the juniper, but anybody walking there can see that the unusually abundant juniper still justifies the Gaelic name.

Place names, like local language and dialect, are an important part of a local community's feelings of identity, and their pronunciation can tell much about changes in language and social change. One can also learn from them about mythology and other aspects, described below.

## Mythology

In our study area the name Carn an Tuirc (hill of the boar) may come from Celtic mythology. Boars featured much in the Irish tales of Fionn or Fingal, which spread through the Highlands (Campbell 1872). Carn an Tuirc stands near Glen Shee (just outside our area), where Diarmaid was said to have been buried on Tom Diarmaid beside the farm of Tomb (Gaelic Tom), after dying from the poisoned bristles of a boar from nearby Ben Gulabin.

In Deeside the second parts of the names Beinn Bhrotain and Clais Bhrodainn (erroneously Clais Rathadan OS) are pronounced the same ('vrǫtɐn) as Loch Bhrodainn south of Kingussie, and probably have the same meaning. MacBain (1922) spelled it as Loch a' Bhrodainn and gave an old legend about Brodainn, a mythical black dog which chased a white fairy deer.

Creag an Fhuathais (crag of the spectre) in Glen Ey looks a forbidding place. Grant (1861) describes a rock of the ghost in Glen Ey, probably meaning Creag an Fhuathais. McConnochie (1891) tells of the priest whose memory lives in the OS map name the Priest's Well at Loch Callater (still known as Fuaran an t-Sagairt to local folk), and in the hill Carn an t-Sagairt nearby. During a severe frost that froze all wells, the priest prayed and the well flowed freely. Cnap a' Chleirich (knob of the clergyman) on Beinn a' Bhuird and Clach a' Chleirich (stone of the clergyman) below it have no story as far as we know.

At Cnoc Chadail (hill of the sleep) up Glen Ey, a man was said to have fallen asleep and lived inside the hill with the fairies, to re-appear seven years later feeling no older. 'The Muir', a house at Inverey, was named from Sliabh Fhearchair (Farquhar's moor); Fearchar fell into the water of Dee while gathering willows upstream, and his body appeared at Sliabh Fhearchair. Mrs Jean Bain gave us both stories, which Diack had mentioned more briefly.

Grant tells of a Cailleach Bheathrach (wild old woman) who roamed the hills. He called her the Thunderbolt Carline and 'the great witch of Glengairn', who milked hinds after attracting them with her voice, like the deer witch in the Lochaber song Cailleach Beinn a' Bhric (Carmichael 1954; Mackinnon 1952). She may be the furthest-east example of the widespread Celtic legend of Cailleach Bheurr in the West Highlands and Cailleach Bhearach in Ireland (McKay 1929). The glacial meltwater channel in Glen Carvie has the name Sloc na Cailliche (pit of the old woman) after Cailleach Bheathrach; legend says that she bit this rocky gap with her teeth to try to make the water of Don flow into Deeside. Buailtean na Cailliche Beathraiche in Glen Fenzie were stone folds for her cattle, and the rocks of Tigh na Cailliche Beathraiche on Morrone her house.

## History

Alexander (1952) wrote that Creag Choinnich at Braemar 'may have been named after the king, Kenneth Macalpine', who once visited the nearby castle of Kindrochit. However, he also noted that the Annals of Ulster in 1014 mention a Cainnech (Kenneth) as Mormaer of Mar. As there is no independent evidence for these derivations from local legends, they are bound to be highly speculative. This illustrates another difficulty in place-name research, that the name could mean something quite different. Coinneach (dative singular Coinnich) also means moss, so the name may simply be crag with the moss (i.e. mossy crag), a good description of Creag Choinnich's cliffs to this day. We have tried to avoid exciting possibilities from distant history, especially when there is a simpler alternative in the form of a descriptive name that is still apt today.

Poll na h-Iuchrach or the Key Pool at Tullich near Ballater figures in one of the many local legends of St Nathalan. Other early saints appear in several names such as Cnoc Chalmac and Poll Ma-Chalmaig. Some old names in Gaelic and English show that many chapels and holy wells were scattered far more widely over the inhabited parts of the area than we see today, as in Eaglais Ceann na Dalach, Chapel Ma-Dheoir, the Chapel of the Seven Maidens, and the Nine Maidens' Well.

Grant tells how Mackenzie of Dalmore hid gold under the fir tree of Craobh an Oir (tree of the gold) in Glen Luibeg, and later on Cairn Geldie, where the OS map shows the name Cnapan Or (little knob of gold). This tale goes back to about the early 1700s, and the tree Craobh an Oir still thrives.

A story from the late 1700s tells of three or more Speyside tailors dying in a snowstorm at Clach nan Taillear (stone of the tailors) in the Lairig Ghru, after they had wagered that they would dance at the Dell of Abernethy, the Dell of Rothiemurchus, and Dail Mhor (now Mar Lodge) in one midwinter day.

Craobh na Croiche (tree of the gallows) at Inverey was last used in the late 1500s when a Lamont was hanged for sheep-stealing. After the laird had refused clemency, Lamont's mother cursed the Farquharson clan, saying it would become extinct, and indeed Grant wrote that the direct line of Farquharsons did come to an end.

At Carn na Cuimhne (cairn of remembrance) west of Crathie, each man who went to fight was said to have put a stone on the cairn, and each who returned removed his stone, so the stones still in the cairn represent the men who fell in battle. Carn na Cuimhne became the war cry of the clan Farquharson. However, early maps and other information show that it should be Carn na Coinnimh (cairn of the assembly), that is, a rally point. This would certainly make a more appropriate war cry. A more recent cairn stands at Tom Sgalan nan Sasunnach (hillock of stage or prop of the Englishmen) on Creag Choinnich; it marks the departure in 1831 of the last English troops from a garrison kept at Braemar Castle since 1748, after the Jacobite war.

Grant (1861) is the best source for legends in Upper Deeside, and several place names go with them. The Colonel's Bed, a concealed shelf of rock above the Ey Burn, commemorates John Farquharson the Black Colonel of Inverey, who hid there from pursuers in the late 1600s. Butan Sasunnach (English butts) by Clunie at Braemar refer to a minor battle with occupation troops after the 1745 Jacobite rising. Grant also tells of Clach Thogalach (the stone of the lifting) in Glen Luibeg. A dispute between the leaders of Rothiemurchus and Mar in 1715 led to a peaceful showdown, a trial of strength to lift and throw this big stone.

The personal name Ruairidh appears in Coire Ruairidh (Rory's corrie) of Beinn a' Bhuird and in Glac Ruighe Ruairidh (hollow of Rory's shieling) near Aberarder. Coutts—a common Deeside name still—features in Clach Choutsaich (Coutts' stone) on Ben Avon. We do not know anything about these people, or about the persons named in James Coull's Cairn on the Monaltrie Moss, or in the Domhnullach Road (the MacDonald's road) near Braemar, or in Ruighe Ealasaid (Elizabeth's shiel) in Glen Geldie, or in many other such names. Their local associations have all been forgotten.

## Ecology

### Plants

Moorland covers most of Upper Deeside, with trees confined to valley bottoms and lower hills. Much of this moorland has been artificially created and maintained by muirburn and by browsing deer and sheep. Fir woods still grow up to 580 m at Coilacriech, birch woods up to 610 m on Morrone, and scattered trees and scrub at higher altitudes on various crags out of reach of deer and sheep. Many tree seedlings start growing on the hill, but soon get eaten. The original natural vegetation would have been a varied woodland up to 600–700 m, a mixture of scrub and moorland for 100 m higher, and short arctic-alpine vegetation above 800 m. The place names reflect this; many tell of trees and scrub where neither exists today and where the nearest woods now lie more than two kilometres away. Good examples are Tom Bealaidh and Moine Bhealaidh (Bealaidh = of broom) north of Corndavon and east of upper Glen Derry, Feith Seileach and An Fheith Seileach (Seileach = willow) north of the Cairnwell and high on Culardoch, and Glen Geusachan (Giubhasach) = pine wood).

Some place names, mostly in the valley, refer to trees of the same species that grow there today. In a few cases where there is woodland now, it is of a different species from that in the place name. Tom Bheithe (hillock of birches) at Micras, which had no trees in 1900–20, now has some small young firs, but no birches, and Am Beitheachan (the little birch place) in Glen Quoich has a fir wood without birch. After vegetation has been burned, birch often comes in first and fir later. At the Muir of Dinnet, birch has colonised the moor since 1940, especially after moor fires, but fir has also begun to grow since 1960.

Most tree species have special requirements, such as fairly fertile damp ground for willow and banks of streams or rivers for alder, and place names show this. Many names with Seileach (willow) refer to wet places. Two hollows formerly called Lochan Seilich, at Tullich near Ballater, now lie on arable fields with no water in summer, but in winter and spring both often hold ponds or tarns.

Usually, juniper grows in big patches only in the woods, but it abounds on the open hill round Morven Lodge, in Glen Fenzie, and around Blairglass, Rineten, and the Coulachan Burn. This reflects the soil underneath, as the underlying rocks are lime-rich, for instance epidiorite on Morven and diorite at Coulachan Burn. More names with Aitionn or juniper occur there than elsewhere.

Lochan Feurach means grassy loch, and several other names probably refer to grass, such as Corrie Feragie, Feuragach, Na Feorachan, and Tom na Feoraich. Fraoch or heather appears in some names, such as Balanreich, Clashinruich, and Allt na h-Easgainne Fraoich. Other plants feature rarely, such as Allt Luachrach (rushes), Croft Muickan and Coire Meacan from Muiceann or Muilceann (baldmoney), and Creit an Roide (bog myrtle). Coirc (oats) appears in several names, such as Loinn a' Choirce, but we have not come across place names with other agricultural plants apart from grass.

### Animals

Only two names refer to invertebrates, Bad nan Cuileag and Allt Ruigh na Cuileige (Cuileag = fly). Although salmon and trout are important to Deeside folk, only one name—Poll an Eisg—mentions fish. Another—the Pass o the Salmon—is obviously a mistranslation (see Language). We found no names about amphibia. Only Creag Asp and Cnapan Nathraichean can be said to refer to adders, but the spellings in old maps suggest that Cnapan Nathraichean (OS) should probably be Cnapan Fhearchair (Farquhar's little knoll).

We found only two names that involved small birds; Preas Bad Smeoraich (thrush), and Tom na Riabhaig (lark). Birds of prey feature more, with Bad an t-Seabhaig and Creag an t-Seabhaig (falcon), and Tom Bad nan Speireag (sparrow-hawk). Several names mention Iolaire or eagle. Golden eagles are strongly traditional when nesting, using the same sites on crags and trees repeatedly over many years; four trees in our area have been used since at least 1880. Two rocks with Iolaire names have no eagle nests now, probably because they stand on grouse-moor country where eagles are disliked and have been persecuted, but eagles still perch there occasionally. Ravens also nest in traditional sites. One crag with a raven name (Fitheach) had ravens nesting for some years in the early 1900s.

Plovers feature in Coire na Feadaige, a good corrie for golden plovers to this day. Three lochs above 700 m have bird names: two cases of Loch nan Eun (loch of the birds), and Loch nan Stuirteag (loch of the black-headed gulls). All three have had small colonies of nesting seagulls since at least 1880, and no other loch above 700 m has had seagull colonies in recent decades.

Ailean nan Cearc (green of the hens), on a grassy flat west of Braemar, may refer to greyhens and to a place for the communal display or lek of the black grouse; lek sites are usually on short vegetation, and black grouse still thrive west of Braemar. Also, Cearc or hen in Irish names often means grouse, not poultry (Joyce 1913). Preas Bad nan Coileach-dubha refers to blackcock, and Balmoral stalkers now call it the Blackcocks' Howe. On Abergeldie, the Blackcocks' Wall (Scots = well) flows near another lek. The Coileach in Tom nan Coileach (hillock of the cocks) of Glen Girnock probably means red grouse because it is a heathery hillock, but the old map giving the Burn of Bad nan Coileach in Ballochbuie adds 'or Woodcocks Burn'. Ptarmigan feature only in Lochan an Tarmachain west of Lochnagar.

We found no Gaelic names to do with hares, though mountain hares have abounded this century in lower Glen Muick, Morven, Glen Gairn and Corndavon. Only one name—Ruighe Choinean—refers to rabbits. The Gaelic noun Cat appears in several names of crags or hollows often used by wild cats today. These occur up to 530 m at Creagan Chait near Inverey, but up to 600 m at Clais nan Cat near the Sleach and Clais nan Cat near Braemar. Graham Sturton at Ballater told us that one of the biggest wild cats he ever saw came from Clais nan Cat near the Sleach. The word Cat also appears in several place names on farmland, but here the derivation may be Cata, a sheep-cot.

Foxes feature in some names, sometimes as Sionnach, as in Allt an t-Sionnaich, but more often as Balgair (a common term in the east Highlands), or Saobhaidh (fox den). Several dog names occur, with Moine nan Con, Loch Vrotachan, and Allt Bhrot-choin.

Some old names refer to deer, such as Fuaran nan Aighean, Carn an Daimh, or Sron an Daimh, but Coire an Daimh Mhoile got its name in Victorian times. Many names with Gabhar show that goats must have been widespread at one time, but no feral goats occur today. All goat names on the open hill are in places with small cliffs or broken rocks.

A few names may involve animals now extinct. Names with Madadh possibly refer to foxes or dogs, but probably to wolves, and Madadh-allaidh certainly to wolves; all are on remote ground in the upper glens, and not on high hills. Tom Glady probably came from Gleadaidh or Gleddie, or red kite, a bird formerly common in Deeside but becoming extinct in the 19th century.

Each (horse) names feature in Ach Eich and Ach Eich an Easa, and Lair (mare) in Preas na Laire. Old estate papers (G) refer to small areas up Glen Geldie where grazing was let for colts or mares. Searrach (colt or foal) appears several times, for instance at Feith Shearrach, Capall (mare, horse) in Capel Mounth, and Marc (horse, charger) in field names (Marcach).

Some lamb, sheep and wether names occur, such as Meall nan Uan, Feith nan Caorach, and Cnoc nam Mult. Cattle names are more common, such as Bo (cow) in Dalnabo and Meall na Ba. There are several names with Laogh (calf) including Cnapan an Laoigh and Allt nan Laogh; some names with Laogh may refer to deer calves, especially those high on the hills. An old map gives 'ox how' at Lag an Daimh, but Daimh can also mean stag. Stirk names appear in Allt nan Gamhainn and Clais nan Gamhainn.

## Social changes since the 19th century

Some place names reflect changes in the way of life. Many people once farmed up glens that now lie empty. Hundreds of names refer to farms whose buildings today are mere heaps of stones. Even many of these have disappeared, as roadmen used them in the early 1900s for road metal.

Up to the 19th century, farming folk summered with their beasts on hill pastures miles away. The ruins of their shielings and enclosures lie in many high glens. Numerous names with Ruighe refer to these shielings and their grazings, as do anglicised names with Shiel or Shieling.

There are two cases of Carn nan Clach-mhuilinn or the Millstone Cairn at Auchallater and Conachcraig, a Carn Clach-mhuilinn in Glen Gairn, and a Carn Cloich-mhuilinn on Beinn Bhrotain. These hills had stones suitable for making millstones, and indeed a partly finished millstone still lies high on the Millstone Cairn near Auchallater.

Many names feature tracks, such as the Kirk Roads that local people used for travelling to church. The late Jimmy Stewart told us that people at Etnach in Glen Tanar formerly walked to their parish church at Ballater along a Kirk Road across peaty moors reaching 550 m altitude. In the early 1900s, gamekeepers at Etnach used this Kirk Road to walk to the nearest bars at Pannanich Inn or the Tink in Ballater. Many travellers once walked the old kirk roads and drove roads, but in recent decades very few have done so. Though some are now hard to find, these rights of way should not be forgotten.

Most bridges have been built since the mid 19th century. Before that, people crossed rivers at fords or by boat. We found names for several fords over Dee, for example at Ballater, Athan Phuill near Abergeldie, McPeder's Causeway west of Balmoral, Clagganghoul west of the Inver, Dalgowan west of Braemar, and An Athan Leathan at Inverey. McPeder's Causeway was a prepared route, to judge from a map of 1807–9. Fords on smaller rivers are Athan a' Gharain Shuas on the upper Gairn, at Balnaan near Gairnshiel, the Fuird o Inchnabobart on Muick, and Beul-ath na Lairige Dhru in Glen Luibeg. Several names such as Cobletoun, Boat of Clachanturn, and Bata an Duinidh (boat of the Dinnet) show that ferries regularly crossed Dee. Boat Puils refer to salmon pools best fished from a boat.

A few pool names are ancient (see History), but most more recent. Angling for salmon became fashionable only in the late 1800s and early 1900s. Ghillies named some pools after people who fished there (Farley's Cast), or lived nearby (Robertson Puil), but others from physical features nearby (Red Brae Puil, Poll Choich). Local folk told us of a Mary who drowned in Poll Mairi of Gairn, but did not know the year of this tragedy.

Place names show the great diversity of trades and occupations in local communities during former times. Allt Beart an Tuairneir (burn of lathe of the turner) flows down a remote hillside in upper Glen Gairn where no trees grow today and where the nearest people now live miles away. Several names contain Gobhann (smith), and others Taillear (tailor), Breabair (weaver), Fucadair (fuller), Muillear (miller), Fleisdear (fletcher), and Fear-bogha (archer). Some names mention Sagart (priest) or Cleireach (clergyman).

Many names refer to meal mills, and a few bobbin mills, bucket mills, saw mills, waulk mills, wool mills, and lint mills, almost all of which no longer exist. Others involve disused rock and slate quarries. Numerous names for the once important peat-mosses exist now only in old records, and very few people still burn local peat. A big rural population, largely self-sufficient and with a great diversity of trades and skills, has virtually gone. The population replacing it lives mostly in towns and villages, depending mainly on tourism, and increasingly includes retired incomers, daily and weekend commuters, and seasonal residents in holiday homes.

Field names show other evidence of social change. We found that most fields have names but on a few farms they are known by recent names invented by the family or workers, who did not know any previous names. We came across such cases mostly where new families had moved in as tenants or buyers from a different part of Scotland. On some farms, people knew fields only by the numbers on large-scale OS maps. We found this where the former tenant–laird relationship of family farms had changed to amalgamations run by the laird as one unit, with paid farm workers. However, at Dinnet Estate the estate owner asked former tenants about old field names with the intention of retaining them after farm amalgamations. Fraser (1978) has noticed in Scotland as a whole that field names are tending to be replaced by map numbers, along with a tendency for agricultural tradition and land tenure to be broken.

Other names are also being lost. The oldest deer stalkers told us that the previous generation had names for every hillock and burn, and that many of these had been forgotten. Old estate maps from the 18th and early 19th centuries show numerous names that are no longer in use today. Job mobility speeds up this change. Where once the deer stalker or farmer had been reared locally and learned names from parents and other local folk, today many have been reared in other parts of Scotland, and often they stay only a few years before moving on again. Furthermore, where one person formerly was gamekeeper or farmer on a small beat or farm, today each one looks after more ground, which gets bigger year by year as employers cut staff to raise productivity and as each farmer adds more land so as to make more money. The bigger the area a person looks after, the less his detailed knowledge of it and the fewer place names he needs to know. These decreases in the number of place names and the social changes that accompany them are also paralleled by changes in language.

## Related pairs or trios

Many names form pairs, such as Allt Mor and Allt Beag, which lie near each other. Although not a big burn, Allt Mor exceeds Allt Beag in size, so the name indicates a relative difference, not an absolute size. Many lowland Scots or English names begin with Little, and most of them pair with a nearby name beginning with Muckle, as in Little Pap and Muckle Pap (Meikle Pap of the OS map). Allt an Aitinn air Bheul runs down the front of a hill on Ben Avon, and Allt an Aitinn air Chul down the back.

Many pairs have Wester and Easter, and some trios West, Mid and East. On Beinn a' Bhuird lie a pair of corries, Ear (East) Choire an t-Sneachda and Iar (West) Choire an t-Sneachda. In Deeside to this day, up means west and down means east, and some names with Suas (up) and Sios (down) have been so translated, as in Lairig Shios or East Lairig. Easter Allt a' Chlaiginn runs into Callater slightly further west than Wester Allt a' Chlaiginn. We explain this apparent paradox by suggesting, as has been noted in some other parts of the East Highlands, that the words Easter and Wester arose as translations of Sios and Suas (lower and upper). As Glen Callater actually runs north-west, the burn joining it lower down (Sios) is farther west than the upper one (Suas), but the Gaelic words have been translated to English with the Deeside understanding of Sios = down = east, and Suas = up = west.

Many names are associated in pairs or trios of a different sort. For instance, many burns take their names from the corries that they run through, as in Allt Coire an t-Saighdeir from Coire an t-Saighdeir. A few corries carry the burn names, as in Coire Alltan na Beinne from Alltan na Beinne. In a few pairs, corrie and burn take their name from a third feature common to both, as in Coire Clach nan Taillear, Allt Clach nan Taillear and Clach nan Taillear. Combinations also appear in lowland Scots or English names, as in the Beinn Iutharns Corrie, the Front o the House Park, and the even more complex the Auld Wifie's Housie Park.

## Language

Numerous farms have some field names of Gaelic and others of lowland Scots origin, and sometimes also English names. There is a higher proportion of English names than in Buchan. Scots has been the main language in Upper Deeside for a much shorter time than in Buchan, and so its development involved rather fewer Scots words. Nether occurs frequently in names in lowland Buchan, but seldom in Upper Deeside, where the more common Lower indicates a later, English influence.

Lowland Scots and English names occur most commonly near Dinnet, and least frequently on Mar. Similarly Gaelic died soonest at Dinnet and latest at Inverey on Mar. The fishing pools show this change well. Lowland Scots and English names predominate east of Ballater, with few Gaelic ones, but become scarcer from Ballater to Ballochbuie as Gaelic names increase. Gaelic names of pools west of Ballochbuie are common, lowland Scots names scarce, but English names still quite common as translations of former Gaelic ones. The word for a pool itself changes, in the east nearly always Scots Puil (phonetic pronunciation pil), but west of Inverey nearly always English Pool or Gaelic Poll.

Similarly, most field names in Cromar are Scots, but at Crathie many are Gaelic. Auchnerran in Cromar has the Cairt Shed Park, the Cornyard Park, the Creagaidh Larach Park, the Gallow Hill Park, the Moss Park and the Tofts Park. Near Auchnerran lies the Mosstown, with the Brig Park, the Lang Straucht, the Mill Course Park, the Mosstown Haugh, and the Smiddie Park. Townhead, east of the Mosstown, has the Auld Wifie's Housie Park, the Gairden Park and the Wall Park. Ballabeg north of Auchnerran has the Barn Park, the Bog Park, the Cornyard Park, the Front o the House Park, Howmies, the Kiln Park, Lang Toman a' Bhothain, the Middle Park, the Mill Park, and Square Toman a' Bhothain. Further up Deeside, the Lebhall east of Crathie has fields with more Gaelic names: the Black Wood Park, A' Bhruach Chorrach, the Bog Park, the Brae Park, the Chapel Park, Dail Iaruinn, the East and West Park, An t-Eilean, Eilean Fhearn, the Haugh, the Lang Back, An Raon, An Roinn Chruaidh, the Three-cornered Park, and An t-Uchd. Most lowland Scots field names take the form 'the . . . Park', whereas Gaelic ones have more variety.

Many names remained Gaelic but with scotticised or anglicised pronunciation; only a few old people still pronounce them according to the Deeside dialect of Gaelic. Others became translated or otherwise changed into lowland Scots or English. Many lowland Scots names have also altered, to English ones. All three processes still continue, as one can see by comparing how old and young people pronounce the same names.

Gaelic names frequently become scotticised or anglicised as translations, such as Clach nan Taillear also being known as the Tailors' Stane. The translations are usually correct, and so probably occurred when people still knew much Gaelic. Incorrect translations probably arose where an uncommon word resembled a different, well-known word. For example, Lairig nam Braighdean or Braidean (pass of the pack saddles) became Pass o the Salmon, probably because the obscure Braighdean resembles the more commonly known Bradan (salmon).

Gaelic names of rivers, farms, villages and high hills have generally not been anglicised or altered to lowland Scots. However, many small hills and lochs in east Scotland have become Hill of ____ and Loch of ____ (Nicolaisen 1965), including some from Gaelic, and also Allt ____ has changed often to Burn of ____ (Nicolaisen 1976), or to the ____ Burn (many examples in our list).

Influential outsiders imposed some anglicisations. Local stalkers used Coire Bhearn-uisge (corrie of the water gap), but an English-speaking deer-shooting tenant suggested Big Corrie. The local stalkers now call it that, even though they would prefer Coire Bhearn-uisge. Some have said our study may help to stop or reverse this process, as they could then point to the book as a reference. No languages or names stay still. However, some of these changes have arisen not spontaneously from local people, but from outsiders paying no regard to local identity or culture. A few Braemar people recently objected to their familiar Milne's Brae being marked as Castleton Place on a street sign. The local authority said it must remain Castleton Place because that was the name on large-scale maps, yet Braemar folk have told us they never heard this name before. Some outsiders' translations or anglicisations did not last, however. The English-speaking Earl of Fife in the 1700s wrote often of the Green Burn of Derry, meaning Glas Allt Mor, but we have never heard anyone call it Green Burn.

A few anglicised names may be due to prudery. The hill Lochnagar takes its name from a tarn at its foot, replacing the older Beinn nan Ciochan or hill of the paps. Michie (1897) passed a revealing, narrow-minded judgement, 'It would, however, be most unwise to go back on these old and obsolete names, and try to re-establish them again. Everything noble, grand, sublime, historic, and poetic, is associated with the name Lochnagar, now given to the mountain. Let the old name Binchichins die in peace'! Another example of this is Devil's Point. It is not the 'literal translation of the Gael. Bod an deamhain' (Alexander 1952); Bod an Deamhain means penis of the demon.

## Pronunciation

We confirm Alexander's (1952) statement that aspiration in Gaelic names has often disappeared in Upper Deeside; for instance, A' Bhruach Mhor (classic Gaelic pronunciation ə͵vruɐχˈvoːr) has become ðɪˈbruɐχˈmoˑr. He also wrote that eclipsis had usually disappeared, and we found many cases of this, for instance karnˈdauḷ and karnˈdagɐrtʃ become karnˈtʌuḷ and karnˈtagɐrt, and often kerṇˈtul and kerṇˈtagɐrt. Only Mrs Jean Bain said karnˈdagɐrtʃ, the sole person with a fair amount of Deeside Gaelic left. Two others who used karnˈdauḷ had heard it from their father who spoke Deeside Gaelic fluently. Nevertheless, many other cases of eclipsis still continue, as at Coire nan Clach ͵kọrnɐˈglɑχ and Coire nam Fiadh ͵kọrnɐˈvio (erroneously Coire an Fheidh (OS)).

The pronunciation of simple Gaelic names like Allt Mor has usually remained relatively unchanged, but the more complex Coire na Fuath-chlais, Coire Cadha an Fhir Bhogha, Allt na h-Easgainne Fraoich, and Allt nan Cuigeal sometimes not (peculiar versions that we have heard, each from only one person and even then not consistently on return visits) are ͵kọrnɐˈfuʒələç, ˈkọrˈkarneˈvu, ˈaltnɐˈfrʌskënˈhu and ˈgʌlpnɐˈgwigəl).

Many Scots names are pronounced in the same way as in lowland Aberdeenshire, but there are a few differences. In place names and ordinary speech, White is fɛit in Buchan, but in Upper Deeside west of Cromar hwɛit. Buchan people pronounce School like the English squeal (skwil), but Upper Deeside folk west of Cromar give the English pronunciation (skul). As in Buchan, old local people in Upper Deeside pronounce Lodge as lʌʤ, and younger ones as lọʤ, but some old folk brought up at Inverey say lœʤ using a vowel more typical of places further west in the Highlands.

Alexander (1952) noticed that people in Upper Deeside pronounced the diphthong sound in Dry as ʌɪ and ʌi. He did not say which parts of Upper Deeside, though on p 356, referring to Cromar people, he wrote that this unusual sound was characteristic of the district, presumably meaning Cromar. We found it commonly in old people brought up at Tullich, Cambus o' May, Inchmarnoch, and Cromar, and one from Inverenzie on Gairn, in place names and ordinary speech, but noted it as the diphthong ɛi. Another interesting pronunciation in Cromar is that a few old folk pronounce the word Stone as sten and not the usual Aberdeenshire phonetic stin. This had already been noticed in another part of Cromar (Ellis 1869–89; Grant 1925), at Tarland, which is near but outside our study area.

In common with many English words, some Gaelic names have had vowel sounds altered to the lowland Scots pronunciation, as in ͵ẹbërˈẹrdër for Aberarder and blərˈglẹs for Blairglass, whereas some people still give the more Gaelic ͵abërˈardër and blərˈglas. Similarly, with Scots and English names, some folk give a Scots pronunciation and others a more English one. Many pronounce Croft as kraft but others krọft, some say pil for Pool but others pul, some say wɑˑl for Well but others wẹl, and some say wɑst for West but most wẹst. Braehead is breˈhid to some, but breˈhẹd to most. People raised at Braemar, Crathie and Ballater generally use the more English pronunciation, whereas those raised in Cromar, mid Deeside and Donside use the less English, more Scottish type. Even in Cromar, however, a few locally-reared people interviewed by us chose to speak English habitually, though they understood Scots well enough. Such people knew very few place names, and tended to use anglicised pronunciations for them. We have chosen not to give their pronunciations in our list. Phonetic data in the list rest entirely on information from the majority of people, who spoke lowland Scots by choice or habit.

During interviews with even habitual Scots speakers, we came to realise the key importance of the OS map in influencing their pronunciations. In many instances where informants gave us traditional pronunciations, they quickly added what they called the 'proper' pronunciation. Nearly always this was what appears on maps, road signs, telephone directories, post office names, and electoral registers, which of course follow the OS maps. Examples:—ðɪˈmʌkəlˈkënër, 'but it should really be ˈmikəlˈkinˈọrd (Meikle Kinord), that's on maps', or ͵ɪnvërˈɪɲi, 'but it's really ͵ɪnvërˈɛˑnzi (Inverenzie), that's printed on the maps', or not far outside our area aˈbɛin, now often distorted to aˈbɔin (Aboyne) as on maps and village signs. The map spelling Coilacriech Inn leads to the frequent ͵kɔilɐˈkriəç instead of the traditional ͵kɛilɐˈçriç, Cambus o' May becomes ˈkambəsoˈme instead of ͵kamɐsɐˈmɛiˑ, and Ballaterach becomes baˈlaˑtërɐχ instead of bɐˈlẹtrɐç.

# APPENDIX 4

## RHYMES AND POEMS

Place names are more than a convenient way of identifying locations. They are also an important part of a local community's culture and feelings of identity. This is well illustrated by the popularity of some local rhymes and poems that emphasise place names.

The earliest recorded song that we have found is the Gaelic one of 'Allt an Lochain Uaine' by William Smith or Gow, the Strathspey poet of the late 18th century who had a poacher's bothy by this burn above Glen Derry. Shaw (1859) gave the full poem, later printed again by Sinton (1906). The first verse goes,

Aig allt an Lochan Uaine,
Bha mi uair 'tamh,
Ged bha 'n t-aite fuar
Bha 'n fhardach fuasach blath,
Ged thigeadh gaoth 'o thuath orm
'Us cathadh luath o'n aird,
Bha Allt an Lochan Uaine,
Le' fhuaim ga m' chuir gu pramh.

Sinton (1906) gives a slightly different version,

Aig Allt an Lochain Uaine,
Gu 'n robh mi uair a' tamh,
'S ged bha 'n t-àite fuar,
Bha 'n fhàrdach fuathasach blàth;
Ged thigeadh gaoth 'o thuath orm,
'Us cathadh luath o 'n àird,
Bhiodh Allt an Lochain Uaine,
Le 'fhuaim ga m' chuir gu pràmh.

A fairly direct translation (Watson 1975) gave,

At the burn of the green tarn,
I was staying a time,
And though the place was cold
The dwelling was wonderfully warm,
Though wind from the north would come on me
And fast drifting from the height
The burn of the green tarn would be
Putting me to slumber with its sound.

The chorus and other verses, given below, mention more place names in the Derry area, which the reader will recognise as the current OS names of Lui and Carn a' Mhaim.

### Luinneag (Chorus)

Mo chailin bhoidheach chuach-bhuidhe,
Na biodh ort gruaim no greann,
Ged tha mi dol as 'm eolas
Ma's beo dhomh thig mi ann,
'S nuair bhios damh na croic
Ri boilich anns a' ghleann,
Cha d-thoirins blas do phoige
Air stor nan Innsean thall.

Oidhche dhomh 's mi a' m' aonar
'S mi comhnuidh anns a ghleann,

Ann am bothan beag na'n sgod,
Far an cluinnear boilich mheann.
Air leam fhein gun cuala mi,
Fuaim a dol fo m' cheann,
Ag innseadh dhomh 'bhi seolta
Gun robh an tòir 's a ghleann.

Dh' eirich mi le buaireadh,
'Us thog mi suas mo cheann,
Gach badag 'bha mu'n cuairt domh,
Chuir mi mu'm ghuaillnibh teann,
Bha "Nigh 'n a chornail" shuas uam,
A choisinn buaidh 's gach am
'Us thuirt i "na biodh gruaim ort
Ma 's ruaig e na bi mall."

Shiubhail mi gach caochan,
O Laoighe gu Carn-Mhaim,
'Us bheachdaich mi gach aon diubh,
Nach bitheadh daoine annt,
Mu 'n d'eirich grian 's na speuraibh,
'S mu 'n d' fheuch i air aon charn,
Ghrad dh' aithnich mi san uair sin.
Am "Madadh Ruadh", 's a' ghleann.

Labhair mi le ceille,
'Us dh' eisd mi ris gach allt,
Mar fhreagradh iad d 'a cheile,
'Us iad gu leir gun chainnt,
Labhair mi ri m' Uachdaran,
'Thug uillt a' cruas nam beann;
Le comhnadh 'n Fhir 'chaidh cheusadh,
Cha bhi mi fein a 'm fang.

Sinton (1906) wrote 'there has probably been no Gaelic song more popular throughout Badenoch and Strathspey during last century than this'. Sung to a well known Gaelic air, this was 'for several generations probably the most popular of all songs, not only in Braemar but throughout the eastern Highlands' (Alexander 1938). Subsequently, as Gaelic died, the song was forgotten. Only one of our oldest Deeside informants—Ian Grant of Inverey—remembered any of it, and could not complete the first verse without reading it. Ian died in 1981. Probably there is now nobody brought up in Upper Deeside who learned and can recite this song from oral tradition.

In verse 4 of his 'Hunting Song', Smith wrote,

'N uair dh' eir'as mi 'sa mhadain
Air Ghlas-Allt bheir mi ruaig,
'S mar fhaigh mi ansa Ghlas-Allt,
Na fir aigeannach bhios uam,
Bheir mi'n sin an leacann orm,
'Us gu 'm beachdaich mi mu'n cuairt,
'Us gu 'm faic mi na daimh-chabarach,
Ann 'n leth taobh' Meall-an-uan.

Ghlas-Allt and Meall-an-uan can be recognised as the OS names of Glas Allt and Meall nan Uan in Glen Derry and Glen Lui.

After 'Allt an Lochain Uaine', the next place-name rhyme that we have come across is in Grant (1861),

'Jarnie is Dai's air da thaobh Gheaullie
The Jarney, the Davy, and both banks of Geldie',

referring to Allt Iarnaidh, Allt Dhaidh and Geldie Burn. And also,

'Theid sinn mach air Gleanneidh,
Agus stigh air Gleann Dee,
Bho Ghleannan gu Gleannan,
Sior leanail an fheidh.'

English translation by us,

We will go out by Glen Ey,
And in by Glen Dee,
From glens to glens,
Continually chasing the deer.

Milne (1897) published the following poem, adding three stanzas of his own to the old locally-known first stanza,

We'll up the muir of Charleston,
   An' owre the water o' Dee,
An' hyne awa to Cean-na-coil,
   It's there that I would be!

Ballaterach braes are bonny
   Wi' the birks a' scattered owre;
And how sweet from Little Tulloch
   Loch Kennor's woody shore!

The muir fowl crops the heather bloom
   An' bickers on the brae;
The Black Cock spreads his glossy wing,
   And everything is gay.

The deer they bound in Etnach,
   And the salmon leap in Dee;
An' hyne awa' to Cean-na-coil,
   It's there that I would be!

Mrs Elizabeth Watt at Newton gave three verses to us like this,

wil'ʌpðr'mi·rɐ'tʃarlstən
ɪn'ʌu.ɐ̈rðr'watɐ̈rɐ'di·
ɪn'hɛɪn‚a'wa·tɪ'kjanɐ'kɛɪl
ɪts'ðɛ̯r‚ðɐt'ae‚wɪd'bi·

bɐ'lɛ̯trɛ̈çs'brez‚ar'bo̯ne
wɪðr'bɐ̈rksa·'skatɐ̈rd'ʌu.ɐ̈r
ɪnhʌu'switfe'lɛ̈təl'tʌlǝç
lo̯χ'kɪnɐ̈rz'wudi'ʃo̯r

ðr'dir‚ðe'bʌund‚ɪn'ɛ̯tnɐχ
ðr'sa·mǝn'lip‚ɪn'di·
‚bɪt‚ɪts'hɛɪn‚a'wa·tɪ'kjanɐ'kɛɪl
ɪts'ðɛ̯r‚ðɐt'ae‚wɪd'bi·

An old saying (Aberdeen Journal Notes & Queries) goes,

Cushnie for cauld, Culbleen for heat, and Clashanreech for heather.

Cushnie is outside our study area, Culblean south of Morven, and Clashanreech in Glen Gairn (Clashinruich in our list).

Several Gaelic poems that the Rev Robert MacGregor had collected in the Glen Gairn–Crathie area around the turn of the 18th–19th centuries were published by Robertson (1932) and by Watson (1983). Several of these mentioned local place names, and 'Oran a rinn fear do Shionnach a bha marbhadh nan caorach aige' referred to quite a number.

Verse 5 goes,

A mhearlaich fàg am Bràigh so,
'S na tamh ann a ghairidhean,
Eadar ruidhean Obaràrdair,
Is bràigh Bad-a-chailean so;
Mur ghabhas sin 'san Làiric,
Cul-Ardoch 's Tom a charraidh thall,
O Easan Ruidh-nan-àiridh,
Gu àthan uisge Gharain shuas.

Diack (ms) recorded a local place-name rhyme about Inchmarnoch,

Balletrach's shepherds watched their sheep,
On Torrykee by nicht;
The Caesar dog cam barkan' by
An' pat them a' to flicht.

It's they did to the Milton gang
Far they had been afore;
The vrichtie he did turn them there,
An' pat them to Rinnmore.

He also noted this one at Dinnet,

There's the Easter bog an' the Waster bog
   An' the bog o' the Trimmlin' tree,
Camasa gate an' Dunkie's Leys,
   An' the Berry bog tee.

Diack wrote 'The "bog o' the Trimmlin' tree" was where Dinnet village is; "Camasa gate" at the river beside Dinnet House; the others I cannot locate'.

Diack also collected a large amount of Gaelic poems and rhymes mentioning place names from various parts of Upper Deeside. We do not give these here as they are readily accessible; he included them in his book 'The Inscriptions of Pictland' (1944).

A poem in 'The Deeside Field' (Second Series, Number 4, 1962) mentions many place names,

### Balmoral's Neighbours

There's places up in Crathie wi' a lilt in
   ilka name
A' clustered roon that bonnie hoose the
   Royal Hielan' hame,
An' prood they richtly are tae be the
   neibours o' the Queen.
There's Tullochcoy, Balchlaggan, an' Belnoe,
   an' Cairnaquheen,
An' Tynabaich an' Crathienaird, the Street
   an' Clachanturn,
Tornauran an' Monaltrie Mains an' Crystal's
   by the burn.
Drumargettie, the Micras an' "John Begg"
   o' Lochnagar,
The Buailteach, Aberarder an' The Bush an'
   Corbieha'.
Alas! Aw doot ma rhyme begins tae hyter
   an' tae falter—
Bit na! here's Lawsie, Piperhole, the
   Inver an' Torgalter.

183

Aye, names that lilt an' sing in herts that
    lang syne kent them weel
Fan they meant Hame an' couthie folks, sae
    friendly, kind an' leal.

G.M.L.
(probably George M. Leys)

The last two lines show the strong feeling that local people have for their place names.

The late Calum Mackie at Ballater composed this place-name rhyme, published in the 'People's Journal' probably in the 1970s, and recited it to us,

Up the Darach,
An ower Stranyarrich,
Up ower the Shenval,
Lift up yir kilt,
Tomintoul an time til't.

ˈʌpðɪˈdarɐχ
ɪnˈʌu.ɐ̈rˌstrɒnˈjarəç
ˈʌpˌʌu.ɐ̈rðɪˈʃɛ̩nˌvɐl
lɐ̈ftˈʌpjɪrˈkɐ̈lt
ˌtamənˈtʌu̩lˌɪnˈtɛimˌtɐ̈lt

Several other poems and rhymes that emphasise place names have been handed down orally and have apparently not been published before now.

A Mr Grant from Glen Muick went abroad last century and composed a poem about his native glen. Mrs Euphemia Downie at Ballater could still recite it at the age of 103 years, but since her death in January 1974 only bits of it are now remembered, and the order and words of some lines are uncertain. We give it in Scots, using spellings as in the Scottish National Dictionary, followed by the pronunciation in phonetics.

Frae the braes o Tom nam Buachaillean
An the rigs o Aultonrea,
Frae the . . . o . . . Loinn Muighe,
Wi its aulden rodden tree,
Up an doon the glen o Muick,
Aa ma friends o memory
Will aye be cherished wi delicht,
When thocht upon by me.

feðɪˈbrezɐˈtamnəˈbaχlən
ɪnðɪˈrɪgzɐˈaltənˈriˑ
feðɪ ɐ ˌlɪnˈmui
wiɪtsˈaˑldɪnˈrɒdɪnˈtri
ˌʌpɪnˈdunðɪˈglɛ̩nɐˈmɐ̈k
ˌaˑmɐˈfrɪnzɐˈmɛ̩mərˈi
wɪlˈɛibiˈtʃɛ̩rɪʃtˌwidɪˈlɐ̈çt
hwɛnˈθɒ̩χtˌʌˈpɒ̩nˌbaeˈmi

At Crathie you can still hear,

Piper Hole, Scutter Hole, Crichienaird,
    an Lawsie.

Doon below the Muckle Craig, ye'll see
    the kirk o Crathie.

ˈpɛipɐ̈rˈholˈskʌtɐ̈rˈholˌkrɪçeˈnerdən
    ˈlaˑzi
ˈdunbəˈloðɪˈmʌkəlˈkregˌjɪlˈsiðɪ
    ˈkɐ̈rkɐˈkraˑθe

A crude, later version runs,

Piper Hole, Scutter Hole, Airse Hole,
    an Lawsie.

ˈpɛipɐ̈rˈholˈskʌtɐ̈rˈholˈɛ̩rsˈholən
    ˈlaˑzi

Another Crathie rhyme goes,

Piper Hole for Scutter Hole,
Inver Inn for skitter an din,
An Crathie for wee bonny bairns.

ˈpɛipɐ̈rˈholˌfɒ̩rˈskʌtɐ̈rˈhol
ˈɪnvɐ̈rˈɛnˌfɒ̩rˈskɛtɐ̈rənˈdɛn
ɪnˈkraˑθeˌfɒ̩rˈwiˌbɒ̩neˈbɐ̈rn̩z

A local expression for any remote place is 'The back o the Buailteach' ðɪˈbakɪðɪˈbultʃɒ̩ç, the Buailteach being the last farm out on the hill road from Balmoral to upper Glen Muick.

The children from the Tomintoul crofts high on Morrone used to be cat-called by the more affluent Braemar children,

Tomin, Tomintoulers,
Oatmeal devourers.

ˌtɒ̩mənˌtɒ̩mənˈtʌulɐ̈rz
ˈotˈmilˌdɪˈvʌurɐ̈rz

A verse about a Ballater man runs,

When Sheridan was herdin
His sheeps at Birkha
The lambies were bleatin
An Sheridan was greetin
An five o the best o the sheep ran awa.

ˈhwənˈʃɐ̈rdɪnˌwɪzˈhɐ̩rdɪn
ˌhɪzˈʃipsˌɐtˌbɐ̈rkˈhaː
ðɪˈlamezˌwɒ̩rˈblitɪn
ɪnˈʃɐ̈rdɪnˌwɪzˈgritɪn
ɪnˈfaevɪðɪˈbɛ̩stɪðɪˈʃipˌrɐnɐˈwaː

Within living memory, Sheridan tended the local butcher's sheep. The story behind the rhyme has been forgotten, but it is an interesting illustration of the local pronunciation of Birkhall.

The number of place-name rhymes and poems, and the affection in which they are held locally, clearly show how important place names are to local tradition and culture.

# REFERENCES

**Publications and unpublished notes**

*Publishers' names are given only for books in the last few decades*

Aberdeen Journal (1908–15) Aberdeen Journal Notes and Queries, Vols 1–8 (Aberdeen)

Abergeldie papers. Unpublished papers formerly in the Abergeldie charter chest, referred to by Macdonald (1899)

Aboyne, Earl of (1894) *The Records of Aboyne* (Aberdeen)

Act of Parliament (1776) The Road from Aberdeen to Braemarr, and from Aberdeen to Durris and Banchory Ternan by the South Side of Dee River. Published according to Act of Parliament, February 8th 1776.

Adair, I (1901) *The Hall of Memories* (Edinburgh)

Alexander, H (1925) Hill excursions from Braemar, *Deeside Fld* **2**, 7–11

—— (1938) *The Cairngorms*, Scottish Mountaineering Club Guide (Edinburgh)

Alexander, W M (1931) An Aberdeenshire cairn and its tradition, *Scott Gaelic Stud* **3**, 200–2

—— (1942) The Mounth Roads, *Scott Gaelic Stud* **5**, 154–60

—— (1945) Some name-pronunciations, *Cairngorm Club Jnl* **15**, 265–8

—— (1952) *The Place-names of Aberdeenshire*, Third Spalding Club (Aberdeen)

—— (1954) The place-names on and around Lochnagar. *Cairngorm Club Jnl* **16**, 60–4. Place-names west of Braemar, *Cairngorm Club Jnl* **16**, 128–33

—— Unpublished notes, Archives Dept, King's College library, Univ of Aberdeen.

Allan, J (1925) Chips from a Deeside lumberman's log, *Deeside Fld* **2**, 36–8

Allardyce, J (1895) *Historical Papers relating to the Jacobite Period 1699–1750*, Vol 1. (1896) Vol 2 (Aberdeen)

Anderson, P J (ed) (1889) *Fasti Academiae Mariscallanae Aberdonensis*, Vol 1 (Aberdeen)

Anderson, R (1922) Scenic view-points on Deeside, *Deeside Fld* **1**, 9–11

Anonymous (1564) *Carta Jacobi Morauie comitis de terris et dominiis de Bramar et Straithdee 1564*, In Robertson (1804) and Robertson (1847)

Anonymous (1672) Book of the Valuationes of the Shyre of Aberdene as they were sett down in the years 1644, 1649 & 1667. At Archives Dept, King's College library, Univ of Aberdeen.

Anonymous (1696) The Book or List of Poleable persons within the Shire off Aberdein & Burghs within the same. Original at Archives Dept, King's College library, Univ of Aberdeen.

Anonymous (1750) The Valuation of the Shire of Aberdeen for the year 1750. At Archives Dept, King's College library, Univ of Aberdeen.

Anonymous (1802) Valuation Book of Lands in Aberdeen-shire 1802 (including 1634 or 1635, 1644, 1649, 1674). At Archives Dept, King's College library, Univ of Aberdeen.

Anonymous (1856) *The Imperial Gazetteer of Scotland* (London)

Anonymous (prob. 1920s) *Tourist's Guide to Deeside* (Aberdeen). In Central Library, Aberdeen.

Anonymous (1924, 1928) *Index to Particular Registers of Sasines for Sheriffdom of Aberdeen.* Vol 1 1599–1609, 1617–1629. Vol 2 1630–1660. Record Office, Scotland. (Her Majesty's Stationery Office, Edinburgh)

Anonymous (1955) Foggo's Fence. *Book of the Braemar Gathering*, p 175

Anonymous (1972) *Fisherman's Map of Salmon Pools on the Aberdeenshire Dee* (Waverley Press, Aberdeen)

Anonymous (1973) *Statistics of the Annexed Estates 1755–1756* (Her Majesty's Stationery Office, Edinburgh)

Armstrong, R A (1825) *Gaelic Dictionary* (London)

Arrowsmith, A (1807) *Map of Scotland* (London)

Astor, G (1971) *Tapestry of Tillypronie*. No publisher stated.

Avery, John & Co (after 1928) *Ballater in Royal Deeside*. Official Guide (Aberdeen)

Bacon, G W & Co (probably before 1900) *New Survey Map* (Manchester)

Balfour, J (1630–57) Collection on the Severall Shires. MS, Advocates' Library, Edinburgh, quoted by Robertson (1843)

Barrow, G W S (1981) Popular courts in early medieval Scotland: some suggested place-name evidence, *Scott Stud* **25**, 1–24

Bellamore Ledger (1857–70s) Ledger of sales of meal from the Mill of Bellamore. Unpublished notebooks held by Miss M A McGregor

Bentinck, C D (1927) Dornoch place names, *Trans Gaelic Soc of Inverness* **31**, 98–115

Blaeu, J (1654) *Atlas Novus.* V (Amsterdam). *Scotiae et Hiberniae Pars Quinta. Duo Vicecomitatus Aberdonia & Banfia.* Also *Braid-Allaban, Atholia, Marria Superior, Badenocha, Strath-Spea, Lochabria.* Compiled from survey of Timothy Pont by Robert Gordon of Straloch. Recently reprinted by J Bartholomew & Sons, Edinburgh. See Cash (1901) and Stone (1970)

Blundell, O (1909) *The Catholic Highlands of Scotland* (Edinburgh & London)

Braemar Ratepayers and Amenities Association (*c.* 1970) *The Official Guide to Royal Braemar* (Herald Press, Arbroath)

Bremner, A (1931) The valley glaciation in the district round Dinnet, Cambus o' May, and Ballater, *Deeside Fld* **5**, 15–24

—— (1933) Geological notes, *Deeside Fld* **6**, 4–7

Brown, J (1831) *A Guide to the Highlands of Deeside* (Aberdeen)

—— (1835) *The Guide to Deeside* (Aberdeen)

—— (1869) *New Deeside Guide* (Aberdeen)

—— (1885) *The Deeside Guide* (Aberdeen)

Buchan, D (1979) The legend of the Lughnasa musician in lowland Britain, *Scott Stud* **23**, 15–37

Bulloch, J M (1903) *The House of Gordon* (Aberdeen)

Burn, R (1924) A Gaelic glossary, *An Gaidheal* **20**, 35–7

—— (1925) Finishing the three thousanders in the Cairngorms, *Cairngorm Club Jnl* **11**, 147–53

—— (1925) A Gaelic glossary, *An Gaidheal* **20**, 107

Campbell, J F (1972 edn) *Leabhar na Feinne* (Irish Univ Press, Shannon)

Carmichael, A (1954) *Ortha nan Gaidheal. Carmina Gadelica.* Vol 5, ed by A Matheson (Oliver & Boyd, Edinburgh)

Cash, C G (1901) The first topographical survey of Scotland, *Scott Geogr Mag* **17**, 399–414

—— (1911) Some early notices of the Avon and Upper Deeside, *Cairngorm Club Jnl* **6**, 18–24

Catholic Register Braemar (1703–36) Braemar Baptismal and Marriage Register, also St Andrews Braemar Baptisms book, 1736–1845, Ballater Baptismal Register 1782–1845, and Ballater Baptisms 1844–1967, held by priest at Braemar. Also St Andrews Catholic Church Braemar Register of Baptisms

1703–57, typed abstract in Archives Dept, King's College library, Univ of Aberdeen.

Catholic Register Glen Gairn. Glengairn and Braemar Baptisms. Register of baptisms administered in the Catholic congregations of Glengairn and Braemar from the year 1782 by me Lachlan McIntosh 1782–1845, typed abstract in Archives Dept, King's College library, Univ of Aberdeen. Also included is Register of Glengairn 1703–57, MS in Archives Dept. Also List of Catholicks in Glengairn 1830, MS book in possession of William Ross, Candacraig, Glengairn, copy in Archives Dept.

Christie, James (1817) *Instructions for Hunting* (Banff)

Committee (1843) *The Statistical Account of Aberdeenshire* (Edinburgh)

Congregation of Gairnside papers (1850) List of the Congregation of Gairnside with Communions by James Forbes, Easter 1850. Unpublished papers formerly held by the late Mrs M J Grant, Pinewood, Inverey.

Crathie Parish Books (1726–1946). Unpublished notebooks giving accounts, minutes, and communion rolls. At Manse of Crathie.

Crathie Presbytery Records (1784–) Unpublished papers formerly held by the late Mrs M J Grant, Pinewood, Inverey.

Crombie, J M (1861) *Braemar, its Topography and Natural History* (Aberdeen)

—— (1875) *Braemar and Balmoral* (Aberdeen)

Davidson, C (1920s) *Deeside Lyrics*. Privately printed.

Diack, F C (1911–35) Unpublished Notes (Da in Table 2) on place names of the eastern Highlands, copied by W M Alexander, held at the Archives Dept, King's College library, Univ of Aberdeen.

—— (1920–21) Place-names of Pictland, I. *Revue Celtique* **38**, 109–32

—— (1922) Place-names of Pictland, II. *Revue Celtique* **39**, 125–74

—— (1924) Place-names of Pictland, III. *Revue Celtique* **41**, 107–48

—— (1926) Aber and inver in Scotland, *Scott Gaelic Stud* **1**, 83–98

—— (1930s) Unpublished typed MS on the history of Glen Tanar. Copy at Archives Dept, King's College library, Univ of Aberdeen.

—— (1944) *The Inscriptions of Pictland*, Third Spalding Club (Aberdeen)

—— Unpublished notes by Rev C M Robertson, from Diack's letters to him, held in Nat Library of Scotland.

Dieth, E (1932) *A Grammar of the Buchan Dialect* (Cambridge)

Dilworth, A (1962) Strathavon in Banffshire, Srath Athfhinn or Srath Abhainn? *Scott Gaelic Stud* **9**, 136–45

Dilworth, M (1956) Catholic Glengairn in the early nineteenth century, *Innes Rev* **7**, 11–23, 87–100

Dinnie, R (1865) *An Account of the Parish of Birse* (Aberdeen)

Dorian, N C (1976) Gender in a terminal Gaelic dialect. *Scott Gaelic Stud* **12**, 279–82

Duff, J (1978) The Goring Hut, *Book of the Braemar Gathering*, pp 97–103

—— (1981) Man of Mar—Bob Scott, *Book of the Braemar Gathering*, p 107

Duguid, J (1931) The beginnings of Ballater, *Deeside Fld* **5**, 87–8

Dwelly, E (1901–11) *The Illustrated Gaelic-English Dictionary*. Reprinted 1971 (Gairm Publications, Glasgow)

Edward, R (1678) The County of Angus. Map on p 18 of D Fraser (1973)

Ellis, A J (1869–89) *On Early English Pronunciation*, Vols 1–5 (London)

Erskine, R (1912) Aberdeen Daily Journal, 4 September

Erskine, S. (1898) *Braemar* (Edinburgh)

Farquhar, A M (1925) The Dee, *Deeside Fld* **2**, 1–4

Fife, Earl of (1783–92) Journal of the Weather at Marr Lodge, during Shooting Season 1783–. Unpublished diary held at Archives Dept, King's College library, Univ of Aberdeen.

Forbes, A P (1872) *Kalendars of Scottish Saints*. (Edinburgh)

Forbes, S (1716–17) Description of Aberdeenshire. In Robertson (1843), pp 31–59

Forsyth, W (1894) Place names of Abernethy. *Inverness Scient Soc* 372–9

Fowler, H W & Fowler, F G (eds) (1911) *The Concise Oxford Dictionary of Current English*. Fourth edn 1956, revised by E McIntosh. (Clarendon Press, Oxford)

Fraser, A S (1973) *The Hills of Home* (Routledge & Kegan Paul, London)

—— (1977) *In Memory Long* (Routledge & Kegan Paul, London)

Fraser, D (1973) *Glen of the Rowan Trees* (Standard Press, Montrose)

Fraser, G M (1921) *The Old Deeside Road* (Aberdeen)

Fraser, I A (1977) Place names from oral tradition, *Tocher* **25**, 53–4

—— (1978) Place names from oral tradition (5), *Tocher* **29**, 334–5

Gaffney, V (1960) *The Lordship of Strathavon*, Third Spalding Club (Aberdeen)

Geddie, W (ed.) (1959) *Chambers's Twentieth Century Dictionary* (Chambers, Edinburgh)

Gibb, A & Hay, M F (1884) *The Scenery of the Dee* (Aberdeen)

Gibson, C (1958) *Highland Deer Stalker* (Seeley, Service & Co, London)

Glen Tanar Right of Way Litigation (1931). Unpublished record of this legal case, held at Central Public Library, Aberdeen.

Gordon, R (1641–48) Map of Badenoch, reproduced in MacBain (1922)

—— (1654) *Praefecturarum Aberdonensis et Banfiensis in Scotia Ultra-Montana Nova Descriptio*. In Blaeu (1662), *Atlas Scotiae* (Amsterdam) and Robertson (1843), pp 1–30

Gordon, S (1912) *The Charm of the Hills* (London)

—— (1920) *Land of the Hills and the Glens* (London)

—— (1921) *Wanderings of a Naturalist* (London)

—— (1925) *The Cairngorm Hills of Scotland* (London)

—— (1948) *Highways and Byways in the Central Highlands* (Macmillan, London)

—— (1951) *Highlands of Scotland* (Robert Hale, London)

Grampian Regional Council (late 1970s) *Hillwalking in the Grampian Region* (Dept of Leisure, Recreation & Tourism, Aberdeen)

Grant, J (1861) *Legends of the Braes o' Mar* (Aberdeen)

Grant, W (1925) The speech of Deeside, *Deeside Fld* **2**, 57–60

Grant, W & Murison, D D (1929–76) *The Scottish National Dictionary* (Scott Nat Dictionary Assn, Edinburgh)

Grub, G (ed.) (1869) *Illustrations of the Topography and Antiquities of the Shires of Aberdeen and Banff*, Vol 1 (Aberdeen)

Harper, J & Son (1906–07) *The Highlands of Scotland. Ballater Balmoral and Braemar*. Publisher not stated.

Humphrey, F P (1893) *The Queen at Balmoral* (London)

Huntly Estate Rental Book Cropt (1784) Notes made by F C Diack, Aboyne-Glen Tanar papers

Huntly rentals. MS referred to by Macdonald (1899)

Innes, C (ed.) (1845) *Registrum Episcopatus Aberdonensis*, 2 vols (Edinburgh)

—— (ed) (1854) *Fasti Aberdonenses* (Aberdeen)

International Phonetic Association (1963) *The Principles of the International Phonetic Association* (University College, London)

Invercauld other papers. Miscellaneous unpublished estate papers, held at Invercauld House.

Jackson, K (1972) *The Gaelic Notes in the Book of Deer* (Univ Press, Cambridge)

Jamieson, J (1867) *Jamieson's Dictionary of the Scottish Language* New edn by J Longmuir (Edinburgh)

Jervise, A (1879) *Epitaphs & Inscriptions* Vol 2 (Edinburgh)

Johnston, A K (1855) Sketch Map of the Valley of the Dee and Braemar. In MacGillivray (1855)

Johnston, J B (1934) *Place-names of Scotland*, Third edn, (London) Reprinted 1970 (S R Publishers, Wakefield)

Joyce, P W (1869, 1871) *Irish Names of Places*, Vols 1 & 2 (Dublin). (1913) Vol 3 (Dublin). All three republished 1976 (E P Publishing, Wakefield)

Keddie, W (late 1800s) *The Valley of the Dee* (Glasgow)

Keith, G S (1811) *General View of the Agriculture of Aberdeenshire* (Aberdeen)

Knox, J (1831) *Map of the Basin of the Tay* (Edinburgh)

Kyd, J G (1958) *Drove Roads around Braemar* (Cunningham, Alva)

Laing, A (1819) *The Caledonian Itinerary* (Aberdeen)

Lamont, A (1932) Place-names of the Knockdow Estate, *Trans Gaelic Soc of Inverness*, 33, 203–24

Lamont, D & Fimister, J (1860) *Valuation Roll of the County of Aberdeen* (Aberdeen)

Ledger from Mill of Auchendryne (1870s). Unpublished, held by J E M Duff, Mill of Auchendryne, Braemar

Legal printed papers. Miscellaneous papers relating to legal cases and Acts of Parliament, held at Scottish Record Office, and at the charter rooms of Invercauld House and Mar Estate Office.

Lindsay, P (1902) *Recollections of a Royal Parish* (London)

List of Catholicks in Glengairn (1830). Unpublished notebook. See Catholic Register Glen Gairn.

Logie, A (1746) Map of Aberdeen and Banff Shires. MS map.

Lothian, J (1838) *County Atlas of Scotland* (Edinburgh) Re-issued A & C Black (1848)

Lyall, J W (1892) *The Sportsman's & Tourist's Time-Tables and Guide to the Rivers, Lochs, Moors, and Deer-Forests of Scotland* (London)

McArthur, M (1982) Ghost evidence, *Scots Mag* 118, 160–5

MacBain, A (1890) Badenoch: its history, clans, and place names, *Trans Gaelic Soc of Inverness* 16, 148–97

—— (1894) The Gaelic dialect of Badenoch, *Trans Gaelic Soc of Inverness* 18, 79–96

—— (1922) *Place Names Highlands & Islands of Scotland* (Stirling)

McConnochie, A I (1885) *Ben Muich Dhui and his Neighbours* (Aberdeen)

—— (1891) *Lochnagar* (Aberdeen)

—— (1895) *Deeside* (Aberdeen)

—— (1896) The Cairngorm Mountains. I. The Eastern Cairngorms, *Cairngorm Club Jnl* 1, 236–58

—— (1898) *The Royal Dee* (Aberdeen)

—— (1923) *The Deer and Deer Forests of Scotland* (London)

—— (1932) *Deer Forest Life* (London)

M'Coss, J (1927) Some walks from Ballater, *Deeside Fld* 3, 10–12

Macdonald, D J (1915) West Kintyre field names, *Trans Gaelic Soc of Inverness* 27, 31–40

Macdonald, J (1892) *Place-names in Strathbogie* (Aberdeen)

—— (1899) *Place Names of West Aberdeenshire* (Aberdeen)

MacGillivray, W (1855) *The Natural History of Dee Side and Braemar* (London)

McKay, J G (1929) Comh-abartachd eadar Cas-Shiubhal-an-t-Sléibhe agus A' Chailleach Bheurr, *Scott Gaelic Stud* 3, 10–51

MacKinlay, J M (1896) Some further notes on the hagiology of Ballater district, *Scott Notes & Queries* 9, 186–7

MacKinnon, D (1887–8) Place names and personal names in Argyll, *The Scotsman* (Edinburgh)

Mackinnon, L (1952) *Cascheum nam Bard*. Earrann I (Highland Printers, Inverness)

Mackintosh, A M (1913, 1914, 1918) *Farquharson Genealogies*, Nos 1, 2, 3 (Nairn)

Macleod, J (ed) (1899) *Register of Testaments 1715–1800* (Scott Record Soc, Edinburgh)

MacPherson, J (1906) *Royal Braemar*. Fourth edn (Arbroath)

—— (1930) *John von Lamont*. Privately printed.

MacPherson, J (1977) Place names in the parish of Daviot and Dunlichity, *Trans Gaelic Soc of Inverness* 49, 1–8

MacQueen, J (1979) Pennyland and Davoch in south-western Scotland: a preliminary note, *Scott Stud* 23, 69–77

MacRae, A M (1983) A manuscript by John Crerar (1750–1840). *Trans Gaelic Soc of Inverness* 52, 198–221

Mar Estate papers. Unpublished papers held in charter room at Mar Estate Office

Mar map. OS 6-inch map with annotations, originally used on Mar Estate, now held by Aberdeen Mountain Rescue Team.

Mathieson, J M (1953) Place-names of Strathspey: Abernethy and Kincardine, *Trans Gaelic Soc of Inverness* 41, 219–41

Michie, C (1922) 'Piperhole', *Deeside Fld* 1, 28–9

Michie, J G (1877) *Loch Kinnord*. Revised edn 1910 (Aberdeen)

—— (1896) *History of Logie Coldstone and Braes of Cromar* (Aberdeen)

—— (1897) The Benchinnans, *Cairngorm Club Jnl* 2, 34–7

—— (1901) *The Records of Invercauld* (Aberdeen)

—— (1908) *Deeside Tales* (Aberdeen)

Milne, J (1897) *Poems in the Aberdeenshire dialect* (Aberdeen)

—— (1908) Kirkmichael (Banffshire) place names, *Cairngorm Club Jnl* 5, 93–114

—— (1912) *Celtic Place-names in Aberdeenshire* (Aberdeen)

Mitchell, A (ed) (1907) *Geographical Collections relating to Scotland, made by Walter Macfarlane*, Vol 2 (Edinburgh)

Mitchell, R L (1968) Maps of mountains, *Cairngorm Club Jnl* 93, 252–5

Moir, D G (1973) *The Early Maps of Scotland* (Royal Scottish Geogr Soc, Edinburgh)

—— (1975) *Scottish Hill Tracks. 2. Northern Scotland* (Bartholomew, Edinburgh)

Moll, H (1725) A Set of Thirty-six New and Correct Maps of Scotland divided into Shires. Copy at Nat Library of Scotland. Facsimile published Shearer, Stirling (1896)

Murison, D D (1963) Local dialects. *The North-East of Scotland* (ed by A C O'Dell & J Mackintosh), pp 197–202 (Central Press, Aberdeen)

Murray, W H (1947) *Mountaineering in Scotland* (London)

Neil, C G (1933) Glengairn, *Deeside Fld* 6, 72–4

—— (1947) *Glengairn Calling* (Univ Press, Aberdeen)

Nethersole-Thompson, D & Watson, A (1974) *The Cairngorms* (Collins, London). (1981) Revised edn Melven Press, Perth

Nicolaisen, W F H (1960) Notes on Scottish place-names, 14, Avon, *Scott Stud* 4, 187–194

—— (1961) Notes on Scottish place-names, *Scott Stud* 5, 85–96

—— (1965) Notes on Scottish place-names, 25, "Hill of ___" and "Loch of ___", *Scott Stud* 9, 175–82

—— (1976) *Scottish Place-names* (Batsford, London)

—— (1979) Field-collecting in onomastics, *Names* 27, 162–78

O'Connor, J D (1978) *Phonetics* (Pelican Books, Harmondsworth)

Ó Dónaill, N (1977) *Foclóir Gaeilge-Béarla* (Oifig an tSoláthair, Baile Átha Cliath)

Ogston, A (1931) *The Prehistoric Antiquities of the Howe of Cromar* (Third Spalding Club, Aberdeen)

OPR. Old Parochial Registers, 1717–1854, Births, Deaths and Marriages for parishes of Crathie & Braemar, and Glenmuick, Tullich & Glengairn, at Register House, Edinburgh.

Ordnance Survey. Original object name books for Scotland, Aberdeenshire Books 1–91, on microfilm at Register House, Edinburgh.

Ordnance Survey (1869). 1:10560 (6 inches = 1 mile) survey of Scotland, and subsequent resurveys.

Ordnance Survey (1973) *Place Names on Maps of Scotland and Wales*. Ordnance Survey, Southampton.

Parish Registers. Parish Registers of Aberdeenshire. Held at Register House, Edinburgh, referred to by Alexander (1952).

Parker, M (1931) *Fisherman's Map of Salmon Pools on the River Dee*. Printed, no location given.

Paul, F A J (1930s) *Sketches of Deeside* (London)

Paul, W (1881) *Past and Present Aberdeenshire* (Aberdeen)

Pennant, T (1769) *A Tour in Scotland*. (1772) *A Tour in Scotland and Voyage to the Hebrides*. (1790) 3 vols (Chester & London)

Philip, W W (1894) *Crathie Churches and Royal Bazaar at Balmoral* (Aberdeen)

Population on the estate of Invercauld (1851). Unpublished notebook, held at Invercauld Estate Office (included under Io in our abbreviations list).

Press & Journal (1973–83). Names seen in the newspaper 'The Press and Journal' (Aberdeen)

Record Office Grants (G). G in our abbreviations represents GD, E and other categories in unpublished papers in the Scottish Record Office, Register House, Edinburgh.

Reid, J & Tewnion, A (1949) *Walks around Ballater*. Third revised edn 1956 (Langstane Press, Aberdeen)

Rental of the Lands and Barrony of Invercauld (1763). Papers formerly held by the late Mrs M J Grant, Pinewood, Inverey.

Robertson, A E (1933) *General Guide-book* (Scottish Mountaineering Club, Edinburgh)

Robertson, C M (1898) Perthshire Gaelic, *Trans Gaelic Soc of Inverness*, **22**, 4–42

—— (1929) Studies in place names, *Trans Gaelic Soc of Inverness*, **32**, 206–19

—— (1932) Gaelic poems collected in Braemar, and original songs composed by the Rev Robert MacGregor and Mr Alex MacGregor, *Trans Gaelic Soc of Inverness*, **33**, 2–43

Robertson, J (1822) *Topographical and Military Map of the Counties of Aberdeen, Banff and Kincardine* (London)

—— (1843) *Collections for a History of the Shires of Aberdeen and Banff* (Aberdeen)

—— (1847) *Illustrations of the Topography and Antiquities of the Shires of Aberdeen and Banff*, Vol 2 (Aberdeen)

Robertson, W (ed) (1798) *An Index, drawn up about the year 1629, of many records of charters, granted by the different Sovereigns of Scotland between the years 1309 and 1413* (Edinburgh)

—— (ed) (1804) *The Parliamentary Records of Scotland* (Edinburgh)

Ross, H (1845) Unpublished typed letters about stalking at Mar Lodge (Captain Horatio Ross). Formerly held by the late Mrs M J Grant, Pinewood, Inverey.

Royal Archives (Ra in Table 2). Unpublished papers in archives at library, Windsor Castle.

Russell, J (1892) *Valuation Roll—County of Aberdeen, 1893* (Aberdeen)

School of Scottish Studies. Tape-recordings 209, PN 1963/12, and 849, of discussions with Gaelic speakers in Braemar, by F MacAulay, W F H Nicolaisen and T P McCaughey.

Scott, I (1959) *Fishermans Map of Salmon Pools on the River Dee*. Printed, no publisher stated.

Scottish Development Department (1967). *Cairngorm Area*. Report of the Technical Group on the Cairngorm Area, chairman F J Evans (HMSO, Edinburgh)

Scrope, W (1894) *Days of Deer-stalking* (Glasgow)

Seymour, W (1815) An account of observations upon some geological appearances in Glen Tilt, and the adjacent country, *Trans R Soc Edinb* **7**, 303–75

Shaw, D (1859) *Highland Legends* (Edinburgh)

Shepherd, N (1962) James McGregor and the Downies of Braemar, *Deeside Fld, 2nd ser*, **4**, 45

Sim, G (1903) *The Vertebrate Fauna of "Dee"* (Aberdeen)

Simpson, I J (1947) *Education in Aberdeenshire before 1872* (Univ of London Press)

Simpson, W D (1929) Beattie at Dee Castle, *Deeside Fld* **4**, 77–9

—— (1943) *The Province of Mar* (Univ Press, Aberdeen)

Sinclair, J (ed) (1791–99) *A Statistical Account of Scotland* (Edinburgh)

Sinton, T (1906) *The Poetry of Badenoch* (Inverness)

Sissons, J B (1966) *The Evolution of Scotland's Scenery* (Oliver & Boyd, Edinburgh)

Skene, W F (1886–90) *Celtic Scotland: a History of Ancient Alban* (Edinburgh)

Smith, A (ed) (1875) *A New History of Aberdeenshire, Part 1* (Aberdeen)

Smith, M (1961) *Climbers' Guide to the Cairngorms Area. 1 The Cairngorms. (1962) 2 Lochnagar, Broad Cairn, Clova* (Scottish Mountaineering Club, Edinburgh)

Smith, R (1980) *Grampian Ways* (Melven Press, Perth)

Smith, W. (1911) *Deeside* (Painted by W Smith, described by R Anderson) (London)

Stirton, J (1925) *Crathie and Braemar* (Aberdeen)

Stobie, J (1783) *The Counties of Perth and Clackmannan* (London)

Stockdale, J (1806) *Map of Scotland* (London)

Stone, J C (1970) The preparation of the Blaeu maps of Scotland: a further assessment, *Scott Geogr Mag* **86**, 16–24

—— (1972) A Locational Guide to the Pont, Gordon and Blaeu Maps of Scotland, *O'Dell Memorial Monogr* **3** (Dept of Geography, Univ of Aberdeen)

—— (1974) A map of Deeside in the late sixteenth century, by Timothy Pont, *Deeside Fld, 3rd ser*, **1**, 61–6

Stuart, J (ed) (1844) List of Pollable Persons within the Shire of Aberdeen. Aberdeen. Original list made in 1696

—— (ed) (1846) The Book of the Annual rentaris and Wedsettaris within the Schirrefdome of Abirdein, *Miscellany of the Spalding Club*, Vol 3, pp 71–139 (Aberdeen)

—— (ed) (1849) The Rentaill of the Lordschipe of Huntlye, *Miscellany of the Spalding Club*, Vol 4, pp 261–319 (Aberdeen)

—— (1865) Notices of a group of artificial islands in the loch of Dowalton, Wigtonshire, and of other artificial islands or 'crannogs' throughout Scotland, *Proc Soc Antiquities of Scotland* **6**

—— (1874) Section on Farquharson of Invercauld. In Fourth Report of the Royal Commission on Historical Manuscripts, pp 533–35 (Edinburgh)

—— (1877) Section on Gordon of Abergeldie. In Sixth Report of the Royal Commission on Historical Manuscripts, pp 712–13 (Edinburgh)

Tayler, A & Tayler, H (1928) *Jacobites of Aberdeenshire & Banffshire in the Forty-Five* (Aberdeen)

—— (1932) *A Jacobite Cess Roll for the County of Aberdeen in 1715* (Third Spalding Club, Aberdeen)

—— (1933) *The Valuation of the County of Aberdeen for the Year 1667* (Third Spalding Club, Aberdeen)

—— (1934) *Jacobites of Aberdeenshire & Banffshire in the Rising of 1715* (Edinburgh)

Taylor, E (1869) *The Braemar Highlands* (Edinburgh)

Taylor, G & Skinner, A (1776) *Survey of the Roads of North Britain or Scotland* (London)

Thomson, J (1826) *Atlas of Scotland* (Edinburgh)

Thomson, J M and others (eds) (1882–1914) *Registrum Magni*

*Sigilii Regum Scotorum* (The Register of the Great Seal of Scotland 1306–1659) (Edinburgh)

Thomson, T (ed) (1811–16) *Abstract of the Records of Retours of Services 1546–1700.* 3 vols (Edinburgh)

—— (ed) (1817–45) *Accounts of the Great Chamberlains of Scotland, 1326–1453* (Bannatyne Club, Edinburgh)

——(ed) (1841) *Liber Cartarum Prioratus Sancti Andree in Scotia* (Bannatyne Club, Edinburgh)

Valuation Roll—County of Aberdeen 1870 (1870) (Aberdeen)

Valuation Roll—County of Aberdeen, 1880 (1879) (Aberdeen)

Victoria, Queen (1868) *Leaves from the Journal of our Life in the Highlands* (London)

—— (1884) *More Leaves from the Journal of a Life in the Highlands* (London)

Wade, General. Map of proposals for a road from Deeside to Speyside via Glen Feshie. Illustrated on p 185 of Wyness (1968)

Watson, A (1975) *The Cairngorms* (Scottish Mountaineering Club District Guide, Edinburgh)

—— (1983) Old Gaelic poems from Aberdeenshire, *Scott Gaelic Stud* **14**, 25–58

Watson, A & Clement, R D (1983) Aberdeenshire Gaelic, *Trans Gaelic Soc of Inverness* **52**, 373–404

Watson, W J (1904) *Place-names of Ross and Cromarty* (Inverness)

—— (1904–5) The study of Highland place-names, *Celtic Rev* **1**, 22–31

—— (1905–6) Some Sutherland names of places, *Celtic Rev* **2**, 232–42, 360–8

—— (1908–9) Topographical varia, *Celtic Rev* **5**, 148–54; **6**, 68–81; **7**, 361–71; **8**, 235–45

—— (1916) Some place-names in the Cairngorm region. *Cairngorm Club Jnl* **8**, 133–6

—— (1924) Place-names of Strathdearn, *Trans Gaelic Soc of Inverness* **30**, 101–21

—— (1926) *The History of the Celtic Place-names of Scotland* (Edinburgh)

—— (1935) The place-names of Breadalbane, *Trans Gaelic Soc of Inverness* **34**, 248–79

—— (1939) Place-names of Perthshire. The Lyon basin, *Trans Gaelic Soc of Inverness* **35**, 277–96

Wills, V (ed) (1973) *Reports on the Annexed Estates 1755–1769* (Her Majesty's Stationery Office, Edinburgh)

Wilson, G W (1866) *Photographs of English and Scottish Scenery: Braemar* (Aberdeen)

Wyness, F (1968) *Royal Valley* (Reid, Aberdeen)

—— (1971) *Spots from the Leopard* (Impulse Books, Aberdeen)

**Unpublished plans at Register House and elsewhere**

*Abergeldie Castle*

Innes map (1806) Copy at Royal Archives, see Ram 1 below.

*Balmoral Estate Office and properties*

Abergeldie map (1848) Plan of the Lands of Birkhall and Abergeldie Forming No 12 of the Inventory of Writs and Title Deeds. Probably drawn by John Innes, Aberdeen. Formerly at Birkhall.

Balmoral map (1857) Plan of the Estate of Balmoral, Surveyed by James Forbes Beattie, Aberdeen.

Balmoral Stalkers' Map (probably early 1900s) Balmoral Estate map, based on a published map, with annotations and a list of place names.

*Blair Castle*

Atholl map (1780) Plan of Blair in Atholl, Forests of Tarff, Benechrombie etc in Perth Shire. Surveyed by James Stobie.

Atholl map (1784) Plan of the north east quarter of Perth-shire. Surveyed by James Stobie.

Atholl map (1815) 1784 map, copied by James Stirton.

Atholl map (1823) Scroll plan Forrest of Atholl.

Atholl map (1827) North-east part of Perthshire from Mr Stobie's survey. 1784 map copied by William Johnson.

*British Library Maps, Blm in Table 2*

Blm 1. K Top XLVIII.68 Campbell, G (1750) A drawn Survey from the Water Aveun to Braemarr Castle, measuring twenty-seven miles.

Blm 1a. 48.66b Caulfield, Major (1750) Ms Report by Major Caulfield of the Roads made in the Highlands in the year 1750.

Blm 2. XLVIII.73 Campbell, G (1751) A drawn Survey from the Castle of Cargarff to that of Braemarr, three different Roads.

Blm 3. XLVIII.74 Gordon, G (1753) A drawn Plan of part of the Road from Perth to Fort George, between Braemarr and Corgarff Barrack.

Roy. XLVIII.25 Roy, W (1747–55) The Military Survey of Scotland. Survey by Col Watson. Copy at Nat Library of Scotland.

*Cairngorm Club Library, Aberdeen*

Cairngorm Club Map of the Cairngorm Mountains (1895). Based on OS 1 inch to 1 mile map, with annotations. Referred to by Mitchell (1968).

*Dinnet Estate Office*

Johnston, T Ruddiman (1885) Plan of the Estates of Aboyne and Glentanar in the County of Aberdeen. Lithographed, Edinburgh.

*Invercauld House (Im in our abbreviations list)*

Im 1. Early, undated plan of Glenmuick and upper Tanar. In Box 13 in charter room.

Im 2. (probably 1700s) Sketch plan of the Braemar area. In Box 23 in charter room.

Im 3. (1743) River Dee from the boat of Braemar up to the Foord called Dee Ford. Hanging in a hall.

Im 4. (c. 1750) Plan of proposed plantings of woods. Hanging in a hall.

Im 5. (1775) An Eye Sketch of Brae Marr to Strath Dee anno 1775. Hanging in a hall.

Im 6. Sketch plan of Auchichness and Calders property. In Box 23 in charter room.

Im 7. (1787) A Draught of the River Gairn from opposite the Kirk of Gairn to opposite the Farmhouses of Pronie. In Box 3 in charter room.

Im 8. (probably late 1700s) A provisional sketch plan of the Corndavon part of Invercauld estate. In Box 2 in charter room.

Im 9. (1798) Plans of estate of Monaltrie. William Panton. In Box 3 in charter room.

Im 10. (1810) Plans of division of Moss of Morven. In Box 3 in charter room.

Im 11. (1826) Plans of Dee above Pannanich. J Hay.

*Macdonald Collection, Dept of Geography, Univ of Aberdeen*

Md 1. (1854) Plan of Aboyne, Braemar and Ballater Turnpike Road. Two separate maps, including one in pencil.

Md 2. (1863) Plan of Part of the Estate of Balmoral. James F Beattie, Aberdeen.

Md 3. (c. 1856–63) Plans of Balmoral estate. Nos I & II on one sheet, No III on another. Referred to by us under Bogus Gaelic names from maps of Balmoral Estate.

Md 4. (1856) Plan of Balmoral. Sheet III. J C Law, Dundee. Different from above Sheet III. Referred to by us under Bogus Gaelic names etc as above.

Md 5. (1800s) A Plan of the Aboyne and Braemar Road.

Md 6. (1883) Plan of Braemar. Report to the Local Authority. Beattie.

Md 7. (1884) Plan of Braemar Sewage Works. Beattie.

Md 8. (1884) Plan of Braemar Water Works. Beattie.

Md 9. (1880s) Braemar Water Supply Section from Gray-Moss Reservoir to Tom-na-loine Reservoir.

Md 10. (1880s) Plan of Braemar Water Works.

Md 11. (late 1800s) Plan of Braemar Drainage.

Md 12. (late 1800s) Plan of Deviation of Braemar Water Works Channel, Deeside District Committee.

*Mar Estate Office*

OS 6 inch to the mile Map of Mar Estate, with annotations. Different from the 'Mar map' in the Publications list.

*National Library of Scotland*

Blaeu, J (1654) MS map with some differences from Atlas Novus.
Gordon, R (1600s) MS maps. See Stone (1970).
Pont, T (1600s) MS maps. See Stone (1970).
Farquharson, J (1703) Plan of the Forest of Mar.

*Register House (RHP), R, I and Ma in Table 2*

R1. RHP 22506 (1725) Map of the five parishes above Colblean.

R1a. RHP 3491 (c. 1735) Plan of Castleton of Braemar.

R2. RHP 31322 (mid 1700s) Plan of Allanaquoich.

R2a. RHP 1767 (1700s) Map of the Lordships of Strathaven, Glenlivat and Achendown.

R2b. RHP 2489 (1773) Plan of Strathavon.

R3. RHP 3647 (1788) Plan of the Lands of Monaltrie Crathienaird Daldounie and Lawsie.

R4. RHP 3498 (1790) Scroll Plan of the Lands of Tullich within dykes, the property of Wm Farquharson Esqr of Monaltrie.

R5. RHP 3499 (probably late 1700s) Scetch of the Marches betwixt the Lands of Crathenard and Monaltrie.

R6. RHP 30741 (c. 1800) Un-named plan of upper Glen Muick.

R6. RHP 30742 (c. 1800) Un-named plan of lower Glen Muick, upper Glen Tanar, and Pannanich.

R6a. RHP 3695 (1804) Plan of the Lands of Crathynard Lawsie and Daldownie Surveyed and Divided. Colin Innes.

I RHP 3897 (1807–9) Plans of the Estate of Invercauld in Aberdeen-shire. Surveyed and delineated by George Brown (Invercauld map in Table 2).

Ma. RHP 3896 (1808) Plans of the Estate of Invercauld in Perth-shire. Surveyed and delineated by George Brown (Marlee map in Table 2, includes Marlee and also lands in Glen Shee bordering Aberdeenshire).

R7. RHP 3645 (1808) Plan of the Mains and Forest of Invercauld together with the Farms of Clunie, Kiloch &c.

R9. RHP 3696 (1826) Scetch of the Lands of Monaltrie.

R10. RHP 811 (1826) Sketch of part of Mar Forest in Aberdeenshire with the Woods divided into Lots.

R11. RHP 2219 (1826) Southern part of Aberdeen and Banff-shrs. A I Ross. Very similar to Robertson (1822).

R12. RHP 3596 (1827) Plan of the Lands of Rhinetten, Crathienaird and Micras &c together with the common hills adjoining Belonging to Mrs Farquharson of Invercauld. By Geo McWilliam.

R13. RHP 3697 (1827) Plan of the Lands of Acalater with the Grazing of Glen Calater belonging to Mrs Farquharson of Invercauld. By Geo McWilliam.

R14. RHP 3512 (1828) Sketch of the Manor Place of Invercauld with that part of the Entail'd Estate Surrounding it etc.

R14a. RHP 3719 (1865) Plan of the estates of Candacraig and Glencarvie. Reduced from original plan in 1825. Taylor & Henderson.

R15. RHP 931 (1864) Plans & Sections of the Proposed Railway from the Charleston of Aboyne to the Castletown of Braemar. David Nimmo, Edinburgh.

R16. RHP 3330 (1867) Map of the Invercauld shooting grounds and deer forests.

R17. RHP 3303 (late 1800s) Aboyne Estate Deeside Aberdeenshire.

R18. RHP 31373 (1895) Fife Estates Plan of Auchindryne Village Lands. Walker & Duncan, Aberdeen.

*Royal Archives (RA), Windsor Castle, Ram in Table 2*

Ram 1. Vol II/160 (1806) Plan of the Estates of Abergeldie and Birkhall. John Innes.

Ram 2. Vol I/66 (late 1800s) Sketch of The Proposed Deeside Railway from Aberdeen to Banchory. Geo Cornwall, Lithographer.

Ram 3. Vol I/9 (late 1800s) Map of Part of the Grampian Mountains. G Cumming, Dundee.

*Note.* Some plans at Register House and the Royal Archives were only photocopies, and a few names were indistinct. In such cases, we subsequently studied the original maps at estate offices and houses to get better definition, as in RHP 3498 and 3499 at Invercauld House, the Invercauld and Marlee maps at Invercauld Estate Office, and the Innes map at Abergeldie Castle.

# ADDENDA

## Further information on published sources

Ach nan Cuithe Iomlan Auchnagymlinn (A).
An t-Alltan Buidhe, 044852 Alltan Buidhe (A).
Allt an Eas Bhig The Little Essie (A).
Allt Bhrot-choin Allt Bhrottachan (A).
Allt nan Gamhainn Allt a ghown (D).
Bad a' Chabair Badhabber (A).
The Bad a' Chabair Moss The Moss of Badhabber (A).
Bad nan Cuigeal Badnagiúgal (M). M noted that a Cuigeal
  could mean a marsh plant (W).
Baile an Eilein Belnallen (A), Bal-nyellan (D in A).
Baile na Coille Balnacoil (A).
Baile nan Gabhar Balnagower (A).
A' Bhruach Ruadh, 280930 Brochroy (A).
Caitir Fhrangach's Cairn Kitty Rankie's Cairn (A).
Carn an t-Sagairt Carn Taggart (A).
The Castletoun Castletoun (Ab 19).
The Chapel House Chapel house (Vr 1904).
Clais Ghiubhas Clais Ghiubhais (A).
Clais Poll Bhathaidh Clais Poll Bha (A).
Cnocan Dubh Knockandhu (A).
Coble Seat of Tullich Appendix 1, Mc.
The Crooked Wreath The Crookit Vrythe (A).
East Toun Eastoun (Ab 3).
The Falls o Muick The Falls of Muick (McC).
An Garbh-choire, 262927 Garchory (A).
The Garbh-choire Burn, 262929 The Garchory Burn (A).

The Glas-choille Road The Glas Choille road (Moi).
The Haughs o Creag an Dail The Haughs of Craigendall (A).
Hospital Haugh The Hospitall hauch (Ri 13).
Little Athan Phuill Little Ann (P).
The Little Cadha Chuirn The Little Ca Carn (A).
The Lower Bobbie Puil Lower Bobbie's (P).
The Manse o Glen Gairn Manse of Glengairn (Vr 1904).
Manse of Glenmuick Manse, Glenmuick (Vr 1904).
The Middle Bobbie Puil Middle Bobbie's (P).
Moor of the Inver The Muir of Inver (McC).
The Muir, 290005. Muir, Glengairn (Vr 1924).
A' Mheall Odhar Bheag Meall Odhar Beag (Wa).
The Mill Craft Mill Croft (Vr 1899).
Milltoun of Inchmarnoch Mylnetoune of Inchemarnocht
  (Ab 13).
Milltoun of Ballachlaggan Milton of Balchlaggan (Vr 1).
Muckle Carn an t-Sagairt Muckle Cairn Tagart (Ri 30).
Ruighean Dubh-chroite Appendix 1, Ri.
Ruighe an Loin (farm) Rinloan (A).
The Sron Ghearraig Road The Strone Yarrick road (A).
Torr an Fhraoich Appendix 1, Ri.
Tigh na Criche Tynacreich (Vr 1).
Tom o Loinn Mhor Tom a lin mor (Mg).
The Upper Bobbie Puil Upper Bobbie's (P).
Waird-Head Wairdhead (Ab 19).

## Extra names added in proof

Abergairns Abergardens (Ab 19). A collective name.
Abergelder See Invergelder.
Allt an Eas Eacartach See Allt Eacartach.
Allt Bhreac-achaidh* (3, 338872), burn of the speckled field. Ald
  vrechachy (G 5). The middle part of Allt an t-Sneachda (OS)
  in Glen Muick. Perhaps Allt an t-Sneachda was the top part,
  which holds much snow; the main glen is not very snowy.
Allt Laoigh See Feith an Laoigh.
The Back Latch To a few (U), this is not the burn, which to
  them is the Burn o the Back Latch, but refers to ground
  about 225823 in Coire Uilleim Mhoir.
The Ben Macdui Lochan Uaine* See Lochan Uaine.
Bert's Loch* (F, 418968), 'bɛrts'lᴏχ. A pool dammed by Bert
  Robertson, near Inchmarnoch.
The Big Criosdaidh See Allt Cristie Mor.
The Big Damhaidh See Allt Dhaidh Mor.
The Big Easaidh See Allt an Eas Mhoir.
The Big Knap* (Ra 15), another name for Cnap a' Choire
  Bhuidhe.
The Big Meall Odhar* See Meall Odhar.
The Brown Cow's White Calf See the White Calf.
The Burn of Bad na h-Earba* See Allt Bad na h-Earba.
Burn of Bad na h-Earba's Inver* (389027). Burn of Badnearb's
  Inver (Io 20), Inver probably Scots = mouth, borrowed from
  Gaelic Inbhir. South-east of Morven.
The Burn of Beinn Fhiubharainn* See Allt Beinn Iutharn.
The Burn of Cadha an Fhir Bhogha* See Allt Coire an Fhir
  Bhogha.

Burn of Clais nan Cat* See Allt Clais nan Cat.
The Burn o Coire an t-Slugain* See Allt Coire an t-Slugain.
The Burn of Little Beinn Fhiubharainn* The Burn of Little
  Benurin (Io 79). Another name for Allt Cac Dubh.
The Burn o the Back Latch* (U), ðɪ'bʌrnɪðɪ'bak'latʃ, same as
  Allt Coire Uilleim Mhoir.
The Burn o the Point o the Lair* (U), ðɪ'bʌrnɪðɪ'pointɪðɪ'leṛ.
  Same as the Mid Grain.
Cadhach Dubh See Allt Cac Dubh.
Cairn Toul Burn See Allt Coire an t-Sabhail.
The Callater (Al). See Callater Burn.
Chapel Ma-Naoimhir Chapel-Monire (S). Same as St Manir's
  Church at Crathie; Stirton incorrectly put it at Micras.
The Chappell of the Hermits (Vd), same as Chapel Ma-Dheoir.
Churraich Pool See Poll Churraich.
The Clais Mhor Burn See Allt na Clais Moire.
The Clunie (Al). See Clunie Water.
Cnoc Phìobair* (3, U, south of 294967), knᴏk'fiˑpër, knoll of
  the piper. East of Crathie.
The Coire an t-Sagairt Burn See Allt Coire an t-Sagairt.
The Coire Chrid Burn* See Allt Coire Chrid.
The Coire Gorm Burn* See Allt a' Choire Ghuirm.
Coire of the Little Easaidh* See Coire an Easaidh Bhig.
The Connie (Al). See Allt Connie.
Conor Mor See Carn an Fhir Bhogha.
Dail Mhorair Muir* See Dail Mhorair.
The Daldownie Brig* (C, 245008), ðɪˌdal'duni'brɪg. A bridge in
  upper Glen Gairn.

191

**The Dee Valley** (Ky).

**An Duibhir** See Allt na Duibhre.

**The Duke's Craig*** (Me 15 in 1813). Another name for Creag an Diuchd.

**The Duke's Path** (Wa, F, 966001), ðɪˈdjuksˈpaθ. On Braeriach.

**The East Grain o Allt Darrarie** (U), ðɪˈistˈgrenɐˌaltˈdarəre, same as the Easter Grain of Allt Darrarie.

**The East Grain o Allt Deas** See the East Grain.

**The Ey** (Al). See Ey Burn.

**The Fairy Dell** (A Tewnion 1948, *Cairngorms Guide*, Scott. Youth Hostels Assn), same as Fairy Glen.

**The Falls of Corriemulzie** (McC).

**The Feardar** (Gf). See Feardar Burn.

**The Foggy Burn*** See Allt Coire na Coinnich.

**Foggy Mill*** Scots Foggy = mossy. Foggy Miln (Io 34). On Invercauld estate; possibly within our study area.

**The Games Park** (Wa). See Moine nan Gall.

**The Garbh-choire Burn** See Allt a' Gharbh-choire.

**The Garbh-choire Burn*** See Allt a' Gharbh-choire.

**The Geallaig** (Gf). A former school at Micras, also called 'the college' (WD, in Watson & Clement 1983), ðɪˈkọləʤ.

**(The) Gelder** (A). See Gelder Burn.

**The Geldie** (Al) See Geldie Burn.

**(The) Girnock** (A). See Girnock Burn.

**An Gocan*** (3, U, 150909), ðɪˈgokɐn, the little pipe. A fast part of Clunie Water.

**The Head of Sron Fhionn*** (134825). The Head of Stronfinne (G 2). At Baddoch.

**Hill of the Knock*** (G 35), same as Knock (OS), 348957.

**Horse Moss*** See Moine an Eich.

**House of Monaltrie** See Mains of Monaltrie.

**Linn of Dee Cottage** (OS, 062896), locally just the Linn of Dee (Er, C), ðɪˈlënɐˈdiˑ. Porter's Lodge (R 10) in 1826.

**The Little Criosdaidh*** See Allt Cristie Beag.

**The Little Damhaidh*** See Allt Dhaidh Beag.

**The Little Easaidh** See Allt an Eas Bhig.

**The Little Knap*** (Ra 15), same as Little Cnap a' Choire Bhuidhe.

**The Little Meall Odhar*** See A' Mheall Odhar Bheag.

**The Loard*** (R 6a, 262968), probably an alternative of Scots Loan = a common pasture, which this was. A field north of Crathie.

**The Loinn Bheag Park*** See An Loinn Bheag.

**Lourde's Cottage*** (Ce 6, in parish of Glenmuick, Tullich & Glengairn), Lourde's doubtful as handwriting unclear. Between Laggan and Ardoch in a Glen Gairn list.

**The Lui** (Al). See Lui Water.

**The Meikle Cairn*** See the Mid Cairn.

**Meikle Craig*** See A' Chreag Mhor.

**Meikle Creag Mhor*** See (A') C(h)reag Mhor.

**Middlefield*** See Mid Park.

**The Mid Grain o Allt Darrarie*** (U), ðɪˈmɪdˈgrenɐˌaltˈdarəre. Same as the Mid Grain.

**Millcroft of Renatton** See Renatton.

**Millhouse*** See the Milltoun, 426964.

**The Mill House*** See the Mill of Castleton.

**The Milton o the Braes*** Milton of Breas (H). Same as Milton of Whitehouse.

**The Minister's Pot*** Same as the Minister's Puil.

**Moss of Moine an Eich*** See Moine an Eich.

**The Muckle Damhaidh*** See Allt Dhaidh Mor.

**The Muckle Easaidh** The Meikle Eas (Cj 1). See Allt an Eas Mhoir.

**Muckle Tom Sgonnach** See Tom Sgonnach Mor.

**The Muckle Whistle*** See Am Feadan Mor.

**The Point o the Lair*** (F), ðɪˈpointɪðɪˈleɾ, a more frequent name for the East Point o the Lair.

**Porter's Lodge*** See Linn of Dee Cottage.

**The Princess Royal and Duke of Fife Memorial Park** See Moine nan Gall.

**Am Punnd*** (3, U, 241010), ðɪˈpọnd, the pound. A ruined former enclosure in Glen Gairn.

**The Quoich** (Al). See Quoich Water.

**The Red Brae*** See A' Bhruach Ruadh.

**The Robbers' Copse*** See Preas nam Meirleach.

**The Sgreuchaig Burn*** See Allt Coire na Sgreuchaig.

**Na Sliabhach** (3), the Sleachs. Na slyiach (D). A collective name.

**The Snowy Burn*** See Allt an t-Sneachda.

**St Comb's Chapel** See Chapel Ma-Chalmaig.

**The Strone*** See Sron Eirbhidh.

**The Stuic Corrie** (Al, 1950 edn). Another name for Coire Lochan nan Eun.

**Tammie's Stripe*** (U, 325833). See Burn of Mohamed.

**The Tobar*** See Tobar Mhoire.

**The Tom of Blar Charraid*** See the Tom o Loinn Mhor.

**The Tom o the Buailteach*** See Tom Buailteach.

**Tom Sionnaich** A collective name, see Tom Sgonnach Beag and Mor.

**Turner Burn*** See Allt Beart an Tuairneir.

**The Uchd Park*** See An t-Uchd.

**Upper Knock*** Upper and Nether Knocks (G in 1779), i.e. Knocks probably plural. Same as Muckle Knock or Over Knock.

**The Water Splash*** See the Splash.